W9-BZA-379

# DK DICTIONARY THESAURUS

A DK Publishing Book

www.dk.com

A DK Publishing Book
www.dk.com

Produced for DK Publishing by
PAGE*One*, Cairn House, Elgiva Lane, Chesham,
Buckinghamshire HP5 2JD

| **PAGE*One* team** | Marion Dent, Chris Stewart,<br>Charlotte Stock, Sophie Williams |
| --- | --- |
| **DK Managing editor**<br>**DK Managing art editor** | Jayne Parsons<br>Gillian Shaw |
| **Thesaurus compilers** | Roz Combley, Jessica Feinstein, Fred McDonald,<br>Elaine Pollard, Laura Wedgeworth, John Williams |
| **Dictionary/Thesaurus editor** | Sheila Dignen |

First American Edition, 1999
6 8 10 9 7

Published in the United States by DK Publishing, Inc.
95 Madison Avenue, New York, New York 10016

**Library of Congress Cataloging-in-Publication Data**
Concise dictionary/thesaurus. – 1st American ed.
p. cm.
Summary: A combined dictionary and thesaurus for school-aged children.
ISBN 0-7894-3949-2
1. English language–Dictionaries. Juvenile. 2. English language–Synonyms and
antonyms–Juvenile literature. [1. English language–Dictionaries. 2. English
language–Synonyms and antonyms.] I. DK Publishing Inc.
PE1628.C66 1999
423–dc21                                            98-52899
                                                    CIP
                                                    AC

Printed and bound in Italy by Printer Trento s.r.l.

# LIST OF ABBREVIATIONS

| | | | | | |
|---|---|---|---|---|---|
| *adj(s)* | adjective(s) | *geog* | geography | *pp* | past participle |
| *abbr* | abbreviation | *geol* | geology | *prep* | preposition |
| *adv(s)* | adverb | *geom* | geometry | *pron(s)* | pronoun(s) |
| *Am* | American | *Ger* | German | *pr p* | present participle |
| *anat* | anatomy | *Gk* | Greek | *psych* | psychology |
| *ar* | archaic | *gram* | grammar | *pt* | past tense |
| *arch* | architecture | *her* | heraldry | *rad* | radio |
| *astron* | astronomy | *hist* | historical | *reflex* | reflexive |
| *Aust* | Australian | *hort* | horticulture | *sb('s)* | somebody('s) |
| *aut* | cars, motoring | *idm* | idiom | *Scot* | Scottish |
| *aux* | auxiliary | *inf* | informal | *sing* | singular |
| *avia* | aviation | *interj* | interjection | *sl* | slang |
| *bio* | biology | *interrog* | interrogative | *Sp* | Spanish |
| *bot* | botany | *It* | Italian | *sth* | something |
| *Brit* | British | *Lat* | Latin | *sup* | superlative |
| *cap* | capital (initial) | *leg* | legal | *tech* | technical |
| *chem* | chemistry | *ling* | linguistics | *telecom* | tele-communications |
| *coll* | colloquial | *lit* | literary | | |
| *comm* | commerce | *masc* | masculine | [TM] | trademark |
| *comput* | computing | *math* | mathematics | TV | television |
| *conj* | conjunction | *mech* | mechanical | *usu* | usually |
| *dated* | old-fashioned | *med* | medicine | *v(s)* | verb(s) |
| *dem* | demonstrative | *met* | meteorology | | |
| *det(s)* | determiner(s) | *mil* | military | | |
| *dram* | drama, theater | *mus* | music | | |
| *eccl* | ecclesiastical | *myth* | mythology | | |
| *econ* | economics | *n(s)* | noun(s) | | |
| *eg* | for example | *naut-* | nautical | | |
| *elec* | electrical, electronics | *opp* | opposite | | |
| | | *phot* | photography | | |
| *esp* | especially | *phr v(s)* | phrasal verb(s) | | |
| *fem* | feminine | *pl* | plural | | |
| *fig* | figurative(ly) | *polit* | politics | | |
| *fml* | formal | *poss* | possessive | | |

**aardvark** *n* S African ant-eating mammal
**aback** *adv* **be taken aback** be startled
**abacus** *n pl* **-uses** counting frame
**abandon** *v* 1 desert; forsake 2 give up
altogether; *n* **abandon, -ment** freedom
from inhibition; *adj* **-ed** 1 deserted
2 unrestrained; depraved

> **abandon** *v* 1 (desert sb) dump, jilt, leave,
> run out on, throw over. 2 (desert a place)
> evacuate, quit, vacate. 3 (give up
> altogether) cede, forfeit, resign, surrender

**abashed** *adj* ashamed; embarrassed
**abate** *v* make or become less intense
**abattoir** *n* slaughterhouse
**abbey** *n* (dwelling place of a) community
of monks or nuns
**abbot** *n* head of abbey or monastery
**abbreviate** *v* shorten; *n* **abbreviation**

> **abbreviate** *v* abridge, condense, curtail, cut,
> précis, reduce, summarize, trim, truncate

**abdicate** *v* give up (power, position,
responsibility); *n* **abdication**
**abdomen** *n* belly; *adj* **abdominal**
**abduct** *v* carry off unlawfully; *n* **abduction**

> **abduct** *v* carry off, kidnap, make off with,
> run away with, seize, snatch

**aberration** *n* thing deviating from what is
normal; *adj* **aberrant**
**abeyance** *n* temporary suspension
**abhor** *v* detest, loathe
**abhorrent** *adj* detestable; *n* **abhorrence**

> **abhorrent** *adj* abominable, disgusting,
> execrable, hateful, horrible, loathsome,
> obnoxious, odious, offensive, repellent,
> repugnant, repulsive, revolting

**abide** *v* tolerate; **abide by** be faithful to

> **abide** *v* 1 (tolerate) accept, bear, endure, put
> up with, stand, stomach, suffer. 2 **abide by**
> adhere to, comply with, conform to,
> follow, keep to, obey, stick to

**abiding** *adj* lasting
**ability** *n* power to do something

> **ability** *n* adeptness, aptitude, bent, capability,
> capacity, cleverness, competence,
> expertise, facility, faculty, flair, gift, knack,
> know-how, power, proficiency, skill, talent

**abject** *adj* miserable, cast down, servile
**ablaze** *adj* 1 burning 2 very bright
**able** *adj* 1 having the power or skill to do
a thing 2 clever; talented; *adv* **ably**

> **able** *adj* (clever) accomplished, capable,
> competent, expert, gifted, masterly,
> proficient, qualified, skilled, strong,
> talented

**able-bodied** *adj* strong and fit
**abnormal** *adj* out of ordinary; deviating from
normal; *adv* **-ly**; *n* **-ity**

> **abnormal** *adj* aberrant, atypical, bizarre,
> extraordinary, idiosyncratic, irregular,
> odd, peculiar, perverted, queer, strange,
> unnatural, unorthodox, unusual, weird

**aboard** *adv* on a ship, train, etc

a
b
c
d
e
f
g
h
i
j
k
l
m
n
o
p
q
r
s
t
u
v
w
x
y
z

**A**

B
C
D
E
F
G
H
I
J
K
L
M
N
O
P
Q
R
S
T
U
V
W
X
Y
Z

**abode** *n* home; dwelling place
**abolish** *v* do away with; *n* **abolition**

> **abolish** *v* annul, ax, cancel, destroy, eliminate, end, eradicate, extinguish, get rid of, put an end to, revoke, stop, terminate

**abominable** *adj* very bad or unpleasant

> **abominable** *adj* abhorrent, awful, despicable, detestable, disgusting, foul, hateful, horrible, loathsome, nasty, obnoxious, odious, offensive, repellent, revolting, terrible, vile

**abort** *v* 1 (to cause) to miscarry (of a fetus) 2 to end prematurely (of a mission or plan); *n* **abortion** miscarriage
**abortive** *adj* unsuccessful

> **abortive** *adj* failed, fruitless, futile, ineffective, ineffectual, pointless, useless, vain, worthless

**abound** *v* be plentiful, well supplied
**about** *prep* 1 concerning; on the subject of 2 around; *adv* 1 nearby; all around 2 nearly; **just about** very nearly; **be about to** be going to
**about-face** *n* change to opposite direction, opinion, or policy
**above** *prep* over; higher than; more than; *adv, adj* overhead
**aboveboard** *adj* open and honest
**abracadabra** *n* magic formula; spell
**abrade** *v* rub or wear off; *n, adj* **abrasive**; *n* **abrasion** place where skin is scraped off, sore so caused
**abreast** *adv, adj* side by side; on a line with
**abridge** *v* shorten, condense

> **abridge** *v* abbreviate, compress, cut, cut down, précis, prune, reduce, summarize, trim, truncate

**abroad** *adv* in another country; outdoors
**abrupt** *adj* 1 rude 2 sudden; *adv* **-ly**

> **abrupt** *adj* 1 (rude) blunt, brusque, curt, direct, gruff, impolite, rough, short, snappish, terse, uncivil. 2 (sudden) hasty, hurried, quick, rapid, sharp, swift, unexpected

**abscess** *n* inflamed infected swelling
**abscond** *v* run away secretly
**abseil** *v* make controlled rapid descent of steep rock face by means of rope
**absent** *adj* 1 not present 2 inattentive; *v* **absent oneself (from)** stay away; *adv* **absently**; *ns* **absence; absentee** one who is not present

> **absent** *adj* 1 (not present) away, elsewhere, gone, missing, out, unavailable, wanting. 2 (inattentive) absentminded, blank, day-dreaming, distracted, faraway, oblivious, preoccupied, unaware, vacant, vague

**absentminded** *n* inattentive; forgetful; *adv* **-ly**; *n* **-ness**
**absolute** *adj* 1 complete 2 definite; *adv* **absolutely**

> **absolute** *adj* 1 (complete) out-and-out, outright, perfect, sheer, thorough, total, unmitigated, unqualified, utter. 2 (definite) categorical, certain, conclusive, decided, positive, sure, undoubted, unequivocal

**absolve** *v* pronounce free from sin; *n* **absolution**
**absorb** *v* 1 take in 2 engross; *adj* **absorbing** engrossing; *ns* **absorbent, absorption**

> **absorb** *v* 1 (take in) assimilate, digest, draw in, draw up, mop up, soak up, suck up. 2 (engross) captivate, engage, enthral, fascinate, occupy, preoccupy, rivet

**abstain** *v* 1 refrain from (*esp* alcohol or food) 2 refuse to vote; *n* **abstainer;** *adj* **abstinent** refraining from food, etc; *n* **abstinence** self-denial, **abstention** not using a right to vote

**abstemious** *adj* temperate; not given to excess, *esp* in food and drink

**abstract** *adj* theoretical; *n* summary; *v* steal; take away; *adj* **abstracted** absentminded; *n* **abstraction**

> **abstract** *adj* complex, conceptual, deep, general, intellectual, metaphysical, obscure, philosophical

**absurd** *adj* unreasonable; ridiculous; *adv* **absurdly;** *ns* **absurdity, absurdness**

> **absurd** *adj* crazy, daft, farcical, foolish, idiotic, illogical, laughable, ludicrous, nonsensical, paradoxical, preposterous, silly, stupid

**abundant** *adj* plentiful; *n* **abundance**

**abuse** *v* 1 misuse 2 behave cruelly to 3 insult; *n* **abuse** 1 misuse 2 cruel behavior 3 insults

> **abuse** *v* 1 (misuse) misapply, mishandle. 2 (behave cruelly to) batter, beat, harm, hurt, ill-treat, injure, maltreat, manhandle, mistreat, molest. 3 (insult) call sb names, curse, denigrate, disparage, malign, revile, swear, vilify
>
> **abuse** *n* 1 (misuse) corruption, misapplication, mishandling. 2 (cruel behavior) beating, cruelty, exploitation, harm, ill-treatment, maltreatment, mistreatment. 3 (insults) curses, defamation, expletives, invective, obscenity, slander, swearing, vilification, vituperation

**abusive** *adj* using insulting language

**abut** *v* to be adjacent to

**abysmal** *adj* very bad

**abyss** *n* bottomless pit

**academic** *adj* 1 to do with education 2 scholarly

> **academic** *adj* 1 (to do with education) educational, instructional, pedagogical, scholastic. 2 (scholarly) cultured, intellectual, learned, literary, well-read

**academy** *n* 1 place of higher education 2 society for advancement of learning

**accede** *v* 1 succeed to 2 give consent or support 3 comply with

**accelerate** *v* increase speed; *n* **accelerator** device for increasing speed in machines, etc

> **accelerate** *v* go faster, hurry, speed up

**accent** *n* stress or emphasis; mark used to indicate sound of vowel

**accept** *v* 1 agree to 2 receive 3 believe *adj* **-able;** *n* **-ability, acceptance**

> **accept** *v* 1 (agree to) accede, acknowledge, admit, approve, comply, concur, consent, cooperate, go along with, undertake. 2 (receive) acquire, come by, gain, obtain, secure, take. 3 (believe) be convinced, credit, have faith, trust

**access** *n* means of approach; right of entry; *v* *comput* retrieve or input (information); *adj* **-ible** easy to reach, approach; *n* **-ibility; accession** coming to throne, office

**accessory** *n* 1 additional equipment; 2 *n* *leg* person who helps to commit a crime

**accident** *n* 1 unfortunate event 2 road collision 3 chance; *adj* **accidental;** *adv* **-ally**

> **accident** *n* 1 (unfortunate event) calamity, catastrophe, disaster, mishap, misfortune, tragedy. 2 (road collision) crash, pile-up, smash. 3 (chance) coincidence, fate, fluke, luck, serendipity, twist of fate

**acclaim** *n* loud applause; welcome; approval; *v* applaud; *n* **acclamation**

**A**

B
C
D
E
F
G
H
I
J
K
L
M
N
O
P
Q
R
S
T
U
V
W
X
Y
Z

**acclimatize** v adapt to a new climate
**accolade** n supreme reward
**accommodate** n 1 give room to 2 help;
*adj* **accommodating** obliging

> **accommodate** v 1 (give room to) board,
> cater for, house, lodge, put up, shelter, take
> in. 2 (help) aid, assist, lend a hand, meet
> sb's needs, oblige, do sb a favor

**accommodation** n lodgings
**accompany** v 1 go with 2 play music
supporting (a soloist)

> **accompany** v (go with) attend, chaperon,
> conduct, escort, guide

**accomplice** n partner in crime
**accomplish** v bring to successful conclusion;
n **accomplishment**
**accomplished** *adj* talented

> **accomplished** *adj* able, capable, competent,
> expert, gifted, skilful, skilled

**accord** v 1 be in harmony; agree 2 bestow; *adj*
**according to** *prep* 1 as stated by 2 following
**accordion** n musical instrument with bellows,
keys, and metal reeds
**accost** v speak to
**account** n 1 report 2 record of financial
transactions 3 consideration (**take into
account**); *prep* **on account of** because of;
*phr v* **account for** explain

> **account** n 1 (report) chronicle, description,
> explanation, history, portrayal, record,
> statement, story, tale. 2 (financial)
> balance sheet, books, reckoning, tally

**accountant** n professional person appointed
to keep or inspect financial accounts;
n **accountancy**
**accredited** *adj* officially recognized
**accrue** v increase, *esp* interest on invested
money

**accumulate** v amass; increase in mass or
number; n **accumulation**

> **accumulate** v accrue, assemble, build up,
> collect, gather, grow, hoard, increase, pile
> up, stash away *inf*, stockpile

**accurate** *adj* exact in detail; precise; *adv* **-ly**

> **accurate** *adj* careful, correct, meticulous,
> reliable, right, scrupulous, sound, strict,
> sure, true

**accuse** v bring charge against; blame

> **accuse** v censure, charge, denounce, hold
> sb responsible

**accustom** v get used to; *adj* **accustomed**
**ace** n 1 single spot on dice or cards 2 highest
3 best
**ache** v suffer dull, continuous pain; n dull,
continuous pain

> **ache** v be painful, be sore, hurt, pound,
> smart, sting, throb

**achieve** v finish; gain; win; n **-ment**

> **achieve** v accomplish, arrive at, attain, bring
> about, carry out, do, earn, effect, execute,
> fulfill, get, manage, obtain, reach, realize

**acid** n sour substance with pH less than 7;
usually having corrosive effect; *adj* 1 sour
and sharp to taste 2 sharp tempered
**acid rain** n rain polluted by industrial smoke
**acknowledge** v 1 notice or greet 2 indicate
receipt of 3 admit as true

> **acknowledge** v 1 (notice or greet) address,
> hail, recognize, respond, say hello to *inf*.
> 2 (indicate receipt of) answer, reply,
> respond. 3 (admit as true) accept, allow,
> concede, own, recognize

**acne** *n* skin disease common in adolescence, causing pimples on the face and neck

**acorn** *n* the fruit of the oak tree

**acoustic** *adj* 1 connected with hearing or sound 2 *mus* (of instruments) not electric; *adv* **acoustically**

**acquaint** *v* inform; make aware of; *idm* **be acquainted (with)** have some knowledge (of)

**acquaintance** 1 person slightly known 2 slight knowledge; **acquaintanceship**

> **acquaintance** *n* 1 (person) associate, colleague, contact. 2 (knowledge) awareness, familiarity, understanding

**acquiesce** *v* agree passively or tacitly

**acquire** *v* get or gain possession of; *n* **acquisition** 1 act of gaining 2 object gained; *adj* **acquisitive** desirous of gain

> **acquire** *v* amass, appropriate, buy, collect, come by, gain, gather, get, earn, obtain, pick up, procure, purchase, receive, win

**acquit** *v* **-quitting, -quitted** declare not guilty (of offence); *n* **acquittal**

> **acquit** *v* absolve, clear, discharge, exonerate, find innocent, free, liberate, reprieve, set free, vindicate

**acre** *n* measure of land 4,046 sq m (4,840 sq yd)

**acrimony** *n* bitter feeling

**acrimonious** *adj* full of bitter feelings

> **acrimonious** *adj* bad-tempered, cutting, harsh, hostile, hot-tempered, petulant, quarrelsome, spiteful, unpleasant, vitriolic

**acrobat** *n* skilled gymnast; *n* **acrobatics**

**acronym** *n* word formed by the initial letters of other words, *eg* NATO

**across** *adv, prep* 1 on the other side (of) 2 from one side to the other (of)

**acrylic** *n* type of synthetic material

**act** *v* 1 do something 2 behave 3 perform on stage 4 have an effect; *n* 1 thing done 2 law 3 piece of entertainment; *n* **actor**, *fem* **actress** one who acts (stage, TV, or film)

> **act** *v* 1 (do sth) be active, function, get involved, move, react, strike, take action, take steps. 2 (behave) carry on. 3 (perform on stage) act out, appear as, dramatize, enact, mime, perform, play a part, portray, represent, tread the boards *inf*. 4 (have an effect) operate, take effect, work
> **act** *n* 1 (thing done) accomplishment, achievement, action, deed, exploit, feat, move. 2 (law) bill, decree, edict, judgment, measure, ruling, statute. 3 (piece of entertainment) item, performance, routine, sketch, show, turn

**acting** *adj* functioning temporarily as

**action** *n* 1 act 2 movement 3 excitement; main events 4 war; fighting 5 lawsuit

> **action** *n* 1 (act) accomplishment, achievement, deed, effort, endeavor, initiative, measure, move, operation, step. 2 (movement) activity, energy, force, forcefulness, liveliness, spirit, vigor, vitality. 3 (excitement) activity, bustle, drama, events, happenings, incidents. 4 (war) battle, combat, conflict, fighting. 5 (lawsuit) case, litigation, proceedings

**active** *adj* 1 lively 2 in action; *adv* **-ly**; *v* **activate** make active; set in motion

> **active** *adj* 1 (lively) animated, bustling, busy, energetic, enthusiastic, industrious, quick, sprightly, spry, vibrant, vigorous, vivacious. 2 (in action) effective, effectual, functioning, in force, live, operating, operative, running, working

**activist** *n* one taking active part in politics

**activity** *n* 1 busy action 2 task

a
b
c
d
e
f
g
h
i
j
k
l
m
n
o
p
q
r
s
t
u
v
w
x
y
z

**A**

B
C
D
E
F
G
H
I
J
K
L
M
N
O
P
Q
R
S
T
U
V
W
X
Y
Z

**activity** n 1 (busy action) commotion, flurry, hustle and bustle, life, movement, stir. 2 (task) hobby, pastime, project, venture

**actual** adj 1 existing 2 real; true; adv **-ly** 1 in fact 2 surprisingly

**acupuncture** n treatment of pain or disease by sticking needles into the patient's body

**acute** adj 1 sharp 2 severe (of pain)

**acute** adj 1 (sharp) alert, astute, clever, keen, observant, penetrating, perceptive, quick, smart. 2 (severe) excruciating, fierce, intense, piercing, racking, sharp, stabbing, shooting, sudden, violent

**AD** abbr anno Domini (Lat = in the year of the Lord)

**adamant** adj stubbornly determined

**adamant** adj firm, inflexible, intransigent, resolute, stubborn, unbending, unyielding

**adapt** v 1 modify; make fit for new use 2 get used to new circumstances; adj **adaptable**; n **adaptability**; **adaptation**; **adapter** 1 person who adapts (also **adaptor**) 2 device used to link equipment, esp electrical plugs

**adapt** v 1 (modify) adjust, alter, change, convert, remodel, reorganize, reshape, tailor, transform. 2 (get used to) accommodate, adjust, become hardened

**add** v 1 put sth together with sth 2 combine numbers and find the sum total 3 say further; n **additive** something added

**add** v 1 (put together) attach, affix, append, combine, include, integrate, join. 2 (combine numbers) add up, compute, count, reckon, total, tot up inf

**adder** n small venomous snake belonging to the viper family

**addict** n 1 person unable to stop taking drugs, alcohol, etc 2 person with a passionate interest; adj **addicted (to)** 1 dependent **(on)** 2 keenly interested (in); n **addiction**; adj **addictive** habit-forming

**addition** n thing added; adj **additional**

**addition** n adjunct, appendage, appendix, attachment, augmentation, enlargement, extension, extra, gain

**addled** adj 1 (of brains) confused 2 (of eggs) rotten

**address** n 1 identification of residence or place of work 2 speech to an audience 3 comput details about storage location of data; v 1 speak to 2 write on a letter, parcel, etc details of its destination

**adenoids** n pl mass of tissue at back of nose, near throat

**adept** adj expert; n skilled person; expert; adv adeptly

**adequate** adj 1 sufficient 2 good enough; adv **-ly**; n **adequacy**

**adequate** adj acceptable, ample, enough, fair, mediocre, OK, passable, presentable, reasonable, satisfactory, suitable

**adhere** v stick; phr v **adhere to** remain loyal to; n **adherence**

**adhesive** n a (substance) which causes things to be stuck together

**adipose** adj fatty; n **adiposity**

**adjacent** adj lying near to; adjoining

**adjective** n word used to qualify a noun; adj **adjectival**

**adjoin** v be next to; adj **adjoining** neighboring

**adjourn** v put off, postpone; n **-ment**

**adjudge** v 1 decide by law 2 grant or award

**adjudicate** v judge; n **adjudicator, adjudication**

**adjunct** n thing added

**adjust** v 1 change slightly 2 become accustomed; adj **-able**; n **-ment**

**adjust** *v* **1** (change slightly) adapt, alter, modify, move, position, rearrange. **2** (become accustomed to) acclimatize, assimilate, get used to, settle in

**administer** *v* **1** manage **2** dispense; give out; *n* **administrator, administration**
**admirable** *adj* worthy of esteem

**admirable** *adj* commendable, creditable, exemplary, fine, good, great, honorable, marvelous, praiseworthy, wonderful

**admiral** *n* high-ranking naval officer; *n* **admiralty** board that controls naval affairs
**admire** *v* view with pleasure or respect
*n* **admirer, admiration**

**admire** *v* applaud, esteem, have a high opinion of, hero-worship, idolize, like, look up to, love, praise, revere, think highly of, value, venerate, wonder at, worship

**admissible** *adj* allowable; *adv* **-ibly**; *n* **admissibility**
**admission** *v* **1** being allowed to enter **2** acknowledgment of fact; confession
**admit** *v* **1** let in **2** acknowledge; confess; *n* **admittance** right of entry

**admit** *v* **1** (let in) allow in, give access to, give admission to. **2** (acknowledge) allow, concede, declare, own up, recognize

**ado** *n* fuss; bother; trouble; bustle
**adolescence** *n* state of growing up; *adj, n* **adolescent** boy, girl growing up
**adopt** *v* **1** take and bring up as one's own child **2** accept formally; *n* **adoption**; *adj* **adopted**; *n* **adoptability**
**adorable** *adj* lovely

**adorable** *adj* appealing, charming, delightful, gorgeous, lovable, sweet

**adore** *v* worship, love; *n* **adoration**

**adore** *v* cherish, dote on, idolize, love, praise, revere

**adorn** *v* beautify; embellish; *n* **adornment** decoration
**adrenalin** *n* hormone produced by adrenal glands
**adrift** *adj, adv* loose on water
**adult** *adj, n* grown-up; mature (person)

**adult** *adj* full-grown, full-size, fully developed, fully grown, of age

**adulterate** *v* corrupt; make impure
**adultery** *n* sexual infidelity in marriage
**advance** *v* **1** move forward **2** develop **3** lend money **4** help; *n* **1** forward move; progress **2** money paid before due **3** loan **4** increase in amount; *adj* early; before the due time; *idm* **in advance** beforehand; *adj* **advanced** **1** beyond; intermediate **2** far on in life

**advance** *v* **1** (move forward) forge ahead, gain ground, go ahead, make headway, move along, press on, proceed, push forward. **2** (develop) evolve, flourish, grow, improve, progress, thrive. **3** (lend money) give, loan, provide. **4** (help) assist, benefit, boost, facilitate, further, promote

**advantage** *n* **1** favorable condition **2** superior position

**advantage** *n* **1** (favorable condition) asset, benefit, blessing, boon, convenience, gain, good point, help. **2** (superior position) edge, head start *inf*, lead, upper hand

**advantageous** *adj* helpful

**advantageous** *adj* beneficial, constructive, convenient, invaluable, positive, profitable, useful, valuable, worthwhile

**A**

**advent** *n* coming, *esp* of Christ; (*usu* CAP) four weeks preceding Christmas

**adventure** *n* **1** exciting incident **2** excitement; *n* **adventurer**

> **adventure** *n* **1** (exciting incident) escapade, experience, exploit, incident, occurrence. **2** (excitement) danger, risk, uncertainty

**adventurous** *adj* seeking adventure

> **adventurous** *adj* bold, brave, courageous, daredevil, daring, intrepid

**adverb** *n* word qualifying verb, adjective, or another adverb

**adversary** *n* **1** enemy **2** opponent

**adverse** *adj* unfavorable; *adv* **-ly**; *n* **adversity** unfavorable circumstances

**advertise** *v* **1** praise in order to sell **2** make known publicly; *n* **advertisement, advertiser, advertising**

> **advertise** *v* **1** (praise in order to sell) market, plug *inf*, promote, push. **2** (make known) announce, broadcast, proclaim, publish

**advice** *n* information given as guidance

> **advice** *n* counseling, guidance, help, recommendation, suggestion, tip, warning

**advise** *v* give advice to; inform of; *n* **adviser**

> **advise** *v* (give advice to) advocate, argue for/against, counsel, encourage, give guidance, help, recommend, urge, warn

**advocate** *v* speak in favor of; recommend; *n* **1** person who speaks in support **2** defense lawyer

> **advocate** *v* advise, argue for, back, campaign for, plead for, promote, recommend, speak for, uphold, urge

**aerial** *adj* of, in, like air; *n* antenna for receiving or sending electromagnetic waves

**aerobatics** *n* spectacular display by aircraft; *adj* **aerobatic**

**aerobics** *n* system of exercise to increase oxygen in the blood

**aerodynamics** *n* branch of physics dealing with forces exerted by moving air or gases; science of flight

**aeronaut** *n* flyer of balloon or aircraft

**aeronautics** science of air navigation

**aerosol** *n* (container of) pressurized liquid for releasing as a spray

**aerospace** *n* (technology related to) earth's atmosphere and space beyond

**aesthetics** *n* study of beauty, *esp* in art; *adj* **aesthetic**; *adv* **-ally**

**affair** *n* **1** event or series of events **2** extramarital sexual relationship; *pl* **affairs** business matters

> **affair** *n* **1** (event) business, case, episode, issue, matter, question, subject, thing, topic. **2** (sexual) attachment, intrigue, liaison, relationship, romance

**affect** *v* **1** have an effect on **2** upset

> **affect** *v* **1** (have an effect on) alter, change, have an impact on, impinge on, influence, sway. **2** (upset) concern, distress, disturb, grieve, move, stir, touch, trouble

**affection** *n* love

> **affection** *n* devotion, fondness, friendliness, friendship, liking, tenderness, warmth

**affectionate** *adj* showing love

> **affectionate** *adj* caring, friendly, kind, loving, tender, warm, warm-hearted

**affiliate** *v* accept persons, societies as members of institution; *n* **affiliation**

**affinity** *n* close relationship

**affirm** *v* confirm; *n* **affirmation**; *n, adj* **affirmative**

> **affirm** *v* assert, attest, avow, confirm, declare, say, state, swear, testify

**afflict** *v* cause to suffer; *n* **affliction**
**affluent** *adj* wealthy; *n* **affluence**

> **affluent** *adj* 1 (of people) loaded, moneyed, prosperous, rich, well-heeled, well-off, well-to-do. 2 (of lifestyle) comfortable, lavish, luxurious, opulent, sumptuous

**afford** *v* 1 have means for 2 supply
**affront** *v* insult; offend; *n* defiant act
**afoot** *adj* happening
**afraid** *adj* frightened

> **afraid** *adj* alarmed, anxious, apprehensive, fearful, nervous, scared, terrified, terror-stricken, timid, worried

**afresh** *adv* again; anew; once more
**after** *prep* 1 later than 2 following 3 as a result of 4 in pursuit of 5 in the style of 6 despite; *conj* 1 later than 2 although; *adv* 1 later 2 behind
**aftermath** *n* period following an event
**afternoon** *n* period of day between noon and evening
**aftershave** *n* lotion used on face after shaving
**afterthought** *n* something thought or added later
**afterward** *adv* later on
**again** *adv* 1 once more 2 as before
**against** *prep* close to; opposite
**age** *n* 1 length of time thing or person has existed 2 historical period 3 closing years of life; *v* grow old; *adj* **aged**

> **age** *n* 1 (historical period) date, days, epoch, era, generation, time. 2 (closing years of life) advancing years, declining years, dotage, maturity, old age, senility, seniority

**ageism, agism** *n* discrimination because of age; *adj, n* **ageist, agist**
**agency** *n* business providing service
**agenda** *adj* list of things to be discussed at meeting
**agent** *n* 1 one who acts for person or company 2 spy
**aggravate** *v* 1 make worse 2 annoy; *adj* **aggravating** annoying; *n* **aggravation**

> **aggravate** *v* 1 (make worse) compound, exacerbate, inflame, intensify. 2 (annoy) exasperate, get on sb's nerves, hassle *inf*, irritate, provoke, rub sb up the wrong way

**aggressive** *adj* rude; offensive; *adv* **-ly**; *n* **aggression**; **aggressor**

> **aggressive** *adj* argumentative, assertive, belligerent, forceful, hostile, provocative, pugnacious, pushy, quarrelsome, warlike

**aggrieve** *v* hurt; cause distress to
**aghast** *adj* shocked
**agile** *adj* active; nimble; *n* **agility**

> **agile** *adj* fit, graceful, lithe, quick, sprightly, spry, supple

**agitate** *v* shake violently; stir up unrest
**agitated** *adj* disturbed, upset

> **agitated** *adj* alarmed, anxious, confused, excited, flustered, nervous, unnerved, unsettled, worked up, worried

**agnostic** *n* one believing that nothing can be known concerning God
**ago** *adv* gone by; in the past
**agog** *adj, adv* excited; eagerly anticipating
**agonize** *v* suffer great anxiety
**agonizing** *adj* unbearably painful

> **agonizing** *adj* distressing, harrowing, racking, tormenting

**A**
B
C
D
E
F
G
H
I
J
K
L
M
N
O
P
Q
R
S
T
U
V
W
X
Y
Z

**agony** n anguish of mind or body

> **agony** n anguish, distress, hurt, misery, pain, suffering, torment, torture, woe

**agoraphobia** n marked fear of open spaces; adj **agoraphobic**

**agrarian** adj relating to land

**agree** v 1 consent 2 be of the same opinion

> **agree** v 1 (consent) accept, acknowledge, acquiesce, admit, allow, concede, grant 2 (be of the same opinion) be of the same mind, concur, get on, see eye to eye

**agreeable** adj pleasant; adv **agreeably**

> **agreeable** adj amiable, charming, congenial, delightful, friendly, lovely, nice, satisfying

**agriculture** n art and theory of farming; adj **agricultural**

**aground** adj, adv grounded; beached

**ahead** adv 1 in front 2 forward

**aid** v help; n 1 help 2 money loan

> **aid** v assist, benefit, encourage, facilitate, lend a hand, relieve, support
> **aid** n (help) assistance, cooperation, encouragement, guidance, support

**aide** n assistant

**AIDS, Aids** abbr Acquired Immune Deficiency Syndrome

**ail** v be out of health; adj **-ing**; n **-ment**

**aim** v 1 point weapon at 2 try to do sth; n 1 action of aiming 2 purpose; adj **aimless**

> **aim** v 1 (point weapon at) direct, focus, line up, take aim, train. 2 (try to do sth) aspire, attempt, endeavor, hope, intend, resolve, seek, set your sights on, strive
> **aim** n (purpose) ambition, aspiration, desire, dream, end, focus, goal, hope, intention, objective, plan, target, wish

**air** n gas around earth 2 manner 3 tune; pl **airs** affected manner; v **air** 1 ventilate 2 dry 3 make known (one's views)

**air-condition** v treat air to ensure purity and even temperature; n **-ing**

**aircraft** n any kind of flying machine

**airfield** n place where aircraft land or take off

**airlift** n transport of people or supplies to or from a place of difficult access

**airline** n company operating aircraft; **airliner** passenger aircraft

**airmail** n mail carried by aircraft

**airplane** n **aircraft**

**airport** n place from where aircraft operate

**airspace** n atmosphere above a country, regarded as its legal property

**airtight** adj impermeable to air

**airworthy** adj fit or safe to fly

**aisle** n passageway between seats

**ajar** adj partly open

**akin** adj 1 related by blood 2 similar

**alacrity** n speed; briskness; eagerness

**alarm** n 1 fear 2 warning of danger; v fill with fear; n **alarmist**

> **alarm** n 1 (fear) anxiety, apprehension, consternation, fright, horror, nervousness, panic, shock, terror, worry. 2 (warning of danger) bell, distress signal, flare, siren
> **alarm** v dismay, distress, frighten, make sb nervous, panic, perturb, scare, shake, shock, terrify, trouble, unnerve, worry

**alarming** adj very worrying

> **alarming** adj, daunting, distressing, disturbing, dreadful, frightening, scary, shocking, startling, ominous, terrifying

**alas** interj expressing dismay or grief

**album** n 1 book of blank pages for stamps, photographs, etc 2 long-playing record with several tracks

**alchemy** n medieval chemistry

**alcohol** n intoxicating liquor; adj **alcoholic**; ns **alcoholism, alcoholic**

**alcove** *n* recess in room or garden

**ale** *n* kind of beer

**alert** *adj* **1** ready to respond **2** having a lively mind; *n* **alertness**

> **alert** *adj* **1** (ready to respond) attentive, awake, on your guard, prepared, ready, sharp-eyed, vigilant, watchful, wide-awake **2** (with a lively mind) bright, on the ball, perceptive, quick, sharp-witted

**algae** *n sing* **algae** lowly organized group of plant, as seaweed, etc

**algebra** *n* branch of mathematics using symbols for numbers and quantities

**alias** *adv* otherwise; *n* false name; *pl* **aliases**

**alibi** *n* proof of being elsewhere when crime was committed; *pl* **alibis**

**alien** *adj* **1** foreign **2** repugnant; *n*; *v* **alienate** estrange; *n* **alienation**

**align** *v* bring into line; *n* **alignment**

**alight** *a* lit; *v* dismount; come to rest

**alike** *adj* similar; *adv* to same degree

> **alike** *adj* comparable, duplicate, equivalent, identical, parallel, resembling, uniform

**alimony** *n* allowance to spouse after legal separation

**aliment** *n* food; *adj* **alimentary** of food channel in body

**alimentary canal** *n* passage from mouth to anus along which food passes and is digested

**alive** *adj* **1** living **2** continuing **3** lively **4** aware **5** full of people or things

> **alive** *adj* **1** (living) alive and kicking, animate, breathing, in the land of the living, **2** (continuing) current, in action, in existence, in operation, ongoing. **3** (lively) active, alert, energetic, full of life, sprightly, vibrant, vigorous, vivacious **4** (aware of) alert to, conscious of, sensitive to. **5** (full of) bustling, crawling, heaving, swarming, teeming

**alkali** *n* substance neutralizing acid

**all** *adj* whole of; full number of; total; *n* everything, everyone; *adv* entirely

**all-around** *adj* with wide range of skills

**all clear** *n* **1** signal of no danger **2** permission to go ahead

**allege** *v* state or suggest; *adj* **alleged**

> **allege** *v* accuse, assert, aver, contend, claim, declare, insist, maintain, profess, say

**allegation** *n* accusation

**allegiance** *n* loyalty

**allergy** *n* abnormal sensitiveness to any substance; *adj* **allergic**

**alleviate** *v* lighten; relieve (pain)

> **alleviate** *v* allay, assuage, ease, lessen, moderate, reduce, relieve, soothe

**alley** *n* narrow passage between houses

**alliance** *n* treaty or agreement between countries or people

> **alliance** *n* affiliation, association, coalition, confederation, federation, league, pact, partnership, relationship, treaty, union

**alligator** *n* reptile of crocodile family

**allocate** *v* grant; assign (to); *n* **-ation**

> **allocate** *v* allot, dish out *inf*, distribute, dole out *inf*, earmark, give, give out, set aside, share out

**allot** *v* **-lotting, -lotted** assign as lot; *n* **allotment 1** share **2** plot of land

**allow** *v* **1** permit **2** give, grant; *n* **allowance**

> **allow** *v* **1** (permit) approve, authorize, give the go-ahead *inf*, let, sanction. **2** (give, grant) allocate, allot, assign, set aside

**alloy** *n* mixture of two or more metals

**all right** *adj* **1** safe **2** acceptable; *adv* **1** agreed **2** for certain

**A**

**allude** *v*; *phr v* **allude to** refer to
**ally** *n* person or state acting in support of
another; *pl* **allies**

> **ally** *n* accomplice, associate, collaborator,
> colleague, co-worker, friend, partner

**almighty** *adj* omnipotent
**almond** *n* kernel of fruit of almond tree
**almost** *adv* very nearly; not quite
**alms** *n* money given in charity to poor
**alone** *adj, adv* **1** apart from others **2** without
help **3** lonely

> **alone** *adj, adv* **1** (apart from others) apart,
> by yourself, detached, isolated, lone,
> separate, solitary, unaccompanied,
> unattended. **2** (without help) by yourself,
> single-handed, solo, unassisted, unaided.
> **3** (lonely) abandoned, deserted, forsaken

**along** *prep* beside whole or part of length of;
*adv* lengthwise
**aloof** *adj* haughty
**aloud** *adv* in an audible voice; loudly
**alphabet** *n* **1** set of letters used in written
language **2** the ABC; *adj* **alphabetical**
**alpine** *adj* of the mountains, *esp* the Alps
**already** *adv* before this; by this time
**also** *adv, conj* besides; in addition; as well
**altar** *n* **1** Communion table **2** slab used for
sacrifices
**alter** *v* change; *adj* **alterable**; *n* **-ation**

> **alter** *v* adapt, adjust, amend, convert, do
> sth differently, make sth different,
> modify, remodel, reshape, revise,
> transform, vary

**alternate** *v* occur by turns; *adj* **alternate**
every second; *adv* **-ly**
**alternative** *n* other possible (choice)
**alternative medicine** *n* forms of treatment
offered instead of conventional medicine
**although** *conj* even though
**altitude** *n* height above sea level

**altogether** *adv* completely; wholly; in the
main
**altruism** *n* unselfishness; *adj* **altruistic**
**aluminum** *n* very light white metal
**always** *adv* **1** every time **2** continually
**3** forever

> **always** *adv* **1** (every time) consistently,
> invariably, without exception, without fail.
> **2** (continually) constantly, incessantly,
> interminably, perpetually, repeatedly.
> **3** (forever) eternally, endlessly, more

**amalgamate** *v* join, unite; *n* **amalgamation**

> **amalgamate** *v* combine, fuse, incorporate,
> integrate, link, merge, mix, unify,

**amass** *v* heap together; pile up
**amateur** *n* *Fr* person following pursuit
for love of it, not to make money;
*adj* **amateurish** not well done
**amaze** *v* surprise; *n* **amazement**

> **amaze** *v* astonish, astound, bowl sb over,
> dumbfound, leave sb speechless, shock,
> stagger, stun, take sb's breath away

**amazed** *adj* surprised, astounded

> **amazed** *adj* astonished, dumbfounded, *inf*,
> left speechless, shocked, staggered,
> stunned, thunderstruck

**amazing** *adj* **1** very good **2** surprising

> **amazing** *adj* **1** (very good) brilliant,
> excellent, fabulous, fantastic, great,
> incredible, marvelous, tremendous,
> wonderful. **2** (surprising) astonishing,
> astounding, shocking, staggering

**ambassador** *n* diplomat representing his
country at foreign court
**ambidextrous** *adj* able to use both hands
equally

**ambient** *adj* entirely surrounding
**ambiguous** *adj* not clear in meaning; *adv* **-ly**;
*n* **ambiguity**

> **ambiguous** *adj* cryptic, double-edged,
> enigmatic, equivocal, obscure, puzzling,
> unclear, vague, with a double meaning

**ambition** *n* strong desire for success
**ambitious** *adj* keen to succeed

> **ambitious** *adj* determined, eager,
> enterprising, go-ahead, keen, motivated

**ambivalent** *adj* undecided; unclear
**amble** *v* move at easy pace
**ambulance** *n* vehicle for carrying sick and
wounded
**ambush** *n* surprise attack; *v* waylay
**amen** *interj* 'So be it'; *n* word of assent
**amenable** *adj* tractable; submissive
**amend** *v* improve; correct
**amendment** *n* change, correction

> **amendment** *n* addendum, adjustment,
> alteration, improvement, modification,
> revision

**amenity** *n* desirable feature
**amiable** *adj* kindly; lovable; *adv* **-bly**

> **amiable** *adj* affable, agreeable, approachable,
> endearing, engaging, friendly, genial, good-
> natured, likeable, pleasant, sociable

**amicable** *adj* friendly; *adv* **-ably**

> **amicable** *adj* amiable, civil, cordial,
> courteous, good-humored, good-natured,
> peaceable

**amid** *prep* in middle of; among
**amiss** *adv* wrongly; *adj* faulty
**ammonia** *n* pungent, colorless gas
**ammunition** *n* bullets, shells, etc
**amnesia** *n* loss of memory

**amnesty** *n* pardon given to offenders against
State
**amok, amuck** *adj* in a frenzy
**among** *prep* in midst of; by mutual action of
**amoral** *adj* without morals; *n* **amorality**
**amorous** *adj* prone to love

> **amorous** *adj* adoring, ardent, doting,
> enamored, erotic, in love, lecherous,
> lovesick, loving, lustful, passionate, sexy

**amount** *n* sum total; quantity; *phr v* **amount
to** add up to
**amp** *abbr* ampere
**ampere** *n* electric unit of force
**amphetamine** *n* stimulant drug
**amphibian** *n* animal or vehicle able to
live or operate on land and in water;
*adj* **amphibious**
**ample** *adj* **1** adequate **2** plentiful **3** large

> **ample** *adj* **1** (adequate) enough, more than
> enough, plenty, sufficient. **2** (plentiful)
> abundant, generous, lavish. **3** (large) big,
> expansive, full, roomy, spacious,
> substantial, voluminous

**amplify** *v* **-fying, -fied** make louder;
*n* **amplifier, amplification**
**amputate** *v* cut off part of body
**amuse** *v* **1** provoke amusement or mirth
**2** entertain; *n* **-ment**

> **amuse** *v* **1** (provoke mirth) entertain,
> make sb laugh, make sb smile, regale sb
> with. **2** (entertain) keep sb happy, occupy

**amusing** *adj* funny; provoking mirth

> **amusing** *adj* comical, droll, hilarious,
> humorous, ludicrous, ridiculous, witty

**anachronism** *n* thing or event placed in the
wrong context of time
**anagram** *n* word made by rearranging letters
in another word

a
b
c
d
e
f
g
h
i
j
k
l
m
n
o
p
q
r
s
t
u
v
w
x
y
z

**analogy** *n* similarity; *adj* **analogous**
**analyze** *v* examine carefully; *adj* **analytical**
(*adv* **-ly**); *n* **analysis, analyst**

> **analyze** *v* evaluate, examine, investigate,
> study, test, work out

**anarchy** *n* no supreme power in State;
lawlessness; *n* **anarchism** practice of
anarchy; *n* **anarchist**
**anathema** *n* curse; hateful thing; *v* **-ematize**
**anatomy** *n* science of structure of body;
*adj* **anatomical; n anatomist**
**ancestor** *n* forebear; *adj* **ancestral**;
*n* **ancestry** lineage

> **ancestor** *n* family, forefather, previous
> generation

**anchor** *n* mass of iron, securing ships to sea-
bed; *v* fasten by anchor
**anchovy** *n* type of small fish
**ancient** *adj* 1 very old 2 old-fashioned
3 belonging to distant past

> **ancient** *adj* 1 (very old) aged, ageing,
> antiquated, elderly. 2 (old-fashioned)
> antiquated, archaic, behind the times,
> dated, obsolete, outmoded, out-of-date
> 3 (belonging to distant past) early, pre-
> historic, primeval, primitive, primordial

**ancillary** *adj* subordinate; auxiliary
**and** *conj* also; as well as
**anecdote** *n* trivial story of isolated event;
*adj* **anecdotal**

> **anecdote** *n* account, cautionary tale,
> reminiscence, story, tale

**anemia** *n* lack of red corpuscles in blood;
*adj* **anemic**
**anemone** *n* wind-flower; **sea-anemone** small
sea creature
**anesthetic** *n* drug causing loss of sensation;
*n* **anesthetist** one who gives anesthetic

**anew** *adv* again; afresh
**angel** *n* celestial being; old gold coin;
*adj* **angelic**
**anger** *n* rage; *v* provoke to anger

> **anger** *n* annoyance, exasperation,
> displeasure, fury, irritation, outrage

**angina** *n* heart spasm
**angle** space between two lines that meet;
corner; *adj* **angular**
**angling** *n* fishing
**Anglican** *adj* member of the Church of
England
**anglicize** *v* give English form to (a foreign
word)
**angry** *adj* 1 full of anger 2 (of a wound or
rash) inflamed; *adv* **angrily**

> **angry** *adj* (full of anger) annoyed, cross,
> mad, fuming, furious, heated, hopping
> mad, hot under the collar, incensed,
> infuriated, irate, irritated, mad, outraged

**angst** *n* state of acute anxiety; anguish
**anguish** *n* acute pain of body or mind

> **anguish** *n* agony, angst, distress, grief,
> heartbreak, misery, pain, sorrow,
> suffering, torment, trauma

**angular** *adj* 1 with sharp corners 2 not
vertical or horizontal; slanting
**animal** *n* living creature
**animate** *v* give life to; *adj* living;
*adj* **animated**

> **animated** *adj* enthusiastic, excited, lively,
> passionate, vehement, vigorous

**animosity** *n* enmity; hatred

> **animosity** *n* acrimony, antagonism, bad
> feeling, bitterness, conflict, disapproval,
> distaste, hostility, loathing, resentment

**aniseed** *n* aromatic seed used for flavoring

**ankle** *n* the joint between foot and leg

**annals** *n* yearly chronicle of events

**annex**[1] *v* join to; steal; *n* **annexation**

**annex**[2] *n* supplementary building

**annihilate** *v* destroy utterly; *n* **annihilation**

> **annihilate** *v* decimate, defeat, eradicate, exterminate, extinguish, take out, wipe out

**anniversary** *n* yearly celebration of an event

**annotate** *v* make explanatory notes on

**announce** *v* declare publicly; *n* **announcer**

> **announce** *v* give out, go public on, make known, publicize, publish, release, reveal

**announcement** *n* public declaration

> **announcement** *n* bulletin, communiqué, disclosure, notice, statement, press release, pronouncement, report, revelation

**annoy** *v* vex; irritate

> **annoy** *v* aggravate, anger, bother, exasperate, get on sb's nerves, infuriate, madden, make sb mad, pester

**annoyed** *adj* angry

> **annoyed** *adj* cross, exasperated, fuming, furious, hot under the collar, incensed, irate, irritated, mad, outraged

**annoying** *adj* provoking anger

> **annoying** *adj* aggravating, exasperating, infuriating, irritating, maddening, tiresome

**annual** *adj* yearly; *n* plant living for year only; yearly publication of book; *adv* **annually**

**anomaly** *n* irregularity; *adj* **anomalous**

**anon** *adv abbr* soon; presently

**anonymous** *adj* not named; *adv* **-ly**; *abbr* **anon**; *n* **anonymity**

**anorexia** *n* medical condition characterized by complete loss of appetite; *adj* **anorexic**

**another** *adj* 1 additional 2 different; *pron* one more

**answer** *v* 1 give a reply to 2 solve; *n* 1 reply 2 solution; *adj* **answerable** responsible

> **answer** *v* 1 (give a reply) acknowledge, react to, respond to, retort. 2 (solve) find a solution to, resolve. 3 (satisfy a need) fit the bill, fulfill, meet, suit

**answering machine** *n* machine for taking telephone messages

**ant** *n* industrious small insect

**antagonist** *n* adversary; opponent; *v* **antagonize** render hostile; *n* **antagonism;** *adj* **antagonistic**

> **antagonize** *v* alienate, annoy, bother, estrange, infuriate, irritate, offend, pester, rub sb up the wrong way

**antarctic** *adj* of region near S Pole

**antelope** *n* deerlike animal

**antenatal** *adj* occurring before birth

**antenna** *n* 1 feeler of insect 2 radio aerial; *pl* **antennae**

**anthem** *n* sacred words set to music

**anthology** *n* collection of poems, stories, etc

> **anthology** *n* collected works, collection, compendium, compilation, selection

**anthropology** *n* science of man; *adj* **anthropological**; *n* **anthropologist**

**anti-** *prefix* Gk against

**antiballistic** *adj* against missiles

**antibiotic** *adj* destroying growth, *esp* of bacteria; *n* such a substance

**antibody** *n* natural antidote to infection produced in blood

**antic** *n* playful, comic gesture *pl* **-s** playful or ridiculous behavior

**anticipate** *v* take action in advance; *n* **anticipation**; *adj* **anticipatory**

**anticipate** *v* assume, count on, expect, forecast, foresee, look forward to, predict

**anticlimax** *n* disappointing turn to an exciting situation; *adj* **anticlimactic**

**anticlimax** *n* comedown, failure, flop, disappointment, letdown, wash-out *inf*

**anticyclone** *n* state of high atmospheric pressure, tending to produce fine weather; *adj* **anticyclonic**

**antidote** *n* chemical that counteracts effects of poison

**antidote** *n* antitoxin, cure, remedy

**antifreeze** *n* chemical added to water to prevent it freezing in winter

**antihistamine** *n* type of drug used to treat allergies

**antipasto** *n* Italian appetizers

**antiperspirant** *n* substance applied to the body to prevent sweating

**antiquated** *adj* old-fashioned

**antiquated** *adj* ancient, archaic, dated, obsolete, out-of-date, outmoded, passé

**antique** *adj* old; *n* relic of past age; *n* **antiquity** remote past; **antiquities** ancient museum pieces

**anti-Semite** *n* hater of Jews; *n* **anti-Semitism**

**antiseptic** *n* substance for preventing infection; *n* **antisepsis** method of preventing infection

**antisocial** *adj* 1 avoiding the company of others 2 unpleasant or aggressive

**antisocial** *n* 1 (avoiding company) cold, standoffish, unapproachable, unfriendly, unsociable, withdrawn. 2 (unpleasant or aggressive) offensive, unacceptable

**antler** *n* a branched horn of deer

**anus** *n* opening at lower end of alimentary canal

**anvil** *n* iron block on which blacksmith works

**anxious** *adj* 1 worried 2 eager to do (something); *adv* **-ly**; *n* **anxiety**

**anxious** *adj* apprehensive, bothered, concerned, nervous, on tenterhooks, stressed-out, tense, uneasy

**any** *adj, pron* some; every; *prons* **anybody, anyone, anyway, anywhere**

**apart** *a, adv* separate; separately

**apartheid** *n* segregation of races practised in S Africa 1948–1992

**apartment** *n* room; set of rooms, *usu* leased

**apartment** *n* living quarters, penthouse, pied-à-terre, rooms, studio flat

**apathy** *n* indifference

**apathetic** *adj* indifferent

**apathetic** *adj* lazy, lethargic, listless, uninterested

**ape** *n* monkey, *esp* tailless kind

**aperitif** *n* drink taken as an appetizer

**aperture** *n* hole; opening

**apex** *n* tip; top; peak; *pl* **apexes, apices**

**aphid** *n* small insect such as a whitefly that feeds on sap of plants

**aphrodisiac** *n* drug exciting sexual desire

**aplomb** *n* self-possession

**apocryphal** *adj* not genuine; fictitious

**apologetic** *adj* expressing regret

**apologetic** *adj* contrite, repentant, sorry

**apologize** *v* express regret

**apologize** *v* eat humble pie *inf*, eat your words, grovel *inf*, make an apology, say sorry, take back what you said

**apology** n expression of regret

**apostle** n one sent out to preach; reformer; adj **apostolic**

**apostrophe** n a mark (') showing omission of letter(s) or the possessive form

**appall** v **-palling, -palled** horrify

> **appall** v disgust, dismay, outrage, shock

**appalling** adj horrifying

> **appalling** adj atrocious, awful, dreadful, foul, ghastly, grim, horrendous, horrific, outrageous, shocking, terrible

**apparatus** n equipment

**apparent** adj visible; adv **apparently** seemingly

**apparition** n supernatural visual impression

**appeal** v 1 ask earnestly 2 seem attractive; n act of appealing; adj **appealing** attractive

> **appeal** v 1 (ask earnestly) ask for, beg for, call for, implore, petition for, put in a request for. 2 (seem attractive) attract, draw, fascinate, interest, please, tempt

**appear** v 1 become visible 2 seem 3 perform in a play or film

> **appear** v 1 (become visible) arrive, come into view, come out, come to light, crop up, emerge, materialize, pop up, show up, turn up. 2 (seem) look like. 3 (perform) play, star, take part

**appearance** n 1 becoming visible 2 outward impression

> **appearance** n 1 (becoming visible) arrival, emergence, materialization. 2 (outward impression) air, aspect, demeanor, dress, expression, impression, look

**appease** v soothe; pacify; satisfy; n **appeasement**

**append** v add; attach; n **appendage**

**appendicitis** n inflammation of appendix

**appendix** n **appendixes, appendices** addition to book; anat small tube attached to intestine

**appertain** v be appropriate or relate (to)

**appetite** n enjoyment of food; desire; n **appetizer** anything giving relish for a meal; adj **appetizing**

> **appetite** n craving, hunger, keenness, relish, stomach, will

**applaud** v express approval by clapping hands; n **applause**

> **applaud** v clap, bring the house down, give a standing ovation to, give sb a big hand, put your hands together for, raise the roof

**apple** n firm, fleshy fruit with seeds

**appliance** n device; gadget; machine

**apply** v **-plying, -plied** 1 be relevant 2 use 3 put on; phr vs **apply for** request; n **application** act of applying; close attention; **applicant** person applying; adj **applicable** relevant, suitable

> **apply** v 1 (be relevant) be appropriate, be valid, concern, involve, pertain, relate. 2 (use) carry out, employ, implement, make use of, put into practice, utilize. 3 (put on) cover with, rub in, spread on

**appoint** v select for office; n **-ment** 1 arrangement to meet 2 job

> **appointment** n 1 (arrangement to meet) date, engagement, meeting, rendezvous. 2 (job) position, post, role, situation

**apportion** v share out; allot; n **-ment**

**appraise** v assess; n **appraisal**

**appreciate** v 1 be grateful 2 estimate highly 3 realize; n **-ation**; adj **-iative** grateful (adv **-ly**); adj **appreciable** noticeable

**A**

B C D E F G H I J K L M N O P Q R S T U V W X Y Z

**appreciate** *v* 1 (be grateful) be appreciative of, be thankful for, value. 2 (estimate highly) like, prize, rate, respect, think a lot of, value. 3 (realize) accept, be aware of, be conscious of, recognize, understand

**apprehend** *v* 1 arrest 2 understand
**apprehension** *n* 1 fear 2 arrest

**apprehension** *n* 1 (fear) alarm, anxiety, concern, nervousness, unease, worry. 2 (arrest) capture, detention, seizure

**apprehensive** *v* fearful

**apprehensive** *adj* afraid, alarmed, anxious, concerned, frightened, mistrustful, nervous, scared, uneasy, worried

**apprentice** *n* one learning a trade
**approach** *v* 1 come near 2 talk to 3 ask sb for sth 4 deal with a task; *n* drawing near

**approach** *v* 1 (come near) advance, arrive, catch up, come close, draw near, gain on, go toward, meet, move toward, near, reach. 2 (talk to) address, greet, hail. 3 (ask sb for sth) appeal, apply, ask, broach the matter with, make a proposal, proposition, solicit, sound out. 4 (deal with a task) commence, embark on, make a start on, set about, tackle, undertake

**approachable** *adj* willing to be consulted

**approachable** *adj* accessible, affable, amicable, easygoing, friendly, informal, kind, open, relaxed, sympathetic, understanding

**appropriate** *v* filch; *adj* suitable to

**appropriate** *adj* apt, correct, fitting, pertinent, proper, relevant, well-suited

**approve** *v* 1 think highly of 2 agree to; *n* **approval**; *adj* **approved, approving**

**approve** *v* 1 (think highly of) acclaim, admire, applaud, appreciate, commend, esteem, favor, have a high regard for, like, praise, regard highly, respect, think well of. 2 (agree to) accept, authorize, consent to, endorse, give the go-ahead, give the OK to, give your backing to, go along with, pass, permit, recommend

**approximate** *adj* very near; about correct; *v* make or come close to; *n* **approximation**
**approximately** *adv* very nearly; about

**approximately** *adv* around, close to, give or take *inf*, in the region of, just about, loosely, more or less, not far off, roughly

**apricot** *n* orange-red fruit allied to peach
**April** *n* 4th month of year
**apron** *n* garment to protect clothes
**apropos** *adv* with reference to
**apt** *adj* 1 appropriate 2 skilled; *adv* **aptly**; *n* **aptness**; **aptitude** fitness; capacity

**apt** *adj* 1 (appropriate) applicable, correct, fitting, pertinent, proper, relevant, suitable, to the point. 2 (skilled) able, adept, astute, bright, clever, competent, gifted, intelligent, quick, sharp, talented

**aquarium** *n* tank where fish are kept; *pl* **aquaria, aquariums**
**aquatic** *adj* living or taking place in water
**aqueduct** *n* conduit for water; bridgelike structure supporting conduit
**Arab** *n* member of a group of people who live throughout Middle East and N Africa; *adj* **Arabian**; *n* **Arabic** language of Arabs
**Arabic numeral** *n* any of the numerals 0, 1, 2, 3, 4, 5, 6, 7, 8, 9
**arable** *adj* suitable for tilling, cultivation
**arbiter** *n* person recognized as able to make a decisive judgment

**arbitrary** *adj* based on impulse or chance

> **arbitrary** *adj* erratic, irrational, personal, random, subjective

**arbitrate** *v* make judgment or settle a dispute between others; *n* **arbitration**
**arc** *n* part of circumference of circle
**arcade** *n* passage with arched roof lined with stores
**arch** *n* curved structure acting as support; curve itself; *v* build arch over; form an arch
**arch-** *prefix* chief
**archaic** *adj* out of date; *adv* **-ally**

> **archaic** *adj* ancient, old, old-fashioned, outdated, outmoded

**archangel** *n* chief angel
**archbishop** *n* chief bishop
**archdeacon** *n* priest next below bishop in rank
**archeology** *n* study of prehistoric cultures; *adj* **-ological**; *n* **-ologist**
**archer** *n* one shooting with bow and arrows; *n* **archery**
**archetype** *n* prototype; *adj* **archetypal**
**archipelago** *n pl* **-oes** group of islands
**architecture** *n* art and science of building; *adj* **architectural** (*adv* **-ly**); *n* **architect** one who designs buildings
**archives** *n* place where records are kept; records themselves
**arctic** *adj* of region of the N Pole
**ardent** *adj* fiery; eager; *adv* **-ly**; *n* **ardour**

> **ardent** *adj* emotional, enthusiastic, fervent, intense, keen, passionate, zealous

**arduous** *adj* difficult; strenuous; *adv* **-ly**

> **arduous** *adj* back-breaking, demanding, exhausting, grueling, hard, taxing, tiring

**area** *n* **1** region **2** surface measured in sq units **3** branch of knowledge

**area** *n* **1** (region) district, environment, neighborhood, patch *inf*, quarter, sector, space, surroundings, territory, turf *sl*. **2** (measured surface) acreage, expanse, extent, measurements, size. **3** (branch of knowledge) branch, discipline, field, province, realm, sphere, world

**arena** *n* place of combat or conflict
**argue** *v* **1** dispute **2** debate **3** assert

> **argue** *v* **1** (dispute) be at each other's throats, bicker, clash, disagree, fall out, feud, fight, pick a fight, quarrel, row, squabble, wrangle. **2** (debate) discuss, dispute, reason, remonstrate. **3** (assert) claim, insist, put forward, say, state, suggest

**argument** *n* **1** dispute **2** assertion

> **argument** *n* **1** (dispute) clash, controversy, difference of opinion, disagreement, discussion, fight, quarrel, row, showdown, squabble, tiff. **2** (assertion) case, claim, contention, hypothesis, idea, plea, proposition, reasoning, statement, view

**arid** *adj* completely dry
**arise** *v* **arising, arose, arisen** happen

> **arise** *v* appear, begin, come to light, crop up *inf*, emerge, occur, originate

**aristocracy** *n* ruling class; nobility
**aristocratic** *adj* of the ruling class

> **aristocratic** *adj* blue-blooded, elite, noble, privileged, upper-class, titled, well-born

**arithmetic** *n* science of numbers; *n* **arithmetician;** *adj* **arithmetical**
**ark** *n* flat-bottomed boat
**arm**[1] *n* **1** upper limb of human body **2** anything extending from main body (arm of tree, chair, etc)

**A**

**arm**[2] n weapon; branch of military forces;
v supply with weapons

**armada** n fleet of warships, *esp* Spanish

**armadillo** n S American burrowing mammal

**armaments** n pl war equipment

**armchair** n chair with armrests

**armistice** n truce pending a formal peace
treaty

**armor** n protective covering for the body in
battle; protective plating of ship or vehicle

**armored** adj protected by armor

---

**armored** adj armor-plated, bombproof,
bulletproof, fortified, protected,
strengthened

---

**armpit** n hollow under the arm below the
shoulder

**arms** n pl 1 weapons 2 coat of arms

---

**arms** n 1 (weapons) armaments, firearms,
guns, ordnance, weaponry. 2 (coat of
arms) crest, emblem, insignia, shield

---

**army** n 1 military force that operates on land
2 large group of people or animals

**aroma** n pleasant smell; adj **aromatic** fragrant

**aromatherapy** n the use of scented oils in
massage; n **aromatherapist**

**arose** pt of **arise**

**around** prep 1 in a circle round 2 at or to
various places within 3 (at) approximately,
about; adv 1 here and there 2 somewhere
nearby 3 turning in a circle 4 on all sides

**arouse** v 1 awaken 2 stimulate; excite

**arrange** v 1 put in order 2 agree 3 adapt
(novel, music)

---

**arrange** v 1 (put in order) align, grade,
group, lay out, line up, order, organize,
rank, set out, sort, tidy. 2 (agree) decide,
fix up, make an appointment, organize,
pencil in, plan, schedule, settle on

---

**arrangement** n 1 way of ordering
2 agreement 3 adaptation

**arrangement** n 1 (way of ordering)
alignment, classification, design, display,
formation, grouping, layout, organization,
pattern, ranking, set-up, structure, system.
2 (agreement) appointment, date, plan

---

**array** n impressive display

**arrears** n debt not paid

**arrest** v 1 seize by legal authority 2 gain
(attention) 3 stop; adj **arresting** striking;
n **arrest**

**arrive** v reach destination; n **arrival**

---

**arrive** v appear, come, come along, come
on the scene, enter, make an entrance,
put in an appearance, show up, turn up

---

**arrogant** adj haughty; proud; n **arrogance**

---

**arrogant** adj big-headed, boastful, brash,
cocky, conceited, egotistical, high-and-
mighty, overbearing, patronizing,
pompous, self-important, smug, superior,
supercilious, vain

---

**arrow** n feathered rod with sharp point shot
from bow

**arsenal** n place where weapons and
ammunition are made or stored

**arsenic** n metallic poison

**arson** n deliberate setting on fire of property

**art** n 1 creative skill and its application 2 craft
or trade; pl humanities as opposed to sciences

**arteriosclerosis** n disease where hardening of
the walls of the arteries impedes circulation
of the blood

**artery** n blood vessel conveying blood from
the heart; adj **arterial**

**artful** adj cunning; crafty

**arthritis** n painful inflammation of joints;
adj **arthritic**

**artichoke** n plant with edible roots or flower
base

**article** n 1 item; object 2 short piece of
writing 3 words *the, a, an*

**article** n 1 (item) artifact, object, piece, thing. 2 (piece of writing) account, essay, feature, item, piece, report, story, write up

**articulate** adj 1 able to express ideas clearly 2 clearly expressed; v 1 join 2 utter distinctly; adv **-ly**; n **articulateness** ability to communicate

**articulate** adj 1 (able to express ideas) eloquent, expressive, fluent, lucid, silver-tongued. 2 (clearly expressed) clear, coherent, comprehensible, eloquent, fluent, intelligible, lucid, understandable

**artifact** n any object made by human skill
**artifice** n ingenuity; trickery
**artificial** adj 1 not natural 2 not real 3 not genuine

**artificial** adj 1 (not natural) man-made, manufactured, synthetic. 2 (not real) bogus, counterfeit, ersatz, fake, false, imitation, mock, phony, pseudo-, sham, simulated. 3 (not genuine) affected, assumed, fake, false, feigned, forced, insincere, put on, unnatural, unreal

**artillery** n guns; branch of army which uses heavy guns
**artist** n 1 person who practices any fine art, esp painting 2 very skillful worker or performer; adj **artistic**
**artiste** n professional entertainer
**artistic** adj 1 good at art, esp painting 2 attractive to look at

**artistic** adj 1 (good at art) accomplished, creative, cultured, gifted, talented. 2 (attractive) beautiful, decorative, elegant, exquisite, graceful, ornamental, stylish, tasteful

**as** adv, conj 1 when 2 because 3 equally, in the capacity of 4 like

**asbestos** n fireproof mineral substance
**ascend** v go; rise to higher rank; climb; n **ascent**

**ascend** v climb up, float up, fly up, gain height, move up, scale, soar, take off

**ascertain** v 1 find out 2 get to know for certain

**ascertain** v 1 (find out) determine, discover, establish, ferret out inf, learn. 2 (get to know for certain) confirm, establish, identify, make sure, settle, verify

**ascetic** adj self-denying; austere
**ascorbic acid** n vitamin C
**ascribe** v attribute (to)
**asexual** adj 1 without sex 2 having no interest in sex
**ash** n gray powdery residue of anything burnt; pl **ashes** cremated human remains
**ashamed** adj troubled by sense of guilt or shame

**ashamed** adj apologetic, chastened, conscience-stricken, contrite, embarrassed, guilty, mortified, red-faced, remorseful, repentant, shamefaced, sheepish, sorry

**ashore** adj, adv on shore; to shore
**Asian** adj, n native of Asia; adj **Asiatic**
**aside** adv on, to, or at one side; apart; n phrase spoken in an undertone
**ask** v 1 seek an answer to 2 request information from 3 request sth 2 invite

**ask** v 1 (seek an answer to) enquire, make inquiries, query, question. 2 (request information from) fire questions at, give sb the third degree, grill, interrogate, interview, pick sb's brains, question, quiz. 3 (request sth) appeal, apply, beg, call upon, claim, demand, petition, plead, pray, seek, solicit. 4 (invite) summon

a
b
c
d
e
f
g
h
i
j
k
l
m
n
o
p
q
r
s
t
u
v
w
x
y
z

**askew** *adj*, *adv* sideways
**asleep** *adv*, *adj* into or in a state of sleep

> **asleep** *adj* catnapping, comatose, dormant, dozing, having a nap, hibernating, resting, sleeping, slumbering, snoozing

**asparagus** *n* plant whose shoots are eaten as vegetable
**aspect** *n* view; look
**aspersion** *n* derogatory remark
**asphalt** *n* bituminous substance for surfacing roads
**asphyxiate** *v* cause or undergo suffocation; *n* **asphyxia, asphyxiation**
**aspiration** *n* strong desire
**aspire** *v* seek eagerly; *adj* **aspiring**

> **aspire** *v* aim, be ambitious, desire, dream of, hanker after, hope, pursue, seek, set your sights on, wish, yearn

**aspirin** *n* drug used for relief of pain
**ass** *n* 1 member of horse family 2 stupid person
**assail** *v* attack; *n* **assailant**
**assassin** *n* political murderer

> **assassin** *n* contract killer, executioner, hit man *inf*, killer, murderer, slayer

**assassinate** *v* murder

> **assassinate** *v* eliminate, execute, hit *sl*, kill, liquidate, slay

**assault** *n* sudden attack; *v* make an assault

> **assault** *v* 1 (a place) assail, attack, invade, storm. 2 (a person) attack, do over, fly at, hit, lay into, set about, set upon

**assemble** *v* 1 come together 2 collect together 3 fit parts together; *n* **assembly** 1 gathering of persons 2 collection of parts

**assemble** *v* 1 (come together) congregate, convene, flock, gather, get together, meet, rally. 2 (collect together) amass, gather. 3 (fit parts together) build, connect, construct, erect, join, make

**assembly line** *n* sequence of machines and workers for assembling parts in a factory
**assent** *v* agree; *n* agreement
**assert** *v* state strongly; *n* **assertion**

> **assert** *v* affirm, allege, announce, argue, claim, contend, declare, insist, maintain, profess, say, state, stress

**assertive** *adj* 1 confident 2 aggressive; *adv* **-ly**

> **assertive** *adj* 1 (confident) decided, firm, insistent, positive, strong-willed. 2 (aggressive) dogmatic, domineering

**assess** *v* estimate; *n* **assessment, assessor**

> **assess** *v* appraise, calculate, determine, evaluate, gauge, judge, rate, size up, value

**asset** *n* thing of value

> **asset** *n* advantage, benefit, blessing, boon, help, resource, support

**assets** *n* all property, etc owned

> **assets** *n* capital, estate, funds, goods, means, money, possessions, property, reserves, resources, wealth

**assign** *v* make over; allot; *n* **assignment** allotted task; **assignation** secret meeting
**assimilate** *v* 1 absorb 2 fit in; *n* **assimilation**
**assist** *v* help; *n* **assistance**

> **assist** *v* aid, collaborate, cooperate with, lend a hand, rally round, support

**assistant** *n* 1 helper 2 subordinate

> **assistant** *n* 1 (helper) accessory, accomplice, ally, associate, collaborator, colleague, comrade, partner. 2 (subordinate) aide, auxiliary, deputy, helper, henchman, mate, right-hand man, second in command

**assize** *n* judicial inquest

**associate** *v* join; connect; combine; *n* partner; member of a society; *adj* linked in function

**association** *n* union of persons for common purposes

> **association** *n* alliance, band, body, club, coalition, company, confederation, corporation, federation, group, league, order, partnership, society, syndicate

**assonance** *n* rhythm of vowel sounds

**assorted** *adj* of mixed kinds

> **assorted** *adj* different, diverse, heterogeneous, miscellaneous, mixed, motley, multifarious, sundry, varied, various

**assortment** *n* mixture

> **assortment** *n* choice, collection, jumble, mixed bag, range, selection, variety

**assuage** *v* soothe; quench; *n* **-ment**
**assume** *v* 1 believe 2 take upon oneself

> **assume** *v* 1 (believe) deduce, expect, guess, imagine, infer, presume, presuppose, reckon, surmise, suspect, think, understand. 2 (take upon oneself) accept, shoulder, undertake

**assure** *v* state positively; *adj* **assured** confident; *n* **assurance** pledge

> **assure** *v* convince, guarantee, persuade, promise, reassure, soothe, swear, vow

**asterisk** *n* symbol (*) used by printers
**asteroid** *n* small planet; *adj* star-shaped
**asthma** *n* chronic condition of the lungs
**astonish** *v* fill with wonder; *n* **astonishment**

> **astonish** *v* amaze, astound, bewilder, daze, dazzle, shock, stagger, stun, surprise, take your breath away

**astonished** *adj* very surprised

> **astonished** *adj* amazed, astounded, dumbfounded, shocked, speechless, staggered, taken aback

**astonishing** *adj* very surprising

> **astonishing** *adj* amazing, astounding, bewildering, mind-boggling *inf*, shocking, striking, stunning

**astound** *v* fill with amazement
**astounding** *adj* amazing

> **astounding** *adj* astonishing, bewildering, impressive, staggering, striking, surprising

**astray** *adj*, *adv* off right path
**astride** *adv* with one leg on each side
**astro-** *prefix* of the stars and outer space
**astrology** *n* prediction of events by stars; *n* **astrologer**; *adj* **astrological**
**astronaut** *n* traveler in space
**astronomy** *n* science of heavenly bodies; *n* **astronomer;** *adj* **astronomical** 1 of astronomy 2 unusually large in number or quantity
**astrophysics** *n* study of physics and chemistry of stars
**astute** *adj* shrewd

> **astute** *adj* artful, calculating, clever, crafty, cunning, discerning, knowing, perceptive, sharp, wily

**asylum** *n* sanctuary; place for care of insane

a
b
c
d
e
f
g
h
i
j
k
l
m
n
o
p
q
r
s
t
u
v
w
x
y
z

**A**

B
C
D
E
F
G
H
I
J
K
L
M
N
O
P
Q
R
S
T
U
V
W
X
Y
Z

**at** *prep* expressing general position
**ate** *pt of* **eat**
**atheism** *n* belief that there is no God;
  *n* **atheist**
**athlete** *n* one skilled in physical exercises;
  *n* **athletics**
**athletic** *adj* skilled in physical exercises

> **athletic** *adj* active, brawny, energetic, fit,
> muscular, powerful, robust, sporty,
> strapping, strong, well-built

**atlas** *n* book of maps
**atmosphere** *n* 1 air surrounding earth
  2 general mood; *adj* **atmospheric**

> **atmosphere** *n* 1 (around the earth) air,
> ionosphere, sky, stratosphere. 2 (general
> mood) air, ambience, character, climate,
> feel, feeling, mood, quality, spirit, tone,
> vibes *inf*

**atom** *n* smallest particle of an element
**atomizer** *n* device for changing liquids into
  fine spray
**atomic** *adj* pertaining to atoms. *Hence:*
  **a. bomb; a. energy; a. reactor;**
  **a. warfare; a. weight**
**atop** *adv, prep* at the top (of)
**atrocious** *adj* awful

> **atrocious** *adj* abominable, appalling, bad,
> dreadful, ghastly, grim, horrendous *inf*,
> horrific, unspeakable

**atrocity** *n* brutal deed

> **atrocity** *n* abomination, barbarity, brutality,
> crime against humanity, killing, massacre,
> outrage, slaughter, war crime

**attach** *v* fasten; *n* **attachment**

> **attach** *v* add, add on, affix, append, connect,
> fit, join, link, pin, secure, stick, tie

**attack** *v* assault; assail; *n* **attack** assault;
  **attacker**

> **attack** *v* 1 (a place) invade, raid, storm.
> 2 (a person) assail, assault, beat, beat up,
> lay into, mug, rape
> **attack** *n* 1 (against place) act of aggression,
> assault, incursion, invasion, onslaught,
> raid, storming. 2 (against person) assault,
> beating, mugging, rape

**attain** *v* achieve; *adj* **attainable**

> **attain** *v* accomplish, acquire, arrive at,
> earn, fulfill, gain, get, obtain, reach,
> realize, secure, win

**attempt** *v* try; *n* an effort, try

> **attempt** *v* aim, do your best, endeavor,
> have a bash at, have a go at, make an
> effort, strive, venture
> **attempt** *n* crack, effort, endeavor, go, shot,
> stab

**attend** *v* 1 give heed (to) 2 be present
  3 escort; *n* **attendance** 1 act of being
  present 2 those present; *adj, n* **attendant,**
  **attention**
**attentive** *adj* paying attention

> **attentive** *adj* alert, awake, aware, listening,
> looking, mindful, observant, on guard, on
> the lookout, vigilant, watchful, watching,
> wide awake

**attest** *v* testify; *n* **attestation**
**attic** *n* small room under roof of house
**attire** *n* dress; clothing
**attitude** *n* 1 mental approach 2 posture

> **attitude** *n* 1 (mental approach) approach,
> disposition, feeling, opinion, outlook.
> 2 (posture) pose, position

**attorney** *n* lawyer

**attract** *v* draw towards; *n* **attraction**
**attractive** *adj* pleasant; agreeable

> **attract** *v* allure, captivate, charm, draw, enchant, entice, fascinate, interest, intrigue, pull, tempt

> **attractive** *adj* **1** (of person) alluring, beautiful, captivating, enchanting, good-looking, gorgeous, handsome, lovely, pretty, sexy, striking, stunning. **2** (of things) appealing, charming, engaging, fascinating, interesting, inviting, pleasing, tempting

**attribute** *n* characteristic quality of thing or person; *v* ascribe (to)
**au pair** *n* Fr young person, *usu* foreign, living and helping in a family home
**aubergine** *adj* dark purple color
**auburn** *adj* reddish- or golden-brown
**auction** *n* public sale in which articles are sold to highest bidder; *v* sell by auction
**audacious** *adj* bold; *n* **audacity**

> **audacious** *adj* adventurous, brave, cheeky, intrepid, reckless

**audible** *adj* able to be heard; *adv* **audibly**
**audience** *n* **1** group of people present or looking on **2** formal meeting

> **audience** *n* **1** (group of people) assembly, congregation, crowd, fans, listeners, public, spectators, turnout, viewers. **2** (meeting) consultation, reception, hearing, interview

**audio** *adj* of sound signals
**audio-** *prefix* of, for, or using sound
**audit** *v* official scrutinizing of accounts
**audition** *n* test for singer, actor, etc; *v* conduct such a test
**auditorium** *n pl* **-ums, -ia** building in which an audience gathers
**auditory** *adj* of the sense of hearing

**augment** *v* cause to increase
**August** *n* the eighth month of the year
**aunt** *n* mother's or father's sister; uncle's wife
**aural** *adj* of the ear; *adv* **aurally**
**auspices** *n*, *pl* patronage
**auspicious** *adj* favorable

> **auspicious** *adj* bright, encouraging, hopeful, opportune, promising, propitious, timely

**austere** *adj* **1** harsh **2** avoiding pleasure

> **austere** *adj* **1** (harsh) hard, plain, Spartan. **2** (avoiding pleasure) abstemious, ascetic, frugal, puritan, sober, solemn, stern, strict

**austerity** *n* hardship

> **austerity** *n* belt-tightening, frugality, poverty, recession

**authentic** *adj* genuine; reliable; *n* **authenticity**

> **authentic** *adj* authenticated, bona fide, kosher, real, true

**author** *n* writer
**authoritarian** *n*, *adj* (person) expecting complete obedience from others

> **authoritarian** *adj* autocratic, despotic, dictatorial, disciplinarian, strict, totalitarian, tyrannical, undemocratic

**authority** *n* **1** power to command **2** right to do sth **3** controlling body **4** one with special knowledge

> **authority** *n* **1** (power to command) control, charge, influence, jurisdiction, prerogative, rule, sovereignty, supremacy. **2** (the right to do sth) authorization, clearance, permission, sanction. **3** (controlling body) board, executive, institution

a
b
c
d
e
f
g
h
i
j
k
l
m
n
o
p
q
r
s
t
u
v
w
x
y
z

A
B
C
D
E
F
G
H
I
J
K
L
M
N
O
P
Q
R
S
T
U
V
W
X
Y
Z

**authorize** *v* give authority or approval

> **authorize** *v* agree to, allow, assent to, clear, countenance, give the go-ahead to, give the green light to, let, permit, sanction

**autism** *n* psychological disorder where one is unable to relate to or communicate with others; *adj*, *n* **autistic**

**auto-** *prefix* 1 self 2 car; motor

**autobiography** *n* life of person written by him/herself; *adj* **autobiographic(al)**

**autocrat** *n* absolute monarch

**autograph** *n* person's own signature; *v* write one's signature (in)

**autoimmune** *adj* (of a disease) caused by antibodies produced against substances naturally present in the body

**automate** *v* cause to work by automation

**automatic** *adj* 1 working by itself 2 behaving mechanically; *adv* **-ally**

> **automatic** *adj* 1 (working by itself) mechanical, electronic, remote-control 2 (behaving mechanically) instinctive, involuntary, unconscious

**automatic pilot** *n* device that automatically maintains an aircraft's course

**automation** *n* control of industrial processes by machine

**automobile** *n* car

**autonomy** *n* self-government; *adj* **autonomous**

**autopsy** *n* examination of dead body by dissection

**autumn** *n* third season of the year

**auxiliary** *adj* helping; additional; supplementary; *n* verb helping to make up tense, mood, etc of another

**available** *adj* able to be used; *n* **availability**

> **available** *adj* accessible, free, handy, in plentiful supply, obtainable, on hand, ready, to hand, vacant

**avalanche** *n* mass of snow, ice rushing down a mountain

**avant-gard** *n* favoring progressive ideas

**avarice** *n* greed; *adj* **avaricious**

> **avarice** *n* acquisitiveness, meanness, miserliness, parsimony, selfishness, stinginess

**avenge** *v* inflict retribution for a wrong

**avenue** *n* 1 way of approach 2 road bordered by trees 3 wide street

**average** *n* mean proportion; *adj* ordinary; *v* estimate average of or average rate of

> **average** *adj* everyday, medium, middle-sized, moderate, normal, run-of-the-mill, standard, typical, unexceptional, usual

**averse** *adj* opposed to

**aversion** *n* dislike

**avert** *v* turn aside; prevent

**aviary** *n* large cage for keeping birds

**aviation** *n* art of flying aircraft; *n* **aviator** a pilot

**avid** *adj* eager; greedy; *adv* **avidly**

> **avid** *adj* enthusiastic, hungry, keen, thirsty

**avocado** *n pl* **-dos** pear-shaped tropical fruit

**avoid** *v* 1 keep away from 2 refrain from; *adj* **avoidable**; *n* **avoidance**

> **avoid** *v* 1 (keep away from) escape, evade, shun, stay away from. 2 (refrain from) abstain from, get out of

**avow** *v* own publicly to; admit openly

**await** *v* wait for; expect; be ready for

**awake** *adj* no longer sleeping; *v* rouse from sleep or inaction; *pt* **awoke;** *pp* **awoken**

> **awake** *adj* alert, aware, compos mentis, conscious, vigilant

**award** *v* grant after due judgment; *n* **1** prize
**2** something awarded after judgment

> **award** *v* accord, allot, assign, bestow,
> confer, give, grant, hand out, present
> **award** *n* **1** (prize) decoration, presentation,
> reward, trophy. **2** (sth awarded after
> judgement) adjudication, compensation,
> damages, grant, order

**aware** *adj* **1** conscious **2** knowing; *n* **-ness**

> **aware** *adj* **1** (conscious) attentive, alert,
> awake. **2** (knowing) conscious of,
> familiar with, mindful of, wise to

**away** *adv* at or to a distance; absent
**awe** *n* fear with respect; *v* fill with awe;
*adj* **awesome** causing awe

> **awe** *n* admiration, amazement, fear, wonder

**awful** *adj* very bad; *adv* **awfully** very

> **awful** *adj* abominable, appalling, atrocious,
> deplorable, disgusting, dire, dreadful,
> frightful, ghastly, grim, horrendous,
> horrific, shocking, sickening, terrible

**awkward** *adj* **1** clumsy; ungainly **2** difficult to
manage **3** ill at ease; embarrassment

> **awkward** *adj* **1** (clumsy) embarrassed, ill-at-
> ease, nervous, uncoordinated, ungainly.
> **2** (difficult) embarrassing, thorny, tricky

**awoke** *pt* **awoken** *pp of* **awake**
**awry** *adj, adv* crooked; twisted
**ax** *n* chopping tool with iron head; *pl* **axes**
**axis** *n* imaginary line about which a body may
rotate real or imaginary line dividing figure
into two equal parts; *pl* **axes**
**axle** *n* rod or bar connecting two wheels and
on which wheel revolves
**azalea** *n* flowering shrub of rhododendron
family

a
b
c
d
e
f
g
h
i
j
k
l
m
n
o
p
q
r
s
t
u
v
w
x
y
z

**BA** *abbr* Bachelor of Arts
**baa** *n* the bleat of a sheep; *v* bleat
**babble** *v* **1** talk indistinctly **2** reveal (secrets);
*n* **1** foolish talk **2** murmur of stream
**baboon** *n* kind of large ape
**baby** *n* young child or animal; infant;
*adj* **babyish** childish; *n* **babyhood**

> **baby** *n* babe, infant, newborn, toddler, tot

**baby-sit** *v* care for children when parents are
out; *ns* **baby-sitter**, **baby-sitting**
**bachelor** *n* unmarried man
**back** *n* **1** part opposite the front **2** (part of
body containing) the spine; *v* **1** move
backward **2** support; *adj* **1** behind **2** of the
past **3** overdue; *adv* **1** away from the front
**2** in or to an earlier condition **3** in return;
*phr v* **back down** yield; *n* **backup 1** support
**2** *comput* make a spare copy

> **back** *v* **1** (move backward) back away, back
> up, backtrack, retreat, reverse. **2**
> (support) advocate, agree with, approve
> of, champion, encourage, endorse, favor,
> finance, invest in, sanction, sponsor

**backache** *n* lower back pain
**backbiting** *n* malicious gossip; *n* **backbiter**
**backbone** *n* spine, vertebrae; courage,
firmness
**backbreaking** *adj* exhausting

**backer** *n* one who supports another, *esp* with
money

> **backer** *n* advocate, champion, investor,
> promoter, sponsor, supporter

**backfire** *n*, *v* **1** *aut* (emit) loud explosion due
to premature ignition of fuel **2** (of plans) go
wrong

> **backfire** *v* (go wrong) fail, miscarry,
> misfire, rebound

**backgammon** *n* board game played with
checkers and dice
**background** *n* **1** part of picture behind main
figures **2** person's past history

> **background** *n* **1** (part of a picture) backdrop,
> distance, scenery. **2** (person's past history)
> credentials, culture, education, experience,
> origins, past, qualifications, upbringing

**backhand** *n* shot played with back of hand
toward opponent
**backing** *n* **1** anything used to cover back of
object **2** support

> **backing** *n* (support) agreement, approval,
> assistance, cooperation, finance, help,
> encouragement, sponsorship

**backlash** *n* hostile (*esp* political) reaction
**backlog** *n* accumulation of work
**backpack** knapsack; *v* hike with backpack
**backside** *n* rear part of person or animal
**backslide** *v* relapse into bad habits
**backspace** *n*, *v* (key to) move typewriter
carriage back
**backstage** *adj*, *adv* behind the stage
**backstroke** *n* swimming on one's back
**backup** *n* **1** person who supports another
**2** alternative kept in reserve
**backward** *adv* toward rear; with back first;
*adj* **1** turned back **2** retarded mentally;
underdeveloped

**bacon** n salted and smoked pork
**bacterium** n one-celled plant organism;
    pl **bacteria**; adj **bacterial**
**bad** adj 1 of low quality 2 unpleasant
    3 serious; severe 4 evil 5 rotten adv **-ly**

---

**bad** adj 1 (of low quality) appalling,
atrocious, awful, inferior, mediocre, poor,
substandard, worthless. 2 (unpleasant)
adverse, disagreeable, distressing, grim,
nasty, uncomfortable, unfavorable,
unfortunate, unlucky, unsatisfactory. 3
(serious, severe) acute, chronic, critical,
disastrous, dreadful, grave, terrible. 4
(evil) base, corrupt, criminal, delinquent,
depraved, dishonest, immoral, nasty,
naughty, sinful, unscrupulous, vile,
villainous, wicked. 5 (rotten) moldy, off,
putrid, rancid, sour, spoiled

---

**bade** v pt of **bid**
**badge** n emblem of membership or office
**badger** n nocturnal burrowing animal
**bad-off** adj not having enough
**badminton** n game played with shuttlecock
    and racquets
**baffle** v confuse; adj **baffling**

---

**baffle** v bewilder, confound, flummox,
mystify, perplex, puzzle, stump

---

**bag** n pouch; sack; adj **baggy** loosely hanging

---

**bag** n basket, case, container, handbag,
holdall, rucksack, satchel

---

**baggage** n luggage

---

**baggage** n belongings, cases, kit, suitcases

---

**bagpipes** n pl musical wind instrument
**baguette** n long thin loaf of French bread
**bail** n 1 sum paid as security for person's
    reappearance in court 2 cricket one of two
    small sticks laid across top of wicket;
    v release on bail; **bail (out)** scoop water out

**bailiff** n sheriff's officer; land agent
**bait** n anything used to lure prey; v torment
**bake** v cook; ns **baker; bakery**
**balaclava** n close-fitting woolen hood
**balance** n 1 weighing instrument 2 fairness
    3 remainder; v weigh; be equal in weight to;
    adjust; be in state of equilibrium

---

**balance** n 1 (weighing machine) scales.
2 (fairness) equanimity, even-
handedness, objectivity, stability,
steadiness. 3 (remainder) difference,
outstanding amount, residue, rest

---

**balanced** adj considering both sides equally

---

**balanced** adj fair, objective, unbiased

---

**balcony** n projecting platform outside
    window; tier of seats in theater
**bald** adj having no hair

---

**bald** adj hairless, receding, thin on top

---

**bale** n bundle of hay bound with cord or wire;
    phr v **bale out** jump from aircraft by
    parachute in emergency
**ball**[1] n 1 roundish body of any size 2 bullet or
    shot
**ball**[2] n social gathering for dancing
**ballad** n traditional story in song
**ball bearings** n steel balls used to relieve
    friction on bearings
**ballerina** n a female ballet dancer
**ballet** n story expressed by dancing; form of
    dance
**balloon** n gas- or hot air-filled bag that rises
    in air; inflatable rubber bag; n **balloonist**
**ballot** n printed sheet used in voting; act of
    voting; v vote by ballot; n **ballot box** 1 box
    for deposit of voting slips 2 system of
    democratic elections

---

**ballot** n election, franchise, plebiscite, poll,
polling, referendum, vote, voting

---

**ballpoint** n pen that dispenses ink by a rollerball

**ballroom** n large room for dancing

**bamboo** n giant grass with hard stem

**ban** n prohibition; v **banning, banned** forbid; exclude

> **ban** n boycott, embargo, moratorium, prohibition, veto
> **ban** v abolish, banish, bar, criminalize, end, forbid, outlaw, prohibit, stop, suppress

**banal** adj trivial

> **banal** adj bland, clichéd, commonplace, humdrum, meaningless, ordinary, pedestrian, stale, tired, trite, trivial

**banana** n tropical fruit tree; its fruit

**band** n 1 narrow piece of material 2 group 3 group of musicians; v unite; gather together

> **band** n 1 (narrow piece of material) bar, line, ribbon, sash, streak, strip, stripe. 2 (group) brigade, bunch, clique, company, gang, mob, pack, set, troop. 3 (group of musicians) ensemble, group, orchestra

**bandage** n strip of cloth, etc used to bind up wounds; to apply a bandage to

**bandit** n outlaw, robber, or brigand

**bang** n sudden loud noise; sharp blow; v thump; beat, shut noisily; explode

> **bang** n boom, detonation, explosion, gunshot, thud, thump

**bangle** n bracelet for arm or ankle

**banish** v 1 drive into exile 2 dismiss (feeling)

> **banish** v 1 (drive into exile) ban, bar, boot out inf, cast out, deport, drive away, eject, evict, exclude, expel, kick out. 2 (dismiss a feeling) dispel, get rid of, shake off

**banister** n rail and supports along a stairway

**banjo** n pl **-jos** or **-joes** musical instrument of guitar family

**bank**[1] n heap or mound of earth; edge of river etc; v pile up

**bank**[2] n 1 commercial concern engaged in keeping and lending money 2 place where sth is stored; v deposit money in bank; phr v **bank on** rely on; ns **banker, banking**

**bankcard** n credit card issued by bank

**bank holiday** n week day when banks are closed

**bankrupt** adj insolvent; v make bankrupt

> **bankrupt** adj broke, failed, in liquidation, insolvent tech, penniless, poor, ruined

**banner** n flag as symbol of country

**banns** n announcement of intended marriage

**banquet** n Fr ceremonial or official feast

> **banquet** n dinner party, feast, repast

**banter** n good-natured chaff

> **banter** n chaff, gossip, joking, patter, small talk, teasing

**baptism** n ceremony of admitting person to Christian church by immersing in or sprinkling with water; v **baptize** name

**Baptist** n, adj (member of Protestant church) believing in baptism by full immersion

**bar** n 1 rod of solid material 2 legal profession 3 counter at which alcoholic beverages are sold 4 obstruction 5 musical unit 6 nonmaterial obstacle; v fasten with (bar); rule out; prep except

**barb** n backward-curving point on arrow, fishhook, etc; adj **barbed**

**barbarian** n uncivilized person

> **barbarian** n boor, brute, hooligan, lout, monster, ruffian, savage

**barbaric** adj cruel

**barbaric** *adj* barbarous, brutal, primitive, savage, uncivilized, uncouth

**barbecue** *n* grid for roasting meat over charcoal fire; outdoor feast; *v* cook in such manner

**barber** *n* one who cuts hair

**bare** *adj* 1 naked 2 empty 3 simple; *v* reveal

**bare** *adj* 1 (naked) exposed, in the buff, in the nude, in your birthday suit, nude, stark naked, stripped, undressed. 2 (empty) austere, plain, spare, unfurnished, vacant

**barely** *adv* hardly

**barely** *adv* just, only just, scarcely

**bargain** *n* 1 agreement 2 something obtained at small price; *v* discuss or argue about terms

**bargain** *n* 1 (agreement) arrangement, contract, deal, negotiation, pact. 2 (sth obtained at small price) good buy, good deal, good value, give-away, reduction

**barge** *n* broad flat-bottomed boat

**bark**[1] *n* outside covering of trees

**bark**[2] *n* sharp cry or noise made by dog

**bark** *v* bay, growl, howl, snarl, yap, yelp

**barley** *n* cereal plant; its seed or grain

**bar mitzvah** *n* (ceremony for) Jewish boy of 13, taking on adult religious responsibilities

**barn** *n* building for storing hay, grain, etc

**barometer** *n* instrument for recording atmospheric pressure

**baron** *n* lowest rank in peerage; *fem* **baroness**

**baronet** *n* lowest hereditary title

**baroque** *n* style of music, architecture, or art

**barrack** *n* (usually *pl*) building in which soldiers live

**barrage** *n* 1 continuous gunfire 2 continuous criticism

**barrage** *n* 1 (continuous gunfire) battery, bombardment, salvo, shelling, volley, wall of fire. 2 (continuous criticism) burst, hail, onslaught, storm, stream, torrent

**barrel** *n* 1 cylindrical vessel or cask with bulging sides 2 metal tube of gun; *v* pack, stow in barrel

**barren** *adj* 1 sterile 2 bare

**barren** *adj* 1 (sterile) childless, infertile. 2 (bare) desolate, unfruitful, unproductive

**barricade** *n* makeshift barrier

**barricade** *n* barrier, blockade, obstacle, obstruction, roadblock

**barrier** *n* anything obstructing passage or advance

**barrier** *n* bar, barricade, blockade, fence, obstacle, obstruction, roadblock

**barrister** *n* advocate in British courts of law

**barrow** *n* small wheeled handcart

**bartender** *n* one who serves drinks in a bar

**barter** *n*, *v* trade by exchange of goods

**base**[1] *n* 1 bottom 2 fundamental part 3 place used as center of activity; *adj* **basic**, **baseless**; *n* **basement** floor below ground level; *phr v* **base sth on sth** use sth as a starting point

**base** *n* 1 (bottom) foot, foundation, pedestal, stand. 2 (fundamental part) basis, core, heart, key, origin, principal, source. 3 (place) camp, headquarters

**base**[2] *adj* low, mean, vicious, vile

**baseball** *n* ball game played with two teams of nine players on a diamond-shaped field

**bases** *n pl* of **basis**

**bash** *n* a heavy blow; *v* strike violently

**bashful** *adj* shy, modest; *adv* **-ly**; *n* **-ness**

**basic** *adj* fundamental; essential

> **basic** *adj* central, elementary, indispensable, intrinsic, key, necessary, rudimentary, underlying, vital

**basically** *adv* fundamentally

> **basically** *adv* at heart, essentially, firstly, mainly, mostly, primarily

**basics** *n pl* basic principles

> **basics** *n* essentials, facts, fundamentals, nuts and bolts, practicalities, rudiments

**basin** *n* **1** hollow vessel **2** region drain by river **3** dock; landlocked harbor

**basis** *n* base, foundation, or principle; *pl* **bases**

**bask** *v* luxuriate in (sun, etc)

**basket** *n* container made of woven rushes or canes

**basketball** *n* ball game played with two teams of five players on a rectangular court

**bass** *adj* low in tone

**bassoon** *n* woodwind instrument

**baste** *v* **basting** moisten (roasting meat) with melted fat; tack loosely

**bat**[1] *n* small nocturnal flying mammal

**bat**[2] **1** wooden implement used in ball games **2 batting, batted** blow; *v* strike with bat

**batch** *n* set of things of the same kind

> **batch** *n* accumulation, amount, collection, group, lot, mass, pack, quantity, set

**bath** *n* act of washing; receptacle to wash in

> **bath** *n* dip, shower, soak, wash

**bathe** *v* **1** apply water to **2** swim

> **bathe** *v* (clean) cleanse, moisten, rinse, soak

**bathrobe** *n* loose garment worn before and after having a bath

**bathroom** *n* **1** room with bath **2** lavatory

**baton** *n* stick, *esp* of orchestral conductor

**batsman** *n* cricket player who bats

**battalion** *n* army unit of about 1,000 men

**batter** *v* beat heavily with repeated violent blows; *n* **1** mixture of flour, milk, and eggs beaten together **2** baseball player who bats

> **batter** *v* abuse, assault, bash *inf*, beat, clobber *inf*, hit, smack, whack

**battering ram** *n* beam of wood formerly used in war for breaking down doors and walls

**battery** *n* **1** physical assault **2** artillery unit **3** group of cells for storing electrical energy **4** set of hen coops designed for quick production of eggs

**battle** *n* fight between armies; *v* fight, struggle; *ns* **battlefield** place of battle; **battleship** heavily armed and armored warship

> **battle** *n* action, affray, attack, campaign, clash, combat, conflict, confrontation, encounter, engagement, fight, hostilities, scuffle, skirmish, struggle, war, warfare

**battlements** *n pl* walls of a castle with openings for firing weapons through

**bawl** *v* shout, cry loudly; *n* loud cry

> **bawl** *v* bellow, call, cry, howl, roar, scream, screech, shout, yell

**bay**[1] *n* kind of laurel

**bay**[2] *n* **1** inlet of sea **2** recess in a room

> **bay** *n* **1** (inlet) cove, gulf, harbor. **2** (recess in room) alcove, niche, nook, opening

**bayonet** *n* daggerlike blade attached to rifle; *v* wound with bayonet

**bazaar** *n* **1** Oriental market **2** sale in aid of charity

**BC** *abbr* before the birth of Christ

**be** *v* exist; have quality, feeling, or state; *pt* **was**, **were**; *pp* **been**; *pr p* **being**

**beach** *n* seashore, *esp* if sand
**beacon** *n* signal light or fire

> **beacon** *n* beam, bonfire, flare, lighthouse, sign, signal, warning light, watchtower

**bead** *n* **1** small ball of glass, wood, etc **2** small drop of moisture
**beak** *n* bill of bird
**beaker** *n* large cup or mug
**beam** *n* **1** thick piece of timber **2** shaft of light

> **beam** *n* **1** (piece of timber) girder, joist, plank, rafter, support. **2** (shaft of light) flash, gleam, glimmer, glint, glow, ray

**bean** *n* leguminous plant; its seed and fruit
**beanbag** *n* **1** small bag of dried beans used for games of throwing **2** large cushion
**bear**[1] *n* heavy, fur-clad mammal
**bear**[2] *v* **1** carry **2** endure **3** produce; *pt* **bore**; *phr vs* **bear down 1** overcome **2** press down hard; **bear on** be relevant to

> **bear** *v* **1** (carry) bring, convey, fetch, move, take, transport. **2** (endure) put up with, stand, suffer, tolerate. **3** (produce) breed, bring forth, engender, give birth to, yield

**bearable** *adj* capable of being tolerated

> **bearable** *adj* acceptable, endurable

**beard** *n* growth of hair on man's cheeks/chin
**bearing** *n* **1** behavior **2** part of machine where moving parts revolve
**bearings** *n pl* sense of direction

> **bearings** *n* direction, location, orientation, position, situation, whereabouts

**beast** *n* **1** four-footed animal **2** brutal person

> **beast** *n* **1** (animal) brute, creature, monster. **2** (person) barbarian, fiend, savage

**beat** *v* **1** hit repeatedly **2** defeat; *pt* **beat**; *pp* **beaten**; *n* throb; *adj* **beaten 1** shaped by beating **2** defeated **3** mixed by beating; *idm* **beat time** mark tempo of music

> **beat** *v* **1** (hit) bang, bash, batter, clobber, hammer, pound, pummel, punch, slap, smack, strike, thrash, thump, wallop *inf*. **2** (defeat) conquer, defeat, outdo, overcome, quash, rout, thrash, vanquish

**beautician** *n* person who gives beauty treatment
**beautiful** *adj* very attractive

> **beautiful** *adj* appealing, charming, elegant, exquisite, fair, fine, glamorous, good-looking, gorgeous, handsome, lovely, pleasant, pretty, ravishing, stunning

**beauty** *n* **1** loveliness **2** beautiful person

> **beauty** *n* **1** allure, appeal, attractiveness, good looks, handsomeness, loveliness, prettiness. **2** (beautiful person) belle, charmer, stunner *inf*

**beaver** *n* water-loving rodent; *v* work hard
**became** *pt of* **become**
**because** *conj prep* for the reason that **because of** on account of
**beckon** *v* signal or call by a gesture
**become** *v* come to be; suit
**bed** *n* **1** thing to sleep on **2** piece of ground **3** foundation; **4** mineral stratum **5** bottom of sea or river
**bedlam** *n* noisy scene or uproar

> **bedlam** *n* chaos, commotion, disorder, pandemonium, tumult, turmoil

**bedraggled** *adj* wet and dirty

> **bedraggled** *adj* disheveled, messy, muddy, soaking, tatty, unkempt, untidy

a
b
c
d
e
f
g
h
i
j
k
l
m
n
o
p
q
r
s
t
u
v
w
x
y
z

**bedroll** *n* sleeping blankets rolled up

**bedroom** *n* room where one sleeps

**bedsore** *n* raw spot on skin from lying too long in bed

**bedspread** *n* cover for bed, *usu* decorative

**bee** *n* four-winged insect, producing honey

**beech** *n* species of tree; its wood

**beef** *n* flesh of ox, cow, considered as food

**been** *pp of* **be**

**beer** *n* alcoholic drink make from malted hops, yeast, etc; *adj* **beery**

**beetle** *n* insect with biting mouth parts

**befall** *v* happen to; *pt* **befell**; *pp* **befallen**

**before** *prep* **1** front of **2** preceeding in time, rank; *adv* **beforehand** in advance

**beg** *v* **begging, begged 1** entreat **2** ask for money; *n* **beggar** person who begs

> **beg** *v* **1** (ask for sth) beseech, entreat, implore, importune, plead. **2** (for money) cadge *inf*, scrounge, sponge *inf*

**begin** *v* **-ginning, -gan, -gun** start

> **begin** *v* commence, get going, inaugurate, initiate, instigate, institute, kick off

**beginner** *n* novice

> **beginner** *n* amateur, apprentice, fresher, learner, trainee

**beginning** *n* start

> **beginning** *n* birth, commencement, dawn, inauguration, inception, initiation, outset

**begrudge** *v* envy

**behalf** *idm* **on behalf of** in the name of

**behave** *v* **1** act **2** act with decorum

> **behave** *v* **1** (act) function, operate, perform, work. **2** (act with decorum) be good, be on your best behavior, mind your manners

**behavior 1** conduct **2** manners

**behind** *prep* at back of; in support of; inferior to; *adv* in arrears

**behold** *v* to look at, see; *pt, pp* **beheld**

**beige** *n, adj* (of) light yellowish-brown (color)

**being** *n* **1** existence **2** human creature

**belated** *adj* unduly deferred; *adv* **-ly**

**belch** *v* **1** release wind through mouth **2** pour out under force; *n* release of wind

**belief** *n* **1** idea **2** religious conviction

> **belief** *n* **1** (idea) feeling, impression, opinion, theory, view, viewpoint.
> **2** (religious conviction) credo, creed, doctrine, dogma, faith, ideology, teaching

**believable** *adj* plausible

> **believable** *adj* acceptable, conceivable, credible, imaginable, likely, possible, probable, reliable, trustworthy

**believe** *v* accept as true; *n* **believer**

> **believe** *v* assume, consider, gather, guess, imagine, presume, reckon, speculate, suppose, think, trust, understand

**bell** *n* hollow cup-shaped object giving musical sound when struck

**belligerent** *adj* waging war; aggressive

**bellow** *v* cry out; *n* deep cry or shout

> **bellow** *v* bawl, call, howl, roar, scream, screech, shriek, yell

**bellows** *n* apparatus for producing air

**belly** *n* abdomen; **belly button** *n coll* navel

**belong** *v* **1** be owned **2** be a member of **3** be part of

> **belong** *v* **1** (be owned) be at the disposal of, be held by, be the property of. **2** (be a member of) be affiliated to, be allied to, be associated with. **3** (be part of) attach to, be connected with, fit, go with

**belongings** *n pl* possessions

> **belongings** *n* effects, gear, goods, property, possessions, stuff, things

**beloved** *adj* greatly loved

> **beloved** *adj* adored, cherished, darling, dear, dearest, idolized, loved, precious

**below** *prep* lower than; *adj, adv* beneath
**belt** *n* 1 band of leather or other fabric worn round waist 2 zone 3 endless band used in driving machinery
**bench** *n* 1 long seat 2 worktable 3 judge's seat in court
**bend** *n* curve *v* 1 curve 2 curve body downward; *pt, pp* **bent**; *idm* **round the bend** *coll* insane

> **bend** *n* angle, arc, corner, hook, loop, spiral, turn, twist
> **bend** *v* 1 (curve) bow, buckle, contort, curl, curve, flex, veer, warp. 2 (curve body forwards) crouch, hunch, lean, stoop

**beneath** *adv* below; *prep* underneath
**benediction** *n* blessing; blessing at end of church service
**benefactor** *n* person who gives help or money
**beneficial** *adj* useful

> **beneficial** *adj* advantageous, favorable, good, helpful, profitable, valuable

**benefit** *n* advantage *v* **-fited** or **-fitted** do or receive good; *pt, pp* **benefited**

> **benefit** *n* asset, assistance, blessing, boon, favor, gain, perk, profit
> **benefit** *v* advance, aid, assist, avail, be an advantage to, enhance, further, help, improve, profit, promote, serve

**benevolence** *n* kindliness; generosity; *adj* **benevolent** kind

**benign** *adj* 1 kindly 2 (of diseases) not malignant

> **benign** *adj* 1 (kind) amiable, benevolent, friendly, generous, genial, sympathetic. 2 (of diseases) curable, harmless, innocent

**bent**[1] distorted; *idm* **bent on** determined on
**bent**[2] *n* inclination; aptitude

> **bent** *adj* 1 angled, bowed, contorted, crooked, hunched, stooped, twisted 2 (bent on) insistent, resolved, set

**bequeath** *v* give or leave by will; *n* **bequest**
**bereaved** *adj* having suffered the death of sb close
**beret** *n* small, soft, flat cap
**berry** *n* small fleshy fruit containing seeds
**berth** *n* 1 space for anchoring ship in dock 2 sleeping place on ship or train; *v* moor a ship
**beseech** *v* implore, beg; *pt, pp* **besought**
**beset** *v* **-setting**, *pt* **-set** surround; assail
**beside** *prep* at side of; *adv, prep* **besides** other than; in addition to
**besiege** *v* beset with armed forces

> **besiege** *v* beleaguer, beset, blockade, encircle, lay siege to, surround

**besotted** *adj* foolish
**best** *adj, adv* most excellent(ly)

> **best** *adj* cream, élite, finest, first, foremost, greatest, highest, leading, outstanding, pick, prime, right, supreme, unsurpassed

**bestial** *adj* coarse; brutish
**best man** *n* bridegroom's attendant
**bestow** *v* give, stow away; *n* **bestowal**
**bet** *v* **betting**, **bet**, or **betted** wager; *n* stake given

> **bet** *v* gamble, risk, speculate, venture
> **bet** *n* speculation, stake, wager

**betray** *v* act falsely towards; reveal secret

> **betray** *v* blow the whistle on, break your promise, double-cross, inform on, sell out

**betrayal** *n* act of betraying

> **betrayal** *n* disloyalty, duplicity, falseness, treachery, treason, subversion, trickery

**better** *adj*, *adv* (*comp of* **good**, **well**) (in a) superior or improved (way)
**between** *prep*, *adv* separated by
**beverage** *n* drink (other than water)
**beware** *v* be on one's guard (against)

> **beware** *v* avoid, be careful, be on the alert, look out, mind, steer clear of, watch out

**bewildered** *adj* confused

> **bewildered** *adj* baffled, bemused, muddled, mystified, perplexed, puzzled, surprised

**beyond** *prep*, *adv* **1** to or on the other side (of) **2** exceeding; past the limit of
**bias** *n* **1** slant; prejudice **2** tendency; *v* influence unfairly
**Bible** *n* sacred book of Jews and Christians
**bibliography** *n* study of books; list of books on a particular subject
**biceps** *n* muscle of upper arm
**bicker** *v* quarrel; wrangle
**bicycle** *n* two-wheeled vehicle propelled by foot pedals; *v* ride this vehicle
**bid** *v* **1** offer; *pt*, *pp* **bid**; **2** command; *pt* **bade**; *pp* **bidden**; *n* **1** offer **2** attempt

> **bid** *v* **1** (offer) propose, put forward, submit, tender. **2** (command) ask, instruct, invite, order, summon, tell
> **bid** *n* **1** (offer) price, proposal, submission, tender. **2** (attempt) effort, try, venture

**biennial** *adj* happening every two years; *n* plant lasting two years; *adv* **-ly**

**bifocals** *n* eyeglasses with double lenses to correct both distant and reading vision
**big** *adj* **-gger**, **-ggest 1** possesing great size **2** important

> **big** *adj* **1** (of great size) bulky, colossal, enormous, extensive, gigantic, great, huge, hulking, immense, large, massive, prodigious, sizable, substantial, tall, vast, voluminous. **2** (important) leading, main, powerful, principal, prominent, serious, significant, valuable, weighty

**bigamist** *n* one who marries another while still married; *n* **bigamy**; *adj* **bigamous**
**big bang** *n* explosion of matter from which the universe is believed to have originated
**bighead** *n coll* conceited person
**bigot** *n* narrow-minded, intolerant person
**bigoted** *adj* narrow-minded

> **bigoted** *adj* dogmatic, fanatical, intolerant, opinionated, prejudiced

**big top** *n* circus tent
**bike** *n*, *v coll* bicycle
**bikini** *n* small two-piece bathing costume
**bile** *n* **1** secretion of liver, aiding digestion **2** ill-humor
**bilingual** *adj* of or using two languages
**bilious** *adj* **1** sick; sickly; **2** yellowish
**bill**[1] *n* bird's beak
**bill**[2] *n* **1** statement of money due **2** draft of proposed legislation **3** poster

> **bill** *n* **1** (statement of money due) account, charges, invoice, statement. **2** (legislation) act, measure, proposal

**billboard** *n* large outdoor advertisment
**billiards** *n* game played with cue and balls on cloth-covered table with pockets
**billion** *n* thousand millions
**billow** *v* swell out; *n* large swelling wave; *adj* **billowy, billowing**
**billy goat** *n* male goat

**bin** n container for waste
**binary** adj dual; involving two
**bind** v 1 fasten 2 compel 3 fasten sheets of book into cover; pt, pp **bound**

**bind** v 1 (fasten) attach, chain, fetter, glue, hitch, lash, secure, stick, strap, tether, tie. 2 (compel) force, impel, oblige

**binding** adj compelling person to do sth

**binding** adj compulsory, irrevocable, mandatory, obligatory, unalterable

**binge** n spree; drinking bout
**bingo** n gambling game with random numbers
**binoculars** n field or opera glasses
**biochemistry** n chemistry of living organisms
**biodegradable** adj capable of being decomposed by nature
**biography** n story of person's life written by sb else; **biographer**; adj **biographical**

**biography** n account, life story, memoir

**biology** n study of living organisms; n **biologist;** adj **biological** (adv **-ly**)
**bionic** adj having superhuman power
**biopsy** n analysis of body tissue and fluid to test for disease
**biotechnology** n use of living cells in industry
**biplane** n aircraft with two pairs of wings
**birch** n 1 tree with thin, smooth bark; wood of this tree 2 birch rod used for caning
**bird** n feathered biped that lays eggs
**birdie** n golf score (of) one under par
**birth** n 1 bearing of offspring 2 beginning 3 parentage

**birth** n 1 (bearing of offspring) childbirth, confinement, delivery. 2 (beginning) emergence, origin, rise, start, source. 3 (parentage) ancestry, background, descent, extraction, family, heritage, line

**birth control** n contraception
**birthday** n anniversary of the day of birth
**birthmark** n distinguishing mark on skin from birth
**biscuit** n thin, crisp bread made of eggs, flour
**bisect** v divide into two parts
**bisexual** adj sexually attracted to both sexes
**bishop** n Christian clergyman of high rank
**bison** n large wild ox; American buffalo
**bit** n 1 small portion 2 tool for boring 3 metal mouthpiece of bridle 4 comput smallest unit of information

**bit** n (small portion) chip, chunk, crumb, flake, fragment, grain, lump, morsel, part, particle, scrap, shred, sliver, speck, trace

**bitch** n female dog or wolf, vixen
**bite** v **biting, bit** use teeth upon; n **bite** 1 nip with teeth 2 wound (by teeth) 3 sting 4 taking of bait

**bite** v chew, crunch, gnaw, masticate, munch, nibble, nip, snap, tear

**biting** adj scathingly
**bitter** adj 1 sour 2 angry; n **bitter** light beer

**bitter** adj 1 (sour) acid, pungent, sharp, tart, unsweetened, vinegary. 2 (angry) acrimonious, hostile, resentful, sullen

**bizarre** adj strange

**bizarre** adj abnormal, extraordinary, fantastic, grotesque, ludicrous, outlandish, peculiar, unconventional, unusual, weird

**blab** v reveal secrets
**black** adj 1 very dark in color 2 gloomy

**black** adj 1 (dark color) coal-black, ebony, inky, jet, pitch-black, raven. 2 (gloomy) depressing, dismal, melancholy, mournful, pessimistic, sad, somber

**black belt** n top grade in judo or karate
**black box** n automatic flight recorder in aircraft
**blackcurrant** n bush with small edible black berries; fruit of this
**blackhead** n small black pimple
**black hole** n area in outer space from which light or matter cannot escape
**blacklist** n list of people in disfavor or due for punishment; v **blacklist**

> **blacklist** v ban, bar, boycott, debar, exclude, expel, ostracize, reject

**blackmail** n, v 1 attempt to extort money by threatening to reveal a guilty secret 2 use threats to induce sb to act in a certain way

> **blackmail** v exact, extract, force, hold to ransom, intimidate

**blackout** n failure of electricity; temporary loss of consciousness
**blacksmith** n a smith who forges iron
**bladder** n sac in body for holding secreted liquids
**blade** n cutting edge of knife; flat of oar; bat, propeller, etc; long thin leaf of grass
**blame** v find fault with; n culpability

> **blame** v accuse, censure, charge, condemn, indict, find guilty, reprimand, reproach, reprove, take to task

**blameless** adj innocent

> **blameless** adj above suspicion, beyond reproach, irreproachable, virtuous

**bland** adj 1 mild in flavor 2 dull

> **bland** adj 1 (mild in flavor) flavorless, insipid, plain, tasteless. 2 (dull) boring, insipid, mediocre, nondescript, neutral, safe, uncontroversial, uninteresting, vapid

**blank** n empty space; cartridge without shot; adj 1 without writing 2 without expression

> **blank** adj 1 (without writing) clean, clear, empty, plain, unmarked. 2 (without expression) baffled, bewildered, confused, expressionless, puzzled, uncomprehending

**blanket** n soft woolen bedcover, horse rug, etc
**blare** v utter loudly; n harsh noise

> **blare** v bellow, blast, boom, honk, hoot, peal, resound, roar, trumpet

**blaspheme** v speak profanely of; talk irreverently; n **blasphemy**
**blast** n 1 explosion 2 sudden loud noise; v scorch; shatter by explosion

> **blast** n 1 (explosion) bang, crash, detonation. 2 (loud noise) blare, boom, hoot, trumpeting, wail

**blatant** adj obvious

> **blatant** adj brazen, conspicuous, flagrant, glaring, open, overt, shameless, unashamed

**blaze** n 1 fire 2 intense light; v 1 burn brightly 2 shine brightly

> **blaze** n 1 (fire) bonfire, conflagration, flames, inferno. 2 (intense light) beam, brilliance, flare, flash, glare
> **blaze** v 1 (burn) be ablaze, burst into flames, catch fire. 2 (shine) beam, flash, glow

**blazer** n lightweight sports jacket
**bleach** v whiten, esp of cloth
**bleak** adj 1 bare 2 desolate

> **bleak** adj 1 (bare) barren, exposed, unsheltered, windswept. 2 (desolate) cheerless, dismal, drab, dreary, gloomy, grim, hopeless, miserable, wretched

**bleat** *n* cry of sheep, goat; *v* cry feebly
**bleed** *v* draw blood from; extort money from; lose blood; *pt, pp* **bled**
**bleep** *n, v* (emit a) short high-pitched electronic sound, *esp* as a warning signal; *n* **bleeper**
**blemish** *n* 1 mark 2 moral defect

> **blemish** *n* 1 (mark) blotch, defect, fault, flaw, imperfection, scar, spot, stain. 2 (moral defect) disgrace, fault, flaw, taint

**blend** *v* mix together; *n* mixture

> **blend** *v* amalgamate, combine, cross, fuse, merge, mingle, synthesize, unite
> **blend** *n* alloy, amalgamation, combination, cross, mix, synthesis, union

**bless** *v* pronounce benediction; make holy; make happy; *adj* **blessed**
**blessing** *n* 1 prayer 2 agreement 3 advantage

> **blessing** *n* 1 (prayer) benison, consecration, dedication, grace, praise, thanksgiving. 2 (agreement) approval, assent, backing, consent, permission, sanction, support. 3 (advantage) boon, gift, godsend, favor

**blight** *n* disease or insect pest attacking plants; *v* spoil
**blind** *adj* 1 unable to see 2 unaware; *n* window shade; *v* make blind; *v* **blindfold** put something over the eyes of

> **blind** *adj* 1 (unable to see) sightless, visually impaired. 2 (unaware) heedless, ignorant, insensitive, oblivious, unconscious

**blind date** *n coll* romantic meeting arranged between two people who have never met
**blind spot** *n* 1 part of retina not sensitive to light 2 area not visible to motorist
**blink** *v* flap eyelids rapidly; flicker; *n* wink
**blinkers** *n pl* small flaps on bridle preventing horse from seeing sideways

**blip** *n* 1 spot of light on radar screen 2 short sharp sound
**bliss** *n* perfect happiness

> **bliss** *n* delight, ecstasy, euphoria, heaven, joy, paradise, rapture

**blissful** *adj* extremely happy

> **blissful** *adj* ecstatic, euphoric, heavenly, joyful, rapturous, wonderful

**blister** *n* 1 bubblelike swelling full of liquid under the skin 2 swelling on surface of paint; *v* form blisters
**blitz** *n* sudden attack
**blizzard** *n* blinding snowstorm with high wind
**bloat** *v* swell; *adj* **bloated**

> **bloated** *adj* dilated, distended, enlarged, full, inflated, puffed up, swollen

**blob** *n* spot; drop of liquid

> **blob** *n* ball, bead, dab, dollop, drop, droplet, glob, globule, lump, mass

**block** *n* 1 lump 2 group of buildings 3 obstruction 4 large quantity; *v* 1 prevent movement along 2 prevent

> **block** *n* (lump) bar, brick, chunk, cube, hunk, piece, rectangle, square, wedge
> **block** *v* 1 (prevent movement along) choke, clog, close, obstruct, plug, stop up. 2 (prevent) hinder, impede, stop, thwart

**blockade** *v* stop access by siege; *n* closure of port, etc
**blockage** *n* obstruction

> **blockage** *n* bar, barrier, impediment, jam, obstacle, plug, stoppage

**blockbuster** *n* 1 powerful bomb 2 any successful commercial promotion

a
**b**
c
d
e
f
g
h
i
j
k
l
m
n
o
p
q
r
s
t
u
v
w
x
y
z

**block letters** *n* capital letters

**blond(e)** *adj* fair-colored; *n* person with fair hair and complexion

**blood** *n* 1 red fluid circulating through body 2 kinship; *adj* **bloodless**; **bloodcurdling** terrifying; **bloodshot** suffused with blood; **bloody** bloodstained; murderous

**blood pressure** *n* force of blood on inner walls of blood vessels

**bloodshed** *n* the shedding of blood

> **bloodshed** *n* butchery, carnage, gore, killing, massacre, murder, slaughter, violence

**blood sport** *n* killing of wildlife for sport

**bloodthirsty** *adj* savage

> **bloodthirsty** *adj* barbaric, brutal, cruel, ferocious, murderous, ruthless, vicious

**bloom** *n* 1 flower 2 prime of life

> **bloom** *n* 1 (flower) blossom, bud, flower. 2 (prime of life) blush, flush, freshness, glow, health, luster, radiance, rosiness

**blossom** *n* flower; *v* 1 flower 2 be successful or happy

> **blossom** *v* 1 (flower) be in bloom, burgeon, open. 2 (be successful) bloom, flourish, glow, thrive

**blot** *n* 1 spot 2 disgrace on reputation

> **blot** *n* 1 (spot) blemish, dot, mark, patch, smudge, speck, spatter, speckle, stain. 2 (disgrace on reputation) blemish, dishonor, fault, flaw, imperfection, taint

**blotch** *n* discolored patch; *adj* **blotchy**

**blouse** *n* loose kind of shirt

**blow** *v* 1 expel air from lungs 2 move by wind; *pt* **blew;** *pp* **blown;** *n* 1 hard knock 2 disappointment; *phr v* **blow up** 1 fill with air 2 explode

**blow** *v* 1 (expel air) breathe, exhale, pant, puff. 2 (move by wind) buffet, flap, flutter, toss, waft, wave, whirl, whisk. 3 **blow up** blast, bomb, detonate, explode, shatter

**blow** *n* 1 (knock) bang, bash, clout, hit, punch, rap, slap, smack, stroke, thump, wallop *inf*, whack. 2 (disappointment) bombshell, catastrophe, disaster, jolt, letdown, misfortune, setback, shock, upset

**blown** *pp of* **blow**

**blowtorch** *n* burner for removing old paint

**blubber** *n* fat of whales; *v* weep

**bludgeon** *n* short heavy club; *v* strike with this

**blue** *adj* 1 color of unclouded sky 2 unhappy; *idm* **out of the blue** unexpectedly; *n pl* **the blues** 1 *coll* mental depression 2 sad type of jazz; *n* **bluebell** wild hyacinth

> **blue** *adj* 1 azure, cobalt, indigo, navy, sapphire, sky-blue, turquoise, ultramarine. 2 dejected, depressed, despondent, downhearted, fed up *inf*, glum, low, melancholy, miserable, sad

**bluff**[1] *n* steep headland, bank

**bluff**[2] *v* deceive; *n* deception

> **bluff** *v* con, fake, feign, lie, mislead, pretend, take in, trick

**blunder** *n* mistake; *v* make a mistake

> **blunder** *n* boob *inf*, error, gaffe, oversight, slip

**blunt** *a*1 having dull edge 2 outspoken; *v* dull edge of; *adv* **bluntly;** *n* **bluntness**

> **blunt** *adj* 1 (having dull edge) dull, rounded, unsharpened. 2 (outspoken) abrupt, direct, forthright, frank, honest, outspoken, straight, straightforward

**blur** n sth that cannot be seen or remembered clearly

**blurb** n brief description of book's contents

**blurred** n unclear

> **blurred** adj clouded, dim, faint, foggy, hazy, indistinct, obscure, out of focus, vague

**blush** v grow red; n flush

**blustery** adj windy

**boa** n 1 nonpoisonous snake that kills by crushing 2 fur of feather neck wrap

**boar** n male pig; wild hog

**board** n 1 plank 2 thick, stiff, compressed paper 3 official body; v provide with meals; n **boarder** one who pays for food, lodging; child living at school in term; idm **go by the board** be ignored; idm **on board** on a ship or aircraft

> **board** n 1 (plank) beam, panel, slat, timber. 2 (official body) committee, council, directorate, directors, panel

**boarding school** n school with living accommodations

**boardroom** n room for meetings of company directors

**boast** v 1 praise oneself 2 have; adj **boastful**

> **boast** v 1 (praise yourself) blow your own trumpet, bluster, brag, crow, exaggerate, show off, swagger. 2 (have) enjoy, own, possess, pride yourself on

**boat** n water craft; n **boating**

**bob** n 1 quick up-and-down movement; clumsy curtsy 2 short haircut; v **bobbed** move jerkily up and down

**bobby** n sl Brit policeman

**bobsled** n sledge steered by wheel on movable front portion

**bodice** n part of woman's dress above the waist

**body** n 1 physical shape 2 corpse 3 main part 4 group of people; adv **bodily**

**body** n 1 (physical shape) build, figure, form, flesh, frame, physique, shape, torso. 2 (corpse) cadaver, carcass, remains. 3 (main part) bulk, essence, majority, mass, matter, substance. 4 (group) association, authority, band, committee, corporation, group, organization, society

**bodyguard** n person or persons guarding someone

**boffin** n coll scientific or technical expert

**bog** n marsh; swamp; adj **boggy**; idm **bogged down** coll stuck

> **bog** n fen, mire, morass, quagmire, wetland

**bogus** adj not genuine, sham

> **bogus** adj artificial, counterfeit, dummy, fake, false, forged, imitation, mock, phony inf, pseudo, sham, spurious

**boil**[1] v cook in boiling water

**boil**[2] n inflamed swelling, filled with pus

**boiler** n vessel or tank for heating or boiling

**boiling** adj extremely hot

> **boiling** adj baking, blistering, hot, roasting, scorching, searing, sweltering

**boisterous** adj rough, turbulent

> **boisterous** adj bouncy, exuberant, loud, noisy, riotous, rowdy, spirited, unruly, uproarious, wild

**bold** adj 1 brave 2 bright; adv **boldly**

> **bold** adj 1 (brave) adventurous, audacious, courageous, daring, dauntless, enterprising, fearless, intrepid, valiant. 2 (bright) colorful, eye-catching, flashy, loud, lurid, showy, strong, vivid

**bollard** n mooring post for ship at dockside

a
b
c
d
e
f
g
h
i
j
k
l
m
n
o
p
q
r
s
t
u
v
w
x
y
z

A
**B**
C
D
E
F
G
H
I
J
K
L
M
N
O
P
Q
R
S
T
U
V
W
X
Y
Z

**bolster** *n* long cushion; *v* support

> **bolster** *v* aid, assist, boost, brace, buttress, help, prop up, reinforce, strengthen

**bolt** *n* 1 metal rod used to bar door, etc 2 thunderbolt; *v* 1 secure with bolt 2 gulp food 3 run away

> **bolt** *v* 1 (secure with bolt) bar, fasten, lock. 2 (gulp food) cram, devour, down, gobble, guzzle, stuff, wolf 3 (run away) dart, dash, escape, flee, fly, hurtle, leap, rush, sprint

**bomb** *n* metal shell filled with explosive; *v* attack with bombs; *n* **bomber** bomb-carrying aircraft

> **bomb** *n* charge, device, explosive, grenade, mine, shell, torpedo
> **bomb** *v* attack, blast, blitz, blow up, bombard, destroy, shell, torpedo

**bombard** *v* 1 attack with shells 2 pester

> **bombard** *v* 1 (attack with shells) blast, blitz, bomb, fire on, open fire, pound, shell, strafe, torpedo. 2 (pester) assail, bother, harass, hassle

**bond** *n* 1 strong link 2 ropes or chains for holding sb prisoner 3 written promise

> **bond** *n* 1 (strong link) affinity, attachment, connection, tie, union. 2 (ropes or chains) binding, cord, fetters, manacles, shackles. 3 (written promise) agreement, contract, covenant, deal, guarantee, obligation, pledge, promise, treaty, word

**bondage** *n* servitude, slavery
**bone** *n* substance of which skeleton of vertebrates is made; any part of skeleton; *v* take out bones; *adj* **bony**
**bonfire** *n* open-air fire
**bongo** *n pl* **bongos** small drum

**bonnet** *n* head covering
**bonny** *adj* handsome, comely
**bonsai** *n* dwarf tree or shrub
**bonus** *n* added sum or benefit; *pl* **bonuses**

> **bonus** *n* benefit, boon, bounty, dividend, extra, gift, perk, plus, prize, reward, tip

**boo** *interj used to indicate disapproval, to startle;* *v* make this sound
**book** *n* sheets of paper bound together in cover to form a volume; *v* reserve in advance; *adj* **bookish** scholarly

> **book** *n* leaflet, magazine, manual, publication, text, tome, treatise, work
> **book** *v* arrange, charter, engage, line up, make a reservation, reserve

**bookend** *n* device to stop books falling over
**bookmaker** *n* professional betting man
**boom** *n* 1 loud hollow roar 2 sudden prosperity; *v* 1 make hollow roar 2 be successful

> **boom** *n* 1 (hollow roar) blast, clap, crash, explosion, roll, rumble, shout, thunder. 2 (sudden prosperity) development, expansion, gain, growth, increase, progress, success, upsurge, upturn
> **boom** *v* 1 (make hollow roar) bang, crash, echo, explode, resound, reverberate, roll, rumble, shout, thunder. 2 (be successful) develop, expand, flourish, grow, increase, progress, prosper, succeed, thrive

**boomerang** *n* wooden object returning to thrower
**boost** *v* help; *n* help

> **boost** *v* assist, encourage, facilitate, further, improve, increase, inspire, praise, promote,
> **boost** *n* assistance, encouragement, improvement, increase, praise, promotion, stimulus, support

**boot** n foot and ankle covering; idm **give sb the boot** dismiss from employment
**booth** n temporary stall in market, etc
**booty** n spoils of war; plunder
**border** n 1 edge 2 frontier 3 flower bed; v line; verge (on)

> **border** n 1 (edge) boundary, brink, edging, fringe, limit, margin, perimeter, rim, verge. 2 (frontier) boundary

**borderline** n, adj (on the) dividing line between two categories
**bore** v 1 make hole in 2 weary by being dull; n dull person; n **boredom** state of being bored
**bored** adj fed up

> **bored** adj apathetic, blasé, fed up, jaded, tired, unenthusiastic, uninspired, weary

**boring** adj tedious

> **boring** adj dull, humdrum, monotonous, repetitious, routine, stale, uneventful

**born** v **be born** come into the world
**borne** pp of **bear**
**borough** n town or city
**borrow** v obtain on loan; adopt; use another's material

> **borrow** v acquire, commandeer, filch, pinch, scrounge, take, use

**bosom** n human breast; seat of emotions
**boss** n head person; v direct

> **boss** n chief, employer, foreman, head, master, overseer, owner, supervisor

**bossy** adj arrogant

> **bossy** adj assertive, bullying, domineering, high-handed, officious, overbearing

**botany** n science of plant life; n **botanist**; adjs **botanic, botanical**
**botch** v patch roughly; bungle
**both** adj, pron the two; conj, adv as well
**bother** v 1 annoy 2 make the effort 3 worry; n nuisance

> **bother** v 1 (annoy) exasperate, harass, hassle, irritate, nag, pester, provoke, torment, vex. 2 (make the effort) be concerned, care, go to any trouble, inconvenience yourself, mind, put yourself out. 3 (worry) alarm, concern, perturb, upset, trouble
> **bother** n annoyance, difficulty, effort, fuss, hassle, inconvenience, irritation, trouble

**bottle** n glass container for liquids; v put into bottles; idm **bottle up** suppress (feelings)
**bottleneck** n narrow passage; condition hindering free circulation
**bottom** n 1 lowest part 2 human rump; adj lowest

> **bottom** n 1 (lowest part) base, bed, depth, floor, foot, foundation, underneath, underside. 2 (human rump) backside, behind, buttocks, hindquarters, rear, seat

**bottom line** n essential fact or factor
**botulism** n form of food poisoning
**bough** n limb of tree
**bought** pt, pp of **buy**
**boulder** n large rounded rock or stone
**bounce** v rebound, as ball

> **bounce** v bob, bound, jump, leap, rebound, recoil, ricochet, spring

**bound**¹ v move with sudden spring; n leap

> **bound** v bounce, caper, frolic, gambol, hop, jump, pounce, prance, skip, spring, vault

**bound**² adj tied; idm **bound to 1** certain to **2** obliged to; **bound for** on the way to

**A**
**B**
**C**
**D**
**E**
**F**
**G**
**H**
**I**
**J**
**K**
**L**
**M**
**N**
**O**
**P**
**Q**
**R**
**S**
**T**
**U**
**V**
**W**
**X**
**Y**
**Z**

**bound** *adj* 1 (tied) fettered, lashed, roped, secured, strapped, tethered, trussed. **2 bound to** (certain to) destined, doomed, fated, sure. **3 bound to** (obliged to) committed, compelled, forced, required

**boundary** something fixing limit, area, etc

**boundary** *n* border, bounds, demarcation, edge, end, extremity, frontier, limits, margin, perimeter, threshold

**bouquet** *n* bunch of flowers

**bouquet** *n* arrangement, bunch, buttonhole, garland, posy, spray, wreath

**bout** *n* 1 fight 2 period of illness or activity

**bout** *n* 1 (fight) competition, contest, encounter, match, set-to *inf*. 2 (period) attack, fit, run, spell, stint, stretch

**boutique** *n* shop selling fashionable clothes
**bovine** *adj* pertaining to ox or cow
**bow**[1] *n* inclination of head or body in respect; front end of ship; *v* make bow

**bow** *v* 1 bend, bob, curtsy, genuflect, kowtow, nod, salaam, stoop. **2 bow to** capitulate, give in, give way, submit, surrender, yield

**bow**[2] *n* 1 weapon for shooting arrows 2 implement for playing violin, etc
**bowels** *n* intestines
**bowl**[1] *n* hollow dish

**bowl** *n* basin, dish, tureen, vessel

**bowl**[2] *v* roll or throw ball; *ns* **bowler** one who bowls; hard round felt hat; **bowling** game played on bowling green
**bowlegs** *n pl* legs curving outwards at the knee; *adj* **bowlegged**

**bow tie** *n* small tie with double loop
**box**[1] *n* 1 container 2 private compartment in theater

**box** *n* (container) carton, case, chest, crate, pack, package, trunk

**box**[2] *v* strike with fist or hand; *n* **boxer** one who fights with fists as sport (**boxing**)
**box office** *n* kiosk in cinema, theater, etc, where tickets are sold
**boy** *n* male child, youth; *n* **boyhood**

**boy** *n* fellow, kid *inf*, lad, schoolboy, son, youngster, youth

**boycott** *v* ban; refuse to deal with

**boycott** *v* bar, blacklist, ostracize, place an embargo on, spurn

**boyfriend** *n* male sweetheart

**boyfriend** *n* date, lover, man, sweetheart, young man

**bra** *n coll* brassiere
**brace** *n* 1 support 2 *pl* support for trousers

**brace** *n* 1 (support) buttress, prop, reinforcement, stay, strut, support, truss. 2 (pair) couple, duo, pair, two

**braced** *adj* ready
**bracelet** *n* wrist band or ornament
**bracket** *n* projecting support; *pl* symbols [], (), enclosing word, etc; *v* join, associate
**brag** *v* boast; *n* 1 boast 2 cardgame
**Brahman, Brahmin** *n* member of highest Hindu caste
**braid** *n* plait of hair; band of fabric; *v* plait
**braille** *n* system of printing used by the blind
**brain** *n* 1 mass of nervous substance within skull; intelligence 2 intelligent person; *v* dash out brains of; hit on head; *adj* **brainy**; *n* **brainwave** sudden bright idea

**brain** *n* **1** (intelligence) brainpower, gray matter, intellect, mind, reason, sense, understanding, wit. **2** (intelligent person) genius, intellectual, mastermind, thinker

**braise** *v* cook by simmering in closed pan
**brake** *n* device for checking wheel's motion; *v* apply brake to
**bramble** *n* prickly shrub, blackberry
**bran** *n* husks remaining after grain is ground
**branch** *n* **1** limb of tree **2** part of organization; *v* produce branches

**branch** *n* **1** (limb of tree) arm, bough, stem, twig. **2** (part of organization) department, division, office, part, section

**brand** *n* **1** type **2** trademark; *v* mark with brand

**brand** *n* **1** (type) class, kind, make, quality, sort, variety. **2** (trademark) hallmark, label, marker, sign, stamp, symbol

**brandish** *v* flourish, wave
**brandy** *n* strong spirit distilled from wine
**brash** *adj* impudently self-assertive

**brash** *adj* arrogant, bold, brazen, cocky *inf*, forward, impertinent, insolent, pushy *inf*

**brass** *n* alloy of copper and zinc; *sl* money
**bravado** *n* show of boldness or bluster
**brave** *adj* courageous; *n* N American Indian warrior; *v* face with courage; *adv* **bravely**

**brave** *adj* bold, daring, dauntless, fearless, gutsy *inf*, heroic, intrepid, tough, unafraid

**bravery** *n* courage

**bravery** *n* boldness, daring, fearlessness, gallantry, guts *inf*, heroism, nerve *inf*, pluck, spirit, valor

**bravo** *interj* well done!
**brawl** *n*, *v* quarrel; fight
**brawn** *n* muscle; strength
**bray** *v* cry, as donkey
**brazen** shameless
**breach** *n* **1** break **2** violation of law, contract; *v* **1** make hole in **2** violate law, contract

**breach** *n* **1** (break) aperture, crack, fissure, fracture, opening, slit. **2** (violation) infringement, transgression
**breach** *v* **1** (make hole in) break through, burst through, open up. **2** (violate) break, contravene, defy, disobey, infringe

**bread** *n* food made from flour, water, yeast, and baked
**breadth** *n* **1** distance across **2** wide range

**breadth** *n* **1** (distance across) broadness, span, spread, thickness. **2** (wide range) comprehensiveness, extent, scale, scope

**breadwinner** *n* person supporting family with earnings
**break** *v* **breaking, broke, broken 1** smash **2** fail to comply with **3** pause; *n* **1** fracture **2** pause; *adj* **breakable**; *phr vs* **break down 1** reduce to pieces **2** analyze **3** fail to work **4** lose control of emotions; **break out** start suddenly; **break up 1** divide **2** end a relationship **3** collapse

**break** *v* **1** (smash) bust, chip, crack, damage, demolish, destroy, fracture, fragment, part, separate, sever, shatter, shiver, snap, splinter, split, tear, wreck. **2** (fail to comply with) contravene, defy, disobey, disregard, flout, infringe, violate. **3** (pause) discontinue, interrupt, knock off, rest, stop, take a break, take five
**break** *n* **1** (fracture) breach, breakage, crack, hole, fissure, gap, gash, rent, rift, rupture, split, tear. **2** (pause) breather *inf*, halt, interlude, lull, respite, rest, stop

**breakage** *n* act of breaking; thing broken

**breakdown** *n* 1 failure to operate 2 nervous collapse 3 statistical analysis

**breakfast** *n* first meal of day

**breakthrough** *n* important discovery leading to progress

> **breakthrough** *n* advance, development, discovery, innovation, invention, leap forward, progress, revolution

**breast** *n* bosom; mammary gland

**breastbone** *n* sternum

**breaststroke** *n* style of swimming using a sideways sweep of both arms

**breath** *n* air drawn into or expelled from lungs; slight breeze; fragrance; *idm* **take one's breath away** astonish one; *v* **breathe** inhale and exhale air; live; utter gently; blow lightly; *n* **breather** short rest; *adj* **breath-taking** very exciting

**breathalyze** *n* measure amount of alcohol drunk by driver; *n* **breathalyzer** apparatus for this

**breathless** *adj* 1 out of breath 2 very excited

> **breathless** *adj* 1 (out of breath) exhausted, choking, gasping, gulping, panting, tired out, wheezing, winded. 2 (excited) all agog, eager, on tenterhooks, openmouthed

**breech birth, breech delivery** *n* birth with baby's feet or buttocks emerging first

**breed** *v* bear offspring; give rise to; *pt, pp* **bred**; *n* strain; kind

> **breed** *v* bring up, hatch, increase, multiply, nurture, procreate, produce, propagate, raise, rear, reproduce
> **breed** *n* class, family, line, lineage, pedigree, race, stock, strain, type, variety

**breeze** *n* gentle wind

> **breeze** *n* draft, gust, puff of air, waft

**brevity** *n* briefness; conciseness

**brew** *v* 1 make beer, tea, etc 2 contrive 3 be afoot; *n* aact or product of brewing

> **brew** *n* beer, beverage, blend, concoction, drink, infusion, liquor, mixture, potion, tea

**briar, brier** *n* thorny shrub; wild rose

**bribe** *n* money, favor given to influence person; *v* influence thus; *n* **bribery**

> **bribe** *n* backhander *sl*, enticement, inducement, pay-off, sweetener *inf*
> **bribe** *v* buy sb off, corrupt, get at *inf*, grease sb's palm *inf*, pay sb off

**bric-a-brac** *n* curios; knick-knacks

**brick** *n* oblong block of baked clay used in building; *v* build with bricks; *n* **bricklayer**

**bridal** *adj* of a bride or wedding

**bride** *n* newly married woman; **bridegroom** newly married man; **bridesmaid**

**bridge**[1] *n* card game

**bridge**[2] *n* 1 structure allowing access over river, railway, etc 2 part of ship used by captain and navigating officer

**bridle** *n* head harness of horse; *v* 1 fit with bridle 2 check 3 show disdain, etc

**brief** *adj* 1 concise 2 short; *n* synopsis of law case; *v* give instructions to; *adv* **briefly**

> **brief** *adj* 1 (concise) compact, crisp, incisive, pithy, short, succinct, to the point. 2 (short) fleeting, passing, quick, short-lived, swift, temporary, transient, transitory
> **brief** *n* advice, briefing, guidance, information, instructions, orders
> **brief** *v* advise, fill sb in *inf*, instruct, prepare, prime, put sb in the picture *inf*

**briefs** *n pl* short pants or underpants

**brigade** *n* military unit

**brigadier** *n* officer commanding a brigade

**bright** *adj* 1 shining 2 clever 3 sunny 4 light in colour; *adv* **-ly**; *adv* **-ness**; *v* **brighten** 1 make bright 2 become fine

**bright** *adj* 1 (shining) blazing, brilliant, dazzling, flashing, gleaming, glittering, glowing, incandescent, intense, luminous, radiant, sparkling, vivid. 2 (clever) astute, intelligent, inventive, quick, sharp, smart. 3 (sunny) clear, cloudless, fair. 4 (light in color) bold, brilliant, colorful, fresh, gaudy, intense, rich, vivid

**brighten** *v* 1 (make bright) cheer up, gladden, illuminate, lighten, light up, liven up, perk up, revitalize. 2 (become sunny) clear, clear up

**brilliance** *n* 1 splendor; radiance 2 outstanding talent
**brilliant** *adj* 1 shining brightly 2 very good 3 very clever

**brilliant** *adj* 1 (shining) bright, dazzling, glittering, intense, radiant, sparkling, vivid. 2 (good) excellent, fabulous, great, marvellous, superb, wonderful. 3 (clever) bright, exceptional, famous, gifted, intelligent, remarkable, smart, talented

**brim** *n* rim, edge; *adj* **brimming, brimful**
**brine** *n* salt water used for pickling meat
**bring** *v* 1 take somewhere 2 cause; *pt, pp* **brought**; *phr vs* **bring about** cause to happen; **bring up** 1 rear (children) 2 mention

**bring** *v* 1 (take somewhere) accompany, bear, carry, convey, deliver, escort, fetch, guide, lead, transport. 2 (cause) attract, contribute to, create, generate, give rise to, produce, prompt, provoke, result in. 3 **bring about** accomplish, achieve, cause, create, lead to, produce, result in. 4 **bring up** (rear children) care for, nurture, raise, rear. 5 **bring up** (mention) allude to, broach, refer to, touch on/upon

**brink** *n* edge (of chasm, precipice, etc)
**brisk** *adj* 1 fast 2 good (of business); *adv* **-ly**

**brisk** *adj* 1 (fast) energetic, lively, quick, speedy, vigorous. 2 (of business) active, bustling, busy, hectic

**bristle** *n* short, stiff hair; *v* 1 stand on end, as bristles 2 show indignation; *adj* **bristly**
**British** *adj* of Britain
**Briton** *n* inhabitant of Britain
**brittle** *adj* easily broken

**brittle** *adj* breakable, crumbling, delicate, fragile, frail, hard, splintery, weak

**broach** *n* boring tool; roasting spit; *v* open, begin (a subject)

**broach** *v* bring up, introduce, mention, propose, raise, suggest, touch on

**broad** *adj* 1 wide 2 covering many subjects; *v* **broaden** make wider; *adv* **broadly**

**broad** *adj* 1 (wide) ample, extensive, large, open, spacious, vast. 2 (covering many subjects) comprehensive, encyclopedic, general, wide, wide-ranging

**broadcast** *v* transmit (radio, television); *pt, pp* **broadcast**; *n* such a transmission
**broad-minded** *adj* tolerant

**broad-minded** *adj* enlightened, liberal, open-minded, unbiased, unprejudiced

**broccoli** *n* hardy type of cauliflower
**brochure** *n* pamphlet

**brochure** *n* booklet, catalog, circular, hand-out, leaflet, prospectus

**broke** *adj coll* having no money
**broken** *pp of* **break** 1 in pieces 2 not working

a
**b**
c
d
e
f
g
h
i
j
k
l
m
n
o
p
q
r
s
t
u
v
w
x
y
z

**broken** *adj* **1** (in pieces) cracked, fractured, fragmented, punctured, shattered, smashed, split, torn. **2** (not working) damaged, defective, faulty, kaput, out of order

**brokenhearted** *n* overcome by grief
**broker** *n* one buying for another on commission
**bronchitis** *n* inflammation of bronchial tubes
**bronze** *n* alloy of copper and tin; its color
**brooch** *n* ornamental clasp or pin
**brood** *n* young of animals, *esp* birds; *v* ponder anxiously

**brood** *v* agonize, dwell upon, fret, mope, mull over, muse, ponder, think, worry

**brook** *n* small stream
**broom** *n* **1** flowering shrub **2** sweeping brush
**broth** *n* thin soup
**brother** *n* **1** son of same parents **2** member of religious order, trade union, etc; *n* **brother-in-law** brother of husband or wife
**brought** *pt, pp of* **bring**
**brow** *n* **1** eyebrow; forehead **2** top of hill, etc
**browbeat** *v* bully
**brown** *adj* **1** color made by mixing black, red, and yellow **2** dark (of hair) **3** tanned

**brown** *adj* **1** (color) beige, buff, chocolate, cocoa, copper, coppery, hazel, mahogany, russet, rust, sepia, tan, tawny, terracotta. **2** (of hair) auburn, chestnut, dark, ginger. **3** (tanned) bronze, bronzed, dark, sunburnt

**browse** *v* feed (as animal) on grass, leaves, etc; glance through book
**bruise** *n* injury that discolors skin; *v* inflict this
**brunette, brunet** *n* woman with dark hair
**brunt** *n* chief stress, strain of attack
**brush** *n* **1** implement for sweeping, painting, dressing hair, etc **2** tail of fox; *v* **1** sweep **2** touch lightly; *phr v* **brush up (on)** revive knowledge of

**brush** *v* **1** (sweep) buff, clean, groom, polish, tidy, wash. **2** (touch lightly) caress, flick, graze, stroke **3 brush up** go over, polish up, read up, revise, study

**brusque** *adj* abrupt, curt
**Brussels sprout** *n* (plant with) edible bud-like small cabbage
**brutal** *adj* cruel and violent

**brutal** *adj* barbaric, bloodthirsty, callous, cold-blooded, heartless, merciless, pitiless, ruthless, savage, vicious

**brutality** *n* cruel and violent act

**brutality** *n* atrocity, barbarity, cruelty, ferocity, savagery

**brute** *n* **1** lower animal **2** cruel person

**brute** *n* **1** (lower animal) beast, creature, dumb animal, wild animal. **2** (cruel person) barbarian, beast, bully, devil, fiend, monster, sadist, savage, swine

**BSc** *abbr* Bachelor of Science
**BSE** *abbr* bovine spongiform encephalopathy; fatal disease of cattle that attacks the central nervous system
**bubble** *n* globule of gas, air; *v* form bubbles; make bubbling sound

**bubble** *v* boil, effervesce, fizz, fizzle, foam, froth, gurgle, simmer, sparkle

**buck** *n* **1** male deer, rabbit, etc **2** sudden spring **3** *sl* dollar; *v* leap suddenly
**bucket** *n* vessel for carrying water, etc
**buckle** *n* clasp with catch for fastening; *v* warp; fasten with buckle
**bud** *n* growth from which flower leaf develops
**Buddhism** *n* religion based on teachings of Buddha; *n, adj* **buddhist**
**budge** *v* move position

**budgerigar** *n* small parakeet, lovebird
**budget** *n* estimated financial schedule; *v* plan spending

> **budget** *n* accounts, allowance, cost, finances, financial plan, funds
> **budget** *v* allocate, allow, apportion, cost, estimate, plan, provide, ration, save

**buff** *n* 1 soft leather 2 pale yellow color
**buffalo** *n pl* **-oes** kind of ox; American bison
**buffer** *n* something that protects against or lessens the force of an impact

> **buffer** *n* bulwark, bumper, cushion, fender, guard, safeguard, screen, shield

**buffers** *n* spring-loaded steel pads attached to railway rolling stock and ends of track to cushion impact
**buffet**[1] *n*, *v* bang against
**buffet**[2] *n* refreshment bar
**bug** *n* 1 small insect 2 germ 3 problem in computer program; *v* **bugging, bugged** 1 listen in 2 annoy

> **bug** *n* 1 (insect) creepy-crawly *inf*, mite. 2 (germ) bacterium, infection, micro-organism, virus. 3 (in a computer program) breakdown, defect, error, fault, flaw, gremlin *inf*, mistake, virus
> **bug** *v* 1 (listen in) eavesdrop, spy on, tap. 2 (annoy) anger, irritate

**buggy** *n* 1 light carriage 2 small motor vehicle 3 also **baby buggy** baby carriage
**bugle** *n* kind of small trumpet
**build** *v* **building, built** construct

> **build** *v* assemble, erect, form, make, manufacture, put together, put up

**buildup** *n* steady increase
**built-in** *adj* 1 constructed as part of 2 inherent
**built-up** *adj* with many buildings

**bulb** *n* 1 globular, modified leafbud, *usu* underground; 2 electric lamp
**bulge** *n* rounded swelling; *v* swell

> **bulge** *n* bump, hump, lump, projection, protuberance, rise

**bulk** *n* volume; size; *idm* **in bulk** in large quantities; *adj* **bulky** voluminous

> **bulk** *n* extent, immensity, magnitude, mass, massiveness, quantity, size, weight

**bull** *n* 1 male of ox family, etc 2 speculator in rising stock values
**bulldog** *n* dog with powerful lower jaw
**bulldozer** *n* powerful earthmoving tractor; *v* **bulldoze** overcome opposition by force
**bullet** *n* metal ball or missile fired from gun

> **bullet** *n* missile, pellet, shot, slug

**bulletin** *n* brief official statement

> **bulletin** *n* announcement, communication, communiqué, message, news-flash, notification, report, statement

**bullfinch** *n* songbird with pink breast
**bullion** *n* gold or silver before being coined
**bullish** *adj* 1 like a bull 2 showing promise of success in stock market 3 optimistic
**bullock** *n* castrated bull
**bull's-eye** *n* center of target
**bully** *n* **-lies** overbearing, cruel ruffian; *v* **-lying, -lied** intimidate

> **bully** *n* abuser, oppressor, persecutor, ruffian, thug, tormentor, tyrant
> **bully** *v* coerce, frighten, persecute, pick on, terrorize, threaten, tyrannize

**bulrush** *n* large rush of sedge family
**bumble** *v* speak incoherently
**bumblebee** *n* large wild humming bee
**bump** *n* 1 blow 2 lump; *v* 1 collide with 2 jolt

A
**B**
C
D
E
F
G
H
I
J
K
L
M
N
O
P
Q
R
S
T
U
V
W
X
Y
Z

**bump** n 1 (blow) bang, collision, crash, knock, smash, thud, thump. 2 (lump) bulge, hump, knob, protuberance, swelling
**bump** v 1 (collide with) bang, crash, hit, hurt, injure, jar, knock, smash into, strike, thump. 2 (jolt) bounce, jerk, rattle, shake

**bun** n small cake; small round bunch of hair
**bunch** n, v 1 group of things tied together 2 handful of flowers 3 group of people

**bunch** n 1 (group) batch, bundle, cluster, collection, heap, load, mass, pack, quantity, set. 2 (of flowers) bouquet, clump, posy, sheaf, spray. 3 (of people) band, crowd, gang, knot, party

**bundle** n number of things tied together; v 1 tie in a bundle 2 hustle (someone) away

**bundle** n assortment, batch, bunch, collection, heap, pack, package, pile, roll

**bung** n cork, wooden stopper, *esp* for cask
**bungalow** n one-storied house
**bungle** v do sth badly; n sth done badly

**bungle** v blunder, botch, fudge, make a mess *inf*, mess up *inf*, ruin, spoil
**bungle** n blunder, botch, error, fiasco, mess, mistake, mix-up, muddle, pig's ear *sl*

**bunion** n inflamed swelling, *esp* on big toe
**bunker** n 1 large bin, *esp* for fuel 2 military dugout 3 hazard on golf course
**bunny** n (child's word for) rabbit
**bunting** n colored flags
**buoy** n floating object anchored in water to mark channel, rocks, etc
**buoyant** *adj* 1 able to float 2 cheerful

**buoyant** *adj* 1 (able to float) floating, light. 2 (cheerful) blithe, bouncy, bright, jaunty, lighthearted, upbeat

**burden** n 1 something carried 2 trouble; v worry

**burden** n 1 (sth carried) cargo, load, weight 2 (trouble) anxiety, difficulty, responsibility, sorrow, stress, trial, worry
**burden** v bother, impose, load, overload, strain, tax, trouble, weigh down, worry

**bureau** n Fr pl **-eaux,** or **-eaus** 1 information office 2 government department
**bureaucracy** n government by state officials; n **bureaucrat;** *adj* **bureaucratic**

**bureaucracy** n administration, ministry, officialdom, red tape, rules and regulations

**burglar** n one who breaks into house to steal
**burglary** n crime of breaking into a house to steal

**burglary** n break-in, breaking and entering, housebreaking, robbery, theft, thieving

**burial** n burying; funeral; n **burial ground**
**burly** *adj* of sturdy build

**burly** *adj* beefy, brawny, hefty, muscular, powerful, stocky, strong, sturdy, well-built

**burn** v 1 be on fire 2 damage by fire

**burn** v 1 (be on fire) blaze, flame, flare, glow, go up in flames, ignite, kindle, set alight, set on fire, smoke, smolder, spark. 2 (damage by fire) blister, char, reduce to ashes, shrivel, singe, toast

**burnout** n mechanical failure through overheating or exhaustion of fuel
**burrow** n hole scooped in ground by animal; v make hole; dig, search

**burrow** n den, earth, hole, lair, shelter, tunnel, warren

**bursar** n treasurer, *esp* of college
**burst** v **bursting, burst** explode; puncture; n explosion; sudden spurt

> **burst** v blow up, break, crack, disintegrate, erupt, explode, fly open, fragment, pop, puncture, rupture, shatter, split, tear

**bury** v **burying, buried** 1 conceal 2 inter

> **bury** v 1 (conceal) cover, enclose, engulf, enshroud, hide, immerse, sink, submerge. 2 (inter) entomb, inter, lay to rest

**bus** n large passenger motor vehicle
**bush** n 1 shrub; thicket 2 wild country; *adj* **bushy**; n **bushiness**
**business** n 1 firm 2 trade 3 affair; **businessman, businesswoman**

> **business** n 1 (firm) company, enterprise, industry, organization, outfit, partnership, venture. 2 (trade) buying and selling, commerce, marketing, merchandising, selling, transactions. 3 (affair) case, issue, matter, problem, question, subject, topic

**businesslike** *adj* efficient

> **businesslike** *adj* efficient, methodical, neat, organized, professional, systematic

**busing, bussing** n transporting schoolchildren to other districts to effect racial equality
**bust** n upper part of human body; sculpture of such part; *adj* **bust, busted** *coll* broken
**bustle** n noisy movement; v move quickly

> **bustle** n activity, agitation, commotion, excitement, flurry, fuss, haste, hurry, movement, toing and froing *inf*

**busy** *adj* **busier, busiest** 1 occupied 2 hectic; v **busying, busied** occupy (oneself); *adv* **busily**

**busy** *adj* 1 (occupied) active, employed, engaged, engrossed, industrious, working. 2 (hectic) chaotic, energetic, frantic

**but** *conj* on the contrary; **all but** almost
**butcher** n 1 tradesman dealing in meat 2 brutal murderer; v kill for food, or indiscriminately
**butt** n 1 barrel 2 end; stub 3 figure of fun; v push with head; *phr* v **butt in** interrupt
**butter** n solidified fat obtained from cream by churning; v spread with butter
**buttercup** n yellow cup-shaped wild flower
**butterfly** n insect with brightly colored wings; *pl* **butterflies**
**buttocks** n the rump
**button** n small flat disk for fastening clothing, etc; small knob; v fasten with button
**buttonhole** n 1 slit in lapel 2 worn in this; v detain and force sb to hear what one has to say
**buttress** n support giving extra strength to anything; v support, prop
**buy** v obtain by paying; bribe; *pt, pp* **bought**; n **buyer**

> **buy** v acquire, come by, get, invest in *inf*, obtain, pay for, procure, purchase

**buzz** n low humming noise, as of bee; v make such sound; n **buzzer** mechanical device that buzzes
**by** *prep* 1 near; close to 2 through; over 3 not later than; *adv* 1 at hand 2 past
**bygone** *adj* past, gone by
**bypass** n 1 route avoiding busy area 2 *med* alternative passage for blood during surgical operation; v go around; avoid

> **bypass** v avoid, circumvent, detour around, evade, go around, sidestep, skirt

**by-product** n subsidiary product or result
**bystander** n one standing near; onlooker
**byte** n *comput* unit of information (= 8 bits)

a
**b**
c
d
e
f
g
h
i
j
k
l
m
n
o
p
q
r
s
t
u
v
w
x
y
z

**cab** n 1 taxi 2 driver's shelter on lorry or bus
**cabal** n intrigue; secret plot
**cabaret** n Fr entertainment in nightclub
**cabbage** n green edible vegetable
**cabin** n 1 hut 2 room on ship for sleeping

> **cabin** n 1 (hut) chalet, lodge, log cabin, shack, shed, shelter. 2 (room on a ship) berth, compartment, quarters, room

**cabinet** n 1 case or set of drawers 2 body of ministers governing country
**cable** n thick strong rope or line
**cable car** n mountain car on high cable
**cable television** n satellite TV system with multiple channels
**caboose** n last car of train for crew's use
**cache** n secret store or hiding place
**cackle** n 1 noise made by hen, goose 2 shrill chatter; v make such noise
**cactus** n, pl **-tuses**, **-ti** prickly plant with fleshy stem
**cadet** n student training for commissioned rank
**cadge** v beg; sponge on others
**café** n Fr restaurant serving light meals; n **cafeteria** self-service cafe

> **café** n cafeteria, coffee bar, coffee shop, diner, restaurant, snack bar, tearoom

**caffeine** n stimulant found in coffee and tea

**cage** v to confine to cage; n structure for confining animals, etc

> **cage** v coop up, fence in, lock up, pen

**cajole** v flatter with ulterior motive
**Cajun** n Louisiana inhabitant descended from Acadian immigrant
**cake** n kind of sweet dough, baked in tin; v to form hard mass, as of clay, etc
**calamine** n pink lotion to soothe sore skin
**calamity** n terrible, disastrous event
**calcium** n metallic element, base of lime
**calculate** v 1 work out by arithmetic 2 judge; ns **calculation**, **calculator**

> **calculate** v 1 (work out by arithmetic) add, compute, count, estimate, measure, total. 2 (judge) assess, consider, determine, evaluate, gauge, rate, weigh up, work out

**calculating** adj scheming

> **calculating** adj crafty, cunning, devious, manipulative, shrewd, sly

**calendar** n official list of dates
**calf**[1] n young of cow and other mammals
**calf**[2] n fleshy back of leg below knee
**caliber** n diameter of bore of gun; quality of mind or character
**calico** n cloth made of cotton
**call** v 1 speak loudly to 2 telephone 3 visit 4 give a name to 5 convene; n cry or shout **caller**; phr v **call off** cancel

> **call** v 1 (speak loudly to) cry out, exclaim, hail, shout, yell. 2 (telephone) call up, contact, give sb a ring, phone. 3 (visit) drop in, pay a call, stop by. 4 (give a name to) christen, designate, entitle, label, name. 5 (convene) announce, convoke, gather, order
> **call** n exclamation, roar, shout, shriek, whoop, yell

**callous** *adj* hard-hearted
**calm** *adj* 1 still 2 relaxed; *n* 1 stillness 2 state of being relaxed; *v* become, make still or peaceful; *adv* **-ly**

> **calm** *adj* 1 (still) airless, motionless, peaceful, quiet, tranquil, windless. 2 (relaxed) composed, cool, level-headed, patient, unfazed, unmoved, unruffled, untroubled
> **calm** *n* 1 (stillness) peacefulness, quietness, restfulness, serenity, tranquillity. 2 (state of being relaxed) composure, equanimity, impassivity, poise, self-control

**calorie** *n* unit of heat, *esp* in relation to value of food; *adj* **calorific** heat making
**calves** *pl of* **calf**
**camaraderie** *n* comradeship
**camcorder** *n* video camera with recorder
**came** *pt of* **come**
**camel** *n* large, ruminant, humped animal
**camera** *n* photographic apparatus
**camomile** *n* herb
**camouflage** *v* disguise appearance of objects; *n* disguise

> **camouflage** *v* cloak, conceal, cover, disguise, hide, mask, obscure, screen
> **camouflage** *n* cover, façade, guise, markings, mask, mimicry

**camp** *n* 1 temporary shelter for travelers 2 place where tents or huts are erected for troops 3 faction or party; *v* build, lodge in camp; *ns* **camping, camper; camp-cot** narrow folding bed
**campaign** *n* 1 action to achieve sth 2 military operations; *v* organize actions to achieve sth

> **campaign** *n* 1 (action to achieve sth) action, crusade, drive, effort, fight, movement, promotion, struggle. 2 (military operations) attack, battle, offensive, push, war
> **campaign** *v* agitate, battle, canvass, crusade, fight, push, struggle, work

**campus** *n* chief grounds of university, school
**can't** *v coll* cannot
**can**[1] *v aux* be able, be allowed to; *pt* **could**; *pp* **been able**
**can**[2] *n* tin vessel used for holding food for preserving; *v* preserve in can
**canal** *n* 1 artificial waterway 2 duct in body
**canary** *n* yellow songbird
**cancel** *v* 1 stop arrangements for 2 cross out; *n* **cancellation**

> **cancel** *v* 1 (stop arrangements for) abandon, abort, call off, postpone, scrap. 2 (cross out) delete, erase, strike out

**cancer** *n* malignant tumour or growth in body; *adj* **cancerous**
**candelabra** *n pl* ornamental candleholder
**candid** *adj* frank; *adv* **candidly**; *n* **candour**

> **candid** *adj* blunt, honest, open, outspoken, plain, straightforward, truthful

**candidate** *n* 1 person standing for election 2 person taking examination

> **candidate** *n* applicant, competitor, contender, contestant, entrant, nominee

**candle** *n* stick of wax with wick, for giving light; *n* **candlestick** candleholder
**candor** *n* frankness
**cane** *n* hard stem of bamboo, etc; walking stick; *v* beat with stick; *n* **caning**
**canine** *adj* of, related to dog
**canister** *n* box, usually of metal
**cannabis** *n* drug extracted from hemp
**canned** *adj* put into cans or sealed jars
**cannibal** *n* human who eats human flesh
**cannon** *n* large mounted gun
**cannot** *v* can not
**canoe** *n* light boat propelled by paddling; *pl* **canoes**; *n* **canoeist**
**canon** *n* 1 rule, law, *esp* of church 2 ecclesiastical dignitary 3 list of saints; *v* **canonize** declare officially to be a saint

a
b
**c**
d
e
f
g
h
i
j
k
l
m
n
o
p
q
r
s
t
u
v
w
x
y
z

**canopy** n overhead covering

**cantankerous** adj ill-natured; quarrelsome

**canteen** n 1 restaurant (in factory, school, etc) 2 camper's water flask

**canter** n easy gallop

**canvas** n strong coarse hempen cloth used for sails or painting pictures on

**canvass** v 1 seek votes 2 discuss 3 seek opinions

> **canvass** v 1 (seek votes) campaign, drum up support, electioneer. 2 (discuss) analyze, examine, investigate, study. 3 (seek opinions) ask for, discuss, poll, solicit

**canyon** n deep gorge between cliffs

**cap** n 1 brimless head covering 2 lid

**capability** n ability

**capable** adj able

> **capable** adj adept, clever, competent, efficient, experienced, gifted, proficient, qualified, skillful, skilled, talented

**capacity** n 1 size 2 ability

> **capacity** n 1 (size) amplitude, dimensions, magnitude, room, space, volume. 2 (ability) aptitude, cleverness, competence, intelligence, skill, talent

**cape** n 1 sleeveless cloak 2 headland

**capillary** n very narrow blood vessel

**capital** n 1 accumulated wealth 2 chief city; adj 1 large (of letters) 2 chief (of cities); ns **capitalism** system of individual ownership of wealth; **capitalist**; phr v **capitalize on** take advantage of

> **capital** n 1 (accumulated wealth) assets, cash, finance, funds, investments, money, property, resources, savings, stock, wealth. 2 (chief city) first city, seat of government

**capital punishment** n punishment by death

**capitulate** v surrender

**capitulate** v acquiesce, admit defeat, back down, concede, give in, submit, yield

**cappuccino** n Italian coffee made with hot, frothy milk

**capsicum** n red or green pepper

**capsize** v overturn, esp of boats

> **capsize** v flip over, keel over, tip over, turn over, turn upside down, upset

**capsule** n 1 part of spaceship in which astronaut travels 2 small case containing drug or medicine

**captain** n naval or military officer; leader of team; v act as leader of team

> **captain** n boss, chief, commander, head, leader, master, officer, pilot, skipper

**caption** n title of picture, etc; heading

**captivate** v enchant, fascinate

**captive** n person held as prisoner; adj unable to escape; n **captivity**

> **captive** n convict, detainee, hostage, internee, prisoner, slave
> **captive** adj captured, confined, fettered, imprisoned, incarcerated, interned, jailed, locked up, under lock and key

**capture** v take prisoner; n act of taking

> **capture** v apprehend, arrest, catch, corner, ensnare, nab, seize, trap
> **capture** n apprehension, arrest, imprisonment, seizure

**car** n automobile

**carafe** n bottle for water, wine

**caramel** n candy; burned sugar for flavoring

**carat** n measure of purity of gold

**caravan** n covered vehicle, used as home

**carbohydrate** n energy-giving food containing sugar or starch

**carbon** *n* nonmetallic element occurring as graphite, diamond, etc

**carbonated** *adj* fizzy

**carbon dioxide** *n* gas formed by burning of carbon or by breathing of animals

**carbon monoxide** *n* poisonous gas emitted in exhaust fumes of gas engines

**carbuncle** *n* inflamed boil

**carcass** *n* dead body

**carcinogen** *n* any substance likely to cause cancer; *adj* **carcinogenic**

**carcinoma** *n* type of cancer

**card** *n* thin pasteboard; visiting card; playing card; postcard; *also* **cardboard**

**cardiac** *adj* concerning heart; *n* **cardiograph** record of heart action

**cardigan** *n* knitted woolen or cotton jacket

**cardinal** *adj* of chief importance; *n* prince of RC Church, next in rank to Pope; *n* **cardinal numbers** 1,2,3, etc

**care** *n* 1 worry 2 carefulness 3 supervision; *v* feel concerned; *idm* **have a care/take care** be careful; *phr v* **care for** 1 look after 2 like

> **care** *n* 1 (worry) anxiety, hardship, problem, sorrow, trouble, woe. 2 (carefulness) attention, caution, concentration, forethought, heed, prudence, thought, watchfulness. 3 (supervision) charge, control, custody, guardianship, keeping, protection, safekeeping
> **care** *v* 1 (feel concerned) be concerned, be troubled, bother, concern yourself with, mind, worry. 2 **care for** (look after) cherish, foster, mind, mother, nurse, protect, provide for, take care of, tend, watch over. 3 **care for** (like) be fond of, cherish, hold dear, love

**career** *n* occupation; *v* rush wildly

> **career** *n* business, calling, employment, livelihood, living, métier, profession, trade, vocation, work

**carefree** *adj* free from anxiety

> **carefree** *adj* cheerful, easygoing, happy-go-lucky, laid-back, light-hearted, relaxed

**careful** *a* 1 paying attention 2 attentive to danger; *adv* **-ly**

> **careful** *adj* 1 (paying attention) conscientious, methodical, meticulous, neat, painstaking, particular, precise, rigorous, thorough, well-organized. 2 (attentive to danger) alert, attentive, cautious, circumspect, heedful, mindful, observant, on guard, vigilant, wary

**careless** *a* 1 not paying attention 2 sloppy

> **careless** *adj* 1 (not paying attention) absent-minded, forgetful, inattentive, irresponsible, negligent, rash, reckless, scatterbrained, thoughtless. 2 (sloppy) disorganized, hasty, inaccurate, messy, shoddy, slapdash, untidy

**caress** *n* mark of affection, kiss, embrace, etc; *v* fondle, embrace

**caretaker** *n* person employed to look after a building

**cargo** *n* freight or load of ship, etc

> **cargo** *n* baggage, consignment, freight, goods, haul, load, merchandise, shipment

**caricature** *n* grotesque, laughable drawing of person; *v* represent in caricature

**caring** *adj* showing concern for others

> **caring** *adj* altruistic, compassionate, concerned, considerate, helpful, kind, loving, sympathetic, thoughtful, understanding, unselfish, well-meaning

**carnage** *n* severe slaughter; massacre

**carnation** *n* cultivated variety of clove pink

**carnival** *n* organized festivities

**carnivore** *n* flesh-eating mammal

**carob** n bean used as substitute for cocoa

**carol** n joyful song, *esp* Christmas hymn

**carousel** n merry-go-round

**carpel** n female reproductive organ of a flowering plant

**carpenter** n woodworker in housebuilding, etc; n **carpentry** craft of carpenter

**carpet** n fabric for covering floor, etc; v cover with carpet

**carriage** n 1 vehicle 2 transportation of anything 3 deportment 4 bearing cost of carriage

**carrier** n 1 person or thing that carries 2 one that passes a disease to others

**carrot** n edible reddish orange root

**carry** v 1 take 2 support; *phr v* **carry on** continue

> **carry** v 1 (take) bear, bring, cart, convey, ferry, fetch, haul, lug, move, remove, ship, transfer, transport. 2 (support) bear, hold, sustain, underpin. 3 (carry on) continue, endure, go on, keep, keep going, last, maintain, persevere, persist

**cart** n two- or four-wheeled vehicle

**cartilage** n strong, elastic tissue, gristle

**carton** n box made of cardboard

**cartoon** n topical drawing in newspaper; animated film

**cartridge** n metal case containing charge for gun

**cartwheel** n sideways somersault

**carve** v 1 cut and shape wood, stone, etc; engrave 2 cut meat; n **carving** piece of carved work

> **carve** v 1 (cut and shape wood) cut, chisel, engrave, etch, scratch, sculpture, shape. 2 (cut meat) cut up, serve, slice

**cascade** n small waterfall

**case** n 1 container 2 suitcase 3 situation 4 legal action; *idm* **in any case** whatever happens; *idm* **in case of** 1 in the event of 2 as a precaution against

> **case** n 1 (container) box, chest, crate, holder. 2 (suitcase) bag, briefcase, hand luggage, trunk. 3 (situation) circumstances, example, illustration, instance, occasion. 4 (legal action) dispute, hearing, inquiry, lawsuit, proceedings, trial, tribunal

**cash** n money; v exchange for notes and coins

> **cash** n change, coins, currency, funds, money, notes, resources, small change

**cash card** n card enabling bank-account holders to get cash from a machine

**cashew** n small kidney-shaped edible nut

**cashmere** n soft woolen material woven from goat's hair

**cashpoint** n cash dispensing machine

**cash register** n machine in a shop with a drawer for safekeeping of money

**casing** n protective covering

**casino** n public room for gambling

**cask** n barrel, mainly used for liquids

**casket** n 1 small box for jewels 2 coffin

**casserole** n fireproof dish for cooking and serving food; food cooked in this way

**cassette** n container for film or tape

**cast** v 1 throw 2 throw a light 3 mold (metal, etc) 4 assign parts in a play; *pt, pp* **cast**; n 1 actors in a play 2 mold

> **cast** v 1 (throw) chuck *inf*, fling, heave, hurl, lob, scatter, sling, toss. 2 (throw a light) direct, emit, give off, send out, shed **cast** n 1 (actors) characters, company, dramatis personae *tech*, performers, players, troupe. 2 (mold) casting, impression, shape

**castanets** n *mus* instrument of two wooden shells clicked rapidly together in the hand

**castaway** n person adrift after a shipwreck

**caste** n division of Indian society

**castellated** adj with battlements

**caster, castor** n small wheel on swivel fixed to leg of chair, etc

**castigate** *v* chastise; punish severely

**cast iron** *n* hard brittle type of iron; *adj* **cast-iron** 1 of cast iron 2 tough; unbreakable

**castle** *n* 1 fortress; stronghold 2 piece in chess (rook)

> **castle** *n* (fortress) citadel, chateau, fort, fortress, mansion, pile, stronghold

**castrate** *v* remove testicles, geld, emasculate, expurgate (book, etc); *n* **castration**

**casual** *adj* 1 relaxed 2 not planned; *n* **casualty** person injured or killed

> **casual** *adj* 1 (relaxed) carefree, easygoing, free and easy, happy-go-lucky, informal, laid-back, nonchalant, unconcerned. 2 (not planned) accidental, chance, impromptu, occasional, random, unexpected, unintentional, unplanned

**cat** *n* any animal of genus *Felix*

**cataclysm** *n* violent upheaval

**catalog** *n* 1 list of names, objects arranged in order 2 book showing goods for sale; *v* make such list

> **catalog** *n* 1 (list) classification, directory, inventory, record, register. 2 (book) booklet, brochure, guide, leaflet

**catalyst** *n* 1 substance causing chemical change without itself changing 2 person, thing facilitating change

**catalytic converter** *n aut* device for converting harmful exhaust fumes into carbon dioxide

**catapult** *n* sling for shooting pellets, stones

**cataract** *n* disease of eye

**catarrh** *n* inflammation of mucous membrane, *esp* of nose

**catastrophe** *n* disaster

> **catastrophe** *n* blow, calamity, crisis, devastation, fiasco, mishap, tragedy

**catch** *v* 1 take hold of; seize 2 be infected by (disease) 3 be in time for; *pt, pp* **caught**; *n* 1 fastener 2 disadvantage 3 act of catching; *idm* **catch fire** begin burning; *phr v* **catch on** 1 understand 2 become fashionable; **catch up** 1 make up for lost time 2 draw level with

> **catch** *v* 1 (take hold of) apprehend, arrest, capture, grab, nab, seize, snatch. 2 (be infected by) contract, get, develop. 3 (be in time for) get, go by, take, travel by
>
> **catch** *n* 1 (fastener) clasp, clip, hook, latch, lock. 2 (disadvantage) difficulty, downside, drawback, problem, snag

**catching** *adj* infectious

> **catching** *adj* contagious, communicable, transmissible, transmittable

**catchphrase** *n* widely-used saying

**categorical** *adj* absolute; positive

**categorize** *v* divide into classes

**category** *n* classification

> **category** *n* class, division, group, grouping, heading, kind, nature, section, sort, type, variety

**cater** *v* provide food, pleasure for

**caterpillar** *n* larva of butterfly, moth

**cathedral** *n* chief church of diocese; *adj* belonging to, containing such

**catheter** *n* tube introduced into passage of body, to draw off fluid, or to dilate

**catholic** *adj* 1 universal 2 of Roman Catholic Church; *ns* **Catholic** a Roman Catholic; **Catholicism**

**catkin** *n* furry flower of willow, birch, etc

**cattle** *n* bovine animals

**catty** *adj* spiteful

> **catty** *adj* bitchy, malicious, nasty, vicious, vindictive

**catwalk** *n* long narrow raised footpath
**caught** *pt of* **catch**
**cauldron, caldron** *n* large metal pot
**cauliflower** *n* white, fleshy, edible flower-head, variety of cabbage
**cause** *n* 1 reason 2 sth campaigned for; *v* bring about

> **cause** *n* 1 (reason) basis, grounds, motive. 2 (sth campaigned for) aim, end, movement, objective, purpose, struggle, **cause** *v* bring on, create, generate, give rise to, instigate, lead to, make, produce, provoke, result in, set off, spark off, trigger

**caution** *n* carefulness; warning; *v* warn

> **caution** *n* 1 (carefulness) circumspection, discretion, prudence, vigilance, wariness. 2 (warning) reprimand, telling-off. **caution** *v* admonish, advise, counsel, reprimand, reprove, tell off, urge

**cautious** *adj* careful

> **cautious** *adj* alert, chary, guarded, tentative, vigilant, wary

**cavalry** *n* horse soldiers
**cave** *n* hollow in earth with lateral extension; den; *n* **cavern** deep cave; *adj* **cavernous;** *n* **cavity** hole; *phr v* **cave in** 1 collapse 2 give up
**cave man** *n* primitive man
**caviar(e)** *n* delicacy of salted sturgeon roe
**cavity** *n* hole, *esp* in a tooth
**cavort** *v* prance about noisily
**cc** *abbr* cubic centimetre(s)
**CD** *abbr* compact disc
**CD-ROM** *n comput* compact disc on which information can be stored
**cease** *v* stop; *adj* **-less**

> **cease** *v* break off, come to an end, die away, end, fizzle out, grind to a halt, finish, quit

**cease-fire** *n* truce
**cedar** *n* large coniferous evergreen tree
**ceiling** *n* 1 lining of upper surface of room 2 upper limit
**celebrate** *v* 1 commemorate 2 have a good time
**celebrated** *adj* well-known

> **celebrated** *adj* acclaimed, eminent, famous, illustrious, legendary, renowned

**celebration** *n* 1 commemoration 2 party
**celebrity** famous person

> **celebrity** *n* big name, bigwig, dignitary, luminary, personality, star, VIP, worthy

**celery** *n* vegetable with juicy edible stalks
**celibacy** *n* unmarried state; abstinence from sexual relations
**cell** *n* 1 small room, in monastery, prison, etc 2 biological basic unit
**cell phone** *n* mobile telephone used on cellular network
**cellar** *n* underground part of house
**cello** *n mus* stringed instrument of violin type held between the knees; *pl* **cellos;** *n* **cellist**
**Cellophane** [TM] transparent plastic for wrapping
**cellular** *adj* 1 of living cells 2 *telecom* based on communications network; *n* **c. handset** mobile phone
**cellulite** *n* type of body fat that causes dimpling of the skin
**Celsius** *adj* = centigrade
**Celtic** *adj* of the Celts
**cement** *n* powdery substance which, mixed with water, sets hard; *v* fix with cement
**cemetery** *n* burial-ground
**censor** *n* one authorized to watch films read books, mail and decide whether the contents are offensive; *v* remove parts considered offensive; *n* **censorship**

> **censor** *v* ban, cut, edit, expurgate, remove

**censure** v criticize; blame; n reproof

**census** n official periodic counting of population of a state

**cent** n hundredth part of dollar; **per cent** in every hundred

**centenary** n hundredth anniversary; adj celebration of this

**centigrade** adj having 100 equal parts; esp **c. thermometer** freezing point 0 and boiling point 100

**centimetre** n measure of length, hundredth part of metre

**centipede** n crawling insect with many feet

**central** adj 1 at the centre 2 most important; adv **-ly**; **central heating** n heating system from a central boiler

> **central** adj 1 (at the centre) mid, middle, inner, interior. 2 (most important) basic, chief, core, fundamental, important, key, main, pivotal, principal

**centralize** v put under central control

> **centralize** v amalgamate, centre, consolidate, converge, focus, rationalize

**centre** n middle or central point

> **centre** n core, crux, focal point, heart, hub, middle, mid-point, nucleus

**centrifugal** adj moving away from the centre; n **c. force** tendency for objects to fly outwards from circular motion

**centurian** n Roman officer commanding 100 men

**century** n 1 100 years 2 100 runs in cricket

**ceramic** adj pertaining to pottery; n pl **ceramics** art of making pottery

**cereal** n edible grain

**cerebral** adj pertaining to brain; n **cerebral palsy** disability caused by damage to the brain before or after birth

**ceremony** n public observance of solemn event; n, adj **ceremonial**

**ceremony** n celebration, commemoration, formal occasion, function, rite, service

**certain** adj 1 sure in your mind 2 definite

> **certain** adj 1 (sure in your mind) confident, convinced, positive, satisfied. 2 (definite) beyond question, clear, evident, irrevocable, obvious, plain

**certainty** n 1 confidence 2 something bound to happen

> **certainty** n 1 (confidence) assurance, conviction, sureness. 2 (something bound to happen) foregone conclusion, inevitability, safe bet

**certificate** n written declaration

> **certificate** n authorization, award, degree, diploma, document, licence, pass, qualification, voucher, warrant

**certify** v attest in written document

> **certify** v authorize, confirm, declare, guarantee, license, validate, verify

**cervix** n pl **cervixes, cervices** narrow part of womb joined to vagina; adj **cervical**

**cessation** n stopping; pause; ceasing

**CFC** abbr chlorofluorocarbon

**chaffinch** n small wild bird

**chain** n 1 series of connected metal links 2 connected series of things; v restrain with chains

> **chain** n (connected series of things) progression, sequence, series, string, succession, train
> **chain** v bind, fetter, shackle, secure, tie

**chainstore** n one of a group of shops owned by one firm

a
b
**c**
d
e
f
g
h
i
j
k
l
m
n
o
p
q
r
s
t
u
v
w
x
y
z

**chair** n 1 single seat 2 professorship; seat of authority, etc; v preside at

**chalk** n soft limestone; crayon; v mark with chalk; phr v **chalk up** 1 write with chalk 2 record success

**challenge** n 1 invitation to do sth difficult 2 difficult task; v 1 invite to do sth difficult 2 question

> **challenge** n 1 (invitation) dare, taunt. 2 (difficult task) hurdle, obstacle, test, uphill struggle
> **challenge** v 1 (invite to do sth difficult) dare, defy, test, throw down the gauntlet. 2 (question) contest, dispute, object to, stand up to

**chamber** n 1 room; apartment 2 body of persons composing legislative assembly; n pl lawyer's office

**chameleon** n lizard able to change color

**chamois leather** n soft pliable leather

**champagne** n French white sparkling wine from Champagne region

**champion** n 1 winner 2 upholder of cause; v act as champion

> **champion** n 1 (winner) gold-medallist, title-holder, victor. 2 (upholer of cause) backer, campaigner, defender, promoter, supporter

**chance** n 1 fate 2 risk 3 likelihood 4 opportunity

> **chance** n 1 (fate) accident, coincidence, destiny, fluke, fortune, luck, providence. 2 (risk) gamble. 3 (likelihood) odds, probability, prospect. 4 (opportunity) opening, possibility, prospect

**chancellor** n 1 head of university 2 chief finance minister

**chandelier** n branched support for lights, hanging from ceiling

**change** v 1 alter 2 swap 3 put on different clothes; n 1 alteration 2 small money

**change** v 1 (alter) do an about-face inf, modify, rearrange, reform, reorganize, restyle, shift, transform, vary. 2 (swap) exchange, replace, substitute.
**change** n (alteration) about-turn, metamorphosis, modification, mutation, transformation, variation, volte-face

**changeable** adj variable

> **changeable** adj changing, erratic, fickle, fluctuating, fluid, irregular, mercurial, shifting, uncertain, unpredictable, unstable, vacillating, volatile

**channel** n 1 riverbed; body of water joining two seas 2 groove 3 that through which liquid flows more 4 means of communication 5 frequency band for transmission of TV, radio; v form, supply through channel

**chant** n sacred hymn; v sing in monotone

**chaos** n confusion

> **chaos** n bedlam, disorder, disarray, pandemonium, mayhem, shambles, tumult, turmoil

**chaotic** adj muddled

> **chaotic** adj confused, disordered, disorganized, messy, untidy

**chap** v **chapped** split, become sore from exposure to cold, etc; n man, boy

**chapel** n private church; cathedral antechamber with small altar

**chaperon** n older person accompanying younger one in public or on social occasion; v act in this way

**chaplain** n clergyman attached to institution, armed forces, etc

**chapter** n 1 main division of book 2 stage in history

**char** v scorch, burn; adj **charred**

**character** n 1 nature 2 person

**character** *n* 1 (nature) disposition, manner, personality, quality, temperament. 2 (person) eccentric, individual, sort

**characteristic** *adj* typical; *n* typical feature

**characteristic** *adj* distinctive, distinguishing, individual, peculiar
**characteristic** *n* attribute, idiosyncrasy, mannerism, peculiarity, quality, quirk, trait

**charcoal** *n* form of carbon, made from charred wood
**charge** *v* 1 demand as price 2 rush 3 accuse; *n* 1 price 2 accusation 3 protection; *idm* **in charge** responsible

**charge** *v* 1 (demand as price) ask, bill, debit, demand, invoice, set a price, want. 2 (rush) dash, hurtle, run, stampede, storm, tear, zoom. 3 (accuse) arraign, indict, put on trial
**charge** *n* 1 (price) cost, fare, fee, levy, rate, rent, toll. 2 (accusation) allegation, indictment. 3 (protection) care, custody, safe hands, safekeeping

**chariot** *n* ancient two-wheeled cart
**charitable** *adj* 1 generous 2 relating to charity

**charitable** *adj* 1 (generous) compassionate, forgiving, kind, sympathetic, tolerant, understanding. 2 (relating to charity) benevolent, humanitarian

**charity** *n* organization giving help; help given

**charity** *n* aid, alms, assistance, handouts, relief, welfare

**charm** *n* appeal; *v* attract

**charm** *n* allure, attraction, charisma, fascination, lure, magic, magnetism

**charming** *adj* lovely

**charming** *adj* attractive, delightful, enchanting, picturesque, pleasant, sweet

**chart** *n* map; graph; *v* make map, graph
**charter** *n* document granting rights; *v* hire
**chase** *v* 1 pursue 2 drive away; *n* pursuit

**chase** *v* 1 (pursue) follow, hound, run after, set off after, shadow, tail, track. 2 (drive away) see off, send packing

**chasm** *n* deep abyss; fissure
**chaste** *adj* sexually innocent

**chaste** *adj* celibate, innocent, pure, undefiled, virgin, virginal

**chastise** *v* punish by beating
**chastity** *n* restraint from sexual intercourse

**chastity** *n* celibacy, innocence, purity, virginity, virtue

**chat** *n* easy, informal talk; *v* talk idly; *phr v* **chat up** talk pleasantly to; *adj* **chatty**

**chat** *n* chit-chat, confab *inf*, discussion, gossip, heart-to-heart, small talk, talk
**chat** *v* chatter, discuss, gossip, have a heart-to-heart, talk

**château** *n Fr* arge country house; *pl* **-s** *or* **-x**
**chatter** *n* rapid, trivial talk; *v* talk idly; rattle teeth; *n* **chatterbox** incessant chatterer
**chauffeur** *n Fr* paid driver of automobile
**chauvinism** *n* perverted, blind patriotism
**cheap** *adj* 1 of low price 2 of poor quality; *adv* **-ly**; *v* **cheapen**

**cheap** *adj* 1 (of low price) budget, cut-price, discounted, economical, inexpensive, low-cost, reasonable, reduced. 2 (of poor quality) shoddy, tacky, trashy

a
b
**c**
d
e
f
g
h
i
j
k
l
m
n
o
p
q
r
s
t
u
v
w
x
y
z

**cheat** *v* swindle; *n* swindler

> **cheat** *v* con, deceive, defraud, double-cross,
> fleece, hoodwink, overcharge, rip off,
> take sb for a ride, trick
> **cheat** *n* con man, fraud, shark

**check**[1] *v* **1** verify **2** look carefully at **3** stop;
*n* **1** careful look **2** control **3** call in chess
**4** pattern in squares; *ns* **checkmate** final
winning move in chess; defeat; **checkout**
pay desk in supermarket; **checkpoint** place
where documents, vehicles, etc are
inspected, *eg* at a frontier

> **check** *v* **1** (verify) confirm, make sure, see.
> **2** (look at) check out, check over,
> examine, give sth the once-over *inf*,
> inspect, test. **3** (stop) curb, halt, inhibit,
> limit, obstruct, restrain, slow down, stem
> **check** *n* **1** (careful look) examination,
> inspection, test, spot-check. **2** (control)
> brake, curb, delay, halt, slow-down,
> stoppage

**check**[2] *n* paper form for withdrawing money
from bank; *n* **check book**
**Cheddar** *n* firm smooth, yellow cheese
**cheek** *n* **1** side of face below eye
**2** impudence; *v* address rudely;

> **cheek** *n* audacity, effrontery, gall, nerve,
> temerity

**cheeky** *adj* impertinent, insolent

> **cheeky** *adj* discourteous, impudent, rude

**cheer** *n* **1** state of mind **2** rich food and drink
**3** applause; *v* applaud vocally; *phr v* **cheer
up** encourage

> **cheer up** *v* bring a smile to sb's face, buck
> up *inf*, buoy up, console, liven up, make
> sb happier, raise sb's spirits, perk up

**cheerful** *adj* happy

> **cheerful** *adj* bright and breezy, chipper,
> contented, enthusiastic, in a good mood,
> optimistic, perky, smiling, upbeat

**cheese** *n* consolidated milk curd used as food
**cheetah** *n* fast-running predator of the cat
family with spotted skin
**chef** *n* professional cook
**chemist** *n* specialist in chemistry
**chemistry** *n* natural science dealing with
composition, reaction of substances;
*n, adj* **chemical**
**chemotherapy** *n* treatment of disease,
*esp* cancer, by use of chemicals
**chenille** *n* tufted cord of silk or worsted
**cherish** *v* hold dear; take care of
**cheroot** *n* kind of cigar, open at both ends
**cherry** *n* edible, small-stoned fruit either red,
black, or white; tree bearing this fruit
**cherub** *n* heavenly being, rosy-faced child
**chess** *n* game of skill, played with 32
chessmen; *ns* **chessmen, chessboard**
**chest** *n* **1** large box **2** upper front of body

> **chest** *n* (large box) box, case, casket,
> coffer, crate, trunk

**chestnut** *n* tree bearing nuts (**sweet c.**
edible; **horse c.** inedible)
**chew** *v* move jaws to eat food

> **chew** *v* champ, chomp, crunch, gnaw,
> masticate, munch

**chewing gum** *n* flavoured substance for
chewing, *usu* made of chicle
**chic** *adj* smart, elegant
**chick** *n* **1** newly hatched bird **2** affectionate
name for child; *n* **chicken** young hen;
*n* **chicken pox** mild contagious disease,
chiefly of children
**chicory** *n* blanched salad vegetable
**chief** *n* leader; *adj* most important;
*adv* **chiefly**

**chief** n boss, controller, director, head, manager, number one, principal, ringleader, ruler, superior, supremo
**chief** adj central, foremost, key, leading, main, primary, principal, top, uppermost

**child** n young human being; pl **children**

**child** n baby, boy, daughter, girl, infant, juvenile, kid, kiddie, little one, minor, mite, offspring, son, teenager, toddler, tot, youngster

**childhood** n period of life to puberty

**childhood** n adolescence, babyhood, boyhood, formative years, girlhood, infancy, school days, teens, youth

**childish** adj silly

**childish** adj babyish, immature, infantile, juvenile, naïve, puerile

**chili** n hot red pepper
**chill** n coldness; illness; v make cold
**chilly** adj 1 cold 2 unwelcoming
**chime** n set of bells
**chimney** n outlet for smoke
**chimpanzee** n type of ape
**chin** n part of jaw below mouth
**china** n fine porcelain ware; adj made of this
**chink**1 n slit; cleft
**chink**2 n tinkling, metallic sound
**chip** n 1 small notch 2 small piece 3 pl fried potatoes; v **chipping, chipped** break small piece off

**chip** n 1 (notch) break, nick. 2 (small piece) fragment, bit, shaving, shard, flake, sliver, splinter. 3 (fried potatoes) fries, sautéed potatoes

**chipmunk** n small striped mammal
**chiropody** n care of feet; n **chiropodist**

**chiropractor** n person who treats disease by massage and manipulation of joints
**chirp, chirrup** v utter short piping note (of birds); n this sound
**chisel** n cutting tool; v to use chisel
**chivalry** n courteous behavior; adj **chivalrous** courteous
**chive** n herb with thin onion-flavored leaves
**chlorine** n nonmetallic element
**chlorofluorocarbon** n compound gas used as a refrigerant and a propellant gas in aerosols and believed to be harmful to the ozone layer
**chloroform** n volatile liquid used as anesthetic; v to make insensible with this
**chock** n wooden wedge
**chocolate** n sweet made from ground cacao beans
**choice** n 1 option 2 selection; adj of high excellence

**choice** n 1 (option) alternative, decision, pick, possibility, preference. 2 (selection) array, assortment, range, variety

**choir** n group of singers, esp in church
**choke** v 1 smother 2 cough

**choke** v 1 (smother) asphyxiate, strangle, suffocate. 2 (cough) gag, gasp for air, retch

**cholera** n infectious disease of bile
**cholesterol** n fatty substance, believed in excess to cause hardening of the arteries
**choose** v select; pt **chose**; pp **chosen**

**choose** v decide on, fix on, name, opt for, pick, prefer, single out, vote for

**chop** v **chopping, chopped** cut with knife, etc; make quick blow; n piece of lamb, pork with rib bone
**chopsticks** n pair of sticks designed for taking food to the mouth in Asian countries
**choral** adj of a choir; sung by a choir
**chord** n blending of notes in harmony

a
b
**c**
d
e
f
g
h
i
j
k
l
m
n
o
p
q
r
s
t
u
v
w
x
y
z

**chore** *n* tedious job of work

> **chore** *n* job, daily grind, duty, hack work, housework, task, toil

**chorus** *n* group of singers; refrain of song

**chose** *pt* **chosen** *pp of* **choose**

**christen** *v* 1 make a member of the Christian church by baptism 2 name at official ceremony

**Christian** *n* follower of Christ; *adj* pertaining to Christians; **C. name** baptismal name; *n* **Christianity** teaching of Christ

**Christmas** *n* feast day (December 25th) celebrating the nativity of Jesus Christ

**chromosome** *n* tiny rods carrying genes in living cells

**chronic** *adj* 1 very bad 2 lasting a long time

> **chronic** *adj* 1 (bad) appalling, awful, dire, dreadful, terrible. 2 (lasting a long time) constant, incessant, incurable, lifelong, long-term, nonstop, persistent

**chronicle** *n* record of events in order of time; *v* register (events, dates)

**chronology** *n* table or list of dates; *adj* **chronological** in order of time

**chrysalis** *n, pl* **chrysalises** sheath enclosing insect larva during resting stage

**chubby** *adj* fat; stumpy

**chuck** *v* throw

**chuckle** *v* laugh softly; *n* low laugh

**chunk** *n* thick piece

> **chunk** *n* bit, hunk, lump, piece, wedge

**church** *n* 1 place of Christian worship 2 whole body of Christians; clergy; *n* **churchyard**

**churn** *n* vessel for making butter; *v* shake liquid violently

**chute** *n* inclined slope for sending down logs, water, any heavy thing

**chutney** *n* hot, sweet-tasting pickle or relish

**cider** *n* drink made of fermented apple juice

**cigar** *n* roll of tobacco leaves for smoking

**cigarette** *n* finely cut tobacco, rolled in thin paper

**cinder** *n* remains of burned-out coal

**cinematographic** *adj* projecting film

**cinnamon** *n* spice

**cipher** *n* secret way of writing

**circle** *n* 1 round flat shape; ring 2 group of people united by common interest; *v* move round, surround

> **circle** *n* 1 (round shape) ball, band, disk, hoop, ring, sphere. 2 (group of people) band, clique, crowd, gang, group, set

**circuit** *n* 1 distance round 2 path of electric current; *adj* **circuitous** indirect

**circular** *adj* forming or moving in a circle; *n* letter circulated to many people

> **circular** *adj* ring-shaped, round, spherical

**circulate** *v* 1 (cause to) move round a closed system 2 move round freely 3 make known or available; *n* **circulation** 1 flow through a system 2 passing of money 3 number of people receiving a publication

> **circulate** *v* (make known or available) broadcast, disseminate, distribute, pass round, promulgate, send around, spread, transmit

**circumcize** *v* cut off foreskin

**circumference** *n* boundary of a circle

**circumstance** *n* event; fact; *pl* financial condition; *adj* **circumstantial** incidental

> **circumstance** *n* accident, factor, occasion, position, situation

**circus** *n* 1 entertainment with, clowns, animals, etc 2 round open space in city

**cistern** *n* 1 water tank 2 natural reservoir

**citadel** *n* fortress protecting a town

**cite** *v* 1 summon 2 quote an authority

**citizen** n one living in city or town

> **citizen** n civilian, man/woman in the street, resident, subject, taxpayer, voter

**citric acid** n weak acid found in many fruits
**citrus fruit** n pl lemons, oranges, etc
**city** n large-sized town
**civic** adj of a city or citizens
**civil** adj 1 relating to citizens 2 nonmilitary 3 polite 4 not criminal; ns **civility** politeness; **civilian** nonmilitary person; v **civilize** bring from barbarism; n **civilization;** adj **civilized**

> **civil** adj 1 (relating to citizens) civic, domestic, internal, municipal, public, state. 2 (polite) cordial, courteous, pleasant, well-mannered

**civil engineering** n building of public works
**civil service** n government departments; n **civil servant**
**claim** v 1 suggest 2 ask for; n 1 suggestion 2 demand; n **claimant**

> **claim** v 1 (suggest) allege, assert, declare, maintain, profess, say, state. 2 (ask for) demand, request, send off for
> **claim** n 1 (suggestion) allegation, assertion. 2 (demand) application, call, request

**clamber** v climb clumsily or laboriously

> **clamber** v climb, scrabble, scramble, shin

**clammy** adj moist and cold to touch, sticky
**clamor** n loud outcry; noise
**clamp** n tool for holding things together; phr v **clamp down on** suppress
**clampdown** n imposing of restrictions
**clan** n group of families or people
**clandestine** adj guiltily secret, surreptitious
**clang** n loud, metallic ring; v make sound
**clank** n sharp metallic sound; v to make such sound

**clap** v **clapping, clapped** applaud with hands; n sudden burst of thunder
**clarify** v **-fying, -fied** make clear; ns **clarification, clarity**

> **clarify** v disambiguate, elucidate, explain, simplify, spell out what you mean, resolve

**clarinet** n woodwind musical instrument
**clash** v 1 come together with loud noise 2 disagree; n 1 metallic sound 2 conflict

> **clash** v (disagree) come into conflict, come to blows, confront, fall out, fight, quarrel, squabble, wrangle
> **clash** n (conflict) brush, confrontation, disagreement, dispute, fight, quarrel, row

**clasp** n hook, bolt for fastening; v grasp
**class** n 1 type 2 school lesson or group 3 social division

> **class** n 1 (type) category, classification, division, grade, group, league, set, sort, status, variety. 2 (lesson) period, seminar, study group, tutorial

**classic** adj 1 excellent 2 typical; n work of art or literature; pl Greek or Latin language; adj **classical** of high quality

> **classic** adj 1 (excellent) brilliant, definitive, fine, first-rate, great, superlative. 2 (typical) archetypal, copybook, model, prototypical

**classification** n 1 way of grouping 2 group

> **classification** n 1 (way of grouping) arrangement, cataloging, grading, grouping, ordering, organization, taxonomy. 2 (group) category, class, division, grade, rank

**classified** adj (of information) limited to authorized persons

A
B
C
D
E
F
G
H
I
J
K
L
M
N
O
P
Q
R
S
T
U
V
W
X
Y
Z

**classify** *v* arrange according to type

> **classify** *v* arrange, categorize, catalog, class, grade, group, order, rank, rate

**clatter** *n* series of dull, hard noises; rattle; noisy talk; *v* make clatter
**clause** *n* short sentence, part of main one; article in treaty, will, contract, etc
**claustrophobia** *n* fear of enclosed spaces
**claw** *n* sharp nails or talons of animals and birds; *v* seize, scratch with claws
**clay** *n* sticky earth
**clean** *adj* 1 free from dirt 2 pure; *v* make clean

> **clean** *adj* 1 (free from dirt) hygienic, immaculate, pristine, scrubbed, shining, spick and span, spotless, sterile, washed. 2 (pure) clear, fresh, unpolluted
> **clean** *v* dust, polish, scrub, sterilize, sweep, vacuum, wash, wipe

**clean-cut** *adj* neat and presentable
**cleanse** *v* remove impurity from
**clear** *adj* 1 obvious 2 transparent 3 not cloudy 4 not blocked; *phr vs* **clear off/out** go away; **clear up** tidy; *adv* **clearly**; *v* 1 remove blockages 2 acquit 3 brighten; disentangle; *ns* **clearance** 1 act of clearing 2 riddance of surplus stock 3 permission to procede 4 clear space between two objects; **clearing** land cleared of trees

> **clear** *adj* 1 (obvious) apparent, beyond doubt, coherent, distinct, evident, lucid, plain, unambiguous. 2 (transparent) colorless, see-through, unclouded. 3 (not cloudy) bright, cloudless, sunny, starlit. 4 (not blocked) free, open, unobstructed
> **clear** *v* 1 (remove blockages) clean out, empty, get rid of, remove, unblock, unclog. 2 (acquit) absolve, exonerate, vindicate

**cleavage** *n* hollow between a woman's breasts seen above neckline of dress
**clef** *n* sign of pitch of stave in music

**cleft palate** *n* genetic defect of fissure in the roof of the mouth
**clench** *v* close (fist); set closely together
**clergy** *n* body of ordained minister in Christian churchs; *ns* **clergyman**; **cleric** any person in Holy Orders; *adj* **clerical** of clergy
**clerk** *n* official in government corporation service; office subordinate; *adj* **clerical** pertaining to office work
**clever** *adj* intelligent, able; *adv* **-ly**

> **clever** *adj* astute, brainy, bright, competent, educated, ingenious, knowledgable, quick, sharp, shrewd, smart, streetwise, talented

**cliché** *n* hackneyed phrase
**click** *v* 1 make slight, sharp sound; 2 *coll* become instantly friendly or popular 3 be understood; *n* thin, rapid, sharp sound
**client** *n* customer of professional person or tradesman; *n* **clientele** body of clients
**cliff** *n* steep rock face, *esp* facing sea
**climate** *n* weather conditions of region
**climax** *n* culminating point; point of greatest tension in film, story, etc; *v* to reach this

> **climax** *n* crowning point, culmination, finale, height, peak, pinnacle, zenith

**climb** *v* ascend; *phr v* **climb down** admit one was wrong

> **climb** *v* clamber, climb up, go up, move up, mount, rise, scale, shin up, shoot up, soar

**clinch** *v* make fast; decide; *n* grip; lock
**cling** *v* stick to; *pt, pp* **clung**

> **cling** *v* adhere, grip, hold, hold on, stick

**clinic** *n* place for medical examination, treatment; *adj* **clinical** 1 of the treatment of patients 2 efficient and objective; without feeling
**clink** *n* tinkling sound; *v* make this sound

**clip** *n* 1 device for fastening 2 short extract from film or video; *n* **clipboard** board with clip for holding papers

> **clip** *n* 1 (device for fastening) clasp, fastener, pin. 2 (extract) clipping, cutting, excerpt, passage, scene, snippet

**clip** *v* **clipping**, **clipped** cut with shears or scissors

> **clip** *v* crop, cut, lop, prune, shear, shorten, snip, trim

**clique** *n Fr* select and snobbish group

**cloak** *n* outer sleeveless garment

**clock** *n* device for measuring time, not intended for wearing; *v* **clock in**, **out** record automatically arrival, departure from work; *phr v* **clock up** 1 record the time taken 2 manage to score

**clockwise** *adv* in the direction of a clock's hands

**clockwork** *idm* **like clockwork** smoothly and easily

**clod** *n* lump of earth

**clog** *n* wooden-soled shoe; *v* **clogging**, **clogged** cause to jam

> **clog** *v* block, block up, choke, congest, jam, obstruct, stop up

**cloister** *n* covered arcade in monastery

**clone** *n* animal or plant produced asexually from the cells of another

**close** *adj* 1 near 2 happening soon 3 well-loved 4 sultry ( of weather); *n* precinct of cathedral; *adv* **-ly**

> **close** *adj* 1 (near) adjacent, adjoining, handy, nearby, neighboring. 2 (happening soon) at hand, imminent, impending. 3 (well loved) dear, devoted, intimate, loving. 4 (sultry) humid, muggy, oppressive

**close** *v* 1 shut 2 conclude 3 get nearer; *n* end

**close** *v* 1 (shut) bolt, fasten, lock, seal, slam. 2 (conclude) bring to a close, cease, complete, end, finish, terminate, wind up. 3 (get nearer) approach, chase, pursue

**closed** *adj* 1 shut 2 concluded

> **closed** *adj* 1 (shut) bolted, fastened, locked, sealed. 2 (concluded) completed, ended, finished, over, resolved, settled

**closed-circuit television** *n* system transmitting within an institution

**closet** *n* small, private room; cupboard

**closure** *n* closing

**clot** *n* coagulated mass of blood; *v* **clotting**, **clotted** coagulate

**cloth** *n* woven fabric

**clothe** to dress; *pt*, *pp* **clothed**

**clothes** *n* garments; *n* **clothing**

> **clothes** *n* attire, costume, dress, garb, gear, kit, outfit, togs *inf*

**cloud** *n* mass of condensed water vapor in sky; mass of smoke; dust in air; *v* make dark, dim, become cloudy

**cloudy** *adj* 1 with clouds 2 not clear

> **cloudy** *adj* 1 (with clouds) dull, hazy, misty, overcast. 2 (not clear) frosted, misty, murky, opaque, smoky, steamed up

**clover** *n* plant, trefoil grown as fodder

**clown** *n* buffoon in circus; *v* play the fool

**club** *n* 1 group of people associated for benefit or pleasure 2 place for dancing, drinking, etc 3 short thick stick 4 black trefoil on playing card; *v* **clubbing**, **clubbed** beat with club

> **club** *n* 1 (group of people) association, fraternity, group, league, society, team, union. 2 (place for dancing) cabaret, nightclub. 3 (stick) baton, truncheon

a
b
**c**
d
e
f
g
h
i
j
k
l
m
n
o
p
q
r
s
t
u
v
w
x
y
z

**cluck** *n* noise of hen; *v* make such noise
**clue** *n* guide to solution of mystery, crime

> **clue** *n* hint, idea, inkling, key, pointer, sign

**clump** *n* group of trees, plants
**clumsy** *adj* not graceful

> **clumsy** *adj* awkward, blundering, bumbling, bungling, gawky, graceless, ham-fisted, lumbering, uncoordinated, ungainly

**clung** *pt, pp of* **cling**
**cluster** *n* bunch or group; *v* form a group
**clutch** *v* grasp; *n* device permitting gradual engagement of mechanism; *idm* **in sb's clutches** under sb's control

> **clutch** *v* clasp, cling to, hang on to, hold

**clutter** *n* things left untidily; *v* make untidy
**cm** *abbr* centimeter
**coach** *n* railroad car; horse-drawn carriage; instructor; tutor; *v* teach

> **coach** *v* direct, drill, exercise, guide, instruct, manage, prepare, train

**coagulate** *v* clot; form moss; curdle
**coal** *n* combustible carbonized vegetable matter, used as fuel
**coalition** *n* alliance, *esp* political

> **coalition** *n* association, bloc, confederacy, confederation, league, merger, pact, union

**coarse** *adj* **1** rough **2** vulgar

> **coarse** *adj* **1** (rough) crude, tough, uneven, unrefined. **2** (vulgar) boorish, common, crude, gross, ill-mannered, uncouth

**coast** *n* edge of land at seashore; *v* free wheel

> **coast** *n* coastline, seaside, shoreline

**coaster** *n* small mat for glasses
**coast guard** *n* official employed to enforce maritime law, prevent smuggling, and save lives at sea
**coat** *n* **1** outer garment with sleeves **2** natural covering of animals **3** layer of paint, etc applied to surface; *v* cover with layer; *n* **coat of arms** heraldic device

> **coat** *n* **1** (outer garment) anorak, cloak, duffel coat, fleece, jacket, mac *inf*, mackintosh, overcoat, parka, raincoat, topcoat. **2** (covering of animal) fleece, fur, hair, pelt. **3** (layer of paint) covering, film, finish, glaze, patina

**coat hanger** *n* shaped piece of wood, wire, or plastic with hook for hanging coats
**coax** *v* persuade by flattery

> **coax** *v* cajole, encourage, entice, induce, inveigle, talk sb into/out of sth

**cobbled** *adj* paved with round stones
**cobbler** *n* shoe mender
**cobra** *n* venomous hooded snake
**cobweb** *n* spider's web
**Coca-Cola** [TM] *n* sweet carbonated drink
**cocaine** *n* illegal drug
**cock** *n* male bird; *v* set cock of gun
**cockerel** *n* young cock
**cockle** *n* edible bivalve; weed; small boat
**cockpit** *n* small space in aircraft for pilot
**cockroach** *n* insect, blackbeetle
**cocktail** *n* **1** mixed alcoholic drink **2** mixture of fruits or seafoods **3** *coll* mixture of dangerous substances
**cocoa** *n* fine powder made from cacao beans; drink
**coconut** *n* tropical palm with edible nut
**cocoon** *n* sheath of silk, silklike thread enclosing chrysalis
**cod** *n* large edible sea fish
**coddle** *v* pamper, cosset
**code** *n* **1** system of rules **2** words or symbols used for sending secret messages

**code** n 1 (system of rules) convention, custom, ethics, etiquette, manners, oath, rules. 2 (for sending secret messages) coding system, cipher, key, notation

**coeducation** n education of boys and girls together; adj **-ational**

**coerce** v force; n **coercion** compulsion

**coerce** v compel, constrain, intimidate, make, persuade

**coexist** v exist together; n **coexistence**

**coffee** n 1 ground roasted beans of coffee plant; drink made from this 2 light brown color

**coffer** n chest; money-box

**coffin** n case for dead body

**cog** n toothlike projection on wheel

**cogitate** v ponder; think deeply; n **-ation**

**cognac** n Fr high-quality French brandy

**cohabit** n live together as man and wife

**coherent** adj clear and easy to understand

**coherent** adj articulate, clear, cogent, consistent, intelligible, logical, lucid, organized, reasoned, sound, systematic, well-ordered, well-structured

**coil** n series of spiral loops; v wind in rings, spiral folds

**coil** v curl, entwine, loop, snake, spiral, twine, twist, wind

**coin** n piece of money; v mint; invent new word, etc

**coincide** v happen at same time; correspond exactly

**coincide** v accord, agree, be the same, come together, concur, correspond, match, tally

**coincidence** n thing that happens surprisingly by chance

**coincidence** n accident, chance, fluke, stroke of luck

**coke** n 1 substance left when gas and tar have been extracted from coal 2 coll Coca-Cola

**cola** n soft drink containing cola nut extract

**colander** n strainer used in cooking

**cold** adj 1 without heat 2 unfriendly; n lack of heat 2 infection causing nasal catarrh; idm **get cold feet** coll lose one's nerve

**cold** adj 1 (without heat) arctic, bitter, chilly, cool, drafty, freezing, fresh, frosty, frozen, glacial, icy, nippy inf, refrigerated, wintry. 2 (unfriendly) aloof, cool, distant, forbidding, frigid, frosty, heartless, indifferent, inhospitable, insensitive, reserved, standoffish, uncaring, unsympathetic, unwelcoming
**cold** n (infection) bug inf, chill, flu, influenza, sniffle inf, virus

**cold-blooded** adj 1 bio with varying blood temperature 2 cruel

**coleslaw** n salad of shredded cabbage, carrot, etc with salad dressing

**colic** n acute pain in bowels

**collaborate** v work together

**collaborate** v assist, collude, connive, conspire, cooperate, help, join forces, team up

**collage** n picture made by pasting various materials on a flat surface

**collapse** v 1 fall down or inwards 2 become ill or unconscious 3 fail; n **collapse**

**collapse** v 1 (fall down or inwards) cave in, come apart, fall apart, fall to pieces, give way, implode, subside. 2 (become ill) crumple, faint, fall over, keel over, pass out. 3 (fail) break down, disintegrate, fall apart, fall through, fold, founder

a
b
c
d
e
f
g
h
i
j
k
l
m
n
o
p
q
r
s
t
u
v
w
x
y
z

**collar** *n* band on garment, round neck
**colleague** *n* associate in work

> **colleague** *n* associate, comrade, fellow worker, partner, peer, workmate

**collect** *v* 1 accumulate 2 gather, come together; *adjs* **collected** not distracted, gathered; **collective** viewed as whole

> **collect** *v* assemble, gather, hoard, marshal, stock, stockpile, store

**collectible** *n* object collected
**collection** *n* group of articles of same nature

> **collection** *n* accumulation, anthology, array, assembly, assortment, cluster, compilation, gathering, group, heap, hoard, pile, set, stock, stockpile, store

**college** *n* institution of higher learning
**collide** *v* crash into

> **collide** *v* bang, bump into, meet head-on, smash into, strike, strike against

**collie** *n* type of sheepdog
**collier** *n* coal miner; *n* **colliery** coal mine
**collision** *n* crash
**colloquial** *adj* used in common speech

> **colloquial** *adj* common, everyday, idiomatic, informal, popular, slang, spoken

**cologne** *n* perfume
**colon** *n* part of large intestine; punctuation mark (:)
**colonel** *n* commander of regiment
**colony** *n* body of people in new country, who remain subject to fatherland; area so settled; *n* **colonist**; *adj* **colonial**; *v* **colonize**
**colossus** *n* huge statue; *adj* **colossal**
**color** *n* 1 tint 2 excitement; *pl* 1 badge, ribbons symbolic of party, school etc 2 flag of ship, regiment; *v* 1 paint 2 influence 3 blush

> **color** *n* 1 (tint) coloration, coloring, hue, pigment, pigmentation, shade, tinge, tone. 2 (excitement) interest, spice, vividness

**color-blind** *adj* unable to distinguish certain colors
**colorful** *adj* 1 with bright colors 2 exciting

> **colorful** *adj* 1 (with bright colors) bright, gaudy, multicolored, psychedelic, vibrant, vivid. 2 (exciting) exotic, graphic, lively, stimulating, striking, vivid

**column** *n* 1 pillar 2 article in newspaper 3 line of people; *n* **columnist** journalist

> **column** *n* 1 (pillar) monument, pile, pole, post, shaft, support, strut, upright. 2 (article in newspaper) article, diary, editorial, feature, leader, leading article, section. 3 (line of people) crocodile, file, line, procession, queue

**coma** *n* deep unconsciousness
**comb** *n* toothed instrument for dressing hair; *v* apply comb to
**combat** *n* fighting; *v* oppose

> **combat** *n* battle, conflict, hostilities, war
> **combat** *v* defeat, fight, resist, struggle against, wage war against

**combination** *n* mixture

> **combination** *n* blend, fusion, integration, merger, mix, mixing, union

**combine** *v* 1 put together 2 come together

> **combine** *v* 1 (put together) amalgamate, blend, fuse, integrate, intertwine, join, merge, mingle, pool, synthesize, unite. 2 (come together) coalesce, conspire, co-operate, interweave, mix, team up, unite

**combine harvester** n machine that reaps and threshes grain

**combustion** n process of burning

**come** v 1 move toward 2 attend; pt **came**; pp **come**; prp **coming**; phr vs **come about** happen; **come across** find by chance; **come forward** offer help or information; **come in for** be exposed to; **come off** 1 become detached 2 succeed; phr vs **come on** progress; **come out** 1 appear 2 go on strike; **come out against** declare opposition to; **come out with** say unexpectedly

> **come** v 1 (move toward) advance, appear, approach, come up, draw nearer, enter, reach. 2 (attend) arrive, be present, get (to), show up, turn up, visit. 3 (come about) come to pass, fall out, happen, occur, take place. 4 (come across) encounter, find, meet, see

**comeback** n 1 recovery 2 redress

**comedian** n comic actor

**comedy** n 1 amusing entertainment 2 amusing play 3 humor

> **comedy** n 1 (amusing entertainment) clowning, humor, slapstick, stand-up comedy. 2 (amusing play or performance) sitcom, situation comedy, sketch, turn. 3 (humor) absurdity, amusement, funny side, ridiculousness, silliness

**comet** n luminous heavenly body, with gaseous tail

**comfort** v reassure; console; n well-being; bodily ease; consolation;

**comfortable** adj 1 pleasant to the body 2 relaxed

> **comfortable** adj 1 (pleasant to the body) comfy inf, cozy, de luxe, easy, homely, luxurious, opulent, padded, plush, relaxing, snug, soft, warm. 2 (relaxed) at ease, comfy, cozy, snug

**comfy** adj coll comfortable

**comic** adj funny; n comedian; comic paper; adj **comical**

> **comic** adj absurd, amusing, droll, facetious, funny, hilarious, humorous, joking, light, rib-tickling, side-splitting, silly, waggish, whimsical, witty

**comma** adj punctuation mark (,), separating words, phrases, etc

**command** v 1 order 2 be in charge of; n 1 words to be obeyed 2 power to command; n **commander**

> **command** v 1 (order) ask, decree, direct, instruct, tell. 2 (be in charge of) control, dominate, have authority over, direct, govern, head, lead
>
> **command** n 1 (words to be obeyed) commandment, decree, directive, edict, injunction, instruction, order. 2 (power to command) authority, charge, control, direction, domination, dominion, government, leadership, mastery, power, superiority, supremacy

**commando** n type of soldier

**commemorate** v celebrate solemnly

**commence** v begin; start

**commend** v entrust; praise; adj **commendable**; n **commendation**

**comment** n remark; v express view; ns **commentary** series of critical remarks; **commentator** radio or TV reporter

> **comment** n mention, note, observation, opinion, reaction, remark, response
>
> **comment** v express an opinion, interpose, note, observe, remark, respond, say

**commerce** n business trading

> **commerce** n business, buying and selling, dealing, money-making, trade, trading

a
b
c
d
e
f
g
h
i
j
k
l
m
n
o
p
q
r
s
t
u
v
w
x
y
z

A
B
C
D
E
F
G
H
I
J
K
L
M
N
O
P
Q
R
S
T
U
V
W
X
Y
Z

**commercial** *adj* to do with business;
*v* **commercialize** make business of

> **commercial** *adj* business, capitalist,
> entrepreneurial, financial, mercenary,
> money-making, profit-making

**commiserate** *v* express sympathy

> **commiserate** *v* comfort, console,
> empathize, sympathize

**commission** *n* 1 warrant giving authority to
officer in armed forces 2 body appointed to
hold enquiry 3 authority to act as agent,
agent's percentage; *v* authorize;
*n* **commissioner** member of commission
**commit** *v* **-mitting, -mitted** 1 perpetrate
2 entrust 3 send for trial; *n* **committal**

> **commit** *v* 1 (perpetrate) carry out, do, effect,
> execute, perform. 2 (entrust) assign, certify,
> consign, deliver, give, hand over, send

**commitment** *n* 1 dedication 2 sth one has
agreed to do

> **commitment** *n* 1 (dedication) devotion,
> fervor, loyalty, passion, perseverance,
> resolution, single-mindedness, support,
> zeal. 2 (sth one has agreed to do)
> engagement, oath, promise, undertaking

**committed** *adj* dedicated

> **committed** *adj* active, ardent, confirmed,
> determined, devoted, diehard, earnest,
> fervent, firm, loyal, militant, passionate,
> resolute, single-minded, staunch, sworn,
> wholehearted, zealous

**committee** *n* group appointed to consider
particular activity
**commodity** *n* article of commerce
**common** *n* tract of public land; *adj* 1 ordinary
2 not rare 3 shared 4 vulgar; *adv* **-ly**

> **common** *adj* 1 (ordinary) customary,
> everyday, familiar, habitual, plain,
> routine, run-of-the-mill, standard,
> traditional, typical, unexceptional, usual.
> 2 (not rare) frequent, numerous,
> plentiful, popular, widespread. 3 (shared)
> collective, communal, general, joint,
> reciprocal. 4 (vulgar) coarse, crude, ill-
> bred, lower-class, plebeian, uneducated

**commotion** *n* agitation

> **commotion** *n* bedlam, chaos, confusion, din,
> disorder, disturbance, excitement, ferment,
> fray, furore, fuss, hubbub, hullabaloo *inf*,
> pandemonium, rumpus, sensation, stir,
> trouble, tumult, turmoil, unrest, uproar

**communal** *adj* for common use

> **communal** *adj* collective, common,
> general, joint, public, shared

**commune** *n* 1 smallest unit of local
government (*eg* in France) 2 community
living and working together
**communicate** *v* 1 be in contact 2 express;
*n* **-ation**

> **communicate** *v* 1 (be in contact) be in
> touch, contact, get through to, interact,
> speak to, talk to. 2 (express) convey, get
> across, get over, impart

**communism** *n* extreme form of socialism;
*n*, *adj* **communist**
**community** *n* body of people sharing locality,
religion, etc, fellowship

> **community** *n* colony, commune, group,
> neighborhood, settlement, society

**commute** *v* exchange, travel daily to work;
*n* **commuter** daily traveler to work
**compact**[1] *n* agreement; contract

**compact**[2] *adj* neatly packed into small space;
*n* small case holding face powder

**compact disk** *n* recording disk from which
sounds are reproduced by laser

**companion** *n* friend; *n* **companionship**

**companion** *n* assistant, associate, chaperon,
comrade, colleague, confidant,
confidante, escort, partner, servant

**company** *n* 1 business 2 group of people
3 companionship

**company** *n* 1 (business) concern,
corporation, enterprise, establishment,
firm, organization. 2 (group of people)
assembly, audience, band, crew, crowd,
gang, gathering, group, troop, troupe.
3 (companionship) friendship, guests,
society, visitors

**compare** *v* 1 judge by sth else 2 observe
similarity; *adj* **comparable**; *n* **comparison**

**compare** *v* 1 (judge by sth else) contrast,
differentiate, juxtapose, set against.
2 (observe similarity) draw a parallel,
equate, liken, match

**compartment** *n* part divided off by partition,
*esp* in railroad car

**compass** *n* boundary; extent; range;
instrument showing N and directions from
it; *pl* instrument drawing circles

**compassion** *n* sympathy

**compassion** *n* concern, consideration,
heart, humanity, kindness, leniency,
mercy, pity, understanding

**compassionate** *adj* sympathetic

**compassionate** *adj* considerate, gentle,
humane, kind, merciful, understanding

**compatible** *adj* 1 able to agree 2 consistent

**compatible** *adj* 1 (able to agree) in-tune,
like-minded, similar, suitable, suited,
well-matched. 2 (consistent) in keeping,
reconcilable

**compatriot** *n* countryman

**compel** *v* enforce; force; *adj* **compelling**
1 very interesting 2 urgent; *n* **compulsion**

**compendium** *n* 1 full information in concise
form 2 box of games; *adj* **compendious**

**compensate** *v* make amends;
*n* **compensation**

**compensate** *v* atone, balance, counteract,
indemnify, make up for, pay back, pay
compensation, recompense, refund,
reimburse, repay

**compete** *v* contend with; *n* **competitor**

**compete** *v* challenge, contend, contest,
fight, oppose, participate, pit yourself
against, rival, take part, vie

**competent** *adj* skilled; *n* **competence**

**competent** *adj* able, accomplished, adept,
capable, clever, experienced, good,
proficient, qualified, skillful, trained

**competition** *n* 1 game 2 state of competing

**competition** *n* 1 (game) championship,
contest, heat, match, race, rally,
tournament. 2 (state of competing)
conflict, contention, opposition, rivalry,
strife, struggle

**competitive** *adj* keen to win

**compile** *v* collect together from various
sources, *eg* as a book

**complacent** *adj* self-satisfied

**complacent** *adj* satisfied, self-assured, smug

a
b
c
d
e
f
g
h
i
j
k
l
m
n
o
p
q
r
s
t
u
v
w
x
y
z

A B **C** D E F G H I J K L M N O P Q R S T U V W X Y Z

**complain** v grumble

> **complain** v bellyache *inf*, carp, find fault, fuss, go on about *inf*, gripe, moan, nag, object, protest, remonstrate, whine

**complaint** n 1 grumble 2 medical condition

> **complaint** n 1 (grumble) criticism, grievance, gripe, grouch, grouse, moan, objection, protest. 2 (medical condition) affliction, ailment, condition, disease, disorder, illness, infection, sickness

**complement** n that which completes; full allowance; *adj* **complementary**
**complete** *adj* 1 entire 2 finished 3 total; v finish; n **completion**

> **complete** *adj* 1 (entire) comprehensive, exhaustive, full, intact, whole. 2 (finished) achieved, completed, concluded, done, ended, over. 3 (total) absolute, downright, out-and-out, outright, thorough, unmitigated, utter
> **complete** v accomplish, achieve, conclude, do, end, finalize, fulfill, realize, settle, terminate

**completely** *adv* totally

> **completely** *adv* absolutely, altogether, entirely, fully, perfectly, thoroughly, utterly, wholly

**complex** *adj* complicated; n psychological obsession; n **complexity**

> **complex** *adj* convoluted, difficult, elaborate, intricate, involved, sophisticated, tortuous
> **complex** n fixation, hang-up, mania, neurosis, obsession, phobia

**complexion** n color, texture of face
**complicate** v to make difficult; n **-ation**
**complicated** *adj* difficult

**complicated** *adj* complex, convoluted, elaborate, intricate, involved, knotty, problematic, sophisticated

**complicity** n partnership in crime, etc
**compliment** n expression of esteem; v pay compliment to; *adj* **-ary**

> **compliment** n accolade, commendation, endorsement, eulogy, flattery, honor, plaudits, praise, tribute

**comply** v **-plying, -plied** obey

> **comply** v abide by, adhere to, conform, consent, follow, fulfill, heed, keep, meet, observe, respect

**component** n constituent part
**compose** v create musical or literary work; ns **composer, composition**

> **compose** v concoct, devise, invent, make up, produce, think up, write

**composed** *adj* calm

> **composed** *adj* at ease, cool, poised, relaxed, self-possessed, unfazed, unperturbed, unruffled, together

**compost** n rotten vegetable matter
**compound** v make worse; *adj* not simple; composite; n 1 mixture 2 enclosure
**comprehend** v understand; n **comprehension**
**comprehensive** *adj* taking in wide range

> **comprehensive** *adj* all-embracing, all-inclusive, broad, complete, exhaustive, extensive, full, inclusive, thorough, wide

**comprise** v include; contain
**compromise** v 1 come to agreement 2 damage a reputation; n agreement

**compromise** *v* 1 (come to agreement) concede, make concessions, meet halfway, negotiate a settlement, strike a balance. 2 (damage a reputation) bring into disrepute, damage, discredit, jeopardize, risk, weaken
**compromise** *n* bargain, concession, deal, settlement, trade-off, understanding

**compulsion** *n* 1 strong urge to do sth 2 sth which forces action; *adj* **compulsive**
**compulsory** *adj* required by law or rules

**compulsory** *adj* mandatory, necessary, obligatory, required, requisite, statutory

**compute** *v* calculate; *n* **computation**
**computer** *n* electronic machine for storing, classifying, and reproducing information and relaying instructions; *v* **computerize**; *n* **-ization**
**comrade** *n* friend, companion
**con** *v* **conning, conned** trick, swindle
**concave** *n* hollow; curved inwardly
**conceal** *v* 1 hide 2 keep secret

**conceal** *v* 1 (hide) camouflage, cloak, cover, disguise, mask, obscure, screen, secrete, shelter. 2 (keep secret) cover up, gloss over, hush up, keep quiet, keep the lid on

**concede** *v* surrender; admit truth of; allow; *n* **concession** that which is conceded
**conceit** *n* vanity
**conceited** *adj* vain

**conceited** *adj* arrogant, big-headed, boastful, egotistical, immodest, puffed up, self-important, smug

**conceive** *v* 1 think of; imagine 2 become pregnant; *adj* **conceivable**
**concentrate** *v* direct to single center; increase strength; fix efforts on one point, object; *n* **concentration**

**concentric** *adj* having common center
**concept** *n* idea; *adj* **conceptual**

**concept** *n* hypothesis, notion, theory, view

**conception** *n* 1 beginning of pregnancy 2 plan; planning 3 understanding
**concern** *v* 1 be relevant to 2 worry; *n* 1 worry 2 affair

**concern** *v* 1 (be relevant to) affect, apply, involve, regard, relate to. 2 (worry) bother, disturb, perturb, preoccupy, trouble
**concern** *n* 1 (worry) anxiety, apprehension, distress, fear, malaise. 2 (affair) business, department, interest, job, matter, problem, responsibility, task

**concerned** *adj* 1 worried 2 interested; *prep* **concerning** regarding, about

**concerned** *adj* 1 (worried) anxious, bothered, distressed, disturbed, fearful, perturbed, troubled, uneasy, unhappy, upset. 2 (interested) affected, implicated, involved

**concert** *n* 1 agreement 2 musical show; *adj* **concerted** planned in common
**concession** *n* 1 yielding after argument 2 reduced price; 3 special permission; *adj* **concessionary**
**conciliate** *v* pacify; win over; *n* **conciliator**; *adj* **conciliatory**
**concise** *adj* brief

**concise** *adj* compact, condensed, pithy, short, succinct, terse, to the point

**conclude** *v* 1 end; finish 2 arrange 3 infer; *n* **conclusion**; *adj* **conclusive** decisive
**concoct** *v* invent; *n* **concoction**

**concoct** *v* contrive, devise, formulate, make up, plan, plot, prepare, think up

a
b
**c**
d
e
f
g
h
i
j
k
l
m
n
o
p
q
r
s
t
u
v
w
x
y
z

**concord** n agreement; harmony

**concourse** n broad open space, *esp* in airport buildings

**concrete** n mixture of sand and cement; *adj* 1 of concrete 2 real; *v* cover with concrete

> **concrete** *adj* (real) actual, definite, existing, explicit, factual, firm, material, palpable, solid, specific, substantial, tangible, visible

**concur** *v* **-curring, -curred** agree; happen at same time; *adj* **concurrent**

**concuss** *v* shake violently; injure brain by blow on head; *n* **concussion**

**condemn** *v* 1 criticize 2 find guilty 3 declare unfit for use

> **condemn** *v* 1 (criticize) blame, castigate, censure, chide, damn, denounce, rebuke, reproach, reprove. 2 (find guilty) convict, judge, pass sentence, punish, sentence

**condense** *v* 1 make shorter 2 concentrate 3 reduce gas, etc to liquid; *n* **condensation**

**condescend** *v* deign, patronize, be affable; *adj* **-ing**; *n* **condescension**

**condiment** *n* spicy seasoning for food

**condition** *n* 1 situation 2 sth necessary 3 state 4 illness; *adj* **conditional** subject to conditions

> **condition** *n* 1 (situation) circumstances, plight, position, predicament, state. 2 (sth necessary) demand, necessity, precondition, prerequisite, proviso, requirement, stipulation, terms. 3 (state) fitness, form, health, order, shape. 4 (illness) affliction, ailment, disease, disorder, infection

**condole** *v* offer sympathy; *n* **condolence**

**condom** *n* contraceptive sheath

**condone** *v* find excuses for

> **condone** *v* accept, approve, excuse, forgive, ignore, overlook, tolerate

**conduct** *v* 1 be in charge of 2 lead 3 transmit (heat, electricity); *n* behavior; *n* **conductor** 1 guide 2 fare collector on train 3 director of orchestra 4 substance capable of transmitting electricity

> **conduct** *v* 1 (be in charge of) administer, command, control, direct, govern, handle, head, lead, manage, organize, oversee, regulate, rule, run, steer, supervise. 2 (lead) accompany, escort, guide, pilot, take, usher

**cone** *n* 1 solid circular shape tapering to apex 2 fruit of conifers; *adj* **conical**

**confection** *n* candy, preserve

**confederate** *n* accomplice; *v* ally with; *ns* **-ation, confederacy**

**confer** *v* **-ferring, -ferred** 1 discuss 2 give

> **confer** *v* 1 (discuss) consult, converse, debate, put your heads together. 2 (give) award, bestow, grant, invest, present

**conference** *n* meeting to discuss

> **conference** *n* congress, convention, forum, meeting, seminar, symposium

**confess** *v* admit; *n* **confession**

> **confess** *v* acknowledge, come clean, concede, disclose, divulge, own up, plead guilty, reveal

**confetti** *n* small pieces of colored paper thrown at wedding, etc

**confide** *v* trust in; tell, as secret

**confidence** *n* 1 trust 2 self-assurance 3 secret

**confident** *adj* 1 self-assured 2 certain

> **confident** *adj* 1 (self-assured) assertive, brave, composed, courageous, fearless, outgoing, self-confident. 2 (certain) convinced, positive, satisfied, sure

**confidential** *adj* secret

**confidential** *adj* classified, hush-hush *inf*, intimate, personal, private

**configuration** *n* figure, form
**confine** *v* imprison; limit; *n* **-ment** 1 imprisonment 2 childbirth; *n pl* **confines** boundaries

**confine** *v* bind, cage, coop up, detain, enclose, hem in, imprison, incarcerate, intern, jail, lock up, restrain, restrict

**confirm** *v* 1 show to be true 2 formalize; *n* **confirmation** rite to confirm vows made at baptism

**confirm** *v* 1 (show to be true) back up, bear out, corroborate, endorse, establish, give credence to, prove, show, substantiate, verify. 2 (formalize) authorize, establish, fix, settle, ratify

**confirmed** *adj* habitual
**confiscate** *v* seize by authority; *n* **-ation**
**conflict** *n* 1 fight 2 disagreement; *v* contend, be incompatible

**conflict** *n* 1 (fight) battle, clash, combat, confrontation, encounter, engagement, war, warfare. 2 (disagreement) antagonism, bad blood, discord, friction, hostility, opposition

**conform** *v* comply; *n* **conformity**
**confound** *v* confuse, perplex, dismay
**confront** *v* meet boldly in opposition

**confront** *v* challenge, defy, face up to, oppose, resist, stand up to, tackle

**confrontation** *n* conflict

**confrontation** *n* battle, clash, encounter, showdown

**confuse** *v* 1 bewilder 2 mix up; *n* **confusion**

**confuse** *v* 1 (bewilder) baffle, disconcert, flummox, fluster, perplex, puzzle. 2 (mix up) jumble, mess up, muddle

**confused** *adj* 1 bewildered 2 mixed up

**confused** *adj* 1 (bewildered) baffled, dazed, mystified, perplexed, puzzled. 2 (mixed up) chaotic, disordered, disorganized, jumbled, messy, muddled, untidy

**confusing** *adj* difficult to understand

**confusing** *adj* baffling, bewildering, complex, complicated, contradictory, difficult, incomprehensible, jumbled, misleading, puzzling, unclear

**conga** *n* dance performed in a long line
**congeal** *v* freeze, solidify
**congenital** *adj* from birth
**conger** *n* large salt-water eel
**congested** *adj* blocked; *n* **congestion**

**congested** *adj* clogged, crammed, crowded, jammed, obstructed, overcrowded, overfilled, packed

**conglomeration** *n* jumble of things
**congratulate** *v* wish joy; express pleasure at; *n* **-ation**; *adj* **-atory**
**congregate** *v* assemble; *n* **-ation** gathering of persons, *esp* for worship; *adj* **-ational**
**congress** *n* formal assembly; *adj* **congressional**

**congress** *n* assembly, chamber, conference, convention, council, delegates, gathering, house, legislature, meeting, parliament, representatives

**conical** *adj* cone-shaped
**conifer** *n* cone-bearing tree, shrub, pine, fir
**conjecture** *v* guess; surmise; *n* guesswork

a
b
c
d
e
f
g
h
i
j
k
l
m
n
o
p
q
r
s
t
u
v
w
x
y
z

**conjugal** *adj* pertaining to marriage; between husband and wife

**conjunction** *n* **1** part of speech, as *and, but*; **2** simultaneous occurrence

**conjunctivitis** *n* inflammation of the eye

**conjure** *v* perform tricks by sleight-of-hand; cast spells; *n* **conjurer, -or**

**conker** *n coll* fruit of horse chestnut; *pl* children's game with this on string

**connect** *v* **1** join **2** associate

> **connect** *v* **1** (join) affix, attach, combine, couple, fasten, fix, link, relate, tie, unite. **2** (associate) equate, identify, link, relate

**connection** *n* **1** joining **2** link **3** person known to you; *idm* **in connection with** regarding

> **connection** *n* **1** (joining) attachment, coupling, fastening, junction, link. **2** (link) alliance, association, bond, equivalence, relation, relationship. **3** (person known) acquaintance, associate, contact, friend

**connoisseur** *n Fr* expert

**conquer** *v* overpower, subjugate, prevail; *ns* **conqueror, conquest**

> **conquer** *v* beat, crush, defeat, invade, master, occupy, overcome, overthrow, rout, seize, take, triumph, vanquish, win

**conscience** *n* sense of right and wrong; *adj* **conscientious** thorough; *n* **-ness**

> **conscience** *n* better nature, ethics, morals, principles, qualms, scruples

**conscious** *adj* **1** awake **2** deliberate; *n* **-ness** awareness

> **conscious** *adj* **1** (awake) alert, aware, responsive. **2** (deliberate) calculated, intentional, premeditated, studied, willful

**conscript** *v* enroll by compulsion for military service; *n* one so enrolled

**consecrate** *v* render holy; set apart as sacred; *n* **-ation**

**consecutive** *adj* following in regular order; expressing consequence

**consensus** *n* general agreement

> **consensus** *n* agreement, common consent, common ground, concord, concurrence, general opinion, harmony, unanimity

**consent** *v* agree to; *n* permission

> **consent** *v* accept, allow, assent, comply, concede, concur, condone, go along with, permit, sanction, support

**consequence** *n* outcome; *adv* **consequently** therefore

> **consequence** *n* aftermath, by-product, effect, end, repercussion, result, reverberation, side-effect, upshot

**conservative** *adj* unwilling to change

> **conservative** *adj* careful, cautious, conventional, narrow-minded, old-fashioned, orthodox, reactionary, right-wing, straitlaced, traditionalist

**conservatory** *n* greenhouse joined to house

**conserve** *v* protect from change, waste, etc; *n* **conservation**

> **conserve** *v* be economical with, hoard, keep, maintain, preserve, protect, safeguard, save, store

**consider** *n* **1** think about **2** take into account **3** think; *adj* **considering** in view of; *n* **consideration 1** thought; reflection **2** concern **3** fact worth remembering **4** payment; *idm* **take into consideration** keep in mind when judging

**consider** *v* 1 (think about) contemplate, deliberate, examine, meditate, mull over, ponder, reflect, study, think. 2 (take into account) allow for, bear in mind, have regard for, make allowances for, reckon with, remember, respect, take into consideration. 3 (think) believe, be of the opinion, deem, judge, reckon, regard

**considerate** *adj* thoughtful for others

**considerate** *adj* attentive, aware, caring, compassionate, concerned, helpful, kind, obliging, sensitive, thoughtful, unselfish

**consign** *v* commit; entrust; send goods; *n* **consignment** goods consigned

**consist in** *phr v* be a matter of (doing certain things)

**consist of** *phr v* be composed of

**consist of** *v* be made up of, comprise, contain, include, incorporate, involve

**consistent** *adj* reliable; *ns* **consistence**, **consistency** degree of density; relevance

**consistent** *adj* constant, dependable, predictable, regular, stable, steady, true, unchanging, unvarying

**console** *v* comfort; make up for; *adj* **consolable**; *n* **consolation**

**console** *v* cheer, encourage, placate, soothe, support, sympathize

**consolidate** *v* make, become solid, firm; combine; *n* **-ation**

**consonant** *n* letter other than vowel

**consort** *n* husband, wife, *esp* of monarch; *phr v* **consort with** associate with

**consortium** *n* temporary association of (commercial, education, etc) institutions for a common purpose; *pl* **-s** *or* **consortia**

**conspicuous** *adj* obvious

**conspicuous** *adj* clear, evident, glaring, loud, noticeable, prominent, striking, visible

**conspire** *v* plot; join another in secret, *usu* for unlawful purpose; *ns* **conspiracy**, **conspirator**; *adj* **conspiratorial**

**constable** *n* high-ranking officer; *n* **constabulary** police force

**constant** *adj* 1 never stopping 2 steadfast; *n math* unvarying term, factor

**constant** *adj* 1 (never stopping) ceaseless, continuous, endless, everlasting, incessant, interminable, perpetual, persistent, relentless, sustained, 2 (steadfast) dependable, even, faithful, firm, loyal, reliable, staunch, true, trusty

**constellation** *n* group of fixed stars

**constipation** *n* inactivity of bowels; *v* **constipate** make bowels sluggish

**constituent** *adj* component; entitled to elect; *n* essential part; voter in constituency; *n* **constituency** place represented in legislature; body of voters

**constitute** *v* make into; set up; give form to; *n* **constitution** structure; natural state of body, mind, etc; principles of government; *adj* **constitutional** pertaining to constitution

**constrain** *v* bring force to bear on person; *n* **constraint** compulsion, embarrassment

**constrict** *v* contract; compress

**construct** *v* build; *n* **construction**

**construct** *v* assemble, create, design, devise, erect, establish, form, formulate, make, manufacture, produce, put together, put up

**constructive** *adj* helpful

**constructive** *v* cooperative, creative, positive, practical, useful, valuable

a
b
**c**
d
e
f
g
h
i
j
k
l
m
n
o
p
q
r
s
t
u
v
w
x
y
z

**construe** v 1 translate 2 analyze grammatically 3 deduce

**consul** n official appointed by state, living in foreign country; n **consulate**

**consult** v discuss with; ns **consultant**, **consultation**

> **consult** v ask, compare notes, confer, debate, deliberate, discuss, interrogate, question, refer to, seek advice, turn to

**consume** v 1 use up 2 destroy by fire; n **consumer** buyer, user of commodity

> **consume** v (use up) absorb, devour, drain, eat up, exhaust, finish off, polish off, spend

**consumer durable** n manufactured article of fairly long life, eg washing machine

**consummate** v make complete

**consumption** n 1 using of food or resources 2 amount used 3 tuberculosis (TB)

**contact** n being in touch; close proximity; v get in touch with

> **contact** v approach, call, communicate, correspond, notify, reach, ring, speak, talk, telephone, write

**contagious** adj spreading

> **contagious** adj catching, communicable, infectious, transmissible, transmittable

**contain** v hold, compromise, enclose, restrain (oneself); n **container** box, jar, etc holding something

**contaminate** v make impure; n **-ation** pollution

> **contaminate** v adulterate, corrupt, debase, dirty, foul, infect, poison, pollute, stain, sully, taint, tarnish

**contemplate** v gaze on, consider, intend, meditate; n **-ation**; adj **-ative**

**contemporary** adj living, existing, made at same time; n one having same age

**contempt** n scorn

> **contempt** n abhorrence, derision, disdain, disregard, disrespect, distaste, loathing, mockery, ridicule

**contend** v struggle, fight, assert

**content** adj satisfied; n holding capacity; real meaning; pl that which is inside; list of topics in book; v satisfy; adj **contented** pleased

> **content** adj at ease, at peace, cheerful, comfortable, contented, fulfilled, gratified, happy, pleased, relaxed

**contentment** n satisfaction

> **contentment** n cheerfulness, comfort, ease, fulfillment, happiness, peace, pleasure

**contest** v 1 fight for 2 disagree with; n competition; n **contestant**

> **contest** v 1 (fight for) battle, compete, contend, fight over, struggle, vie. 2 (disagree with) argue, call into question, challenge, debate, dispute, doubt, oppose
> **contest** n battle, fight, game, match, rivalry, tournament, trial

**context** n things surrounding sth

> **context** n background, circumstances, conditions, environment, framework, milieu, setting, situation, surroundings

**continent** n one of large land areas of earth

**continental drift** n geol theory that continents once belonged to a single land mass and then separated

**contingency** n possibility, chance occurrence; adj **contingent** possible, dependent on; n quota, esp of troops

**continual** adj never stopping

**continual** *adj* ceaseless, constant, endless, everlasting, incessant, interminable, never-ending, nonstop, perpetual, persistent, regular, relentless, sustained, unceasing, unending, unrelenting

**continue** *v* persist, remain

**continue** *v* carry on, go on, keep on, live on, persevere, proceed, resume, survive

**contortionist** *n* acrobat
**contour** *n* outline; shape
**contraband** *n* smuggled goods
**contraception** *n* birth-control;
  *n, adj* **contraceptive** (that) which prevents conception
**contract** *n* binding agreement; *v* 1 enter into agreement 2 become smaller 3 incur 4 catch (disease); *adj* **contractual**

**contract** *n* agreement, arrangement, bargain, commitment, convention, covenant, deal, lease, pact, settlement, transaction, treaty, understanding

**contradict** *v* show or say to be not true;
  *adj* **contradictory**

**contradict** *v* argue, be at odds, be at variance, challenge, deny, disagree, dispute, dissent from, oppose, refute

**contradiction** *n* disagreement

**contradiction** *n* clash, conflict, counter, incompatibility, inconsistency, paradox

**contralto** *n* female voice of deep tone; singer with such a voice
**contraption** *n* eccentric device
**contrapuntal** *n* *mus* of or involving counterpoint
**contrary** *n* exact opposite, of object, fact, quality; *adj* 1 different 2 refusing to agree

**contrary** *adj* 1 (different) clashing, conflicting, contradictory, opposed, opposite. 2 (refusing to agree) awkward, headstrong, intractable, intransigent, obstinate, perverse, stubborn, uncooperative, wayward, willful

**contrast** *v* compare, show difference;
  *n* striking difference

**contrast** *n* clash, comparison, difference, dissimilarity, distinction, opposition

**contravene** *v* infringe; disobey (law)
**contribute** *v* give to common fund; write for the press; have share in producing result
**contribution** *n* donation

**contribution** *n* gift, grant, offering, payment, present, subscription

**contrite** *adj* penitent; sorrowful for sin
**contrive** *v* 1 invent; devise; scheme
  2 manage; *n* **contrivance** device
**control** *v* **-trolling, -trolled** 1 be in charge of 2 steer 3 restrain; *n* 1 authority
  2 restraint; *pl* instruments guiding machine;
  *adj* **controllable**; *n* **controller** person regulating expenditure

**control** *v* 1 (be in charge of) administer, direct, dominate, govern, handle, lead, look after, manage, manipulate, oversee, preside, rule, run, supervise. 2 (steer) command, pilot. 3 (restrain) check, constrain, curb, hold back, master
**control** *n* 1 (authority) charge, command, dominance, influence, leadership, power, rule, supervision, supremacy. 2 (restraint) direction, grip, hold

**controversy** *n* argument; *adj* **controversial** liable to provoke controversy
**conundrum** *n* riddle; difficult problem
**conurbation** *n* large urban area

a b **c** d e f g h i j k l m n o p q r s t u v w x y z

**convalesce** *v* regain health gradually
**convene** *v* summon; convoke; *n* **convention**
1 formal assembly 2 custom, usage
**convenience food** *n* food sold ready to eat
**convenience store** *n* small variety store that
stays open latet
**convenient** *adj* 1 easy to use 2 suitable;
*n* **convenience** personal comfort; ease

> **convenient** *adj* 1 (easy to use) at hand,
> available, labor-saving, nearby. 2
> (suitable) appropriate, helpful, opportune

**convent** *n* community of monks or nuns
**conventional** *adj* 1 standard 2 conservative

> **conventional** *adj* 1 (standard) accepted,
> customary, expected, mainstream, normal,
> ordinary, orthodox, proper, straight,
> traditional, usual. 2 (conservative)
> conformist, reactionary, unadventurous

**converge** *v* meet at given point
**conversation** *n* talk

> **conversation** *n* chat, dialogue, discussion,
> gossip, heart-to-heart, tête-a-tête

**converse**[1] *adj* opposite; *n* the opposite
**converse**[2] *v* talk with someone
**convert** *v* 1 change 2 convince; *ns* **convert**
one who has been convinced; **conversion**

> **convert** *v* 1 (change) alter, modify, reshape,
> transform, turn, switch. 2 (convince)
> change sb's mind, persuade, reeducate,
> reform, rehabilitate, save, win over

**convex** *adj* curving outward
**convey** *n* 1 carry 2 impart; *n* **conveyancing**
business of transferring property
**conveyor belt** *n* continuous moving belt
**convict** *v* prove, find guilty of crime;
*ns* **convict** criminal serving sentence of
imprisonment; **conviction** act of
convicting; assured belief

**convince** *v* persuade, arouse belief in, by
argument or proof

> **convince** *v* assure, persuade, satisfy, win over

**convincing** *adj* believable

> **convincing** *adj* compelling, credible, likely,
> logical, plausible, probable, valid

**convoy** *n* group of ships, vehicles, etc
traveling together
**convulse** *v* cause sudden violent muscular
spasms; *n pl* **convulsions** hysterical fits of
emotion; spasms
**cook** *n* one who prepares food for eating;
*v* prepare food; *ns* **cookery** art of cooking;
**cookhouse** camp kitchen
**cool** *adj* 1 pleasantly cold 2 calm 3 unfriendly;
*v* make, become cool; *n* **coolness** 1 state of
being cool 2 unfriendliness

> **cool** *adj* 1 (pleasantly cold) chilled, cold,
> fresh, iced. 2 (calm) collected, composed,
> dignified, self-possessed, sensible, unruffled.
> 3 (unfriendly) aloof, offhand, unwelcoming

**coop** *n* wooden cage; *v* confine
**cooperate** *v* act together for common aim;
*ns* **cooperation** working together;
**cooperative** profit sharing concern
(*adj* working together; helpful)

> **cooperate** *v* assist, collaborate, combine,
> help, join forces, unite, work together

**coordinate** *v* adjust so as to harmonize

> **coordinate** *v* arrange, integrate, match,
> organize, synchronize

**cope** *v* handle successfully

> **cope** *v* get by, get through, make, manage,
> muddle through, survive

**copier** n machine that makes copies
**copious** adj plentiful

> **copious** adj abundant, ample, extensive, full, generous, profuse, rich

**copper** n reddish, ductile, malleable metal; sl policeman
**coppice**, **copse** n small wood
**copulate** v join, unite sexually
**copy** n 1 imitation 2 single specimen of book, etc; v **copying, copied** 1 make a copy of 2 imitate; n **copyright** legal exclusive right to reproduce book, music, work of art, etc

> **copy** n (imitation) clone, counterfeit, double, duplicate, facsimile, fake, forgery, imitation, model, photocopy, print, replica, reproduction
> **copy** v 1 (make a copy of) counterfeit, duplicate, forge, photocopy, replicate, reproduce, transcribe. 2 (imitate) crib, plagiarize, steal

**coral** n hard red or white substance made by marine polyps and which forms reefs
**cord** n 1 thin rope 2 ribbed cloth
**cordial** adj hearty, friendly, sincere; n stimulating, warming drink
**cordon** n line of troops or police
**cords** n pl coll corduroy trousers
**corduroy** n ribbed cotton material
**core** n 1 central part 2 seed case of some fruits

> **core** n (central part) center, crux, essence, gist, heart, inside, kernel, middle, nub

**corgi** n breed of small Welsh dog
**cork** n bark of cork oak; piece used as stopper for bottle, etc; v stop up with a cork; adj **corked** (of wine) tasting of decayed cork; n **corkscrew** tool for extracting corks
**cormorant** n large seabird
**corn**[1] n grain; seed of cereals
**corn**[2] n hardened, thickened skin causing pain, usually on toe

**corner** n meeting place of two converging lines; hidden remote place; angle formed by meeting walls, sides (of box, etc); v 1 force into difficult position 2 buy up all available stocks of; adj **cornered**
**cornet** n trumpet having valves; cone-shaped wafer holding ice cream
**cornflakes** n breakfast cereal of crisp flakes from corn
**cornucopia** n symbolic horn of plenty; fig abundance
**corny** adj sl (of jokes, stories) unoriginal
**coronary** adj anat relating to arteries supplying heart muscle; **c. thrombosis** formation of clot in coronary artery
**coronation** n act of crowning a sovereign
**coroner** n leg officer holding inquiry as to cause of any unnatural death
**corporal** n NCO ranking below sergeant
**corporation** n business; civic authority

> **corporation** n company, conglomerate, firm, organization, partnership, trust

**corps** n largest tactical military unit; any organized group of persons
**corpse** n dead body, usu human
**corpulent** adj stout, obese, fat
**corpuscle** n red and white constituent particles of blood
**correct** v put right; adj 1 acceptable (of behavior) 2 right

> **correct** v adjust, alter, amend, cure, fix, improve, mark, rectify, redress, remedy, repair, right
> **correct** adj 1 (acceptable) appropriate, conventional, proper, seemly, suitable. 2 (right) accurate, exact, faultless, flawless, perfect

**correction** n change made to put sth right

> **correction** n adjustment, alteration, amendment, improvement, revision

A
B
**C**
D
E
F
G
H
I
J
K
L
M
N
O
P
Q
R
S
T
U
V
W
X
Y
Z

**correspond** v 1 write to 2 be equivalent to;
ns **correspondent**, **correspondence**
1 similarity 2 exchange of letters

> **correspond** v 1 (write) communicate,
> exchange letters, keep in touch. 2 (be
> equivalent) agree, be consistent, be
> similar, coincide, compare, fit, match

**corridor** n 1 passage in building, railroad car,
etc 2 strip of land (or air route) passing
through state to which it does not belong
**corroborate** v confirm; make more certain;
n **corroboration**; adj **corroborative**
**corrode** v eat into; wear away gradually,
esp by chemical action; adj **corrosive**
**corrugated** adj with ridges or folds
**corrupt** adj not honest; v make corrupt;
adj **-ible**; n **-ion**

> **corrupt** adj bent, crooked, depraved, dirty,
> dishonest, fraudulent, immoral, unethical,
> unprincipled, untrustworthy, wicked
> **corrupt** v bribe, buy off, deprave, influence,
> lead astray, pervert, subvert, tempt

**corset** n close-fitting undergarment
**cosmetic** n preparation for beautifying hair,
complexion, skin; adj **cosmetic**
**cosmic** adj relating to universe and laws
governing it
**cosmonaut** n astronaut, space traveler
**cosmopolitan** adj 1 well traveled 2 of many
nationalities

> **cosmopolitan** adj 1 (well traveled) cultured,
> sophisticated, urbane, worldly, worldly-
> wise. 2 (of many nationalities)
> international, multiracial

**cosset** v pamper, fondle, pet
**cost** n 1 price of purchase 2 harm done by sth;
pl **costs** expenses; idm **at all costs** whatever
happens; v 1 cause expenditure of 2 cause
loss of 3 estimate cost of production;
pt, pp **cost**

**cost** n 1 (price of purchase) charge, expense,
fare, outlay, payment, price, rate, tariff,
value, worth. 2 (harm done) damage,
harm, hurt, loss, sacrifice, suffering

**costly** adj expensive
**costar** n famous actor/actress in the same film
as another such actor/actress
**costume** n mode of dress, esp if peculiar to
nation, period, etc; theatrical clothes
**cot** n child's bed; n **cot death** the sudden
death of an infant from no apparent illness
**cottage** n small house
**cotton** n type of fabric; adj made of cotton;
idm **cotton to** take a liking to
**couch** n sofa, long seat for reclining on
**couch potato** n sl inactive person who spends
a lot of time watching television
**counterfeit** adj forged; v imitate with intent
to deceive; n **counterfeiter**

> **counterfeit** adj artificial, copied, faked,
> false, fraudulent, imitation, phony, sham

**counterfoil** n part of check, receipt, etc, kept
by issuer as record
**counterpart** n person or thing exactly
resembling another; duplicate
**counterproductive** adj achieving opposite of
desired effect
**countersign** v fig ratify
**countless** adj innumerable

> **countless** adj endless, immeasurable,
> incalculable, infinite, numerous, untold

**country** n 1 land with definite boundaries,
occupied by one nation 2 land of your birth
3 rural areas; n **countryside** rural area

> **country** n 1 (land) empire, nation, state.
> 2 (land of your birth) fatherland,
> motherland, native land. 3 (rural areas)
> countryside, farmland, green belt, wilds

**county** n political division of a state

**coup** n Fr achievement

**coup** n 1 (achievement) accomplishment, deed, exploit, feat, maneuvre, tour de force. 2 (overthrow of government) coup d'état, overthrow, revolt, revolution

**couple** n two objects or persons; v join, unite

**coupon** n negotiable ticket or voucher

**courage** n bravery

**courage** n boldness, daring, determination, fearlessness, fortitude, gallantry, heroism, nerve, pluck, resolution, spirit, valor

**courageous** adj brave

**courageous** adj bold, daring, fearless, heroic, indomitable, intrepid, plucky, stout-hearted, unafraid, undaunted, valiant

**courier** n express messenger; person conducting travelers on tour

**course** n 1 movement 2 path followed by moving object 3 race track 4 programme of study 5 part of meal served at one time

**course** n 1 (movement) advance, flow, march, progress, succession. 2 (path followed by moving object) circuit, direction, line, orbit, passage, path, road, route, track, trail, trajectory. way. 3 (race track) circuit, lap, racecourse. 4 (program of study) curriculum, lectures, program, studies, syllabus

**court** n 1 open space, paved yard enclosed by buildings or walls 2 space marked out, for playing games like tennis 3 household of sovereign 4 place of justice where trials are held 5 body with judicial powers; v woo; n **court-martial**, pl **courts-martial** court of officers trying military or naval offenses; ns **courtroom**, **courthouse** room, place where courts of law are held

**courteous** adj polite

**courteous** adj attentive, civil, considerate, gallant, gracious, refined, respectful,

**courtesy** n politeness

**cousin** n son or daughter of uncle or aunt

**cove** n small sheltered bay or inlet

**covenant** n formal agreement, contract; v grant, promise by covenant

**cover** v 1 place (sth) over 2 include 3 report on 4 stand in for; n 1 sth that covers 2 individual table setting

**cover** v 1 (place (sth) over) blanket, carpet, bury, cloak, clothe, coat, conceal, encase, enclose, envelop, hide, house, mask, obscure, screen, shade, sheathe, shelter, shroud, veil, wrap. 2 (include) contain, encompass, incorporate, involve. 3 (report on) describe, investigate, recount, write up. 4 (stand in for) fill in, relieve, replace, take over
**cover** n (sth that covers) blanket, canopy, cap, case, coating, covering, lid, roof, top

**covering** n sth that covers

**covering** n blanket, canopy, casing, cladding, coat, cover, film, layer, rind, sheet, skin, surface, veneer, wrapping

**cover-up** n concealment of illegal activity or a mistake

**covet** v **coveting**, **coveted** desire

**cow** n adult female of bovine and various other animals

**coward** n one lacking courage; n **cowardice**

**coward** n chicken, scaredy-cat inf, wimp

**cowardly** adj fearful

**cowardly** adj faint-hearted, scared, soft, spineless, weak, wimpish, yellow inf

**cowboy** *n* man, *usu* on horseback, who grazes cattle

**cower** *v* shrink fearfully from

> **cower** *v* cringe, crouch, flinch, grovel, hide, quail, recoil, shrink, skulk, tremble

**cowrie** *n* small shell used as money in parts of S Asia and Africa

**cowslip** *n* wild plant of primrose family

**coxswain** *n* one steering boat; (*naval*) petty officer in charge of ship's boat

**coy** *adj* affecting shyness

> **coy** *adj* bashful, demure, diffident, evasive, flirtatious, modest, reticent, shy

**cozy** *adj* 1 warm and snug 2 friendly

> **cozy** *adj* 1 (warm and snug) safe, secure, sheltered. 2 (friendly) intimate, reassuring

**crab** *n* edible shellfish, with eight legs and two pincers

**crab apple** *n* wild apple

**crack** *v* 1 break 2 make sharp noise 3 bump part of body 4 suffer breakdown; *n* 1 break 2 sharp sound; *ns* **cracker** firecracker; brittle thin breadlike snack; **crackle** sound of small cracks; **crackling** crisp, browned skin of roast pork

> **crack** *v* 1 (break) fracture, fragment, snap, splinter, split. 2 (make sharp noise) boom, crackle, resound, ring out. 3 (bump part of body) bang, bash, clout, hit, knock, smack, strike, whack. 4 (suffer breakdown) collapse, go to pieces, lose control
>
> **crack** *n* 1 (break) chink, chip, cleft, crevice, fissure, flaw, fracture, gap, opening, rift, slit, split. 2 (sharp sound) burst, clap, crash, explosion, pop

**crackdown** *n* rigorous campaign to control criminal activity

**cradle** *n* baby's bed or cot; supported framework; *v* rock; nurse

**craft** *n* 1 cunning 2 manual dexterity 3 members of skilled trade, guild 4 boat; *ns* **craftsman**, **craftsmanship**

**crafty** *adj* subtly cunning; *adv* **craftily**

> **crafty** *adj* artful, calculating, canny, clever, conniving, deceitful, devious, furtive, scheming, sharp, shrewd, sly, sneaky, wily

**crag** *n* rough, steep mass of rock

**cram** *v* **cramming**, **crammed** stuff, pack tightly into; eat greedily; coach intensively for exams

**cramp** *n* sudden painful muscular spasm; *v* hamper, confine, restrict

**cramped** *adj* with not enough space

> **cramped** *adj* closed in, confined, congested, crowded, narrow, overcrowded, packed, restricted, small, tight, uncomfortable

**crampon** *n* iron spike on climbing boots

**cranberry** *n* small red berry

**crane** *n* 1 slender wading bird with long neck 2 machine for raising heavy weights; *v* stretch out one's neck

**cranium** *n* skull; *adj* **cranial**

**crank** *n* bar with right-angle bend for turning things; *v* wind, turn; start up engine by hand

**cranny** *n* chink, narrow opening

**crash** *v* 1 fall violently with loud noise 2 fail 3 have collision; *n* 1 loud noise 2 collision 3 ruin

> **crash** *v* 1 (fall with loud noise) bang, boom, clash, clatter, smash, splinter. 2 (fail) collapse, fold, go under, plunge, topple, tumble. 3 (have collision) crash into, drive into, hit, plow into, smash into
>
> **crash** *n* 1 (loud noise) bang, boom, clang, clash, din, explosion, racket, thunder. 2 (collision) accident, pile-up, smash. 3 (ruin) bankruptcy, collapse, failure

**crash-land** v avia land in an emergency, with probable damage; n **crash-landing**
**crate** n wooden or wicker packing case
**crater** n hole in ground; mouth of volcano
**cravat** n necktie
**crave** v have strong desire for

> **crave** v be dying for, desire, fancy, hanker after, hope for, hunger after, long for, lust after, need, pine for, require, thirst for, want, yearn for

**craving** n longing

> **craving** n addiction, appetite, desire, hankering, hope, hunger, lust, need, thirst, urge, yearning

**crawl** v 1 creep 2 abase yourself; n 1 creeping movement 2 stroke in swimming

> **crawl** v 1 (creep) clamber, edge, go on all fours, inch, slither, wriggle, writhe. 2 (abase yourself) be obsequious, flatter, grovel, humble yourself, suck up sl

**crayfish**, **crawfish** n fresh water edible shellfish like lobster
**crayon** n stick of charcoal or colored chalk
**craze** n popular fashion

> **craze** n enthusiasm, fad, fashion, infatuation, mania, obsession, passion

**crazy** 1 mad 2 very foolish

> **crazy** adj 1 (mad) berserk, cracked sl, demented, deranged, insane, loopy, lunatic, maniacal, nuts, potty, round the bend, touched, unbalanced, unhinged. 2 (very foolish) bizarre, confused, eccentric, odd, outrageous, peculiar, ridiculous, silly, strange, weird, wild, zany

**creak** v make grating, squeaking noise; n grating, squeaking noise

> **creak** v grate, grind, jar, rasp, scrape, scratch, screech, squeak, squeal

**cream** n 1 fat part of milk 2 best of anything; v 1 skim cream from milk 2 form into a cream; adj **creamy** like cream
**crease** n wrinkle; ridge made by folding; line marking position of batsman or bowler in cricket; v make creases; become wrinkled
**create** v bring into existence

> **create** v bring into being, build, compose, conceive, concoct, construct, design, develop, devise, establish, forge, formulate, found, generate, hatch, initiate, invent, make, originate, produce, shape

**creation** n 1 making 2 sth made

> **creation** n 1 (making) beginning, birth, building, establishment, formation, foundation, generation, inception, origin, procreation, setting up. 2 (sth made) achievement, brainchild, handiwork, invention, masterpiece, work

**creative** adj having lots of good, new ideas

> **creative** adj artistic, imaginative, inspired, inventive, original, visionary

**creator** n maker
**creature** n living being; animal
**crêche** n public day nursery
**credentials** n pl documents showing authority
**credible** adj worthy of belief

> **credible** adj believable, conceivable, convincing, imaginable, likely, persuasive, plausible, possible, reasonable

**credit** n 1 prestige gained by merit 2 sum in person's bank account; idm **on credit** allowing person to have goods for later payment; v 1 believe 2 acknowledge

a
b
**c**
d
e
f
g
h
i
j
k
l
m
n
o
p
q
r
s
t
u
v
w
x
y
z

**credit** n (prestige) approval, commendation, distinction, esteem, fame, glory, honor, kudos, merit, praise, recognition, thanks

**credit card** n card that permits buying of goods without cash

**credulous** adj easily deceived

**creed** n set of principles; formally phrased confession of faith

**creek** n narrow inlet on seacoast; arm of river

**creep** v 1 crawl 2 flatter; pt, pp **crept**

**creep** v 1 (crawl) edge, inch, slink, slither, sneak, squirm, steal, tiptoe, worm, wriggle. 2 (flatter) bow and scrape, butter up inf, curry favor, grovel, suck up sl

**creepy** adj eerie

**cremation** n burning (corpse) to ashes; v **cremate**; n **crematorium** place where cremation takes place

**creosote** n oily substance used for preserving wood

**crepe paper** n thin, wrinkled paper for decorating and wrapping

**crept** pt of **creep**

**crescendo** adj, adv n gradual increase in loudness, esp of music

**crescent** n 1 shape of new moon 2 curved row of houses

**cress** n plant with edible pungent leaves

**crest** n 1 top 2 tuft on animal's head 3 coat of arms

**crest** n 1 (top) apex, brow, crown, peak, pinnacle, ridge, summit. 2 (tuft on animal's head) comb, plume, tassel, mane, tuft. 3 (coat of arms) badge, emblem, insignia, seal, shield

**crevice** n small chink, fissure

**crew** n ship's, aircraft's company

**crew cut** n very short haircut for men

**crib** n child's bed; v **cribbing**, **cribbed** copy closely

**crick** n painful spasm of back or neck muscles

**cricket**[1] n chirping insect

**cricket**[2] n game played by teams of eleven a side, with wickets, bats, and ball

**cried** pt of **cry**

**cries** 3rd sing present of **cry**

**crime** n 1 action that breaks law 2 lawbreaking

**crime** n 1 (action that breaks law) felony, misdeed, misdemeanor, offense, outrage, transgression, wrong. 2 (lawbreaking) delinquency, dishonesty, lawlessness

**criminal** adj 1 against the law 2 wrong; n one who has broken law

**criminal** adj 1 (against law) corrupt, crooked, dishonest, evil, illegal, illicit, immoral, unlawful, villainous, wicked, wrong. 2 (wrong) deplorable, immoral, reprehensible, scandalous, shameful
**criminal** n convict, crook inf, culprit, delinquent, felon, jailbird, law-breaker, miscreant, offender, outlaw, villain

**crimson** n deep, slightly bluish red color

**cringe** v cower

**cringe** v draw back, flinch, quail, recoil, shrink, shy away, tremble, wince

**crinkle** v wrinkle; rumple; n undulation

**cripple** n lame, disabled, or maimed person; v maim, impair

**crisis** n time of acute danger or difficulty

**crisis** n calamity, catastrophe, dilemma, dire straits, disaster, emergency, predicament, quandary, trouble

**crisp** adj dry and brittle

**crisp** adj breakable, crispy, crumbly, crunchy, firm, fresh

**criterion** n standard of judgment; test

**critic** n 1 professional reviewer of plays, books, art, etc 2 fault finder

**critical** adj 1 finding fault 2 very important 3 very dangerous

> **critical** adj 1 (finding fault) carping, criticizing, derogatory, disapproving, disparaging, judgmental, nagging, niggling, nit-picking, uncomplimentary, unfavorable. 2 (very important) crucial, decisive, important, key, momentous. 3 (very dangerous) crucial, dangerous, grave, perilous, risky, serious, urgent

**criticize** v find fault with; n **criticism**

> **criticize** v blame, censure, complain, condemn, disapprove, disparage, find fault, knock, nit-pick inf, slam inf

**croak** v emit hoarse, dismal cry, as frog, raven; n sound itself; adj, n **croaking**

**crochet** n Fr kind of fancy-work done with small hooked needle; v make such work

**crock** n 1 earthenware pot 2 old worn-out person, horse

**crocodile** n large amphibious reptile

**crocus** n pl -ses small spring-flowering plant

**croissant** n Fr flaky crescent-shaped pastry

**crone** n hideous, withered old woman

**crony** n old friend, close companion

**crook** n 1 shepherd's staff; long hooked stick 2 coll criminal

**crooked** adj 1 not straight 2 not even 3 dishonest

> **crooked** adj 1 (not straight) bent, bowed, curved, deformed, distorted, gnarled, irregular, misshapen, twisted, twisting, warped, winding, zigzag. 2 (not even) askew, asymmetric, at an angle, lopsided, off-center, slanting, sloping, tilted. 3 (dishonest) corrupt, criminal, deceitful, dubious, fraudulent, shady, shifty

**crop** n season's produce or yield of any cultivated plant; v **cropping, cropped** 1 reap, gather 2 clip hair; phr v **crop up** occur

**cross** n 1 upright stake with transverse bar, used for execution; 2 the Cross, on which Christ died; symbol of Christian faith 3 mark made by intersecting lines 4 mixture of breeds; mongrel, hybrid, etc 5 affliction; v 1 place or lay across 2 traverse 3 interbreed; phr v **cross off/out** delete; adj angry

> **cross** adj angry, annoyed, bad-tempered, disagreeable, fractious, fretful, grouchy, grumpy inf, irritable, irritated, ratty, short-tempered, sullen, upset, vexed

**cross-country** adj proceeding over fields, through woods, etc, rather than on a track

**cross-examine** v interrogate closely

**cross-eyed** adj squinting

**crossroads** n 1 place where two roads intersect 2 decisive point in time

**cross section** n 1 (image of) surface formed by cutting across, usu at right angles 2 representative sample

**crossword** n puzzle built up of intersecting words in numbered squares

**crotch** n place where legs fork from body

**crotchety** adj irritable

**crouch** v stoop low

> **crouch** v bend, bow, kneel, squat, stoop

**croup** n throat disease of children

**crow** n large black bird of raven family

**crowbar** n heavy iron bar for levering

**crowd** n large number of people; v cram into small place

> **crowd** n army, bevy, bunch, circle, clique, flock, gang, group, herd, horde, host, lot, mass, mob, multitude, pack, rabble, throng
> **crowd** v assemble, congregate, cram, flock, gather, huddle, jam, pile inf, press, push, squeeze, surge, swarm, throng

a b **c** d e f g h i j k l m n o p q r s t u v w x y z

**crowded** *adj* full of people

> **crowded** *adj* busy, congested, cramped, full, packed, swarming, teeming

**crown** *n* 1 royal headdress 2 wreath worn on head 3 sovereignty; supreme power; *v* place crown on; make king

**crucial** *adj* very important

> **crucial** *adj* central, critical, decisive, essential, important, major, momentous

**crucify** *v* **-fying**, **-fied** put to death by nailing or binding to cross; *ns* **crucifixion**; **crucifix** figure of Christ on the Cross

**crude** *adj* 1 obscene 2 in natural state 3 not sophisticated

> **crude** *adj* 1 (obscene) coarse, dirty, gross, indecent, indelicate, lewd, smutty, vulgar. 2 (in natural state) natural, unprocessed, unrefined. 3 (not sophisticated) clumsy, inelegant, primitive, rough, rudimentary, sketchy, undeveloped, unfinished

**cruel** *adj* 1 willing to cause pain 2 very harsh; *n* **cruelty**

> **cruel** *adj* 1 (willing to cause pain) barbaric, barbarous, brutal, callous, cold-blooded, hard-hearted, heartless, inhuman, merciless, murderous, pitiless, ruthless, sadistic, savage, spiteful, unfeeling, unkind, vengeful, vicious. 2 (very harsh) atrocious, bitter, fierce, grim, hard, harsh, hellish, painful, raw, severe, unrelenting

**cruise** *v* travel at leisurely speed; *n* sea voyage for pleasure

**crumb** *n* very small piece

> **crumb** *n* bit, bite, grain, morsel, particle, scrap, shred, speck

**crumble** *v* break into crumbs; disintegrate

**crumple** *v* make creases or folds; fall into wrinkles; *adj* **crumpled**

**crunch** *v* chew, crush noisily with teeth; tread heavily on gravel, etc

**crusade** *n* 1 campaign 2 holy war

**crush** *v* 1 squash 2 press out of shape 3 defeat; *idm* **a crush (on sb)** *coll* strong but brief adolescent infatuation (with sb)

> **crush** *v* 1 (squash) break, bruise, compress, grind, mangle, mash, pound, press, pulp, pulverize, shatter, smash, squeeze. 2 (press out of shape) crease, crinkle, crumple, rumple, wrinkle. 3 (defeat) conquer, overcome, overpower, put down, quash, quell, stamp out, subdue, vanquish

**crust** *n* hard outer part; dry piece of bread; hard covering of anything; *v* form crust

**crustacean** *n* animal having hard crustlike shell, *eg* lobster, crab, etc

**crutch** *n* staff with crosspiece to go under arm, to help lame to walk; support; crotch

**crux** *n* knotty point; important or critical point; puzzle

**cry** *n* 1 loud call 2 slogan 3 characteristic call of animal; *v* **crying**, **cried** 1 weep 2 shout

> **cry** *v* 1 (weep) bawl, blubber, howl, shed tears, sob, wail, whimper. 2 (shout) bawl, bellow, roar, scream, screech, shriek, yell

**cryogenics** *n* study or use of extremely low temperatures; *adj* **cryogenic**

**crypt** *n* underground vault, *esp* of church

**cryptic** *adj* mysterious

> **cryptic** *adj* coded, enigmatic, hidden, obscure, puzzling, secret, unclear, veiled

**cryptogam** *n* plant reproducing without seed

**crystal** *n* clear transparent quartz; solidified inorganic substance of geometrical form; fine, hard glassware

**crystal ball** *n* glass sphere used by fortune tellers

**crystal gazing** n 1 looking into a crystal ball 2 trying to predict future events
**cub** n young fox, bear, etc
**cube** n 1 regular geometric solid shape with six equal square faces; anything cube-shaped; 2 *math* third power; v calculate cube of; adj **cubic**
**cubicle** n small, enclosed part in larger room, sleeping car, etc
**cuckoo** n migratory bird, with characteristic call, which lays eggs in another bird's nest
**cucumber** n long fleshy green fruit of plant of gourd family, used in salads
**cuddle** v hug; n a hug

> **cuddle** v clasp, embrace, hold closely, pet

**cue**[1] n word serving as signal to another to act or speak; *fig* hint, lead
**cue**[2] n long tapering rod used in billiards
**cuisine** n quality, style of cooking
**cul-de-sac** n *Fr* dead end
**culinary** adj connected with cooking
**cull** v 1 gather 2 kill selectively
**culminate in** *phr* v end in
**culprit** n one guilty of crime

> **culprit** n bad guy *inf*, delinquent, guilty party, miscreant, offender, wrongdoer

**cult** n system of religious belief; devotion to person or cause; fashion
**cultivate** v till, work land; grow (crops); improve; seek acquaintance of
**cultivated** adj educated and well mannered
**culture** n 1 way of life 2 education; adjs **cultured** refined; **cultural** pertaining to culture

> **culture** n 1 (way of life) civilization, customs, lifestyle, mores, society. 2 (education) erudition, good taste, refinement, sophistication

**cumulative** adj increasing in force, value, etc by successive additions

**cunning** n slyness; adj cleverly sly

> **cunning** adj astute, clever, crafty, devious, imaginative, ingenious, resourceful, sharp, shrewd, subtle, wily

**cup** n 1 small drinking vessel with handle 2 trophy in shape of cup, *usu* silver
**cupboard** n small closet with shelves
**cupid** n figure of winged boy with bow and arrow, representing love
**curable** adj able to be cured
**curate** n rector's or vicar's assistant
**curative** n, adj (substance) effecting a cure
**curator** n person in charge of a museum
**curb** n stopping or prevention; v restrain

> **curb** v check, constrain, contain, control, hinder, hold back, impede, inhibit, limit, repress, restrict, suppress

**curd** n thick substance separated from milk by acid action; v **curdle** turn into curd; coagulate
**cure** v 1 restore to health 2 put right 3 preserve (food) by salting; n sth that restores sb to health

> **cure** v 1 (restore to health) heal, treat. 2 (put right) correct, fix, rectify, remedy, repair, solve. 3 (preserve food) dry, kipper, preserve, salt, smoke
> **cure** n antidote, medication, medicine, panacea, prescription, remedy, solution, therapy, treatment

**curfew** n regulation requiring all persons to be indoors by stated hour
**curio** n small unusual, collector's item; *pl* **-s**
**curiosity** n 1 interest 2 interesting object

> **curiosity** n 1 (interest) inquisitiveness, interference, meddling, nosiness, prying, snooping. 2 (interesting object) freak, novelty, oddity, rarity

a b **c** d e f g h i j k l m n o p q r s t u v w x y z

**curious** *adj* 1 interested 2 nosy 3 strange

**curious** *adj* 1 (interested) inquiring, inquisitive, probing, puzzled, questioning. 2 (nosy) inquisitive, interfering, intrusive, meddlesome, meddling, prying, snooping. 3 (strange) bizarre, exotic, mysterious, novel, odd, puzzling, unusual

**curl** *n* coiled lock of hair; ringlet; spiral or similar shape; *adj* **curly**; *v* twist, roll, or press into spirals; *n* **curling** game like bowls, played on ice

**curlew** *n* wading bird of snipe family

**currant** *n* small dried grape; edible fruit of various shrubs

**current** *adj* modern; in general use; *n* 1 flow of body of water, air 2 movement of electricity; *n* **currency** state of being current; money in circulation

**current** *adj* alive, contemporary, continuing, fashionable, living, modern, popular, present, prevailing, up-to-date

**curriculum** *n* **-la** *or* **-lums** course of study at a school, college, etc

**curriculum vitae** *n* (document with) details of one's qualifications and experience

**curry** *n* highly spiced, hot flavored food; *v* make into a curry; *pl* **-ries**; *n* **curry powder** mixture of turmeric and other spices

**curse** *v* 1 swear 2 put bad luck on; *n* 1 bad language 2 jinx

**curse** *v* 1 (swear) blaspheme, take God's name in vain, use bad language. 2 (put bad luck on) jinx, put a jinx on, put the evil eye on

**cursor** *n* mark on a computer screen that shows where you are working

**cursory** *adj* not careful or detailed

**curt** *adj* short, abrupt, rudely brief

**curtail** *v* cut short

**curtail** *v* abbreviate, break off, reduce, restrict, shorten, stop, trim

**curtain** *n* sheet of material hung to screen window, doo, etc; screen separating stage and audience; *v* cover with a curtain

**curtain call** *n* reappearance of actor(s) to acknowledge applause at end of play

**curtsy** *n* bending of knees as sign of respect; *v* make such gesture

**curve** *n* line of which no part is straight; *v* form a curve

**curve** *n* arc, arch, bend, bow, bulge, camber, circle, crescent, curvature, half-moon, loop, spiral, twist, undulation
**curve** *v* arc, arch, bend, bow, coil, curl, loop, meander, snake, swerve, turn, twist, wind

**cushion** *n* pillow, soft pad to sit or rest on

**cushy** *adj sl* easy, light, profitable

**custard** *n* dessert made of milk, eggs, sugar, that is baked or boiled

**custody** *n* 1 detention 2 safekeeping; *n* **custodian** keeper, curator

**custody** *n* 1 (detention) arrest, imprisonment, incarceration. 2 (safekeeping) care, charge, guardianship, possession, protection, supervision

**custom** *n* habit; practice; *pls* duties on imports; place where these are collected

**custom** *n* (habit) convention, etiquette, form, formality, manner, observance, practice, ritual, routine, tradition, way

**custom-built** *n* made to customer's own specifications

**customer** *n* buyer

**customer** *n* client, consumer, patron, purchaser, regular *inf*, shopper

**ustomize** *v* adapt to customer's requirements

**ut** *v* 1 injure 2 shape by cutting 3 reduce; *pt, pp* **cut**; *n* 1 wound 2 reduction; *phr vs* **cut both ways** have both pros and cons; **cut back** 1 prune 2 reduce; **cut down** 1 fell 2 reduce; **cut off** 1 separate 2 disconnect 3 deprive of inheritance

**cut** *v* 1 (injure) gash, graze, knife, lacerate, lance, nick, open, sever, slash, snick, stab, wound. 2 (shape by cutting) carve, chisel, chop, cleave, crop, dissect, divide, engrave, grate, guillotine, hack, hew, lop, mow, notch, pare, pierce, prune, saw, score, sculpt, shave, shear, shred, slice, slit, whittle. 3 (reduce) abbreviate, abridge, condense, curtail, cut back, decrease, delete, economize, edit, excise, lessen, rationalize, shorten, slash, slim down, trim, truncate

**cut** *n* 1 (wound) gash, graze, incision, laceration, nick, opening, rent, rip, slash, slit, snip, split, tear. 2 (reduction) cutback, economy, fall, lowering, saving

**utback** *n* reduction
**ute** *adj* pretty; charming; cheeky
**uticle** *n* skin at base of nails
**utlass** *n* short, broad-bladed sword
**utlery** *n* implements for eating with
**utlet** *n* small meat chop
**utthroat** *adj* 1 murderous 2 fiercely competitive; *n* very sharp razor
**utting** *adj* sharply critical

**cutting** *adj* acerbic, acid, barbed, biting, hurtful, sarcastic, scathing, sharp, stinging, spiteful, trenchant, wounding

**v** *abbr* curriculum vitae
**wt** *abbr* hundredweight
**yanide** *n* prussic acid
**yberspace** *n* the environment through which electronic information and pictures travel when they are sent from one computer to another

**cycle** *n* 1 period of time during which there is regular orderly series of events 2 *coll* bicycle; *v* ride bicycle; *n* **cyclist** bicycle rider
**cyclone** *n* rotating winds surrounding regions of low pressure; *adj* **cyclonic**
**cylinder** *n* solid or hollow roller-shaped body; *adj* **cylindrical**
**cymbal** *n* one of two brass plates struck to make clashing sound
**cynic** *n* skeptical, mocking person; *n* **cynicism** being a cynic
**cynical** *adj* scornful

**cynical** *adj* doubting, full of doom and gloom, negative, pessimistic, skeptical, sneering

**cypress** *n* dark evergreen coniferous tree
**cyst** *n* *med* abnormal sac containing pus, fluid; *n* **cystitis** inflammation of the bladder
**cystic fibrosis** *n* hereditary disease
**czar, tsar** *n* former emperor of Russia

**dab** *v* **dabbing, dabbed** touch lightly;
 *n* slight tap

**dabble** *v* **1** dip in and out of water **2** engage
 in halfheartedly (study, etc)

**dachshund** *n* type of long-bodied, short-
 legged dog

**dad, daddy** *n* childish word for father

**daddylonglegs** *n* spider with very long legs

**daffodil** *n* spring-flowering bulb, narcissus

**daft** *n* foolish, feeble-minded

**dagger** *n* short two-edged knife

**daily** *adj, adv* happening every day
 *n* newspaper published on weekdays

> **daily** *adj,adv* common, day-to-day,
> everyday, regular, routine, usual

**dainty** *adj* delicate

> **dainty** *adj* elegant, fine, graceful, neat,
> petite, pretty

**dairy** *n* place where milk and its products are
 dealt with and sold

**daisy** *n* type of common wild flower

**dale** *n* valley, *esp* in N England

**Dalmatian** *n* large black-spotted, white dog

**dam** *n* barrier holding back water flow;
 *v* **damming, damned** hold back by dam

> **dam** *n* barrage, barricade,wall, weir

**damage** *v* harm; *n* injury to persons, property,
 etc; *pl* money claimed, or paid as
 compensation for injury libel, etc

> **damage** *v* bend, break, bruise, bump, bust,
> chip, crack, crash, deface, dent, hurt,
> impair, injure, rip, ruin, sabotage, scratch,
> spoil, tear, vandalize, warp, wreck
> **damage** *n* abuse, devastation, harm, havoc,
> hurt, injury, sabotage, vandalism

**dame** *n* lady; *cap* title of lady member of
 Order of British Empire

**damn** *v* condemn to eternal punishment;
 curse

**damp** *adj* slightly wet; *n* moisture; *v* **dampen**
 make damp

> **damp** *adj* clammy, dank, humid, misty,
> moist, muggy, soggy, steamy, wet
> **damp** *n* clamminess, dampness, humidity,
> mist, steaminess, wetness

**dance** *v* move with rhythmic sequence of
 steps, usually to music; *n* social gathering
 organized for dancing; form of dance

> **dance** *v* cavort, do a jig, jive, leap about,
> shake a leg *inf*, smooch, sway, take the
> floor, twirl, waltz
> **dance** *n* ball, ballet, bop *inf*, dancing, disco,
> hop, jig, square dance

**dandelion** *n* common yellow wild flower

**dandruff** *n* small scales of dead skin on scalp

**danger** *n* menace, risk of death

> **danger** *n* hazard, jeopardy, peril, pitfall,
> risk, threat

**dangerous** *adj* likely to cause harm or death

> **dangerous** *adj* chancy, daredevil, foolhardy,
> hairy *inf*, hazardous, life-threatening,
> nasty perilous, risky, ugly, unsafe

**dangle** *v* hang, sway loosely
**dank** *a* disagreeably damp
**dapper** *a* neat and trim in appearance
**dare** *v* 1 challenge 2 have courage for; *n* challenge

**dare** *v* 1 (challenge) defy, goad, provoke, taunt, throw down the gauntlet.
2 (have courage for) brave, have the guts or nerve, risk, take the plunge or risk
**dare** *n* provocation, taunt

**daren't** *contracted form of* dare not
**daring** *adj* bold; *n* audacity

**daring** *adj* adventurous, audacious, brave, fearless, rash, wild

**dark** *adj* 1 without light 2 (of complexion) deep in shade 3 (of colors) deep; *v* **darken** make or become darker; *ns* **dark, darkness**, absence of light

**dark** *adj* 1 (without light) black, cloudy, dim, dingy, gloomy, inky, overcast, poorly lit, shadowy, unlit. 2 (of complexion) black, brown, dark-skinned, olive, swarthy, tanned. 3 (of colors) deep, dense, rich
**dark** *n* blackness, darkness, dusk, gloom, murkiness, night, nightfall, nighttime, shade, shadows, twilight

**darling** *n* dearly loved person

**darling** *n* dear, dearest, love, pet, sweetheart, sweetie

**darn** *v* repair hole with interlacing stitches; *n* part so mended
**dart** *n* 1 light pointed missile 2 sudden rapid forward movement; *pl* indoor game played with target and small darts; *v* move quickly

**dart** *v* bolt, dash, fly, hop, hurtle, nip, race, run, rush, scuttle, shoot, sprint, tear

**dash** *v* 1 rush 2 throw violently; *n* 1 rush 2 small quantity (of liquid)

**dash** *v* 1 (rush) bolt, charge, fly, hurry, hurtle, race, run, speed, sprint, tear, zoom. 2 (throw violently) crash, fling, hurl, pitch, slam, smash, throw

**dashboard** *n* instrument panel inside car
**data** *n pl* known facts from which conclusion can be drawn; *sing* **datum**

**data** *n* details, facts, figures, information, statistics

**database** *n comput* large store of data for reference
**date**[1] *n* 1 particular day in the calendar 2 arrangement to meet; *idm* **out of date** old fashioned; *idm* **up to date** modern; *phr vs* **date from/back to** be applicable from

**date** *n* 1 (day) age, day and age, epoch, era, period, time, vintage, year. 2 (arrangement to meet) appointment, assignation, engagement, meeting, rendezvous

**date**[2] *n* sweet fruit of date palm
**dated** *a* old-fashioned

**dated** *adj* ancient, antiquated, fuddy-duddy *inf*, fusty, obsolete, old, old-hat, outmoded, passé, stale, unfashionable

**daub** *v* smear; coat; plaster; paint roughly; *n* unskillful painting; smear
**daughter** *n* female child or offspring; *adj* **daughterly**; *n* **daughter-in-law** son's wife
**daunting** *adj* frightening

**daunting** *adj* disconcerting, discouraging, intimidating, overwhelming, scary, terrifying, unnerving

a
b
c
d
e
f
g
h
i
j
k
l
m
n
o
p
q
r
s
t
u
v
w
x
y
z

**dawdle** v walk slowly; waste time

> **dawdle** v amble, dilly-dally, hang about, lag behind, linger, loiter, drag your feet, saunter, shilly-shally, take your time

**dawn** v begin to grow light; *phr v* **dawn on** gradually become evident to; n 1 daybreak 2 start

> **dawn** n 1 (daybreak) cock-crow, crack of dawn, daylight, first light, start the day, sunrise, sun-up. 2 (start) advent, beginning, birth, genesis, onset

**day** n 1 period between sunrise and sunset 2 epoch; **daybreak** dawn; **daylight** natural light; **daytime** hours between sunrise/sunset

> **day** n 1 (period between sunrise and sunset) daytime, daylight. 2 (epoch) age, date, day and age, era, generation, period, point in time, time

**daydream** n reverie
**day-to-day** a 1 everyday 2 one day at a time
**daze** v confuse
**dazed** adj confused

> **dazed** adj bemused, bewildered, dizzy, floored, muddled, numbed, shocked, staggered, stunned, stupefied

**dazzle** v confuse vision; blind by brilliant light; daze by hope of success
**dazzling** adj brilliant

> **dazzling** adj amazing, glittering, magnificent, sensational, sparkling, splendid, stunning, terrific

**deacon** n ordained person, lower order than priest; *fem* **deaconess**
**dead** adj 1 no longer living 2 obsolete 3 unresponsive 4 not lively; v **deaden** reduce force of; muffle; benumb

**dead** adj 1 (no longer living) deceased, departed, late, lifeless, no more, passed away, pushing up the daisies, six feet under. 2 (obsolete) extinct, obsolete. 3 (unresponsive) cold, emotionless, indifferent, inert, lifeless, numb, paralyzed, without feeling, wooden. 4 (not lively) boring, dreary, dull, flat, lifeless, uninteresting

**dead end** n impasse
**dead heat** n race where two runners reach finish simultaneously
**deadline** n time limit for finishing a job
**deadlock** n situation in dispute when neither opposing party will give way, so progress is impossible

> **deadlock** n checkmate, dead end, impasse, logjam, stalemate, standoff, standstill

**deadly** adj 1 causing death 2 very boring

> **deadly** adj 1 (causing death) fatal, lethal, malignant, noxious, poisonous, virulent. 2 (very boring) awful, dire, dull, tedious

**deadpan** adj without sign of emotion
**dead weight** n heavy, lifeless mass
**deaf** adj unable to hear; v **deafen** make deaf

> **deaf** adj hard of hearing, stone deaf, with a hearing problem, with impaired hearing

**deafening** adj very loud

> **deafening** adj at full blast, at full volume, blaring, ear-splitting, loud, roaring, thudding, thunderous

**deal** v share out; *pt, pp* **dealt**; *phr vs* **deal in** buy and sell; **deal with** handle; n agreement; *idm* **a good/great deal** a lot; n **dealing** trading; n pl **dealings (with)** relations (with), *esp* business

**deal** *v* 1 (share out) allocate, allot, dish out, distribute, dole out, give, hand out. **2** (**deal in**) buy and sell, do business, handle, trade, traffic. **3** (**deal with**) attend to, do, fix, handle, see to, sort, sort out, tackle, take care of, take on, take responsibility for
**deal** *n* arrangement, bargain, business deal, contract, pact, transaction, understanding, venture

**dealer** *n* one who buys and sells sth

**dealer** *n* agent, broker, buyer, handler, retailer, seller, trader, vendor, wholesaler

**dean** *n* head of chapter of cathedral; head of university faculty
**dear** *adj* 1 expensive 2 beloved; *n* lovable person; *adv* **dear, dearly** at high price

**dear** *adj* 1 (expensive) costly, exorbitant, extortionate, high-priced, luxury, over-priced, pricey, steep *inf*, top-rate, up-market, upscale. 2 (beloved) close, close to your heart, darling, intimate, loved, much-loved

**death** *n* 1 dying; killing 2 end; *idm* **put to death** execute; *idm* **sick to death (of)** *coll* absolutely fed up with; *adj*, *adv* **deathly** like death

**death** *n* 1 (dying, killing) bloodshed, curtains *inf*, decease, demise, end, fatality, loss of life, massacre, slaughter. 2 (end) annihilation, destruction, downfall, end, eradication, extermination, finish, obliteration, ruin

**death row** *n* place where condemned prisoner awaits execution
**debar** *v* **-barring, -barred** prevent; exclude; prohibit
**debase** *v* lower in value, *esp* of coinage; render base (dignity, morals); *n* **-ment**

**debatable** *adj* questionable

**debatable** *adj* arguable, controversial, doubtful, dubious, open to question

**debate** *v* discuss; *n* formal discussion

**debate** *n* argument, deliberation, disagreement, discussion, dispute

**debauch** *v* corrupt; *n* **debauchery**
**debit** *n* entry in account, of sum owing; *v* charge as due
**debit card** *n* payment card with which money is paid directly from bank account
**debonair** *adj* genial, affable, cheerful
**debrief** *v* question sb in detail about a mission or task after completion
**debris** *n* broken remains

**debris** *n* detritus, dross, garbage, litter, remains, rubbish, rubble, waste

**debt** *n* something owed, liability; *n* **debtor**

**debt** *n* arrears, credit, dues, hire purchase, loan, money owing, mortgage, overdraft

**debug** *v* 1 remove hidden microphones from (*eg* house) 2 identify and remove faults from computer program
**début** *n* *Fr* first appearance in public
**decade** *n* period of ten years
**decadent** *adj* corrupt

**decadent** *adj* debauched, decaying, declining, degenerate, depraved, dissipated, dissolute, immoral

**decaffeinate** *v* remove caffeine from
**decahedron** *n* solid with ten faces
**decamp** *v* 1 break camp 2 run away; abscond
**decant** *v* pour off gently, leaving sediment; *n* **decanter** stoppered glass container for decanted wine
**decapitate** *v* cut off head; behead

**decathlon** *n* athletic contest for the best overall result in ten events

**decay** *v* rot; *n* rotting, gradual breaking up

> **decay** *v* corrode, crumble, decline, decompose, die, disintegrate, go bad, mold, perish, putrefy, shrivel, waste away, wither
>
> **decay** *n* collapse, corrosion, crumbling, death, decline, decomposition, disintegration, going bad, rot, putrefaction, withering away

**decease** *v* die; *n* death

**deceased** *n* the dead person

**deceit** *n* act of deceiving, fraud, sham

> **deceit** *n* cheating, deception, dishonesty, disloyalty, double-dealing, duplicity, false pretenses, lying, pretense, subterfuge, treachery, trickery

**deceitful** *adj* giving false idea

> **deceitful** *adj* crooked, dishonest, disloyal, double-dealing, false, fraudulent, lying, sham, two-faced, underhand, untruthful

**deceive** *v* mislead; cheat

> **deceive** *v* double-cross, dupe, fool, hoodwink, lead sb on, pull a fast one, swindle, take for a ride, take in, trick

**decelerate** *v* decrease speed

**December** *n* twelfth month of year

**decennial** *adj* 1 ten yearly 2 lasting ten years; *n* tenth anniversary

**decent** *adj* 1 honest 2 adequate; *n* **decency**

> **decent** *adj* 1 (honest) dependable, good, honorable, nice, proper, respectable, suitable, trustworthy, upright, worthy. 2 (adequate) acceptable, fair, good, reasonable, sufficient

**decentralize** *v* remove from central control; *n* **-ization**

**deception** *n* 1 deceiving 2 trick

> **deception** *n* 1 (deceiving) cheating, deceit, dishonesty, double-dealing, duplicity, fraud, lying, misrepresentation, pretense, subterfuge, treachery, trickery, untruthfulness. 2 (trick) con *inf*, cover-up, dodge, fiddle, hoax, lie, pretense, ruse, sham, swindle

**deceptive** *adj* misleading

> **deceptive** *adj* deceiving, false, illusory, unreliable

**decibel** *n* unit of loudness of sounds

**decide** *v* make up one's mind; *adj* **decided** determined, definite

> **decide** *v* choose, conclude, determine, give your verdict, make a decision, make up your mind, opt for, resolve, settle, settle for, settle on, take the plunge

**deciduous** *adj* shedding leaves annually

**decimal** *adj* based on number ten; *n* decimal fraction; *v* **decimalize** reduce to decimal fractions or system

**decimate** *v* kill large proportion of

**decipher** *v* make out meaning of

**decision** *n* conclusion

> **decision** *n* choice, finding, judgment, outcome, pronouncement, resolution, result, ruling, verdict

**decisive** *adj* 1 definite opinion 2 important

> **decisive** *adj* 1 (definite opinion) definite, firm, forceful, positive, resolute, self-confident, unfaltering, unwavering. 2 (important) critical, crucial, deciding, definitive, key, pivotal, significant

**deck** n 1 horizontal flooring of ship, bus, etc. 2 pack of cards; v 1 cover with deck 2 adorn; decorate

**deck chair** n folding portable seat for reclining on a beach

**declaration** n announcement

> **declaration** n assertion, decree, disclosure, edict, notice, press release, proclamation, revelation, statement

**declare** v announce formally

> **declare** v affirm, assert, claim, contend, disclose, maintain, make known, proclaim, profess, reveal, say, state

**decline** v 1 deteriorate 2 refuse 3 slope downwards; n deterioration

> **decline** v 1 (deteriorate) degenerate, diminish, dwindle, fade, fall, fall off, get worse, go downhill, peter out, sink, tail off, wane, weaken. 2 (refuse) reject, send your apologies, turn down
> **decline** n degeneration, downturn, downward trend, drop, fall, reversal, slump

**decode** v translate from cipher or code

**decomission** v take out of service

**decompose** v decay

**decongestant** n, adj, med relieving congestion, eg of nose, chest

**decontaminate** v free from contamination

**décor** n Fr decorative scheme

**decorate** v 1 paint, paper a room 2 make attractive by additions; adj **-ative**

> **decorate** v 1 (paint, paper) do up, refurbish, smarten up, wallpaper. 2 (make attractive) deck, embellish, garnish, festoon, trim

**decoration** n 1 decorative scheme 2 ornament

**decorous** adj seemly; sober; decent; n **decorum** propriety

**decoy** v lure into danger; n thing or person used as a lure or bait

> **decoy** v attract, entice, induce, inveigle
> **decoy** n bait, distraction, lure, trap

**decrease** v grow, make less; n lessening

> **decrease** v abate, cut, cut back on, decline, diminish, downsize, dwindle, go down, lessen, lower, reduce, subside, taper off
> **decrease** n cutback, decline, downsizing, downturn, drop, fall, reduction, shrinkage

**decree** v order by decree; n formal order

> **decree** v announce, dictate, direct, lay down, prescribe, ordain, order, proclaim, pronounce, rule, say, state
> **decree** n announcement, command, dictum, directive, edict, injunction, judgment, law, order, policy statement, ruling

**decrepit** adj old, feeble, tottery; n **decrepitude**

**decriminalize** v declare no longer illegal

**dedicate** v devote solemnly; inscribe (book, etc) to a person; n **dedication**

**dedicated** adj devoted

> **dedicated** adj committed, enthusiastic, keen, loyal, single-minded, wholehearted, zealous

**deduce** v draw as conclusion from given facts; n **deduction** conclusion reached

> **deduce** v conclude, infer, gather, realize, surmise, understand, work out

**deduct** v subtract, take away; n **deduction** amount subtracted

> **deduct** v cut, discount, knock off inf, subtract, take away, take off

**deed** n 1 action; 2 legal document

**deed poll** n leg document registering a change of name

**deem** v believe; consider; regard

**deep** adj 1 extending far down, 2 extending far back 3 low in pitch 4 dark in color 5 strongly felt; v **deepen**; n **depth** distance from surface

> **deep** adj 1 (extending far down) bottomless, cavernous. 2 (extending far back) broad, large. 3 (low in pitch) bass, booming. 4 (dark in color) intense, rich, vivid. 5 (strongly felt) heartfelt, passionate

**deep-freeze** v freeze (food) quickly; pt **deep-froze**; pp **deep-frozen**; n freezer

**deep-fry** n fry in deep pan of oil or fat

**deer** n family of antlered ruminants; pl **deer**

**deface** v disfigure; mar; obliterate

**defame** v speak evil of; n **-ation**; adj **-atory**

**default** v leg fail to appear, pay, or act

**defeat** v conquer; n 1 conquest 2 failure; n **defeatism** acceptance of defeat; n **-ist**

> **defeat** v annihilate, beat, get the better of, hammer, get the upper hand, overthrow, rout, thwart, topple, trounce, vanquish
> **defeat** n 1 (conquest) rout, thrashing, trouncing, victory, win. 2 (failure) collapse, downfall, frustration, ruin

**defect** n fault; v desert ones country, duty; n **defector** one who defects; adj **defective** faulty; imperfect

> **defect** n blemish, bug, deficiency, error, failing, flaw, mistake, shortcoming, weakness, weak spot

**defend** v 1 protect 2 stand up for

> **defend** v 1 (protect) fortify, guard, secure. 2 (stand up for) champion, espouse, justify, speak up for, stand by, support

**defense** n 1 protection 2 justification

> **defense** n 1 (protection) barricade, bastion, cover, deterrent, fortification, fortress, shelter, shield. 2 (justification) case, excuse, explanation, vindication

**defensive** protecting

**defer** v **-ferring**, **-ferred** 1 delay, put off 2 yield to another's wishes

**defiant** adj standing up to others

> **defiant** adj belligerent, challenging, disobedient, intransigent, noncompliant, rebellious, stubborn

**deficiency** n shortage; lack

**deficient** adj lacking, incomplete

**deficit** n excess of liabilities over assets

**defile** v pollute; corrupt; desecrate

**define** v show or explain clearly; n **definition** exact description

**definite** adj 1 sure 2 obvious

> **definite** adj 1 (sure) certain, confident, confirmed, guaranteed, positive. 2 (obvious) clear, clear-cut, explicit, marked, precise, unmistakable

**deflate** v 1 let out air, gas from 2 reduce inflated currency

**deflect** v change course of

**deforest** v clear land of trees

**deform** v spoil shape, beauty of; n **-ity**

**deformed** adj misshapen

> **deformed** adj contorted, damaged, disfigured, distorted, injured, maimed, malformed, mutilated, twisted

**defraud** v cheat; swindle

**defrost** v remove ice from; unfreeze

**deft** adj skilful; neat; competent

**defunct** adj dead, deceased

**defuse** v 1 remove fuse; render (bomb, etc) harmless; 2 make less tense or dangerous

**defy** *v* **-fying, -fied** challenge; disobey

> **defy** *v* confront, disregard, flout, foil, frustrate, rebel against, resist, withstand

**defiant** *adj* disobedient; *n* **defiance**
**degenerate** *v* decline from higher to lower state or condition; *adj* depraved

> **degenerate** *v* deteriorate, get worse, go downhill, go from bad to worse, sink, slide

**degrade** *v* humiliate
**degrading** *adj* humiliating

> **degrading** *adj* demeaning, embarrassing, mortifying, shameful, undignified

**degree** *n* **1** unit of measurement **2** grade in any series **3** extent **4** university rank
**dehydrate** *v* remove water from
**deign** *v* condescend to do

> **deign** *v* bother, condescend, consent, stoop

**deity** *n* a god
**déjà vu** *n Fr* **1** sense that a new event has been experienced before **2** *coll* sense of boredom with familiar situation
**dejected** *adj* depressed

> **dejected** *adj* despondent, discouraged, disgruntled, dispirited, downhearted, gloomy, miserable, out of sorts, sad

**delay** *v* **1** postpone **2** keep back; *n* postponement

> **delay** *v* **1** (postpone) adjourn, defer, hold over, put on ice, put on the back burner, shelve. **2** (keep back) detain, hold up, make late, slow down
> **delay** *n* break, hiatus, hitch, holdup, interruption, lull, setback, suspension, time-lag, wait

**delectable** *adj* delightful, enjoyable
**delegate** *v* **1** send as representative **2** entrust with duties, etc; *n* representative
**delegation** *n* body of delegates
**delete** *v* erase, remove, obliterate; *n* **deletion**
**deleterious** *adj* harmful, injurious
**deliberate** *v* **1** think about **2** discuss; *adj* **1** intentional **2** careful

> **deliberate** *v* **1** (think about) consider, evaluate, mull over, ponder, reflect, review, ruminate, think, think over, weigh. **2** (discuss) consider, debate
> **deliberate** *adj* **1** (intentional) calculated, cold-blooded, conscious, knowing, preconceived, premeditated, willful. **2** (careful) determined, measured, methodical, painstaking, patient, ponderous, resolute, slow

**deliberately** *adv* on purpose

> **deliberately** *adv* consciously, intentionally, knowingly, willfully, wittingly

**delicate** *adj* **1** small and elegant **2** pastel **3** sensitive **4** weak (of health); *n* **delicacy 1** fineness; refinement **2** weakness (of health) **3** tasty food

> **delicate** *adj* **1** (small and elegant) dainty, elegant, fine, flimsy, fragile, graceful, intricate. **2** (pastel) muted, pale, soft, subtle, understated. **3** (sensitive) awkward, difficult, diplomatic, discreet, tactful, tricky

**delicatessen** *n* shop selling specially imported foods, *eg* cheese, cooked meats, etc; *coll* **deli**
**delicious** *adj* very tasty

> **delicious** *adj* appetizing, gorgeous, mouth-watering, scrumptious, tasty, tempting

a b c d e f g h i j k l m n o p q r s t u v w x y z

A
B
C
D
E
F
G
H
I
J
K
L
M
N
O
P
Q
R
S
T
U
V
W
X
Y
Z

**delight** n great pleasure; v give great pleasure

> **delight** n amusement, ecstasy, elation,
> enjoyment, enthusiasm, excitement,
> happiness, joy, jubilation, pleasure, thrill
> **delight** v amuse, captivate, cheer, enchant,
> entertain, excite, please, thrill, tickle

**delighted** adj very pleased

> **delighted** adj captivated, ecstatic,
> enchanted, glad, happy, in raptures,
> jubilant, on top of the world, overjoyed,
> pleased, thrilled, tickled pink inf

**delightful** adj lovely

> **delightful** adj agreeable, appealing,
> attractive, captivating, charming, cute,
> enchanting, engaging, enjoyable,
> entertaining, fascinating, nice, pleasant,
> pleasurable, thrilling, wonderful

**delineate** v depict; describe
**delinquent** n person committing illegal acts
**delirious** adj 1 feverish 2 very happy
**delirium** n mental disturbance due to illness,
esp fever causing wildness of speech
**deliver** v 1 hand over 2 utter 3 aim (blow,
etc); n **delivery**

> **deliver** v 1 (hand over) bring, dispatch,
> produce, send, supply, take, transfer,
> transport. 2 (utter) announce, declare,
> give, make, pronounce, read. 3 (aim)
> administer, deal, direct, hit, hurl, inflict,
> send, throw

**delphinium** n genus of plants, including
larkspur
**delta** n alluvial land at river mouth
**delude** v deceive; mislead; n **delusion**
**deluge** v inundate; flood; overwhelm; n flood;
torrent (of words, etc); downpour
**deluxe** adj luxurious
**demagogue** n political agitator

**demand** v 1 ask for 2 ask a question
3 necessitate; n 1 urgent claim 2 question
3 need

> **demand** v 1 (ask for) appeal, ask, call for,
> claim, clamor for, cry out for, insist on,
> lay claim to, make a claim for, press for,
> request, urge. 2 (ask a question) ask,
> challenge, inquire, interrogate, question.
> 3 (necessitate) call for, entail, involve,
> need, require, take, want
> **demand** n 1 (claim) appeal, entreaty,
> insistence, pressure, request, requisition.
> 2 (question) challenge, interrogation.
> 3 (need) necessity, requirement

**demanding** adj difficult

> **demanding** adj arduous, challenging,
> daunting, exacting, exhausting, grueling,
> hard, taxing, tiring, tough, trying

**demarcation** n boundary line; limit
**demean** v **demean oneself** lower, degrade
oneself; adj **demeaning**
**demeanour** n bearing, conduct
**demented** adj insane; n **dementia** form of
insanity
**demerara** n kind of brown sugar
**demise** n death
**democracy** n rule by the people; state so
governed
**democrat** n supporter of democracy
**democratic** adj supporting or using
democracy

> **democratic** adj autonomous, classless,
> egalitarian, free, of the people, popular,
> populist, representative, republican

**demolish** v destroy; n **demolition**

> **demolish** v bulldoze, dismantle, flatten,
> knock down, level, pull down, raze, ruin,
> tear down, trash inf, wreck

**demon** n 1 evil spirit 2 wicked, cruel person
**demonstrate** v 1 prove 2 show 3 protest;
ns **-ation** 1 proof 2 exhibition of method 3
public protest; **-ator** one who demonstrates

> **demonstrate** v 1 (prove) confirm, indicate,
> show, testify, verify. 2 (show) describe,
> explain, illustrate, show how, teach.
> 3 (protest) lobby, march, parade, picket

**demoralize** v discourage
**demote** v reduce in order, rank, etc
**demur** v hesitate; raise objections to
**demure** adj modest and serious
**den** n lair of wild animals; cage; small room
**denial** n negation; refusal
**denigrate** v sneer at; defame
**denim** n coarse cotton, cloth
**denominate** v name; designate; ns **-ation**
name of particular class, religion, etc
**denote** v stand for

> **denote** v express, indicate, mark, mean,
> represent, show, signify, symbolize

**denounce** v 1 criticize 2 accuse

> **denounce** v 1 (criticize) attack, castigate,
> condemn, damn, decry, revile, stigmatize,
> vilify. 2 (accuse) betray, blame,
> incriminate, report

**dense** adj 1 compact 2 unintelligent;
n **density**

> **dense** adj 1 (compact) close, compressed,
> concentrated, condensed, impenetrable,
> solid, substantial, thick. 2 (unintelligent)
> clueless, dim, dumb, ignorant, stupid, thick

**dent** v make, mark with dent; n slight hollow
made by blow, etc

> **dent** v buckle, crumple, depress, knock in,
> press in, push in

**dental** adj relating to teeth or dentistry
**dentist** n surgeon who cares for teeth;
ns **dentistry** art of dentist; **denture(s)** set
of false teeth
**denunciation** n denouncing
**deny** v 1 declare untrue 2 refuse request;
n **denial**.

> **deny** v 1 (declare untrue) refute, retract,
> take back. 2 (refuse) prohibit, rebuff,
> reject, revoke, turn down, veto, withhold

**deodorize** v remove smell from;
n **deodorant**
**depart** v go away; leave; n **departure** starting
out; leaving

> **depart** v abscond, be off, clear off, disappear,
> emigrate, exit, go, make tracks, migrate,
> move away, move off, quit, retire, retreat,
> split, take your leave, vanish, withdraw

**department** n 1 branch 2 area of knowledge;
**department store** large shop selling variety
of goods; adj **departmental**

> **department** n 1 (branch) agency, bureau,
> division, office, section, sector, subdivision,
> unit. 2 (area of knowledge) area, concern,
> domain, field, function, job, line, realm,
> responsibility, speciality, sphere

**depend** v 1 rely on 2 be based on

> **depend** v 1 (rely on) bank on, be dependent
> on, cling to, count on, lean on, need, put
> your faith in, trust in, turn to. 2 (be based
> on) be dependent on, be determined by,
> be subject to, hinge on, pivot on, rest on

**dependable** adj reliable

> **dependable** adj consistent, faithful,
> reputable, responsible, sensible, staunch,
> steadfast, trustworthy, trusty, unfailing

a
b
c
d
e
f
g
h
i
j
k
l
m
n
o
p
q
r
s
t
u
v
w
x
y
z

**dependent**[1] n person relying on another
**dependent**[2] adj 1 depending on 2 needing someone else for support
**depict** v describe; represent
**deplete** v empty out, exhaust
**deplorable** adj terrible

> **deplorable** adj abominable, atrocious, awful, despicable, disgraceful, disreputable, dreadful, reprehensible, scandalous, shameful, shocking

**deplore** v disapprove of
**deploy** v use; n **deployment**
**deport** v expel; n **deportation** expulsion
**depose** v remove from office
**deposit** v 1 entrust for safekeeping 2 leave (as sediment); n 1 sediment 2 money deposited at bank or given as pledge
**depot** n storehouse, bus garage
**depraved** adj corrupt

> **depraved** adj debauched, degenerate, dissolute, evil, immoral, indecent, lewd, obscene, perverted, sinful, vile, wicked

**deprecate** v express disapproval of
**depreciate** v lose value or quality
**depress** n 1 press down 2 make dejected; weaken
**depressed** adj dejected

> **depressed** adj blue, despondent, discouraged, disheartened, dismayed, dispirited, down, down in the dumps, downcast, fed up, gloomy, glum, low, melancholy, miserable, moody, morose, sad, saddened, unhappy, upset

**depressing** adj making you feel dejected

> **depressing** adj black, bleak, discouraging, disheartening, dismal, dispiriting, distressing, dreary, gloomy, hopeless, melancholy, miserable, sad, somber

**depression** n 1 concavity 2 despondence 3 low atmospheric pressure 4 slump in trade; adj, n **depressant** sedative
**deprive** v take away from; n **deprivation**.
**depth** n degree of deepness; idm **in/out of one's depth** 1 able/unable to touch bottom with head above water 2 able/unable to cope or understand; pl **depths** deepest part or feeling
**deputation** body of representatives
**deputy** n assistant

> **deputy** adj proxy, representative, second in command, sidekick, under-study, vice-chairman, vice-president

**derail** v cause to leave rails; n **-ment**
**derange** v upset; disturb; drive mad
**deregulate** v free from legal control
**derelict** adj deserted

> **derelict** adj abandoned, crumbling, decrepit, dilapidated, falling-down, neglected, ramshackle, ruined, rundown, tumbledown

**deride** v mock at, ridicule; n **derision**; adj **derisive**; adv **-ly**; adj **derisory** mocking, ironical
**derive** v get from; n **derivation**

> **derive** v acquire, collect, draw, elicit, extract, gain, gather, get, glean, infer, lift, obtain, pick up, procure, receive

**dermatitis** n inflammation of skin
**dermatology** n study of skin diseases
**derogatory** adj full of criticism

> **derogatory** adj damaging, defamatory, disapproving, disparaging, injurious, insulting, offensive, uncomplimentary, unfavorable, unflattering

**derrick** n crane, latticed tower over oil well
**desalinate** v remove salt from; n **-ation**

**descend** v 1 move, slope down 2 be derived; *idm* **be descended from** have as ancestor(s) n **descendent** offspring

**descend** v come down, dip, drop, fall, go down, incline, move down, plummet, plunge, sink, slope, tumble

**descent** n 1 downward movement 2 ancestry

**descent** n 1 (downward movement) dip, drop, fall, plunge, slump, swoop. 2 (family background) ancestry, background, blood, extraction, genealogy, heredity, lineage, origin, parentage, stock

**describe** v give account of, depict in words

**describe** v define, depict, detail, explain, express, give details of, illustrate, narrate, outline, portray, put into words, recount, relate, report, sketch, specify, tell

**description** n account in words

**description** n account, chronicle, depiction, explanation, illustration, narrative, outline, portrayal, representation, sketch

**descriptive** *adj* giving an account in words
**desecrate** v damage the sacredness of
**desert** n barren, uninhabited land
**desert** v abandon; *mil* abscond from service; n **desertion**

**desert** v forsake, give up, jilt, leave, leave in the lurch, maroon, strand, walk out on

**deserted** *adj* abandoned

**deserted** *adj* derelict, desolate, empty, forlorn, godforsaken, isolated, lonely, neglected, solitary, unoccupied, vacant

**deserve** v be worthy of; *adj* **deserving** worthy of

**deserve** v be entitled to, earn, gain, have a claim to, have a right to, justify, merit, rate, warrant, win

**deshabille** n partial undress
**desiccated** *adj* dried
**design** v invent and plan out; n 1 way sth is planned out 2 pattern; *pl* **designs** *idm* **have designs on** be planning to get or win by unscrupulous means; n **designer** one who makes artistic designs; *adj* made by a notable designer

**design** v conceive, create, devise, draft, draw, draw up, hatch, invent, originate, outline, plan, sketch, think up

**designate** v specify; nominate for office, specify; *adj* nominated but not installed
**desire** v long for; n strong longing; *adj* **desirable** worth having

**desire** v aspire to, covet, crave, dream of, fancy, hanker after, hope for, hunger for, lust after, set your heart on, strive for, want, wish for, yearn for
**desire** n ambition, appetite, aspiration, craving, hunger, inclination, longing, lust, need, passion, preference, wish, yearning

**desist** v stop, cease
**desk** n table or other piece of furniture used for reading or writing on
**desolate** *adj* waste, dismal; forsaken; lonely, forlorn; v lay waste; make lonely, sad
**despair** v lose hope; n hopelessness

**despair** v give in, give up, lose heart, quit, resign yourself, surrender
**despair** n defeatism, dejection, depression, desperation, despondency, distress, gloom, misery, pessimism, wretchedness

**despatch, dispatch** v 1 send off 2 finish off speedily 3 kill; n official report, message

**desperate** *adj* **1** despairing **2** very serious; *n* **desperation**

> **desperate** *adj* **1** (despairing) frantic, inconsolable, wretched. **2** (very serious) acute, critical, drastic, grave, hopeless, irretrievable, pressing, risky, severe, urgent

**despicable** *adj* contemptible
**despise** *v* feel contempt for

> **despise** *v* abhor, detest, hate, loathe, revile

**despite** *prep* in spite of
**despondent** *adj* depressed; dejected
**despot** *n* tyrant, oppressor
**dessert** *n* sweet served at end of meal
**dessert spoon** *n* medium-sized spoon
**destination** *n* place where sb/sth is going, being sent
**destine** *v* determine future of; intend
**destined** *adj* **1** fated **2** intended
**destiny** *n* preordained fate

> **destiny** *n* chance, doom, fate, fortune, lot, providence

**destitute** *adj* extremely poor; *n* **destitution**
**destroy** *v* ruin; demolish; *n* **destruction**

> **destroy** *v* annihilate, break, crush, decimate, devastate, dismantle, knock down, level, obliterate, ravage, raze, shatter, smash, spoil, trash, wipe out, wreck

**destructive** *adj* causing damage
**detach** *v* unfasten; disconnect; *adj* **-ed**; separate; impartial; aloof; *n* **-ment** **1** separation **2** unconcern **3** number of troops, etc detached for special duty

> **detach** *v* cut loose, cut off, disengage, disentangle, free, isolate, loosen, part, pull off, release, remove, sever, take off, tear off, uncouple, undo

**detail** *n* small part; *v* **1** deal with item by item **2** select for duty

> **detail** *n* aspect, component, element, fact, factor, feature, intricacy, item, part, particular, point, respect, technicality
> **detail** *v* **1** (deal with item by item) catalog, cite, enumerate, itemize, list, point, set out, specify, spell out, relate. **2** (select for duty) allocate, appoint, assign, charge, commission, delegate, detach, send

**detailed** *adj* containing a lot of information
**detain** *v* hinder; withold; retain in custody; *n* **detention** forced delay; keeping in custody
**detainee** *n* person detained, *esp* by police
**detect** *v* discover; *ns* **detection**, **detective** police investigator of crime

> **detect** *v* ascertain, catch, discern, distinguish, find, find out, identify, note, notice, observe, recognize, scent, spot, uncover

**détente** *n Fr* reduction of international political tension
**detention** *n* being kept in a place, *esp* as prisoner or pupil in school
**deter** *v* **-terring, terred** discourage; *adj*, *n* **deterrent**

> **deter** *v* daunt, dissuade, frighten, inhibit, intimidate, prevent, put off, scare, stop, talk sb out of, warn off

**detergent** *adj* cleansing; *n* cleansing, purifying substance
**deteriorate** *v* become worse

> **deteriorate** *v* crumble, decay, decline, decompose, degenerate, depreciate, disintegrate, fade, fall apart, go downhill *inf*, weaken, worsen

**determinant** *n* that which decides result

**determination** n resolution

> **determination** n backbone, commitment, conviction, dedication, doggedness, drive, fortitude, grit, guts, perseverance, persistence, resolve, single-mindedness, staying power, tenacity, willpower

**determine** v decide, resolve

**determined** adj 1 intent on 2 strong-willed

> **determined** adj 1 (intent on) bent on, fixed on, resolved, set on. 2 (strong-willed) dedicated, dogged, firm, insistent, persistent, purposeful, resolute, resolved, single-minded, steadfast, tenacious, tough, unwavering

**deterrent** n, adj (thing) which deters
**detest** v hate; adj **-able**

> **detest** v abhor, abominate, despise, disdain, dislike, loathe, scorn

**dethrone** v remove from throne
**detonate** v explode (bomb, etc)
**detour** v remove poison from
**detoxify** n going round; alternative route
**detract (from)** v take away from; also **detoxificate**; n **detoxification**
**detriment** n harm, loss, injury
**detrimental** adj damaging
**detritus** n debris
**deuce** n 1 die or playing card with two spots 2 score 40-all, in tennis
**devalue** v reduce in value; n **devaluation**
**devastate** v 1 destroy 2 shock greatly; n **-ation**

> **devastate** v 1 (destroy) demolish, flatten, level, obliterate, ravage, raze, ruin, spoil, wreck. 2 (shock) disappoint, horrify, overwhelm, traumatize

**develop** v 1 grow 2 expand on 3 get (illness)

**develop** v 1 (grow) advance, enlarge, evolve, expand, flourish, mature, progress, ripen, spread. 2 (expand on) amplify, augment, broaden, dilate on, elaborate, enlarge on, expand. 3 (get) acquire, catch, contract, pick up

**developing country** n poor country trying to improve economy and living conditions
**development** adj **developmental** involved in development; adv **-ly**
**deviate** v turn aside; diverge; n **-ation**; adj **devious** rambling; crooked; fig shifty
**device** n 1 tool 2 trick

> **device** n 1 (tool) apparatus, appliance, contraption, gadget, gizmo, implement, instrument, machine, utensil, widget. 2 (trick) con, expedient, fraud, gambit, machination, plan, ploy, ruse, scheme, stratagy, subterfuge, tactic

**devil** n spirit of evil, Satan, wicked person
**devil may care** adj reckless
**devious** adj cunningly dishonest

> **devious** adj artful, calculating, crafty, crooked, cunning, deceitful, evasive, guileful, indirect, insidious, insincere, misleading, scheming, sly, sneaky, underhand, wily

**devise** v invent, contrive

> **devise** v arrange, come up with, conceive, concoct, construct, create, design, dream up, engineer, form, formulate, frame, imagine, plan, plot, prepare, scheme, think up, work out

**devoid (of)** adj lacking, without
**devolution** n transfer of power to others
**devolve** v transfer; delegate
**devote** v set apart, dedicate; addict oneself to; n **devotion** strong affection

a
b
c
d
e
f
g
h
i
j
k
l
m
n
o
p
q
r
s
t
u
v
w
x
y
z

**devoted** *adj* dedicated

> **devoted** *adj* adoring, ardent, attentive, besotted, caring, committed, concerned, conscientious, constant, devout, dutiful, enthusiastic, faithful, fond, loving, loyal, passionate, staunch, steadfast, true, unswerving, zealous

**devour** *v* eat voraciously
**devout** *adj* pious

> **devout** *adj* dutiful, God-fearing, godly, holy, orthodox, prayerful, religious, reverent, righteous, zealous

**dew** *n* condensed moisture from air, falling on earth
**dexterity** *n* manual and mental skill; *adj* **dexterous** skillful; quick
**diabetes** *n* disease characterized by excess sugar in urine; *adj*, *n* **diabetic**
**diabolic(al)** *adj* devilish, fiendish; *sl* very bad, unpleasant
**diadem** *n* fillet, crown
**diagnose** *v* identify disease from symptoms; *n* **diagnosis**; *adj* **diagnostic**
**diagonal** *adj* oblique; *n* line from corner to corner
**diagram** *n* plan, chart

> **diagram** *n* drawing, figure, illustration, outline, picture, representation, sketch, symbol, table

**dial** *n* 1 face of clock 2 graduated face of gauge, meter, compass, etc; *v* use telephone
**dialect** *n* regional form of language
**dialogue** *n* conversation; its representation in writing, in drama, books, etc

> **dialogue** *n* chat, communication, conference, discourse, discussion, exchange, interchange, talk

**dialysis** *n med* process for purifying blood

**diameter** *n* straight line passing from side to side, through center of solid or geometric figure; length of such line
**diamond** *n* 1 hard, brilliant precious stone of crystalized carbon 2 suit of cards 3 rhombus; *adj* made of, set with diamonds
**diaphragm** *n* 1 muscular wall between thorax and abdomen 2 device controlling transmission of light, sound, etc 3 vibrating disk producing sound waves 4 contraceptive device for women
**diarrhoea** *n* excessive, irritable laxity of bowels
**diary** *n* daily record, *esp* of personal events or thoughts
**diatribe** *n* vituperative attack, abusive criticism
**dice** *n pl* (*sing* **die**) cubes marked on each side (1-6 spots), used in game of chance; *v* cut into small cubes
**dictate** *v* 1 order 2 speak aloud; *n* order

> **dictate** *v* 1 (order) command, declare, decree, direct, enjoin, give orders, impose, lay down, ordain, prescribe. 2 (speak aloud) read out, say, recite, transmit, utter

**dictator** *n* despot, absolute ruler
**diction** *n* choice and use of word
**dictionary** *n* book listing words alphabetically, with their meanings, etc
**diddle** *v* cheat, swindle
**didn't** *contracted form of* did not
**die** *v* **dying**, **died** 1 stop living 2 end; wither; *idm* **be dying for/to** want urgently; *phr vs* **die away** fade until no longer noticeable; **die down** subside; **die off** die one by one; **die out** become extinct

> **die** *v* 1 (stop living) be no more, bite the dust, decease, depart, expire, kick the bucket, pass away, perish, snuff out. 2 (end) come to an end, decay, decline, decrease, disappear, dwindle, fade, pass, sink, vanish, wane, wilt, wither

**diesel** *adj* of oil-burning internal-combustion engine

**diet** *n* usual food; planned feeding, for medical reasons; *v* follow prescribed diet to lose weight; *adj* **dietary**; *n* **dietician, dietitian** expert in nutrition and dietary requirements

**diet** *v* abstain, cut down, fast, go on a diet, lose weight, reduce, slim

**differ** *v* disagree; be unlike; quarrel
**difference** *n* 1 dissimilarity 2 argument

**difference** *n* 1 (dissimilarity) contrast, discrepancy, disparity, distinction, divergence, nonconformity, peculiarity, singularity, variation, variety. 2 (argument) altercation, clash, conflict, controversy, disagreement, dispute, objection, quarrel

**different** *adj* 1 not similar 2 not usual

**different** *adj* 1 (not similar) assorted, contradictory, contrasting, dissimilar, distinct, diverse, incongruous, miscellaneous, mixed, separate, singular, various, varying, unlike. 2 (not usual) abnormal, bizarre, distinctive, eccentric, interesting, novel, odd, original, peculiar, singular, special, strange, striking, uncommon, unconventional, unique, unorthodox, unusual, weird

**difficult** *adj* 1 not easy 2 hard to please

**difficult** *adj* 1 (not easy) arduous, challenging, complex, complicated, demanding, daunting, exacting, formidable, grueling, hard, laborious, onerous, painful, problematic, strenuous, taxing. 2 (hard to please) argumentative, awkward, contrary, demanding, fastidious, fractious, intractable, obstreperous, quarrelsome, tiresome, troublesome, trying, uncooperative, unmanageable

**difficulty** *n* 1 problem 2 plight

**difficulty** *n* 1 (problem) adversity, arduousness, awkwardness, challenge, hardship, ordeal, pain, strain, struggle. 2 (plight) dilemma, distress, mess, predicament, quandary, scrape *inf*

**diffident** *adj* shy; self-effacing; timid
**diffuse** *v* scatter, spread around; *adj* not localized
**dig** *v* **digging, dug** 1 make hole (in earth, sand, etc) 2 look for sth 3 prod; **dig up**; *n* **dig** 1 act of digging 2 prod 3 gibe

**dig** *v* 1 (make a hole) burrow, delve, excavate, fork, gouge, grub, harrow, hoe, hollow, mine, penetrate, pierce, plow, quarry, scoop, till, tunnel, turn over. 2 (look for sth) delve, go into, investigate, probe, research, search

**digest** *v* 1 convert food in digestive tract for assimilation into blood 2 summarize, condense 3 absorb mentally; *n* classified summary; magazine containing condensed versions of books, etc; *adjs* **digestive, digestible**; *n* **digestion**
**digit** *n* 1 any figure 1 to 9 2 finger or toe; *adj* **digital** numerical
**dignified** *adj* serious and elegant

**dignified** *adj* ceremonious, distinguished, formal, graceful, gracious, grave, imposing, impressive, lofty, noble, proud, regal, solemn, stately, tasteful

**dignify** *v* do honor to, exalt, ennoble
**dignitary** *n* holder of high office
**dignity** *n* elegant pride

**dignity** *n* ceremony, class, decorum, distinction, elegance, formality, grace, grandeur, gravity, hauteur, honor, majesty, nobility, pride, solemnity

a
b
c
d
e
f
g
h
i
j
k
l
m
n
o
p
q
r
s
t
u
v
w
x
y
z

**digress** v depart from main subject, wander, ramble; n **-ion**

**digs** n coll lodgings

**dihedral** adj having two plane faces

**dike** n ditch; embankment or causeway to prevent flooding

**dilapidated** adj shabby

**dilate** v expand; swell

**dilemma** n very difficult situation

> **dilemma** n catch-22, difficulty, fix, impasse, jam, pickle, plight, predicament, problem, puzzle, quandary, scrape inf, vicious circle

**diligent** adj hardworking and careful

> **diligent** adj assiduous, attentive, busy, conscientious, dutiful, earnest, industrious, meticulous, patient, scrupulous, studious, thorough

**dilute** v weaken, thin down fluid by adding another fluid; adj **diluted**

**dim** adj **dimmer**, **dimmest** 1 not bright 2 unintelligent; adv **-ly**; v **dimming**, **dimmed** make or become dim

> **dim** adj 1 (not bright) bleary, blurred, blurry, cloudy, dark, dingy, dull, dusky, faint, foggy, fuzzy, gloomy, hazy, indistinct, misty, murky, muted, obscure, obscured, shadowy, unclear, vague. 2 (unintelligent) dense, dozy, dull, dull-witted, dumb, obtuse, slow, stupid, thick

**dimension** n length, breadth, thickness; extent; size

**diminish** v weaken

**diminutive** adj tiny

**dimple** n small depression in surface of skin, esp of cheek

**din** n loud continuous noise, clamor

**dine** v eat a meal; phr vs **dine out** eat away from home; n **dining room**

**dinghy** n small boat (usu with sails)

**dingy** adj dull and shabby; n **dinginess**

**dingy** adj cheerless, dark, depressing, dim, dirty, dismal, drab, dreary, faded, gloomy, grimy, murky, rundown

**dinner** n main meal of the day, eaten in the middle of the day or in the evening

**dinosaur** n gigantic, extinct reptile

**dint** n dent, mark; **by dint of** by force of

**diocese** n district under jurisdiction of bishop; adj **diocesan**

**diode** n elec semiconductor for converting alternating current to direct current

**dip** v **dipping**, **dipped** 1 put into liquid 2 go downwards; n 1 act of putting into liquid 2 downward slope 3 reduction

> **dip** v 1 (put into liquid) bathe, douse, drench, duck, dunk, immerse, lower, plunge, rinse, soak, souse, steep, submerge. 2 (go downwards) descend, dive, drop, fall, plunge, sag, slip
>
> **dip** n 1 (act of putting into liquid) bathe, immersion, plunge, rinse, soak, submersion, swim. 2 (downward slope) dent, depression, hole, hollow, incline, slope, valley. 3 (reduction) decline, dive, drop, fall, plunge, slip, slump

**diphtheria** n serious, infectious disease of throat

**diploma** n document attesting holder's proficiency

**diplomacy** n art of management of international relations; tactful skill in dealing with people

**diplomat** n professional employed in diplomacy

**diplomatic** adj tactful

> **diplomatic** adj adept, adroit, careful, considerate, delicate, discreet, judicious, politic, prudent, sensitive, subtle

**dipstick** n rod for measuring level of liquid

**dire** adj terrible

**dire** *adj* alarming, appalling, atrocious, awful, calamitous, catastrophic, chronic, disastrous, dreadful, frightful, ghastly, grievous, horrendous, horrible, horrifying, shocking, unspeakable

**direct** *v* 1 control 2 order 3 show way; *adj* 1 straight 2 frank 3 without intermediary

**direct** *v* 1 (control) administer, be in charge of, conduct, govern, handle, head, manage, orchestrate, oversee, regulate, run, supervise. 2 (order) bid, command, dictate, instruct, tell. 3 (show way) conduct, escort, give directions, guide, indicate, lead, pilot, point, steer, usher
**direct** *adj* 1 (straight) immediate, non-stop, shortest, through, unbroken, uninterrupted. 2 (frank) blunt, candid, clear, explicit, forthright, honest, open, outspoken, plain, plainspoken, straight, straightforward, to the point, unambiguous, unequivocal, upfront

**direction** *n* 1 guiding 2 command 3 course taken by moving object; *pl* **directions** instructions to a place
**directive** *n* official order
**direct mail** *n* publicity material sent to many people
**direct object** *n* *ling* noun or pronoun following a transitive verb
**director** *n* one who controls; member of board managing company
**directory** *n* book listing names and addresses, telephone numbers, etc
**direct speech** *n* actual words spoken
**dirge** *n* lament for dead; mournful song
**dirigible** *n* airship capable of being steered
**dirk** *n* short dagger
**dirndl** *n* Austrian pesant dress with close bodice and full gathered skirt
**dirt** *n* earth; filth
**dirty** *adj* 1 not clean 2 not honest or fair 3 obscene

**dirty** *adj* 1 (not clean) contaminated, dusty, filthy, foul, grimy, grubby, grungy *inf*, impure, marked, messy, mucky *inf*, muddy, nasty, polluted, smudged, soiled, spotted, stained, sticky, sullied, tainted, tarnished, unclean. 2 (not honest or fair) corrupt, crooked, deceitful, dishonest, dishonorable, fraudulent, illegal, treacherous, unfair, unscrupulous, unsporting. 3 (obscene) bawdy, blue, coarse, improper, indecent, lascivious, lewd, offensive, pornographic, ribald, risqué, rude, salacious, sleazy *inf*, smutty, suggestive, vulgar

**disabled** *adj* having a disability
**disability** *n* incapacity
**disadvantage** *n* unfavorable condition or situation

**disadvantage** *n* defect, disability, downside, drawback, fault, flaw, handicap, hindrance, hitch, impediment, inconvenience, minus, obstacle, problem, snag, weakness

**disaffection** *n* disloyalty; *adj* **disaffected** discontented
**disagree** *v* differ, quarrel

**disagree** *v* argue, bicker, clash, contradict, counter, debate, discuss, dispute, dissent, diverge, fall out, fight, object, oppose, question, quibble, squabble, take issue, wrangle

**disagreement** *n* difference of opinion

**disagreement** *n* altercation, argument, clash, conflict, contradiction, controversy, debate, difference, discord, discussion, dispute, dissent, divergence, division, falling out, fight, objection, opposition, quarrel, row, squabble, tiff, wrangle

**disallow** *v* refuse to sanction; prohibit

A
B
C
D
E
F
G
H
I
J
K
L
M
N
O
P
Q
R
S
T
U
V
W
X
Y
Z

**disappear** *v* vanish
**disappearance** *n* vanishing
**disappoint** *v* fail to fulfill the desires or hopes of; *n* **-ment**

> **disappoint** *v* depress, disenchant, dishearten, disillusion, dismay, dispirit, dissatisfy, fail, frustrate, let down, sadden, thwart, upset

**disappointed** *adj* discouraged

> **disappointed** *adj* cast down, depressed, despondent, disenchanted, disheartened, disillusioned, dismayed, dispirited, dissatisfied, downcast, frustrated, let down, sad, saddened

**disappointing** *adj* disheartening

> **disappointing** *adj* depressing, discouraging, disenchanting, dispiriting, frustrating, unsatisfactory, upsetting

**disapprove (of)** *v* show, express unfavorable attitude (to); *adj* **disapproving**
**disarm** *v* deprive of weapons; conciliate; reduce armaments; *n* **disarmament**
**disarrange** *v* make untidy
**disarray** *v* throw into confusion; disturb
**disaster** *n* sudden great misfortune

> **disaster** *n* accident, act of God, adversity, blow, calamity, cataclysm, catastrophe, misadventure, mischance, misfortune, mishap, reverse, ruin, tragedy, trouble

**disastrous** *adj* very unfortunate

> **disastrous** *adj* adverse, appalling, awful, catastrophic, destructive, devastating, dire, dreadful, fatal, fateful, terrible, tragic, unfortunate, unlucky

**disavow** *v* repudiate; deny belief in
**disband** *v* scatter, disperse, break up
**disbelief** *n* lack of belief

**discard** *v* reject as valueless

> **discard** *v* abandon, cast aside, dispense with, dispose of, ditch, get rid of, jettison, reject, repudiate, scrap, throw away

**discern** *v* make out; distinguish (by senses or with mind); *adjs* **discerning** shrewd, discriminating; **discernible** that can be clearly seen
**discharge** *v* 1 fire (gun, etc) 2 emit 3 dismiss 4 release; *n* 1 act of discharging 2 release 3 matter discharged or emitted 4 payment
**disciple** *n* follower, one who learns from another
**discipline** *n* 1 training in obedience, self-control and orderliness 2 maintenance of order and control; *v* control; train mentally, morally, physically

> **discipline** *n* 1 (training in obedience) control, correction, drilling, exercise, punishment, regulation, rules, strictness, training. 2 (maintenance of order) control, organization, restraint, self-control, self-restraint, strength, will-power

**disclaim** *v* disown; *n* **disclaimer**; *leg* renunciation of right, title, etc
**disclose** *v* reveal
**disco** *n* 1 party with dancing to recorded pop music 2 club or place where disco dancing occurs 3 type of music for this dancing (*also* **disco music**)
**discolor** *v* alter, change color of, stain
**discomfit** *v* disconcert, defeat
**discomfort** *n* lack of comfort

> **discomfort** *n* ache, disquiet, distress, hardship, hurt, inconvenience, irritation, nuisance, pain, pang, soreness, trouble, twinge, uneasiness, vexation

**disconcert** *v* discompose, embarrass
**disconnect** *v* 1 detach 2 deprive of service *eg* telephone

**disconsolate** *adj* forlorn, sad, unhappy
**discord** *n* 1 disagreement; strife 2 harsh sound
**discothèque** *n Fr* disco
**discount** *n* sum deducted from debt, for prompt or cash settlement; *v* 1 ignore 2 reduce (price)

> **discount** *v* 1 (ignore) disbelieve, disregard, gloss over, overlook, pass over, pay no attention to, reject, take no notice of. 2 (reduce) cut, lower, mark down, take off, slash

**discourage** *v* 1 demoralize 2 advise against

> **discourage** *v* 1 (demoralize) abash, cast down, dampen, daunt, depress, deter, dishearten, dismay, dissuade, intimidate, put off, unnerve. 2 (advise against) caution against, disapprove, dissuade, deter, frown on, oppose, put off, repress, take a dim view, urge against

**discourse** *n* speech; lecture; conversation; *v* lecture, preach, converse
**discourteous** *adj* impolite
**discover** *v* find out, *esp* something unknown before; *ns* **discovery**, **discoverer**

> **discover** *v* 1 (find) come across, come upon, dig up, light on, locate, track down, turn up, uncover, unearth. 2 (learn) ascertain, detect, find out, identify, perceive, realize, recognize, see, spot, suss out, uncover

**discredit** *v* 1 spoil the good reputation of 2 create doubts about; *adj* -**able** shameful
**discreet** *adj* tactful

> **discreet** *adj* careful, circumspect, diplomatic, judicious, polite, politic, prudent

**discrepancy** *n* inconsistency
**discretion** *n* 1 tact 2 ability to judge well; *idm* **at sb's discretion** according to sb's own decision

**discriminate** *v* make a distinction; *idm* **discriminate against/in favor of sb** treat sb worse/better than other people; *adjs* **discriminating** showing good judgment; **discriminatory** discriminating against; *n* **discrimination**
**discursive** *adj* dealing with wide range of subjects; rambling
**discus** *n* heavy disk thrown in contest of strength
**discuss** *v* argue in detail

> **discuss** *v* argue, confer, consider, converse, debate, deliberate, put your heads together, talk, talk about, talk over

**discussion** *n* detailed talk, argument

> **discussion** *n* conference, conversation, debate, deliberation, dialogue, talk

**disdain** *v* treat with contempt, scorn; *n* scorn; aloofness; *adj* **disdainful**.
**disease** *n* illness, ailment; *adj* **diseased** suffering from or impaired by disease
**disembark** *v* go, put ashore from ship
**disfigure** *v* render unsightly; *n* -**ment**
**disgrace** *v* bring shame on, dismiss from favour; *n* shame, disrepute; dishonor
**disgraceful** *adj* 1 morally shameful 2 terrible

> **disgraceful** *v* 1 (morally shameful) contemptible, corrupt, degrading, disgusting, dishonorable, ignominious, outrageous, shameful. 2 (terrible) appalling, awful, dreadful, pathetic, shocking

**disgruntled** *adj* displeased; sulky
**disguise** *v* conceal identity of; *n* deceptive appearance

> **disguise** *n* camouflage, concealment, costume, cover, false identity, fancy dress, mask

A
B
C
D
E
F
G
H
I
J
K
L
M
N
O
P
Q
R
S
T
U
V
W
X
Y
Z

**disgust** n strong aversion, repugnance; v fill with loathing, nauseate
**disgusting** adj revolting, terrible

> **disgusting** adj appalling, awful, disgraceful, distasteful, gross, horrible, nauseating, obscene, offensive, outrageous, repugnant, repellent, repulsive, sickening, ugly, unpleasant

**dish** n shallow vessel for holding, cooking food; contents of dish; v serve in dish; idm **dish out** coll give away lavishly; phr v **dish up** coll serve up
**dishcloth** n cloth used for washing dishes, wiping tables and kitchen surfaces
**dishearten** v discourage
**dishevelled** adj (of hair) ruffled, untidy, unkempt in appearance
**dishonest** n not honest; n **dishonesty**

> **dishonest** adj cheating, criminal, crooked, deceitful, dishonorable, duplicitous, lying, unscrupulous, untrustworthy

**dishonor)** disgrace; v 1 bring disgrace to 2 (of bank) refuse to cash check; adj **-able**
**dishwasher** n person or machine that washes dishes
**disillusion** v make aware of unpleasant truth; adj **disillusioned;** n **-ment**

> **disillusioned** adj alienated, cynical, disabused, disaffected, disappointed, disenchanted, fed up

**disinfect** v destroy infection; remove harmful germs, etc; n **-ant** substance that disinfects
**disintegrate** v split up, resolve into parts, elements; fall to pieces; n **-ation**

> **disintegrate** v break down, collapse, decay, fall apart, fall to pieces, implode

**disinterested** adj without selfish motives
**disjointed** adj incoherent; disconnected

**disk** n 1 comput disc carrying data 2 round thin object
**disk drive** n comput device for transferring data between disk and computer memory
**diskette** n comput small disk
**disk jockey** n sl radio announcer of program of recorded popular music
**dislike** v not like; n hatred

> **dislike** v be hostile to, be put off by, detest, disapprove of, hate, have an aversion to
> **dislike** n antipathy, aversion, detestation, distaste, hate, hostility

**dislocate** v put out of joint; displace
**dislodge** v remove from resting-place; drive out (enemy)
**disloyal** adj not loyal; n **disloyalty**

> **disloyal** adj disobedient, false, mutinous, perfidious, traitorous, treacherous, seditious, unfaithful

**dismal** adj gloomy

> **dismal** adj bleak, cheerless, dark, demoralizing, depressing, disheartening, dispiriting, miserable, sad

**dismantle** v strip of equipment, furnishings
**dismay** v disappoint; n disappointment

> **dismay** n annoyance, consternation, displeasure, frustration, shock

**dismiss** v 1 send away 2 expel from job 3 banish from mind; n **dismissal**

> **dismiss** v 1 (send away) banish, cast out, chuck out inf, exclude, excuse, send out, throw out. 2 (expel from a job) downsize, fire, get rid of, kick out, remove, sack. 3 (banish from mind) brush aside, brush off, discount, disregard, forget about, ignore, reject, ridicule

**dismount** v get down from saddle
**disobedient** adj not obedient;
n **disobedience**

> **disobedient** adj cheeky, defiant, disrespectful, dissenting, dissident, disloyal, insubordinate, mutinous, naughty, unruly

**disobey** v not obey
**disorder** n lack of order

> **disorder** n anarchy, chaos, clutter, disarray, jumble, muddle, turmoil, untidiness, unrest, unruliness

**disorganized** adj not organized

> **disorganized** adj anarchic, chaotic, disorderly, in disarray, jumbled, muddled, random, uncontrolled, unplanned, unstructured, unsystematic, untidy

**disorient(ate)** v take away sense of direction;
n **-ation**
**disown** v refuse to acknowledge
**disparaging** adj scornful
**dispassionate** adj calm; unbiased
**dispatch** see **despatch**
**dispel** v **-pelling, -pelled** drive away; cause to vanish
**dispense** v give out; phr v **dispense with** do without; n **dispensary** place where medicine is made up

> **dispense** v 1 (give out) distribute, disseminate, hand out, prescribe, provide. 2 (**dispense with**) cancel, do without, eliminate, forget, forget about, get rid of, go without, not bother with, remove, scrap

**disperse** v scatter; adj **dispersed**
**dispirit** v discourage; adj **dispirited**
**displace** v move out of place; oust;
adj **displaced** out of place
**display** v 1 exhibit 2 show feeling; n parade, showing off, exhibition

**display** v 1 (exhibit) arrange, present, put on view, show, show off. 2 (show feeling) betray, reveal, show

**displease** v annoy; offend; n **displeasure**;
anger, indignation
**disposable** adj 1 available 2 to be used once and discarded
**dispose** phr v **dispose of** get rid of;
n **disposal** removal; idm **at one's disposal** available to one for use or for help;
n **disposition** temperament
**disproportionate** adj excessive
**disprove** v refute; show to be false
**dispute** v 1 question 2 compete for;
n 1 argument 2 disagreement between workers and management

> **dispute** v 1 (question) contest, deny, reject, oppose, wrangle over. 2 (compete for) battle for, contend for, contest, fight over, vie for
> **dispute** n 1 (argument) altercation, battle, conflict, controversy, difference of opinion, differences, disagreement, feud, fight, quarrel, row. 2 (disagreement between workers and management) go slow, grievance, industrial action, lock-out, strike

**disqualify** v make ineligible; debar;
incapacitate; n **disqualification**
**disquiet** v make anxious, apprehensive, restless; n **disquietude**
**disregard** v ignore; n lack of concern
**disrepair** n bad condition resulting from negligence
**disreputable** adj of bad repute
**disrespect** n lack of respect
**disrespectful** adj not showing respect

> **disrespectful** adj cheeky, contemptuous, disdainful, disobedient, impertinent, impolite, impudent, insolent, scornful

A B C D E F G H I J K L M N O P Q R S T U V W X Y Z

**disrupt** *v* cause disorder to

> **disrupt** *v* disturb, interfere with, interrupt, sabotage, throw into disarray, upset

**disruptive** *adj* badly behaved

> **disruptive** *adj* distracting, ill-behaved, interfering, naughty, troublesome, unruly

**dissatisfy** *v* fail to satisfy; *adj* **dissatisfied**; *n* **dissatisfaction**

**dissect** *v* cut up for examination

**dissemble** *v* conceal feelings, motives, etc

**disseminate** *v* spread abroad

**dissension** *n* discord

**dissent** *v* disagree; *n* disagreement

> **dissent** *n* argument, defiance, discontent, disobedience, dissension, dissidence, nonconformism, opposition

**dissertation** *n* formal discourse or treatise

**dissident** *n* one who opposes government

**dissimilar** *adj* unlike; *n* **dissimilarity**

**dissipate** *v* 1 scatter, dispel 2 squander

**dissociate** *v* separate; sever, repudiate connection with; *n* **dissociation**

**dissolve** *v* 1 liquefy; melt 2 become faint 3 break up 4 terminate; annul; *adj* **dissoluble** capable of being dissolved; *n* **dissolution** act or process of dissolving

**dissuade** *v* persuade against

> **dissuade** *v* deter, discourage, prevent, put off, stop, talk sb out of

**distance** *n* 1 space between two things 2 remoteness 3 aloofness

**distant** *adj* 1 far off 2 aloof

> **distant** *adj* 1 (far off) faint, far, faraway, remote. 2 (aloof) cold, detached, haughty, preoccupied, unfriendly

**distaste** *n* aversion, dislike

**distasteful** *adj* unpleasant

**distemper** *n* 1 contagious disease of dogs 2 thick paint used for internal walls

**distend** *v* inflate, become blown out

**distil** *v* **-tilling, -tilled** evaporate liquid and condense it again; refine by this method; trickle; *ns* **distillation, distiller** one who distils, *esp* alcoholic spirit; **distillery** place where distillation is carried on

**distinct** *adj* 1 easily seen, heard 2 separate

> **distinct** *adj* 1 (easily seen, heard) audible, clear, definite, discernible, noticeable, perceptible, tangible, unmistakable, visible. 2 (separate) contrasting, independent, individual, unconnected

**distinction** *n* difference; high standing or special quality; mark of favor

**distinctive** *adj* characteristic

> **distinctive** *adj* distinguishing, own, peculiar, specific, tell-tale

**distinguish** *v* 1 see, hear clearly 2 see difference in

> **distinguish** *v* 1 (see, hear clearly) discern, hear, make out, notice, perceive, see. 2 (see difference) differentiate, discriminate, draw a distinction, make a distinction, tell apart, tell the difference

**distinguished** *adj* famous

> **distinguished** *adj* award-winning, celebrated, eminent, experienced, favored, honored, respected

**distort** *v* spoil shape of; misrepresent; *n* **distortion**

> **distort** *v* bend out of shape, change, deform, falsify, misrepresent, pervert, twist, warp

**distract** *v* 1 divert (thoughts) 2 perplex
3 drive mad; *n* **distraction** 1 amusement
2 madness; *adj* **distraught** agitated
**distraught** *adj* extremely distressed
**distress** *n* suffering; *v* cause suffering to

> **distress** *n* agony, anguish, anxiety, grief,
> misery, pain, torment, trauma, worry

**distressed** *adj* upset

> **distressed** *adj* anguished, anxious, distraught,
> grieving, in pain, jumpy, nervous, panicky,
> suffering, traumatized, troubled, worried

**distressing** *adj* upsetting

> **distressing** *adj* difficult, disturbing, painful,
> sad, stressful, traumatic, troubling, trying,
> upsetting, worrisome, worrying

**distribute** *v* share out; disperse; *n* **-ution**

> **distribute** *v* allocate, allot, deal out, deliver,
> dispense, dispatch, disseminate, divide up,
> give out, hand out, issue, share out

**district** *n* region, area, locality
**distrust** *n* doubt; suspicion; lack of
confidence in; *v* feel distrust
**disturb** *v* 1 interrupt 2 upset 3 move; *n* **-ance**

> **disturb** *v* 1 (interrupt) bother, butt in,
> distract, hassle, harass, hinder, intrude,
> pester. 2 (upset) agitate, alarm, concern,
> distress, fluster, perturb, shake, trouble,
> unnerve, unsettle, worry. 3 (move)
> interfere with, mess about *inf*, mix up,
> muddle, rearrange, touch

**disturbing** *adj* worrying

> **disturbing** *adj* alrming distressing,
> frightening, harrowing, troubling,
> unsettling, upsetting

**disused** *adj* no longer used; *n* **disuse**;
*idm* **fallen into disuse** disused
**ditch** *n* narrow trench cut in earth, used for
drainage or defense; *v* throw away
**dither** *v* waver, tremble, hesitate nervously
**ditto** *n* the same, as already said or written
**divan** *n* low backless couch, bed
**dive** *v* 1 plunge into water 2 move suddenly
3 descend through air; *n* act of diving;
*n* **diver** one who dives

> **dive** *v* 1 (plunge into water) go under,
> jump, leap, plunge. 2 (move suddenly)
> dart, disappear, dodge, drop, duck.
> 3 (descend through air) fall, nosedive,
> plummet, swoop

**diverge** *v* branch off set course; separate;
*ns* **divergence**, **diversion** turning aside or
away; alternative route; *adj* **divergent**
**diverse** *adj* dissimilar

> **diverse** *adj* assorted, different, differing,
> distinct, miscellaneous, mixed, separate,
> several, sundry, varied, various

**diversify** *v* make different; give variety to
**diversity** *n* variety
**diversion** *n* 1 rerouting of traffic
2 entertainment 3 distraction of attention
**divert** *v* 1 turn aside 2 distract; amuse;
*n* **diversion** entertainment; *adj* **diverting**
**divide** *v* 1 split into parts 2 share out 3 find
out number of times one number is
contained in another; *n* **dividend**
1 number divided by another 2 profit on
money invested; share of profits, etc

> **divide** *v* 1 (split into parts) cut, detach,
> disconnect, halve, partition, quarter,
> separate, sever, shear, split, subdivide.
> 2 (share out) allocate, deal out, dole out,
> measure out, parcel out

**divine** *adj* relating to God; *n* **divinity**
1 god 2 quality of being divine; *v* guess

**division** n 1 type or part 2 thing which divides 3 part of organization 4 disagreement

> **division** n 1 (type or part) category, class, compartment, department, group, portion, section, sector, segment, share, slice. 2 (thing which divides) border, boundary, frontier, line, partition, wall. 3 (part of organization) branch, department, unit

**divisive** adj causing disagreement
**divorce** v dissolve marriage; separate; n legal dissolution of marriage; separation; n **divorcee** divorced spouse
**divulge** v reveal (secret)
**DIY** abbr **do-it-yourself**
**dizzy** adj giddy; n **dizziness**

> **dizzy** adj dazed, faint, light-headed, muddled, reeling, shaky, staggering, swimming, unsteady, wobbly, woozy inf

**DJ** abbr disk jockey
**do** v pt **did**; pp **done** 1 achieve 2 make 3 be enough 4 coll cheat; phr vs **do away with** 1 abolish 2 kill; **do in** coll 1 kill 2 exhaust 3 wreck; **do over** sl attack; beat up; **do up** 1 fasten; wrap up 2 make improvements to; **do with** idm **can/could do with** need(s); idm **have/be to do with** be connected with; phr v **do without** manage without

> **do** v 1 (achieve) accomplish, carry out, cause, complete, finish, perform, undertake. 2 (make) arrange, create, design, get ready, look after, manufacture, organize, prepare, produce, provide, see to. 3 (be enough) be adequate, be enough, be sufficient, satisfy, serve, suffice. 4 (cheat) con, deceive, defraud, hoodwink, trick

**docile** adj placid

> **docile** adj compliant, co-operative, obedient, passive, submissive

**dock**[1] n coarse, large-leaved weed
**dock**[2] n artificial basin where ships are loaded repaired; v enter, put into dock; ns **dockyard** series of docks, warehouses, etc; **docker** dock laborer
**dock**[3] n enclosure in court, for accused
**docket** n 1 label, ticket 2 list of contents; cases for trial
**Doc Martens** (TM) type of ankle boots or shoes with thick soles
**doctor** n 1 holder of highest degree in any faculty of university 2 medical practitioner
**doctorate** n highest university degree
**doctrine** n accepted belief; n **doctrinaire** narrow-minded, obstinate person

> **doctrine** n belief, canon, conviction, creed, dogma, principle, teaching, theory

**document** n written information, evidence; v bring written evidence; n, adj **documentary** factual (report, film); n **documentation** documentary proof, evidence
**dodder** v move shakily, feebly
**dodge** v 1 escape 2 move away from 3 avoid doing

> **dodge** v 1 (escape) elude, evade, give sb the slip. 2 (move away from) dart, dive, sidestep, swerve, veer, weave. 3 (avoid doing) avoid, get out of, skirk, steer clear of, wriggle out of

**dodo** n **dodos, dodoes** extinct bird
**doe** n female of deer, rabbit, hare, etc
**does** 3rd sing pres of **do**
**dog** n 1 domestic quadruped, related to wolf; 2 male wolf, fox, etc; v **dogging, dogged** to follow and watch constantly, to hamper
**dog collar** n 1 collar for dog 2 coll clergyman's stiff white collar
**dogfish** n small fish related to shark
**doggy bag** n bag for taking home uneaten food from restaurant
**dogma** n article of belief; body of such theories, etc

**dogmatic** *adj* stubborn in opinions;
*n* **dogmatism**

> **dogmatic** *adj* arrogant, assertive,
> authoritarian, dictatorial, hard-line *inf*,
> imperious, insistent, overbearing

**dog paddle, doggie paddle** *n* swimming
stroke of quick, short movements
**dog tired** *adj coll* utterly exhausted
**do-it-yourself** *n* doing one's own repairs,
decorating, etc, not using professional
workmen
**doldrums** *n pl* low spirits
**dole** *n* unemployment benefit; *v* give out
sparingly
**doleful** *adj* woeful, sad, lugubrious
**doll** *n* child's toy, like human figure; *sl sexist*
woman; *n* **dolly** child's name for doll
**dollar** *n* unit of coinage in US, Canada, etc
**dollop** *n* big shapeless lump
**dolphin** *n* sea mammal akin to whale
**domain** *n* land, realm held, ruled over;
*fig* sphere of activity or influence
**dome** *n* convex curved roof
**domestic** *adj* 1 relating to home or family
2 not foreign 3 (of animals) kept by man;
*v* **domesticate** tame animals

> **domestic** *adj* 1 (relating to home or family)
> family, home, personal, private. 2 (not
> foreign) home, internal, national. 3
> (kept by man) domesticated, house-
> trained, pet, tame

**domicile** *n* usual dwelling-place
**dominant** *adj* 1 controlling 2 most important

> **dominant** *adj* 1 (controlling) assertive,
> domineering, leading, most influential,
> ruling, superior. 2 (most important)
> biggest, conspicuous, eye-catching, highest,
> imposing, largest, main, major, tallest

**dominate** *v* 1 have control over 2 tower
above; *adj* **dominating**; *n* **domination**

**dominate** *v* 1 (have control over) be in the
driver's seat, boss, command, control,
direct, govern, influence, lead,
monopolize, rule, tyrannize. 2 (tower
above) dwarf, loom over, overlook,
overshadow, stand over

**domineer** *v* act harshly, arrogantly; tyrannize,
bully; *adj* **domineering**
**dominion** *n* supremacy, sovereignty
**domino** *n* small oblong piece of bone, etc
marked with 1-6 dots; *pl* **dominoes** game
using 28 such pieces
**domino effect** *n* sequence of events each
resulting in another or others
**don** *n* 1 Spanish title 2 college professor
**donate** *v* give
**donation** *n* gift

> **donation** *n* contribution, grant, offering,
> present

**done** *pp of* **do** finished
**donkey** *n* ass; *fig* stupid person
**donor** *n* one who gives
**doodle** *v* draw, scribble idly
**doom** *n* fate; evil destiny
**doomed** *adj* destined to fail or die
**door** *n* structure for closing an entrance;
*n* **doorway** opening so closed

> **door** *n* barrier, doorway, entrance, entry,
> exit, gate, opening

**doormat** *n* mat for wiping dirt from shoes
**dormant** *adj* inactive

> **dormant** *adj* asleep, hibernating,
> motionless, quiet, resting, sleeping,
> sluggish, slumbering

**dormer** *n* vertical window in sloping roof
**dormitory** *n* sleeping room with several beds
**dormouse** *n* small hibernating rodent, like
mouse; *pl* **dormice**

**dose** *adj* amount of drug, etc, taken at one time; *v* give medicine to; *n* **dosage**

> **dose** *n* amount, measure, portion, prescribed amount, quantity

**dossier** *n Fr* set of documents, etc, concerning particular person or subject
**dot** *n* small round mark or spot; *idm* **on the dot** punctually; *v* **dotting, dotted** mark with a dot or dots; *adj* **dotted** made of dots

> **dot** *n* circle, dab, fleck, jot, point, speck, speckle

**dote** *v* love blindly, be foolish over
**doting** *adj* loving too much

> **doting** *adj* adoring, devoted, fond, indulgent

**double** *adj* twice as much; ambiguous; twofold; *n* **1** thing or person exactly like another **2** twice the amount; *v* make, become double; *idm* **at the double 1** running **2** fast; *phr vs* **double back** return by the same route; **double up 1** bend at the waist **2** share a room; *adv* **doubly** twice as much; *n pl* **doubles** match for opposing pairs
**double agent** *n* spy acting for two opposing countries
**double bass** *n mus* largest instrument of violin family
**double cross** *n, v* swindle; *n* **-er**
**double-decker** *n* bus with two floors
**double glaze** *v* fit window with double glass panel for better heat insulation; *n* **double glazing**
**double-jointed** *adj* having very flexible joints
**doubt** *v* be uncertain; *n* uncertainty; *adj* **doubtful**; *adv* **doubtless** probably

> **doubt** *n* apprehension, cynicism, disbelief, fear, hesitation, incredulity, misgivings, mistrust, qualms, reservations, skepticism, suspicion, uneasiness, worries

**dough** *n* flour moistened and kneaded
**doughnut** *n* round or ring-shaped cake
**dour** *adj* stern; grim; obstinate
**douse** *v* **1** dip in water **2** extinguish (light)
**dove** *n* bird of pigeon family
**dowager** *n* woman whose title derives from deceased husband
**dowdy** *adj* dull and unfashionable
**dowel** *n* wooden, metal, or plastic peg
**down**[1] fine soft feathers
**down**[2] *adv* towards lower position, size, quality, etc; *prep* from higher to lower position, along; *idm* **down-and-out** destitute; *idm* **be/go down with** be/fall ill with; *adj, adv* **downward** descending
**downcast** *adj* dejected
**downfall** *n* defeat

> **downfall** *n* collapse, disgrace, fall, overthrow, ruin, undoing

**downgrade** *v* reduce to lower grade
**downhearted** *adj* discouraged
**downhome** *adj* relating to common folk
**download** *v comput* transfer (data)
**downpour** *n* sudden heavy fall of rain

> **downpour** *n* cloudburst, deluge, flood, rainstorm, torrents of rain

**downright** *adj* complete; *adv* absolutely
**downs** *n pl* rolling grassy hills
**downstream** *adj, adv* with the current of a stream
**down-to-earth** *adj* practical; unsophisticated
**downturn** *n* decline, *esp* economic
**dowry** *n* money or property brought by a woman to marriage
**doze** *v* sleep lightly
**dozen** *n* set of twelve; **baker's dozen** thirteen
**drab** *adj* dull

> **drab** *adj* colorless, dingy, dismal, dowdy, dreary, flat, gray, lackluster, mousy, somber

**draft** n 1 rough sketch, outline 2 order for payment 3 current of air 4 body of troops for special duty; v 1 send on special duty 2 make draft; n **draftsman** one who draws up plans; fem **draftswoman**

**drag** v **dragging, dragged** 1 pull along 2 pass slowly; n **drag** 1 air resistance 2 sl boring situation

> **drag** v 1 (pull along) haul, lug, pull, tow, trail, tug, yank. 2 (pass slowly) be tedious, crawl, creep, go on too long, go slowly, move slowly, stretch out

**dragon** n fabulous winged reptile, breathing out fire

**dragonfly** n iridescent long-bodied insect

**drain** v 1 draw off (liquid) gradually 2 exhaust gradually; n 1 pipe; ditch; sewer 2 fig constant strain (on strength, time, etc)

**drainage** n (system for) draining waste water

**drake** n male duck

**drama** n 1 play 2 art of acting 3 exciting situation

> **drama** n 1 (a play) comedy, dramatization, melodrama, play, production, show, tragedy. 2 (art of acting) acting, dramatic art, improvisation, stagecraft, theater. 3 (exciting situation) crisis, excitement, histrionics, scene, spectacle

**dramatic** adj exciting

> **dramatic** adj breathtaking, electrifying, impressive, melodramatic, powerful, sensational, tense, thrilling

**dramatize** v 1 make into play, drama 2 exaggerate; n dramatization

**drank** pt of **drink**

**drape** v arrange in folds; cover loosely

**drastic** adj severe; adv **-ally**

> **drastic** adj desperate, dire, extreme, radical

**draw** v 1 make a picture of 2 attract 3 pull along 4 take out (weapon) 5 score equally; pt **drew**; pp **drawn**; n tie at end of game; n **drawing** art of depicting in pencil, etc

> **draw** v 1 (make a picture of) color, depict, design, make a drawing, paint, pencil, sketch, trace. 2 (attract) coax, entice, lure, persuade, pull. 3 (pull along) haul, pull, tow. 4 (take out weapon) bring out, produce, pull out, remove, take out, unsheathe. 5 (score equally) be equal, be neck and neck, tie

**drawback** n disadvantage

**drawer** n 1 one who draws 2 lidless, sliding box in table, etc

**drawbridge** n lifting bridge over a moat

**drawing room** n room for entertaining people

**drawl** v speak slowly and affectedly; n such manner of speech

**drawn** pp of **draw**; adj pale and tired

**dray** n low sideless cart used for heavy loads

**dread** v feel fear at; n fear

> **dread** v be afraid of, be terrified of, fear, shrink from, worry about
> **dread** n alarm, apprehension, cold feet, dismay, foreboding, fright, horror, terror, trepidation, uneasiness, worry

**dreadful** adj terrible

> **dreadful** adj appalling, awful, dire, disgusting, distressing, fearful, frightful, ghastly, grim, hideous, horrible, horrifying, nasty, repugnant, revolting, shocking

**dreadnought** n battleship

**dreadlocks** n long curled strands of hair

**dream** n illusion of senses occurring in sleep, fantasy; v have dreams; phr v **dream up** invent; imagine; pt, pp **dreamed, dreamt**; n **dreamer**

**dreamboat** n coll attractive person

A B C **D** E F G H I J K L M N O P Q R S T U V W X Y Z

**dreary** *adj* gloomy and dull

> **dreary** *adj* boring, colorless, dark, depressing, dismal, drab, flat, funereal, joyless, melancholy, miserable, monotonous, mournful, sad, somber, uninteresting

**dredge** *v* bring up (mud, etc) from under water; *n* type of net, scoop, etc
**dredger** *n* ship used for dredging
**drench** *v* soak thoroughly

> **drench** *v* douse, drown, flood, saturate, wet

**dress** *v* 1 put clothes on 2 decorate 3 apply dressing to (wound); *n* frock; formal clothes; *phr v* **dress up** dress smartly, dress in costume

> **dress** *v* 1 (put clothes on) don, get changed, get dressed, put on, slip on. 2 (decorate) adorn, trim. 3 (apply dressing to) attend to, bandage, bind, cover, put a plaster on, tend, treat

**dressage** *n* training of horse to make exact movements; performance of these
**dressing down** *n* reprimand
**dressing gown** *n* loose garment worn at home (over night clothes or underwear)
**drew** *pt of* **draw**
**dribble** *v* trickle; *n* drop
**dried** *pt, pp of* **dry**
**drift** *v* move aimlessly; *n* 1 deviation from course 2 something driven by wind, water 3 general meaning

> **drift** *v* be carried, coast, float, ramble, roam, stray, waft, wander

**drill**[1] *n* instrument for boring holes, narrow furrow for seeds; *v* bore hole
**drill**[2] *n* regular exercise; military training; *v* perform, cause to perform drill
**drily** = **dryly**

**drink** *v* **drinking, drank, drunk** 1 swallow liquid 2 drink alcohol; *n* 1 amount of liquid swallowed 2 alcoholic beverage; *n* **drinker**

> **drink** *v* 1 (swallow liquid) gulp, guzzle, knock back, sip, suck, swig. 2 (drink alcohol) booze, carouse, get drunk, have a few, hit the bottle, indulge, take a drop
> **drink** *n* 1 (amount of liquid swallowed) dram, glass, gulp, pint, sip, slug, swig, tot. 2 (alcoholic beverage) alcohol, booze, grog, hard stuff, hooch, liquor, spirits

**drip** *v* **dripping, dripped** trickle; let fall drop by drop; *n* act of dripping; *adj* **dripping** very wet
**drive** *v* 1 force into movement 2 go in vehicle 3 force; *pt* **drove**; *pp* **drive**; *n* 1 ride in vehicle 2 determination 3 private road to house; *n* **driver** one who drives

> **drive** *v* 1 (force into movement) direct, guide, herd, move, propel, push, send, steer, urge. 2 (go in vehicle) chauffeur, give sb a lift, go by car, ride, run. 3 (force) coerce, compel, goad, impel, oblige, prod, put pressure on, spur
> **drive** *n* 1 (ride in vehicle) excursion, jaunt, journey, outing, ride, run, spin *inf*, trip. 2 (determination) ambition, energy, enterprise, enthusiasm, initiative, motivation, vigor

**drivel** *n* talk foolishly; *n* nonsense
**driveway** *n* path in front of house
**drizzle** *v* rain finely; *n* very fine rain
**droll** *adj* funny
**dromedary** *n* camel with one hump
**drone** *n* 1 male honey bee 2 low humming sound; *v* speak monotonously
**drool** *v* slaver over
**droop** *v* hang down limply

> **droop** *v* bend, dangle, drop, fall, flop, hang, sag, sink, slump, stoop, wilt

**drop** n 1 small globule of liquid 2 small amount 3 reduction; v **dropping, dropped** 1 let fall 2 become less 3 go downward 4 give up 5 leave out of team; *phr vs* **drop off** go to sleep; **drop out** choose not to participate; n *pl* **drops** liquid medicine taken a few drops at a time

**drop** n 1 (small globule of liquid) bead, blob, drip, droplet, globule, pearl, tear. 2 (small amount) dab, dash, mouthful, sip, smidgen, splash, spot, taste, trace, trickle. 3 (reduction) cut, decline, decrease, dip, downturn, fall-off
**drop** v 1 (let fall) let go. 2 (become less) collapse, decrease, dip, fall, lessen, plummet. 3 (go downward) descend, dip, dive, fall, fall away, go downhill, plummet, plunge, sink, subside, tumble. 4 (give up) abandon, chuck, discontinue, ditch, finish with, give up, kick *inf*

**dropout** n 1 person opting out of conventional society 2 person failing to complete academic course
**drought** n long period without rain
**drove** *pt of* **drive**
**drown** v 1 die, kill by suffocation in water 2 overwhelm 3 muffle (sound)
**drowsy** adj sleepy, lethargic
**drudge** n overworked servant; v work like drudge
**drudgery** n hard, dull work

**drudgery** n chores, grind *inf*, hard work, labor, slavery, slog, toil

**drug** n any vegetable, mineral substance used in medicine; v **drugging, drugged** give drug (*esp* narcotic) to
**drum** n 1 percussion instrument 2 various hollow cylindrical objects 3 part of ear; v **drumming, drummed** play drum; beat, sound continuously; *phr vs* **drum sth into sb** say sth repeatedly until it is understood; n **drummer**

**drumstick** n 1 stick used by drummer 2 lower leg of cooked chicken, turkey, etc
**drunk** adj intoxicated by alcohol; *pp* of **drink**; n **drunkard** habitual heavy drinker

**drunk** adj blind drunk, inebriated, loaded *sl*, merry, out of it *inf*, paralytic, plastered *inf*, sloshed *inf*, smashed *inf*, tight, tipsy, under the influence

**drunken** adj intoxicated
**dry** v **drying, dried** remove or lose moisture; adj 1 without moisture 2 subtle (of humor) 3 (of wine) not sweet; adv **drily, dryly** without emotion; n **dryness**

**dry** v dehydrate, desiccate, drain, dry off, dry out, dry up, make dry, parch, sear, shrivel, wither, wilt
**dry** adj 1 (without moisture) arid, baked, barren, dead, dehydrated, desiccated, dried up, moistureless, parched, shriveled, waterless, wilted, withered, wizened. 2 (subtle) deadpan, droll, ironic, laconic, sarcastic

**dryad** n wood nymph
**dry-clean** v clean with chemicals, without washing ns **dry-cleaner, dry-cleaning**
**dryer** n machine for removing moisture
**dry goods** n 1 grain, fruit, etc 2 haberdashery
**dual** adj of two, double, twofold; n **duality**
**dub** v 1 confer knighthood on 2 (of films, etc) re-record sound track, with additions, etc
**dubious** adj 1 not certain 2 not clear

**dubious** adj 1 (not certain) doubtful, hesitant, skeptical, suspicious, uncertain, unconvinced, undecided, unsure. 2 (not clear) ambiguous, debatable, indefinite, obscure, problematical, unclear, unresolved, unsettled, vague

**duchess** n 1 wife of duke 2 female peer with status of duke
**duchy** n land owned by duke or duchess

a
b
c
d
e
f
g
h
i
j
k
l
m
n
o
p
q
r
s
t
u
v
w
x
y
z

**duck**[1] n 1 water bird 2 heavy cotton fabric; n **duckling** young duck

**duck**[2] v 1 plunge person, thing into liquid 2 bob down (to avoid blow); n **ducking**

**duct** n tube for conveying liquid, air

**dud** n unsuccessful person, thing

**due** adj 1 (of money) owing 2 adequate 3 scheduled to arrive; idm **due to** resulting from; adv (of direction) exactly

> **due** adj 1 (owing) in arrears, outstanding, owing, payable, unpaid. 2 (adequate) appropriate, decent, deserved, fit, fitting, merited, proper, right. 3 (scheduled to arrive) awaited, expected, scheduled

**duel** n contest (physical or intellectual) between two persons; v fight duel

**duet** n musical work for two performers

**duffel coat** type of thick woolen coat

**dug** pt, pp of **dig**

**dugout** n 1 hollowed out canoe 2 underground shelter

**duke** n holder of highest hereditary rank of peerage; fem **duchess**

**dull** adj 1 stupid 2 tedious 3 not bright 4 overcast; v make, become dull

> **dull** adj 1 (stupid) dense, dim, dim-witted, obtuse, slow, unintelligent. 2 (tedious) boring, dreary, mind-numbing, tame, unexciting, unimaginative, uninteresting. 3 (not bright) dark, dingy, drab, dreary, faded, flat, matt, muted, somber, toned down, washed-out. 4 (overcast) cloudy, dark, dismal, gloomy, gray, murky

**duly** adv 1 as expected 2 punctually

**dumb** adj 1 unable to speak 2 unintelligent

> **dumb** adj 1 (unable to speak) at a loss for words, inarticulate, mute, silent, soundless, speechless, tongue-tied. 2 (unintelligent) dense, dim, slow, stupid

**dummy** n 1 sham object 2 tailor's model

**dummy run** n practice attempt

**dump** v 1 unload roughly 2 dispose of (refuse); n rubbish heap, place for depositing refuse, depot for ammunition

> **dump** v 1 (unload roughly) deposit, drop, fling down, sling, throw. 2 (dispose of refuse) ditch inf, get rid of, jettison, scrap, throw away, throw out

**dumper** n vehicle used on building sites

**dumpling** n piece of boiled suet, dough

**dunce** n dullard; pupil slow to learn

**dune** n wind-driven sand hill

**dung** n excrement of animals; manure

**dungarees** n pl overalls

**dungeon** n dark, underground prison cell

**duo** n mus 1 pair of players 2 piece for two

**dupe** v deceive, trick; n victim of duping

**duplicate** v make double; do again; n replica; n **duplication**

> **duplicate** v clone, copy, double, photocopy, print, repeat, replicate, reproduce
> **duplicate** n carbon copy, clone, copy, double, facsimile, imitation, photocopy, spitting image inf, twin

**duplicity** n deception

**durable** adj long-lasting; n pl **durables** goods expected to last; n **durability**

**duration** n length of existence

**duress** n compulsion

**during** prep 1 in the course of 2 throughout

**dusk** n late twilight

**dust** n powdery particles (of earth, etc) suspended in air; v remove dust; sprinkle with powder, etc; n **duster** cloth for wiping away dust; phr v **dust off** start to use again after long disuse

> **dust** n dirt, earth, grime, grit, powder, smut, soil, soot

**dust bowl** n area suffering from loss of vegetation through drought

**dust jacket** *n* protective cover of book

**dustpan** *n* flat container for collecting dust

**dust-up** *n coll* noisy quarrel, brawl

**dusty** *adj* covered in dust

dusty *adj* dirty, dust-covered, filthy, grimy, sooty, unswept

**Dutch courage** *n coll* courage gained by taking alcohol

**Dutch oven** *n* covered pan for slow cooking

**dutiful** *adj* showing respect

**duty** *n* **1** sth you have to do **2** moral obligation **3** tax on goods

duty *n* **1** (sth you have to do) assignment, chore, job, mission, obligation, responsibility, task. **2** (moral obligation) allegiance, loyalty, obligation, respect, responsibility. **3** (tax on goods) charge, customs, dues, levy, tariff, tax, toll

**duvetcover** *n* fabric cover for comforter

**dwarf** *n* person, animal, or plant much below usual size; *pl* **dwarfs** or **dwarves**; *v* make look small

dwarf *v* dominate, overshadow, tower above, tower over

**dwell** *v* live; *phr v* **dwell on** keep thinking, talking about; *pt, pp* **dwelling, dwelled,** or **dwelt**

**dwelling** *n* abode

**dwindle** *v* become smaller, less

**dyad** *n* two units considered as one

**dye** *v* **dyeing, dyed** impart color to; tint; *n* coloring matter used for dyeing

**dyed-in-the-wool** *adj* unchangeable

**dying** *pr p of* **die**

**dynamic** *adj* energetic

dynamic *adj* active, enterprising, enthusiastic, forceful, high-powered, lively, motivated, powerful, spirited

**dynamite** *n* high explosive made with nitroglycerine; *v* blow up with dynamite

**dynasty** *n* succession of rulers of same family; *adj* **dynastic**

**dysentery** *n* disease of large intestine

**dyslexia** *n* pathological inability to spell or read; word-blindness; *adj* **dyslexic**

**dyspepsia** *n* indigestion; *adj* **dyspepsic**

a
b
c
d
e
f
g
h
i
j
k
l
m
n
o
p
q
r
s
t
u
v
w
x
y
z

**E number** *n* number used to identify additive to food

**each** *adj, pron* every one considered separately

**eager** *adj* impatient to act

> **eager** *adj* anxious, bursting, enthusiastic, excited, greedy, hungry, impatient, intent, itching, keen, longing, thirsty

**eagle** *n* large bird of prey

**ear**[1] *n* **1** organ of hearing **2** sense of tune

**ear**[2] *n* spike, cluster of seeds of cereal

**earl** *n* rank in peerage below marquis

**earlobe** *n* soft lobe of outer ear

**early** *adj, adv* **1** before the time stated **2** near start of a period of time

> **early** *adj* (before the time stated) advanced, ahead of time, before time, forward, precocious, premature, untimely

**earmark** *v* note or set aside for a purpose

**earn** *v* **1** gain by labor **2** win **3** deserve; *n pl* **earnings** wages; salary

> **earn** *v* **1** (gain by labor) bring in, gain, get, make, net, pocket, pull in, realize, receive, take home. **2** (win) accumulate, collect, gain, qualify for, receive. **3** (deserve) be entitled to, be worthy of, gain, have a right to, merit, rate, secure, win

**earnest** *adj* **1** sincere **2** serious

> **earnest** *adj* **1** (sincere) committed, conscientious, dedicated, determined, grave, hard-working, intense, purposeful, resolved, solemn, studious, zealous. **2** (serious) heartfelt, impassioned, passionate, sincere, wholehearted

**earphones** *n pl* headphones

**earring** *n* item of jewelry worn on ear

**earshot** *n* **within/out of earshot** within/out of range of audibility

**earth** *n* **1** planet inhabited by man **2** land; soil **3** lair of fox **4** conductor of electricity to earth; *v* connect electric wire with earth; *adj* **earthly** belonging to earth

**earthenware** *n* coarse pottery

**earthquake** *n* tremor of earth's surface

**earthworm** *n* burrowing worm

**earwig** *n* small insect with pincers at rear

**ease** *n* **1** comfort **2** absence of difficulty; *v* relieve pain, anxiety, strain

> **ease** *n* **1** (comfort) calmness, contentment, enjoyment, happiness, leisure, peace, relaxation, serenity, tranquillity. **2** (absence of difficulty) casualness, dexterity, easiness, effortlessness, nonchalance

**easel** *n* frame to hold paintings, blackboard

**east** *n* one of four cardinal points; part of horizon where sun rises; eastern countries; *adj* situated in, coming from east; *adjs* **easterly** from, to east; **eastern** of living in the east; *adj, adv* **eastward** toward east

**Easter** *n* annual festival commemorating Resurrection

**easy** *adj* **1** not difficult **2** without problems

> **easy** *adj* **1** (not difficult) cushy *inf*, light, simple, soft, straightforward, undemanding. **2** (without problems) carefree, comfortable, cozy, peaceful, pleasant, troublefree, uncomplicated,

**eat** *v* **eating, ate, eaten 1** partake of food **2** consume **3** corrode

> **eat** *v* **1** (partake of food) bolt, chew, consume, devour, digest, gobble, graze *inf*, munch, nibble, put away *inf*, stuff yourself *inf*, swallow, wolf

**eating disorder** *n* illness characterized by compulsive dieting or overeating
**eau de cologne** *n Fr* scented toilet water
**eaves** *n pl* projecting edge of roof
**eavesdrop** *v* listen secretly
**ebb** *n* going out of tide; *idm* **at a low ebb** depressed; *v* **1** flow back **2** decrease
**ebony** *n* hard, black wood; jet black color
**ebullient** *adj* exuberant; *n* **ebullience** act of boiling over, exuberance
**eccentric** *adj* unconventional

> **eccentric** *adj* bizarre, cranky, dotty, freakish, idiosyncratic, irregular, nutty, odd, peculiar, strange, uncommon, unusual, weird

**ecclesiastic(al)** *adj* relating to church or clergy; *n* clergyman
**echo** *n* **1** reflected sounds **2** imitation; *pl* **echoes;** *v* **-oing; -oed** reverberate; imitate
**éclair** *n Fr* finger-shaped iced cake
**eclectic** *adj* selecting from many sources, not exclusive; *n* philosopher who collects doctrines
**eclipse** *n* obscuring of light of sun, moon by another heavenly body
**ecology** *n* study of relation of living things to the environment; *adj* **ecological;** *n* **ecologist**
**economical** *adj* **1** cheap **2** careful with money

> **economical** *adj* **1** (cheap) cost-effective, efficient, inexpensive, money-saving, time-saving. **2** (careful with money) careful, economizing, frugal, mean, miserly, parsimonious, prudent, scrimping, sparing, thrifty

**economics** *n pl* scientific study of production and distribution of wealth
**economize** *v* cut down expenses
**economy** *n* management of affairs of household or state; avoidance of waste; *n* **economist** student of economics
**ecosystem** *n* ecological unit with all forms of life that interact within it
**ecstasy** *n* **1** great joy **2** stimulant drug; *adj* **ecstatic**
**eczema** *n* inflammatory disease of skin
**eddy** *n* **eddies** small whirlpool; spiral current of air, etc
**edge** *n* **1** boundary **2** cutting side of knife, etc; *idm* **have the edge on** be (slightly) superior (to); *idm* **on edge** nervous; *adj* **edgy** nervous

> **edge** *n* (boundary) border, brim, brink, circumference, fringe, limit, line, lip, margin, outline, perimeter, periphery, rim, side, threshold, verge

**edible** *adj* suitable, wholesome to eat
**edict** *n* formal order
**edifice** *n* large building
**edit** *v* prepare for publication, broadcasting; direct policies of editing; *ns* **editor; edition** one of several forms in which a book, etc. is published; total number of copies published at one time; **editorial** leading article; *adj* **editorial** of editor

> **edit** *v* adapt, amend, annotate, arrange, assemble, censor, check, compile, correct, polish, prepare, rephrase, revise, rewrite

**educate** *v* **1** teach **2** cultivate mind; *n* **education;** *adj* **educational;** *n* **educationalist** expert in teaching

> **educate** *v* **1** (teach) coach, discipline, drill, indoctrinate, inform, instruct, lecture, nurture, prepare, school, train, tutor. **2** (cultivate mind) civilize, cultivate, develop, edify, enlighten, inform

**educated** *adj* knowledgeable

> **educated** *adj* civilized, cultivated, cultured, enlightened, informed, learned, literate, well-informed, well read

**eel** *n* long snakelike fish
**eerie, eery** *adj* strange and frightening
**effect** *v* cause; bring about; *n* 1 result 2 mental impression

> **effect** *n* 1 (result) aftermath, conclusion, consequence, outcome, repercussion, upshot. 2 (mental impression) feeling, illusion, impression, sensation, sense

**effective** *adj* 1 producing good result 2 working well 3 in force

> **effective** *adj* 1 (producing good result) compelling, convincing, impressive, moving, noticeable, persuasive, powerful, striking, strong. 2 (working well) capable, competent, efficacious, efficient, powerful, productive, strong, successful, useful. 3 (in force) active, current, valid

**effeminate** *adj* unmanly, weak, womanish

> **effeminate** *adj* feminine, girlish, wimpish *inf*, womanly

**effervesce** *v* 1 bubble 2 be excited *adj* **effervescent**
**efficacy** *n* effectiveness; *adj* **efficacious** having desired effect
**efficient** *adj* 1 working well 2 not wasteful; *n* **efficiency**

> **efficient** *adj* 1 (working well) able, businesslike, capable, competent, effective, organized, productive. 2 (not wasteful) cost-effective, economic, effective, productive, profitable

**effigy** *n* image; representation

**effluent** *n* liquid sewage
**effort** *n* 1 exertion 2 attempt; *adj* **effortless**

> **effort** *n* 1 (exertion) application, challenge, diligence, endeavor, energy, force, labor, muscle, power, strain, stress, struggle, trouble, work. 2 (try) attempt, crack, shot, stab

**effrontery** *n* impudence, audacity
**eg** *abbr Lat* exempli gratia (for example)
**egalitarian** *n, adj* (person) concerned with social equality; *n* **-ism**
**egg** *n* oval body, containing embryo, reptile, etc; female cell for producing young
**ego** *n* conscious awareness of self; *ns* **egoism** selfishness; **egoist**; *adj* **egoistic(al)**; *ns* **egotism** self-conceit; **egotist**; *adj* **egotistical** conceited
**eider** *n* arctic sea-duck; *n* **eiderdown** soft down of eider; comforter stuffed with this
**eight** *n, pron, det, dets* cardinal number, one above seven; *n* crew of eight-oar boat; *adjs, ns* **eighth** ordinal number; eighth part; **eighteen** eight plus ten; **eighteenth**; **eighty** eight tens; **eightieth**
**either** *adj, pron* one of two; *adv, conj* choice of
**ejaculate** *v* 1 exclaim 2 eject (semen)
**eject** *v* 1 expel from place 2 emit

> **eject** *v* 1 (expel from place) banish, boot out, chuck out, deport, discharge, dismiss, evict, exile, expel, get rid of, kick out, oust, remove, sack, throw out, turn out. 2 (emit) disgorge, excrete, expel, exude, release, send out, shoot out, spew, spout, throw out, vomit

**elaborate** *v* add detail to; *adj* complicated

> **elaborate** *v* amplify, develop, embellish, expand, fill out, flesh out, improve, polish
> **elaborate** *adj* careful, complex, detailed, exact, exhaustive, fancy, fussy, intricate, involved, painstaking, precise, thorough

**elapse** *v* (of time) pass

**elastic** *adj* resuming normal shape after stretching; *n* fabric having rubber woven in it

> **elastic** *adj* bendy, bouncy, flexible, plastic, pliable, resilient, rubbery, springy, stretchy, supple, yielding

**elasticity** *n* resilience

**elated** *adj* very happy; in high spirits; *n* **elation** exaltation, high spirits

**elbow** *n* joint between forearm and upper arm; *v* push, jostle with elbows

**elder** *adj* (*comp* of **old**) older; as **elderly** growing old; (*sup* of **old**) **eldest** oldest

**elder** *n* tree having white flowers and producing small black berries

**elect** *v* choose by voting; *adj* selected, but not yet in office; *ns* **election; elector; electorate** body of voters; *adj* **electoral**

> **elect** *v* adopt, appoint, choose, decide upon, nominate, pick, select, vote for

**electricity** *n* form of energy, produced by friction, magnetism, etc; supply of electrical current, for lighting, etc; *adj* **electric(al)**; *n* **electrician** mechanic who works with electricity

**electrocardiogram** *n* tracing of electrical activity of the heart; *n* **electrocardiograph** instrument for doing this (*abbr* **ECG**)

**electrocute** *v* kill by electricity

**electrode** *n* either of a pair of conductors of electric current

**electromagnet** *n* iron or steel core with wire wound round that becomes magnetic when electric current is passed through it

**electron** *n* particle of matter bearing negative charge, revolving round atom

**electronic** *adj* related to, operated by movement of electrons, by electric current

**electronic mail** *n* transmission of information between computer terminals (*abbr* **E-mail**)

**electronics** *n* study of behavior of electrons and application of this to technology

**elegant** *adj* graceful; *n* **elegance**

> **elegant** *adj* beautiful, chic, debonair, fashionable, genteel, refined, sophisticated, stylish, suave, tasteful

**elegy** *n* song of mourning, sad poem; *adj* **elegiac** mournful

**element** *n* basic constituent; natural, suitable environment; *pl* **the elements 1** basic facts of subject **2** (inhospitable) weather

**elementary** simple

> **elementary** *adj* basic, easy, plain, rudimentary, straightforward, understandable

**elephant** *n* very large mammal with trunk and ivory tusks

**elevate** *v* lift, raise up; exalt

**eleven** *n, pron, det* cardinal number one above ten; team of eleven players; *adj, det* **eleventh** ordinal number of eleven

**elf** *n* small woodland sprite; *pl* **elves**

**elicit** *v* bring, draw out (information), obtain

**eligible** *adj* qualified to be chosen

> **eligible** *adj* acceptable, allowed, authorized, fit, qualified, suitable, suited, worthy

**eliminate** *v* remove; *n* **elimination**

> **eliminate** *v* cut out, exclude, get rid of, leave out, reject, take out

**elite** *n* select body of persons, aristocracy

**elixir** *n* powerful invigorating remedy

**ellipsis** *n* omission of word, usually understood, from sentence

**elm** *n* kind of deciduous tree; its wood

**elocution** *n* art and manner of speaking

**elongate** *v* make longer

**elope** *v* run away secretly, with lover, *esp* in order to marry; *n* **elopement**

**eloquent** *a* fluent in speech;
*n* **eloquence**

> **eloquent** *adj* articulate, graceful, moving, persuasive, plausible, powerful, well-expressed

**else** *adv* besides; instead; otherwise;
*adv* **elsewhere** in, to, another place
**elucidate** *v* explain, make clear
**elude** *v* dodge, baffle; *adj* **elusive** evasive; difficult to catch, to remember
**elves** *pl of* **elf**
**emaciated** *adj* very thin
**E-mail** *abbr* electronic mail
**emanate** *v* issue forth; originate from
**emancipate** *v* set free; *n* **-ation** freedom
**embalm** *v* preserve corpse from decay, by use of preservatives; *n* **-ment**
**embankment** *n* artificial bank carrying road, railway, etc or damming water
**embargo** *n* order prohibiting movement of ships; official ban on trade, etc

> **embargo** *n* ban, bar, boycott, prohibition, restriction, seizure, stoppage

**embark** *v* 1 go on board ship 2 start

> **embark** *v* 1 (board a ship) board, go on board, go aboard. 2 (start) begin, enter into, go into, set about, set out, take on, undertake, venture into

**embarrass** *v* shame; *n* **-ment**

> **embarrass** *v* fluster, humiliate, make sb feel awkward, mortify, show up

**embarrassed** *adj* ashamed

> **embarrassed** *adj* awkward, blushing, flustered, humiliated, mortified, red, red-faced, self-conscious, shamefaced, sheepish

**embarrassing** *adj* causing shame

> **embarrassing** *adj* awkward, humiliating, mortifying, tricky, uncomfortable

**embassy** *n* residence of ambassador
**embed** *v* **-bedding, bedded** implant deeply, firmly
**embellish** *v* adorn, improve
**embers** *n pl* glowing ashes; cinders
**embezzle** *v* steal money in trust
**emblem** *n* badge, symbol
**embody** *v* represent; *n* **embodiment**
**embrace** *v* 1 hug 2 include; *n* hug

> **embrace** *v* 1 (hug) clasp, cuddle, fold sb in your arms, hold. 2 (include) comprise, embody, encompass, incorporate, take in, subsume

**embroider** *v* ornament with needlework;
*n* **embroidery**
**embroil** *v* involve in quarrel, confusion
**embryo** *n* **-bryos** unborn, not fully developed animal; any rudimentary object, idea, etc
**emerald** *n* bright green precious stone; this color
**emerge** *v* 1 come into view 2 become apparent; *n* **emergence**

> **emerge** *v* 1 (come into view) appear, come out, emanate, materialize, surface. 2 (become apparent) arise, become known, crop up, come out, come to light, develop, get around, transpire, turn out

**emergency** *n* crisis

> **emergency** *n* accident, danger, disaster, fix, hole, predicament, red alert

**emeritus** *n* title given to retired professor, etc
**emery board** *n* paper coated with ground emery, used for filing nails
**emigrate** *v* leave one's country to live in another; *ns* **-ation**; **emigrant**

**éminence grise** n Fr person who secretly wields great influence

**eminent** adj famous, outstanding

> **eminent** adj celebrated, distinguished, esteemed, important, notable, prominent, renowned, respected

**emit** v **emitting, emitted** give out, send out; ns **emissary, emission** one sent on mission

**emote** v display exaggerated emotion

**emotion** n strong feelings

> **emotion** n excitement, feeling, fervor, passion, sentiment

**emotional** adj showing or feeling strong emotions

> **emotional** adj ardent, demonstrative, excitable, fervent, fiery, heated, hot-blooded, impassioned, poignant, sensitive, sentimental, warm

**emotive** adj stimulating emotion

**empathy** n ability to identify with another person's feelings; v **empathize**

**emperor** n ruler of an empire

**emphasis** n special importance

> **emphasis** n attention, force, importance, priority, significance, stress, weight

**emphasize** v give special importance to

> **emphasize** v accentuate, bring out, feature, focus on, highlight, stress, underline

**emphatic** adj definite; adv **-ally**

**emphysema** n med disease of lungs affecting breathing

**empire** n (group of states, under) supreme rule (of an emperor.)

**empirical** adj (of knowledge) based on experience and observation, not theory

**employ** v 1 hire 2 use

> **employ** v 1 (hire) commission, engage, put on the payroll, recruit, sign up, take on. 2 (use) exercise, make use of

**employee** n one employed by another

**employer** n one who employs another

**employment** n work; use of

> **employment** n business, job, livelihood, living, occupation, profession, trade, vocation

**emporium** n **-s** or **-ia** large general store

**empower** v authorize, enable

**empress** n 1 female ruler of empire 2 wife of emperor

**empty** adj **-tier, -tiest** 1 containing nothing 2 pointless; v **-tying, -tied** make empty; n **emptiness**

> **empty** adj 1 (containing nothing) bare, barren, blank, clear, deserted, unfilled, vacant, with nothing inside. 2 (pointless) futile, hollow, meaningless, purposeless, senseless, trivial, worthless

**emu** n large flightless Australian bird

**emulate** v try to equal; imitate

**emulsion** n globules of one liquid suspended in another; v **emulsify**

**enable** v make able; empower; give means to

> **enable** v allow, authorize, entitle, equip, facilitate, make sth possible, open the way for, prepare, qualify

**enamel** n hard, glossy coating, paint, used to preserve surface; outer coating of tooth

**enamored (with)** adj very fond (of)

> **enamored** adj besotted, captivated, infatuated, in love, keen on, smitten

**encapsulate** n summarize

**A B C D E F G H I J K L M N O P Q R S T U V W X Y Z**

**encase** *v* cover entirely
**encephalitis** *n* inflammation of the brain
**enchanted** *adj* 1 delighted 2 under spell

> **enchanted** *adj* 1 (delighted) bewitched, captivated, charmed, entranced, fascinated, spellbound. 2 (under spell) charmed, magic, magical

**enchanting** *adj* delightful

> **enchanting** *adj* alluring, attractive, captivating, charming, fascinating

**encircle** *v* surround; form circle round
**enclave** *n* district surrounded by foreign territory
**enclose** *v* surround completely; insert
**encore** *n* call for repetition (of song, etc); repetition; *v* ask for encore
**encounter** *v* meet face to face; *n* meeting

> **encounter** *v* be faced with, bump into, come across, come up against, confront, meet, run into

**encourage** *v* support

> **encourage** *v* be conducive to, bolster, buoy up, cheer on, foster, give courage to, give hope to, inspire, reassure, spur on, stimulate, strengthen, urge

**encouragement** *n* support
**encouraging** *adj* reassuring

> **encouraging** *adj* heartening, hopeful, inspiring, optimistic, promising, supportive, uplifting

**encroach** *v* advance on; trespass
**encyclopedia** *n* book, set of books, of information on one or all subjects
**end** *n* 1 stopping 2 edge 3 death 4 aim; *v* 1 stop 2 finish; *idm* **put an end to** terminate; *phr v* **end up** finish

**end** *n* 1 (stopping) cessation, climax, close, completion, conclusion, culmination, finale, finish. 2 (edge) boundary, extent, limit, margin, terminus, tip. 3 (death) curtains *inf*, demise, destruction, downfall, extermination, extinction, ruin. 4 (aim) goal, intention, motive, objective, purpose
**end** *v* 1 (stop) abolish, conclude, finish, halt, phase out, terminate, wind up. 2 (finish) break off, cease, close, conclude, culminate, stop, terminate

**endearing** *adj* lovely
**endeavor** *v* try hard; *n* vigorous effort
**endemic** *adj* (of disease) regularly occurring in an area
**endive** *n* kind of chicory, used in salads
**endless** *adj* never ending

> **endless** *adj* continual, continuous, everlasting, incessant, interminable, limitless, nonstop, perpetual, unbroken, unending

**endorse** *v* 1 give approval to 2 write name on back of (document, etc.)
**endure** *v* 1 tolerate 2 last; *n* **endurance**

> **endure** *v* 1 (tolerate) bear, cope with, face, go through, put up with, stand, stick. 2 (last) carry on, continue, exist, live, persist, prevail, survive

**enema** *n* liquid medicine for the bowels
**enemy** *n* hostile person

> **enemy** *n* adversary, foe, rival, the opposition

**energetic** *adj* full of strength and activity

> **energetic** *adj* active, animated, brisk, dynamic, forceful, hard-working, lively, spirited, tireless, vigorous

**energy** *n* power; strength
**enforce** *v* demand, insist on
**enfranchise** *v* grant right to vote
**engage** *v* 1 employ 2 occupy attention of 3 join in battle; *idm* **engage in** take part in
**engaged** *adj* 1 busy 2 promised in marriage to sb; *n* **-ment** betrothal

**engaged** *adj* 1 (busy) occupied, tied up, unavailable. 2 (promised in marriage) betrothed, spoken for

**engender** *v* cause; arouse, stir up
**engine** *n* any machine converting physical force into mechanical energy
**engineer** *n* one skilled in mechanical science; *v* cause to happen

**engineer** *n* architect, designer, mechanic, planner, technician
**engineer** *v* bring about, create, devise, effect, manage, mastermind, orchestrate, plan

**engineering** *n* practical application of physics, chemistry, etc
**English** *adj, n* relating to England; language, people of England
**engrave** *v* cut lines or pattern in; *ns* **engraving** print taken from engraved plate; **engraver**

**engrave** *v* carve, chisel, cut, etch, gouge, inscribe, scratch

**engrossed** *adj* absorbed

**engrossed** *adj* fascinated, immersed, intent, involved, preoccupied, rapt, riveted, wrapped up

**engulf** *v* overwhelm
**enhance** *v* add to, improve
**enigma** *n* mystery
**enigmatic** *adj* mysterious
**enjoy** *v* gain pleasure from; *idm* **enjoy oneself** have fun

**enjoy** *v* (gain pleasure from) adore, get a kick out of, like, love, relish, revel in

**enjoyable** *adj* giving pleasure

**enjoyable** *adj* brilliant, entertaining, fun, good, good fun, great, lovely, nice, pleasant, super, superb, wonderful

**enjoyment** *n* pleasure

**enjoyment** *n* amusement, delight, entertainment, fun, gratification, joy, relish, satisfaction

**enlarge** *v* make larger; *phr v* **enlarge upon** explain in detail

**enlarge** *v* add to, blow up, broaden, deepen, expand, extend, increase, inflate, lengthen, let out, magnify, stretch, widen

**enlighten** *v* make meaning clear to
**enlist** *v* get help or support of
**enmity** *n* hatred
**enormity** *n* seriousness
**enormous** *adj* huge; *adv* **-ly**

**enormous** *adj* astronomic, big, colossal, excessive, giant, gigantic, immense, jumbo, mammoth, massive, vast

**enough** *adj* as much as necessary

**enough** *adj* adequate, ample, as much as you need, plenty, sufficient

**enrapture** *v* delight; entrance with joy
**enrich** *v* make richer
**enroll** *v* **-rolling, -rolled** register name on list as member; *n* **-ment**
**en route** *adv* Fr on the way
**ensemble** *n* parts considered as whole; *mus* combination of soloists and chorus
**ensign** *n* naval, military flag

Alphabet sidebar: a b c d **e** f g h i j k l m n o p q r s t u v w x y z

A
B
C
D
**E**
F
G
H
I
J
K
L
M
N
O
P
Q
R
S
T
U
V
W
X
Y
Z

**enslave** *v* reduce to slavery
**ensnare** *v* entangle, catch in trap
**ensue** *v* follow
**ensure** *v* guarantee

> **ensure** *v* certify, confirm, make certain, make sure, secure

**en suite** *adv Fr* forming a unit
**ENT** *abbr med* ear, nose, and throat
**entail** *v* necessitate
**entangle** *v* involve; entrap
**entente** *n* friendly understanding, *esp* between nations
**enter** *v* **1** go inside **2** add (information) **3** become member

> **enter** *v* **1** (go inside) board, come in, get into, get onto, go in, penetrate. **2** (add information) add, document, log, note, put down, register, take down, write down, write in. **3** (become member) enlist, enroll, go in for, join, participate in, sign up for, take part in

**enterprise** *n* plan, project, *esp* daring, difficult venture; ability to take initiative; *adj* **enterprising**
**entertain** *v* amuse

> **entertain** *v* divert, keep sb happy, keep sb's attention, occupy

**entertainer** *n* one who performs to amuse
**entertaining** *a* amusing

> **entertaining** *adj* diverting, funny, hilarious, interesting, witty

**entertainment** *n* amusement

> **entertainment** *n* distraction, diversion, enjoyment, fun, pleasure, treat

**enthralled** *adj* completely absorbed
**enthrone** *v* put on throne

**enthusiasm** *n* great eagerness and energy

> **enthusiasm** *n* commitment, eagerness, excitement, exuberance, fervor, gusto, keenness, passion, relish

**enthusiast** *n* someone very keen on sth
**enthusiastic** *adj* keen

> **enthusiastic** *adj* avid, crazy *inf*, eager, excited, fanatical, mad about, passionate, vehement, wholehearted

**entice** *v* attract, allure, tempt
**entire** *adj* whole, complete, perfect; *adv* **entirely**
**entitle** *v* give right, claim to; *n* **-ment**
**entity** *n* real thing in itself; being, existence
**entomology** *n* study of insects
**entourage** *n* group of associates
**entrails** *n pl* internal organs
**entrance** *n* **1** way in **2** admission **3** act of entering

> **entrance** *n* **1** (way in) access point, door, doorway, entry, foyer, gate, gateway, lobby, mouth, opening, portal, threshold, way in. **2** (admission) access, admittance, entry, right of entry

**entrant** *n* person entering race, competition
**entreat** *v* beg earnestly; *n* **entreaty** urgent request
**entrenched** *adj* firmly established
**entrepreneur** *n Fr* person organizing commercial venture, *esp* with risk
**entrust** *v* give into care of; charge with
**entry** *n* **1** way in **2** admission **3** act of entering

> **entry** *n* **1** (way in) access point, door, doorway, entrance, foyer, gate, gateway, lobby, opening, threshold, way in. **2** (admission) access, admittance, entrance, right of entry

**entwine** v twist together; wind one round the other

**enumerate** v count

**enunciate** v say, speak clearly

**envelop** v **enveloping**, **enveloped** wrap round, obscure

**envelope** n outer covering, *esp* of paper for enclosing letters, etc; wrapper

**enviable** adj to be envied

**envious** adj full of envy

> **envious** adj green-eyed, green with envy, jealous, resentful

**environs** n pl immediate surroundings

**environment** n conditions of life; surroundings; adj **-mental**; n **-mentalist** person concerned with protecting, improving the environment

> **environment** n conditions, context, environs, habitat, locale, locality, milieu, setting, situation

**envisage** v visualize; contemplate

**envoy** n one sent as representative

> **envoy** n agent, ambassador, consul, delegate, emissary, go-between, intermediary, messenger, representative

**envy** n jealousy; v feel jealous of another's success, possessions, etc

> **envy** n enviousness, resentfulness, resentment

**enzyme** n chemical ferment

**epaulet, epaulette** n *mil* shoulder decoration

**ephemeral** adj of short duration

**epic** n long, narrative poem; book or film

**epicene** adj having characteristics of both sexes

**epicenter** n center of earthquake

**epicure** n person who enjoys good food and drink

**epidemic** adj (of disease) prevalent in one community; n such disease

> **epidemic** adj global, pandemic, prevalent, rampant, rife, spreading, sweeping, universal, widespread
> **epidemic** n outbreak, plague, rash, scourge, wave

**epidural** n *med* anesthetic injected into spine, *esp* to counter pain during childbirth

**epigram** n brief, pointed, witty saying

**epilepsy** n medical condition characterized by fits and unconsciousness; adj **epileptic**

**epilogue** n concluding lines of play or book

**episcopal** adj relating to bishop

**episode** n 1 event 2 installment of story

> **episode** 1 n (event) affair, chapter, escapade, experience, incident, interlude, matter, occasion, occurrence.
> 2 (installment) edition, part, scene, section

**epitaph** n memorial inscribed on tomb

**epitome** n thing that embodies a quality

**epoch** n period of time

**equable** adj steady, uniform; unvarying

**equal** adj 1 similar 2 even 3 fair; n one having same rank, qualities, etc as another; v be equal to

> **equal** adj 1 (similar) alike, comparable, identical, equivalent, on a par, the same, uniform. 2 (even) evenly matched, fifty-fifty, level, neck-and-neck. 3 (fair) egalitarian, even-handed, impartial, just, unbiased

**equality** n condition of being equal

> **equality** n egalitarianism, equal opportunity, fairness, impartiality, justice

**equalize** v make even or fair

**equanimity** n tranquillity; composure

A
B
C
D
**E**
F
G
H
I
J
K
L
M
N
O
P
Q
R
S
T
U
V
W
X
Y
Z

**equate** *v* consider as equal; reduce to common standard; associate; *n* **equation** *math* statement of equality between known and unknown quantities

**equator** *n* imaginary circle dividing earth into two equal parts

**equestrian** *adj* relating to horseback riding; *n* horseman

**equidistant** *adj* equally distant

**equilibrium** *n* state of perfect balance

> **equilibrium** *n* balance, evenness, stability, symmetry

**equine** *adj* of or like a horse

**equinox** *n* time of year when day and night are of equal length

**equip** *v* **equipping, equipped** provide with kit or supplies

> **equip** *v* arm, fit out, furnish, kit out, prepare, provide, supply

**equipment** *n* kit, machinery needed for task

> **equipment** *n* apparatus, gear, instruments, machinery, materials, rig, stuff, supplies, tackle, things, tools, trappings

**equitable** *adj* just, reasonable

**equivalent** *adj* equal in value, amount, meaning, etc

> **equivalent** *adj* alike, analogous, comparable, corresponding, equal, identical, interchangeable, similar

**equivocal** *adj* not certain

**era** *n* period of time; epoch

**eradicate** *v* destroy completely

> **eradicate** *v* abolish, annihilate, destroy, eliminate, expunge, exterminate, get rid of, obliterate, remove, root out, stamp out, take out, weed out, wipe out

**erase** *v* rub out; *n* **eraser**

> **erase** *v* cancel, cross out, delete, remove, scratch out, scrub out, wipe out

**erect** *v* set upright; build; *adj* upright; *n* **erection**

**erg** *n* unit of work, energy

**ERM** *n* Exchange Rate Mechanism

**ermine** *n* common stoat in winter coat; such fur

**erode** *v* wear away; *n* **erosion**

> **erode** *v* abrade, corrode, eat away, rub away, wash away, weather

**erotic** *adj* pertaining to sexual desire, love

**err** *v* go astray, make mistakes, be wrong

**errand** *n* short journey undertaken to perform a task

**erratic** *adj* irregular

> **erratic** *adj* changeable, chaotic, fickle, inconsistent, meandering, sporadic, unpredictable, unreliable

**erroneous** *adj* mistaken, incorrect

**error** *n* mistake

> **error** *n* blunder, boo-boo *inf*, bug, fault, gaffe, howler, miscalculation, misprint, oversight, slip-up *inf*

**erudite** *adj* learned; *n* **erudition** learning

**erupt** *v* burst out, become active; *n* **eruption** bursting out, *esp* of volcano

**escalate** *v* increase by stages

> **escalate** *v* accelerate, climb, get worse, grow, heighten, increase, intensify, mount, rise, spiral, step up

**escalator** *n* moving stairway

**escapade** *n* daring adventure, prank

**escape** *v* 1 get free 2 avoid 3 leak; *n* 1 evasion of capture 2 leak

**escape** *v* 1 (get free) abscond, bolt, break loose, break out, flit, get away, get out, run away, run off. 2 (avoid) dodge, duck, evade. 3 (leak) bleed, discharge, drain, ooze, seep

**escarpment** *n* steep hillside, inland cliff
**eschew** *v* shun, avoid
**ESL** *abbr* English as a Second Language
**escort** *v* accompany; *n* person, persons escorting another

**escort** *v* conduct, go with, guide, lead, partner, shepherd, take
**escort** *n* attendant, bodyguard, chaperon, companion, date, entourage, guard, outrider, partner, retinue

**especially** *adv* in particular
**espionage** *n* spying
**esplanade** *n* leveled terrace, *esp* promenade along sea front
**espouse** *v* support (a cause, etc)
**espresso** *n* **-os** strong black coffee
**esquire** *n* title of respect used on letter, abbreviated to Esq
**essay** *n* piece of discursive writing; *n* **essayist**

**essay** *n* article, assignment, comment, composition, critique, paper, piece, treatise, review, writings

**essence** *n* 1 most important quality 2 extract from plant; *idm* **of the essence** vitally important
**essential** *adj* vitally important

**essential** *adj* critical, crucial, important, indispensable, key, necessary, vital. 2 basic, cardinal, fundamental, inherent, intrinsic, principal

**establish** *v* 1 set up 2 prove; *n* **establishment** act of establishing; household; permanent civil, military force

**establish** *v* 1 (set up) create, form, found, put in place, start. 2 (prove) confirm, demonstrate, show, verify

**established** *adj* accepted

**established** *adj* deep-rooted, entrenched, ingrained, long-standing, orthodox, official, settled, traditional

**estate** *n* property, possessions
**estate car** *n* car with rear doors and luggage area behind folding seats
**esteem** *v* consider highly; *n* respect
**estimate** *v* 1 guess cost 2 believe; *n* calculation of approx. cost

**estimate** *v* 1 (guess cost) assess, calculate, evaluate, gauge, judge, reckon, value, work out. 2 (believe) appraise, assess, consider, judge, rate, reckon, surmise, think, view
**estimate** *n* approximation, assessment, ballpark figure, calculation, guess, guesstimate *inf*, reckoning, rough figure

**estimation** *n* opinion; esteem
**estrange** *v* alienate; hurt feelings of; *n* **estrangement** decrease in affection
**estuary** *n* mouth of river, where tide enters
**ETA** *abbr* Estimated Time of Arrival
**etc** *abbr* et cetera (and the rest)
**etch** *v* make designs on metal, by eating away by acid; *n* **etching**
**eternal** *adj* 1 everlasting 2 constant

**eternal** *adj* 1 (everlasting) abiding, deathless, immortal, infinite, permanent, perpetual, timeless, unceasing, undying, without end. 2 (constant) ceaseless, continual, continuous, endless, incessant, interminable, never-ending, nonstop, perpetual, unending

**eternity** *n* the afterlife, very long time

a b c d e f g h i j k l m n o p q r s t u v w x y z

A
B
C
D
E
F
G
H
I
J
K
L
M
N
O
P
Q
R
S
T
U
V
W
X
Y
Z

**ethical** *adj* moral

> **ethical** *adj* correct, decent, fair, good,
> honest, honorable, just, principled,
> proper, right, upright, virtuous

**ethics** *n pl* system of morally correct conduct
**ethnic** *adj* of race
**ethos** *n fml* characteristic spirit or ideas
**etiquette** *n Fr* 1 politeness 2 convention

> **etiquette** *n* 1 (politeness) civility, courtesy,
> decorum, good manners, propriety.
> 2 (convention) code of behavior, code of
> conduct, code of practice, custom,
> manners, propriety, protocol, the
> proprieties

**etymology** *n* branch of philology dealing with
derivation of words
**eucalyptus** *n* genus of Australasian trees,
yielding pungent, volatile oil
**eulogy** *n* praise, written or spoken
**eunuch** *n* castrated man
**euphemism** *n* mild word used in place of
unpleasant one; *adj* **euphemistic**
**euphoria** *n* great happiness; *adj* **euphoric**
**eureka** *interj* expressing triumph of discovery
**European** *n, adj* (inhabitant) of Europe
**euthanasia** *n* deliberate killing of one with
incurable illness to avoid suffering
**evacuate** *v* withdraw from; *ns* **evacuation**

> **evacuate** *v* abandon, desert, flee, go away
> from, leave, move out of, pull out of *inf*,
> quit, retreat from, vacate

**evade** *v* 1 avoid 2 not answer (question);
*n* **evasion** avoidance

> **evade** *v* 1 (avoid) dodge, elude, escape, give
> sb the slip, shake off, sidestep, steer clear
> of. 2 (not answer a question) avoid, beat
> about the bush, dodge, equivocate, fudge,
> hedge, prevaricate

**evaluate** *v* find value of; appraise
**evangelic, evangelical** *adj* of, based on the
Gospels; *n* **evangelism** spreading of the
Gospel
**evaporate** *v* turn into vapor; expel moisture,
by heating; *n* **-ation**
**evasive** *adj* 1 avoiding sth in cunning way
2 not clear or direct

> **evasive** *adj* 1 (avoiding sth in cunning
> way) artful, cagey *inf*, cunning, devious,
> disingenuous, elusive, shifty. 2 (not clear
> or direct) ambiguous, disingenuous,
> equivocal, indirect, misleading, oblique

**eve** *n* evening or day before event
**even** *adj* 1 level 2 constant 3 equal 4 fair
5 divisible by two; *v* 1 make even 2 equalize;
*phr v* **even out** 1 become level 2 become
balanced; *adv* **evenly** 1 smoothly 2 equally

> **even** *adj* 1 (level) flat, flush, horizontal,
> plane, smooth. 2 (constant) consistent,
> regular, stable, steady, unbroken, uniform,
> unvarying. 3 (equal) alike, all square,
> balanced, identical, level, similar, the
> same, tied. 4 (fair) balanced,
> disinterested, equitable, evenhanded,
> impartial, just, unbiased

**evening** *n* part of day between afternoon and
night
**event** *n* 1 incident 2 race, contest

> **event** *n* 1 (incident) episode, experience,
> happening, occasion, occurrence,
> phenomenon. 2 (race, contest)
> competition, fixture, game, match,
> round, tournament

**eventful** *adj* with much happening

> **eventful** *adj* action-packed, active, busy,
> exciting, full, lively, never a dull moment

**eventual** *adj* final

**eventuality** *n* possible event
**eventually** *adv* finally

> **eventually** *adv* after all, at last, at the end
> of the day, in the end, in the long run, in
> time, sooner or later, one day, one fine
> day *inf*, some day, sooner or later

**ever** *adv* at any time; in any degree; *idm* **ever
so/such** extremely
**evergreen** *adj* with green leaves all year
**everlasting** *adj* 1 lasting for ever 2 continual
**every** *adj* each one of all
**everybody** *n* all people
**everyday** *adj* usual
**everyone** *n* all people
**everything** *n* all things
**everywhere** *adv* in all places
**evict** *v* put out of a property; expel by legal
process; *n* **eviction**

> **evict** *v* chuck out, dislodge, dispossess, drive
> out, eject, expel, give notice to quit, kick
> out, oust, put out, remove, show sb the
> door, throw out, turn out

**evidence** *n* 1 supporting facts 2 testimony;
*idm* **(be) in evidence** (be) clearly seen

> **evidence** *n* 1 (supporting facts)
> confirmation, corroboration, data, facts,
> indication, information, mark, proof,
> sign, substantiation, support, verification.
> 2 affidavit, declaration, deposition,
> statement

**evident** *adj* 1 easy to see or understand 2 true

> **evident** *adj* 1 (easy to see or understand)
> apparent, clear, easy to see, manifest,
> noticeable, palpable, perceptible, plain,
> self-explanatory, tangible, transparent,
> unmistakable, visible. 2 (true) clear,
> incontestable, incontrovertible,
> indisputable, obvious, undeniable

**evil** *adj* wicked; *n* evil thing or act

> **evil** *adj* atrocious, bad, base, corrupt, cruel,
> demonic, diabolic, depraved, fiendish,
> foul, immoral, iniquitous, malicious,
> malevolent, shameful, sinful, vicious,
> vile, villainous

**evil eye** *n* power to harm sb by a look
**evince** *v* show, demonstrate
**eviscerate** *v* disembowel
**evoke** *v* 1 cause (response of emotion)
2 bring to mind; *adj* **evocative**

> **evoke** *v* 1 (cause response or emotion)
> arouse, cause, give rise to, induce, inspire,
> kindle, provoke, stimulate, stir up.
> 2 (bring to mind) call to mind, conjure
> up, invoke, inspire, recall, summon up

**evolve** *v* develop naturally; *n* **evolution**
course of development of species

> **evolve** *v* change, develop, grow, expand,
> improve, mature, open out, progress

**ewe** *n* female sheep
**ewer** *n* large water pitcher
**exacerbate** *v* make worse, irritate, embitter;
*n* **-bation** irritate
**exact** *adj* completely accurate; *v* demand,
extort, insist on; *adj* **-ing** severe, exhausting;
*ns* **-itude**, **-ness** accuracy

> **exact** *adj* accurate, careful, correct,
> explicit, faithful, literal, meticulous,
> precise, spot on, strict, true

**exactly** *adv* 1 quite right 2 very carefully

> **exactly** adv 1 (quite right) absolutely,
> certainly, definitely, indeed, precisely,
> quite, quite right, quite so. 2 (carefully)
> accurately, correctly, faithfully, precisely,
> strictly, to the letter, word for word

a b c d **e** f g h i j k l m n o p q r s t u v w x y z

**exaggerate** *v* overemphasize, overstate, enlarge; *n* **-ation** overstatement

**exaggerate** *v* amplify, embellish, embroider, magnify, make a mountain out of a molehill, overrate, stretch the truth

**examination** *n* **1** study **2** careful check **3** questioning of witness **4** test

**examination** *n* **1** (study) appraisal, analysis, consideration, exploration, inspection, investigation, observation, perusal, probe, review, scrutiny. **2** (careful check) checkup, inspection. **3** (questioning of witness) cross-examination, interrogation, questioning. **4** (test) assessment, exam

**examine** *n* **1** study **2** look carefully at **3** question **4** test knowledge of

**examine** *v* **1** (study) analyze, appraise, assess, check out, consider, explore, look into, scrutinize, weigh, weigh up. **2** (look carefully at) check, go over, inspect, look at, look over, observe, peruse, scan, take a look at. **3** (question) cross-examine, grill *inf*, interrogate, test. **4** (test knowledge of) assess

**example** *n* **1** sample **2** model; *idm* **make an example of** single out for reward or punishment to encourage others

**example** *n* **1** (sample) case, case in point, illustration, instance, specimen. **2** (model) ideal, paragon, pattern, standard

**exasperate** *v* make angry, aggravate, provoke; *n* **-ation**; *adj* **-ating** very annoying

**exasperate** *v* anger, annoy, enrage, get on your nerves, incense, infuriate, irk, irritate, madden, needle, rouse, try the patience of, vex, wind up

**Ex Calibur** *n* King Arthur's sword
**excavate** *v* dig out; hollow out; unearth; *ns* **-ation; -ator**
**exceed** *v* go beyond (limit, etc); surpass; *adv* **exceedingly** extremely
**excel** *v* **-celling, -celled** be very good at
**excellency** *n* title given to ambassadors
**excellent** *adj* very good; *n* **excellence**

**excellent** *adj* ace, brilliant, exceptional, exquisite, fabulous, fantastic, great, marvelous, outstanding, perfect, superb, superior, wonderful

**except** *v* exclude; *prep* omitting; *conj* unless
**exception** *n* thing excluded
**exceptional** *adj* **1** unusually good **2** unusual
**excerpt** *n* selected passage, extract from book, etc
**excess** *n* amount, sum over normal, usual quantity, etc; overindulgence
**excessive** *adj* extreme

**excessive** *adj* exaggerated, extravagant, inordinate, lavish, needless, overdone, over the top, superfluous, uncalled-for, unnecessary, unreasonable

**exchange** *v* give (something), receive (another thing) in return; interchange; *n* act of exchanging; place where brokers, merchants transact business
**excise** *n* duty on goods manufactured, consumed within a country
**excitable** *adj* easily excited
**excite** *v* rouse up; agitate; stimulate
**excited** *adj* thrilled

**excited** *adj* agog, animated, aroused, boisterous, enthusiastic, exhilarated, exuberant, high, in high spirits, intoxicated, turned on

**excitement** *n* **1** agitation, animation, anticipation, elation, enthusiasm, tumult **2** adventure, thrill

**exciting** *adj* thrilling

> **exciting** *adj* dramatic, electrifying, exhilarating, fast-moving, gripping, heady, stimulating, stirring

**exclaim** *v* cry out suddenly, loudly; *n* **exclamation** interjection of surprise, etc
**exclamation mark** *n* punctuation mark (!)
**exclude** *v* 1 keep out 2 not include; *n* **exclusion**

> **exclude** *v* 1 (keep out) ban, bar, blacklist, debar, forbid, ignore, leave out, ostracize, prohibit, refuse, reject, shut out. 2 (not include) be aprt from, be exclusive of, except

**exclusive** *adj* limited; selective; *adv* **-ly**
**excommunicate** *v* expel from Church
**excrement** *n* waste matter from bowels; *v* **excrete** discharge waste matter
**excruciating** *adj* acutely painful
**excursion** *n* journey, *esp* pleasure trip; digression
**excuse** *v* 1 forgive 2 overlook (fault, etc); 3 release from obligation; *n* apology; pretext

> **excuse** *v* 1 (forgive) absolve, exonerate, let off, make allowances for, pardon. 2 (overlook) condone, defend, explain, forgive, ignore, justify, pardon. 3 (release from obligation) exempt, free sb from, let sb off, relieve, spare
> **excuse** *n* defense, explanation, justification, mitigation, reason

**execute** *v* 1 perform; carry out 2 kill 3 complete legal instrument; *ns* **execution**, **executioner** one who carries out capital punishment
**executive** *adj* administrative; *n* one charged with administrative work
**exemplar** *n* model, example; *adj* **exemplary** worthy, commendable
**exemplify** *v* **-fying, -fied** serve as example

**exempt** *v* free from duty, obligation; *adj* not liable to; *n* **exemption**
**exercise** *n* healthy physical activity; use of (rights, etc); *mil* maneuvres; *v* 1 do physical activity 2 use

> **exercise** *n* activity, effort, exertion, games, gym, gymnastics, keep fit, movement, sport, training, workout
> **exercise** *v* 1 (do physical activity) do exercises, drill, exert yourself, take exercise, train, work out. 2 (use) apply, employ, exert, practice, utilize

**exert** *v* make an effort; put into action; *n* **exertion** activity, mental or physical
**exhale** *v* breathe out; *n* **exhalation**
**exhaust** *v* 1 tire 2 use up; *n* waste gas, steam discharged from engine

> **exhaust** *v* 1 (tire) debilitate, drain, enervate, fatigue, knock out, ire out, wear out, weary. 2 (use up) consume, deplete, drain, empty, finish off, finish up, run out of, spend, squander, waste

**exhausted** *adj* very tired

> **exhausted** *adj* all in, dead beat, dog-tired, drained, fatigued, ready to drop, shattered, spent, tired out, worn out

**exhaustion** *n* intense fatigue
**exhausting** *adj* very tiring

> **exhausting** *adj* arduous, back-breaking, debilitating, enervating, fatiguing, grueling, laborious, punishing, tiring, taxing, wearing, wearying

**exhaustive** *adj* comprehensive
**exhibit** *v* show in public; give evidence of; *n* thing exhibited, *esp* in museum, or as material evidence in court
**exhibition** *n* display of works of art, etc
**exhilarate** *v* raise spirits of

A
B
C
D
**E**
F
G
H
I
J
K
L
M
N
O
P
Q
R
S
T
U
V
W
X
Y
Z

**exhume** *v* dig up corpse
**exile** *n* 1 banishment 2 one banished;
*v* banish

> **exile** *n* 1 (banishment) deportation,
> explusion, 2 (one banished) deportee,
> displaced person, outcast, refugee
> **exile** *v* bar, deport, drive out, eject, evict,
> expel, send into exile, uproot

**exist** *v* be

> **exist** *v* be found, be in existence, be real,
> happen, live, occur, remain, survive

**existence** *n* 1 fact of living 2 way of life
**exit** *n* 1 act of leaving, going out 2 way out;
*v* leave stage; go out
**exodus** *n* departure, *esp* of many people
**exonerate** *v* free from blame
**exorbitant** *adj* excessive in price
**exorcise** *v* expel (evil spirit)
**exotic** *adj* foreign; rare, unusual
**expand** *v* 1 make bigger 2 become bigger;
*phr v* **expand on** explain in more detail;
*n* **expansion**

> **expand** *v* 1 (make bigger) broaden, build
> up, develop, distend, elaborate, enlarge,
> extend, fill out, increase, inflate, open up,
> widen. 2 (become bigger) grow, increase
> in size, open out, stretch, swell, widen

**expanse** *n* wide, open tract of land
**expect** *v* 1 believe 2 wait for 3 require;
*adj* **expectant** awaiting; *n* **expectation** that
which is expected; future prospects

> **expect** *v* 1 (believe) assume, calculate,
> guess, imagine, presume, suppose, suspect,
> think, think likely, trust. 2 (wait for)
> anticipate, await, be prepared for,
> envisage, foresee, hope for, look forward
> to, predict. 3 (require) call for, consider
> necessary, demand, insist on, want

**expectorate** *v* spit, cought up (phlegm, etc);
*n* **-pation**
**expedient** *adj* suitable, advantageous,
convenient; *n* means to an end;
*n* **expediency** convenience
**expedite** *v* speed up
**expedition** *n* journey for set purpose
**expel** *v* **-pelling, -pelled** 1 send away
2 emit

> **expel** *v* 1 (send sb away) ban, banish, cast
> out, chuck out, deport, drive out, eject,
> evict, exile, kick out, oust, remove, send
> away, throw out, turn out. 2 (emit)
> belch, discharge, eject, force out, give off,
> push out, send out, spew out

**expend** *v* give out, spend, use up
**expendable** *adj* inessential, of little value
**expenditure** *n* amount spent
**expense** *n* cost; *pl* **expenses** costs incurred
**expensive** *adj* costly

> **expensive** *adj* dear, exorbitant,
> extortionate, overpriced, pricey,

**experience** *n* 1 sth that happens to you
2 knowledge gained by doing sth; *v* undergo,
meet with

> **experience** *n* 1 (sth that happens to you)
> encounter, episode, event, incident,
> occurrence, perception, sensation.
> 2 (knowledge gained by doing sth)
> competence, expertise, familiarity,
> grounding, knowledge, maturity, record,
> track record, wisdom

**experienced** *adj* competent through practice

> **experienced** *adj* competent, expert,
> familiar, knowledgeable, mature, wise

**experiment** *n* trial, undertaken to test theory,
discover new facts; *v* make experiments;
*adj* **-al**

**expert** *adj* skilled, dextrous; *n* one having special knowledge; *n* **expertise**

**expert** *adj* adept, advanced, capable, competent, experienced, practiced, proficient, qualified, skillful, specialist
**expert** *n* authority, connoisseur, professional, pundit, specialist

**expiate** *v* atone for, make amends for
**expire** *v* die, come to an end; *n* **expiry** conclusion
**explain** *v* give reasons for, show meaning
**explanation** *n* account giving reasons

**explanation** *n* account, answer, clarification, defense, elucidation, excuse, explication, hypothesis, interpretation, justification, reason, reply

**expletive** *n* exclamation, oath
**explicable** *adj* able to be explained
**explicit** *adj* clearly stated
**explode** *v* 1 burst violently 2 cause to explode

**explode** *v* 1 (burst violently) blow up, burst, erupt, fly apart, go bang, go off, go up, implode. 2 (cause to explode) blast, blow up, detonate, drop, let off, set off, trigger

**exploit** *n* bold, adventurous deed; *v* make unfair use of, *esp* to one's own benefit, develop resources of; *ns* **-ation, -er**
**explore** *v* 1 travel in strange region 2 study; *ns* **exploration; explorer**

**explore** *v* 1 (travel in strange region) discover, journey, look around, travel, visit, voyage. 2 (study) analyze, consider, discuss, examine, go into, investigate, look into, probe, research, survey

**explosion** *n* 1 violent release of energy resulting from a chemical or nuclear reaction 2 sudden increase

**explosion** *n* 1 (violent release of energy) bang, blast, boom, burst, detonation, eruption, gunshot, mushroom cloud, report. 2 (sudden increase) escalation, expansion, flowering, growth, increase, outbreak, mushrooming

**explosive** *n*, *adj* (substance) which explodes; *adv* **-ly**
**exponent** *n* person explaining a belief
**export** *v* send (goods) abroad for trade; *ns* **exportation, exporter**
**expose** *v* lay bare, leave unprotected, display, reveal; *n* **exposure**
**exposé** *n* revealing of wrongdoing
**expostulate** *v* remonstrate, protest against
**expound** *v* explain, set forth; *n* **exponent**
**express** *v* make known by speech, visual image, etc; *adj* explicit; *n* fast train service;

**express** *v* announce, articulate, communicate, convey, declare, describe, display, give vent to, indicate, make known, manifest, put into words, say, show, speak, state, utter, verbalize, voice

**expression** *n* 1 expressing of ideas, emotions 2 group of words 3 look on face

**expression** *n* 1 (expressing of ideas, emotions) announcement, articulation, communication, declaration, demonstration, description, display, exhibition, indication, manifestation, reflection, statement, voicing. 2 (group of words) figure of speech, idiom, phrase, proverb, saying, utterance. 3 (look on face) air, appearance, countenance, face, look, mien

**expressive** *adj* showing emotions
**expulsion** *n* act of expelling
**expurgate** *v* remove offensive material from text (of books, etc)
**exquisite** *adj* extremely beautiful

A
B
C
D
E
F
G
H
I
J
K
L
M
N
O
P
Q
R
S
T
U
V
W
X
Y
Z

**extant** *adj* still surviving, still in existence
**extempore** *adj, adv* without preparation;
*adj* **extemporary**; *v* **extemporize** improvise,
make up speech, song, etc on spur of
moment
**extend** *v* 1 make bigger 2 cover 3 offer

> **extend** *v* 1 (make bigger) add to, augment,
> elongate, enlarge, expand, increase,
> lengthen, prolong, spread, stretch, stretch
> out. 2 (cover) range, reach, span, spread,
> stretch. 3 (offer) advance, give, grant,
> hold out, impart, make available, proffer

**extension** *n* stretching out, expansion,
addition
**extensive** *adj* widespread, comprehensive
**extent** *n* scope

> **extent** *n* area, breadth, dimensions, expanse,
> length, magnitude, range, spread

**extenuate** *v* lessen guilt or blame;
*adj* **extenuating**
**exterior** *adj* outside; external; *n* outward
appearance
**exterminate** *v* wipe out; extirpate; destroy;
*ns* **extermination, exterminator**
**external** *adj* outside; *adv* **-ly**; *v* **externalize**
give outward expression to
**extinct** *adj* 1 having died out 2 inactive
(of volcano); *n* **extinction**

> **extinct** *adj* (having died out) dead, defunct,
> died out, exhausted, extinguished, gone,
> lost, vanished, wiped out

**extinguish** *v* 1 destroy 2 put out;
*n* **extinguisher** device for putting out fire

> **extinguish** *v* 1 (destroy) end, eradicate,
> kill, quench, snuff out, stifle, suppress.
> 2 (put out a fire, light) blow out, put off,
> put out, smother, snuff out, switch off,
> turn off, turn out

**extol** *v* **-tolling, -tolled** praise highly
**extort** *v* obtain money by threats;
*n* **extortion**
**extortionate** *adj* unreasonably expensive
**extra** *adj* additional; *n* 1 something extra;
2 (in a film) walk-on part

> **extra** *adj* added, bonus, further,
> more, supplementary, surplus
> **extra** *n* 1 (something extra) accessory,
> addition, additive, add-on, bonus,
> supplement, surplus. 2 (in a film) bit
> part, chorus girl, non-speaking part

**extract** *v* 1 pull, draw out, *esp* by force
2 select; distill; *n* thing extracted;
*ns* **extraction, extractor**
**extracurricular** *adj* not part of course of
study
**extradition** *n* surrender of an alleged
criminal, by one state to another;
*v* **extradite** give, obtain such surrender
**extramarital** *adj* (of sexual behavior) outside
marriage
**extramural** *adj* outside walls of; associated
with, not taking place in university
**extraneous** *adj* unrelated to, not essential;
foreign
**extraordinary** *adj* exceptional; *adv* **-arily**

> **extraordinary** *adj* amazing, astonishing,
> incredible, marvelous, outstanding, rare,
> remarkable, singular, striking, unique,
> unusual, wonderful

**extrapolate** *v* deduce or guess from known
facts or personal observation
**extrasensory perception** *n* ability to
acquire information not through the physical
senses
**extraterrestrial** *adj* (from) beyond the earth
**extraterritorial** *adj* (from) outside limits,
jurisdiction of country
**extravagant** *adj* excessive; *n* **extravagance**
**extravaganza** *n* elaborate and costly
entertainment

**extreme** *adj* 1 great 2 remote 3 radical;
*adv* **-ly**; *ns* **extremist** one holding extreme
views (in politics); **extremity** boundary,
danger, edge, end, great distress, limit;
*pl* **-ies** hands and feet

> **extreme** *adj* 1 (great) absolute, acute,
> drastic, high, intense, severe, utmost.
> 2 (remote) furthest, furthest away, most
> distant, outer, remotest. 3 (radical)
> drastic, exaggerated, excessive, fanatical,
> harsh, over-the-top, uncompromising,
> unreasonable

**extricate** *v* free from; disentangle;
*n* **extrication**
**extrinsic** *adj* not belonging to; from outside;
*adv* **-ally**
**extrovert** *n* one whose interests are directed
outwards from self; vigorous personality
**extrude** *v* thrust out; expel; *n* **extrusion**
**exuberant** *adj* full of vitality
**exude** *v* ooze out; discharge through pores;
*n* **exudation**
**exult** *v* rejoice greatly, triumph
**exultant** *adj* jubilant
**exultation** *n* great joy
**eye** *n* 1 organ of sight 2 power of observation
3 hole in needle 4 ring for a hook to fit
5 calm spot in center of storm; *idm* **easy
on the eye** good-looking; *idm* **have an eye
for** be capable of judging; *idm* **in the eyes
of** in the opinion of; *idm* **keep an eye on**
watch closely; *idm* **make eyes at** flirt with;
*idm* **see eye to eye** understand one another,
agree; *idm* **up to one's eyeballs in** *coll*
extremely busy with; *idm* **with an eye toward**
1 keeping in mind 2 with the intention of; *v*
**eyeing or eying, eyed** look at, stare at
**eyeball** *n* (*idm* **eyeball to eyeball** *coll* face to
face)
**eye cup** *n* small optic cup for washing or
applying medicine to the eyeball
**eyebrow** *n* ridge of hair above eye
**eyeglasses** *n* lsnzsz aodn fo `ix izion
**eyelash** *n* hair fringing eyelid

**eyelid** *n* skin covering eyeball
**eye-opener** *n* thing, event revealing
surprising new facts
**eye shadow** *n* make-up used on eyelids
**eyesight** *n* power of seeing
**eyesore** *n* ugly object, *esp* spoiling landscape

> **eyesore** *n* blemish, blight, disfigurement,
> monstrosity, scar

**eyewash** *n coll* deceptive nonsense
**eyewitness** *n* person actually present at event
**eyrie** *n* eagle's nest

a
b
c
d
e
f
g
h
i
j
k
l
m
n
o
p
q
r
s
t
u
v
w
x
y
z

A B C D E **F** G H I J K L M N O P Q R S T U V W X Y Z

**fable** n short story with moral; myth; fiction
**fabled** adj legendary
**fabric** n structure, framework; woven cloth
**fabricate** v 1 manufacture 2 invent falsely;
  n **fabrication**
**fabulous** adj 1 wonderful 2 imaginary

> **fabulous** adj 1 (wonderful) brilliant,
> fantastic, good, great, super, superb.
> 2 (imaginary) fantastic, invented,
> legendary, make-believe, mythical

**façade** n Fr front of building; outward
  appearance
**face** n 1 front part of head 2 visual
  expression; v 1 look at 2 look toward
  3 meet in contest 4 deal with; idm **face to
  face** close up; in direct contact, opposition;
  idm **in the face of** (going) against; in spite
  of; idm **on the face of it** judging by
  appearances phr v **face up to** 1 meet
  courageously 2 be realistic about

> **face** v 1 (look at) gaze at, stare at, turn
> to, turn toward. 2 (look toward) be
> opposite, front onto, give onto, have a
> view of, look out on, overlook. 3 (meet
> in contest) be opposed to, confront, meet,
> play, play against. 4 (deal with) accept,
> come to terms with, confront, face up to

**face card** n king, queen, jack in deck of cards

**faceless** adj of unknown identity or character
**face-lift** n plastic surgery to improve face; fig
  (of building) renovation
**face-saver** n thing which saves sb from
  embarrassment; adj **face-saving**
**facet** n aspect, side
**facetious** adj not serious, flippant; adv **-ly**;
  n **-ness**
**face value** n (of money) value shown;
  idm **take sth at its face value** assume sth
  is what it seems to be
**facial** adj of the face; n beauty treatment of
  face
**facile** adj too simple
**facilitate** v make easier
**facility** n ease, dexterity; pl **facilities**
  equipment and resources
**facing** n decorative or protective lining
**facsimile** n exact copy
**fact** n thing known to be true; idm **in fact**
  actually

> **fact** n 1 actuality, certainty, reality, truth.
> 2 (in fact) actually, as a matter of fact, as
> it happens, in actual fact, indeed, in
> point of fact, in reality, in truth, really

**faction**[1] n group within a political party
**faction**[2] n TV dramatized version of factual
  events
**factious** adj causing trouble
**factor** n contributory force to a result

> **factor** n aspect, component, consideration,
> detail, element, facet, influence,
> ingredient, part

**factory** n building in which goods are
  manufactured
**facts of life** n 1 facts of sexuality 2 true
  nature of situation
**factual** adj based on or containing facts
**faculty** n aptitude; inherent ability; natural or
  special function (of mind or body); division
  of university
**fad** n whim; passing craze

**fade** *v* 1 lose color 2 lose strength; *phr v* **fade away** die; **fade in/out** 1 bring slowly into/out of view 2 make more/less clearly audible

> **fade** *v* 1 (lose color) become pale, dim, dull, grow pale. 2 (lose strength) decline, die away, disappear, dwindle, grow faint, vanish, wane

**fag end** *n* 1 remnant 2 untwisted end of rope
**fagot** *n* bundle of sticks for firewood
**Fahrenheit** *adj* scale of temperature, having boiling point 212°, and freezing point 32°
**fail** *v* 1 be unsuccessful 2 not do sth 3 let down 4 not function properly

> **fail** *v* 1 (be unsuccessful) be defeated, break down, collapse, fall flat, fall through, founder, go bankrupt, go under, lose, miscarry, misfire, miss. 2 (not do sth) avoid, decline, neglect, omit, refuse. 3 (let down) abandon, desert, disappoint

**failing** *n* fault
**failure** *n* 1 lack of success 2 act of not doing sth 3 unsuccessful person 4 unsuccessful thing

> **failure** *n* 1 (lack of success) bankruptcy, breakdown, collapse, defeat, malfunction. 2 (not doing sth) dereliction of duty, inability, omission, oversight, refusal. 3 (unsuccessful person) incompetent, loser. 4 (unsuccessful thing) disaster, dud, flop, washout

**faint** *adj* 1 weak 2 dizzy; *v* swoon

> **faint** *adj* 1 (weak) barely audible, barely perceptible, barely visible, blurred, dim, feeble, indistinct, quiet, soft, unclear. 2 (dizzy) giddy, light-headed, weak, woozy

**fair**[1] *n* market for sale of goods, often with sideshows, etc.; trade exhibition

**fair**[2] *adj* 1 impartial 2 (of hair) not dark 3 (of skin) not dark 4 quite good; *adv* **-ly** 1 in an honest way 2 quite; *n* **-ness**

> **fair** *adj* 1 (impartial) balanced, even-handed, honest, just, legitimate, objective, reasonable, right, unbiased, unprejudiced. 2 (of hair) blond, blonde, flaxen, yellow. 3 (of skin) light, pale, white

**fairy** *n* imaginary being with magic powers; *n* **f.-tale** story of magic
**faith** *n* 1 trust 2 religious belief
**faithful** *adj* loyal

> **faithful** *adj* committed, reliable, true, trusting, trusty

**fake** *v* make imitation of something rare; pretend; *n* sham; *adj* not genuine

> **fake** *adj* artificial, counterfeit, fabricated, false, forged, fraudulent, imitation, sham

**falcon** *n* bird of prey
**fall**[1] *v* 1 move downward 2 slip to ground 3 decrease 4 lose position of power 5 be killed or wounded 6 hang loosely; *pt* **fell** *pp* **fallen**; *phr vs* **fall apart** disintegrate; **fall behind** fail to keep up; **fall flat** collapse; fail; **fall for** 1 be attracted by 2 be deceived by; **fall out** quarrel; **fall through** (of plans) fail

> **fall** *v* 1 (move downward) collapse, descend, drop, plop, plummet, sink, stumble, tip over, topple over, trip, tumble. 2 (slip to ground) collapse, fall down, fall over, keel over, lose your balance, slip, stumble, trip, tumble. 3 (decrease) come down, decline, drop, fall off, go down, plummet, slump, tumble. 4 (lose position of power) be defeated, be dismissed, be ousted, be voted out, fall from grace, lose office, lose power, resign, stand down

**fall**[2] n 1 act of falling 2 failure; *pl* **falls** waterfall

**fallacy** n 1 false belief 2 false reasoning; *adj* **fallacious**; *adv* **-ly**

**fallible** *adj* liable to error; *n* **fallibility**

**falling star** n shooting star

**fallopian tube** n tube by which egg passes from ovary to womb

**fall out** n 1 radio-active dust in air following nuclear explosion 2 effects of this

**false** *adj* 1 wrong 2 dishonest 3 not genuine

> **false** *adj* 1 (wrong) erroneous, fallacious, incorrect, invalid, mistaken, unfounded, untrue. 2 (dishonest) deceitful, disloyal, insincere, unfaithful. 3 (not genuine) artificial, counterfeit, fake, forged, imitation, mock, synthetic

**falsetto** n (use by man of) high-pitched head voice as of female

**falsify** v alter with intent to deceive

**falter** v stumble, stammer; hesitate; *adj* **faltering**

**fame** n renown; *adj* **famed** well-known

> **fame** n celebrity, distinction, eminence, esteem, greatness, importance, notoriety, pre-eminence, reputation, stardom

**familiar** *adj* 1 well known 2 friendly; **familiar with** conversant with; *n* **familiarity**

> **familiar** *adj* 1 (well-known) common, commonplace, customary, everyday, frequent, habitual, household, mundane, normal, ordinary, predictable, recognizable, regular, routine, usual. 2 (friendly) amiable, close, confidential, cordial, easy, free, informal, intimate, open, relaxed, sociable. 3 (familiar with) acquainted with, at home with, aware of, conscious of, conversant with, expert in, informed about, trained in, versed in, well up in

**familial** *adj* of the family

**familiarize** v accustom someone to something

**family** n 1 group of people related by blood, marriage 2 one's children 3 people with a common ancestor

**famine** n acute shortage of food

**famished** *adj* extremely hungry

**famous** *adj* widely known; *adv* **-ly**; *coll* extremely well

> **famous** *adj* acclaimed, big, celebrated, eminent, famed, illustrious, legendary, notorious, prominent, renowned, well-known

**fan**[1] n 1 device causing flow of air 2 outspread tail feathers of bird; v **fanning, fanned** cause a rush of air with a fan

**fan**[2] n enthusiastic supporter

> **fan** n adherent, admirer, aficionado, buff, devotee, enthusiast, fanatic, follower, lover, nut, zealot

**fanatic** n one with extreme views; *n* **fanaticism**

**fanatical** *adj* having unreasoning belief in

**fan belt** n *aut* belt connecting engine drive to fan for cooling engine

**fanciful** 1 imaginary 2 imaginative

**fancy** n 1 imagination 2 thing imagined 3 desire; v 1 believe 2 desire sth 3 be attracted to

**fancy** *adj* elaborately decorated

> **fancy** *adj* decorative, elaborate, elegant, embellished, embroidered, intricate, jazzy, lavish, ornamental, ornate, posh, showy, snazzy *inf*

**fancy-free** *adj* not committed to any relationship

**fandango** n (*pl* os) lively Spanish dance

**fanfare** n flourish of trumpets

**fang** n long, pointed tooth

**fanlight** n small window

**fantasia** n imaginative composition in free form, *esp* music
**fantasize** v have fantasies
**fantastic** adj 1 wonderful 2 strange

> **fantastic** adj 1 (wonderful) brilliant, excellent, fabulous, first-class, first-rate, great, magnificent, marvelous, outstanding, phenomenal, sensational, splendid, super, superb, terrific, tremendous. 2 (strange) absurd, amazing, eccentric, exaggerated, exotic, fanciful, far-fetched, freakish, grotesque, incredible, odd, peculiar, quaint, queer, weird, whimsical

**fantasy** adj 1 imagination 2 wild idea
**far** adj, adv 1 at a distance 2 very much

> **far** adv 1 (at a distance) afar, a good way, a great distance, a long way, deep. 2 (very much) considerably, decidedly, greatly, incomparably

**farce** n Fr boisterous comedy; absurd situation
**farcical** adj 1 very amusing 2 ridiculous
**fare** n sum charged for conveyance of passenger; v get on
**farewell** n leave-taking; *interj* good-bye
**far-fetched** adj unbelievable

> **far-fetched** adj doubtful, dubious, improbable, ridiculous, unconvincing, unlikely, unnatural, unrealistic

**farm** n 1 area of land for growing crops and rearing animals 2 house and buildings near this; v cultivate land; ns **farmer**, **farming**
**far-off** adj distant
**far-reaching** adj having extensive influence
**farsighted** adj 1 aware of possible future developments 2 longsighted
**farther** adj, adv = further
**farthest** adj, adv = furthest
**fascinate** v interest greatly; n **fascination**
**fascinated** adj very interested

> **fascinated** adj absorbed, captivated, enchanted, engrossed, enthralled, hypnotized, intrigued, mesmerized, riveted, spellbound, transfixed

**fascinating** adj very interesting

> **fascinating** adj absorbing, captivating, compelling, engrossing, enthralling, gripping, interesting, intriguing, riveting

**fashion** n 1 latest style 2 method; v form, shape, make
**fashionable** adj stylish and modern

> **fashionable** adj à la mode, chic, current, in fashion, in vogue, latest, trendy, up-to-date, with it

**fast**[1] adj 1 speedy 2 firmly fixed 3 (of clock) ahead of actual time; adv 1 rapidly 2 securely; *idm* **fast asleep**

> **fast** adj (speedy) breakneck, brisk, hasty, high-speed, hurried, nippy, quick, rapid, supersonic, swift

**fast**[2] v abstain from food or some kinds of food; n act of fasting
**fasten** v attach; ns **fastener**, **fastening**

> **fasten** v affix, anchor, bind, bolt, buckle, chain, clamp, connect, couple, do up, fix, hitch, join, link, seal, secure, tether, tie

**fast food** n food that can be cooked easily and eaten quickly or taken away
**fastidious** adj difficult to please; fussy
**fat** adj **fatter**, **fattest** plump; n oily substance; v **fatten** (of animals) make fat for slaughter

> **fat** adj beefy, chubby, corpulent, flabby, heavy, obese, overweight, portly, pudgy, rotund, squat, stocky, stout, tubby, weighty

a
b
c
d
e
f
g
h
i
j
k
l
m
n
o
p
q
r
s
t
u
v
w
x
y
z

**fatal** adj 1 resulting in death 2 resulting in sth unpleasant

> **fatal** adj 1 (resulting in sb's death) deadly, final, incurable, killing, lethal, malignant, mortal, pernicious, terminal. 2 (resulting in sth unpleasant) catastrophic, dire, disastrous, lethal, ruinous

**fatalism** n doctrine that all events are preordained; adj, n **-ist**
**fatality** n death by accident
**fate** n 1 destiny 2 outcome

> **fate** n 1 (destiny) chance, doom, fortune, lot, predestination, providence. 2 (outcome) end, future, result, upshot

**fateful** adj disastrous
**Father Christmas** n Brit old man with red robe and white beard giving presents to children at Christmas (also **Santa Claus**)
**father** n male parent; adj **-ly**; ns **fatherhood**, **f.-in-law** wife's, husband's father
**fathom** n measure of depth, 6 ft; v understand; adj **fathomless** very deep
**fatigue** n Fr exhaustion; v tire
**fatten** v make fatter
**fatty** adj 1 like fat; 2 full of fat
**fault** n 1 imperfection 2 mistake 3 break in earth's surface; idm **at fault** to blame

> **fault** n 1 (imperfection) blemish, defect, deficiency, drawback, failing, flaw, shortcoming, snag, weakness. 2 (mistake) blunder, boob inf, error, faux pas, gaffe, howler inf, inaccuracy, miscalculation, omission, oversight, slip

**faulty** adj not working properly

> **faulty** adj bad, broken, damaged, defective, flawed, imperfect, malfunctioning, out of order, unusable, weak, wrong

**faun** n imaginary creature with horns and goat's feet
**fauna** n all animal life of region or period
**faux pas** n Fr embarrassing mistake
**favor** n 1 act of good will 2 partiality; idm **in favor of** supporting; idm **in sb's favor** to sb's advantage; v 1 approve of 2 have special liking for

> **favor** v 1 (approve of) advocate, back, be in sympathy with, endorse, promote, recommend, sanction, support. 2 (have special liking for) indulge, pamper, reward, show favoritism towards, spoil

**favorable** adj 1 beneficial 2 complimentary
**favorite** n preferred person or thing; adj preferred; n **favoritism** undue partiality

> **favorite** adj best, best-loved, choice, chosen, dearest, favored, ideal, most-liked, selected

**fawn** n young deer; adj pale, grayish brown
**fax** n message sent along a telephone line, then printed on a special machine; v send a message in this way; n **fax machine**
**fear** n great anxiety; v be afraid of

> **fear** n alarm, apprehension, dread, fearfulness, foreboding, fright, horror, nervousness, panic, qualms, shivers, terror, timidity, trepidation, uneasiness
> **fear** v be scared of, dread, live in fear/terror of, shrink from, shudder at, take fright, tremble at, worry about

**fearful** adj apprehensive, awful
**fearless** adj courageous
**fearsome** adj horrible
**feasible** adj possible; n **feasibility**

> **feasible** adj achievable, attainable, doable, likely, practicable, realizable, reasonable, viable, workable

**feast** n lavish meal; *idm* **feast one's eyes on** enjoy looking at

**feat** n act of bravery, skill, etc

**feather** n one of quilled, soft appendages forming plumage of birds

**feature** n 1 part 2 special article in newspaper 3 part of face; v 1 give prominence to 2 be present in

**feature** n 1 (part) aspect, attribute, characteristic, detail, facet, factor, mark, peculiarity, point, property, quality, side, trait. 2 (article in newspaper) column, item, piece, report, story
**feature** v 1 (give prominence to) accentuate, emphasize, focus on, highlight, play up, present, promote, spotlight, stress. 2 (be present in) act, appear, figure, participate, perform, star

**feature-length** *adj* (of film) full-length

**February** n second month of year

**feces** n excrement

**feckless** *adj* irresponsible

**fed** *pt* and *pp* of **feed**

**fed up** *adj* bored, dejected, dissatisfied

**fed up** *adj* annoyed, depressed, down, gloomy, glum, miserable, sad, weary

**federal** *adj* relating to states which unite for external affairs, but remain internally independent; n **federate** unite to form federation; n **-ation** federal union, society

**fee** n charge for services

**fee** n bill, cost, dues, payment, price, rate, subscription, tariff, toll

**feeble** *adj* weak; *adv* **feebly**

**feed** v give food to; eat; *pt*, *pp* **fed**

**feed** v (give food to) cater for, nourish, nurture, provide for, provision, suckle, support, supply, sustain

**feedback** n 1 information from user back to originator of idea or product 2 *elec* output from, *eg* amplifier, returned as new input

**feeding bottle** n bottle with small aperture for feeding liquid to babies or small animals

**feel** v **feeling, felt 1** explore by touch 2 have sensation or emotion 3 believe; *idm* **feel like** want; *idm* **feel for** sympathize with; n 1 exploration by touch 2 sensation; *idm* **get the feel of** become used to

**feel** v 1 (explore by touch) caress, finger, fondle, handle, manipulate, maul, paw, stroke, thumb, touch. 2 (have sensation or emotion) be aware of, be conscious of, detect, discern, endure, enjoy, experience, go through, have, know, notice, observe, perceive, suffer, undergo. 3 (believe) be convinced, be of the opinion that, consider, have a (funny) feeling, intuit, judge, sense, think. 4 (feel like) desire, fancy, want, wish for, would like, yearn for

**feeler** n insect's antenna; *idm* **put out feelers** test people's opinions

**feel-good factor** n general feeling of optimism among the population of a country

**feeling** n 1 sensation 2 emotion 3 awareness 4 belief

**feet** *pl* of **foot**

**feign** v pretend, assume, simulate

**felicity** n happiness, bliss, contentment

**feisty** *adj coll* 1 spirited 2 quarrelsome

**feline** *adj* of cats; catlike

**fell**[1] v 1 *pt* of **fall** 2 cut down

**fell**[2] n bare rocky hillside or moorland in N England

**fellow** n companion; man; associate; member of university

**fellowship** n 1 companionship 2 society 3 position of fellow in university

**felony** n grave crime; n **felon** criminal; *adj* **felonious**

**felt**[1] n fabric made of compressed wool

**felt**[2] *pt* of **feel**

**felt-tip** *adj*, n (pen) with felt nib

a b c d e f g h i j k l m n o p q r s t u v w x y z

**female** *adj* 1 of the sex that bears offspring or fruit 2 of women; *n* woman or female animal

**feminine** *adj* of women; delicate and graceful; *ns* **femininity**, **feminism** advocacy of equality between sexes

> **feminine** *adj* elegant, gentle, girlish, ladylike, soft, tender

**femme fatale** *n Fr* woman attractive but dangerous to men

**femur** *n* thighbone; *adj* **femoral**

**fen** *n* low, flat, marshy land; *adj* **fenny**

**fence** *n* railing; *v* enclose, protect with fence; fight with sword; *n* **fencing** protective fences; art of sword play

> **fence** *n* barricade, barrier, defense, fencing, hedge, hurdle, paling, palisade, railings, rampart, stockade, wall, wire

**fend** *phr vs* **fend for** look after; protect; **fend off** ward off; push away

**fennel** *n* fragrant herb used in cooking

**feral** *adj* fatal, gloomy, undomesticated, wild

**ferment** *v* undergo chemical process involving effervescence

**fern** *n* plant with fronds, feathery or plain

**ferocious** *adj* fierce; *n* **ferocity**

**ferret** *n* small animal of weasel family

**ferric**, **ferreous**, **ferrous** *adj* of, containing iron

**ferrule** *n* metal cap protecting end of stick

**ferry** *v* **-rying**, **-ried** convey; *n* **-ies** boat, raft used for ferrying across river, channel

**fertile** *adj* capable of producing offspring; fruitful; rich in ideas; *n* **fertility**

**fertilize** *v* make fertile; *n* **-ization**

**fertilizer** *n* substance used to improve soil

**fervent** *adj* intense; *n* **fervor**

> **fervent** *adj* ardent, avid, devout, eager, earnest, emotional, enthusiastic, excited, fanatical, fiery, heartfelt, heated, keen, passionate, vehement, zealous

**fester** *v* become septic; feel aggrieved

**festival** *n* celebration; series of organized musical, dramatic performances

**festive** *adj* joyous, convivial

> **festive** *adj* celebratory, cheerful, gay, happy, jolly, jovial, joyful, merry

**festivity** *n* gaiety, joyousness; *pl* **festivities** joyful celebration

**festooned** *adj* decorated with ribbons, garlands

**fetch** *v* 1 bring 2 be sold for; *adj* **fetching** attractive; *adv* **-ly**

> **fetch** *v* 1 (bring) carry, conduct, convey, deliver, escort, get, go and get, import, obtain, retrieve, transport. 2 (be sold for) bring in, earn, make, raise, realize, sell for

**fête** *n* festival, usually open-air; *v* honor with festivities

**fetid** *adj* stinking

**fetish** *n* object of worship or devotion; *n* **fetishism**; *n*, *adj* **-ist**

**fetter** *n* shackle for feet; *pl* restraint

**fetus** *n* distinctly developed embryo in womb or egg; *adj* **fetal**

**feud** *n* bitter, long-standing hostility between two persons, families, etc

**feudal system** *n* medieval system of land tenure

**fever** *n* 1 disorder characterized by high temperature 2 extreme nervous excitement

**feverish** *adj* 1 with high temperature 2 frantic

> **feverish** *adj* 1 (with high temperature) delirious, flushed, hot. 2 (frantic) desperate, distracted, excited, frenetic, frenzied, hectic

**few** *adj*, *n* not many; small number of

**fez** *n* felt cap

**fiancé** *n Fr* betrothed man; *fem* **fiancée**

**fiasco** *n* total, utter failure

**fib** n mild untruth; v **fibbing**, **fibbed** tell fib
**fiber**) thread of animal, plant tissue;
threadlike substance that can be spun; adj
**fibrous**; ns **fiberboard** board of compressed
wood fibers; **fiberglass** material from glass
fibers and resin for bodywork in cars, boats,
etc; **fiber optics** transmission of date by
infrared signals along thin glass fibre;
adj **fiber-optic**
**fibrositis** n inflammation of fibrous tissue,
esp muscle
**fibula** n outer bone of lower leg; adj **fibular**
**fickle** adj not loyal

> **fickle** adj capricious, changeable, disloyal,
> erratic, fitful, flighty, inconstant,
> unpredictable, vacillating, volatile

**fiction** n 1 literature of the imagination 2 sth
not true

> **fiction** n 1 (literature of the imagination)
> fable, fantasy, legend, make-believe,
> myth, romance, story, tale. 2 (sth not
> true) deception, fabrication, falsehood,
> fancy, fantasy, fib, imagination,
> invention, lie, tall story, untruth

**fictional** adj not true

> **fictional** adj fictitious, imaginary, invented,
> made-up, make-believe, pretend,
> nonexistent, unreal

**fictitious** adj imaginary
**fiddle** n 1 violin 2 sl swindle; idm **as fit as a
fiddle** completely healthy; v 1 fidget
2 swindle 3 play violin; ns **fiddler**,
**fiddlestick** violin bow; interj **fiddlesticks**
dated nonsense

> **fiddle** v 1 (fidget) fuss, meddle, play,
> tamper, tinker, toy, trifle. 2 (swindle)
> cheat, falsify, fix, maneuver, wangle

**fiddly** adj awkward to manipulate or do

**fidelity** n 1 faithfulness 2 exactitude
**fidget** v move restlessly; n one who fidgets

> **fidget** v fiddle, fuss, have ants in your
> pants, mess about, mess around, play
> about, shuffle, squirm, twitch, wriggle

**fidgety** adj nervous
**fiduciary** adj of trustee; held in trust
**field** n 1 area of land for crops or pasture
2 area for sporting activity 3 area of interest;
v 1 deal successfully with difficult questions
2 sport select (people to play) 3 cricket:
1 play against the batting team 2 stop the
ball to prevent scoring of runs; n **fielder**

> **field** n 1 (area for crops or pasture)
> clearing, enclosure, grassland, green,
> meadow, paddock, pasture. 2 (area for
> sports) arena, court, ground, pitch,
> playing field, recreation ground, stadium,
> turf. 3 (area of interest) area, discipline,
> domain, line, province, speciality, sphere,
> subject, territory

**field event** n athletic contest other than
running
**field glasses** n binoculars
**field test** n educational visit
**field-work** n academic work outside class
**fiend** n demon, devil; excessively evil person;
adj **fiendish** cruel, malevolent
**fierce** adj 1 savage 2 intense; n **fierceness**

> **fierce** adj (savage) barbaric, brutal, cold-
> blooded, cruel, dangerous, fearsome,
> ferocious, menacing, murderous,
> passionate, ruthless, threatening,
> uncontrollable, untamed, vicious,
> violent, wild

**fiery** adj 1 of, resembling fire 2 flaming,
glowing 3 showing anger easily
**fiesta** n festival, esp religious one in Spanish
speaking countries
**fifteen**, **fifth**, **fifty** see **five**

a
b
c
d
e
f
g
h
i
j
k
l
m
n
o
p
q
r
s
t
u
v
w
x
y
z

**fifty-fifty** *adj*, *adv* (shared) equal(ly) between two

**fig** *n* soft, sweet with many seeds, eaten fresh or dried; tree bearing this

**fight** *v* 1 do battle with 2 oppose 3 argue with; *pt*, *pp* **fought**; *phr vs* **fight back** 1 retaliate 2 recover from losing situation; *n* 1 battle 2 argument

> **fight** *v* 1 (do battle with) attack, battle, box, brawl, clash, come to blows, engage, grapple, joust, scrap, skirmish, struggle, tussle, war, wrestle. 2 (oppose) challenge, contest, defy, dispute, resist, struggle against, take a stand against, withstand. 3 (argue with) be at odds, bicker, clash, dispute, feud, quarrel, squabble, wrangle
> **fight** *n* 1 (battle) action, affray, attack, bout, brawl, clash, conflict, contest, engagement, fracas, fray, joust, punch-up, scrap, skirmish, struggle, tussle, war, wrestle. 2 (argument) altercation, brush, disagreement, dispute, falling out, feud, quarrel, squabble, wrangle

**fighter** *n* one who fights; aircraft for fighting

**figment** *n* fantasy; something imagined

**figure** *n* 1 number 2 outward shape 3 diagram; *v* 1 imagine; depict 2 calculate 3 be conspicuous; *phr vs* **figure out** calculate

> **figure** *n* 1 (number) amount, cipher, digit, integer, numeral, sum, value. 2 (outward shape) body, build, form, frame, outline, physique, shape, silhouette. 3 (diagram) chart, graph, illustration, symbol, table

**figurative** *adj* metaphorical, symbolic

**file**[1] *n* tool with rough surface for cutting or smoothing; *v* use file on

**file**[2] 1 *n* stiff wire, box or folder for storing documents 2 collection of documents so kept for reference; *v* place in or on file

**file**[3] *n* line of persons one behind another; *v* march, move in file

**filial** *adj* of, concerning son or daughter

**fill** *v* make/become full; *phr vs* **fill in** complete with details; give information to; **fill out** 1 become fatter 2 complete in writing; *n* full supply

> **fill** *v* block, cram, crowd, gorge, jam, load, pack, refill, replenish, satisfy, stock, stuff

**fillet** *n* piece of boneless meat, fish; *v* slice and remove bones

**filling** *n* something used to fill cavity in

> **filling** *n* contents, insides, middle, padding, stuffing, wadding

**filly** *n* female foal, young mare

**film** *n* 1 thin layer 2 thin flexible sensitized strip or roll used in photography, cinematography 3 motion picture; *v* make, direct, produce motion picture

**film star** *n* famous film actor/actress

**filter** *n* 1 cloth, etc used for straining liquids 2 device eliminating some light or electrical frequencies; *v* 1 strain liquid through filter; percolate 2 *fig* leak out; *n* **filtration**

> **filter** *v* (strain liquid) clarify, filtrate, purify, refine, screen, sieve, sift, strain

**filter tip** *n* cigarette with filter at one end

**filth** *n* 1 dirt 2 obscenity

**filthy** *adj* 1 very dirty 2 obscene

> **filthy** *adj* 1 (dirty) contaminated, defiled, foul, grimy, grubby, mucky, polluted. 2 (obscene) bawdy, blue, coarse, impure, indecent, lewd, licentious, pornographic, raunchy, rude, smutty, sordid, vulgar

**fin** *n* winglike organ by which fish swim

**final** *adj* last; *n* last examination, game, or heat of series; *ns* **finalist** competitor in final of race, game, etc; **finality**, **finale** end; concluding movement, number of symphony, opera, etc

**final** *adj* closing, concluding, dying, end, eventual, finishing, parting, ultimate

**inance** *n* 1 management of money 2 money; *v* supply money for; *adj* **financial**

**finance** *v* back, fund, guarantee, invest in, pay for, subsidize, support, underwrite

**inch** *n* small seed-eating birds

**ind** *v* 1 discover 1 retrieve sth lost 3 notice; *pt, pp* **found**; *n* thing found; valuable or pleasing discovery; *phr vs* **find against** *leg* give judgment against; **find for** *leg* give judgment in favor of; **find out** learn; **finding** *esp pl* 1 things found by official enquiry 2 *leg* decision or verdict

**find** *v* 1 (discover) chance upon, come across, encounter, happen on, hit on, light on, spot, turn up, uncover, unearth. 2 (retrieve sth lost) get back, locate, recoup, recover, rediscover, regain, trace, track down. 3 (notice) become aware, conclude, discover, note, observe, perceive, realize. 4 (find out) detect, discover, expose, learn, observe, realize, reveal, see

**ine arts** *n pl* painting, sculpture, music, etc

**ine**[1] *n* sum exacted as penalty; *v* punish by fine

**ine**[2] *adj* 1 of good quality 2 satisfactory 3 sunny 4 subtle; *ns* **fineness, finery** elaborate dress

**fine** *adj* 1 (of good quality) beautiful, classic, elegant, excellent, exceptional, exquisite, first-class, first-rate, good, high-class, high-quality, magnificent, outstanding, rare, refined, select, splendid, superb, superior, top-notch, world-class. 2 (satisfactory) acceptable, adequate, agreeable, all right, OK *inf*, suitable. 3 (sunny) balmy, bright, clear, cloudless, dry, fair, pleasant

**finger** *n* one of five (or four, excluding thumb) members at end of hand; anything finger shaped; *v* touch with fingers, handle; *ns* **f.-nail, fingertip** end of finger

**finical, finicking, finicky** *adj* fussy, overfastidious

**finish** *v* 1 bring to an end; complete 2 stop 3 defeat; *phr vs* **finish off** 1 complete, terminate 2 kill; **finish with** 1 have as final item 2 have no further use for 3 end relationship with; *n* end; final appearance

**finish** *v* 1 (bring to an end) close, complete, conclude, culminate, discharge, end, execute, finalize, fulfill, get done, perfect, settle, wrap up. 2 (stop) break off, cease, desist, discontinue, halt, interrupt, pack up, phase out, suspend, terminate, wind up. 3 (defeat) annihilate, beat, conquer, destroy, dispose of, exterminate, get rid of, kill, overcome, overpower, ruin

**finished** *adj* accomplished, perfect
**finite** *adj* having limits
**Finnish** *adj, n* of finland
**fir** *n* coniferous, evergreen tree
**fire** *n* 1 thing burning 2 shooting of weapons 3 passion; *idm* **open/cease fire** begin/stop shooting; *idm* **on fire** burning; *idm* **under fire** being shot at; *v* 1 set fire to 2 shoot 3 dismiss from post 4 bake (pottery) in kiln; *ns* **f.-alarm, f.-arm** gun; **f.-brigade** body of firefighters; **f. drill** practice routine for ensuring safe escape from fire; **f.-fighter, f.-fighting, fireman** (*pl* **firemen**); **f.station** HQ of fire brigade; **firework** chemical container, emitting bright colored light or exploding when ignited

**fire** *n* 1 (thing burning) blaze, combustion, flame, inferno, pyre. 2 (shooting of weapons) bombardment, gunfire, salvo, shelling, shooting, sniping. 3 (passion) ardor, energy, fervor, intensity, spark, spirit, vehemence, vigor, vivacity, zeal

a
b
c
d
e
f
g
h
i
j
k
l
m
n
o
p
q
r
s
t
u
v
w
x
y
z

**fire** v 1 (set fire to) burn, ignite, kindle, put a match to, set sth alight, set sth on fire, torch. 2 (shoot) detonate, discharge, launch, let off, pull the trigger, set off. 3 (dismiss) discharge, get rid of, give sb the boot, let sb go, make sb redundant, sack

**firefly** n nocturnal beetle that produces light
**fireplace** n a recess for a fire
**fireproof** adj safe against fire
**fireside** n area close to fireplace; hearth
**firing squad** n execution by shooting
**firm** adj 1 solid 2 stable 3 determined; v make firm; n business

**firm** adj 1 (solid) compact, compressed, condensed, dense, hard, inflexible, resilient, resistant, rigid, set, strong, taut, tight, stiff, unyielding. 2 (stable) anchored, braced, fast, fixed, immovable, rooted, secured, solid, steady, strong, sturdy, tight, unmoving. 3 (determined) adamant, certain, definite, intransigent, resolute, resolved, set, settled, staunch, steadfast, stubborn, sure, unbending, unshakable, unswerving, unwavering, unyielding

**first** adj 1 earliest 2 highest; best 3 principal 4 basic, elementary; adv before all else, all others; n, pron 1 best person or thing 2 top result; ns **f. aid** emergency medical treatment; **f. person** form of pronoun used when speaker refers to himself/herself
**first-class** adj excellent
**firstly** adv first of all
**firsthand** (of information) direct from source
**firth** n estuary; inlet of sea
**first-rate** adj excellent
**fiscal** adj concerned with public revenue
**fish** n cold-blooded vertebrate, with fins, living in water; flesh of fish used as food; v 1 catch fish 2 try to get information; ns **fisher**; **f. farm** place for breeding of fish; **f. fry** picnic, dinner serving fried fish; **fishing**; **fishnet** netlike fabric

**fissure** n cleft, esp in rock
**fist** n clenched hand; v strike with fist
**fit**[1] n sudden sharp attack of illness
**fit**[2] adj 1 healthy 2 good enough; v **fitting**, **fitted** 1 suit; be adapted to, of correct size 2 supply; furnish 3 be properly adjusted to; n that which fits; adjustment; phr vs **fit in** harmonize

**fit** adj 1 (healthy) energetic, in shape, robust, strapping, strong, toned, vigorous, well. 2 (good enough) able, adequate, capable, competent, correct, decent, eligible, equipped, fitting, qualified, proper, right, suitable, up to the job, worthy

**fitted** adj made to size and shape 2 fixed in position
**fitting** adj suitable, proper, seemly
**five** n, pron, det cardinal number after four; adjs, ns, dets **fifth** ordinal number; a fifth part; **fifteen** five plus ten; **fifteenth**, **fifty** five tens; **fiftieth**
**fix** v 1 make secure 2 agree 3 repair

**fix** v 1 (make secure) anchor, attach, connect, embed, fasten, fit, install, stick, tie. 2 (agree) arrange, arrive at, conclude, decide, determine, establish, finalize, limit, name, resolve, set, settle, specify. 3 (repair) mend, patch up, put right, restore, sort out

**fixation** n obsession
**fixture** n 1 sth fixed in a building 2 arranged sports event
**fizz** v hiss, splutter, effervesce; phr v **fizzle out** become feeble and ineffective
**fizzy** adj containing bubbles of air
**fjord** n narrow coastal inlet, esp in Norway
**flabbergasted** adj astonished
**flabby** adj hanging loosely; limp
**flag** n piece of cloth bearing emblem; v signal

**flag** n banner, bunting, colors, ensign, pennant, standard, streamer

**agon** n vessel for serving wine

**agrant** adj open and obvious

**flagrant** adj barefaced, blatant, bold, brazen, glaring, ostentatious, outrageous, overt, scandalous, shameless, shocking, unashamed, unconcealed, undisguised

**air** n natural ability

**flair** n ability, aptitude, facility, feel, genius, gift, knack, skill, talent

**ake** n small piece; particle of snow; v come off in flakes; adj **flaky**

**lamboyant** n showy

**lame** n 1 burning gas or vapor; jet of fire 2 ardent passion, imagination; v emit flames; blaze; flare

**lamenco** n lively Spanish dance

**laming** adj 1 burning 2 brightly colored

**lamingo** n scarlet-feathered aquatic bird, with long legs and neck

**lammable** adj easily set on fire

**lan** n open pie with sweet fillings

**lank** n part of side of body between hip and ribs; side of hill, building, or body of troops; v guard, attack flank; be at side of

**lannel** n soft, woolen or cotton cloth; pl trousers, esp casual, sporting; n **flannelette** lightweight cotton flannel

**lap** v **flapping, flapped** 1 move up and down 2 panic; n act of flapping; flat piece of material partly attached and hanging; idm **flapjack** pancake

**flap** v 1 (move up and down) agitate, beat, flail, flutter, oscillate, shake, swing, swish, thrash, wag, waggle, wave. 2 (panic) be in a state, fuss, get flustered

**lappable** adj able to beeasily upset

**lare**[1] n 1 bright, unsteady flame 2 vivid signal light 3 outburst of anger; v blaze up; spread outwards

**lare**[2] v be wider at bottom; n flare shape

**flare-up** n outbreak of violent activity

**flash** v emit sudden bright light; n 1 sudden brief gleam of light 2 moment; idm **in a flash** instantly; ns **flashback** episode going back in time; **flashbulb** device for taking photos in bad light; **flashlight** small, battery-run handheld light

**flash** v beam, blaze, dazzle, flare, flicker, glare, gleam, glimmer, glint, glisten, glitter, light up, reflect, shimmer, shine, sparkle, twinkle

**flash** n 1 (gleam of light) beam, blaze, bolt, burst, flare, flicker, glare, glimmer, glint, ray, shaft, shimmer, shine, spark, sparkle, twinkle. 2 (moment) instant, jiffy, minute, second, split second, twinkling of an eye

**flashy** adj bright and showy

**flask** n small, pocket bottle for spirits; small narrow-necked bottle for scientific use

**flat** adj 1 level and smooth 2 lying down 3 dull 4 deflated 5 mus below pitch indicated 6 (of denial) absolute; idm **flat out** at full speed; n 1 flat tire 2 flat part of sth 3 mus sign indicating a semitone lower; adv 1 mus below pitch 2 at full extent; level with the ground 3 absolutely

**flat** adj 1 (level and smooth) even, horizontal, plane, unbroken. 2 (lying down) outstretched, prone, prostrate, reclining, recumbent, sprawling, spread-eagled, stretched out, supine. 3 (dull) bland, boring, dead, dry, insipid, lackluster, lifeless, monotonous, prosaic, stale, tedious, uninteresting, unvarying

**flatten** v 1 make or become flat 2 defeat

**flatten** v 1 (make, become flat) compact, compress, even out, iron out, level out, plane, press down, smooth out. 2 (defeat) crush, demolish, destroy, knock down, level, raze, squash, trample

**flatter** *v* praise insincerely

> **flatter** *v* butter up, compliment, crawl, fawn, gush, lick sb's boots, pander to, pay court to, praise, suck up to, sweet-talk

**flattery** *n* insincere praise
**flatulence, flatulency** *n* gas in stomach or intestines; *adj* **flatulent** caused by, affected with flatulence; *fig* vapid
**flaunt** *v* make display of
**flavor)** 1 taste (also **flavoring**) 2 special characteristic; *v* give taste to

> **flavor** *n* 1 (taste) piquancy, relish, savor, seasoning, smack, tang, tastiness, zest. 2 (special characteristic) ambience, atmosphere, character, essence, feel, feeling, nature, quality, soul, spirit, tone

**flaw** *n* defect; *v* crack; make flaw in
**flawed** *adj* imperfect
**flax** *n* plant, whose fibers are spun into linen
**flaxen** *adj* (of hair) pale yellow
**flea** *n* small bloodsucking jumping insect
**fleck** *n* spot, freckle
**flee** *v* run away; *pt, pp* **fled**

> **flee** *v* abscond, beat a retreat, beat it *inf*, bolt, decamp, disappear, escape, fly, make off, run off, take flight, take off, vanish

**fleece** *n* sheep's wool; *v* swindle, plunder; *adj* **fleecy** soft, wooly
**fleet**[1] *n* number of warships under one command; number of ships, aircraft, cars owned by one company or person
**fleet**[2] *adj* speedy; *adj* **fleeting** brief
**flesh** *n* 1 soft tissue of body, beneath skin, covering bones 2 edible animal tissue; meat 3 pulp of vegetable or fruit 4 sensuality; *idm* **in the flesh** physically present; in person
**flew** *pt* of **fly**
**flex** *v* bend, be bent; *n* flexible, insulated wire
**flexibility** ability to bend
**flexible** *adj* 1 able to bend 2 able to change

**flexible** *adj* 1 (able to bend) bendable, ductile, giving, elastic, malleable, plastic, pliable, springy, stretchy, supple, yielding. 2 (able to change) adaptable, amenable, biddable, compliant, open, responsive, tractable, yielding

**flextime** *n* system of variable working hours
**flick** *v* tap lightly; *n* sharp light blow
**flicker** *v* burn, shine unsteadily; *n* unsteady gleam or movement

> **flicker** *v* blink, flash, flutter, glimmer, glint, glitter, oscillate, quiver, tremble, twinkle, vibrate, waver, wink, wobble

**flier** *n* aviator
**flight** *n* 1 act of flying; distance flown; journey by air 2 act of fleeing 3 series of stairs
**flighty** *adj* giddy, fickle, frivolous
**flimflam** *n* deception
**flimsy** *adj* 1 thin and fragile 2 not good

> **flimsy** *adj* 1 (thin and fragile) breakable, brittle, delicate, fine, frail, insubstantial, lightweight, makeshift, ramshackle, rickety, shaky, slight, weak. 2 (not good) feeble, implausible, inadequate, pathetic, poor, thin, trivial, unconvincing, unsatisfactory, weak

**flinch** *v* draw back in pain, fear

> **flinch** *v* baulk, blench, cower, cringe, dodge, duck, flee, jump, recoil, retreat, shrink, shy away, start, swerve, wince

**fling** *v* throw, hurl; move with haste; lash out; flounce; *pt, pp* **flung**; *n* 1 throw 2 vigorous dance 3 brief amorous relationship.
**flint** *adj* very hard dark gray quartz
**flip** *v* **flipping, flipped** flick; jerk; *n* **flipper** limb or fin for swimming
**flippant** *adj* not serious; *n* **flippancy**

**flippant** *adj* casual, cheeky, disrespectful, facetious, flip, frivolous, glib, light-hearted, impertinent, impudent, jokey, offhand, pert, shallow, superficial

**flirt** *v* pay amorous attentions without serious intent

**flirtatious** *adj* flirting

**flit** *v* **flitting**, **flitted** pass lightly, rapidly, and quietly; *sl* move house secretly

**float** *v* **1** rest on surface of liquid **2** glide through air **3** start; set going; launch (loan, company, etc); *n* **1** anything that floats, *esp* supporting something else on liquid **2** wheeled motorized platform decorated for parades **3** cork on fishing net **4** sum of cash for running expenses

**float** *v* (rest on liquid) bob, drift, glide, hang, hover, poise, sail, slide, slip

**flock** *n* number of animals (*esp* sheep) or birds, as unit; congregation; *v* crowd together

**flock** *v* assemble, congregate, converge, gather, group, herd, huddle, mass, swarm, throng, troop

**floe** *n* sheet of ice floating on sea

**flog** *v* **flogging**, **flogged** beat hard; *idm* **flog a dead horse** *coll* persist in unprofitable activity

**flood** *n* **1** overflow of water in usually dry place **2** sudden excess; *v* inundate, overflow, overwhelm

**flood** *n* **1** (overflow of water) deluge, downpour, flash flood, overflow, tidal wave, tide, torrent. **2** (sudden excess) abundance, excess, flow, glut, plethora, profusion, rush, stream, surfeit, surge

**floodlight** *n* powerful artificial lighting; *v* illuminate by floodlights

**floor** *n* lower surface of room, etc; story

**flop** *v* **flopping**, **flopped 1** move, fall limply **2** fail utterly; *adv* **floppily**; *n* failure

**flop** *v* **1** (move, fall limply) collapse, dangle, droop, drop, fall, flag, hang, sag, slump, topple, tumble, wilt. **2** (fail) bomb *inf*, close, fall flat, founder
**flop** *n* disaster, dud *inf*, fiasco, loser, no-hoper *inf*, nonstarter, washout

**floppy disk** *n* *comput* disc for storing data

**flora** *n* flowers, plants, collectively

**florist** *n* seller or flowers

**flotation** *n* starting of a new company

**flotsam** *n* floating wreckage or goods on the sea

**flounce** *v* go, move jerkily, impatiently

**flounder** *v* struggle helplessly

**flour** *n* finely ground meal, *esp* of wheat; any very fine, soft powder; *v* cover with flour

**flourish** *v* **1** thrive **2** hold up; *n* fanciful curved line; fanfare

**flourish** *v* **1** (thrive) be fruitful, be successful, bloom, blossom, burgeon, grow, prosper, succeed. **2** (hold up) brandish, shake, swing, swish, twirl, wave, wield

**flout** *v* defy

**flow** *v* **1** (of water) glide along **2** (of blood) circulate **3** (of fabric) fall in loose folds; *n* that which flows; rising tide; steady, copious supply

**flow** *v* (of water) cascade, course, dribble, drip, ebb, glide, gush, leak, move, ooze, pour, roll, run, rush, seep, slide, slip, spill, spout, squirt, stream, surge, sweep, swirl, trickle, well, whirl

**flower** *n* blossom, bloom; *v* **1** produce blooms **2** reach highest state of development; *adjs* **flowery** abounding in flowers; florid; **flowered** decorated with floral pattern

**flown** *pp* of **fly**

**flu** *n* influenza

**fluctuate** *v* rise and fall; *adj* **-ating**

> **fluctuate** *v* alternate, be unsteady, change, hesitate, oscillate, move, seesaw, shift, swing, vacillate, vary, veer, waver, yo-yo

**flue** *n* tube, pipe, shaft conveying air, smoke
**fluent** *adj* flowing; able to speak easily
**fluff** *n* light soft mass of wool, dust; *v* make into fluff; *sl* bungle; *adj* **fluffy**
**fluid** *n* liquid; not solid; *adj* flowing easily
**fluke** *n* lucky chance event
**flummox** *v* bewilder, abash, disconcert
**flung** *pt, pp* of **fling**
**fluorescent** *adj* reflecting light in a particular way
**fluoride** *n* chemical protecting teeth against decay, *v* **fluoridate**; *n* **-ation**
**flurry** *n* sudden gust
**flush** *v* 1 redden 2 clean by rush of water; *n* 1 rush of water 2 blush; sudden emotion; *adj* 1 level with 2 *sl* having plenty (of money)

> **flush** *v* 1 (redden) blush, color, glow, go red. 2 (clean by rush of water) clean out, flood, hose down, rinse, wash out

**fluster** *v* muddle, worry
**flute** *n* wind instrument, with side mouthpiece, and holes stopped by keys or fingers
**flutter** *v* move wings quickly, nervously; quiver; *n* 1 act of fluttering 2 *sl* small bet
**fly**[1] *n* two-winged insect; imitation used as fish bait
**fly**[2] *v* 1 move through air 2 control plane 3 blow in wind 4 pass quickly 5 rush; *pt* **flew**; *pp* **flown**

> **fly** *v* 1 (move through air) flit, glide, hover, sail, soar, swoop, take wing. 2 (control plane) maneuver, operate, pilot. 3 (blow in wind) flap, flutter, raise, show, wave. 4 (pass quickly) elapse, race, roll on, slip away, slip past. 5 (rush) dart, dash, hurry, race, rush, shoot, sprint, tear, zoom

**foal** *n* young of horse, ass, etc
**foam** *n* mass of small bubbles, froth, on surface of liquid; *v* form, emit foam; emit thick saliva, or sweat; *adjs* **-y**, **-ing**
**focus** *n* center of activity or intensity; *pl* **focuses, foci**; *v* 1 adjust to see clearly 2 concentrate attention

> **focus** *n* center, core, focal point, heart, hub, pivot, target

**fodder** *n* dried food for cattle, horses, etc
**foe** *n* enemy
**fog** *n* thick mist

> **fog** *n* cloud, gloom, haze, mistiness, murk, murkiness, smog

**foible** *n* weakness of character
**fogy, fogey** *n* fussy, old-fashioned person
**foggy** *adj* covered in fog; not clear
**foil**[1] *n* thin sheet of metal
**foil**[2] *v* baulk; frustrate; repel (attack)
**foist** *v* palm off; impose fraudulently
**fold** *v* 1 bend 2 clasp in arms 3 (of business) fail; *n* crease made by folding; piece of folded material; hollow in hill

> **fold** *v* 1 (bend) crease, crimp, crinkle, crumple, double, gather, jackknife, overlap, pleat, pucker, tuck, turn. 2 (clasp in your arms) embrace, enclose, enfold, entwine, envelop, hold, wrap. 3 (fail) close, collapse, crash, go bankrupt, go bust *inf*, go under *inf*

**folder** *n* container for documents
**foliage** *n* leaves
**folk** *n* 1 nation 2 people in general; *ns* **folk dance** traditional dance; **folklore** traditional beliefs, etc
**follow** *v* 1 go behind 2 obey 3 come after 4 understand; *idm* **follow suit** do likewise; *phr vs* **follow through** pursue to the end; **follow up** 1 investigate 2 take further action on

**follow** v 1 (go behind) chase, hound, hunt, pursue, shadow, stalk, tag along, tail, track, trail. 2 (obey) abide by, comply with, conform, honor, observe, stick to. 3 (come after) replace, step into sb's shoes, succeed, supersede, take sb's place

**follower** n one who believes in sb
**following** a 1 next 2 (of wind) favorable; n group of supporters
**folly** n 1 foolishness 2 useless building
**foment** v stir up (trouble, etc)
**fond** adj loving; idm **fond of** have affection/liking for; n **fondness**

**fond** adj 1 (loving) adoring, affectionate, caring, devoted, warm. 2 (fond of) attached to, enamored of, hooked on, in love with, keen on, mad about, partial to

**fondle** v caress
**font** n bowl for baptismal holy water, in church
**food** n any substance consumed to support life and growth
**fool** v stupid, silly person; v 1 deceive 2 clown

**fool** n blockhead, clot, dope, half-wit, idiot, moron, nerd, nincompoop, nit, nitwit, twerp, twit
**fool** v 1 (deceive) bamboozle, bluff, cheat, con, delude, dupe, hoax, hoodwink, kid, make a fool of, mislead, play a trick on, take sb in, trick. 2 (clown) act the fool, joke, mess about, play tricks, tease

**foolhardy** adj rash
**foolish** adj stupid, unwise

**foolish** adj brainless, crazy, daft, dumb, hare-brained, idiotic, ill-advised, ludicrous, mad, ridiculous, senseless, silly, simple, thoughtless, unintelligent

**foot** n 1 lowest part of leg below ankle 2 bottom end of sock, stocking 3 base; bottom of sth 4 end of bed opposite to head 5 measure of 12 inches; pl **feet**
**football** n game played with pointed leather ball on a large field
**foothill** n low hill
**foothold** n secured position for further progress
**footnote** n note at the bottom of page
**footpath** n a path for people going on foot
**footprint** n mark left by foot
**for** prep suitable to; because of; toward; in favor of; instead of; during; at price of; in spite of; in search of; conj because
**forage** v search for food
**foray** n raid
**forbid** v prevent; pt **forbade**; pp **forbidden** adj **forbidding** threatening, sinister

**forbid** v ban, deny, exclude, inhibit, prohibit, refuse, rule out, stop

**forbidden** adj not allowed

**forbidden** adj against the law, banned, outlawed, out of bounds, prohibited, restricted, secret, taboo, wrong

**force** n 1 power 2 compulsion 3 effectiveness 4 strength of feeling 5 body of people; idm **in force** operational; idm **join forces (with)** unite (with); v 1 compel 2 break open 3 cause plants to flower, fruit before natural season 4 produce by effort

**force** n 1 (power) effort, energy, impact, might, muscle, pressure, stamina, strength. 2 (compulsion) arm-twisting, coercion, pressure. 3 (effectiveness) influence, persuasiveness, power, validity, weight. 4 (strength of feeling) drive, emphasis, feeling, intensity, passion, persistence. 5 (body of people) army, battalion, corps, division, group, squadron, troops, unit

a
b
c
d
e
f
g
h
i
j
k
l
m
n
o
p
q
r
s
t
u
v
w
x
y
z

A B C D E F G H I J K L M N O P Q R S T U V W X Y Z

**force** *v* 1 (compel) coerce, constrain, dragoon, impose, make, oblige, press-gang, pressurize, twist sb's arm. 2 (break open) blast, prise, thrust, use force, wrench

**forced** *adj* produced by special effort
**forceful** *adj* powerful, impressive
**forcible** *adj* done by force
**forceps** *n* surgical pincers or tweezers
**ford** *n* shallow place in river; *v* cross by means of ford
**forearm** *n* arm between elbow and wrist
**foreboding** *n* feeling that trouble is near
**forecast** *v* estimate (result) beforehand; *n* prediction of future event

**forecast** *v* divine, foresee, foretell, forewarn, predict, prophesy
**forecast** *n* guess, outlook, prognosis, projection, prophecy, speculation

**forefather** *n* ancestor
**forego** *v* -**going**, -**went**, -**gone** go without
**foregone conclusion** *n* certain outcome
**foreground** *n* nearest part of picture or view
**forehand** *n* tennis shot where player has palm of hand facing opponent
**forehead** *n* part of face above eyes
**foreign** *adj* 1 of a country other than one's own 2 concerning other countries 3 alien

**foreign** *adj* 1 (of a country other than one's own) alien, distant, exotic, faraway, outlandish, remote, strange, unfamiliar, unknown. 2 (concerning other countries) external, international, outside, overseas

**foreigner** *n* person of other nationality
**foreman** *n* 1 leading worker 2 leader of jury; *fem* **forewoman**
**foremost** *adj* most distinguished
**forename** *n* first name
**forensic** *adj* related to lawcourts **f. medicine** medical evidence used in lawcourts
**forerunner** *n* harbinger, precursor

**foresee** *v* -**seeing**, -**saw**, -**seen** predict

**foresee** *v* anticipate, envisage, expect, forebode, forecast, foretell, prophesy

**foresight** *n* ability to see and plan ahead

**foresight** *n* anticipation, care, farsightedness, forethought, vision

**foreskin** *n* loose skin covering tip of penis
**forest** *n* large tract of land covered with trees; *n* **forestry** art of managing forests
**forever** *adv* always; *n* eternity
**forewarn** *v* warn in advance
**foreword** *n* preface
**forfeit** *v* lose as penalty; *n* anything lost as penalty in law or game
**forge** *v* 1 soften, shape (metal) by heating 2 imitate deceitfully, counterfeit; *idm* **forge ahead** progress quickly; *n* workshop for working red-hot metal; *n* **forger** counterfeiter
**forgery** *n* fraudulent making or alteration of signature, document, etc

**forgery** *n* copy, counterfeit, fake, imitation, replica, reproduction

**forget** *v* -**getting**, -**got**, -**gotten** fail to remember

**forget** *v* disregard, ignore, lose sight of, neglect, omit, overlook

**forgetful** *adj* having bad memory

**forgetful** *adj* absentminded, distracted, dreamy, inattentive, oblivious, preoccupied

**forgive** *v* **forgiving**, **forgave** pardon; *n* **forgiveness**

**forgive** *v* absolve, acquit, condone, excuse, exonerate, ignore, let off, overlook

**forgiving** *adj* liable to forgive people

> **forgiving** *adj* compassionate, lenient, magnanimous, merciful, mild, soft-hearted, tolerant, understanding

**fork** *n* 1 pronged tool for digging, lifting 2 pronged tool for eating 3 junction of two roads, rivers 4 meeting of bough and trunk of tree; *v* 1 dig, lift, toss with fork 2 divide into branches; *idm* **fork out** *coll* pay reluctantly

**forlorn** *adj* 1 unhappy 2 empty 3 (of hope) very faint

**form** *n* 1 shape 2 type 3 document with spaces for information to be added 4 class; *v* 1 make 2 come into being 3 think up 4 act as

> **form** *n* 1 (shape) configuration, design, formation, pattern, structure. 2 (type) kind, sort, variety. 3 (document) paper, sheet. 4 (class) grade, group
>
> **form** *v* 1 (make) build, concoct, create, fashion, forge, model, mold, produce, shape. 2 (come into being) appear, come into existence, develop, grow, materialize, take shape. 3 (think up) devise, draw up, dream up, formulate, plan

**formal** *a* 1 dignified behavior 2 very polite 3 serious

> **formal** *adj* 1 (dignified behavior) ceremonial, elaborate, official, ritualistic, sophisticated. 2 (very polite) aloof, conventional, correct, prim, reserved, rigid, stuffy, unfriendly. 3 (serious) binding, contractual, legal, official, proper

**formality** *n* 1 propriety 2 *esp pl* conventional procedure 3 ceremony, *esp* one without real meaning or use

**format** *n* 1 shape of book 2 general plan of sth 3 *comput* arrangement of data; *v* comput **-matting, -matted** prepare with a format

**formation** *n* 1 act or instance of forming 2 thing formed 3 pattern of people or vehicles moving together.

**former** *adj* of earlier time; *n* thing or person referred to first; *adv* **-ly** in the past

**Formica** [TM] hard, laminated, heat-resistant plastic sheet

**formidable** *adj* terrifying; overwhelming; presenting obstacles; huge

**formula** *n* 1 set form of words, prescribed for use on particular occasion 2 definition of dogma 3 recipe; prescription 4 method of solving problem; *pl* **formulae, formulas**

**formulate** *v* 1 express 2 make; *n* **formulation**

> **formulate** *v* 1 (express) articulate, define, frame, give form to, set out, specify. 2 (make) create, devise, draw up, evolve, map out, plan, work out

**forsake** *v* abandon; *pt* **forsook**; *pp* **forsaken**

**fort** *n* fortified place; stronghold

**forte** *n* special ability; strong point

**forth** *adv* forward, onward

**forthcoming** *adj* 1 coming soon 2 communicative

> **forthcoming** *adj* 1 (coming soon) approaching, imminent, impending, prospective, upcoming. 2 (communicative) talkative, voluble

**forthright** *adj* outspoken, candid

**fortieth** *pron, det* ordinal number of 40

**fortification** *n* defensive works, walls, etc

**fortify** *v* **-fying, -fied** strengthen

**fortitude** *n* sustained courage

**fortnight** *n* *Brit* two weeks; *adv* **fortnightly**

**fortress** *n* fortified place; stronghold

**fortuitous** *adj* due to chance; accidental

**fortunate** *adj* lucky

> **fortunate** *adj* blessed, favored, happy, jammy, prosperous, successful

a b c d e f g h i j k l m n o p q r s t u v w x y z

**fortune** n 1 wealth 2 chance

> **fortune** n 1 (wealth) affluence, assets, inheritance, money, prosperity, riches, treasure. 2 (chance) accident, destiny, fate, kismet, luck, providence

**forty** adj, n four tens; **fortieth**

**forum** n Lat place where ideas can be discussed

**forward** adj 1 advanced 2 too bold; adv toward front; at, in fore part (of ship, etc.); onward (in direction, time); n sport one of players in front line; v send, mail on farther

> **forward** adj 1 (advanced) early, precocious, premature, well-developed. 2 (too bold) brash, brazen, impudent, insolent, overfamiliar, presumptuous, shameless

**forwent** pt of **forgo**

**fossil** n petrified remains of prehistoric animal, vegetable organism found preserved in earth or rocks; v **fossilize**

**foster** v 1 rear another's child as one's own 2 encourage; ns **foster-child**, **f.-mother**, **f.-father**

**foul** adj 1 dirty and disgusting 2 unpleasant 3 obscene; n, v act against the rules

> **foul** adj 1 (dirty, disgusting) contaminated, fetid, filthy, impure, infected, polluted, rank, repugnant, repulsive, revolting, rotten, smelly, squalid, stinking, unclean. 2 (unpleasant) atrocious, cruel, disgraceful, evil, horrible, scandalous, sordid, vicious, violent, wicked. 3 (obscene) blasphemous, coarse, filthy, offensive, rude, vulgar

**found** v 1 establish, institute 2 base; n **foundation** 1 founding 2 substructure of building 3 basis

**founder** v (of ship) fill with water and sink; fail

**fountain** n artificial, ornamental jet of water; jet of drinking water

**four** n, pron, det cardinal number next after three; adjs, ns, dets **fourth** a fourth part; ordinal number; **fourteen** four plus ten; **fourteenth;** n **four-poster** bed with four posts for curtains

**fowl** n bird; domestic cock or hen

**fox** n 1 reddish bushy-tailed animal 2 crafty person; v act cunningly; mislead

**foyer** n large hall, anteroom of theater

**fracas** n brawl; noisy quarrel

**fraction** n numerical quantity less or more than integer; small piece; fragment

> **fraction** n division, part, portion

**fracture** n break; v break

**fragile** adj easily broken

> **fragile** adj breakable, brittle, delicate, feeble, flimsy, frail, insubstantial, thin, weak

**fragment** n piece broken off; unfinished part

> **fragment** n bit, chip, crumb, fraction, morsel, part, particle, piece, portion, remnant, scrap, shard, shred, sliver

**fragrant** adj sweet-scented; n **fragrance**

**frail** adj 1 not in strong health 2 easily broken

> **frail** adj 1 (not in strong health) delicate, feeble, fragile, ill, infirm, puny, sickly, unwell, vulnerable, weak. 2 (easily broken) breakable, dainty, easily damaged, flimsy, fragile, insubstantial, rickety, thin

**frame** v 1 construct; contrive 2 express in words; 3 cause to appear guilty 4 surround with, serve as, frame; n structure; border of wood, etc round picture setting; wood and glass structure protecting plants, etc; idm **frame of mind** mood; n **framework** substructure, skeleton

**franc** n French, Belgian, Swiss, etc coin, monetary unit

**franchise** n 1 voting rights of citizen 2 right to sell company's goods or services; v grant such; adj right

**frank** adj direct and sincere; adv **-ly** openly

> **frank** adj blunt, candid, forthright, honest, open, outspoken, plain, straight, straightforward, truthful, upfront

**frankfurter** n small smoked sausage

**frankincense** n sweet resin used in incense

**frantic** adj violenty excited, esp with rage, pain

> **frantic** adj agitated, beserk, beside yourself, crazy, desperate, distracted, distraught, frenetic, frenzied, furious, hectic, hysterical, mad, raving, wild

**fraternal** adj pertaining to brother; brotherly; n **fraternity** association of men with common interest; v **fraternize** be on friendly terms

**fraud** n 1 criminal deception 2 trick 3 impostor

> **fraud** n 1 (criminal deception) cheating, dishonesty, double-dealing, sharp practice, skulduggery, treachery, trickery. 2 (trick) con, deception, hoax, ruse, scam. 3 (impostor) cheat, con man, fake, hoaxer, phony, quack, scoundrel, swindler

**fraudulent** adj dishonest

**fraught** adj charged; teeming; full of

**fray**[1] n noisy fight

**fray**[2] v become ragged (as cloth) by rubbing

**freak** n abnormal form; adj abnormal

> **freak** adj atypical, bizarre, exceptional, extraordinary, freakish, odd, peculiar, queer, rare, unexpected, unpredictable, unusual, weird

**freckle** n small brown spot on skin; adj **freckled**

**free** adj 1 given without payment 2 at liberty 3 independent 4 available for use; idm **free with** generous in giving; adv **-ly**; v liberate

> **free** adj 1 (given without payment) at no cost, complimentary, for nothing, on the house. 2 (at liberty) allowed, at large, clear, liberated, loose, unchained, unhindered, unobstructed, unrestrained. 3 (independent) autonomous, democratic, self-governing. 4 (available for use) empty, extra, spare, unoccupied, unused, vacant
> **free** v cut loose, discharge, emancipate, extricate, let go, let out, loose, release, rescue, save, turn loose, unchain, undo, unleash, untie

**freedom** n 1 right to do sth 2 liberty

> **freedom** n 1 (right to do sth) carte blanche, flexibility, free rein, latitude, leeway, license, opportunity, scope. 2 (liberty) autonomy, deliverance, emancipation, home rule, independence, sovereignty

**free kick** n kick awarded for infringement of rule

**freelance** n self-employed independent worker

**freeman** n person given freedom of the city

**freeze** v 1 become ice; 2 congeal with cold 3 refrigerate; chill keep (wages, interest, etc) fixed at present level 4 fig become rigid 5 pt **froze**; pp **frozen**; n **freezer** refrigerator; adj **frozen** (food) preserved by freezing; (assets, etc) unrealizable

**freezing** adj extremely cold

> **freezing** adj arctic, biting, bitter, cutting, frosty, ice-cold, icy, raw, snowy, wintry

**freight** n hire of ship for conveyance of goods; any load of goods for transport, esp ship's cargo; v hire, load (vessel)

**French** n, adj (the language) of France; pl people of France

a b c d e f g h i j k l m n o p q r s t u v w x y z

**frenetic** a very busy; frantic
**frenzied** *adj* wildly, violently agitated
**frenzy** *n* violent excitment; rage, grief, etc
**frequency** *n* repeated occurrence; *elec*
number of cycles per second of alternating
current; **high f., medium f., low f.**
*rad* rate of vibration of sound waves
**frequent** *adj* happening often; common
*adv* **-ly**; *v* visit habitually

> **frequent** *adj* common, constant, continual,
> customary, everyday, familiar, habitual,
> incessant, innumerable, many, numerous,
> persistent, recurrent

**fresco** *n* wall painting on damp plaster
**fresh** *adj* 1 (of food) not stale or previously
cooked 2 (of water) clear 3 new 4 lively
5 (of wind) bracing 6 clean; *adv* **-ly**;
*n* **-ness**; *v* **freshen** make, become fresh

> **fresh** *adj* 1 (of food) crisp, healthy, natural,
> raw, unprocessed, untreated. 2 (of water)
> clean, clear, drinkable, pure, refreshing,
> sweet, uncontaminated. 3 (new)
> different, innovative, modern, novel,
> original, up-to-date. 4 (lively) alive,
> awake, bright, energetic, invigorated,
> refreshed, restored, revived, tingling.
> 5 (of wind) bracing, brisk, chilly, cool,
> invigorating, strong. 6 (clean) crisp,
> laundered, starched, unused, washed

**freshwater** *adj* of inland (not salinated)
water
**fret** *v* **fretting, fretted** worry
**friar** *n* monk
**fricative** *n adj* (consonant) made by air
passing through narrow space between teeth,
tongue, lips, etc
**friction** *n* resistance met when surface of
body moves across another; *fig* antagonism
**Friday** *n* sixth day of week
**fridge** *n coll* refrigerator
**friend** *n* person for whom one feels affection
and respect

**friendly** *n* kind, amiable

> **friendly** *adj* affectionate, agreeable,
> amicable, approachable, civil, helpful,
> hospitable, intimate, kindhearted, kindly,
> neighborly, sociable, sympathetic, warm,
> welcoming

**friendship** *n* kindly feeling
**frieze** *n* ornamental horizontal band in room
or building
**frigate** *n* light warship; sailing warship
**fright** *n* sudden alarm; fear; terror
**frighten** *v* scare

> **frighten** *v* 1 alarm, petrify, spook, startle,
> terrify, terrorize, unnerve, upset

**frightened** *adj* scared

> **frightened** *adj* afraid, alarmed, anxious,
> apprehensive, cowardly, fearful, horrified,
> horror-struck, panicky, panic-stricken,
> petrified, shocked, startled, terrified,
> trembling, unnerved, upset

**frightening** *adj* causing fear

> **frightening** *adj* alarming, blood-curdling,
> creepy, daunting, dreadful, eerie, fearful,
> fearsome, ghostly, hair-raising, horrifying,
> intimidating, menacing, scary, shocking,
> sinister, spine-chilling, terrifying

**frightful** *adj* shocking, horrible
**frigid** *adj* cold; devoid of feeling
**frill** *n* pleated, flounced ornamental trimming
on edge of dress, curtains, etc
**fringe** *n* 1 ornamental edging of threads,
loops, tassels, etc 2 outer edge; border; limit;
*v* adorn with, act as fringe
**Frisbee** [TM] saucer-shaped plastic disk for
throwing
**frisk** *v* gambol, frolic; *coll* search (suspect);
*n* **-iness**
**frisky** *adj* lively

**fritter**[1] n slice of fruit, etc, fried in batter
**fritter**[2] v waste, dissipate money, time, etc
**frivolous** adj silly
**frock** n woman's dress
**frog** n tailless amphibian, developed from tadpole; ns **frogman** swimmer equipped and trained for underwater operations; **frog spawn** frog's eggs
**frolic** v gambol, play pranks
**from** prep expressing source, distance, divergence, cause; opp of to; not near to
**front** n 1 forward part 2 battle area, forward line 3 area of land on beach 4 face of building 5 something, person acting as cover for illegal activities 6 forward part of weather change; v face; stand opposite to; idm **in front of** 1 ahead of 2 in the presence of; idm **up front** paid in advance
**frontage** n wide th building or plot at front
**frontier** n boundary between states

> **frontier** n border, confines, edge, limit

**frontispiece** n illustration at front of book
**frost** n particles of frozen moisture on earth's or other surface; air temperature causing this; adj **frosty** freezing; not genial; n **frostbite** gangrenous injury to tissues, due to exposure to extreme cold; adj **frostbitten**
**froth** n light mass of small bubbles; foam; v cause to emith froth
**frothy** adj bubbly
**frown** v wrinkle forehead in concentration or anger

> **frown** v glare, glower, knit your brows, look sullen, scowl

**frugal** adj 1 sparing; thrifty 2 inexpensive
**fruit** n 1 edible part of plant containing seed 2 usu pl result of effort
**fruitcake** n cake with dried fruit
**fruitful** adj successful
**fruitless** adj vain
**fruit salad** n mixture of fruits in syrup
**fruition** n fulfillment, enjoyment

**frump** n plain, dowdy woman; adj **-ish**
**frustrate** v baffle, irritate

> **frustrate** v annoy, defeat, disappoint, discourage, dishearten, embitter, foil, hinder, prevent, spoil, stymie, thwart, vex

**frustrated** adj irritated

> **frustrated** adj annoyed, disappointed, discontented, discouraged, disheartened, embittered, resentful, unfulfilled, unsatisfied

**frustration** n resentment
**fry** v **-ying, -ied** cook, be cooked in hot fat
**frying pan** n shallow pan for frying
**fuchsia** n ornamental flowering shrub
**fuddy-duddy** n, adj fussy person
**fudge**[1] n 1 soft, sugary candy 2 nonsense
**fudge**[2] v coll 1 perform clumsily 2 evade 3 falsify
**fuel** n any material used for burning; v **fueling, fueled** provide with, take in fuel
**fugitive** adj fleeing; n one fleeing from captivity
**fugue** n musical contrapuntal composition with recurring themes
**fulcrum** n point on which lever moves
**fulfil** v **-filling, -filled** satisfy; comply with; carry out; perform; n **-ment**
**fulgent** adj shining, radiant, blazing; n **fulgency**
**full** adj 1 unable to hold more 2 detailed 3 crowded 4 plump

> **full** adj 1 (full of sth) brimful, brimming, bursting, filled, gorged, loaded, overflowing, replete, sated, satisfied, saturated, stuffed, well-stocked. 2 (detailed) complete, comprehensive, copious, entire, exhaustive, thorough, unabridged, whole. 3 (crowded) chock-full inf, crammed, jammed, jam-packed inf, packed

**full-blown** *adj* fully developed
**fully** *adv* completely
**fulminate** *v* 1 flash, explode, detonate
2 denounce violently; *n* highly explosive
compound; *n* **-ation**
**fulsome** *adj* excessive
**fumble** *v* 1 grope clumsily 2 bungle
**fume** *v* 1 emit fumes 2 be angry
**fumes** *n pl* pungent smoke

> **fumes** *n* exhaust, gases, pollution, smog,
> smoke, vapor

**fumigate** *v* disinfect by fumes; *ns* **-ation**,
**-ator**
**fun** *n* enjoyment; *idm* **make f. of** ridicule;
*idm* **in f.** as joke

> **fun** *n* amusement, distraction, diversion,
> entertainment, games, jokes, joking, joy,
> laughter, merriment, pleasure, recreation,
> relaxation, sport

**function** *n* 1 normal purpose 2 official task
3 large social gathering; *v* act, work

> **function** *n* 1 (normal purpose) aim,
> purpose, raison d'être, use. 2 (official task)
> capacity, duty, job, responsibility, role.
> 3 (social gathering) affair, do, event,
> occasion, party, reception, social occasion

**functional** *adj* having special purpose;
*med* affecting function
**functionary** *n* official
**fund** *n* permanent stock; sum set apart for
special purpose; *pl* **-s** money resources;
*v* invest in
**fundamental** *adj* basic; *adv* **-ly**; *n* basic rule;
principle

> **fundamental** *adj* central, crucial,
> elementary, essential, first, important,
> inherent, intrinsic, key, necessary,
> principal, quintessential, underlying, vital

**funding** *n* money given to pay for work
**funeral** *n* burial of dead; *adj* relating to
funeral
**funeral director** *n* undertaker
**funeral parlor** *n* undertaker's premises
**funerary** *adj* of, for funeral
**funereal** *adj* mournful, dismal, black
**fungus** *n* (*pl* **-i**) plant or allied growth
reproducing by spores, *eg* mushroom, mildew,
etc; *adj* **fungoid, fungous**; *n* **fungicide**
substance which destroys fungi
**funky** *adj coll* 1 with simple style
2 fashionable
**funnel** *n* 1 cone-shaped tube for pouring
liquids through to container 2 smoke stack
of ship, locomotive; *v* pour off, as through
funnel
**funny** *adj* 1 amusing 2 strange; *adv* **funnily**

> **funny** *adj* 1 (amusing) comical, daft, droll,
> entertaining, hilarious, humorous, ironic,
> ludicrous, mad, nonsensical, preposterous,
> ridiculous, riotous, satirical, side-splitting,
> uproarious, witty. 2 (strange) curious,
> mysterious, peculiar, puzzling, suspicious

**funny bone** *n* elbow
**fur** *n* 1 short soft hair forming animal coat;
dressed skin of animal; *pl* such skins
collectively 2 coating; deposit (on tongue, in
kettle, etc); *v* cover, become coated, with
fur; *adj* **furry** of, like fur
**furbish** *v* polish, clean up; burnish
**furcate** *adj* branched, forked
**furious** *adj* 1 very angry 2 fierce

> **furious** *adj* 1 (very angry) beside yourself,
> enraged, fuming, incensed, infuriated,
> irate, livid, mad. 2 (fierce) frantic,
> frenetic, intense, stormy, turbulent, violent

**furl** *v* roll up and bind securely (umbrella)
**furlong** *n* ⅛th mile, 220 yards (approx
207 m)
**furnace** *n* enclosed chamber of brick, metal,
in which great heat can be generated

**furnish** *v* provide; equip, *esp* house, office, etc with furniture; *n* **furnisher** one who sells furnitue; **furnishing act of** equipping house

**furniture** *n* movable household equipment

**furor** *n* general excitement

**furrier** *n* dealer in furs

**furrow** *n* **1** groove made in land by plow **2** deep wrinkle on face, etc; *v* make furrows

**further** *v* forward, promote; *adv* besides; *adj, adv* (*comp* of **far**) more distant; to greater degree, extent; *adj, adv* **furthest** to greatest degree, extent; *n* **furtherance** promotion; *adv* **furthermore** besides; **furtive** *adj* secret

> **furtive** *adj* clandestine, conspiratorial, covert, disguised, hidden, secretive, shifty, skulking, slinking, sly, sneaking, sneaky, stealthy, surreptitious, underhand

**fury** *n* **1** extreme anger; rage **2** *cap* avenging, Greek goddess

**furze** *n* thick-growing, yellow-flowered, prickly shrub

**fuse** *n* **1** device to explode shells, mines, etc **2** soft wire with low melting point, used as safety device in electric circuits; *v* **1** melt (metal) with heat **2** fit fuse to

**fuselage** *n* body of aircraft

**fusillade** *n* continuous rapid firing

**fuss** *n* nervous, anxious state of mind; *v* fret

> **fuss** *n* bother, confusion, excitement, flurry, row, trouble, tumult, uproar, upset

**fusspot** *n coll* fussy person

**fussy** *adj* liking only certain things but not others

> **fussy** *adj* choosy, difficult, finicky, hard to please, nit-picking *inf*, picky *inf*

**fusty** *adj* stale and stuffy; old-fashioned

**futile** *adj* vain, useless, ineffectual; *n* **futility**

**futon** *n* padded type of mattress used on bed

**future** *adj* happening hereafter; *n* **1** time to come **2** fate **3** tense of verb indicating future; *pl* **-s** *comm* goods or shares for later delivery paid for at today's prices; *ns* **futurity**, **futurism** non-representational art against tradition; *adj* **futuristic**

> **future** *adj* approaching, awaited, coming, forthcoming, impending, prospective, subsequent, to come

**fuzz** *n* **1** stiff fluffy hair **2** *sl* police

**fuzzy** *adj* fluffy, blurred

**FYI** *abbr* for your information

a
b
c
d
e
f
g
h
i
j
k
l
m
n
o
p
q
r
s
t
u
v
w
x
y
z

**gabardine** *n* woolen fabric; rainproof coat

**gabble** *v* utter rapidly and indistinctly; *n* such talk

**gable** *n* triangular upper part of wall of building enclosed by roof ridges

**gad** *v* **gadding, gadded** wander about aimlessly or seeking pleasure; *n* **gadabout** pleasure seeker

**gadget** *n* ingenious device

> **gadget** *n* appliance, contraption, contrivance, device, instrument, invention, novelty, tool, utensil

**Gaelic** *n* Celtic speech, *esp* of Scotland; *n* **Gael** Scottish, Irish Celt

**gaffe** *n* blunder

**gag** *n* **1** anything thrust into mouth to silence person **2** joke; *v* **gagging, gagged 1** silence by gag **2** retch

**gaggle** *n* flock of geese

**gaiety** *n* cheerfulness

**gaily** *adv* in a cheerful manner

**gain** *v* obtain; earn; *n* sth obtained or earned

> **gain** *v* achieve, acquire, attain, build up, capture, collect, get, make, net, pick up, reach, secure, win, yield
>
> **gain** *n* acquisition, advantage, attainment, benefit, earnings, improvement, income, increase, profit, return, rise, winnings

**gainsay** *v* **gainsaying, gainsaid** dispute, contradict, deny

**gait** *n* manner of walking

**gala** *n* festivity; fête

**galaxy** *n* vast cluster of stars, as Milky Way; *fig* brilliant assembly; *adj* **galactic**

**gale** *n* strong, violent wind

> **gale** *n* blast, cyclone, hurricane, squall, storm, tempest, tornado, typhoon, wind

**galena** *n* natural lead sulfide

**gall** *n* **1** bitter secretion from liver **2** bitterness **3** effrontery

**gallant** *adj* brave; *n* **gallantry**

> **gallant** *adj* bold, chivalrous, courageous, courteous, courtly, daring, dashing, fearless, heroic, honorable, intrepid, manly, noble, polite, valiant

**galleon** *n* three- or four-decked sailing ship

**gallery** *n* **1** upper tier of seats in theater **2** room, building for showing works of art

**galley** *n* **1** ship with sails and oars **2** ship's kitchen

**Gallic** *adj* of, relating to Gaul; French; *n* **Gallicism** French word, idiom used in another language

**gallivant** *v* gad about

**gallon** *n* liquid or dry measure of capacity

**gallop** *v* move, ride very fast; *n* fastest pace of horse, etc; quick ride; *fig* hurry

**Gallop poll** *n* survey of public opinion

**gallows** *n* structure for hanging criminals

**galore** *adv* plentifully; in great abundance

**galvanize** *v* stimulate into activity

**gambit** *n* opening, first move

**gamble** *v* **1** bet money **2** take a chance; *n* risky chance; *n* **gambler**

> **gamble** *v* **1** (bet money) bet, have a flutter, lay bets, stake money, wager. **2** (take a chance) speculate, stick your neck out *inf*, take a risk, trust, venture

**game**[1] *n* pastime; sporting contest; jest

**game**[2] *n* birds, animals hunted for sport

**gamesmanship** *n* art of winning by distracting one's opponent without breaking any rules

**gamete** *n* mature sexual reproductive cell that joins with another to form a new organism

**gamut** *n* whole range, extent

**gander** *n* male goose

**gang** *n* group; band of criminals

> **gang** *n* band, clique, crew, crowd, herd, horde, lot, mob, pack, posse, team

**gangling** *adj* awkwardly tall and thin

**gangplank** *n* gangway on ship

**gangrene** *n* decay of living tissue

**gangster** *n* 1 member of criminal gang

> **gangster** *n* bandit, brigand, desperado, gunman, robber, thug, tough

**gangway** *n* movable bridge from ship to shore; way between rows of seats

**gantry** *n* frame structure used for support

**gap** *n* 1 hole 2 interval

> **gap** *n* 1 (hole) aperture, blank, breach, break, cavity, chink, crack, crevice, divide, gulf, opening, rift, space, void. 2 (interval) break, breathing-space, interlude, interruption, lull, pause, respite, rest, suspension, wait

**gape** *v* stare in wonder; open widely

**garb** *n* clothing, dress

**garbage** *n* 1 food waste 2 useless information

**garbled** *adj* confused, jumbled

**garden** *n* area of ground for growing flowers, fruit, or vegetables; *v* cultivate a garden; *ns* **gardener; garden center** place where plants, tools, etc are sold

**gargle** *v* wash or soothe sore throat with liquid held there by blowing gently

**gargoyle** *n* carved head on church

**garish** *adj* gaudy; ostentatious

**garland** *n* wreath of flowers

**garlic** *n* bulbous-rooted plant of onion family

**garment** *n* article of clothing

**garner** *v* store up; accumulate

**garnet** *n* red semiprecious stone

**garnish** *v* decorate, improve appearance of (*esp* food); *n* material for this

**garret** *n* room under roof of house; attic

**garrison** *n* troops defending fortress, town

**garrotte** *v* kill by strangling

**garter** *n* band worn to keep stocking up

**gas** *n* **-es** or **-ses**. 1 vaporous substance 2 liquid distilled from petroleum 3 poisonous vapor used in warfare; *v* **gassing, gassed** use gas upon; *ns* **g. mask, gasworks**; *adjs* **gaseous, gassy**

**gash** *n* deep cut; slash; *v* cut deeply

> **gash** *v* cut, gouge, lacerate, nick, score, slit, split, tear, wound

**gasp** *v* catch breath suddenly, as in surprise or fear; *n* sudden catching of breath

**gastric** *adj* of, relating to stomach

**gastroenteritis** *n* inflammation of stomach

**gastronomy** *n* science of good food

**gate** *n* 1 hinged frame of wood or metal across opening, path, etc 2 sluice 3 way in or out of place; *v* **gate-crash** enter uninvited; *n* **-er**

> **gate** *n* barrier, door, doorway, entrance, exit, gateway, portal, portcullis, turnstile

**gateway** *n* entrance with gate

**gather** *v* 1 collect 2 come together 3 understand 4 pick; *n* **gathers** small pleats

> **gather** *v* 1 (collect) accumulate, amass, heap, hoard, pile up, stockpile. 2 (come together) assemble, congregate, convene, crowd, get together, flock, group, mass, mobilize, swarm, throng. 3 (understand) assume, believe, deduce, guess, hear, infer, learn. 4 (pick) harvest, pluck, reap

a b c d e f g h i j k l m n o p q r s t u v w x y z

**A B C D E F G H I J K L M N O P Q R S T U V W X Y Z**

**gathering** n assembly

**gauche** adj clumsy, tactless, awkward;
n **gaucherie**

**gaucho** n S American cowboy

**gaudy** adj showy; garish

> **gaudy** adj bright, brilliant, flashy, glaring, harsh, loud, ostentatious, tasteless, tawdry, vivid, vulgar

**gauge** n 1 standard of measure 2 instrument for measuring rainfall, force of wind, etc; v 1 measure 2 estimate

> **gauge** n 1 (standard of measure) bore, capacity, depth, height, measure, size, thickness, width. 2 (instrument) dial, indicator, meter

**gaunt** adj lean and haggard

> **gaunt** adj angular, bony, drawn, emaciated, hollow-cheeked, pinched, scrawny, skinny, starving, thin, wasted

**gauntlet** n large glove with protective cuff; idm **throw down g.** issue challenge; idm **run the g.** run (as punishment) between two rows of hostile people

**gauze** n thin, transparent silk fabric

**gawk** v stare at in a stupid way

**gawky** adj awkward; ungainly

**gay** adj 1 cheerful 2 homosexual; n homosexual

**gaze** v look intently

> **gaze** v eye, gape, look, stare, watch

**gazebo** n pavilion structure set on a lawn

**gazelle** n small, delicately formed antelope

**gazette** n newspaper; v publish in gazette; n **gazetteer**

**gazpacho** n cold vegetable soup

**gear** n 1 equipment 2 mechanism transmitting or controlling movement 3 clothes; n **gear-box**

**gear** n 1 (equipment) belongings, bits and pieces, kit, paraphernalia, possessions, stuff, things, tools, trappings. 2 (mechanism controlling movement) cog, cogwheel, gearwheel, machinery. 3 (clothes) clothing, dress, outfit, togs

**gecko** n house lizard

**geese** pl of **goose**

**Geiger counter** n instrument that detects radioactivity

**gelatin** n sticky substance, obtained from animal bones; adj **gelatinous** like jelly

**geld** v castrate; n **gelding** castrated horse

**gelid** adj icy

**gem** n precious stone

**gender** n 1 classification of nouns, pronouns according to sex 2 sex

**gene** n carrier of hereditary factor in chromosome

**genealogy** n line of descent from ancestors; adj **-logical**

**genera** pl of **genus**

**general** adj 1 not specific 2 usual 3 approximate; n army rank above colonel; ns **g. election** national election; **g. practitioner** physician

> **general** adj 1 (not specific) across-the-board, blanket, broad, comprehensive, global, inclusive, overall, universal. 2 (usual) accepted, common, customary, normal, regular, typical. 3 (approximate) ballpark, broad, loose, outline, rough, vague

**generalize** v draw general conclusions; ns **-ization**

**generally** adv 1 usually 2 by most people

> **generally** adv 1 (usually) as a rule, broadly speaking, by and large, commonly, mostly, normally, on the whole, typically. 2 (by most people) commonly, popularly, universally, widely

**generate** *v* be cause of; *n* **generation** 1 act of generating 2 all persons of approximate same age group; *n* **generator** apparatus for producing electricity

**generation gap** *n* lack of understanding between parents and younger generation

**generic** *adj* pertaining to genus or class

**generous** *adj* 1 willing to give 2 large in amount; *n* **generosity**

> **generous** *adj* 1 (willing to give) benevolent, charitable, kind, magnanimous, philanthropic. 2 (large in amount) abundant, huge, large, lavish, plentiful

**genetic engineering** *n* changing of genetic structure to produce new strain

**genetic fingerprint** *n* the genetic information about an individual, used to identify the person or as evidence in court

**genetics** *n* branch of biology studying heredity; *adj* **genetic**

**genial** *adj* 1 kind and friendly 2 (of climate) mild, warm; *n* **-ity**

**genie** *n* Arabian demon or spirit; *pl* **genii**

**genital** *adj* relating to reproductive organs; *n pl* external reproductive organs

**genius** *n* 1 very clever person 2 exceptional ability; *pl* **geniuses**

> **genius** *n* 1 (very clever person) expert, master, mastermind, prodigy, virtuoso, whiz-kid *inf*. 2 (ability) aptitude, brains, brilliance, flair, gift, talent

**genocide** *n* deliberate murder of a people

**genre** *n* 1 kind, style, species 2 painting of rustic life

**genteel** *adj* unnaturally polite or elegant

**gentian** *n* herb usually having vivid blue flowers

**gentile** *n* person who is not Jewish

**gentle** *adj* 1 kind 2 quiet 3 not steep; *ns* **gentleman** well-bred man; honorable, courteous man; **gentleness** quality of being gentle; kindliness

**gentle** *adj* 1 (kind) amiable, mild, placid, soft, tender. 2 (quiet) delicate, easy, light, mild, muted, peaceful, soft, soothing. 3 (not steep) easy, gradual, moderate, slight, smooth, steady

**gentry** *n* upper-class people

**genuine** *adj* 1 true; real 2 sincere; *adv* **-ly**

> **genuine** *adj* 1 (true) authentic, bona fide, guaranteed, kosher, legitimate, original, pukka *inf*, real. 2 (sincere) candid, honest, open, straight

**genus** *n* sort; group of species; *pl* **genera**

**geography** *n* science describing earth's physical features, climate, etc; *n* **geographer**; *adj* **geographic(al)**

**geology** *n* science dealing with earth's crust, its history and structure; *n* **geologist** *adj* **geologic(al)**

**geometry** *n* mathematical science dealing with properties of lines, surfaces, etc

**gerbil** *n* small, burrowing rodent

**geriatrics** *n pl* medical care and treatment of old people; *adj* **geriatric** of old people

**germ** *n* microbe causing illness

> **germ** *n* bacteria, bug *inf*, infection, micro-organism, virus

**German** *n* (native, language) of Germany; **G. measles** contagious disease

**germinate** *v* begin to sprout or develop

**gerund** *n* verbal noun

**gestation** *n* time from conception to birth

**gesticulate** *v* wave hands or arms

**gesture** *n* 1 movement of arms, hands to convey meaning 2 something done for effect

**get** *v* **getting, got** 1 obtain 2 become 3 fetch 4 capture 5 become ill with 6 arrive 7 understand; *phr vs* **get along** be friendly; **get around** 1 avoid 2 be friendly; **get at** 1 criticize 2 imply; **get away** escape; **get on** progress

a b c d e f **g** h i j k l m n o p q r s t u v w x y z

**get** *v* **1** (obtain) achieve, acquire, attain, come by, earn, gain, inherit, lay your hands on, make, procure, receive, secure, win. **2** (become) go, grow, turn. **3** (fetch) collect, pick up. **4** (capture) arrest, collar, grab, nail, seize, trap. **5** (become ill with) be infected by, catch, come down with, contract, develop, fall ill with, go down with, pick up. **6** (arrive) come, reach. **7 get along** (be friendly) be on good terms, get along, hit it off. **8 get at** (criticize) attack, blame, carp, make fun of, nag, pick on, taunt, tease. **9 get at** (imply) hint, insinuate, mean, suggest. **10 get away** (escape) abscond, break free, break out, depart, disappear, get out, leave, run away. **11 get on** (progress) carry on, continue, crack on, press on

**getaway** *n* escape
**getup** *n coll* choice of clothes
**geyser** *n* natural spout of hot water
**ghastly** *adj* terrifying, horrible
**gherkin** *n* small cucumber used in pickles
**ghetto** *n* poor quarter inhabited by one racial or ethnic group of city, town
**ghetto blaster** *n coll* large portable radiocassette player
**ghost** *n* spirit of dead person

**ghost** *n* apparition, ghoul, phantom, shade, specter, spirit, spook *inf*, wraith

**ghostly** *adj* strange and unnatural
**ghoul** *n* ghost; spirit
**giant** *n* huge man, creature

**giant** *n* behemoth, colossus, Goliath, leviathan, monster, titan, whopper *inf*

**gibber** *v* chatter incomprehensibly
**gibberish** *n* meaningless words
**gibbet** *n* gallows for execution by hanging
**gibbon** *n* small, long-armed ape
**giblets** *n pl* edible inner parts of fowl

**giddy** *adj* dizzy; *n* **giddiness**
**gift** *n* **1** present **2** talent

**gift** *n* **1** (present) bequest, contribution, donation, endowment, gratuity, legacy, offering, tip. **2** (talent) ability, flair, genius, knack, power

**gifted** *adj* talented

**gifted** *adj* accomplished, brainy, bright, brilliant, clever, expert, skillful

**gig** *n* performance of pop music
**gigabyte** *n* one billion bytes
**gigantic** *adj* enormous

**gigantic** *adj* colossal, giant, huge, immense, king-size, mammoth, massive, monstrous, towering, vast

**giggle** *v* laugh in nervous way
**gild** *v* **gilding, gilded** or **gilt** coat thinly, with gold; *fig* embellish; *adj* **gilt** gilded; *n* **gilt** gold leaf or paint
**gilt-edged** *adj* (of securities) with fixed, guaranteed interest rate
**gill** *n* fish's breathing organ
**gimmick** *n sl* device for attracting publicity

**gimmick** *n* dodge, gizmo, publicity stunt, stunt, trick

**gin** *n* type of alcoholic drink
**ginger** *n* tropical spice; *adj* sandy red color
**gingerbread** *n* cake flavored with ginger
**gingerly** *adv* carefully
**gingham** *n* checked or striped cotton cloth
**giraffe** *n* very tall African ruminant
**girder** *n* large metal or wooden beam
**girl** *n* female child; young unmarried woman

**girl** *n* daughter, female, kid, lass, schoolgirl, woman, young woman, youngster

**girlfriend** *n* female sweetheart or woman

**girlfriend** n date, lover, sweetheart, young lady, woman

**girth** n bellyband of saddle, etc; circumference
**gist** n main points of speech
**give** v **giving, gave 1** offer **2** say **3** inflict **4** organize **5** yield; *phr vs* **give away 1** sell for no profit **2** betray; **give in** surrender; **give out 1** share out **2** emit; **give up 1** abandon doing **2** stop doing

**give** v **1** (offer) allocate, award, contribute, deliver, dish out, dole out, donate, grant, hand over, prescribe, present, provide, share out, supply. **2** (say) announce, communicate, deliver, make, reveal, tell, utter. **3** (inflict) administer, dish out, dispense, impose. **4** (organize) arrange, have, put on. **5** (yield) buckle, fall, give way, sink. **6** (**give in**) capitulate, comply, concede defeat, give up, quit, submit, succumb, surrender, throw in the towel. **7** **give out** (share out) deal, distribute, dole out, hand out. **8** **give out** (emit) discharge, exude, give off, produce, release. **9** **give up** (abandon doing) capitulate, concede defeat, give in, lose heart, quit, submit, succumb, surrender, throw in the towel

**givaway** n **1** revealing act or remark **2** event where prizes are awarded
**glabrous** adj smooth; hairless
**glacier** n slowly moving mass of ice; adj **glacial** of ice, glaciers, very cold
**glad** adj **1** happy **2** willing; v **gladden**

**glad** adj **1** (happy) cheerful, chuffed, delighted, elated, joyful, over the moon, pleased, satisfied, thrilled, well-pleased. **2** (willing) delighted, eager, happy, keen, pleased, ready

**glade** n opening, clearing in wood, forest
**gladiator** n in ancient Rome, professional fighter with sword, etc in arena

**glamor** n mysterious charm
**glamorous** adj attractive and wealthy

**glamorous** adj appealing, beautiful, beguiling, dazzling, exciting, flash, glittering, glossy, prestigious, smart

**glance** n, v (give) quick look
**gland** n organ that secretes substance for use in body; adj **glandular**
**glare** v **1** emit dazzling light **2** stare angrily; n blinding brightness

**glare** v (stare angrily) frown, glower, look daggers at, scowl, stare

**glaring 1** flagrant **2** dazzling
**glass** n **1** transparent substance used for windows **2** drinking vessel of glass **3** mirror; pl **-es** spectacles
**glaze** v **1** put glass into **2** coat with glassy substance; n glasslike surface; shiny coating for pottery
**gleam** v shine; n flash of light

**gleam** v flash, glimmer, glint, glisten, glow, sparkle, twinkle

**glean** v gather facts
**glee** n lighthearted mirth
**glen** n narrow valley
**glide** v move along smoothly; n action of gliding; n **glider** aircraft without engine

**glide** v coast, drift, sail, skate, skim, slide, slip, soar

**glimmer** v flicker, glow faint;y
**glimpse** adj passing sight; v see briefly
**glint** v flash, shine faintly
**glisten** v shine, sparkle

**glisten** v gleam, glint, glitter, shimmer

**glitter** v shine, sparkle
**glitterati** n fashionable, wealthy people

**glitz** n showy glamor; adj **-y**
**gloat** v boast

> **gloat** v brag, crow about, revel in, rub it in, show off, wallow in

**globe** n 1 ball 2 earth; model of earth; adj **global** 1 worldwide 2 overall; adv **-ly**; n **global warming** increase in temperature of the earth's atmosphere believed to be caused by the greenhouse effect
**globule** n drop of liquid
**glockenspiel** n instrument of metal bars struck by hammers, giving bell-like notes
**gloom** n darkness; melancholy
**gloomy** adj 1 depressed 2 dark

> **gloomy** adj 1 (depressed) dejected, dismal, down, low, miserable, pessimistic, sad. 2 (dark) dim, dull, murky, overcast

**glorious** adj wonderful

> **glorious** adj beautiful, brilliant, fine, gorgeous, lovely, magnificent, splendid, superb, terrific

**glory** n 1 triumph 2 magnificence; v take delight in; boast
**gloss**[1] n shine on surface; phr v **gloss over** conceal (faults); adj **glossy**
**gloss**[2] n explanation; v explain; n **glossary** explanatory list of words
**glove** n covering for hand and fingers
**glow** v shine; n shine
**glower** v scowl
**glowing** adj 1 shining 2 full of praise

> **glowing** adj 1 (shining) bright, flushed, radiant, red, rich, rosy, vivid. 2 (full of praise) complimentary, enthusiastic, warm

**glucose** n sugar found in fruits
**glue** n adhesive; v fasten with glue; idm **glued to** unable to turn one's attention from
**glum** adj morose; sullen; moody

**glut** n too much of sth

> **glut** n excess, overabundance, oversupply, surplus

**gluten** n protein found in wheat flour
**glutinous** adj sticky
**glutton** n greedy feeder; insatiable enthusiast (for work, etc); n **gluttony**
**GMT** abbr Greenwich Mean Time
**gnarled** adj knobby; rugged; weather-beaten
**gnash** v grind teeth with rage
**gnat** n small blood-sucking winged insect
**gnaw** v chew

> **gnaw** v bite, chomp, eat, eat away, munch, nibble, wear away

**gnome** n dwarfish goblin
**gnu** n S African antelope; wildebeest
**go** v **going, went** 1 leave 2 move 3 function 4 lead to 5 pass 6 become 7 proceed; phr vs **go ahead** proceed; **go along with** agree with; **go back on** change one's mind about; **go down** 1 descend 2 be defeated 3 be received; **go down with** fall ill with; **go for** 1 attack 2 like; **go in for** 1 enter (contest) 2 like; **go off** 1 turn bad 2 explode 3 cease to like; **go through** 1 look through 2 endure

> **go** v 1 (leave) beat it, depart, disappear, get away, get going, get moving, retreat, set off, set out, shove off inf, vanish. 2 (move) make for, pass, proceed, progress, travel. 3 (function) be working, operate, run, work. 4 (lead to) continue, extend, reach, spread, stretch. 5 (pass) elapse, fly, slip by. 6 (become) get, grow, turn. 7 (proceed) develop, end up, fare, happen, pan out, turn out, work out. 8 **go for** (attack) assault, launch yourself at, lunge at. 9 **go for** (like) choose, prefer. 10 **go off** (go bad) deteriorate, go moldy, rot, turn sour. 11 **go off** (explode) detonate, go bang

**goad** *n* pointed stick for driving cattle;
*fig* incentive; *v* urge on; *fig* provoke; incite

**goad** *v* egg on *inf*, prod, prompt, provoke,
push, spur, stimulate, urge

**go-ahead** *n* permission to begin
**goal** *n* 1 score posts in football, etc; score so
made 2 ambition; *ns* **goalkeeper** defender
of goal

**goal** *n* (ambition) aim, aspiration, end,
objective, target

**goat** *n* agile ruminant, often horned and
bearded; *n* **goatee** small pointed beard
**gob** *n sl* mouth; *v* **gobble** eat greedily
**gobbledygook** *n* jargon
**go-between** *n* carrier of messages
**goblet** *n* drinking vessel
**goblin** *n* malicious ugly sprite
**go-cart** *n* small, low vehicle for racing
**god** *n* supernatural being with divine powers;
*fem* **goddess**; *ns* **godfather, -mother, -
parent** sponsor at baptism; **godchild** one
who is sponsored at baptism; **godliness**
piety; *adj* **godless**wicked
**godsend** *n* unexpected lucky chance

**godsend** *n* bit of luck, blessing, boon,
miracle, unexpected bonus

**go-getter** *n coll* enterprising person
**goggles** *n pl* protective spectacles
**goings-on** *n pl* mysterious activities
**goitre** *n* enlargement of the thyroid gland
**gold** *n* 1 yellow precious metal 2 the colour of
this; *ns* **goldfish; g. medal, g. medallist,
g. mine**
**golden** *a* 1 of gold color 2 valuable;
*n* **g. wedding** 50th wedding anniversary

**golden** *adj* 1 (of gold color) fair, gilded,
gilt, gold, yellow. 2 (valuable) excellent,
ideal, opportune, perfect, wonderful

**golf** *n* game in which small hard ball is struck
by clubs into series of holes; *v* play golf;
*ns* **golfer** one who plays golf; **golfcourse,
golf links** land laid out for golf
**gondola** *n* Venetian canal boat
**gone** *pt of* **go**
**gong** *n* metal disk giving note when struck
**goo** *n coll* 1 sticky wet mess 2 sentimentality;
*adj* **-ey**; *n* **-iness**
**good** *adj comp* **better** *sup* **best** 1 pleasing
2 kind 3 well-behaved; *idm* **good at**
proficient, clever at; *idm* **a good deal** a lot;
*idm* **a good few** several; *idm* **for good**
forever; *pl* 1 wares 2 possessions; *n* **-ness**

**good** *adj* 1 (pleasing) brilliant, delicious,
enjoyable, excellent, first-class, great,
interesting, lovely, nice, pleasant,
satisfactory, suitable, super. 2 (kind)
caring, considerate, decent, generous,
honest, honorable, kindhearted,
trustworthy, virtuous. 3 (well-behaved)
obedient. 4 (good at) accomplished,
capable, clever, competent, efficient,
professional, proficient, skilled, talented

**good-bye** *interj, n* farewell

**good-bye** *interj* adieu, au revoir, bye, bye-
bye, cheerio, see you, so long

**good-looking** *adj* attractive
**goodly** *adj* numerous; abundant
**goof, goofball** *n sl* stupid, awkward person;
*adj* **goofy** silly or stupid
**goon** *n sl* foolish person
**goose** *n* **geese** large web-footed bird;
*ns* **goose bumps** pimply bristling of skin
due to cold, fear; **goose-step** marching with
stiff legs
**gooseberry** *n* thorny shrub, with hairy, sweet
edible berries
**gore**[1] *n* blood, shed and clotted; *adj* **gory**
**gore**[2] *v* pierce with horn or tusk
**gore**[3] *v* triangular gusset in garment
**gorge** *n* deep, narrow valley; *v* eat greedily

a
b
c
d
e
f
**g**
h
i
j
k
l
m
n
o
p
q
r
s
t
u
v
w
x
y
z

**gorgeous** *adj* wonderful, beautiful

> **gorgeous** *adj* brilliant, glorious, good-looking, handsome, impressive, lovely, magnificent, stunning, superb, terrific

**gorgon** *n* mythical snake-haired woman
**Gorgonzola** *n* Italian blue cheese
**gorilla** *n* largest anthropoid ape
**gorse** *n* spiny yellow-flowered shrub
**gosling** *n* young goose
**gospel** *n* one of books of New Testament
**gossip** *n* idle talk, *esp* about others; *v* spread rumors

> **gossip** *n* 1 (idle talk) hearsay, report, rumor, scandal. 2 (person) busybody, scandalmonger
> **gossip** *v* blab, chat, chatter, talk

**got** *pt, pp of* **get**
**gouge** *n* chisel for making grooves; *phr v* **gouge out** dig out with sharp tool
**goulash** *n* rich stew of meat and vegetables
**gourd** *n* dried rind of pumpkin, etc as vessel
**gourmet** *n* connoisseur of food and wine
**gout** *n* painful disease of joints
**govern** *v* 1 control 2 influence; *adj* **governable**; *ns* **governor** ruler; **governess** private woman teacher

> **govern** *v* 1 (control) administer, look after, manage, oversee, rule, run. 2 (influence) affect, control, decide, determine

**government** *n* ruling of state

> **government** *n* administration, authorities, executive, parliament, regime, ruling party, state, the powers that be

**gown** *n* flowing garment; woman's dress
**GP** *abbr* general practitioner
**grab** *v* **grabbing, grabbed** seize; *n* action of grabbing; *idm* **up for grabs** *coll* available to anyone to take

**grab** *v* catch hold of, collar *inf*, get hold of, grasp, snatch, take hold of

**grace** *n* 1 elegant beauty 2 extra time 3 prayer of thanks for food; *idm* **with good/bad grace** willingly/unwillingly
**graceful** *adj* elegant; *adv* **-fully**

> **graceful** *adj* attractive, charming, deft, natural, polished, tasteful

**gracious** *adj* 1 charming, courteous 2 beneficient; *adv* **-ly**; *n* **-ness**
**graceless** *adj* 1 clumsy 2 rude, boorish; *adv* **-ly**; *n* **-ness**
**grade** *n* standard; *v* classify; arrange in grades; *idm* **make the grade** succeed
**gradient** *n* degree of slope
**gradual** *adj* happening slowly and steadily

> **gradual** *adj* continuous, easy, even, gentle, progressive, regular, steady, step-by-step

**graduate** *v* get university degree; *n* holder of university degree; *n* **graduation**
**graffiti** *n pl* writing, drawing on walls
**graft** *n* 1 cutting from one plant fixed to grow on another 2 skin, bone, etc transferred to grow elsewhere on the body 3 unfair means
**grail** *n* chalice; Holy Grail
**grain** *n* 1 small, hard particle 2 hard seed, *esp* of cereals 3 direction of fibers
**gram** *n* metric unit of weight
**grammar** *n* science dealing with correct use of words; **grammatic(al)** following rules of grammar; *n* **grammar school** type of school
**granary** *n* grain storehouse
**grand** *adj* 1 big 2 dignified; *n* $1000; *ns* **grandchild, granddaughter, grandson** child of daughter/son; **grandad/grandpa** *coll* grandfather; **grandma** *coll* grandmother; **g. master** chess champion; **grandparent, grandfather, grandmother** parent of father/mother; **g. piano** large piano with horizontal strings

**grand** *adj* (dignified) elegant, imposing, impressive, luxurious, magnificent, majestic, palatial, regal, stately

**grandeur** *n* imposing greatness

**grandeur** *n* elegance, luxury, magnificence, opulence, pomp, splendor

**grandiose** *adj* imposing, pretentious
**grange** *n* large country house
**granite** *n* very hard granular igneous rock
**granny** *n coll* grandmother
**grant** *v* allow; *idm* **take for granted** 1 assume to be true 2 fail to show due appreciation to/for; *n* money given to maintain student

**grant** *n* allowance, award, bursary, donation, endowment, scholarship

**granule** *n* small grainlike particle
**grape** *n* fruit of vine; *ns* **grapefruit** citrus fruit; **g. vine** vine on which grapes grow
**graph** *n* diagram showing relative positions, variations (of quantity, temperature, etc)
**graphic** *adj* 1 vivid 2 of visual symbols, writing, drawing; *n* **graphics** 1 drawing by mathematical principles 2 display of information by pictures, etc

**graphic** *adj* (vivid) blow-by-blow, clear, descriptive, detailed, explicit, realistic, striking

**graphite** *n* form of carbon, used in pencils
**grapple** *phr v* **grapple with** struggle with
**grasp** *v* 1 hold firmly 2 understand; *n* 1 firm hold, grip 2 comprehension 3 reach; *adj* **-ing** eager for gain

**grasp** *v* 1 (hold firmly) grab, clutch, grip, hold, seize, take hold of. 2 (understand) comprehend, follow, get, realize, see

**grass** *n* green herbage of fields, lawns etc; *ns* **grasshopper** jumping insect that makes shrill singing noise; **g. roots** *polit* ordinary people; *v* sow with grass
**grate** *n* fire bars and framework of fireplace; *n* **grating** open framework of bars
**grate** *v* 1 rub, scrape with rough surface 2 grind into small pieces 3 make harsh noise, by rubbing; *n* **grater** kitchen utensil
**grateful** *adj* thankful

**grateful** *adj* appreciative, full of gratitude, indebted, pleased

**gratify** *v* **-fying, -fied** please, satisfy
**grating** *n* framework of bars across opening
**gratis** *adj, adv* free of charge
**gratitude** *n* gratefulness

**gratitude** *n* appreciation, thankfulness, thanks

**gratuitous** *adj* freely given; *n* **gratuity** gift, *esp* money, for services rendered
**grave**[1] *n* hole dug in earth for burial; *ns* **gravestone, graveyard**
**grave**[2] *adj* serious
**gravel** *n* small pebbles
**gravitate** *v fig* be attracted by
**gravity** *n* 1 force that attracts objects toward one another 2 seriousness
**gravy** *n* sauce of juice of roasting meat
**gray** *adj* 1 of the color of slate, ash, etc 2 having hair this color; *ns* **g. area** aspect of situation hard to define, hard to deal with; **gray matter** 1 brain cells 2 intelligence
**graze**[1] *v* feed in pastures
**graze**[2] *v* scratch surface; *n* small cut, scratch
**grease** *n* soft, melted animal fat; semisolid oil as lubricant; *v* apply grease to
**greasepaint** *n* theatrical make-up
**greasy** *adj* like or covered in grease; *n* **greasiness**

**greasy** *adj* fatty, oily, slimy, slippery, smeary, waxy

a
b
c
d
e
f
g
h
i
j
k
l
m
n
o
p
q
r
s
t
u
v
w
x
y
z

**great 1** excellent **2** large **3** considerable **4** important; *ns* **great grandparent/grandfather/grandmother/aunt/uncle** parent of grandparent, etc; *adv* **-ly**; *n* **-ness**

> **great** *adj* **1** (excellent) brilliant, classic, gifted, good, marvelous, outstanding, skillful, superb, talented, terrific, wonderful. **2** (large) big, enormous, huge, immense, massive, vast. **3** (considerable) acute, extreme, severe. **4** (important) celebrated, distinguished, eminent, famous, leading, main, prominent, renowned

**Grecian** *n* of ancient Greece
**Greece** *idm coll* **it's all Greek to me** it's incomprehensible
**greedy** *adj* **1** wanting, eating too much food **2** selfish with money; *n* **greed**

> **greedy** *adj* **1** (for food) gluttonous, piggish *inf*, voracious. **2** (with money) avaricious, grasping, miserly, money-grabbing, selfish, tight-fisted

**green** *adj* **1** of the color of grass **2** rich in vegetation *n* **g. belt** area free from urban development **3** unripe; immature **4** inexperienced; gullible **5** envious **6** fertile **7** concerned with conservation of environment; *idm* (**give/get**) **the green light** (give/get) signal of consent; *n* grassy area; *pl* **-s** green vegetables; *ns* **greenery** vegetation; **greenfly** small insect harmful to plants; **greengrocer** seller of fruit, vegetables; **greenhouse** building with glass sides and roof for growing plants; **greenhouse effect** gradual warming of earth's atmosphere due to pollution
**greet** *v* welcome
**greeting** *n* words spoken to welcome sb

> **greeting** *n* good wishes, hello, message, nod, reception, regards, tidings, wave, welcome

**gregarious** *adj* living in herds, flocks; sociable; *n* **-ness**
**gremlin** *n* imaginary creature supposed to be cause of malfunction in machines
**grenade** *adj* small bomb thrown by hand
**grenadier** *n* member of British infantry regiment
**grenadine** *n* **1** thin silk fabric **2** pomegranate syrup **3** red dye
**grew** *pt of* **grow**
**grid** *n* **1** grating **2** national network of electricity supply **3** numbered network of squares on map, as reference
**grief** *n* great sorrow; *idm* **come to grief** have an accident; fail; *v* **grieve** cause, feel grief; *n* **grievance** cause for complaint; *adj* **grievous** painful

> **grief** *n* anguish, bereavement, despair, heartache, misery, mourning, sadness, unhappiness

**grill** *n* **1** gridiron; food cooked on this; *v* cook, be cooked on grill **2** *sl* interrogate closely
**grille** *n* metal framework over opening
**grim** *adj* **1** unpleasant **2** stern

> **grim** *adj* **1** (unpleasant) appalling, awful, dire, dreadful, ghastly, grisly, gruesome, harrowing, horrendous, shocking, terrible. **2** (stern) gloomy, morose, serious, somber, sour, sullen

**grimace** *n* facial contortion, expressing ridicule, pain, etc; *v* make grimaces
**grime** *n* ingrained dirt; *adj* **grimy**
**grin** *v* **grinning, grinned** smile broadly; *n* broad smile
**grind** *v* **grinding, ground** reduce to small pieces or powder by pressure; wear down; make smooth; sharpen; grate; *n* act of grinding; *sl* hard work; *n* **grindstone** hard sandstone used for grinding
**grip** *v* **gripping, gripped 1** hold firmly **2** hold interest of; *n* **1** grasp **2** power **3** handle

**grip** v 1 (hold firmly) clasp, grab, grasp, hold, seize, take hold of. 2 (hold interest of) capture, enthrall, fascinate, hold spellbound, mesmerize

**gripe** v sl complain; n pain in bowels
**gripping** adj thrilling

**gripping** adj absorbing, compulsive, exciting, fascinating, heady, interesting, riveting, sensational

**grisly** adj horrifying; gruesome
**grist** n grain for grinding; idm **(all) grist to the mill** sth useful, that can be turned to profit
**gristle** n cartilage, esp in cooked meat
**grit** n 1 small fragments of stone 2 coarse sand; v **gritting, gritted** treat surface with grit; idm **grit one's teeth** show determination and courage; adj **gritty**; n **grittiness**
**grizzly bear** n large N American bear
**groan** v utter deep sound of pain, grief, etc; n sound made in groaning

**groan** v cry out, moan, object, protest, sigh, wail

**grocer** n dealer in dry and canned goods, household items, etc; n **grocery** grocer's trade; pl **groceries** goods sold by grocer
**grog** n spirit (usu rum) with water
**groggy** adj unsteady; shaky; weak
**groin** n depression between thigh and abdomen
**groom** n servant in charge of horses; v 1 make smart 2 prepare for contest 3 care for horse

**groom** v 1 (make smart) arrange, brush, clean, comb, fix, make tidy, smarten up, spruce up, tidy. 2 (prepare for contest) coach, drill, get ready, instruct, prepare, prime, school, teach, train

**groove** n narrow channel, furrow; v cut groove in; idm **stuck in a groove** fixed in one's habits
**grope** v 1 feel round blindly 2 search cautiously 3 touch in an erotic way
**gross** adj 1 fat 2 obscene 3 very obvious 4 total; adv **-ly**; n **-ness**

**gross** adj 1 (fat) bloated, bulky, heavy, huge, massive, obese, overweight. 2 (obscene) coarse, crude, disgusting, offensive, rude, vulgar. 3 (very obvious) blatant, flagrant, glaring, outrageous, serious, shameful, shocking

**grotesque** adj 1 very strange 2 misshapen; art highly decorated with intertwined animal forms and foliage

**grotesque** adj 1 (very strange) absurd, bizarre, curious, fantastic, outlandish, peculiar, strange, surreal, unnatural, weird. 2 (misshapen) deformed, distorted, gnarled, twisted, ugly

**grotto** n cave; artificial cavern; pl **grottoes**
**grouch** v grumble persistently
**ground** n 1 soil 2 surface of earth 3 area for sports; ns **g. floor, groundcloth** waterproof sheet for camping; **g. swell** 1 heavy slow-moving wave 2 rapid surge of public feeling; **groundwork** work providing for future development; idm **get off the ground** make a successful start; idm **prepare the ground for** make possible; v force to stay on the ground; connect electrically with the earth; adj **-ed**; n **-ing** basic instruction; adj **groundless** without cause; adv **-ly**; pl **grounds** land round building; land designated for a purpose

**ground** n 1 (soil) dirt, earth, mud. 2 (surface of earth) deck inf, earth, floor, terra firma. 3 (area for sports) arena, field, pitch, playing field, stadium

a b c d e f **g** h i j k l m n o p q r s t u v w x y z

185

**group** n 1 number of people 2 club 3 number of things; v make, form group

> **group** n 1 (number of people) assembly, band, bunch *inf*, cluster, company, congregation, crew, crowd, flock, gaggle *inf*, gang, gathering, horde, host, mob, multitude, party, rabble, swarm, team, throng. 2 (club) association, cadre, circle, clique, faction, ring, school, sect, set. 3 (of things) assortment, batch, bunch, bundle, category, class, cluster, collection, lot, set
> **group** v 1 (make group) arrange, assemble, bring together, categorize, classify, collect, gather, marshal, organize, put together, set out. 2 (form group) associate, cluster, come together, congregate, flock, gather, get together, swarm, team up, throng

**groupie** n coll fan following pop groups on tour

**group practice** n group of doctors working as partners

**grouse**[1] n wild game bird; its edible flesh

**grouse**[2] v sl complain; n **grouse**

**grout** n fine mortar; v cover, fill spaces between tiles, etc, with grout

**grove** n small wood

**grovel** v -eling, -eled *fig* humble oneself

**grow** v 1 get bigger 2 become 3 develop 4 cultivate; *pt* **grew**; *pp* **grown**; *phr vs* **grow on** become increasingly attractive to; **grow out of** become too big for; **grow up** become adult; *adj* **grown(-up)** adult

> **grow** v 1 (get bigger) develop, enlarge, expand, extend, fill out, increase, lengthen, multiply, spread, swell, thicken, widen. 2 (become) come to be, get, turn. 3 (develop) expand, flourish, make progress, progress, prosper, thrive. 4 (cultivate) farm, plant, produce, propagate, raise

**growl** v utter deep rumbling sound of anger; n growling sound

**growth** n 1 process of growing 2 success; increase in economic activity 3 abnormal formation on or in the body 4 sth that has grown

> **growth** n 1 (process of growing) development, enlargement evolution, expansion, extension, increase, multiplication. 2 (success) advance, expansion, improvement, progress, proliferation, rise. 3 (abnormal formation on the body) cancer, cyst, lump, swelling, tumor

**grub** v **grubbing, grubbed** dig, uproot; *fig* search arduously; n larva of insect; *sl* food; *adj* **grubby** dirty

**grudge** v be reluctant to give or do sth; n feeling of resentment

**grudging** adj reluctant; adv **-ly**

**gruel** n thin watery oatmeal

**grueling** adj exhausting

**gruesome** adj macabre, horrible

**gruff** adj 1 rough 2 bad-tempered; n **gruffness**

> **gruff** adj 1 (rough) hoarse, husky, rasping, throaty. 2 (bad-tempered) abrupt, brusque, crabby, crotchety, crusty, curt, grumpy, rough, rude, surly, uncivil

**grumble** v complain; murmur angrily; rumble; n complaint

**grumpy** adj bad-tempered; adv **grumpily**; n **grumpiness**

**grungy** adj sl dirty or unkempt

**grunt** v utter deep, sound; n deep snort

**guarantee** n pledge, promise given that conditions of contract will be carried out; manufacturer's undertaking to make good defects in product; v promise

> **guarantee** v assure, give a guarantee, give an assurance, give your word, pledge, vouch for, swear, vow

**guard** n 1 protector of person 2 protector of place 3 prison official 4 rail official in charge of train 5 protective device or part; v 1 watch a person 2 defend a place; idm **be off/on one's guard** be unready/ready to cope with danger; phr v **guard against** take care to prevent; forestall; adj **guarded** 1 protected 2 wary

**guard** n 1 (protector of person) bodyguard, escort, guardian, protector. 2 (protector of place) bouncer inf, custodian, defender, lookout, night watchman, patrol, picket, security guard, sentry, watch, watchman. 3 (prison official) jailer, prison officer, warder
**guard** v 1 (watch a person) escort, keep under guard, keep watch over, mind, protect, save, secure, shelter, shield, tend, watch over. 2 (defend a place) cover, defend, patrol, police, secure, watch over

**guardian** n person looking after a child in lieu of parent
**guava** n tropical tree, having egg-shaped fruit
**gubernatorial** adj of a governor
**gudgeon**[1] n small European freshwater fish
**gudgeon**[2] n piston pin; socket; bearing
**guerney** n rolling stretcher
**guernsey** n breed of tan and white dairy cow
**guerrilla** n one engaged in irregular warfare
**guess** v form opinion without evidence; n estimate; ns **guesstimate** coll rough estimate based on a guess; **guesswork** process of guessing

**guess** v conjecture, estimate, have a feeling, have a hunch, have an idea, postulate, predict, speculate, surmise, suppose, think likely
**guess** n assumption, conjecture, feeling, hypothesis, prediction, speculation, suspicion, surmise

**guest** n person enjoying another's hospitality; one staying in hotel, etc

**guffaw** n burst of loud laughter
**guide** v 1 show way 2 give advice 3 be in charge; n 1 one who shows way 2 one who gives advice 3 thing that shows way 4 book giving information; n **guidance** 1 leadership 2 help with personal problems

**guide** v 1 (show way) accompany, conduct, direct, escort, lead, lead the way, pilot, shepherd, show, steer, usher. 2 (give advice) advise, brief, counsel, give guidance, influence, inform, instruct, make suggestions. 3 (be in charge) command, control, govern, handle, manage, preside over, regulate, steer, ssupervise
**guide** n 1 (one who shows way) attendant, courier, director, escort, leader, usher. 2 (one who gives advice) advisor, counselor, guru, mentor, teacher, tutor. 3 (thing that shows way) beacon, clue, guiding light, key, landmark, sign. 4 (book giving information) directory, guidebook, guidelines, handbook, instructions, manual, tourist guide

**guild** n association of people with common trade, profession, or aim; n **-hall** meeting place of guild or corporation
**guilder** n unit or currency in Netherlands
**guile** n deceit; wiliness; adjs **-ful, -less**
**guillotine** n machine for beheading; one for papercutting; v use guillotine
**guilt** n fact of having committed crime
**guilty** adj 1 having committed crime 2 full of remorse

**guilty** adj 1 (having committed crime) at fault, blameworthy, convicted, criminal, culpable, responsible, to blame. 2 (full of remorse) ashamed, conscience-stricken, contrite, penitent, remorseful, repentant, shamefaced, sheepish

**guinea fowl** n domesticated fowl, like pheasant
**guinea pig** n domestic rodent

**guise** *n* disguise; false appearance
**guitar** *n* six-stringed musical instrument;
  *n* **guitarist**
**gulag** *n* (formerly) Soviet state labor camp
**gulch** *n* deep ravine or torrentbed
**gulf** *n* large, deep, inlet of sea; huge gap;
  *fig* impassable gap; *pl* **-s**
**gull** *n* 1 web-footed seabird 2 dupe, fool;
  *v* deceive, cheat; *n* **gullibility**
**gullet** *n* passage from mouth to stomach
**gullible** *adj* easily duped

> **gullible** *adj* credulous, foolish, innocent,
> naive, silly, simple, trusting, unsuspecting

**gully** *n* channel worn by water
**gulp** *v* swallow noisily; choke back; *n* large
  mouthful
**gum**[1] *n* firm tissue around teeth
**gum**[2] *n* 1 sticky viscid substance exuded by
  certain trees 2 liquid glue 3 chewing gum;
  *v* **gumming, gummed** stick with glue
**gumbo** *n* soup made with okra
**gumdrop** *n* hard jellylike sweet
**gumshoe** *n* *sl* detective
**gumption** *n* common sense
**gumtree** *n* eucalyptus; *idm* **up a gumtree** in
  dificulty
**gun** *n* weapon from which bullets, missiles are
  fired; *idm* **at gunpoint** with threat of
  shooting; *phr vs* **gun down** shoot to kill or
  wound; **gun for** seek chance to attack;
  *ns* **gunfire** (noise of) shooting; **gunman**
  armed criminal; **gunpowder** explosive
  powder
**gung-ho** *adj coll* thoroughly enthusiastic and
  loyal
**gunwale** *n* upper edge of boat's side
**guppy** *n* tiny tropical fish
**gurgle** *v* flow with bubbling sound
**guru** *n* Hindu spiritual teacher
**gush** *v* flow out fast; *n* violent flow

> **gush** *v* burst out, cascade, flood, flow, pour,
> rush, spout, spurt, stream, surge

**gusset** *n* triangular section let into garment,
  to enlarge or strengthen it
**gust** *n* sudden, brief blast of wind
**gusto** *n* relish; zest; enjoyment
**gut** *n* fine thread made from animal intestines;
  *pl* 1 intestines 2 *coll* courage; *adj sl* **gutted**
  disappointed, upset; *v* **gutting, gutted**
  remove guts of; destroy inner contents of
  (house)
**gutter** *n* 1 narrow trough under eaves to carry
  rainwater 2 open channel along road
  3 *fig* lowest social class
**guy**[1] *n* rope used to guide, steady, or secure
**guy**[2] *n coll* fellow, man; *v* mock
**guzzle** *v* drink, eat greedily and to excess

> **guzzle** *v* bolt, cram yourself, devour,
> gobble, gulp down, knock back *inf*,
> stuff yourself, swig *inf*, swill, toss off *inf*,
> wolf down

**gym** *n coll* 1 gymnasium 2 gymnastics
**gymkhana** *n* equestrian event
**gymnasium** *n* hall for physical training and
  gymnastics; *n pl* **gymnastics** physical
  exercises, with or without apparatus;
  *n* **gymnast** one skilled in gymnastics
**gynecology** *n* science dealing with functions
  and diseases of women
**gypsy** *n cap* member of wandering race
**gyrate** *v* revolve; whirl around
**gyroscope** *n* flywheel capable of rotating
  about any axis

**habit** *n* usual behavior; monk's robe

> **habit** *n* convention, custom, practice, procedure, routine, rule, tradition, way

**habitable** *adj* fit to be inhabited
**habitat** *n* natural home of animal
**habitation** *n* place of abode
**habitual** *adj* usual
**hack**[1] *v* 1 cut roughly 2 kick shins of

> **hack** *v* (cut) carve, chop, cut, cut down, gash, hew, lacerate, mutilate, slash

**hack**[2] *n* 1 old, tired horse 2 badlypaid writer
**hacker** *n* person gaining illegal entry to computer system
**hackles** *n pl* hairs on animal's neck
**hackney** *n* medium-sized riding horse
**hackneyed** *adj* overworked and predictable
**had** *pt, pp* of **have**
**haddock** *n* edible salt-water fish, akin to cod
**Hades** *n* abode of dead; underworld
**hadn't** *contracted form of* had not
**haft** *n* handle, hilt; *v* fit haft
**hag** *n* ugly old woman; witch
**haggard** *adj* having worn, wasted look

> **haggard** *adj* drawn, emaciated, gaunt, pinched, tired, wan, wasted, worn out

**haggis** *n* Scottish culinary dish

**haggle** *v* wrangle over price
**hagiology** *n* study of saints or of their lives; *n* **hagiographer** writer of saint's life
**hail** *n* small lumps of ice falling like rain; *v* shower down hail; *n* **hailstone**
**hair** *n* fine threadlike growth from skin of animal; mass of this on human head
**haircut** *n* 1 act of cutting hair 2 style in which hair is cut
**hairdo** *n coll* hair style
**hairdresser** *n* one who cuts people's hair
**hairpin corner** *n* sharp corner on steep road
**hairsplitting** *n* fussing about minute unimportant detail
**hairspray** *n* liquid spray to hold hair in place
**hairy** *adj* 1 covered with hair 2 dangerous

> **hairy** *adj* (covered with hair) bearded, bristly, fleecy, furry, hirsute, long-haired, shaggy, unshaven, wooly

**hake** *n* coarse edible salt-water fish, like cod
**hale** *adj* strong and healthy
**half** *n* one of two equal parts of sth; 50%; *pl* **halves**; *adj* 1 consisting of, equal to half 2 partial; *idm* **sb's better/other half** sb's husband/wife; *n* **h. brother/sister** one with whom one shares one parent
**half-hearted** *adj* done without enthusiasm

> **half-hearted** *adj* apathetic, cool, indifferent, lackluster, lukewarm, unenthusiastic

**half time** *n* short rest midway through sports match
**halibut** *n* large edible flat salt-water fish
**halitosis** *n* foul breath
**hall** *n* 1 large public room 2 lobby at entrance to building 3 large private house; **hallmark** official mark on gold, silver plate

> **hall** *n* 1 (public room) assembly room, auditorium, meeting room. 2 (lobby) entrance hall, entry, foyer, vestibule

**hallelujah** *n, interj* praise the Lord!

**hallow** v make holy; consecrate

**Halloween** n October observed by children who dress in costumes and ask for treats

**hallucination** n fancied perception by senses of some nonexistent thing; v **hallucinate** have hallucinations

> **hallucination** n apparition, delusion, dream, fantasy, figment of the imagination, illusion, mirage, vision

**hallucinogen** n drug causing hallucinations

**halo** n golden circle around head of figure in picture, symbolizing holiness; pl **haloes**

**halt** n stop; v stop; cause to stop

> **halt** v 1 (stop) break off, cease, come to a standstill, come to a stop, draw up, pull up, stand still, wait. 2 (cause to stop) arrest, block, check, crush, end, nip in the bud, put an end to, stop, terminate

**halter** n style of dress with supporting strap around neck, revealing bare back

**halve** v divide in halves; reduce by half

> **halve** v bisect, cut in half, cut in two, divide equally, reduce by fifty percent, share equally, split in half, split in two

**ham** n 1 back of thigh; 2 salted and smoked pork; 3 amateur radio operator

**hamburger** n patty of ground beef on bread roll

**hamlet** n small village

**hammer** n 1 long-handled tool with heavy head, for driving in nails, working metal, etc 2 striking part of gun lock 3 device for striking bell; v strike with, use hammer; knock loudly; phr v **hammer out** solve problem by repeated discussion

**hammerhead shark** n shark with broad flat nose

**hammock** n canvas bed, slung on cords

**hamper**¹ n large basket with lid

**hamper**² v hinder

> **hamper** v block, delay, encumber, frustrate, hold back, hold up, impede, inhibit, obstruct, restrain, slow down, thwart

**hamster** n rodent with cheek pouches

**hamstring** n tendon at back of knee; v render helpless

**hand** n 1 end of arm below wrist 2 style of writing 3 pointer on dial, clock, etc 4 set of cards held by player 5 assistance; idm **at hand** nearby; v give; phr vs **hand down** bequeath; **hand in** deliver; **hand out** issue; n **handout**; phr v **hand over** give possession of, control of

> **hand** v 1 (give) convey, deliver, offer, pass, present. 2 **hand down** bequeath, hand on, leave, pass down, pass on, will. 3 **hand out** deal out, dish out, dispense, distribute, dole out, give out, share out. 4 **hand over** deliver, donate, give, present, surrender, turn over

**handbag** n woman's light bag

**handbook** n manual

**handbrake** n brake used in parked vehicle

**handcuffs** n chain with rings for holding prisoner by the hands

**handful** n 1 amount that the hand can hold 2 small number

**handicap** n disability; disadvantage; v **-capped, -capping** impose handicap

**handicraft** n product made with artistic skill

**handiwork** n sth done using manual skill

**handkerchief** n small cloth for wiping nose

**handle** n part of tool held in hand; v 1 touch, with hands 2 control 3 deal in; n **handler**

> **handle** n grip, haft, hilt, knob, shaft, stock
> **handle** v 1 (touch with hands) feel, finger, grasp, hold, maul, stroke. 2 (control) administer, be in charge of, cope with, deal with, direct, manage, take care of. 3 (deal in) market, sell, trade in, traffic in

**handlebars** *n pl* bar for steering bicycle
**handmade** *adj* made by hand, not machine
**handmaid** *n* personal female servant
(*also* **handmaiden**)
**handsome** *adj* 1 good-looking 2 generous

> **handsome** *adj* (good-looking) attractive, elegant, fine, fine-looking, good-looking, gorgeous, hunky, striking

**handwriting** *n* writing done by hand
**handy** *adj* 1 close by 2 useful 3 skillful

> **handy** *adj* 1 (close by) accessible, at your fingertips, available, close at hand, convenient, nearby, ready, to hand, within reach. 2 (useful) convenient, helpful, practical, serviceable. 3 (skillful) adept, capable, clever, competent, deft, dexterous, good with your hands, nimble-fingered, proficient

**hang** *v* 1 be suspended 2 attach to wall *pt, pp* **hung** 3 execute by hanging from rope round neck; *pt* hung, *pp* hanged; abruptly; *idm* **get the hang of** understand; *idm* **hang one's head** look ashamed; *phr vs* **hang around** *coll* wait; **hang back** show reluctance; **hang on 1** hold on tight 2 wait; **hang in there, hang tough** *coll* persevere; have faith, courage; **hang onto** *coll* keep hold of; **hang out** live, stay; **hang up** 1 suspend 2 end telephone conversation **be hung up on/about** be obsessed about; *adj* **h.dog** dejected, guilty; *n* **hanger** clothes/coathanger

> **hang** *v* 1 (be suspended) dangle, droop, flap, swing. 2 (attach) drape, fix, pin up, put up, suspend. 3 **hang on** (hold on to sth) cling, cling on to, clutch, grasp, grip, hold, hold on to

**hangar** *n* covered shed, *esp* for aircraft
**hang glider** *n* large kitelike frame for flying without engine; **hang gliding** this sport

**hangover** *n* 1 sick feeling the day after drinking too much alcohol 2 lasting effect of something
**hang-up** *n sl* sth causing unusual anxiety
**hank** *n* skein, coil, length, *esp* measure of yarn
**hanker** *phr v* **hanker after** desire strongly
**Hanukkah** *n* annual Jewish festival
**hap** *n* chance; *adj* **-less** unlucky, wretched
**haphazard** *adj* random, accidental
**happen** *v* take place; *n* **-ing** occurrence

> **happen** *v* arise, come about, come to pass, crop up, occur, transpire, turn out

**happiness** *n* feeling of being happy

> **happiness** *n* bliss, cheerfulness, cheeriness, contentment, delight, ecstasy, elation, enjoyment, euphoria, gaiety, gladness, good fortune, high spirits, joy, merriment, pleasure

**happy** *adj* 1 cheerful 2 fortunate; *adv* **happily**

> **happy** *adj* 1 (cheerful) carefree, cheery, contented, delighted, ecstatic, euphoric, glad, in a good mood, in good spirits, jolly, jovial, joyful, light-hearted, merry, overjoyed, pleased, radiant, satisfied, smiling, thrilled, untroubled.
> 2 (fortunate) advantageous, auspicious, beneficial, convenient, lucky, opportune, welcome

**harangue** *n* vehement speech; *v* crticize
**harass** *v* pester; *n* **-ment**
**harbinger** *n* forerunner, precursor, heraldl
**harbor** *n* port; *v* shelter; conceal
**hard** *adj* 1 firm 2 tiring 3 difficult to solve 4 without kindness 5 harsh; *adv* intensively; *idm* **hard up** short of money; *v* **harden** make hard; *ns* **hardback** hard-covered book; **h. copy** printed copy; **h. currency** stable currency; **h. disk** *comput* rigid disk with large storage capacity; **h. labour** hard physical work as punishment

A B C D E F G H I J K L M N O P Q R S T U V W X Y Z

**hard** *adj* 1 (firm) dense, inflexible, rigid, rocklike, solid, solidified, stiff, stony, tough, unyielding. 2 (tiring) arduous, backbreaking, daunting, difficult, exhausting, grueling, heavy, laborious, onerous, strenuous, taxing. 3 (difficult to solve) baffling, complex, complicated, daunting, difficult, perplexing, puzzling, thorny, tough. 4 (without kindness) callous, cold, cruel, hard-hearted, harsh, heartless, implacable, inflexible, merciless, pitiless, ruthless, severe, stern, strict, unbending, unfeeling, unkind. 5 (harsh) austere, bad, difficult, distressing, grim, intolerable, unbearable, unpleasant

**hard-core** *n* 1 graphic, explicit 2 totally committed
**hardhat** *n* 1 worker's helmet 2 working-class conservative
**hardship** *n* suffering

**hardship** *n* adversity, affliction, austerity, deprivation, destitution, difficulty, misery, misfortune, need, poverty, privation, tribulation, trouble, want

**hardware** *n* 1 domestic tools, pots and pans 2 *comput* machines 3 weapons
**hare** *n* swift rodent, resembling rabbit; *adj* **h.brained** rash, flighty
**harem** *n* women's quarters in Muslim house
**haricot** *n* French bean
**hark** *v* listen to; *phr v* **h. back** to revert to (a subject)
**harlequin** *n* comic character in pantomime
**harlot** *n* prostitute
**harm** *n* damage; injury; *v* hurt

**harm** *n* abuse, damage, detriment, disservice, hurt, impairment, injury, loss, misfortune, ruin
**harm** *v* abuse, damage, ill-treat, impair, injure, maltreat, spoil, wound

**harmful** *adj* likely to cause damage or injury

**harmful** *adj* damaging, destructive, detrimental, evil, hurtful, injurious, noxious, poisonous, prejudicial, toxic, unhealthy, unwholesome

**harmless** *adj* not dangerous
**harmony** *n* agreement; melodious sound; *adj* **harmonious** in harmony; melodious; *n* **harmonica** mouth organ; *v* **harmonize** bring into harmony; *n* **-ization**
**harness** *n* straps and fastenings of horse; *v* put into harness; control, use
**harp** *n* musical instrument, with strings plucked by hand; *phr v* **harp on** talk of repeatedly, tediously
**harpsichord** *n* musical instrument like piano
**harpoon** *n* barbed spear with rope attached, for striking whales and large fish
**harpy** *n* 1 mythical monster, half woman, half bird 2 cruel merciless person
**harrow** *n* spiked frame dragged over ground, to break it up; *adj* **-ing** heartrending
**harsh** *adj* 1 rough in tone 2 severe 3 cruel

**harsh** *adj* 1 (rough in tone) croaking, grating, guttural, rasping, raucous, rough. 2 (severe) austere, bleak, difficult, grim, hard. 3 (cruel) brutal, despotic, domineering, draconian, excessive, hard, heavy-handed, severe, stern, strict, unfair, unjust, unkind

**hart** *n* adult male deer
**harvest** *n* gathering in of crops; season for this; results of this; *v* gather in
**has** *3rd person sing pres of* **have**
**has-been** *n coll* person whose success, popularity are all in the past
**hash** *n* 1 dish of chopped cooked meat 2 mess; muddle
**hasn't** *contracted form of* has not
**hasp** *n* metal clasp, or hinged flap for fastening door, etc
**hassle** *n* trouble; bother *v* pester

hassle *n* annoyance, aggravation,
   argument, difficulty, grief, irritation, pain,
   problem, upset
hassle *v* annoy, argue with, bother, harass,
   harry, irritate, plague, trouble

haste *n* speed; hurry; *v* **hasten** move with
   haste; *adj* **hasty**; *adv* **-ily**
hat *n* head covering
hatch[1] *n* trapdoor covering opening
hatch[2] *v* emerge from egg
hatchback *n* car with hinged rear door at top
hatchet *n* small ax; tomahawk
hate *v* dislike intensely; *n* intense dislike

hate *v* abhor, be contempuous of, be
   unable to bear, be unable to stand,
   despise, detest, dislike, loathe
hate *n* abhorrence, antipathy, aversion,
   contempt, detestation, dislike, enmity,
   hatred, hostility, ill-will, loathing, spite

hatred *n* feeling of intense dislike

hatred *n* abhorrence, antipathy, aversion,
   contempt, detestation, dislike, enmity,
   hate, hostility, ill-will, loathing

haughty *adj* proud; disdainful; arrogant
haul *v* drag, pull with effort; transport; *n* act
   of hauling; distance hauled
haunch *n* hind quarter of animal as meat
haunt *v* visit habitually, frequent; *n* habitual
   resort of human or animal
have *v* 1 possess 2 do 3 suffer from 4 receive
   5 experience 6 give birth to; produce; *3rd
   sing pres* **has**, *pt, pp* **had**; *idm* **had to** ought
   to; *idm* **have to** be obliged to

have *v* 1 (possess) be blessed with, enjoy,
   hold, keep, own, retain. 2 (do) enjoy, go
   for, indulge in, manage, partake of, take.
   3 (suffer from) be affected by, experience,
   get, meet with, suffer, sustain, undergo

haven *n* safe place

haven *n* hideaway, hideout, love nest,
   oasis, refuge, retreat, safe haven,
   sanctuary, shelter

haven't *contracted form of* have not
haversack *n* canvas bag for carrying rations,
   camping equipment, etc
havoc *n* anarchy, chaos, devastation,
   destruction, mayhem, trouble, violence
haw[1] *n* red fruit of hawthorn; *n* **hawthorn**
   thorny shrub with white, pink, or red flowers
haw[2] *v* hesitate in speech; *n* inarticulate
   sound expressing doubt
hawk[1] *n* 1 short-winged long-tailed falcon
   2 person who favors aggressive tactics;
   *adj* **hawkish**
hawk[2] *v* sell from door to door; *fig* spread
   around; *n* **hawker** itinerant seller of wares
hawk[3] *v* clear throat noisily
hawk-eyed *adj* possessing excellent vision
hawse *n* part of ship's bows where anchor
   cables pass through holes
hawser *n* large rope or small cable
hay *n* grass mown and dried for fodder;
   *ns* **hayfever** allergic catarrh of nose and
   throat; **hayride** revening ride in hay-filled,
   horse-drawn wagon; **haystack** rick of hay
haywire *n inf* amiss
hazard *n* danger; *v* expose to risk
hazardous *adj* risky
haze *n* mist, vapou
hazel *n* tree with edible nuts; light brown
   color
hazy *adj* 1 misty 2 vague

hazy *adj* 1 (misty) foggy, polluted, smoky,
   steamy, vaporous. 2 (vague) blurred,
   confused, distant, faint, indistinct,
   obscure, unclear

H-bomb *n* hydrogen bomb
he *masc nom pron* (3rd pers sing) male person,
   etc just referred to
he'd *contraction for* 1 he had 2 he would

**he'll** *contracted form of* he will
**he-man** *coll* virile man
**he's** *contracted form of* 1 he is 2 he was
**head** *n* 1 part of body housing brain, eyes, mouth 2 chief person 3 top part 4 mental ability 5 froth on top of beer; *pl* **-s** side of coin showing head of sb; *v* 1 lead 2 be at front, top of list 3 hit with the head; *phr vs* **head for** go toward; **head off** 1 (cause to) change direction 2 prevent; *ns* **headache** pain in head; **headboard** board at head of bed; **header** act of striking ball with head; **h.hunter** 1 tribal warrior who collects heads 2 person recruiting senior staff; **heading** title; **headlight** light on front of vehicle; **headland** promontory; **headline** title in newspaper; **h. master/ mistress** teacher in charge of school; **headphone** listening apparatus, *usu pl;* **headquarters** central office; **headset** headphones with microphone; **headship** post of head teacher; **h. start** early advantage; **headstone** stone placed at head of grave; **head wind** wind in one's face

> **head** *n* 1 (part of body) brain, cranium, face, mind, skull. 2 (chief person) boss, chairman, chief, chief executive, director, headmaster, headmistress, head teacher, leader, manager, principal. 3 (top part) apex, beginning, start, summit, tip, top

**headlong** *adv* 1 head first 2 in haste
**headstrong** *ad* impetuous; self-willed
**heal** *v* make, become sound or healthy

> **heal** *v* cure, make better, mend, remedy, restore to health, soothe, treat

**health** *n* state of well-being; body condition; toast drunk wishing one health and prosperity; *ns* **h. farm** place where people go to stay for help with diet, exercise, etc; **h. food** natural, organic food
**healthy** *adj* 1 in good health 2 good for health

> **healthy** *adj* 1 (in good health) fit, fit as a fiddle, in fine fettle, in good health, sound, strong, vigorous, well. 2 (good for health) health-giving, invigorating, nourishing, nutritious, restorative, wholesome

**heap** *n* piled-up mass of things; *v* form into heap

> **heap** *n* collection, hoard, lot, mass, mound, mountain, pile, quantity, stack

**hear** *v* **hearing, heard** perceive by ear; listen to; *phr vs* **hear from** get news from; *n* **hearing** sense by which sound is perceived; formal, official listening
**hearse** *n* funeral vehicle for coffin
**heart** *n* muscular organ which pumps blood round the body; *fig* seat of human emotions; core; central part; *idm* **by heart** from memory; *idm* **set one's heart on** long for; *ns* **h. attack** malfunction of heart; **heartbeat** pumping of heart
**heartache** *n* sorrow
**heartbreak** *n* anguish
**heartbreaking** *adj* extremely upsetting
**heartbroken** *adj* extremely upset
**heartburn** *n* indigestion pain
**hearten** *v* cheer up, encourage
**heartfelt** *adj* sincere

> **heartfelt** *adj* deep, earnest, emotional, from the heart, genuine, honest, warm

**heartless** *adj* unfeeling, cruel
**heartrending** *adj* deeply moving
**hearty** *adj* 1 cordial; jovial 2 (of meals) big
**hearth** *n* place where domestic fire is made
**heat** *n* 1 hotness; sensation of warmth 2 strong emotion 3 period of sexual desire in female mammals 4 eliminating round or course in race or contest; *ns* **h. rash**; **h.stroke** sunstroke; **h. wave** spell of very hot weather; *n* **-er** machine for heating; *n* **-ing** means of providing heat; *v* make hot

**heat** *v* boil, heat up, microwave, raise the temperature of, reheat, warm, warm up

**heated** *adj* angry; excited

**heated** *adj* emotional, fierce, frenzied, furious, het up, passionate, vehement, vigorous, violent, worked up

**heath** *n* open, shrubby ground; heather
**heathen** *n* one who does not believe in God; barbarous, irreligious person; *adj* savage; unenlightened; *adj* **heathenish** pagan
**heather** *n* plant of heath family, growing in open areas and on mountains
**heave** *v* lift up; drag along; throw (something heavy); utter (sigh)
**heaven** *n* 1 abode of God 2 great happiness; *adj* **heavenly** delightful

**heaven** *n* 1 (abode of God) Elysian Fields, Elysium, heavens, Olympus, paradise, sky, Valhalla. 2 (happiness) bliss, dream come true, heaven on earth, Nirvana, paradise, perfection

**heavy** *adj* 1 of great weight 2 severe 3 serious 4 indigestible; *adv* **heavily**; *n* **heaviness**

**heavy** *adj* 1 (of great weight) big, cumbersome, dense, fat, heavyweight, large, overweight, weighty. 2 (severe) abundant, considerable, great, hard, high, intense, strong. 3 (serious) deep, dense, difficult, profound, solemn, weighty

**heavyweight** *n* 1 heaviest class of boxer 2 very important person
**hebdomadal** *adj* weekly
**Hebrew** *n* language of the Jewish people
**heckle** *v* interrupt public speaker with questions; *n* **heckler**
**hect-, hecto-** *prefix* hundred
**hectare** *n* (area of) 10,000 square meters
**hectic** *adj* exciting, rushed, busy

**hectic** *adj* chaotic, fevered, feverish, frantic, frenetic, frenzied

**hector** *v* bully; browbeat
**hedge** *n* shrubs planted closely as fence or boundary; *v* 1 enclose with hedge 2 refuse to commit oneself; *idm* **hedge one's bets** protect oneself against loss by backing more than one possibility
**hedgehog** *n* small, wild, spiny mammal
**hedgerow** *n* wild hedge enclosing field
**hedonism** *n* theory that pleasure is the chief good; *n* **-ist**
**heed** *v* take notice of; *adj* **-less** careless

**heed** *v* acknowledge, bear in mind, consider, follow, listen to, notice, obey, pay attention to, pay heed to, pay regard to, respect, take account of

**heel** *n* hind part of foot; part of shoe, boot supporting this
**hefty** *adj* big and strong

**hefty** *adj* cumbersome, enormous, heavy, huge, large, weighty, whacking, whopping

**hegemony** *n* leadership; political control
**heifer** *n* young cow that has not yet calved
**height** *n* vertical dimension; loftiness; culmination; hill
**heighten** *v* increase

**heighten** *v* add to, augment, boost, enhance, improve, intensify, stimulate

**heinous** *adj* hateful; atrocious; odious
**heir** *n* one who succeeds to another's rank, property, on the death of the latter; *fem* **heiress;** *n* **heirloom** object inherited from ancestors

**heir** *n* beneficiary, daughter, heiress, inheritor, next in line, son, successor

**helicopter** *n* aircraft deriving lift from horizontally rotating rotors

**heliograph** *n* signaling device using reflected rays of sun

**heliport** *n* base for landing of helicopters

**heliotrope** *n* plant of borage family, with fragrant purple flowers; *adj* color of flowers

**helium** *n* light nonflammable gas

**hell** *n* **1** abode of damned souls **2** place, state of intense suffering

> **hell** *n* **1** (abode of damned souls) Hades, inferno, nether world, other place, purgatory, underworld. **2** (place of suffering) agony, hell on earth, misery, murder *inf*, nightmare, suffering, torture

**hellish** *adj* awful

**hello** *interj* cry of surprise; greeting

**helm** *n* steering wheel of ship, tiller; *idm* **at the helm** in control

**helmet** *n* protective covering for head

**help** *v* **1** give assistance **2** serve **3** alleviate; *n* assistance; *idm* **(not) be able to help (sth)** (not) to avoid (doing sth)

> **help** *v* (give assistance) advise, aid, assist, come to the rescue, contribute, give sb a hand, help out, lend sb a hand, rescue, serve, succor, volunteer
> **help** *n* aid, contribution, donation, hand, helping hand, hint, service, succor

**helper** *n* one who helps

**helpful** *adj* **1** willing to help **2** useful

> **helpful** *adj* **1** (willing to help) accommodating, amenable, benevolent, cooperative, friendly, kind, generous, obliging, supportive. **2** (useful) beneficial, constructive, convenient, handy, positive, practical, productive, profitable, serviceable, valuable

**helpless** *adj* **1** not knowing what to do **2** unable to defend yourself

> **helpless** *adj* **1** (not knowing what to do) at a loss, bewildered, floundering, forlorn, hapless, incapable, incompetent, struggling, uncomprehending, useless. **2** (unable to defend yourself) defenseless, impotent, powerless, vulnerable, weak

**helpmate** *n* comrade, partner, *esp* husband or wife

**helter-skelter** *adv* in disorderly haste

**hem** *n* edge of cloth turned up and stitched; *v* **hemming**, **hemmed** sew thus; *phr v* **hem in** trap

**hemisphere** *n* half of earth's surface

**hemlock** *n* plant producing powerful poison

**hemoglobin** *n* protein substance of red blood corpuscles

**hemophilia** *n* hereditary disease, in which blood fails to clot

**hemorrhage** *n* bleeding; *v med* to bleed

**hemp** *n* plant, whose fiber is used for rope

**hen** *n* female domestic fowl, or any bird; *adj* **henpecked** nagged by wife

**hence** *adv* from this; therefore; *advs* **-forth**, **-forward** from now onward

**henchman** *n* staunch supporter

**henna** *n* red or brown hair dye from plant

**hepatitis** *n* inflammation of liver

**her** *adj object or poss* case of **she**; *pron* **hers** of her; *pron* **herself**

**herald** *n* official who makes public announcements or arranges ceremonies; sth that shows future event; *v* announce; *n* **heraldry** study of coats of arms

**herb** *n* plant used in medicine, or flavoring; *adjs* **-aceous** dying down in winter; perennial flowering; **-al** of herbs; *n* **herbalist** dealer in medicinal herbs

**herbicide** *n* substance for killing weeds

**herculean** *adj* requiring extraordinary strength, effort, courage, etc

**herd** *n* group of animals living, feeding together; mob; *v* huddle together

**here** *adv* in, toward this place; at this point; *adv* **hereafter** in future; *n* life after death

**hereabouts** *adv* somewhere near here

**hereby** *adv fml* by this means

**heredity** *n* passing of body, mental characteristics from parent to child

**hereditary** *adj* 1 passing by heredity 2 passing by inheritance

> **hereditary** *adj* 1 (passing by heredity) congenital, family, genetic, inborn, inherited, innate. 2 (passing by inheritance) ancestral, family, genealogical, handed down, inherited

**heresy** *n* erroneous religious belief; opinion contrary to orthodox on

**heritage** *n* inheritance; characteristic derived from ancestors; *adj* **heritable**

> **heritage** *n* birthright, culture, endowment, legacy, patrimony, tradition

**hermaphrodite** *n* human being, animal, plant with both male and female characteristics

**hermetic** *adj* air-tight; *adv* **-cally** so as to be perfectly closed

**hermit** *n* one living in solitude

**hernia** *n* rupture, *esp* abdominal

**hero** *n* 1 brave person 2 admired person 3 chief male character in story; *pl* **heroes**; *fem* **-ine**

> **hero** *n* 1 (brave person) celebrity, champion, conqueror, daredevil, star, superhero, superman, superstar, victor. 2 (admired person) example, exemplar, ideal, idol, inspiration, role model

**heroic** *adj* courageous; *n* **heroism** courage

> **heroic** *adj* bold, brave, daring, gallant, fearless, intrepid, valiant

**heroin** *n* illegal habit-forming drug

**heron** *n* long-legged wading bird

**herpes** *n* skin disease; shingles

**herring** *n* edible salt-water fish; *n* **h.bone** pattern of crisscross lines

**herself** *reflex or emphatic form of* **she**

**hertz** *n* radio unit of frequency

**hesitant** *adj* undecided; *n* **hesitancy**

> **hesitant** *adj* dithering, doubting, equivocal, evasive, hesitating, indecisive, reluctant, reticent, uncertain, unsure

**hesitate** *v* pause in doubt

> **hesitate** *v* delay, dither, equivocate, falter, hang back, have doubts, have second thoughts, hedge, pause, stall, think carefully, think twice, wait

**hesitation** *n* pause while deciding

> **hesitation** *n* delay, dithering, doubt, evasion, hedging, indecision, pause, reluctance, reticence, uncertainty, wait

**heterogenous** *adj* made up of different kinds

**heterosexual** *adj* attracted to opposite sex

**het up** *adj coll* excited, upset

**hexagon** *n* plane figure with six sides

**heyday** *n* peak, acme, prime

**hiatus** *n* gap, pause

**hibernate** *v* sleep through winter

**hiccup, hiccough** *n* spasm of diaphragm causing sharp sound in throat

**hickory** *n* N American hardwood tree bearing nuts

**hide**[1] *n* raw or dressed animal skin

**hide**[2] *v* **hiding, hid, hidden** 1 conceal 2 hide yourself; *n* **hide-and-seek** game in which players hide

> **hide** *v* 1 (conceal) cover, disguise, hide away, keep secret, mask, obscure, put away, secrete. 2 (hide yourself) go into hiding, go to ground, hole up, lie low, lurk, take cover, take refuge

a b c d e f g **h** i j k l m n o p q r s t u v w x y z

**hideaway** n (also **hideout**) place of escape from other people

**hideous** adj repulsive, horrible

> **hideous** adj disfigured, disgusting, ghastly, gruesome, horrific, nightmarish, ugly, unsightly

**hiding** n sl thrashing

**hierarchy** n graded system of officials

**hieroglyph** n symbol used in ancient Egyptian picture writing; adj **hieroglyphic**

**hi-fi** n equipment for playing recorded music

**higgledy-piggledy** adj, adv completely disordered; jumbled up

**high** adj 1 tall; far above ground 2 senior 3 great in amount 4 raised in pitch 5 coll intoxicated, drugged; n 1 high point 2 met anticyclone 3 state of excitement

> **high** adj 1 (tall, far above ground) lofty, high up, raised, top, upper. 2 (senior) chief, commanding, elevated, high-ranking, high up, influential, leading, powerful, superior, supreme, top. 3 (great in amount) abundant, buoyant, considerable, expensive, extreme, great, intense. 4 (raised in pitch) alto, falsetto, high-pitched, soprano, squeaky, treble

**high jump** n contest of jumping over high bar

**highlands** n pl mountains

**highlight** n most important part; v emphasize

**highly** adv extremely

> **highly** adv abundantly, considerably, greatly, intensely, seriously, severely, very

**highly-strung** adj excitable

**highness** n title used for members of royal family

**high-spirited** adj lively

**highway** n main road

**highwayman** n (formerly) person who robs travelers

**hijack** v take over control of vehicle, esp aircraft by force; stop and rob vehicle; n instance of this; n **-er**

**hike** v walk through country; n walking excursion; n **hiker**

**hilarious** adj extremely funny; n **hilarity**

> **hilarious** adj a great laugh, amusing, comic, comical, funny, humorous, hysterical inf, side-splitting, uproarious, witty, zany

**hill** n small elevation of earth's surface

**hilt** n handle of sword, dagger; idm **up to the hilt** completely

**him** pron objective case of **he**; pron **himself** emphatic form

**hind** adj at back

**hinder** v prevent or make difficult; n **hindrance**

> **hinder** v bar, block, check, curb, delay, deter, encumber, frustrate, get in the way, hamper, handicap, hold back, impede, inhibit, interrupt, limit, obstruct, oppose, restrain, restrict, retard, sabotage, slow down, stop, thwart

**hindquarters** n, pl back legs and rump

**hindsight** n understanding of past mistakes

**Hindu** n follower of Hinduism

**hinge** n joint on which door, lid, etc hangs and turns; v provide hinge; fig depend on

**hint** n 1 indirect suggestion 2 small piece of advice; v suggest

> **hint** n 1 (indirect suggestion) clue, idea, implication, indication, insinuation, intimation, mention, reminder, sign, suggestion, tipoff. 2 (piece of advice) advice, help, pointer, suggestion, tip
>
> **hint** v allude, imply, indicate, insinuate, intimate, mention, signal

**hip** n projecting part of upper thigh

**hippie**, **hippy** n person rejecting conventions of society, esp in 1960s

**hippopotamus** *n* large, ungainly, amphibious African mammal

**hire** *n* payment for services of person, or use of thing; *v* engage for wages; pay for temporary use; *n* **hireling** mercenary person

**hirsute** *adj* hairy

**his** *pron, adj* belonging to him

**Hispanic** *adj* of Spain, Portugal, Latin America

**hiss** *v* 1 make noise like a long *s* 2 express disapproval by this sound

> **hiss** *v* 1 (make noise like long *s*) buzz, purr, rasp, rustle, shrill, sizzle, wheeze, whistle, whizz. 2 (express disapproval) boo, catcall, jeer, mocking, ridicule, scoff, scorn, taunt

**histamine** *n* chemical produced in the body that can cause allergic reactions

**historic** *adj* important and famous

> **historic** *adj* celebrated, extraordinary, memorable, momentous, notable, outstanding, remarkable, significant

**historical** *adj* based on, recorded in history

**history** *n* 1 the past 2 account of past events 3 study of the past; *n* **historian** writer of history

> **history** *n* 1 (the past) antiquity, bygone days, former times, the good old days, the old days, time gone by, yesterday, yesteryear. 2 (account of past events) account, biography, chronicle, diary, memoirs, narration, narrative, recital, record, relation, report, saga, story, tale

**hit** *v* 1 strike deliberately 2 strike accidentally 3 find by design or luck; *pt, pp* **hit;** *phr vs* **hit back** retaliate; **hit out at/against** attack vigorously; *n* 1 well-aimed blow 2 *coll* popular success; *ns* **h. list** list of people against whom action, *esp* killing, is planned; **h. man** hired assassin; **h. parade** list of best-selling pop songs

> **hit** *v* 1 (strike deliberately) bang, bash, batter, beat *sl*, belt, clout *sl*, clobber, cuff, deck *sl*, knock, lay one on *sl*, punch, slap, smack, sock, spank, strike, swat, thump, wallop, whack. 2 (strike accidentally) bang into, bump, clip, collide, crash, run into, smash into
> **hit** *n* 1 (well aimed blow) bang, bash, blow, bump, clash, clout, clip, collision, crash, cuff, impact, knock, punch, slap, smack, smash, spank, strike, swat, thump, wallop, whack. 2 (popular success) sellout, sensation, success, triumph

**hitch** *v* 1 raise with jerk 2 fasten by hook 3 ride free in sb else's car (*also* **hitchhike**); *n* 1 temporary problem 2 jerk; lifting movement; *adj* **hitched** *sl* married

**hi-tech** *adj* using advanced technology

**HIV** *n* virus in the blood responsible for AIDS; *adj* **HIV positive** infected with HIV

**hive** *n* box for honeybees to live in; *idm* **hive of industry** busy place

**hives** *n pl* skin rash

**HMO** *n* health maintenance organization; *adj* health plan providing comprehensive services to subscribers

**hoard** *n* secret store; *v* gather and hide

> **hoard** *n* accumulation, cache, collection, fund, heap, mass, pile, reserve, reservoir, stash, stock, stockpile, store, supply
> **hoard** *v* accumulate, amass, assemble, buy up, collect, deposit, gather, put by, save, stash, stockpile, stock up, store

**hoarding** *n* temporary wooden fence, *esp* one used for posters

**hoarse** *adj* husky; rough; harsh; *n* **-ness**

> **hoarse** *adj* croaky, grating, gravely, growling, gruff, guttural, harsh, husky, rasping, rough, throaty

**hoax** *n* practical joke; *v* play practical joke

**hob** n ledge beside grate to keep things hot

**hobbit** n fictional underground creature

**hobble** v 1 limp, walk clumsily 2 tie two legs (of horse, etc) together to prevent straying; n straps, rope used to hobble animal

**hobby** n leisure occupation; n **h. horse** rocking-horse; fig hobby

**hobnob** v -**nobbing**, -**nobbed** be on familiar terms with

**Hobsons choice** n situation where no choice is given

**hobo** n tramp; migratory worker; pl **hoboes**

**hock** n joint in middle of hind leg of animal

**hockey** n game played with ball or disk and curved sticks, in field or on ice

**hocus-pocus** n trickery, nonsense

**hod** n small trough on handle for carrying bricks, mortar, etc

**hoe** n tool for breaking soil, weeding etc; v **hoeing**, **hoed** use hoe

**hog** n adult male pig; greedy, filthy person

**hoi-polloi** n common people; the masses

**hoist** v raise with tackle; heave, lift up

**hold**[1] v **holding, held** 1 keep in hand 2 keep in arms 3 have 4 imprison 5 maintain (opinion) 6 contain 7 be valid; phr vs **hold on** 1 wait 2 retain one's grip; persevere; **hold out** 1 offer 2 last; **hold out for** persevere until one gets; **hold up** 1 delay 2 rob with threat of violence; n 1 grasp 2 manner of holding; idm **a hold on/over** means of control, influence

---

**hold** v 1 (keep in hand) bear, carry, clasp, clinch, cling to, clutch, grasp, grip, hang on to, hug. 2 (keep in arms) cradle, cuddle, embrace, enfold, hug. 3 (have) keep, maintain, own, possess, retain. 4 (imprison) arrest, bind, confine, detain, impound, incarcerate, lock up, put behind bars, restrain 5 (maintain opinion) assume, believe, consider, deem, esteem, judge, maintain, presume, reckon, regard, think. 6 (contain) accommodate, comprise, have a capacity of, seat, take

---

**hold**[2] n space below deck, for cargo, in ship

**holder** n 1 person in possession 2 container

**holding** n land held by tenant

**hole** n 1 split 2 excavation in ground

---

**hole** n 1 (split) aperture, breach, break, chink, crack, fissure, gap, opening, orifice, perforation, puncture, rift, rip, slit, slot, space, tear, vent. 2 (excavation in ground) abyss, cavity, chasm, crater, dent, depression, dip, excavation, hollow, indentation, pit, pocket, pothole, shaft

---

**holiday** n day, time off from work; time of commemoration; religious festival; adj festive

**holier-than-thou** adj self-righteous

**holistic** adj related to the whole person

**hollandaise** n rich, egg-based sauce

**hollow** n cavity; depression; hole; small valley; adj 1 sunken 2 sounding empty 3 insincere; v make hollow; scoop out

---

**hollow** adj 1 (sunken) cavernous, concave, deep-set, depressed, dimpled, indented. 2 (sounding empty) empty, hollowed-out, unfilled, vacant, void. 3 (insincere) artificial, empty, false, hypocritical, insignificant, meaningless, two-faced

---

**holly** n evergreen shrub with glossy, prickly leaves and red berries

**hollyhock** n tall flowering plant

**Holocaust** n Nazi mass murder of Jewish people during World War II

**hologram** n phot flat image that appears 3-dimensional when lit by laser beam

**holster** n case for pistol, hung from belt

**holt** n copse; wooded hill

**holy** adj 1 sacred 2 good and religious

---

**holy** adj 1 (sacred) blessed, consecrated, divine, hallowed, revered, sacrosanct. 2 (good and religious) devout, faithful, God-fearing, godly, pious, pure, reverent, righteous, saintly, spiritual, virtuous

---

**homage** n honor, respect

**homburg** n man's felt hat with curved brim

**home** n 1 dwelling place 2 native place 3 place where sth lives or exists; *idm* **at home** comfortable; *phr v* **home in on** direct one's aim at; *adj* pertaining to home or country; *ns* **home run** baseball strike enabling batter to complete circuit in one run; **h. rule** self-government; **homestead** house with small farm; **h. truth** unpleasant fact that one has to face up to; **homework** work to be done at home; *adjs* **h.grown**, **h.made**

> **home** n 1 (dwelling place) abode, base, domicile, dwelling, habitation, house, lodging, pad *inf*, quarters, residence. 2 (native place) birthplace, country of origin, fatherland, homeland, home town, motherland, native land

**homeless** adj without a home

> **homeless** adj abandoned, destitute, displaced, dispossessed, down-and-out, evicted, exiled, itinerant, nomadic, of no fixed abode, rootless, vagrant, wandering

**homeopathy** n treatment of disease with very small doses of drugs

**homesick** adj longing for home

**homeward** adj toward home

**homicide** n killing of human being; *adj* **-idal**

**homing** adj able to steer toward home, target

**homogeneous** adj all belonging to same category; *n* **homogeneity**

**homograph** n word having same spelling as another

**homonid** n human or human-like being

**homonym** n word having same spelling and sound as another but a different sense

**homophobia** n hatred or fear of homosexuals; *adj* **homophobic**

**homophone** n word having same sound as another, but different spelling

**Homo sapiens** n *Lat* the human species

**homosexual** adj attracted to one's own sex

**honest** adj 1 not criminal 2 truthful

> **honest** adj 1 (not criminal) aboveboard, decent, ethical, genuine, high-minded, honorable, law-abiding, reliable, reputable, scrupulous, straight, trustworthy, trusty, upright, upstanding, virtuous. 2 (truthful) blunt, candid, direct, forthright, frank, open, outright, plain, sincere

**honesty** n 1 integrity; trustworthiness 2 garden herb, with transparent seed pods

**honey** n sweet sticky fluid made from nectar by bees; *ns* **h.comb** mass of hexagonal wax cells, made by bees, to store honey; **h.dew** sweet deposit on plants

**honeymoon** n vacation spent alone by newly married couple

**honk** n cry of wild goose; similar sound, *esp* of motor horn; *v* to make this sound

**honky-tonk** n, adj (of) ragtime piano music

**honor** n 1 fairness and honesty 2 good reputation; moral dignity, high rank 3 mark of esteem; *pl* distinction in university exam; *v* esteem highly; confer high rank on

**honorable** adj decent and honest

> **honorable** adj admirable, chivalrous, ethical, fair, faithful, good, irreproachable, just, law-abiding, moral, principled, proper, reliable, righteous, true, truthful, trustworthy, upright, upstanding, virtuous

**hood** n soft covering for head and neck; *v* **hoodwink** deceive

**hoodlum** n violent petty criminal

**hoof** n horny sheath protecting animal's foot; *pl* **hoofs** or **hooves**

**hoo-ha** n *coll* fuss

**hook** n 1 curved piece of metal, wood, etc for holding, hanging, or pulling something 2 blow with bent arm in boxing; *v* grasp, hold, fasten with hook; *idm* **off the hook** freed from sth; *adj* **hooked** shaped like a hook; *idm* **hooked (on)** *coll* addicted (to)

a b c d e f g h i j k l m n o p q r s t u v w x y z

A B C D E F G H I J K L M N O P Q R S T U V W X Y Z

**hook-up** n link between electrical circuits, radio, or TV stations

**hooligan** n noisy ruffian

> **hooligan** n bully, delinquent, hoodlum, lout, tearaway, thug *inf*, trouble-maker, vandal

**hoop** n circular band of wood, metal, or plastic

**hooray** *interj expressing delight*

**hoot** n 1 cry of owl 2 sound of car horn 3 cry of derision; v utter hoots

**Hoover** [TM] n vacuum cleaner; v clean with a vacuum cleaner

**hooves** *pl of* **hoof**

**hop**[1] n plant whose flowers are used in making beer

**hop**[2] v **hopping, hopped** jump on one leg; n leap

**hope** n 1 something desired 2 feeling of confident expectation; v 1 desire 2 confidently expect

> **hope** n 1 (something desired) ambition, aspiration, craving, desire, dream, longing, wish, yearning. 2 (feeling of confident expectation) anticipation, assumption, assurance, belief, conviction, expectation
>
> **hope** v 1 (desire) aspire, crave, dream, wish, yearn. 2 (confidently expect) anticipate, assume, await, be hopeful, believe, contemplate, look forward to, trust

**hopeful** adj 1 optimistic 2 encouraging; adv **-ly**

> **hopeful** adj 1 (optimistic) buoyant, confident, expectant, positive. 2 (encouraging) auspicious, cheerful, cheering, favorable, heartening, promising, propitious, reassuring, rosy

**hopeless** adj 1 full of gloom 2 very unlikely to succeed 3 impossible

> **hopeless** adj 1 (full of gloom) defeated, dejected, demoralized, despairing, desperate, despondent, disconsolate, downhearted, forlorn, in despair, negative, pessimistic, resigned. 2 (very unlikely to succeed) beyond (all) hope, helpless, incurable, irremediable, irreparable, irretrievable, irreversible, lost. 3 (impossible) futile, impracticable, no-win, pointless, unattainable, useless, vain

**hopper** n funnellike container for grain, etc

**hopscotch** n children's game of jumping into and across marked squares

**horde** n destructive gang, rabble

**horizon** n line where earth and sky seem to meet; limits of interest, mental outlook; adj **-tal** level (adv **-ly**)

**hormone** n internal secretion by glands, which stimulates body functions

**hormone replacement therapy** n hormone treatment for women, *esp* after the menopause

**horn** n 1 one of hard, bony pointed growths on head of cow, etc 2 wind instrument 3 warning device on vehicle

**hornbill** n tropical bird with big curved beak

**hornblende** n mineral found in granite and other igneous rocks

**hornet** n large species of wasp; *idm* **stir up a hornet's nest** provoke trouble

**horoscope** n calculation of positions of stars and planets at person's birth, to predict fortune, character, etc

**horrendous** adj terrible, dreadful

**horrible** adj very unpleasant

> **horrible** adj abominable, appalling, awful, cruel, disagreeable, disgusting, dreadful, fearful, frightful, ghastly, grim, hateful, heinous, horrendous, horrid, loathsome, macabre, nasty, objectionable, obnoxious, repulsive, shocking, terrible, unkind

**horrific** *adj* terrible

> **horrific** *adj* appalling, atrocious, blood-curdling, disgusting, dreadful, frightening, grisly, gruesome, hair-raising, harrowing, horrendous, horrifying, nauseating, shocking, sickening, unthinkable

**horrified** *adj* 1 terrified 2 very shocked

> **horrified** *adj* 1 (terrified) alarmed, frightened, petrified, scared, scared out of your wits, scared stiff, scared to death. 2 (shocked) appalled, disgusted, dismayed, outraged, revolted, scandalized, sickened

**horrify** *adj* 1 frighten 2 shock and disgust
**horror** *n* 1 terror 2 disgust

> **horror** *n* 1 (terror) alarm, apprehension, consternation, dismay, dread, fear, fearfulness, fright, panic, trepidation, uneasiness. 2 (disgust) abhorrence, antipathy, aversion, dislike, distaste, hatred, loathing, repugnance, revulsion

**hors d'oeuvre** *n Fr* light savory dish served before meal as appetizer
**horse** *n* 1 large four-footed domesticated mammal, used for riding on 2 vaulting block; *ns* **h.chestnut** tree with inedible shiny brown nuts; **horseman**, **horsemanship**; **h.play** rough, noisy play; **horsepower** unit of engine power (*also* **hp**); **horseradish** edible root with hot flavor; **h.-race**; **horseshoe** U-shaped shoe, symbol of good luck; **horsewoman**
**horticulture** *n* study of gardening; *adj* **-tural**
**hose** *n* flexible tube for carrying liquids
**hospice** *n* home for terminally ill
**hospitable** *adj* welcoming to visitors

> **hospitable** *adj* convivial, cordial, courteous, friendly, generous, genial, gracious, kind, neighborly, sociable, warm-hearted

**hospital** *n* place where sick and injured are cared for; *v* **-ize** send, admit to hospital
**hospitality** *n* kindness, generosity to guests

> **hospitality** *n* cheer, conviviality, cordiality, courtesy, friendliness, geniality, graciousness, neighborliness, sociability, warm-heartedness, warmth, welcome

**host**[1] *n* one who entertains a guest; hotelkeeper; emcee on TV
**host**[2] *n* army; great number
**hostage** *n* one given or taken as pledge that promises will be kept
**hostel** *n* lodging house for students, workers, young people, etc
**hostess** *n* 1 female host 2 air hostess 3 female compere on TV
**hostile** *adj* 1 aggressive 2 adverse (conditions); *n* **hostility**; (*pl* **-ies** fighting)

> **hostile** *adj* (aggressive) antagonistic, belligerent, combative, confrontational, contrary, inimical, unfriendly, unkind, unsympathetic

**hot** *adj* 1 of high temperature 2 spicy 3 *coll* (of news) exciting and fresh; *ns* **h.-cross bun** spicy bun eaten on Good Friday; **h. dog** frankfurter in long bread roll; **hothead** rash person; **hot-house** greenhouse; **h. line** direct telephone link between heads of state; **hotplate** surface for cooking; *adjs* **h.-blooded** passionate; **h.-tempered** quick to become angry

> **hot** *adj* 1 (of high temperature) baking, blistering, boiling, burning, fiery, flaming, heated, piping, red-hot, roasting, scalding, scorching, searing, steaming, sultry, sweltering, thermal, torrid, tropical, warm. 2 (spicy) peppery, piquant, pungent, sharp, strong

**hotel** *n* place where guests pay to stay; *n* **hotelier**

**hound** n dog hunting by scent; v pursue; persecute

**hour** n sixty minutes; fixed point of time; pl regular time of work; adv **hourly** every hour; n **h.glass** sand glass that runs out in one hour

**house** n 1 dwelling place 2 business 3 body of people with power to govern; v provide house for; idm **bring the house down** provoke loud laughter or applause; idm **on the house** coll paid for by manager; ns **h. arrest**; **houseboat**; **housebreaker** burglar; **household** people living in a house (**household name/word** well-known name/word); **householder** head of household; **housekeeper** person employed to look after house; **housekeeping** 1 work of running house 2 money for this; **H. of Commons** assembly of elected representatives in UK and Canada; **H. of Representatives** assembly of elected representatives in USA, Australia, New Zealand; **h.-warming** party given by new occupants; **housewife**; adjs **h.-broken** (of animals) trained not to urinate, defecate indoors; **h.-proud** fussy about appearance of home

**house** n 1 (dwelling place) abode, building, domicile, dwelling, edifice, habitation, pad inf, residence. 2 (business) company, concern, corporation, enterprise, establishment, firm, organization,

**housing** n 1 living accommodation 2 cover for machinery

**hove** pt, pp of **heave**

**hovel** n small, shabby dwelling

**hover** v 1 (of birds) float motionless in air 2 linger; n **hovercraft** craft moving along, on cushion of air, over land or water

**hover** v 1 (float in air) be suspended, drift, float, flutter, fly, poise. 2 (linger) hang about, hang around, loiter, wait about

**how** adv in what way; by what means; to what degree; idm **How come?** why?; idm **How do you do?** formal greeting

**however** adv 1 nevertheless 2 in whatever way; to whatever degree 3 by what possible means

**howl** v utter loud dismal cry; n such cry; n **howler** sl stupid mistake

**HQ** abbr headquarters

**HRT** abbr hormone replacement therapy

**hub** n central part of wheel; fig center of activity or importance

**hubbub** n uproar, riot

**hubcap** n metal cover for center of car wheel

**hubris** n excessive pride or self-confidence

**huckleberry** n N American shrub; its fruit

**huddle** v 1 crowd together 2 come close together for warmth; n small group of people all close together

**huddle** v 1 (crowd together) bunch, cluster, converge, cram, flock, gather, group, herd, squeeze, swarm, throng. 2 (come close together for warmth) crouch, cuddle, curl up, hug, nestle **huddle** n band, bunch, cluster, crowd, gang, gathering, group, knot, mass, pack

**hue** n color; tint; complexion

**huff** n sulkiness; adj **huffy** sulky

**hug** v **hugging, hugged** embrace warmly; fig keep close to; n act of hugging

**huge** adj very great, enormous

**huge** adj colossal, extra-large, gargantuan, giant, gigantic, hulking, immense, jumbo inf, large, mammoth, massive, mighty, outsize, vast, whopping

**hulk** n 1 derelict, dismantled ship 2 large person; adj **hulking** big and clumsy

**hull** n body of ship

**hullabaloo** n uproar, din, clamor

**hum** v **humming, hummed** produce low buzzing sound, like bee; sing with closed lips; n continuous low drone

**hum** *v* buzz, murmur, purr, sing, throb, thrum, vibrate, whir

**human** *adj* relating to people
**humane** *adj* kind; merciful

**humane** *adj* altruistic, benevolent, benign, charitable, compassionate, forgiving, gentle, good, humanitarian, kindhearted, lenient, magnanimous, mild, sympathetic, tender, understanding, warmhearted

**humanism** *n* system of thought dealing with human interests; *n* **humanist**
**humanity** *n* human race as whole kindness; *pl* **humanities** classical literary studies
**humanitarian** *adj* given to help suffering people
**humanize** *v* make, become human, humane
**humanoid** *adj* having human characteristics
**humble** *adj* 1 modest 2 of low social rank; *v* put to shame; *adv* **humbly**

**humble** *adj* 1 (modest) deferential, docile, meek, submissive, unpretentious. 2 (of low social rank) common, ignoble, insignificant, low, lowly, modest, ordinary, simple, undistinguished, unimportant

**humbug** *n* 1 nonsense 2 empty, boastful person; *v* deceive, dupe
**humdrum** *adj* dull
**humerus** *n* bone of upper arm
**humid** *adj* damp; *n* **-idity**

**humid** *adj* clammy, close, dank, moist, muggy, steamy, sticky, sultry, wet

**humiliate** *v* put to shame; *n* **-ation**

**humiliate** *v* abase, chasten, crush, deflate, debase, degrade, demean, disgrace, embarrass, humble, make sb feel small, mortify, shame, show sb up *inf*

**humility** *n* quality of being humble
**hummingbird** *n* minute tropical bird with long beak
**hummock** *n* knoll; hillock; ridge of ice
**hummus** *n* Gk puree of chickpeas, tahina, etc
**humorous** *adj* amusing

**humorous** *adj* comic, comical, droll, entertaining, facetious, farcical, funny, hilarious, laughable, ludicrous, ridiculous, satirical, witty

**humor)** 1 fun, amusement 2 mood; *v* indulge moods; *ns* **humorist, humorist** comic writer, artist or actor

**humour** *n* 1 (fun, amusement) banter, comedy, farce, hilarity, jesting, jocularity, jokes, joking, laughter, ludicrousness, merriment, quips, repartee, ridiculousness, satire, wisecracks, wit. 2 (mood) disposition, state of mind, spirits, temper, temperament

**hump** *n* rounded lump, bulge, or mound; *v* carry on back
**humus** *n* decayed organic matter giving fertility to soil
**hunch** *n* intuitive idea; *v* stoop; *n* **-back** one with unnatural lump on back
**hundred** *n, pron, det* cardinal number, ten times ten; *adj* **-th** ordinal number 100th; *n* **hundredweight** measure of weight = 112 lbs. or 1/20 ton
**hung** *pt, pp of* **hang**
**hunger** *n* 1 desire for food 2 desire for sth; *phr v* **hunger after /for** long for; *n* **h. strike** refusal of all food, as protest

**hunger** *n* 1 (desire for food) appetite, emptiness, famine, hungriness, ravenousness, starvation. 2 (desire) appetite, craving, eagerness, greed, hankering, itch, keenness, longing, lust, pining, yearning

a b c d e f g h i j k l m n o p q r s t u v w x y z

**hungry** *adj* feeling hunger; *adv* **hungrily**

> **hungry** *adj* empty, famished, malnourished, peckish, ravenous, starved, starving, underfed, undernourished

**hunk** *n* **1** thick piece **2** *sl* sexually attractive man; *adj* **hunky**

**hunt** *v* pursue (animals) in order to kill, or catch; pursue (person); *n* search; local association of people with their horses, hounds engaged in hunting; *ns* **huntsman** man in charge of hounds; **hunter**; *fem* **huntress**

**hurdle** *n* light wooden fence to jump over; *ns* **hurdler** one who runs in hurdle races; **h. race** race in which hurdles are leaped

**hurdy-gurdy** *n* small barrel organ

**hurl** *v* throw violently; *n* **hurler**

> **hurl** *v* cast, chuck *inf*, fire, fling, heave, launch, lob, pitch, propel, send, sling, toss

**hurly-burly** *n* noisy activity

**hurricane** *n* violent wind-storm, of 120 kmph (75 mph) or more; tropical cyclone; *n* **h. lamp** lamp with well-shielded flame

**hurry** *v* **hurrying**, **hurried** **1** move quickly **2** speed up; *adj* **hurried**; *adv* **-ly**; *n* rush

> **hurry** *v* (move quickly) belt, dash, fly, hasten, get a move on, make haste, run, rush, scurry, speed, step on it

**hurt** *v* **hurting**, **hurt** **1** cause pain or injury to **2** be painful **3** upset; *n* harm; wound; pain; *adj* feeling pain or distress

> **hurt** *v* **1** (cause pain or injury) bruise, cut, damage, disable, harm, impair, injure, mar, spoil, wound. **2** (be painful) ache, be painful, be sore, burn, smart, sting, throb. **3** (upset) aggrieve, cut, distress, grieve, insult, offend, pain, sadden, wound

**hurtful** *adj* unkind and upsetting

**hurtle** *v* move violently; dash against; whirl

**husband** *n* married man

**husbandry** *n* farming and raising livestock

**hush** *v* make, become silent; *phr v* **hush up** keep secret; *n* silence; stillness

**husk** *n* dry covering of certain seeds; *v* strip husk from; *adv* **huskily**; *n* **-iness**

**husky**[1] *adj* dry and harsh (of voice)

**husky**[2] *n* Inuit sledge dog

**hustings** *n pl* electioneering platform; election proceedings

**hustle** *v* hurry; jostle; urge along roughly; *n* bustle, hurry; *n* **hustler** one who gets things done

**hut** *n* small wooden building

> **hut** *n* cabin, hovel, lean-to, refuge, shack, shanty, shed, shelter

**hutch** *n* boxlike coop for rabbits, etc

**hyacinth** *n* bulbous plant with spikes of fragrant, bell-shaped flowers

**hybrid** *n* animal or plant produced by parents of different species; *fig* anything derived from mixed origins; *adj* cross-bred; *v* **-ize** cross-fertilize, interbreed; *n* **-ization**

> **hybrid** *adj* amalgam, blend, composite, compound, cross, crossbreed, half-blood, half-breed, mix, mixture, mongrel

**hydra** *n* **1** *myth* many-headed serpent; **2** *fig* evil that defies destruction **3** freshwater polyp

**hydrangea** *n* shrub with pink, blue, or white flowers

**hydrant** *n* pipe from water main, with attachment for hose

**hydraulic** *adj* conveying water; water-powered

**hydr-**, **hydro-** *prefix; forms compounds with meaning of* water

**hydrocarbon** *n* organic compound of hydrogen and carbon

**hydrochloric** *adj* containing hydrogen and chlorine; *n* **h. acid**

**hydroelectric** *adj* relating to electricity generated by water power

**hydrofoil** *n* boat with vanes that lift hull above water to reduce drag and increase speed

**hydrogen** *n* colorless gas combining with oxygen to form water; **h. bomb** highly destructive atom bomb

**hydrophobia** *n* rabies; abnormal fear of water, *esp* as symptom of this

**hydrotherapy** *n* use of water to treat disease

**hyena** *n* carnivorous doglike animal with cry like wild laughter

**hygiene** *n* science and principles of maintaining health and cleanliness

**hygienic** *adj* clean and not harmful to health

> **hygienic** *adj* aseptic, disinfected, healthy, germ-free, pure, sanitary, sterile, sterilized, uncontaminated, unpolluted

**hygrometer** *n* instrument for measuring humidity of atmosphere

**hymen** *n* membrane partly covering entrance to vagina of a virgin

**hymn** *n* song of praise to God; *adj, n* **-al** (book) of hymns

**hype** *n* exaggerated publicity; *phr v* **hype up** publicize in a wildly exaggerated way; *adj* **hyped up 1** overpromoted **2** overstimulated

**hyper-** *prefix: forms compounds with meaning of* excessive; *eg* **hypersensitive** *adj* too sensitive

**hyperactive** *n* unable to settle down

**hyperbola** *n* curve formed by section of cone when cutting plane makes larger angle with base than side makes

**hyperbole** *n* rhetorical exaggeration

**hypercritical** *adj* overly critical

**hypertension** *n med* **1** abnormally high blood pressure **2** abnormal emotional tension

**hyphen** *n* mark (-) indicating that two words or syllables are connected; *adj* **-ated**

**hypnosis** *n* artificially induced state resembling deep sleep; *adj* **hypnotic** inducing sleep

**hypnotize** *v* put into state resembling deep sleep; *ns* **hypnotism, -ist**

> **hypnotize** *v* entrance, fascinate, mesmerize, put in a trance, spellbind

**hypo-, hyph-, hyp-** *prefix: forms compounds with meaning of* below, less, under

**hypoallergenic** *adj* (of cosmetics) unlikely to cause an allergic reaction on the skin

**hypochondria** *n* morbid obsession with one's health; *n* **-driac** person with this

**hypocrisy** *n* pretending to be better morally than one is

**hypocrite** *n* person pretending to be better morally than they are

**hypocritical** *adj* pretending to be good, honest, etc

> **hypocritical** *adj* deceitful, dishonest, dissembling, duplicitous, fake, false, fraudulent, hollow, inconsistent, insincere, phony, sham, spurious, two-faced

**hypodermic** *adj* under the skin

**hypotenuse** *n* side of right-angled triangle opposite the right angle

**hypothermia** *n* very low body temperature, *esp* in old people

**hypothesis** *n* unproved theory; *pl* **-theses**

**hypothetical** *adj* presumed but not proved

> **hypothetical** *adj* academic, conjectured, notional, possible, proposed, putative, speculative, suggested, theoretical

**hysterectomy** *n* surgical removal of uterus

**hysteria** *n* extreme emotional excitability; *n pl* **hysterics** fit of hysteria

**hysterical** *n* emotionally excited and out of control

> **hysterical** *adj* berserk, beside yourself, crazed, delirious, distracted, distraught, frantic, frenzied, irrational, manic, raving

**I** *pron* (1st per sing nom) myself; (*pl* **we**); **I'd** *abbr* **1** I had **2** I should **3** I would; **I'm** *abbr* I am; **I've** *abbr* I have

**Iberian** *adj* of Spain and Portugal

**ice** *n* **1** frozen water **2** ice cream; *idm* **break the ice** initiate relations; remove embarrassment; *idm* **keep on ice 1** keep chilled **2** (of ideas) hold in reserve; *idm* **skate on thin ice** take unwise risk; *ns* **i. age** very cold prehistoric era on earth; **iceberg** mass of floating ice at sea (*idm* **the tip of the iceberg** only a small part of the problem); **i. cap** permanently frozen polar region; **i. cream** frozen confection of flavoured cream, custard etc; **i. hockey**; **i. pack** tool for breaking ice; **i. pick** tool for breaking ice; **i. rink** artificial sheet of ice for skating, ice hockey, etc; **i. skate** boot with metal blade for skating on ice (*v* **i.-skate, i.-skating**); *v* **1** make cold with ice **2** cover with sugar icing

**ichneumon** *n* smallanimal, like weasel

**icicle** *n* long hanging piece of ice

**icing** *n* (also **frosting**) decorative coating for cake made from icing sugar

**icon** *n* image; sacred portrait

**icy** *adj* **1** extremely cold **2** covered in ice

> **icy** *adj* (extremely cold) arctic, biting, bitter, chill, chilly, freezing, frosty, frozen, glacial, ice-cold, polar, raw

**ID** *abbr* identification; identity

**idea** *n* **1** thought **2** suggestion

> **idea** *n* **1** (thought) belief, concept, hypothesis, image, impression, notion, opinion, principle, theory, understanding, view. **2** (suggestion) brainwave, creation, inspiration, plan, proposal, scheme

**ideal** *adj* perfect; *n* supreme perfection; *ns* **idealism** seeking perfection in all things; **idealist 1** one who believes in perfection in all things **2** impractical person; *v* **idealize** exaggerate good qualities of

> **ideal** *adj* classic, complete, exemplary, faultless, flawless, model, optimum, supreme

**idée fixe** *n Fr* obsession

**identical** *adj* exactly alike

> **identical** *adj* alike, duplicate, equal, indistinguishable, interchangeable, like, matching, the same, twin

**identify** *v* recognize who/what sb/sth is; *idm* **identify with** sympathize with; *n* **identification**

**identity** *n* individuality

**ideogram** *n* symbol to represent ideas (as in Chinese)

**ideograph** *n* symbolic representation of an object, without naming it

**ideology** *n* set of political ideas; *adj* **-ological**

**idiocy** *n* stupidity

**idiom** *n* informal phrase

**idiosyncrasy** *n* individual peculiarity of manner, thought, way of speaking, etc

**idiot** *n* fool

> **idiot** *n* blockhead, bonehead, dimwit, dummy, dunce, halfwit, ignoramus, imbecile, moron, nitwit, numbskull, simpleton, twit

**idiotic** *adj* utterly foolish; senseless

> **idiotic** *adj* daft, dense, dimwitted, dumb, fatuous, foolish, half-witted, inane, moronic, stupid

**idle** *adj* **1** lazy **2** not working **3** not meaningful; *v* **1** waste time **2** (of machine) run at low speed; *n* **-ness**; *adv* **idly**; *n* **idler**

> **idle** *adj* **1** (lazy) apathetic, indolent, loafing, shiftless, slothful, sluggish, torpid, work-shy. **2** (not working) inactive, inoperative, jobless, out of action, out of use, redundant, unemployed, unoccupied, unproductive, unused

**idol** *n* **1** image representing deity **2** false god **3** person, object of extreme devotion; *ns* **idolator** worshiper of false gods (*fem* **idolatress**); **idolatry**

**idolize** *v* love, admire excessively

**idyll** *n* **1** romantic rural place **2** short, simple poem on homely, pastoral subjects; *adj* **-ic**

**i.e.** *abbr* id est *Lat* that is

**if** *conj* supposing that; even though

**igloo** *n* hut of frozen snow blocks

**igneous** *adj* produced by volcanic action; fiery

**ignite** *v* set on fire; start burning; *n* **ignition** setting on fire; means of firing of explosive gaseous mixture by electric spark

> **ignite** *v* burn, catch fire, kindle, light, set alight, set fire to, spark off

**ignoble** *adj* base, degraded, humiliating, shameful; *adv* **-bly**

**ignominy** *n* dishonor

**ignorance** *n* lack of education; inexperience

**ignorant** *adj* uninformed; unaware

> **ignorant** *adj* blind, ill-informed, inexperienced, innocent, naïve, oblivious, stupid, unconscious, uneducated, unenlightened, unknowing

**ignore** *v* not consider

> **ignore** *v* brush aside, discount, disregard, neglect, omit, overlook, pass over, pay no attention, reject, shut your eyes, take no notice, turn a blind eye

**iguana** *n* large, crested S American tree lizard

**ilk** *adj* Scot of that ilk **1** of same name, etc **2** coll of that kind

**ill** *adj* sick; *adjs* **i.-advised** unwise; **i.-mannered**; *v* **i.-treat**

> **ill** *adj* ailing, groggy, infirm, not well, off-colour, out of sorts, poorly, sickly, under the weather, unhealthy, unwell

**illegal** *adj* against the law

> **illegal** *adj* banned, black-market, criminal, felonious, forbidden, illegitimate, illicit, outlawed, prohibited, unauthorized, unlawful, unlicensed, wrongful

**illegible** *adj* difficult to read; *adv* **-ibly**; *n* **-ibility**

**illegitimate** *adj* unlawful; not born in wedlock

**illicit** *adj* prohibited, forbidden

**illiterate** *adj* unable to read; *n* **illiteracy**

**illness** *n* sickness

> **illness** *n* affliction, ailment, attack, bug, complaint, condition, disease, disorder, ill-health, indisposition, infection, infirmity, invalidity, malady, malaise

**illogical** *adj* not rational or logical

> **illogical** *adj* absurd, fallacious, faulty, inconsistent, incorrect, invalid, irrational, meaningless, senseless, spurious, unreasonable, unscientific, unsound

**illuminate** *v* make light; decorate with lights; *adj* **-ating** helpful and revealing

a
b
c
d
e
f
g
h
i
j
k
l
m
n
o
p
q
r
s
t
u
v
w
x
y
z

**illusion** v deceptive appearance; delusion

**illustrate** v 1 make clear; explain 2 furnish (book, etc) with pictures; ns **-ation**; **illustrator**

**illustrious** adj famous, glorious

**image** n 1 picture 2 mental picture 3 popular opinion about a person, company or commercial product; n **imagery** images; mental pictures

> **image** n 1 (picture) depiction, figure, likeness, photograph, portrayal, projection, reflection, representation. 2 (mental picture) conception, idea, notion, perception. 3 (popular opinion) name, reputation, repute, standing, status

**imaginary** adj imagined, not real

> **imaginary** adj dreamed-up, fabulous, fanciful, fantastic, fictional, ideal, illusory, invented, legendary, made-up, mythical, non-existent, unreal

**imagination** n ability to have original ideas

> **imagination** n creativity, fancy, ingenuity, insight, inspiration, inventiveness, originality, vision

**imaginative** adj containing original ideas

**imagine** v 1 form image, idea in mind 2 suppose

> **imagine** v 1 (form idea in mind) conceive, conjure up, create, devise, dream up, envisage, fantasize, invent, make believe, picture, pretend, project, think of, think up, visualize. 2 (suppose) assume, believe, conjecture, deduce, gather, guess, infer, judge, presume, reckon, surmise, suspect, think

**imago** n final state of insect, esp of winged one

**imbalance** n lack of balance or proportion

**imbecile** n fool

**imbibe** v drink

**imbue** phr v **imbue (with)** fill (with)

**IMF** n International Monetary Fund

**imitate** v copy closely

> **imitate** v caricature, copy, duplicate, echo, follow, impersonate, mimic, mirror, mock, parody, repeat, simulate

**imitation** n 1 act of imitating 2 copy

> **imitation** n 1 (act of imitating) copying, impersonation, impression, mimicry, parody. 2 (copy) clone, counterfeit, dummy, duplication, fake, forgery, look-alike, mock-up, model, replica, reproduction, sham, simulation

**immaculate** adj pure, unsoiled, innocent; n **I. Conception** Roman Catholic belief that the mother of Jesus was born without original sin

**immanent** adj inherent; ever present

**immaterial** adj unimportant

**immature** adj 1 not fully developed 2 childish; adv **-ly**; n **immaturity**

> **immature** adj 1 (not fully developed) crude, green, half-formed, raw, undeveloped, unformed, unripe, young. 2 (childish) adolescent, babyish, backward, callow, infantile, juvenile, puerile

**immeasurable** adj too vast to be calculated

**immediate** adj 1 happening now or next 2 nearest in space, in relationship; adv **-ly** 1 at once 2 with nothing between

> **immediate** adj (happening now or next) instant, instantaneous, on the spot, prompt, quick, rapid, speedy, sudden, swift, unhesitating

**immemorial** adj beyond living memory; very ancient

**immense** *adj* very great; *n* **immensity**

> **immense** *adj* colossal, elephantine,
> enormous, extensive, giant, gigantic,
> great, huge, infinite, mammoth, massive,
> mighty, monumental, prodigious,
> stupendous, titanic, tremendous, vast

**immerse** *v* dip, plunge into liquid; *fig* engross;
*n* **immersion**

> **immerse** *v* bathe, cover, douse, drench,
> duck, dunk, lower, sink, soak, submerge

**immigrate** *v* come to foreign country to live;
*ns* **-ation**; **immigrant** person settling in
foreign country
**imminent** *adj* about to happen; *adv* **-ently**

> **imminent** *adj* approaching, at hand,
> close, coming, forthcoming, gathering,
> impending, looming, near, on the
> horizon, threatening

**immobile** *adj* not moving; fixed; *n* **-bility**;
*v* **immobilize** render immobile
**immoderate** *adj* excessive; unrestrained
**immoral** *adj* morally wrong; corrupt
**immortal** *adj* never dying; *n* **-ity**

> **immortal** *adj* abiding, ageless, constant,
> endless, enduring, eternal, everlasting,
> imperishable, indestructible, infinite,
> lasting, never-ending, perennial,
> perpetual, timeless, undying, unfading

**immune** *adj* free from; exempt from; resistant
to (disease); *ns* **i. system** function of body
to combat disease; **immunity**; *v* **immunize**
(*n* **-ization**)
**immure** *v* shut up; enclose; imprison
**immutable** *adj* unchangeable
**imp** *n* little devil; mischievous child
**impact** *n* 1 collision 2 strong impression;
*v* press strongly together
**impair** *v* weaken; *n* **-ment**

**impair** *v* blunt, damage, debilitate,
diminish, disable, enfeeble, harm, hinder,
hurt, impede, injure, lessen, mar, reduce,
spoil, undermine, worsen

**impale** *v* transfix, *esp* on pointed stake;
*n* **-ment**
**impart** *v* transmit; make known
**impartial** *adj* unprejudiced; *adv* **-ly**; *n* **-ity**

> **impartial** *adj* balanced, detached,
> disinterested, dispassionate, equal,
> equitable, evenhanded, fair, fair-minded,
> just, neutral, objective, open-minded,
> unbiased

**impassable** *adj* impossible to cross over
**impasse** *n* deadlock; blind alley
**impassioned** *adj* ardent, passionate
**impassive** *adj* without emotion; calm
**impatient** *adj* 1 waiting irritably 2 eager to do
sth 3 short-tempered; *adv* **-ly**; *n* **impatience**

> **impatient** *adj* 1 (waiting irritably) agitated,
> edgy, fidgety, intolerant, irritable, restive,
> testy. 2 (eager to do sth) anxious, eager,
> keen, longing, raring. 3 (short-tempered)
> abrupt, brusque, hasty, irritable, quick-
> tempered, terse

**impeach** *v* charge with crime; *n* **-ment**
**impeccable** *adj* faultless; *adv* **-ably**
**impecunious** *adj* poor
**impede** *v* obstruct; delay; *n* **impediment**
**impel** *v* **-pelling, -pelled** urge on; force
**impending** *adj* due to happen soon
**impenetrable** *n* 1 impassable
2 incomprehensible
**imperative** *adj* urgent; necessary
**imperfect** *adj* not perfect; *n* **-ion** blemish

> **imperfect** *adj* blemished, broken, chipped,
> cracked, damaged, defective, faulty,
> flawed, incomplete, spoilt, unfinished

A
B
C
D
E
F
G
H
I
J
K
L
M
N
O
P
Q
R
S
T
U
V
W
X
Y
Z

**imperial** *adj* of empire or emperor; *ns* **-ism** belief in colonial empire; **-ist**

**imperil** *v* **-illing, -illed** endanger

**imperious** *adj* dominating; dictatorial

**impersonal** *adj* 1 not distinctive 2 without feelings

**impersonate** *v* pretend to be another; act part of; *ns* **-ation; -ator**

**impertinent** *adj* cheeky; *n* **impertinence**

> **impertinent** *adj* brazen, cocky, disrespectful, forward, impolite, impudent, insolent, irreverent, rude, saucy

**imperturbable** *adj* calm; not liable to be ruffled; *adv* **-ably**

**impervious** *adj* not allowing entry; unaffected

**impetuous** *adj* rash and hasty

> **impetuous** *adj* eager, hot-headed, impulsive, quick, reckless, spontaneous, thoughtless, unthinking

**impetus** *n* momentum; driving force; *fig* stimulus

**impinge** *v* have an effect on

**impious** *adj* without piety; ungodly

**implacable** *adj* relentless

**implant** *v* insert; *n* sth put in body by surgery

**implement** *n* tool; *v* carry into effect

**implicate** *v* involve; include; **-tion**

**implicit** *adj* 1 hinted at 2 unquestioning; *adv* **-ly**

> **implicit** *adj* (hinted at) contained, implied, indirect, inherent, tacit, understood, unspoken

**implore** *v* ask for earnestly

**imply** *v* **-plying, -plied** suggest indirectly

> **imply** *v* hint, indicate, insinuate, intimate, mean, point to, signify, suggest

**import** *v* bring in (*esp* goods from abroad); *n* thing imported; *ns* **-ation; importer**

**importance** *n* significance

> **importance** *n* gravity, momentousness, newsworthiness, prestige, rarity, relevance, seriousness, status, usefulness, value, worth

**important** *adj* 1 significant 2 high-ranking or famous 3 essential; *adv* **-ly**

> **important** *adj* 1 (significant) basic, big, cardinal, central, chief, far-reaching, grave, historic, key, main, major, momentous, principal, salient, serious, urgent, weighty. 2 (high-ranking, famous) celebrated, distinguished, eminent, influential, leading, powerful, prominent, well-known. 3 (essential) critical, crucial, necessary, pressing, vital

**importune** *v* pester with troublesome demands; *adj* **importunate**; *adv* **-ly**; *n* **importunity**

**impose** *v* 1 exact (tax, etc) 2 force sth unwanted on sb; *n* **imposition** 1 act of imposing 2 sth forced on one

**imposing** *adj* impressive

**impossible** *adj* 1 not possible 2 not true; *adv* **-ibly**; *n* **-ibility**

> **impossible** *adj* 1 (not possible) difficult, hopeless, impracticable, impractical, inconceivable, insoluble, out of the question, unattainable, unimaginable, unthinkable, unworkable. 2 (not true) absurd, incredible, outrageous, preposterous, unbelievable

**impostor** *n* person who pretends to be someone else to deceive people

**impotent** *adj* powerless; feeble; lacking sexual capacity; *n* **impotence**

**impound** *v* 1 confiscate 2 enclose in pound

**impoverish** *v* make poor; weaken

**imprecation** *n* curse

**impregnable** *adj* unassailable; invincible

**impregnate** *v* make pregnant; fertilize

**impress** *v* affect deeply

> **impress** *v* affect, be memorable, excite,
> influence, inspire, leave your mark, make
> an impression, make an impact, stick in
> sb's mind, stir, sway, touch

**impression** *n* 1 effect produced on mind
2 belief 3 imitation
**impressionable** *adj* easily influenced
**impressionism** *n* style of painting giving
general effect without detail
**impressive** *adj* exciting or inspiring

> **impressive** *adj* awe-inspiring, awesome,
> formidable, grand, magnificent,
> memorable, moving, powerful, stirring,
> striking, touching

**imprest** *n* loan made to individual by the
state
**imprint** *v* 1 stamp 2 fix in mind; *n* mark,
stamp made by pressure; publisher's, printer's
name, etc in book
**imprison** *v* put in prison; *n* **-ment**

> **imprison** *v* confine, detain, incarcerate,
> jail, lock up, put away, remand, send
> down, send to prison, shut up

**impromptu** *adv, adj* unrehearsed; without
preparation
**improper** *adj* 1 socially unacceptable;
indecent 2 incorrect; *adv* **-ly**;
*n* **impropriety**
**improve** *v* 1 make better 2 get better

> **improve** *v* 1 (make better) correct,
> enhance, enrich, help, mend, modernize,
> put right, rectify, refine, reform, repair,
> revise, touch up, update, upgrade. 2 (get
> better) advance, develop, gain strength,
> increase, look up, make headway, pick
> up, progress, rally, recover

**improvement** *n* gain or progress

**improvement** *n* advance, amendment,
correction, development, enhancement,
growth, increase, recovery, upswing, upturn

**improvident** *adj* not careful or cautious
**improvise** *v* do on spur of moment, *esp* with
makeshift materials; *n* **-ation**
**impudent** *adj* cheeky; *adv* **-ly**; *n* **-dence**

> **impudent** *adj* bad-mannered, bold, brazen,
> disrespectful, forward, impertinent,
> insolent, presumptuous, rude, saucy

**impugn** *v* criticize, challenge
**impulse** *n* sudden inclination to do sth; push;
stimulus; *n* **impulsion** impetus
**impulsive** *adj* rash; acting without thought

> **impulsive** *adj* automatic, hasty, impetuous,
> instinctive, quick, spontaneous, sudden

**impunity** *n* freedom; safety from penalty;
*idm* **with impunity** without being penalized
**impure** *adj* dirty; not pure; *n* **impurity**
**impute** *v* ascribe to; credit;
*n* **imputation** reproach, accusation
**in-** *prefix forming adjs, advs, ns (also **im-** before
**b, m** *or* **p** *and* **il-, ir-** *before* **l** *and* **r**
*respectively*) 1 not 2 lack of; *eg adj*
**inaccurate** not accurate; *n* **inaccuracy**
lack of accuracy
**in** *prep* 1 contained by 2 during 3 into 4 at
end of (time) 5 wearing (clothes);
*adv* 1 inside 2 at home 3 included
4 available; *adj* 1 *coll* fashionable
2 belonging to an exclusive group
**inadequate** *adj* 1 not good enough
2 insufficient

> **inadequate** *adj* 1 (not good enough)
> deficient, disappointing, incompetent,
> incomplete, unacceptable, unqualified,
> unsatisfactory, unsuitable. 2 (insufficient)
> limited, meager, not enough, scanty, scarce

**inadvertent** *adj* unintentional; *adv* **-ly**;
n **inadvertency**
**inalienable** *adj* that cannot be taken away;
n **i. right**
**inane** *adj* foolish, senseless, frivolous;
n **inanity** silly remark
**inarticulate** *adj* not speaking clearly

> **inarticulate** *adj* faltering, hesitant,
> incoherent, incomprehensible, indistinct,
> muffled, shy, stammering, stuttering,
> tongue-tied, unclear, unintelligible

**inasmuch** *conj* as seeing that; since
**inaugurate** *v* install in office with ceremony;
begin, open, *esp* formally; *adj* **-al**; n **-ation**
**inauspicious** *adj* unlucky; unfavorable
**inborn, inbred** *adj* inherent; natural;
n **inbreeding** breeding from close stocks
**inbuilt** *adj* forming an inherent part of sth
**incalculable** *adj* beyond calculation;
unpredictable; uncertain
**incandescent** *adj* luminous with heat
**incantation** n magic spell; charm
**incapable** *adj* not capable

> **incapable** *adj* feeble, helpless, inadequate,
> incompetent, ineffective, inept,
> powerless, unfit, useless, weak

**incapacitate** *v* render unfit; disable;
disqualify; n **incapacity**
**incarcerate** *v* imprison; n **-ation**
**incarnate** *adj* embodied in human form;
personified; n **-ation**
**incendiary** *adj* designed to cause fire
**incense**[1] n fragrant smoke from burning
spices, etc
**incense**[2] *v* anger, enrage
**incentive** n reason for doing sth

> **incentive** n bait, carrot, encouragement,
> impetus, impulse, inducement, lure,
> motivation, motive, reward, spur,
> stimulus, sweetener

**inception** n beginning
**incessant** *adj* constant; unceasing
**incest** n sexual intercourse between close
blood relations; *adj* **-uous**
**inch** n ½th. linear foot; *v* advance by small
degrees
**inchoate** *adj* undeveloped; rudimentary
**incident** n event

> **incident** n adventure, affair, episode,
> experience, happening, matter, occasion,
> occurrence

**incidental** *adj* occurring by chance; *adv* **-ally**
by the way
**incinerate** *v* destroy by fire; n **-ation**
**incipient** *adj* beginning; in early stages
**incision** n cut
**incisor** n cutting tooth
**incisive** *adj* very clear
**incite** *v* rouse sb to take action; n **-ment**

> **incite** *v* drive, egg on, encourage, excite,
> goad, inflame, provoke, whip up, work up

**inclement** *adj* (of weather) cold, severe
**incline** *v* 1 slope; lean; bend 2 tend; be
disposed; n slope; slant; n **-ination** 1 slope
2 bow or nod head 3 tendency; liking
**inclined** *adj* likely to do sth
**include** *v* contain; regard as part of whole;
n **inclusion;** *adj* **inclusive**

> **include** *v* comprise, cover, embrace,
> encompass, hold, incorporate, involve,
> take in

**incognito** *adj* passing under assumed name;
n 1 such a name 2 person adopting it
**incoherent** *adj* not expressing thoughts
clearly

> **incoherent** *adj* confused, garbled, illogical,
> inarticulate, incomprehensible, muddled,
> rambling, unintelligible

**income** *n* money received, *esp* annually, from investments, salary, etc; *n* **i. tax**

**income** *n* earnings, interest, pay, profit, revenue, salary, takings, wages

**incoming** *adj* coming in; next to take office
**incommode** *v* disturb, trouble; *adj* **-modious** inconvenient
**incommunicado** *adv* not allowed to communicate with anyone
**incomparable** *adj* too good to be compared; *adv* **-ly**
**incompatible** *adj* not suited to one another; unable to exist together; *n* **-bility**
**incompetent** *adj* not competent

**incompetent** *adj* clumsy, hopeless, incapable, ineffectual, inept, unqualified, unskillful, untrained, useless

**incomplete** *adj* not complete

**incomplete** *adj* fragmentary, imperfect, insufficient, lacking, partial, short, undeveloped, undone, unfinished

**incongruous** *adj* inappropriate, inconsistent; *n* **incongruity**
**inconsequential** *adj* unimportant, irrelevant; *adv* **-ly**
**inconsiderate** *adj* not thinking about others

**inconsiderate** *adj* careless, insensitive, intolerant, rude, self-centered, selfish, tactless, thoughtless, uncaring, unhelpful, unkind, unsympathetic

**incontestable** *adj* that cannot be disputed; *adv* **-ly**
**incontinent** *adj* unable to control one's bladder; *n* **-ence**
**incontrovertible** *adj* unquestionable; totally indisputable; *adv* **-ibly**
**inconvenient** *adj* causing difficulty or discomfort; *adv* **-ly**; *n* **-ence**; *v* **-ence**

**inconvenient** *adj* annoying, awkward, difficult, disrupting, embarrassing, inappropriate, irritating, tiresome, troublesome, unmanageable, unsuitable

**incorporate** *v* include; blend; *n* **-ration**
**incorrect** *adj* not correct
**incorrigible** *adj* impossible to correct or improve; *adv* **-ibly**; *n* **-ibility**
**increase** *v* 1 make, become larger 2 amplify 3 improve; *n* enlargement; growth; *adv* **increasingly** more and more

**increase** *n* addition, boost, development, escalation, expansion, extension, gain, rise, upturn
**increase** *v* (make, become larger) add to, augment, broaden, build up, enlarge, expand, extend, gain, grow, inflate, lengthen, magnify, maximize, multiply, mushroom, proliferate, prolong, snowball, spread, strengthen, stretch, swell, widen

**incredible** *adj* 1 unbelievable 2 very good

**incredible** *adj* 1 (unbelievable) absurd, beyond belief, far-fetched, highly unlikely, implausible, impossible, improbable, inconceivable, miraculous, preposterous, surprising, unconvincing, unimaginable. 2 (very good) amazing, extraordinary, fantastic, great, wonderful

**incredulous** *adj* unbelieving; *n* **incredulity**
**increment** *n* addition; increase
**incriminate** *v* suggest that sb is guilty

**incriminate** *v* accuse, blame, charge, implicate, involve, point your finger at, put the blame on

**incubate** *v* hatch, sit on eggs; *ns* **-ation**; **-bator** apparatus for artificially hatching eggs, or rearing premature babies
**inculcate** *v* impress on mind

**incumbent** *n* holder of office
**incur** *v* **-curring, -curred** become liable to (debt, etc); *n* **-sion** attack, invasion
**incurable** *adj* that cannot be cured

> **incurable** *adj* fatal, hopeless, inoperable, terminal, untreatable

**indebted** *adj* owing; under obligation
**indecent** *adj* 1 improper 2 offending against sense of decency, morality; *adv* **-ly;** *n* **indecency**
**indecisive** *adj* unable to make a decision

> **indecisive** *adj* dithering, faltering, hesitating, in two minds, tentative, uncertain, undecided, unsettled, wavering

**indecorous** *adj fml* showing lack of manners
**indeed** *adv* truly; in fact; certainly
**indefatigable** *adj* never tiring
**indefensible** *adj* inexcusable
**indefinite** *adj* not precise; *adv* **-ly** for an indefinite period

> **indefinite** *adj* ambiguous, doubtful, inconclusive, open, uncertain, undecided

**indelible** *adj* not capable of being erased
**indelicate** *adj* lacking in refinement
**indemnity** *n* security from loss, injury, etc; compensation for loss, etc; *v* **indemnify** compensate
**indent** *v* place (text) in from margin
**independent** *adj* 1 free 2 separate 3 not dependent on others; *adv* **-ly;** *n* one not attached to any political party; *n* **independence** self-reliance

> **independent** *adj* 1 (free) liberated, neutral, self-governing. 2 (separate) distinct, free-standing, individual, self-contained. 3 (not dependent) carefree, footloose, free, individualistic, liberated, open-minded, self-reliant, self-sufficient, self-supporting

**indescribable** *adj* impossible to describe
**indestructible** *adj* impossible to destroy
**index** *n* 1 pointer; indicator 2 alphabetical list of words, subjects in book; *pl* **indexes** or *math* **indices;** *v* provide with index; enter in index; *n* **i. finger** finger nearest thumb
**indicate** *v* show; imply; *ns* **indication** sign; suggestion; **indicator** one who, that which indicates; *adj* **indicative of** showing

> **indicate** *v* be a sign of, communicate, convey, denote, manifest, mean, point to, reveal, say, signal, signify, stand for, suggest, symbolize

**indict** *v* accuse formally; *n* **-ment**
**indifferent** *adj* 1 not caring 2 mediocre; *n* **indifference**

> **indifferent** *adj* 1 (not caring) aloof, apathetic, blasé, callous, cold, cool, detached, distant, uncaring, unconcerned, unfeeling, uninterested, unmoved, unresponsive. 2 (mediocre) average, fair, ordinary, uninspired

**indigenous** *adj* native; natural to a country
**indigestion** *n* inability to digest food
**indignant** *adj* offended and angry; *ns* **indignation; indignity** insult; humiliating treatment
**indigo** *adj* deep blue; *n* blue dye got from indigo plant
**indirect** 1 not straight 2 not intended 3 not stating openly; *adv* **-ly;** *n* **i. speech** report of what is said, not the actual words spoken

> **indirect** *adj* 1 (not straight) circuitous, crooked, meandering, rambling, roundabout, tortuous, wandering, winding, zigzag. 2 (not intended) accidental, incidental, secondary, unintended. 3 (not stating openly) devious, disguised, euphemistic, implicit, implied, oblique, sneaky, surreptitious

**indiscreet** *adj* not tactful; *n* **indiscretion**
1 lack of tact 2 indiscreet act or remark

**indiscriminate** *adj* done at random, without careful thought; *adv* **-ly**

**indisposition** *n* slight illness; *adj* **indisposed** 1 unwell 2 averse

**indistinct** *adj* 1 not clear 2 not easily heard, understood

**individual** *n* one particular person, animal, or thing; single person; *adj* distinct; characteristic of single person, thing; *adv* **-ly** one by one; *adj* **-ist**; *n* **individuality** personality; individual character

**indoctrinate** *v* teach particular doctrine to; *n* **-ation**

> **indoctrinate** *v* brainwash, drill, instill, reeducate, school, teach, train

**indolent** *adj* lazy; *adv* **-ly**; *n* **indolence**

**indomitable** *adj* unyielding

**indoor** *adj* pertaining to inside of houses, etc; domestic; *adv* **indoors**

**indubitable** *adj* beyond doubt; *adv* **-ably**

**induce** *v* persuade; *n* **-ment** incentive

> **induce** *v* coax, convince, encourage, get, impel, incite, motivate, prompt, talk into, tempt, urge

**induct** *v* install formally; *n* **-ion**

**indulge** *v* gratify; give way to; pamper; *n* **indulgence** gratification of one's desires

**indulgent** *adj* too lenient

> **indulgent** *adj* doting, easygoing, fond, kind, lenient, liberal, permissive, sympathetic, tolerant, understanding

**industrial** *adj* relating to production of goods; *n* **-ist**; *v* **-ize** (*n* **-ization**); *ns* **i. relations**; **i. revolution** change in economy from agricultural to industrial basis

**industrious** *adj* hard-working

**industry** *n* 1 manufacturing or production 2 hard work 3 firm that does this

> **industry** *n* 1 (manufacturing) business, commerce, manufacturing, production, trade. 2 (hard work) activity, application, diligence, effort, energy, industriousness, labor, perseverance, steadiness, tirelessness, toil, zeal

**inebriated** *adj* drunk

**inedible** *adj* not suitable to be eaten

**ineffable** *adj* unutterable; inexpressibly great

**ineffective** *adj* 1 not having any effect 2 powerless

> **ineffective** *adj* 1 (not having any effect) fruitless, futile, ineffectual, unavailing, unsuccessful, vain. 2 (powerless) inadequate, incapable, incompetent, inefficient, inept, useless, weak, worthless

**ineffectual** *adj* unsatisfactory, futile

**inefficient** *adj* unable to work properly; wasteful; incompetent; *n* **-ency**

**ineligible** *adj* unqualified, unsuitable

**ineluctable** *adj fml* inevitable

**inept** *adj* clumsy, unskillful

**inert** *adj* unable to move or act; *ns* **-ness**; **inertia** sluggishness; tendency to resist change; (*ns* **i. reel** reel with tape that resists sudden pull; **i. selling** mailing of unsolicited goods with demand for payment)

> **inert** *adj* comatose, dead, dormant, immobile, inactive, inanimate, lifeless, motionless, passive, stationary, still, torpid, unresponsive

**inestimable** *adj* impossible to estimate

**inevitable** *adj* certain to happen; *adv* **-ably**; *n* **-ability**

> **inevitable** *adj* assured, bound to happen, certain, destined, fixed, inescapable, inexorable, ordained, sure, unavoidable

**inexorable** *adj* relentless

a b c d e f g h i j k l m n o p q r s t u v w x y z

**inexperienced** *adj* not experienced

**inexperienced** *adj* amateur, immature, naïve, new, raw, unpracticed, unqualified, unskilled, untrained, young

**inexplicable** *adj* not able to be explained
**infallible** *adj* never mistaken; *n* **-ibility**
**infamous** *adj* disgraceful; notorious; shameful; *adv* **-ly**; *n* **infamy**
**infant** *n* very young child; *n* **infancy**; *adj* **infantile**
**infantry** *n* foot soldiers
**infatuated** *adj* in love; *n* **-ation**

**infatuated** *adj* besotted, bewitched, captivated, enamored, enchanted, fascinated, obsessed, smitten

**infect** *v* pass disease to; pollute; affect by example; *n* **-ion**
**infectious** *adj* able to spread between people

**infectious** *adj* catching, contagious, spreading, transmissible, transmittable

**infer** *v* **-ferring, -ferred** draw conclusion

**infer** *v* conclude, deduce, gather, presume, read between the lines, understand

**inference** *n* conclusion drawn

**inference** *n* assumption, conclusion, conjecture, deduction, presumption

**inferior** *adj* 1 lower in rank 2 of less value, quality; *n* one lower in rank, etc; *n* **-ity**

**inferior** *adj* 1 (lower in rank) humble, junior, lesser, lower, lowly, minor, secondary, second-class, subordinate, unimportant. 2 (less in value, in quality) cheap, defective, faulty, imperfect, poor, second-rate, shoddy, substandard

**infernal** *adj* devilish, terrible
**inferno** *n*, *pl* **-os** very large fire
**infertile** *adj* not able to produce young

**infertile** *adj* arid, barren, childless, sterile, unfruitful, unproductive

**infest** *v* swarm in; *n* **-ation**
**infidel** *n* unbeliever; pagan; *n* **infidelity** 1 (act of) disloyalty 2 (act of) adultery
**infighting** *n* disagreement within group
**infiltrate** *v* filter through; permeate; penetrate by stealth; *n* **-ation**
**infinite** *adj* without limit; *adj* **infinitesimal** minute; *n* **infinity** unlimited time, space

**infinite** *adj* bottomless, boundless, enormous, eternal, huge, immense, incalculable, inexhaustible, limitless, measureless, never-ending, numberless, unbounded, uncounted, unending, untold, vast, wide, without end, without number

**infirm** *adj* feeble; physically weak; *ns* **-ity**; **infirmary** hospital; sick-quarters
**inflame** *v* anger
**inflammable** *adj* easily set on fire

**inflammable** *adj* combustible, flammable, incendiary, likely to burn, volatile

**inflammation** *n* redness, swelling, pain
**inflate** *v* 1 swell, distend with air, gas 2 increase (currency) in circulation 3 raise (prices) artificially; *adjs* **inflatable, inflated**; *n* **inflation** 1 inflating, being inflated with air, etc 2 upward trend in costs and prices; *adj* **inflationary**
**inflexible** *adj* 1 unwilling to change 2 stiff

**inflexible** *adj* 1 (unwilling to change) adamant, firm, obstinate, pig-headed, strict, stubborn, uncompromising, unhelpful. 2 (stiff) firm, fixed, hard, inelastic, rigid, unyielding

**inflict** *v* cause to undergo; impose;
*n* **infliction** punishment; suffering

**inflorescence** *n* arrangement of flowers on
stem; flowering

**inflow** *n* flowing in

**influence** *v* have an effect on; *n* power over
others; *idm* **under the influence** drunk

> **influence** *v* affect, bias, change, determine,
> manipulate, persuade, prejudice, put
> pressure on, sway
> **influence** *n* authority, clout, control,
> dominance, hold, importance, power,
> prestige, standing

**influential** *adj* having power or influence

**influenza** *n* infectious virus disease

**influx** *n* flowing in, arrival

**info** *n coll* information

**inform** *v* give information to; *phr v* **inform**
**against/on** report to authorities;
*ns* **informant** giver of information;
**informer** one who informs, *esp* against
criminal

> **inform** *v* advise, announce, enlighten, fill
> sb in, leak, let sb know, notify, put sb in
> the picture, teach, tell

**information** *n* facts; knowledge;
*n* **i. technology** use of computers for
collection, storage, and retrieval of
information; *adj* **informative**

> **information** *n* advice, data, evidence,
> intelligence, news, statistics

**information superhighway** *n* means of
transferring information very quickly via an
electronic network

**infrastructure** *n* underlying systems and
installations that enable an organization or
political, social unit to operate

**infrequent** *adj* rare

**infringe** *v* disobey; break; *n* **-ment**

**infuriate** *v* annoy greatly

> **infuriate** *v* aggravate, anger, bug, enrage,
> exasperate, incense, irritate, madden,
> outrage, provoke, rile

**infuriating** *adj* extremely annoying

> **infuriating** *adj* aggravating, annoying,
> exasperating, galling, irritating, maddening

**infuse** *v* steep, soak in liquid; *n* **infusion**
liquid extract so obtained

**ingenious** *adj* very clever; *n* **ingenuity**

> **ingenious** *adj* brilliant, clever, crafty,
> cunning, imaginative, inventive, neat,
> original, smart

**ingenuous** *adj* honest and open

**ingestion** *n* taking (of food) into stomach

**ingle** *n* fire on hearth; *n* **i.nook** chimney
corner

**inglorious** *adj* shameful

**ingot** *n* block of cast metal

**ingrained** *adj* firmly fixed

**ingratiate** *v* obtain another's good will

**ingredient** *n* component; part of mixture

**inhabit** *v* dwell in; occupy

**inhabitant** *n* person living in a place

> **inhabitant** *n* dweller, tenant, occupant,
> householder, citizen, resident, inmate,
> lodger, native

**inhale** *v* breathe in; *n* **inhalation**

**inherent** *adj* innate, natural; *adv* **-ly**

**inherit** *v* derive from parents, ancestors

> **inherit** *v* accede to, be heir to, be left, be
> willed, come into, succeed to, take over

**inheritance** *n* property inherited

> **inheritance** *n* bequest, birthright,
> endowment, estate, heritage, legacy

a
b
c
d
e
f
g
h
**i**
j
k
l
m
n
o
p
q
r
s
t
u
v
w
x
y
z

A B C D E F G H I J K L M N O P Q R S T U V W X Y Z

**inhibit** v restrain; obstruct; n **inhibition** *psyc* suppression of natural urge

**inhospitable** *adj* 1 unfriendly to guests 2 bleak

> **inhospitable** *adj* 1 (unfriendly to guests) aloof, cool, hostile, unfriendly, unsociable, unwelcoming. 2 (bleak) barren, desolate, forbidding, godforsaken, hostile, uninviting

**inhuman** *adj* brutally cruel; n **inhumanity**

> **inhuman** *adj* barbaric, barbarous, cruel, heartless, inhumane, merciless, pitiless, savage, unfeeling, unnatural

**inhumane** *adj* unkind, pitiless
**inimical** *adj* hostile, unfriendly, antagonistic
**inimitable** *adj* unrivaled
**iniquity** n injustice; wickedness, sin; *adj* **iniquitous** unfair, wicked
**initial** *adj* occurring at beginning; *adv* **-ly**; n initial letter; v write, mark with, one's initials
**initiate** v start
**initiative** n 1 ability and motivation to make things happen 2 scheme

> **initiative** n 1 (ability and motivation) ambition, creativity, drive, dynamism, enterprise, resourcefulness, self-motivation. 2 (scheme) plan, program, project, proposal, scheme, suggestion

**inject** v insert drug by needle
**injection** n insertion of drug by needle

> **injection** n booster, fix, immunization, inoculation, jab, shot, vaccination

**injunction** n writ issued to restrain action
**injure** do harm, hurt to

> **injure** v cut, damage, disable, disfigure, fracture, harm, hurt, mutilate, wound

**injury** n hurt, wound

> **injury** n bruising, cut, fracture, gash, laceration, sore

**injustice** n unfairness

> **injustice** n bias, discrimination, favoritism, inequity, offense, one-sidedness, prejudice, wrong

**ink** n colored fluid used for printing and writing
**inkjet printer** n printer in which the characters are produced by tiny jets of ink
**inkling** n hint; vague idea; suspicion
**inland** n interior of country; *adj* away from sea; *adv* in, toward inland
**in-laws** n relations by marriage other than wife/husband
**inlet** n creek, entrance
**inmate** n inhabitant; lodger
**inmost** *adj* most intimate (*also* **innermost**)
**inn** n public house providing lodging, etc, for traveler
**innards** n pl inside parts, *eg* stomach
**innate** *adj* inborn

> **innate** *adj* built-in, inbuilt, inherent, inherited, instinctive, intrinsic, natural

**inner** *adj* inside
**innings** n pl one round of play in baseball, etc
**innkeeper** n landlord, manager of inn
**innocent** *adj* 1 not guilty 2 inexperienced in the world; n **innocence**

> **innocent** *adj* 1 (not guilty) blameless, in the clear. 2 (inexperienced) childlike, credulous, gullible, naïve

**innocuous** *adj* harmless, inoffensive
**innovate** v introduce new methods, changes; n **-ation**; *adjs* **-active, -atory**
**innuendo** n hint; insinuation; pl **-does**
**innumerable** *adj* too many to be counted

**inoculate** *v* make immune by infecting with specific germ; *n* **-action**

**inoffensive** *adj* harmless

**inoperable** *adj* not suitable for treatment by surgical operation

**inopportune** *adj* badly timed

**inordinate** *adj* excessive

**inorganic** *adj* not result of natural growth; of substances without carbon

**in-patient** *n* patient treated in hospital

**input** *n* **1** suggesting of ideas **2** data put into computer; *v* **inputing, inputed,** or **input** *comput* to record data

**inquest** *n* legal, judicial inquiry into a death

**inquire** *v* ask; *phr v* **inquire into** investigate; *adj* **inquiring** showing curiosity, desire for knowledge; *n* **inquiry 1** question **2** investigation

> **inquire** *v* explore, investigate, look into, make inquiries, query

**inquisition** *n* ecclesiastical court for suppression of heresy; *n* **inquisitor**

**inquisitive** *adj* curious

> **inquisitive** *adj* interested, interfering, meddlesome, nosy, prying

**insane** *adj* mad; *n* **insanity** madness

> **insane** *adj* crazy, deranged, disturbed, mentally ill, not all there, off your rocker, out of your mind, unbalanced, unhinged

**insanitary** *adj* unhealthy, filthy

**insatiable** *adj* that cannot be satisfied

**inscribe** *v* write, engrave on

> **inscribe** *v* carve, cut, etch, mark, sign

**inscription** *n* written or carved message

> **inscription** *n* dedication, engraving, legend, lettering, message, signature, words

**inscrutable** *adj* not showing feelings

**insect** *n* invertebrate with six legs and segmented body, *usu* two or four wings; *n* **insecticide** substance for killing insects

**insecure** *adj* feeling vulnerable

> **insecure** *adj* anxious, exposed, lacking confidence, nervous, uncertain, unsafe

**inseminate** *v* make pregnant; *n* **-ation**

**insensate** *adj* unreasoning, inanimate, foolish

**insensible** *adj* unconscious; unaware

**insensitive** *adj* not sensitive to others

> **insensitive** *adj* crass, heartless, indifferent, oblivious, tactless, thoughtless, unaffected, uncaring, unfeeling, unmoved, unsympathetic, unthinking

**insert** *v* put in; *n* **insertion**

> **insert** *v* add, enclose, enter, implant, interject, introduce, pop in, set in, slide in, stick in

**inside** *adj* within; *adv* on the inner side; *n* inner side; *idm* **inside out 1** with the inside part turned outside **2** thoroughly; *n* **insider** person within organization

**insidious** *adj* cunning, treacherous, sly

**insight** *n* understanding

> **insight** *n* acumen, awareness, grasp, intuition, knowledge, perception, perceptiveness, vision

**insignia** *n pl* badges of office; distinguishing marks (of honor, etc)

**insinuate** *v* hint at; *n* **-ation**

**insipid** *adj* **1** lacking flavor, color **2** dull

> **insipid** *adj* **1** (lacking flavor, color) bland, colorless, pale, watery, weak, wishy-washy. **2** (dull) boring, dead, flat, humdrum, lifeless, stale, unimaginative

a b c d e f g h **i** j k l m n o p q r s t u v w x y z

**insist** *v* emphasize; *adj* **-ent**; *n* **-ence**

> **insist** *v* assert, be firm, demand, persist, put your foot down, stand firm, stress

**in situ** *adv Lat* in the correct place
**insofar as** *conj* as far as
**insolent** *adj* rude; *n* **-lence**

> **insolent** *adj* bad-mannered, cheeky, disrespectful, impertinent, impudent, offensive

**insolvent** *adj* without funds to pay debts; *n* insolvency

> **insolvent** *adj* bankrupt, broke, failed, finished, in debt, in the hands of the receivers, in the red, penniless, ruined

**insomnia** *adj* inability to sleep
**insouciant** *adj* unconcerned; *n* **-ance**
**inspect** *v* examine closely; *ns* **inspection**; **inspector**

> **inspect** *v* audit, check out, examine, go over, go through, look at, look over, scrutinize, study

**inspire** *v* 1 make enthusiastic 2 cause feeling of; *n* **inspiration** 1 stimulation of ideas 2 sb/sth that inspires 3 sudden bright idea; *adj* **inspired** brilliant

> **inspire** *v* (make enthusiastic) encourage, enthuse, fire sb's imagination, galvanize, motivate, prompt, spark off, spur, stimulate, trigger

**install** *v* 1 place in office formally; establish 2 put in position for use, etc; *n* **-ation**
**installment** *n* 1 one part-payment of debt 2 one part of thing appearing, supplied at intervals
**instance** *n* 1 example 2 request; *v* cite; refer to

**instant** *adj* immediate; *n* precise moment; *adj* **instantaneous** occurring in an instant; *adv* **instantly**

> **instant** *adj* direct, fast, instantaneous, on-the-spot, quick, rapid

**instead** *adv* in place of; as alternative to
**instep** *n* upper surface of foot in front of ankle
**instigate** *v* incite; urge; stir up; *ns* **instigation, instigator**
**instill** *v* **-stilling, -stilled** teach
**instinct** *n* natural aptitude or feeling

> **instinct** *n* feel, hunch, gut feeling, impulse, intuition, predisposition, sixth sense

**instinctive** *adj* done without thinking

> **instinctive** *adj* automatic, inborn, inbred, innate, intuitive, involuntary, natural, reflex

**institute** *v* set up; begin; *n* scientific, social, etc society; *n* **institution** 1 custom 2 organization 3 act of founding; *adj* **-al**
**instruct** *v* 1 teach 2 order; *adj* **instructive** informative; *n* **instructor**

> **instruct** *v* 1 (teach) coach, drill, educate, inform, train. 2 (order) brief, direct, tell

**instruction** *n* 1 order 2 education 3 *pl* directions

> **instruction** *n* 1 (order) brief, command, direction, injunction, requirement. 2 (education) classes, coaching, drilling, grounding, guidance, lessons, preparation, training, tuition

**instrument** *n* 1 tool; implement 2 device for producing musical sounds; *adj* **instrumental** 1 acting as means, or instrument 2 produced by musical instruments; *n* **instrumentation** arrangement of music for instruments

**insubordinate** *adj* disobedient;
  *n* **insubordination**
**insufficient** *adj* not enough

> **insufficient** *adj* inadequate, meager,
> pathetic *inf*, scant, scanty, skimpy

**insular** *adj* of, like an island; narrow-minded
**insulate** *v* isolate; prevent passage of
  electricity, heat or sound by use of
  nonconducting material; *n* **insulation**
**insulin** *n* extract from animal pancreas, used
  in treating diabetes, etc
**insult** *v* treat with contempt; *n* contemptuous
  remark

> **insult** *v* abuse, affront, be rude to, call
> names, hurt sb's feelings, libel, offend,
> slander, snub
> **insult** *n* abuse, affront, insolence, libel,
> rudeness, slander, slight, slur

**insuperable** *adj* impossible to overcome
**insure** *v* enter into contract to secure
  payment in event of loss of (life, health,
  etc); *ns* **insurance, insurer**
**insurgent** *adj* rebellious; *n* **-ency**
**insurrection** *n* armed revolt
**intact** *adj* entire

> **intact** *adj* in one piece, perfect, sound,
> unbroken, undamaged, unharmed,
> unscathed, whole

**intake** *n* 1 what is taken in 2 group of new
  recruits, members, etc
**intangible** *adj* not visible or concrete; vague
**integral** 1 essential 2 whole, complete
**integrate** *v* make whole; bring into one
  group; *adj* **integrated**; *n* **-ation** integrating;
  being integrated

> **integrate** *v* amalgamate, assimilate,
> combine, fuse, incorporate, interweave,
> knit, merge, mesh, unite

**integrity** *n* 1 honesty 2 state of being
  undivided, unharmed
**intellect** *n* faculty of knowing, reasoning
**intellectual** *adj* using brain rather than body;
  *n* intellectual person; *adv* **-ly**

> **intellectual** *adj* academic, bookish,
> cerebral, mental, scholarly, studious

**intelligence** *n* 1 quickness in learning
  2 information, *esp* military

> **intelligence** *n* aptitude, brains, brilliance,
> cleverness, gumption *inf*, intellect, IQ,
> mental capacity, wit

**intelligent** *adj* clever

> **intelligent** *adj* brainy *inf*, bright, brilliant,
> educated, gifted, knowledgeable,
> learned, quick, sensible, sharp, smart,
> well-informed

**intelligible** *adj* clear in meaning
**intemperate** *adj* unrestrained; given to
  excess; *adv* **-ly**; *n* **-erance**
**intend** *v* have in mind as sth one wants to do
**intense** *adj* 1 extreme 2 violent 3 eager;
  *v* **intensify** increase; make stronger;
  *n* **intensity** strength, depth

> **intense** *adj* acute, deep, fierce, forceful,
> heavy, keen, passionate, powerful, severe,
> strong, vehement

**intensive** *adj* thorough, concentrated
**intensive care** *n* constant medical attention
  for patient in critical condition
**intent** *adj* concentrating; *n* purpose; motive;
  *idm* **to all intents and purposes** virtually;
  *adv* **-ly**
**intention** *n* aim

> **intention** *n* ambition, goal, idea, objective,
> plan, purpose, wish

a b c d e f g h **i** j k l m n o p q r s t u v w x y z

**intentional** *adj* deliberate

> **intentional** *adj* calculated, conscious, intended, meant, on purpose, planned, premeditated

**inter-** *prefix Lat* between; *forms compounds*
**inter** *v* **-terring, -terred** bury; *n* **-ment**
**interact** *v* act upon another; *n* interaction
**interactive** *adj* 1 acting on each other 2 *comput* allowing exchange of information between user and machine during program
**intercede** *v* plead for; mediate
**intercept** *v* prevent passage of; *n* **-ion**

> **intercept** *v* block, catch, cut off, head off, stop

**interchange** *v* exchange; alternate with; *n* 1 (act of) interchanging 2 system of linking roads between highways, other main roads; *adj* **-able**
**intercity** *adj* providing fast transport between cities
**intercom** *n* internal telephone system
**intercourse** *n* 1 mutual dealings, relations 2 sexual act (*also* **sexual i.**)
**interest** *n* 1 attention 2 concern 3 hobby 4 money received on investment; *idm* **in sb's interest** to sb's advantage; *v* hold sb's attention

> **interest** *n* 1 (attention) absorption, curiosity, notice. 2 (concern) consequence, note, relevance, significance. 3 (hobby) leisure activity, pastime, pursuit
> **interest** *v* amuse, appeal to, arouse sb's curiosity, attract, captivate, divert, fascinate, intrigue

**interesting** *adj* holding one's interest

> **interesting** *adj* absorbing, appealing, compelling, curious, entertaining, fascinating, intriguing, thought-provoking

**interface** *n* point where two systems meet, interconnect, and work together
**interfere** *v* meddle; *idm* **interfere with** 1 hinder 2 cause malfunction by touching 3 assault sexually; *n* **-ference** 1 interfering 2 *rad* extraneous noise

> **interfere** *v* 1 butt in, fiddle with, intrude, poke your nose in, pry, stick your oar in

**intergalactic** *adj* between galaxies
**interim** *adj* temporary, meantime
**interior** *adj* inner; inland; *n* inside; inland
**interject** *v* interrupt by saying; *n* **-jection** exclamation
**interlock** *v* lock or fit closely together
**interloper** *n* meddler in another's affairs
**interlude** *n* interval between acts of play
**intermediate** *adj* in the middle; *n* **-mediary** mediator
**interminable** *adj* endless; unduly prolonged
**intermission** *n* interval, respite
**intermittent** *adj* ceasing at intervals
**intern** *v* confine; lock up; *ns* **-ment**; **internee** person interned
**internal** *adj* 1 inside 2 within a country; *adv* **-ly**; *v* **-ize**

> **internal** *adj* 1 (inside) central, core, inland, inner, interior. 2 (within a country) civil, domestic, home, in-house, national

**international** *adj* pertaining to relations between nations; *n* game, match between different countries
**Internet** *n* (TM) international computer network allowing computer users to exchange information
**interplay** *n* reciprocal action; interaction
**Interpol** *n* international police organization
**interpose** *v* interrupt to say sth
**interpret** *v* explain; *n* **-er**

> **interpret** *v* clarify, crack, decipher, decode, elucidate, expound, translate, understand

**interpretation** n way of explaining sth

**interpretation** n analysis, explanation, meaning, reading, sense, translation, understanding, version

**interregnum** n interval between reigns
**interrogate** v ask searching questions of; ns **-ation, -ator**; adj **-ative** questioning
**interrupt** v 1 break in 2 cause to stop; n **-ruption**

**interrupt** v 1 (break in) barge in, butt in, chime in, disturb, heckle, interject, intervene, muscle in. 2 (cause to stop) block, break, break off, bring to a standstill, cut off, obstruct, postpone, punctuate, suspend

**intersperse** v scatter among; diversify
**interval** n 1 pause 2 intervening time

**interval** n 1 (pause) break, delay, gap, intermission, interlude, lull, recess. 2 (intervening time) interim, meantime, period, space, spell, time

**intervene** v come between; interfere; take part in; n **-vention**
**interview** n 1 meeting to assess sb 2 formal meeting and conversation; v question in an interview; n **interviewer**; n **interviewee** person interviewed

**interview** n 1 (meeting to assess sb) assessment, evaluation procedure, oral examination. 2 (formal meeting and conversation) audience, consultation, dialogue, discussion, exchange, face-to-face, one-to-one, press conference

**intestine** n lower part of alimentary canal
**intimate**[1] adj 1 inward 2 closely linked 3 familiar 4 having sexual relationship; n **-macy**
**intimate**[2] v make known

**intimidate** v force sb to do sth by threats; n **-ation**

**intimidate** v browbeat, bully, coerce, cow, frighten, lean on, menace, pressurize, scare, terrify, terrorize, threaten

**into** prep from outside to inside
**intolerant** adj not tolerant of others

**intolerant** adj bigoted, chauvinistic, dogmatic, narrow-minded, one-sided, prejudiced, racist, sexist, small-minded, uncharitable, xenophobic

**intone** v chant; n **intonation** tone of voice
**intoxicate** v make drunk; n **-ation**
**intransigent** adj obstinately hostile; n **-ence**
**intravenous** adj into a vein; adv **-ly**
**intrepid** adj brave; fearless; n **-ity**
**intricate** adj very complicated; n **intricacy**

**intricate** adj complex, convoluted, detailed, elaborate, entangled, fiddly, involved

**intrigue** n secret plot; illicit love affair; v interest greatly
**intriguing** adj fascinating

**intriguing** adj appealing, captivating, exciting, interesting, riveting, tantalizing

**intrinsic** adj inherent, real, genuine
**introduce** v 1 make known formally 2 bring into use 3 announce

**introduce** v 1 (make known formally) acquaint, bring together, familiarize, make acquainted, make known, present. 2 (bring into use) begin, bring in, establish, found, inaugurate, initiate, introduce, institute, launch, organize, originate, pioneer, set in motion, set up, start, usher in. 3 (announce) begin, lead into, lead up to, preface

a
b
c
d
e
f
g
h
i
j
k
l
m
n
o
p
q
r
s
t
u
v
w
x
y
z

**introduction** n 1 words announcing sth
2 first experience of sth 3 start 4 being made known formally to sb

> **introduction** n 1 (words announcing sth) foreword, lead-in, opening, preamble, preface, preliminaries, prelude, prologue. 2 (first experience of sth) baptism, debut, inauguration, induction, initiation, launch, presentation. 3 (start) beginning, establishment, inauguration, institution

**introspection** n self-analysis; adj **-spective** dwelling on one's own thoughts
**introvert** n self-centered, introspective person
**intrude** v force yourself in uninvited; ns **intruder, intrusion**; adj **intrusive**

> **intrude** v barge in, break in, butt in, crash, encroach, interfere, interrupt, invade sb's privacy, poke your nose in, stick your nose in, trespass

**intuit** v fml sense by intuition; n **intuition** (power of) instant understanding without evidence or logical reasoning; adj **intuitive**
**inundate** v flood, overwhelm
**inure** v accustom; harden
**invade** v 1 enter with hostile intent
2 encroach on; n **invader**

> **invade** v (enter with hostile intent) assail, assault, attack, march into, occupy, overrun, penetrate, raid, storm, take over

**invalid**[1] adj not valid; v **-ate**
**invalid**[2] n, adj (person) suffering from ill health, weakness
**invaluable** adj very valuable
**invariable** adj unchanging; adv **-ly**
**invasion** n 1 attack 2 encroachment on

> **invasion** n (attack) assault, foray, incursion, offensive, onslaught, raid

**invective** n verbal abuse
**inveigle** v lure; entice; n **-ment**
**invent** v 1 create for first time 2 make up; adj **-ive** able to create new things; n **-or**

> **invent** v 1 (create for first time) come up with, conceive, contrive, create, design, devise, formulate, frame, improvise, originate, think up. 2 (make up) come up with, concoct, cook up inf, dream up, fabricate, think up

**invention** n 1 act of inventing 2 thing invented 3 ability to create new things 4 sth made up

> **invention** n 1 (act of inventing) coinage, contrivance, creation, design, devising, innovation, origination. 2 (thing invented) brainchild, contraption, contrivance, construction, design, device. 3 (ability to create new things) creativeness, creativity, genius, imagination, ingenuity, inventiveness, resourcefulness. 4 (sth made-up) fabrication, falsehood, fiction, figment of sb's imagination, lie, story

**inventory** n detailed list of stock, etc
**inverse** adj reversed, contrary
**invert** v turn upside down; reverse position of; adj **-ed**
**invertebrate** n animal without backbone
**invest** v use money to earn interest; phr v **invest in** buy; ns **investment** 1 act of investing 2 property purchased; **investor**
**investigate** v study carefully to find out facts; ns **-ation, -ator**

> **investigate** v analyze, consider, inquire into, examine, explore, go into, inspect, look into, make inquiries, probe, research, search, study

**inveterate** adj long-established, confirmed
**invidious** adj giving offenze by injustice

**invigorate** *v* strengthen, refresh
**invigorating** *adj* refreshing

> **invigorating** *adj* bracing, enlivening, exhilarating, rejuvenating, revitalizing, strengthening

**invincible** *adj* unconquerable; *n* **-ibility**
**inviolable** *adj* not to be dishonoured or violated
**invisible** *adj* impossible to see

> **invisible** *adj* camouflaged, concealed, disguised, hidden, indiscernible, obscured, out of sight, unseen

**invite** *v* 1 ask person to come to social gathering, etc 2 request 3 attract; provoke; *adj* **inviting** attractive (*adv* **-ly**); *n* **invitation** 1 act of inviting 2 request to come 3 provocation
**in vitro** *adj Lat* in test tube or by artificial means; *n* **i.v. fertilization**
**invoice** *n* list of goods sent, with prices; *v* make out invoice
**invoke** *v* appeal to
**involuntary** *adj* unintentional; instinctive
**involve** *v* 1 mean 2 include 3 affect

> **involve** *v* 1 (mean) entail, imply, necessitate, require. 2 (include) bring in, comprise, draw in, hold, incorporate, take in. 3 (affect) concern, interest, touch

**inward** *adv* 1 toward interior 2 into the mind; *adj* **inward** 1 internal 2 spiritual; mental; *adv* **-ly** privately
**iodine** *n* nonmetallic element
**ion** *n* electrically charged atom
**iota** *n* very small part, jot
**IOU** *n* signed acknowledgment of debt
**IQ** *abbr* intelligence quotient
**irascible** *adj* easily provoked to anger
**irate** *adj* furiously angry; *adv* **-ly**; *n* **-ness**
**iridescent** *adj* changing in color, like rainbow; *n* **iridescence**

**iridium** *n* hard silvery metallic element
**iris** *n* colored part of eye, around pupil; tuberous-rooted plant
**Irish** *n*, *adj* (language, inhabitant) of Ireland; *n* **I. stew** stew of meat, potatoes, and onions
**irk** *v* weary, worry; *adj* **irksome** tiresome
**iron** *n* 1 very hard metallic element 2 appliance for smoothing cloth 3 metal-headed golf club; *adj* 1 of iron 2 very strong; *v* smooth (clothes) with an iron
**irony** *n* 1 way of speaking, in which the meaning is the opposite of apparent meaning 2 sarcasm 3 perverseness in a situation occurring in the wrong way or at the wrong time; *adj* **ironic** of irony
**irradiate** *v* treat with light or electromagnetic radiation; *n* **-iation**
**irrational** *adj* without reason or judgement

> **irrational** *adj* 1 (of an idea) absurd, crackpot, groundless, illogical, implausible, ridiculous, senseless, unreasonable, unsound, wild, without foundation. 2 (of a person) confused, crazy, demented, illogical, insane, mad, muddled, unintelligent, unstable, unthinking

**irreconcilable** *adj* bitterly opposed
**irregular** *adj* 1 unusual 2 not regular in shape 3 not happening regularly 4 against the rules

> **irregular** *adj* 1 (unusual) abnormal, eccentric, extraordinary, odd, peculiar, quirky. 2 (not regular in shape) asymmetric, bumpy, crooked, craggy, jagged, lumpy, ragged, rough, uneven. 3 (not happening regularly) erratic, fitful, fluctuating, haphazard, intermittent, occasional, patchy, random, shaky, spasmodic, sporadic, uneven, unsteady, varying. 4 (against the rules) against the rules, illegal, improper, out of order, unconventional, unofficial, unorthodox

**irreparable** *adj* impossible to mend or repair
**irrespective** *adj* not taking sth into account

**irresponsible** *adj* not reliable or trustworthy

> **irresponsible** *adj* careless, immature, negligent, reckless, thoughtless, unreliable, untrustworthy, wild

**irrevocable** *adj* impossible to change later
**irrigate** *v* water by artificial channels
**irritable** *adj* bad-tempered

> **irritable** *adj* cantankerous, crabby, cross, crotchety, fractious, grumpy, impatient, irascible, peevish, petulant, querulous, ratty, short-tempered, tetchy, touchy

**irritate** *v* 1 annoy 2 make sore; *n* **-ation**; *adj* **irritant** causing irritation

> **irritate** *v* anger, annoy, bother, exasperate, get on sb's nerves, get sb's back up, pester, provoke, try sb's patience, vex

**irruption** *n* invasion; sudden violent incursion
**ISBN** *abbr* International Standard Book Number
**Islam** *n* Muslim religion; *adj* **Islamic**
**island** *n* piece of land, surrounded by water; *n* **-er** one who lives on island
**isle** *n* island; *n* **islet** small island
**isn't** *abbr* is not
**isobar** *n* line on map joining places with equal mean atmospheric pressure
**isolate** *v* set apart; keep (infected person) away from others; *n* **-ation**; **-ationism** policy of avoiding involvement in world politics; **-ationist**
**isolated** *adj* 1 lonely 2 remote 3 unique

> **isolated** *adj* 1 (lonely) alone, excluded, forlorn, segregated, separated, solitary. 2 (remote) cut off, hidden, lonely, off the beaten track, out of the way, secluded. 3 (unique) anomalous, exceptional, freak, single, solitary

**isosceles** *adj* triangle with two equal sides
**issue** *n* 1 matter 2 edition 3 outcome 4 children; *v* 1 publish 2 emit 3 go out

> **issue** *n* 1 (matter) affair, argument, controversy, point, problem, question, subject, topic. 2 (edition) impression, installment, number, printing, version. 3 (outcome) conclusion, consequence, effect, end, result, upshot

**isthmus** *n* strip of land between two seas
**IT** *abbr* information technology
**it** *pron* 3rd pers. neuter; *referring to inanimate objects* that one, thing; *adj* **its** belonging to it; *pron* **itself** emphatic form
**Italian** *adj, n* native or language of Italy
**it'd** *abbr* 1 it would 2 it had
**it'll** *abbr* it will
**it's** *abbr* it is
**italic** *adj* of type, with letters sloping up to right; *n pl* this type
**itch** *v* 1 feel itch 2 have restless desire; *adj* **itchy**
**item** *n* single detail in list; piece of news; subsection of agenda, etc; *v* **-ize**
**itinerant** *adj* traveling from place to place
**itinerary** *n* route

> **itinerary** *n* journey, plan, programme, schedule, timetable, travel plan

**IVF** *abbr* in vitro fertilization
**ivory** *n* hard white substance from tusks of elephants
**ivy** *n* climbing evergreen plant

**jab** *v* **jabbing, jabbed** poke suddenly, with force; thrust roughly

**jabber** *v* speak rapidly, gabble; chatter

**jabot** *n* frill, ruffle on bodice, shirtfront

**jacaranda** *n* tropical American hardwood tree

**jacinth** *n* reddish orange variety of zircon

**jack** *n* 1 device for raising load from below 2 *cards* knave 3 *bowls* ball used as mark 4 ship's flag; *ns* **jackhammer** pneumatic drill; **j.-in-the-box** box with doll that springs up when lid is released

**jackal** *n* wild scavenging animal, akin to dog

**jackass** *n* male ass; *n* **laughing j.** large Australian kingfisher

**jackdaw** *n* small kind of crow

**jacket** *n* 1 short coat 2 outer casing, covering

**jackpot** *n* pool in poker game; money prize increasing in value until won

**Jacuzzi** *n* [TM] bath with air-jets creating constant bubbles

**jade** *n* hard green gem stone; color green

**jagged** *adj* having sharp or rough edges

**jagged** *adj* angular, barbed, chipped, craggy, indented, irregular, notched, ragged, rough, serrated, sharp, spiky, toothed, uneven, zigzag

**jaguar** *n* large carnivorous S American cat

**jail** *n* prison; *v* put in prison

**jail** *n* can, cooler, lockup, pen *inf*, slammer

**jam** *n* 1 fruit preserve 2 crush 3 traffic hold-up; *v* **jams, jamming, jammed** 1 block, fill up 2 cease to work; *adj* **j.-packed** *coll* very crowded

**jamb** *n* side post of door; window frame

**jamboree** *n* spree; social gathering; Scout rally

**jangle** *v* make harsh, clanging sound; *n* such sound

**janitor** *n* doorkeeper; caretaker

**January** *n* first month of year

**Japanese** *n* native or language of Japan; *adj* **Japanese**

**japonica** *n* type of red-flowered quince tree

**jar** *n* round glass, earthenware vessel

**jar** *n* bottle, container, crock, pot, tub, urn

**jar** *v* **jars, jarring, jarred** 1 be, sound discordant 2 grate upon 3 cause to shake

**jargon** *n* technical language

**jaundice** *n* morbid state, characterized by yellow tint of eyes and skin

**jaundiced** *adj* jealous, biased

**jaunt** *n* short pleasure trip

**jaunty** *adj* care-free, sprightly; *adv* **-ily**

**javelin** *n* light throwing spear, or shaft

**jaw** *n* two bones, in which teeth are set, and their muscles; *pl* **-s** 1 animal's mouth 2 gripping part of pliers or similar tool; *n* **jawbone**

**jazz** *n* syncopated rhythmical music; *phr v* **jazz up** make more lively; *adj* **jazzy** with bright colors or vivid patterns

**jealous** *adj* 1 envious 2 distrustful *n* **jealousy**

**jealous** *adj* 1 (envious) bitter, covetous, green with envy, grudging, jaundiced, resentful. 2 (distrustful) possessive, protective, vigilant, watchful, wary

A
B
C
D
E
F
G
H
I
**J**
K
L
M
N
O
P
Q
R
S
T
U
V
W
X
Y
Z

**jeans** n pl trousers of twilled cotton fabric
**Jeep** n [TM] light, open truck, with four-wheel drive
**jeer** v mock, scoff at; n taunt, gibe

> **jeer** v boo, deride, gibe, heckle, hiss, laugh, make fun of, ridicule, scorn, sneer, taunt

**Jehovah** n God of Old Testament; n **J.'s Witness** member of fundamentalist sect
**jejunum** n middle of small intestine
**jelly** n semisolid, transparent food made with gelatin; v **jell** set; sl take definite form
**jellyfish** n free floating sea creature; medusa
**jenny** n 1 spinning machine 2 female ass
**jeopardize** v imperil
**jeopardy** n hazard; peril; danger
**jerk** n quick pull, sudden, sharp movement; v move with jerk; adj -**y**; adv -**ily**; n -**iness**

> **jerk** v jolt, jump, lurch, pull, rattle, shake, snatch, tug, twitch, waggle, wrench, yank

**jerboa** n small African burrowing rodent; desert rat
**jerry-built** adj hastily, flimsily constructed
**jersey** n close-fitting knitted jumper; breed of cow
**jest** n joke; v make jokes
**jester** n joker

> **jester** n buffoon, clown, comedian, comedienne, comic, entertainer, fool, funny man, joker

**Jesuit** n member of RC religious order
**Jesus** n founder of Christian religion (also **Jesus Christ**)
**jet**[1] n hard black mineral, used for jewelry; adj **j. black**
**jet**[2] n 1 stream, spurt of liquid, gas, forced from small opening 2 nozzle 3 aircraft propelled by jet engine; v **jets, jetting, jetted** gush, give out in jet
**jetsam** n things thrown overboard to lighten vessel, and washed ashore

**jetty** n pier, quay

> **jetty** n breakwater, landing stage, marina, mole, mooring, wharf

**Jew** n member of Hebrew race
**jewel** n precious stone, gem; ornament set with one; precious object; ns **jeweler** dealer in jewels; **jewelry** ornaments containing jewels

> **jewel** n gemstone, item of jewelry, ornament, piece of jewelry, precious stone, semi-precious stone, stone

**jib** n ship's triangular foremost staysail; projecting arm of crane, etc
**jig** n lively dance; v **jigs, jigging, jigged** move jerkily up and down
**jigsaw** n machine saw for cutting curved, irregular patterns; n **j. puzzle** picture mounted on wood, etc and cut in irregular pieces, to be reassembled
**jihad** n Islamic holy war
**jilt** v reject (lover) after encouraging him
**jingle** n 1 light, ringing, tinkling sound, as of small bells 2 verses with simple catchy words; v make, cause to make this sound

> **jingle** v chime, chink, clink, jangle, ping, ring, sound, tinkle

**jingo** n warmonger; n -**ism** aggressive patriotism
**jink** v move with sudden twists and turns; dodge
**jinx** n bringer of bad luck
**jitney** n small shuttle bus
**jitters** n pl sl extreme nervousness; panic; adj **jittery** nervy; jumpy; n **jitterbug** 1 one who dances convulsively 2 one who panics easily
**jive** n lively dance performed to jazz and rock and roll; v dance to this style
**job** n 1 employment 2 occupation 3 task, matter

**job** n 1 (employment) appointment, opening, position, post, situation, vacancy, work. 2 (occupation) business, career, duties, line, profession, trade, vocation. 3 (task) chore, commission, errand, matter, mission, odd job, piece of work, project, undertaking

**jockey** n professional rider in horse racing
**jocular** adj joking
**jocund** adj merry; cheerful
**jodhpurs** n pl riding breeches
**jog** v **jogs, jogging, jogged** 1 push; nudge 2 keep moving steadily; fig stimulate memory
**join** v 1 connect 2 meet 3 become member of; n place of joining

**join** v 1 (connect) attach, bind, bring together, join up, merge, put together, tie, unify, unite. 2 (meet) come together, connect, converge, join up, merge, unite. 3 (become member) enlist, enroll, join up, register, subscribe
**join** n boundary, connection, dividing line, edge, joint, junction, meeting point, seam

**joint** n 1 joining place of bones, of pieces of wood, etc 2 large piece of meat for roasting 3 sl cigarette with cannabis; adj shared; n **j. venture** enterprise by cooperative management

**joint** adj collective, common, communal, concerted, co-operative, mutual, shared

**joist** n one of parallel beams, supporting floor or ceiling
**joke** n jest; something not meant to be serious; v make jokes

**joke** n crack, funny story, gag, jape, laugh, one-liner, practical joke, prank, punch line, quip, riddle, shaggy-dog story, sketch, spoof, story, wisecrack, witticism

**joker** n 1 one who jokes 2 odd card in pack
**jolly** adj 1 jovial; hearty 2 pleasant; v persuade by flattery; n **J. Roger** pirate flag with skull and crossbones; adv coll very; ns **jollity, jollification** merrymaking

**jolly** adj (jovial) bright, cheerful, cheery, happy, hearty, joyful, laughing, merry

**jolt** v shake with sudden jerk; jog; n sudden jerk or bump
**joss** n Chinese idol; n **j. house** Chinese temple; **j. stick** incense
**jostle** v knock or bump against

**jostle** v brush, crowd, elbow, manhandle, push, push out of the way, shove

**jot** n trifle; small amount; v **jots, jotting, jotted** make brief note
**joule** n unite of electrical energy
**journal** n 1 daily record; diary 2 periodical 3 daily newspaper
**journalism** n profession of producing, editing, writing in newspapers, etc
**journalist** n writer for newspapers, etc; adj **-istic**

**journalist** n broadcaster, columnist, critic, correspondent, cub reporter, editor, feature writer, hack sl, newshound, press man, reporter, reviewer

**journey** n act of traveling; distance traveled; v travel

**journey** n crossing, drive, excursion, expedition, flight, hike, holiday, odyssey, passage, pilgrimage, ride, trek, trip, voyage, walk

**journeyman** n 1 trained employee 2 reliable but not brilliant worker; pl **-men**
**joust** n encounter between two armed, mounted knights; v take part in joust
**jovial** adj cheerful, jolly

a b c d e f g h i **j** k l m n o p q r s t u v w x y z

**joy** *n* great pleasure; *adjs* **joyful** (*adv* **-ly**; *n* **-ness**); **joyless**; **joyous**

> **joy** *n* bliss, delight, ecstasy, elation, euphoria, happiness, joie de vivre, jubilation, pleasure, rapture, rejoicing

**joystick** *n* control lever of aircraft or computer

**JP** *abbr* justice of the peace

**Jr** *abbr* junior

**jubilation** *n* rejoicing; *adj* **jubilant** elated

**jubilee** *n* fiftieth anniversary; festive celebration

**Judaism** *n* Jewish religion, custom

**judge** *n* **1** official appointed to preside over court of justice **2** one who decides winner of a competition; *v* **1** form opinion on **2** decide on **3** try (case) in law court

> **judge** *n* **1** (in court) circuit judge, jurist, justice, magistrate, your Honor. **2** (in a competition) adjudicator, assessor, official, referee, umpire
>
> **judge** *v* **1** (form opinion) appraise, assess, calculate, consider, decide, estimate, evaluate, form an opinion, gauge, guess, weigh, weigh up. **2** (decide on dispute, etc) adjudge, adjudicate, arbitrate, decide, referee, umpire. **3** (try case) find, hear, pass sentence, preside, pronounce, rule, sentence, sit in judgment, try

**judgment** *n* **1** sentence of court **2** opinion **3** ability to evaluate **4** divine retribution

> **judgment** *n* **1** (sentence) adjudication, arbitration, award, decision, finding, ruling, verdict. **2** (opinion) appreciation, appraisal, assessment, calculation, consideration, estimate, estimation, evaluation, guess, view. **3** (ability to evaluate) common sense, discretion, discrimination, level-headedness, maturity, objectivity, tact

**judicial** *adj* of, befitting court of law, judge; impartial; **judicious** wise; *n* **judiciary** body of judges

**judo** *n* Japanese system of unarmed combat

**jug** *n* vessel with handle and lip or spout, for holding liquids; its contents

> **jug** *n* carafe, ewer, pitcher, pot, urn, vase

**juggernaut** *n* powerful, relentless destructive force

**juggle** *v* toss and catch objects as entertainment; *n* **juggler**

**juice** *n* liquid part of fruit or vegetable

> **juice** *n* cordial, crush, essence, gravy, liquid, mineral, sap, squash

**juicy** *adj* succulent

> **juicy** *adj* (succulent) dripping, moist, ripe, sappy, squashy, squelchy *inf*, watery

**July** *n* seventh month of Gregorian calendar

**jumble** *v* mix up; *n* disorded heap

> **jumble** *v* confuse, entangle, mix, muddle, shuffle, tangle

**jump** *v* **1** spring into the air by use of leg muscles **2** pass over (obstacle) by jumping **3** react in surprise **4** move suddenly (in specified direction) **5** (of prices, costs, etc) rise steeply **6** malfunction by moving suddenly out of position **7** attack **8** go out of turn (**j. the gun, the line, the (traffic) lights**); *n* **1** act of jumping **2** obstacle to cross **3** sharp rise

> **jump** *v* **1** (spring) bounce, bound, dive, hop, leap, prance, rise, skip, soar, take off, vault. **2** (pass over obstacle) clear, cross, jump over, leap, leapfrog, straddle, traverse. **3** (react in surprise) flinch, jump out of your skin, recoil, shiver, start, twitch

**jump** n 1 (act of jumping) bounce, bound, dive, hop, leap, skip, spring, vault. 2 (obstacle) bar, barrier, ditch, fence, hurdle, wall

**jumper** n 1 one who jumps 2 *aut* electric lead for connecting two batteries
**jumpy** adj nervous

**jumpy** adj agitated, edgy *inf*, fidgety, jittery, nervy, on edge, on tenterhooks, twitchy

**junction** n joining; place, point of union; station where branches of railway meet

**junction** n crossroads, fork, intersection

**June** n sixth month of Gregorian calendar
**jungle** n wild, uncultivated land, with thick undergrowth; *fig* confused, tangled mass
**junior** adj younger; of lower status; n subordinate; one who is younger; n **j. college** educational institution offering a two-year course of studies

**junior** adj inferior, lowly, low-ranking, second, subordinate, young

**juniper** n evergreen tree
**junk** n 1 *sl* useless articles 2 rubbish ns **j. food** snack food that is of little nutritional value; **j. mail** mass-printed, mainly advertising matter sent unsolicited by mail to people's houses
**junket** n 1 milk curdled with rennet 2 *coll* pleasure trip for government official, financed with public money
**Jupiter** n supreme Roman god; the largest planet
**jurisdiction** n authority to administer law; area covered by authority; n **jurisprudence** science, knowledge of law
**jury** n 1 body of persons sworn to return verdict in court of law 2 panel of judges for a contest; ns **juror, juryman** member of jury

**just** adj fair; right; adj, adv 1 exactly (eg **just here, just right, just so**) 2 instantly (eg **just coming**) 3 barely; scarcely (eg **just about, just missed, just in time, only just**) 4 only (eg **just a little, just a minute**)

**just** adj (fair, right) equitable, evenhanded, fair-minded, honest, honorable, impartial, justifiable, justified, legitimate, objective, unbiased, upright

**justice** n 1 fairness 2 administration of law 3 punishment for crime 4 judge; magistrate (n **J. of the Peace**, *also* **JP**)
**justify** v 1 prove to be right; vindicate; exonerate; adj **justifiable** (adv **-ably**) 2 *printing* space letters to give lines of equal length; adj **justified**; n **justification**
**jut** v **juts, jutting, jutted** project; stick out
**jute** n fiber of Indian plant, used for rope, canvas, etc
**juvenile** adj 1 young 2 characteristic of youth; n young person; ns **j. delinquency** criminal activity by young person; **j. delinquent** such a person
**juxtapose** v put side by side; n **-position**

kabab n pieces of meat cooked on skewer

Kabuki n Japanese traditional song-and-dance drama, with stylized costumes

kedgeree n dish of rice, fish, and boiled egg

kaftan n long loose garment with belt

kaiser n German emperor

kaleidoscope n tube containing pieces of colored glass and reflectors, showing varying patterns when tube is moved

kamikaze n (World War II) Japanese suicide pilot

kangaroo n Australian marsupial with powerful hindlegs; n **k. court** sl irregular, illegal court

kapok n soft fiber from silk-cotton tree seeds, used to fill cushions, etc

karaoke n amateur impromptu singing with recorded music

karate n Japanese martial art using hands and feet

karma n fate, destiny

kasha n hulled grain from buckwheat

kayak n Inuit canoe of stretched sealskin

keel n ship's lowest timbers, on which hull is built; *phr v* 1 capsize 2 fall over sideways

keen adj 1 eager 2 sharp

keen adj 1 (eager) ardent, avid, crazy about, desirous, earnest, enthusiastic, fervent, mad, passionate. 2 (sharp) acute, astute, penetrating, sensitive, shrewd, strong

keep v keeps, keeping, kept 1 hold; retain 2 look after 3 do (specified action) continuously 4 fulfill (promise) 5 delay 6 (of food) remain fresh; n 1 cost of day to day living 2 castle tower n **keepsake** memento

keep v 1 (hold, retain) conserve, guard, have, own, possess, preserve. 2 (look after) care for, conserve, feed, maintain, nurture, pay for, provide for, subsidize, sustain, take care of. 3 (do continuously) carry on, continue, go on, keep on, persevere, persist. 4 (fulfill a promise) abide by, adhere to, honor, observe, realize, respect

keeper n guard, guardian

keg n small cask

kelp n large brown seaweed

kelvin n unit of temperature; **K. scale** international temperature scale

kempt adj neat, tidy, well kept

kennel n hut, shelter for dog; *pl* boarding, training establishment for dogs

Kentucky Derby n sthorobred horserace held in Kentucky the first Saturday in May

kept pt, pp of keep

keralin n protein found in nails, claws, etc

kerchief n head-covering; scarf

kernel n inner, germinating part of nut, or fruit stone; *fig* essential, vital part

kerosene n paraffin oil

kestrel n small migratory falcon or hawk

ketch n small two-masted sailing vessel

ketchup n spicy sauce made from tomatoes,

kettle n metal vessel with spout and handle, used for boiling water; *idm* **a fine kettle of fish** a messy, unpleasant situation

kettledrum n cauldron-shaped brass or copper drum, having variable musical pitch

key n 1 metal instrument to fasten/unfasten lock, to wind clockwork mechanism, etc 2 lever, button on keyboard, musical instrument 3 clue; explanation 4 essential factor; adj very important; v comput type; n **keyboard** fingerboard of typewriter, piano

**key** *adj* crucial, essential, important, indispensable, major, vital

**keyhole surgery** *n* surgery performed through a very small incision on the body
**kg** *abbr* kilogram
**KGB** *n* (formerly) Soviet secret police
**khaki** *adj* dull brownish yellow, earth colored; *n* military uniform
**khan** *n* Asiatic ruler in medieval times
**kibbutz** *n* Israeli collective farm settlement
**kibosh** *n sl* rubbish, nonsense; *idm* **put the kibosh on** put an end to
**kick** *v* 1 strike out with foot 2 *sl* give up (harmful habit); *n* 1 act of kicking 2 *coll* force; **k.off** start, *esp* of football game
**kid** *n* 1 young goat; leather made of its skin 2 *coll* child; *v* **kids, kidding, kidded** *sl* tease, hoax
**kidnap** *v* **kidnaps, kidnapping, kidnapped** take sb away by force and demand a ransom in exchange for returning them; *ns* **kidnapper, kidnapping**

**kidnap** *v* abduct, capture, hold to ransom, seize, snatch, take hostage

**kidney** *n* one of a pair of glandular organs, secreting urine; *n* **k. machine** *med* used to save life of patient with diseased kidneys
**kill** *v* 1 cause to die 2 destroy; *n* 1 act of killing 2 thing killed

**kill** *v* (cause to die) assassinate, butcher, cut down, electrocute, execute, exterminate, gas, gun down, hang, massacre, murder, poison, slaughter, put to death, shoot, slay, smother, stone, strangle, suffocate

**killer** *n* person who kills

**killer** *n* assassin, butcher, executioner, gunman, hangman, murderer, murderess, poisoner, strangler

**killing** *n* act of causing death; *idm* **make a killing** have big success with stocks and shares

**killing** *n* assassination, atrocity, butchery, capital punishment, death, death penalty, electrocution, elimination, euthanasia, execution, extermination, hanging, manslaughter, massacre, murder, shooting, slaying, strangulation, suffocation

**kiln** *n* furnace, oven
**kilo-** *prefix* thousand, as in kilobyte *comput* 1000 or 1024 bytes; *n* **kilogram** 1000 grams; **kilometer** 1000 metres; **kilowatt** 1000 watts
**kilohertz** *n* unit of radio frequency
**kilt** *n* short pleated skirt, usually tartan
**kilter** *idm* **out of kilter** not working
**kimono** *n* loose, wide-sleeved Japanese robe
**kin** *n* relatives; *n* **-ship**
**kind**[1] *n* type, sort

**kind** *n* category, class, species

**kind**[2] *adj* friendly; considerate *adj* **k.hearted**; *ns* **kindness, kindliness**; *adv* **kindly**

**kind** *adj* benevolent, compassionate, fair, generous, helpful, kindhearted, kindly, obliging, sympathetic, understanding, warm, welcoming, well-meaning

**kindergarten** *n* first year of school
**kindle** *v* 1 set light to 2 *fig* stir up; *n* **kindling** small sticks to start fire

**kindle** *v* 1 (set light to) get going, ignite, light, set fire to, start. 2 (stir up) excite, inspire, rouse, stimulate, stir

**kindred** *adj, n* (people to whom one is related); *adj* similar; *n* **k. spirit** person with similar interests, tastes, ideals
**kinetics** *n* science of motion in relation to force; *adj* **kinetic**

a b c d e f g h i j k l m n o p q r s t u v w x y z

A
B
C
D
E
F
G
H
I
J
**K**
L
M
N
O
P
Q
R
S
T
U
V
W
X
Y
Z

**king** n 1 male ruler of nation; monarch 2 card with picture of king 3 piece in game of chess; adj **kingly** noble, royal; adj **k.-size** extra large

**king** n (male ruler) crown, head of state, His Majesty, liege, monarch, ruler, sire

**kingdom** n 1 state ruled by king; monarchy 2 domain, sphere, esp of nature

**kingdom** n (state) country, domain, fiefdom, land, monarchy, realm, territory

**kingfisher** n small brilliantly colored fish-eating bird
**kingpin** n 1 swivel-pin 2 fig chief person
**kink** n twist, bend in rope, hair, etc; v make, put kink in
**kinship** n relationship
**kiosk** n open pavilion; refreshment or newspaper stall; telephone booth

**kiosk** n booth, box, office, pavilion, stall, window

**kipper** n 1 smoked, salted herring; 2 salmon at spawning time; v cure fish by smoking, salting
**kirsch** n cherry flavored brandy
**kiss** v caress with lips; n act of kissing; n **k. of life** form of artificial respiration by breathing into patient's mouth

**kiss** v neck inf, peck, smooch inf

**kit** n 1 equipment 2 outfit
**kitchen** n place where food is cooked; **kitchenette** small kitchen
**kite** n 1 bird of prey 2 light framework covered with paper, flown in wind
**kith and kin** n family and relations
**kitsch** n vulgarized, pretentious art or literature with sentimental appeal
**kitten** n young cat; adj **-ish** like kitten; playful

**kittiwake** n kind of seagull
**kitty** n pool of money in some gambling games; jointly held fund
**kiwi** n flightless N Zealand bird
**kiwifruit** n oval fruit with green flesh (also **Chinese gooseberry**)
**Kleenex** n [TM] soft paper handkerchief
**kleptomania** n compulsive impulse to steal; n, adj **-maniac**
**km** abbr kilometer
**knack** n aptitude, talent, trick
**knacker** n dealer in worn-out horses for slaughter; v Brit sl exhaust; adj **-ed**
**knapsack** n small rucksack
**knave** n rogue; rascal; n **knavery** villainy; adj **knavish**
**knead** v squeeze and press with hands, esp to work bread dough; massage

**knead** v manipulate, massage, press, pummel, roll, squeeze, work

**knee** n 1 joint between upper and lower leg 2 part of trousers covering this; adjs **k.-deep**; **k.-high**; **k.-jerk** automatic (**k.-jerk reaction**); n **kneecap** flat bone protecting knee joint
**kneel** v rest on knees; pt, pp **knelt**; n **kneeler**

**kneel** v be on your knees, fall to your knees, genuflect, get down on your knees

**knell** n sound of tolling bell; omen of doom
**knew** pt of **know**
**knickerbockers** n resident of New York; pl loose, baggy breeches
**knickknack** n trifle, trinket
**knife** n cutting implement with blade set in handle; v stab with knife; n **k.-edge** 1 cutting edge 2 any sharp edge; idm **on a k.-edge** in a critical situation

**knife** n blade, carving knife, cutter, dagger, flick-knife, penknife, sheath knife

**knight** *n* one who receives nonhereditary honor, carrying title 'Sir'; *n* **-hood**; *v* create (man) knight; *adj* **-ly**

**knit** *v* **knits, knitting, knitted,** or **knit** make fabric by fastening loops of wool, etc together with needles; draw close together, make compact; *ns* **knitter; knitting** knitted work (**k. needles**); **knitwear**

**knives** *pl* of **knife**

**knob** *n* **1** rounded handle, switch, button, etc **2** small lump; *adj* **knobbly** lumpy

**knock** *v* **1** strike **2** collide with **3** *coll* criticize; *v* **knock out 1** strike unconscious **2** eliminate *n* **1** blow **2** tapping noise **3** *coll* slight misfortune; *ns* **knockout 1** act of rendering unconscious (*n* **k. blow**) **2** contest in which players are gradually eliminated **3** *coll* impressive or attractive person; **-er** hinged bar for knocking on door; *adj* **k.-kneed** having legs that curve in at the knees

> **knock** *v* **1** (strike) bump, collide, hit, push, tap. **2** **knock out** (strike unconscious) anesthetize, floor, knock unconscious, KO

**knoll** *n* small rounded hill, mound

**knot** *n* **1** tightly tied loop of string, rope, etc **2** *fig* difficulty **3** hard lump where branches join trunk **4** unit of ship's speed; *v* **knots, knotting, knotted** tie into, make knot; become entangled; *adj* **knotty** full of knots; *fig* complicated

**know** *v* **knowing, knew, known** **1** understand **2** be acquainted with **3** recognize; *ns* **k.-how; k.-it-all**; *adj* **knowing**

> **know** *v* **1** (understand) be aware, be certain, be conscious, be familiar with, be informed, be sure, comprehend. **2** (be acquainted with) be a friend of, be familiar with, be friends with, get to know

**knowledge** *n* **1** understanding **2** what is known **3** information

**knowledge** *n* **1** (understanding) awareness, certainty, cognition, comprehension, consciousness, erudition, intelligence, learning. **2** (what is known) data, facts, findings, information, learning, lore, observations, scholarship, science

**knowledgable** *adj* well-informed

> **knowledgable** *adj* aware, brainy *inf*, clever, informed, intelligent, learned, scholarly

**knuckle** *n* **1** bone at finger-joint **2** knee-joint of veal, pork, etc

**KO** *n coll* knockout

**koala** *n* small tree-dwelling Australian marsupial, with very sharp claws and gray fur

**kola** *n* bitter, stimulating extract from kola nut

**kooky** *adj coll* crazy, eccentric

**Koran** *n* sacred book of Muslims

**Korean** *adj, n* (inhabitant, language) of Korea

**kosher** *adj* ceremonially fit, pure, clean, as laid down by Jewish law

**kowtow** *n* act of bowing; humble situation; *v* bow to; *fig* be servile to

**krall** *n* **1** African fenced village **2** cattle enclosure

**kudos** *n sl* fame, credit

**kung fu** *n* Chinese martial art combining skills of judo and karate

**kw** *abbr* kilowatt

A B C D E F G H I J K **L** M N O P Q R S T U V W X Y Z

L

**lab** *abbr* laboratory

**label** *n* slip of paper, etc attached to object giving information on it; *v* **labels, labeling, labeled** 1 fix label to 2 *fig* classify as

**labial** *adj* of lips; sound made by lips

**labor** *n* 1 hard work; task 2 act of childbirth 3 body of workers ; *v* 1 work hard; toil 2 (of ship) toss in heavy seas; *n* **-er** manual worker; *adjs* **-ed** lacking in spontaneity; **laborious** tiring

**laboratory** *n* scientific establishment for research and experiment

**Labor Day** *n* a national holiday (first Monday in September) commemorating all workers

**Labrador** *n* large retriever dog

**laburnum** *n* tree with pendulous yellow flowers

**labyrinth** *n* maze; network of winding paths

**lace** *n* 1 patterned netlike fabric 2 string, cord used as fastening, *esp* for shoes; *v* 1 fasten with laces 2 *coll* add spirits to (coffee, etc); *adj* **lacy**

**lacerate** *v* tear, mangle; *fig* distress; *n* **laceration**

**lack** *n* deficiency, absence; *v* be short of; want

> **lack** *n* dearth, insufficiency, need, scarceness, scarcity, shortage, want
> **lack** *v* be lacking in, be without, have need of, miss, need, require

**lackadaisical** *adj* dreamy

**lackey** *n* servile follower

**lackluster** *adj* dull, lifeless

**laconic** *adj* brief; using few words; terse; *adv* **-ally**

**lacquer** *n* hard, glossy varnish; *v* paint with this

**lacrosse** *n* ball game played with long-handled racquet, or crosse

**lactose** *n chem* form of sugar found in milk

**lacuna** *n* 1 gap, hiatus 2 empty space, *esp* in book 3 cavity (in bone or tissue)

**lad** *n* boy; young man

**la-de-da** *adj* feigning refinement

**ladder** *n* 1 climbing device of two poles joined by rungs 2 vertical tear in stockings; *v* (of stockings, etc) develop vertical tear

**lading** *n* cargo; freight

**ladle** *n* long-handled, deep-bowled spoon; *v* serve with ladle

**lady** *n* 1 noblewoman; 2 *coll* any woman 3 *cap* title of wives of knights, baronets, and peers below rank of duke; *prefix* feminine, female; **ladyship** title of lady; *adj* **ladylike**

> **lady** *n* 1 (noblewoman) baroness, countess, dame, duchess, marchioness, peeress, viscountess. 2 (any woman) female, girl, lass *inf*, wife, woman

**ladybug** *n* small reddish beetle with black spot

**lag**[1] *v* **lags, lagging, lagged** walk, move slowly

**lag**[2] *v* wrap boiler, pipes etc to conserve heat

**lager** *n* light beer; glass of this

**lagoon** *n* shallow salt-water channel, enclosed by reef, sandbank, or atoll

**laid** *pt, pp of* lay

**laid-back** *adj coll* relaxed; lacking in sense of urgency

**lain** *pp of* lie

**lair** *n* den; resting place, *esp* of wild animals

**laissez-faire** *n* policy of noninterference, *esp* by government, allowing things to take natural course

**lake** n large sheet of water enclosed by land

> **lake** n lagoon, lido, loch, pool, pond, reservoir, sea, tarn, water

**lam** v sl beat, flog, thrash; n **-ming**

**lama** n Buddhist priest in Tibet; n **lamasery** monastery of lamas

**lamb** n 1 young sheep 2 its meat

**lambast(e)** v attack violently

**lambent** n 1 softly shining 2 light and witty

**lame** adj 1 disabled; unable to walk well 2 unconvincing; v cripple

**lamé** n Fr fabric interwoven with metallic threads

**lament** v feel, express deep grief; n expression of deep grief; dirge; n **-ation**; adj **-able** deplorable

**laminate** v roll, beat into thin plates; cover with thin sheets (of metal, plastic, etc); split into layers; n thin plate, layer

**lamp** n any of various devices for giving light or therapeutic rays

> **lamp** n lantern, light, street light, table lamp, torch

**lampoon** n venomous, abusive personal satire; v satirize in lampoon

**lance** n long, ceremonial cavalry spear; fish spear; v pierce, cut with lance or lancet

**land** n 1 dry solid surface of earth 2 country; nation 3 area; v 1 disembark 2 set (aircraft) down; 3 catch (fish) 4 succeed in getting (job)

> **land** n 1 (dry surface of earth) coast, dry land, earth, ground, shore, solid ground, terra firma. 2 (country) district, nation, province, region, state, territory, tract. 3 (area) acres, estate, grounds, property
> **land** v 1 (disembark) alight, arrive, berth, come ashore, debark, dismount, dock. 2 (set aircraft down) come in to land, touch down

**landing** n 1 coming to dry land from air or sea (ns **l. craft** flat boat; **l. gear** aircraft undercarriage and wheels; **l. stage** platform for landing passengers or cargo) 2 level area at top of staircase

**landlady, landlord** n manager or owner of rented accommodation

**landmark** n 1 feature of area easy to recognize and orientate oneself by 2 important event

**landscape** n 1 scenery of area 2 picture of this (**l. gardening** planned layout of garden for scenic effect)

> **landscape** n (scenery) aspect, countryside, outlook, panorama, prospect, rural scene, scene, view, vista

**landslide** n 1 sudden fall of earth, rocks 2 election win by vast majority (n **l. victory**)

**lane** n 1 narrow road, street 2 regular route for shipping, aircraft 3 marked division on sports track or main road

**language** n 1 speech 2 particular form of speech of nation, race, profession, etc 3 any symbols, gestures expressing meaning

> **language** n 1 (speech) communication, conversation, discourse, expression, parlance, speaking, talk, talking, verbal expression, vocalization, words.
> 2 (particular language) argot, dialect, idiom, jargon, lingo inf, patois, tongue, vernacular, vocabulary

**languish** adj pine; droop from misery, etc; adj **languish** weak, spiritless; n **languor**

**lank** adj 1 limp 2 long and thin; adj **lanky**

> **lank** adj 1 (limp) drooping, dull, lifeless, long, lusterless, straggling, straight.
> 2 (long and thin) bony, emaciated, gangling, gaunt, lanky, lean, scraggy, scrawny, skinny, slender, slim, tall

a
b
c
d
e
f
g
h
i
j
k
**l**
m
n
o
p
q
r
s
t
u
v
w
x
y
z

**lantern** *n* transparent case for lamp, etc

**lap**[1] *n* **1** part between knees and waist of seated person **2** circuit of racetrack; *v* **laps, lapping, lapped** complete one circuit of racetrack

**lap**[2] *v* **1** splash softly **2** drink by scooping up movement of tongue, as animal

**laparoscopy** *n med* internal examination of abdomen through narrow tube

**lapel** *n* front part of coat folded back to shoulders

**lapidary** *n* worker in gems; *adj* meticulous in detail

**lapis lazuli** *n* semiprecious bright blue stone

**Lapp** *n* member of nomadic arctic tribe

**lapse** *n* **1** error **2** passing (of time, etc.); *v* fall away; cease to exist

**laptop** *n* small personal computer

**larceny** *n* stealing, theft

**larch** *n* coniferous tree

**lard** *n* refined, rendered pig fat; *v* **1** insert strips of fat in meat **2** enrich (style of speech) with; *adj* **lardy**

**large** *adj* great in size or amount

> **large** *adj* ample, big, broad, bulky, colossal, considerable, elephantine, enormous, extensive, generous, giant, gigantic, grand, great, huge, immense, jumbo, king-size, liberal, lofty, massive, mighty, monumental, roomy, sizable, spacious, sweeping, substantial, vast, wide

**largo** *adv mus* slowly and nobly; *n* such music

**lariat** *n* long, noosed string or rope

**lark** *n* singing wild bird, skylark

**larva** *n* caterpillar, wormlike stage of butterfly, fly, etc; *pl* **-ae**; *adjs* **larval, larviform**

**larynx** *n* back of throat, containing vocal chords; *n* **laryngitis** inflammation of the larynx

**lasagne** *n It* flat rectangular layers of pasta cooked with layers of meat or vegetables, topped with cheese

**laser** *n* device producing intense concentrated light beam; *n* **l. beam**

**lash** *v* **1** strike with whip **2** strike violently **3** *fig* scold fiercely **4** fasten, bind tightly; *n* **1** whip **2** eyelash

**lass** *n* young girl

**lassitude** *n* weariness, weakness

**lasso** *n* **-os** or **-oes** rope with noose; *v* catch with lasso

**last**[1] *adj* **1** final **2** previous **3** only remaining; *n* **l.rites** religious rites for person about to die

**last**[2] *v* **1** continue **2** suffice (for); *adj* **-ing**

> **last** *v* (continue) abide, carry on, endure, go on, hold, keep, linger, live, persist, remain, survive

**latch** *n* fastening for doors and windows; *v* fasten with latch

**late** *adj* **1** behindtime; **2** no longer living; *comp* **later**; *sup* **last, latest**; *adv* (*also* **lately**) recently

> **late** *adj* **1** (behind the time expected) behind, behind schedule, behind time, belated, delayed, overdue, slow, tardy. **2** (no longer living) dead, deceased, defunct, departed

**latent** *adj* hidden; dormant

**lateral** *adj* at, from side; *adv* **-ly** sideways

**latex** *n* white, milky juice, secreted by plants, *esp* rubber tree

**lath** *n* thin strip of wood, or other material

**lathe** *n* machine used in turning wood, metal

**lather** *n* **1** froth of soap and water **2** (of horse) foamy sweat; *v* form lather; *idm* **in a lather** nervously excited

**Latin** *adj* of ancient Rome; of languages and races descended from this

**latitude** *n* **1** *geog* distance N and S from equator **2** freedom from restriction

**latter** *a, pron* later; second of two; *adj* **l. day** modern; *adv* **-ly** recently

**lattice** *n* structure of criss-cross strips; window with glass crossed by lead strips; *adj* **latticed**

**laud** *v* praise, extol; *adj* **-able** praise-worthy

**laugh** *v* utter sounds expressing amusement, joy, scorn; *n* such sound; *adjs* **laughing**; **laughable** ridiculous (*adv* **-ably**)

> **laugh** *v* be in stitches, burst out laughing, chortle, chuckle, crack up, fall about, giggle, guffaw, roll about, snigger, split your sides, titter
> **laugh** *n* belly laugh, chortle, chuckle, giggle, guffaw, roar of laughter, snigger, titter

**launch**[1] *v* 1 initiate 2 hurl 3 set afloat 4 *fig* embark on

> **launch** *v* 1 (initiate) begin, commence, embark, establish, get going, inaugurate, instigate, introduce, open, set up, start. 2 (hurl) cast, catapult, discharge, dispatch, fire, project, propel, send off, set off, shoot, throw

**launch**[2] *n* large power-driven pleasure boat

**launder** *v* 1 wash and iron (clothes) 2 make source (of stolen money) untraceable by depositing abroad; *ns* **laundry** place where linens, etc are washed; clothes sent there; **laundromat** place where washing machines can be used on playment of fee

**laurel** *n* evergreen, glossy-leaved shrub; *pl* its leaves; symbol of victory, fame

**lava** *n* molten volcanic rock

**lavatory** *n* room with sink andtoilet

**lavender** *n* shrub with fragrant mauve flowers

**lavish** *adj* profuse; extravagant; abundant; *v* bestow; spend recklessly

**law** *n* 1 rule 2 jurisprudence 3 sequence of natural processes in nature 4 sequence of causes and effects; *adjs* **l.-abiding**; **lawful** (*adv* **-ly**; *n* **-ness**); **lawless** (*n* **-ness**); *n* **lawsuit** noncriminal case

> **law** *n* (rule) act, bill, bylaw, code, covenant, decree, directive, edict, enactment, injunction, mandate, order, ordinance, regulation, statute

**lawn**[1] *n* fine linen

**lawn**[2] *n* stretch of close-mown grass; *ns* **l. mower; l. tennis** ball game played on grass or hard court

**lawyer** *n* sb attorney at law

> **lawyer** *n* advocate, attorney, counsel, legal advisor, legal practitioner, member of the bar

**lax** *adj* 1 loose 2 slack, careless 3 (of bowels) relaxed; *adj* **-ative** having lossening effect on bowels; *ns* **-ity, -ness** slackness; lack of moral principles

**lay** *adj* not clerical or professional; *n* **layman/-person/-woman** one who is not expert, not a priest

**lay** *v* **lays, laying, laid** 1 place horizontally; set in position 2 set out formally 3 produce (egg) 4 settle 5 deposit; *phr v* **lay out** 1 set out; arrange (*n* **layout**) 2 knock unconscious;

> **lay** *v* 1 (place) deposit, leave, plant, put, rest, set, settle. 2 (set out) arrange, dispose, organize, position

**layer** *n* 1 one of several thicknesses on a surface 2 hen that lays eggs

> **layer** *n* (one of several thicknesses) bed, coat, coating, covering, film, row, seam, skin, stratum, thickness, tier

**layette** *n* *Fr* outfit of clothes, etc for new - born child

**laze** *v* be idle; rest oneself

> **laze** *v* do nothing, idle, lie around, loaf, lounge, relax, sit around, unwind

**lazy** *adj* unwilling to make effort; *n* **laziness**

> **lazy** *adj* idle, inactive, indolent, laxity, slack *inf*, slothful

**lb** *abbr* pound(s) (in weight)

**lea** *n* meadow; open grassland

**lead**[1] *n* 1 heavy bluishwhite metal element 2 piece of this used for sounding depth of water; 3 graphite (**l. pencil**); *v* cover, space with lead; *adjs* **leaded** containing lead; **leaden** heavy and dull; **l.-free**

**lead**[2] *v* **leads, leading, led** 1 guide 2 govern 3 be ahead; *phr vs* **lead someone on** influence sb to believe or do sth wrong; **lead up to** prepare for; *n* 1 first place 2 guidance 3 clue to mystery 4 *elec* wire connecting source of power to appliance 5 extent of advantage in competition; *ns* **l.-in** introduction; **l. time** *comm* time needed to complete

**lead** *v* 1 (guide) conduct, draw, escort, pilot, show the way, steer, usher. 2 (govern) be in charge of, captain, command, direct, head, manage, supervise. 3 (be ahead) be in the lead, exceed, excel, head, leave behind, outdo, surpass
**lead** *n* 1 (first place) advantage, edge, precedence, priority, vanguard. 2 (guidance) direction, example. 3 (clue) guide, hint, indication, line, suggestion, tip-off. 4 (wire) cable

**leader** *n* sb who leads (*n* **-ship**); *adj* **leading**

**leader** *n* boss, captain, chief, commander, conductor, director, foreman, guide, head, number one, principal, ruler, skipper, supremo

**leaf** *n* 1 one of lateral growths from plant stem 2 page of book; *pl* **leaves**; *n* **leaflet** small printed sheet of paper; *adj* **leafy**

**league** *n* alliance; association, etc with common interest

**leak** *n* crack, hole through which liquid or gas passes; *v* 1 allow liquid, gas to pass out 2 prematurely disclose (news, etc); *n* **leakage** leaking; gradual escape or loss; *adj* **leaky**

**leak** *v* 1 (allow liquid, gas to pass out) discharge, drip, escape, exude, issue, ooze, seep, spill, trickle. 2 (prematurely disclose news) disclose, divulge, give away, let out, let slip, let the cat out of the bag, make known, reveal, spill the beans

**lean**[1] *adj* thin; containing no fat; *n* nonfat part of meat

**lean**[2] *v* 1 bend 2 prop against; *phr vs* **lean on** rely on; **lean toward** be in favor of

**lean** *v* 1 (bend) be at an angle, incline, slant, slope, tilt, tip 2 (prop against) be propped, be supported, recline, repose, rest

**leap** *v* jump (*pt, pp* **leaped** *or* **leapt**); *n* 1 act of leaping 2 sudden increase; **l. year** year of 366 days occurring every fourth year

**leap** *v* bounce, bound, caper, cavort, frisk, gambol, hop, skip, spring

**learn** *v* **learning, learned**. or **learnt** 1 acquire knowledge 2 commit to memory 3 find out; *adj* **learned** well informed; *ns* **learner, learning** knowledge acquired by study

**learn** *v* 1 (acquire knowledge) assimilate, attain, grasp, imbibe, master, pick up. 2 (commit sth to memory) learn by heart, memorize. 3 (find out) ascertain, discover, gather, hear, understand

**lease** *n* contract whereby land, property is rented for stated time by owner to tenant; *v* let, rent by lease; *adj* **leasehold** held on lease

**leash** *n* 1 chain or strap holding dog 2 set of three dogs so held 3 thong holding hawk; *v* hold by leash

**least** *det, pron* the smallest; *adv* in the smallest degree; *idms* **(not) in the least** (not) at all; **not least** especially; in particular

A B C D E F G H I J K L M N O P Q R S T U V W X Y Z

**leather** *n* skin of animal prepared by tanning; *adj* **leathery** tough

**leave** *v* 1 go away 2 allow, cause to remain 3 deposit; (*pt, pp* left); *phr v* **leave out** 1 omit 2 leave outside; *n* 1 permission 2 absence from work or duty; allowance of time for this

> **leave** *v* 1 (go away) be off *inf*, check out, depart, disappear, exit, go, move, quit, retire, split *inf*, withdraw. 2 **leave out** (omit) disregard, exclude, ignore, miss out, neglect, overlook, reject, skip

**leaven** *n* 1 yeast 2 *fig* stimulating, spiritual influence; *v* 1 raise with yeast 2 influence
**leaves** *pl of* leaf
**lecher** *n* lustful, sensual person
**lectern** *n* reading desk in church
**lecture** *n* instructive discourse; admonishment; *v* deliver lecture; reprove *ns* **l. hall, lecturer, lecturing; lectureship**
**led** *pt, pp of* lead
**ledge** *n* narrow shelf projecting from wall, cliff face, etc

> **ledge** *n* mantle, overhang, projection, protrusion, ridge, shelf, sill, step

**ledger** *n* principal account book of business, etc; flat stone
**leech** *n* blood-sucking worm
**leek** *n* vegetable of onion family
**leer** *v* glance lustfully; slyly; *n* such a look
**left**[1] *pt, pp of* leave
**left**[2] *adj* 1 on the side of the body where the heart is 2 toward this side 3 *polit* tending to liberal or radical views; *n* 1 left side 2 *polit* left wing; *adjs* **l.-hand** situated on the left; **l.-handed** using left hand (*n* **l.-hander**); *adjs* **leftist; left-wing** *polit*
**leg** *n* 1 limb supporting body 2 part of trousers, etc covering this 3 support for chair, bed, etc 4 joint of meat 5 stage of journey, of relay race

**legacy** *n* gift, bequest by will; *fig* something handed down

> **legacy** *n* bequest, endowment, estate, heirloom, inheritance

**legal** *adj* pertaining to law; *adv* **-ly**; *ns* **legality; legalistic**; *v* **-ize** make legal

> **legal** *adj* aboveboard, allowed, approved, authorized, decriminalized, lawful, legalized, legitimate, licensed, permissible, proper, sanctioned, valid

**legate** *n* ambassador of pope
**legation** *n* diplomatic body; chief of such body and his staff; his official residence
**legato** *adv mus* smoothly, without breaks
**legend** *n* traditional story

> **legend** *n* epic, fable, fairy tale, fiction, folk tale, myth, narrative, saga, story, tale

**legendary** *adj* famous

> **legendary** *adj* acclaimed, celebrated, famed, glorious, great, immortal, proverbial, world-famous

**legerdemain** *n Fr* conjuring trick; sleight of hand
**legible** *adj* easily read

> **legible** *adj* clear, decipherable, distinct, easy to read, intelligible, neat, plain, readable

**legion** *n* unit of ancient Roman infantry; body of troops; multitude; large organized group; *adj, n* **legionary**
**legislator** *n* maker of laws; *v* **legislate** make laws; *adj* **legislative**; *n* **legislature** legislative body
**legitimate** *adj* lawful; justifiable; born in wedlock; *v* make lawful; *n* **legitimacy** state of being legitimate; *vs* **legitimatize, legitimize** to legitimate

**Lego** [TM] construction toy of studded, interlocking, colored plastic bricks and other shapes

**leguminous** *adj* pod-bearing (pea, bean, etc)

**leisure** *n* freedom from work; free time

**leisurely** *adj* unhurried

> **leisurely** *adj* comfortable, easy, gentle, laid-back, lazy, relaxed, relaxing, restful, slow

**leitmotif** *n mus* recurring theme; *fig* recurrent association of ideas

**lemming** *n* small arctic ratlike animal

**lemon** *n* very acid pale yellow fruit; its color; *ns* **lemonade** drink flavoured with lemon; **l. sole** flat fish

**lemur** *n* small monkeylike animal

**lend** *v* 1 grant temporary use of 2 let out for hire 3 give; *pt, pp* **lent**; *n* **lender**

**length** *n* 1 distance from end to end 2 quality of being long 3 duration in time; extent 4 long piece of sth; *adv* **lengthways/ lengthwise**; *adj* **lengthy**; *adv* **-thily**; *n* **-thiness**

**lengthen** *v* make longer

> **lengthen** *v* continue, drag out, draw out, elongate, expand, extend, increase, prolong, protract, stretch

**lenient** *adj* merciful; *n* **leniency**

> **lenient** *adj* charitable, clement, forbearing, forgiving, gentle, humane, indulgent, kind, lax, magnanimous, mild, soft, sparing, tolerant

**lenitive** *adj, n* soothing (drug)

**lens** *n* 1 curved disk of glass or transparent plastic which magnifies (*eg* **camera lens; contact lens**) 2 part of eye which does this

**Lent** *n* period of penance and fasting from Ash Wednesday to Easter

**lent** *pt, pp of* lend

**lentil** *n* dried seed of leguminous food plant

**lento** *adv mus* slowly

**leopard** *n* large spotted carnivore of cat tribe

**leotard** *n* close-fitting, stretchy garment worn by dancers

**leper** *n* sufferer from leprosy; *n* **leprosy** infectious chronic skin disease

**lepidoptera** *n pl* insects with four scaly wings, including moths and butterflies

**leprechaun** *n* Irish sprite

**lesbian** *n* female homosexual; *n* **lesbianism** homosexuality between women

**lesion** *n* injury

**less** *a, adv* (*comp* of **little**) not so much; to a lesser degree, amount; *n* smaller amount, quantity; *prep* with deduction of

**lessen** *v* reduce

> **lessen** *v* abate, assuage, curtail, decline, decrease, die down, diminish, ease, ease off, ebb, let up, lighten, lower, mitigate, moderate, relieve, slacken, subside, tail off, tone down, weaken

**lesser** *adj* 1 smaller 2 less important

**lesson** *n* 1 sth taught 2 warning 3 portion of scripture read in Church

> **lesson** *n* 1 (sth taught) class, coaching, drill, instruction, period, schooling, seminar, session, teaching, tutoring. 2 (warning) admonition, deterrent, example, exemplar, message, model, moral

**lest** *conj* for fear that

**let** *v* 1 allow 2 rent out (property) (*pt, pp* **let**); *phr vs* **let down** 1 lower 2 deflate 3 disappoint; **let off** 1 cause to explode 2 release 3 excuse; **let on** tell (secret); **let out** 1 reveal 2 utter 3 release; **let up** become less intense (*n* **letup**); *n* 1 leasing of property; 2 *tennis* service touching net before landing in court; *n* **letting** renting out

> **let** *v* (allow) agree to, authorize, consent, give leave, give permission, give the go-ahead, grant, permit, sanction, tolerate

**lethal** *adj* fatal, deadly
**lethargic** *adj* drowsy and not enthusiastic

> **lethargic** *adj* apathetic, dull, enervated, fatigued, heavy, inactive, indolent, inert, languid, languorous, lazy, listless, passive, sleepy, slothful, slow, sluggish, somnolent, torpid, weary

**lethargy** *n* abnormal drowsiness; apathy; indifference
**letter** *n* **1** written symbol expressing a sound of speech **2** written message **3** *pl* literary culture; literature; *v* mark with letters; *adj* **-ed 1** having education **2** marked with letters; *ns* **l.head** printed heading on stationery; **l.press** printing from type
**lettuce** *n* plant used for salads
**leucocyte** *n* white blood corpuscle
**leukemia** *n* malignant disease in which the body produces too many white blood cells
**level** *adj* **1** horizontal **2** equal **3** of same height; *n* **1** plane surface **2** usual height **3** moral, intellectual, social standard **4** horizontal passage in mine **5** instrument for testing horizontal plane; *v* **levels, leveling, leveled 1** make flat **2** bring to same level **3** aim (gun)

> **level** *adj* **1** (horizontal) even, flat, flush, smooth, straight, true, uniform. **2** (equal) aligned, balanced, comparable, equivalent, identical, in line, matching, on a par, proportionate, the same

**lever** *n* rigid bar (usually supported at fixed point) that lifts or moves weight at one end when power is brought to bear on the other; *n* **-age** action, power of lever; *v* use lever
**leveret** *n* young hare
**leviathan** *n* **1** sea monster of the Bible **2** something very large or powerful
**levitation** *n* power of raising solid body into air by nonphysical means; *v* **levitate** cause to do this
**levity** *n* frivolity, facetiousness, lightness

**levy** *n* **1** collection of tax; sum thus collected **2** forced military enlistment; *v* **levies, levying, levied** impose tax, etc
**lewd** *adj* indecent; obscene
**lexical** *adj* of words; *adv* **-ly**
**lexicography** *n* art, process of making dictionaries; *n* **-grapher**
**lexicon** *n* dictionary
**liable** *adj* legally responsible; *n* **liability** obligation
**liaison** *n* **1** connection **2** cooperation **3** illicit sexual relationship; *v coll* **liaise** act as means of coordination with
**liar** *n* untruthful person
**libation** *n* drink, offering to gods
**libel** *n* written, printed statement likely to damage person's reputation; *v* **libels, libeling, libeled** publish libel; defame character

> **libel** *n* aspersion, calumny, defamation, denigration, lie, obloquy, slander, slur, smear, vilification

**libelous** *adj* defamatory; *n* **-ness**
**liberal** *adj* **1** generous **2** tolerant
**liberal arts** *n* college study of the arts, humanities, natural and social sciences
**liberate** *v* set free; *ns* **-ation, -ator**

> **liberate** *v* deliver, discharge, emancipate, free, let go, let out, redeem, release, rescue, unchain, untie

**llibertine** *n* debauched, dissolute man; *adj* dissolute
**liberty** *n* freedom

> **liberty** *n* autonomy, emancipation, independence, release, self-determination, sovereignty

**libido** *n* sexual desire; *adj* **libidinous**
**library** *n* collection of books; place where books are kept, or may be borrowed; *n* **librarian**

a b c d e f g h i j k l m n o p q r s t u v w x y z

**libretto** *n* words of an orpera or musical play; *pl* **libretti** or **-s**

**lice** *pl of* **louse**

**license**[1] *n* permission granted by authority; document granting it

**license**[2] *v* grant license to; *n* **licensee** holder of license

**licentious** *adj* dissolute, immoral

**lichen** *n* flowerless, mosslike plant growing on trees, rocks, etc

**lick** *v* **1** pass tongue over **2** flicker round **3** *sl* beat; defeat; *adj* act of licking; *n* **licking** *sl* beating, thrashing

**licorice** *n* black, very sweet candy

**lid** *n* **1** movable cover **2** eyelid

**lie**[1] *v* **lying, lay, lain 1** be in resting position **2** be situated, placed; *n* **1** direction **2** way sth lies; *phr vs* **lie around** be idle; **lie behind** be the real explanation of

> **lie**[1] *v* (be in resting position) be horizontal, be lying, be prone, be prostrate, be recumbent, be supine, lean back, lounge, recline, repose, rest, sprawl, stretch out

**lie**[2] *v* **lying, lied** make false statement; *n* deliberate untruth

> **lie**[2] *v* bear false witness, bluff, deceive, dissemble, equivocate, fabricate, falsify, fib *inf*, invent, make up, misrepresent, perjure, pretend, tell a falsehood, tell a lie
> **lie** *n* bluff, deceit, deception, fabrication, falsehood, fib *inf*, fiction, invention, mendacity, misrepresentation, perjury, pretense, story, untruth, whopper

**liege** *n* bound to render feudal service; *n* lord, sovereign; *n* **liegeman** vassal, subject

**lien** *n leg* right to hold property of another until debt is paid

**lieutenant** *n* deputy; rank below naval lieutenant commander or army captain

**life** *n* **1** animate existence **2** duration of this **3** vitality **4** biography; *pl* **lives**; *adjs* **lifeless** (*adv* **-ly**; *n* **-ness**); **l.-size/-sized**

**life** *n* **1** (existence) being, breath, entity, living. **2** (duration of life) career, days, lifespan, lifetime, time on earth. **3** (vitality) activity, animation, dynamism, energy, enthusiasm, exuberance, liveliness, oomph, spark, sparkle, spirit, sprightliness, verve, vigor, vivacity, zest

**lifelike** *adj* looking like the real thing

> **lifelike** *adj* authentic, convincing, exact, faithful, graphic, natural, real, realistic, true-to-life, vivid

**lift** *v* raise to higher position; take up; (of fog) disperse; *phr v* **lift off** *avia* leave the ground (*n* **liftoff**) *n* that which lifts

**ligament** *n* band of fibrous tissue connecting bones; connecting band

**light**[1] *adj* **1** not heavy **2** trivial **3** loose **4** friable **5** mild; *adv* in light manner; *adv* **-ly** *n* **-ness**

> **light** *adj* **1** (not heavy) airy, delicate, flimsy, gossamer, lightweight, portable, slight. **2** (trivial) amusing, easy, entertaining, diverting, fun, frivolous, simple, superficial, undemanding

**light**[2] *n* **1** form of energy, acting on optic nerve, making vision possible **2** source of brightness **3** knowledge; *v* **1** set fire to **2** illuminate (*pt, pp* **lighted** *or* **lit**); *phr v* **light up 1** make or become bright **2** light a cigarette; *adj* **1** bright **2** pale (*eg* **l. brown**)

> **light** *n* **1** (form of energy) beam, blaze, brightness, brilliance, flare, flash, glare, gleam, glint, glitter, glow, illumination, incandescence, luminescence, luminosity, luster, phosphorescence, radiance, ray, scintillation, shaft, shine, sparkle, twinkle. **2** (source of brightness) beacon, bulb, candle, lamp, lantern, taper, torch

**light** *v* (set fire to) fire, flame, ignite, kindle, put a match to, set alight
**light** *adj* (bright) full of light, glowing, illuminated, lit-up, sunny, well-lit

**lighten** *v* become light; make light
**lightning** *n* electrical discharge in atmosphere seen as flash in sky
**light-year** *n* distance traveled by light in one year, approx six million million miles
**ligneous** *adj* like, made of wood; *n* **lignite** soft woody brown coal
**like**[1] *adj* similar; *adv* in same way; *prep* in manner of

**like** *adj/prep* akin, alike, allied, analogous, corresponding, equal, equivalent, identical, matching, parallel, relating, resembling, same

**like**[2] *v* be fond of; be attached to; *n* **liking**

**like** *v* admire, appreciate, approve of, be keen on, be partial to, cherish, delight in, enjoy, esteem, love, prize, relish, revel in, take pleasure in

**likeable** *adj* agreeable, attractive
**likely** *adj* probable (*n* **likelihood**)

**likely** *adj* anticipated, expected, feasible, in the cards, plausible

**liken** *v* compare
**likeness** *n* resemblance, portrait
**lilac** *n* flowering shrub; pale mauve color
**Lilliputian** *adj* diminutive
**lilt** *v* sing sweetly with spirit; *n* well-marked beat or rhythm in music; swing; *adj* **lilting**; *adv* **-ly**
**lily** *n* bulbous flowering plant
**limb** *n* 1 leg or arm; wing 2 bough of tree
**lime** *n* kind of citrus tree; its round acid fruit
**limelight** *n* *fig* glare of publicity
**limestone** *n* kind of rock, calcium carbonate

**limerick** *n* nonsense verse of five lines
**limit** *n* boundary; *v* restrict; *n* **-ation**; *adj* **-ed**

**limit** *n* border, bound, brim, brink, confines, edge, end, extent, frontier, perimeter, periphery
**limit** *v* cap, check, circumscribe, confine, control, curb, delineate, demarcate, fix, put a limit on, ration, restrain

**limitless** *adj* without limit

**limitless** *adj* boundless, countless, endless, everlasting, immeasurable, incalculable, inexhaustible, infinite, innumerable, never-ending, numberless, unbounded, unconfined, unending, unlimited

**limousine** *n* large, closed type of car
**limp**[1] *adj* flaccid; not firm; *n* **-ness**

**limp** *adj* drooping, flabby, floppy, loose, relaxed, sagging, slack, soft, wilting

**limp**[2] *v* walk lamely; *n* lameness

**limp** *v* be lame, falter, hobble, shamble, shuffle, totter

**limpet** *n* rock-clinging marine shellfish
**line** *n* 1 thin mark, made by pen, etc 2 wrinkle 3 string 4 row 5 occupation; hobby 6 lineage 7 type of goods; *v* 1 mark with lines 2 insert lining 3 bring into line; *n* **lining** material used to cover inner surface

**line** *n* 1 (thin mark) band, bar, border, boundary, contour, dash, hyphen, mark, rule, streak, striation, strip, stripe, stroke, trail, underscore. 2 (wrinkle) channel, corrugation, crease, fold, furrow, groove. 3 (string) cable, cord, filament, lead, rope, strand, thread, wire. 4 (row) chain, column, cordon, crocodile, file, parade, procession, queue, rank, series

a
b
c
d
e
f
g
h
i
j
k
l
m
n
o
p
q
r
s
t
u
v
w
x
y
z

**linear** *adj* in lines

**linen** *n* cloth made of flax; underclothes, bed linens, tablecloths, etc; *adj* made of linen

**liner** *n* 1 large passenger ship 2 thing used for lining sth 3 thing used for making line (*eg* **eyeliner**)

**linger** *v* 1 delay; loiter 2 be slow to disappear

> **linger** *v* 1 (delay) dally, dawdle, hang around, hover, lag, loiter, pause, remain, stay, stop, take your time, tarry, wait. 2 (be slow to disappear) abide, continue, endure, persist, remain

**lingerie** *n* women's underwear

**linguist** *n* expert in a language or languages

**link** *n* 1 connection 2 loop, ring of chain; *v* join together, as with link; connect

> **link** *n* (connection) affiliation, association, attachment, bond, relationship, tie

**lint** *n* soft material for dressing wounds

**lintel** *n* horizontal stone or timber bar over doorway or window

**lion** *n* large powerful carnivore of cat tribe; *fem* **lioness**

**lip** *n* 1 one of fleshy flaps of tissue round mouth 2 edge; rim; 3 *coll* impertinence; *v* **lip-read** decipher speech when deaf by watching speaker's lip movements; *n* **lipstick** make-up for lips

**liposuction** *n* surgical removal of excess fat from under skin

**liquefy** *v* become, make liquid; melt

**liqueur** *n Fr* strong, sweetened alcoholic liquor

**liquid** *n* substance between solid and gas, fluid; *adj* 1 flowing smoothly 2 (of sounds) harmonious; fluid 3 easy to realize as money (*ns* 1. **assets, liquidity**)

> **liquid** *adj* (flowing smoothly) flowing, fluid, liquefied, melted, molten, running, runny, sloppy

**liquidate** *v* 1 pay (debt) 2 wind up financial affairs and dissolve company 3 *coll* kill; *ns* **-ation, -ator** official appointed to liquidate business

**liquor** *n* liquid substance, *esp* alcoholic one

**lira** *n* unit of currency in Italy and Turkey

**lisle** *n* fine cotton thread or fabric

**lisp** *v* speak with imperfect pronunciation of sibilants

**list**[1] *n* roll, catalog of names, words, etc; inventory; *v* make, write list

> **list** *n* directory, file, index, inventory, listing, record, register, schedule, table, tally

**list**[2] *n* leaning (of ship, etc) toward one side; *v* slope, lean

**listen** *v* pay attention so as to hear; *idm* **listen in** 1 listen to radio 2 eavesdrop; *n* **-er**

> **listen** *v* attend, concentrate, hark, hear, heed, mind, note, observe, take notice

**listeria** *n* bacteria causing food poisoning

**listless** *adj* apathetic

**litany** *n* prayer with responses from congregation

**literacy** *n* ability to read and write

**literal** *adj* 1 of letters 2 based on exact words of original; accurate; word for word; *adv* **literally** *coll* absolutely

**literary** *adj* concerned with literature or writers

**literate** *adj* educated, able to read and write

**literati** *n pl fml* experts on literature

**literature** *n* writings of country or period; written works on any subject

**lithe** *adj* supple; flexible

**lithium** *n* light metal

**lithography** *n* art of printing copies from designs on prepared stone or metal plates; *ns* **-graph** print so made; **-grapher**; *adj* **-graphic**

**litigate** *v* contest at law; make subject of lawsuit; *ns* **litigant, litigation**; *adj* **litigious** fond of litigation

**litmus** n vegetable substance turned red by acids and blue by alkalis; n **l.-paper**

**litmus test** fig use of single issue or factor as basis for judgment

**liter** n metric unit of capacity (about 1 ¾ pints)

**litter** n 1 scattered oddments of garbage 2 portable stretcher 3 all young born at one time 4 straw, etc as bedding for animals; v make untidy with litter

> **litter** n (garbage) clutter, debris, detritus, jetsam, junk, mess, refuse, trash, waste

**little** adj small, brief; n small amount; adv slightly

> **little** adj baby, compact, diminutive, dinky inf, dwarf, infinitesimal, Lilliputian, microscopic, midget, mini inf, miniature, minuscule, minute, petite, short, teeny inf, tiny, wee inf

**littoral** adj pertaining to seashore; n coastal region

**liturgy** n prescribed public worship; adj **-ical**

**live**[1] v 1 exist 2 dwell 3 subsist 4 pass one's life

> **live** v 1 (exist) be, be alive, breathe, draw breath, have life. 2 (dwell) abide, have your home, inhabit, lodge, occupy, reside, settle. 3 (subsist) exist, get by inf, make a living, make ends meet, support oneself, survive

**live**[2] adj 1 having life; vital 2 flaming, glowing 3 not prerecorded; v **liven** (**up**) make more lively

> **live** adj 1 (having life) active, actual, alive, animate, breathing, existing, living, sentient

**livelong** adj lasting throughout the day

**lively** adj full of life and energy (n **-iness**)

**lively** adj active, alert, animated, bouncy, bubbly inf, buoyant, bustling, cheerful, chirpy, energetic, enthusiastic, exuberant, frisky, high-spirited, irrepressible, jolly, nimble, perky inf, quick, spirited, sprightly, spry, vigorous, vital, vivacious

**liver** n organ secreting bile

**liverwurst** n liver sausage

**livery** n 1 servants of one employer 2 food allowance for horses; n **l. stable** one where horses are boarded or hired out

**lives** pl of **life**

**livid** adj of bluish pale color, as by bruising; sl very angry

**living** adj 1 alive 2 active; in use (eg **l. language**); n **l. memory** period recalled by oldest person alive; **l. room** main room of house; n 1 livelihood 2 way of life 3 position of clergyman; his income

> **living** n (livelihood) daily bread, employment, income, job, keep, means of support, occupation, subsistence, sustenance, wage, work

**lizard** n four-footed reptile

**llama** n woolly S American ruminant

**load** n 1 sth carried 2 burden 3 elec amount of energy drawn from source; v 1 place burden on, in 2 charge (gun)

> **load** n 1 (sth carried) bale, cargo, charge, consignment, freight, shipment. 2 (burden) cross, duty, encumbrance, millstone, pressure, responsibility, strain, trouble, weight, worry

**loaf**[1] n mass of bread of definite size, weight; pl **loaves**

**loaf**[2] v loiter; work lazily; n **loafer**

**Loafer** [TM] slip-on casual shoe

**loam** n rich vegetable soil

**loan** n something lent; act of lending; money lent; v lend

a b c d e f g h i j k **l** m n o p q r s t u v w x y z

**loathe** v detest; hate; n **loathing** great disgust, repulsion; adj **loathsome** disgusting

**loaves** pl of **loaf**

**lob** n high-pitched underhand ball in cricket; high ball in tennis; v **lobs, lobbing, lobbed** throw, hit in high shot

**lobby** n hall; anteroom; v **lobbies, lobbying, lobbied** try to influence MPs (to favour particular group, interests etc); n **-ing** frequent lobby for such purpose; n **lobbyist**

**lobe** n soft lower part of ear

**lobelia** n herbaceous plant

**lobotomy** n med operation to remove brain tissue

**lobster** n large edible marine crustacean

**lobworm** n large worm used as fish bait

**local** adj of, in, confined to particular place, region, part of body; n person belonging to district; ns **locale** scene of event; **locality** position, district; v **localize** restrict to particular area; give local character to

**locate** v discover, set in, particular place

**location** n 1 position 2 outdoor set where scenes for film are shot

**loch** n Scottish lake or arm of sea

**lock**[1] n tress of hair

**lock**[2] n 1 device for closing door, safe, etc, operated by key 2 enclosure on river, canal in which boats can be moved from one level to another 3 mechanism for firing gun 4 blockage; idm **lock, stock, and barrel** altogether; v 1 close with a lock 2 become fixed, immobile

> **lock** n (device for closing door) bolt, catch, clasp, fastening, latch padlock
> **lock** v (close) bolt, fasten, padlock, secure, shut

**locker** n lockable small closet

**locket** n small metal case for photograph, etc, worn as ornament

**locksmith** n maker, repairer of locks

**locomotive** n steam, diesel, electric engine moving by its own power; n **locomotion** action, power of moving

**locust** n destructive winged insect

**locum (tenens)** n Lat one acting temporarily as deputy, esp of doctor or priest

**locus** n 1 exact place 2 math line tracing path of pint through space

**locution** n mode, style of speech; phrase

**lodestone** n magnet; magnetic iron oxide

**lodge** n gatekeeper's house v 1 house 2 deposit 3 be embedded 4 lay (accusation, charge against) 5 occupy lodgings

**lodger** n one who pays rent for part of another's house

**lodgings** n room(s) let to lodger

> **lodgings** n accommodation, apartment, a roof over your head, boarding house, digs inf, pad inf, somewhere to live

**lofty** adj of great height; fig noble; sublime; haughty; adv **-ily**

**log** n 1 unhewn piece of timber 2 daily record of ship's voyage, aircraft flight, etc; v **logs, logging, logged** enter in logbook; phr v **log off/out** comput finish on-line operation; ns **logbook** daily record of journey

**logarithm** n exponent of power to which invariable number must be raised to produce given number, tabulated for use in calculation

**logic** n art of reasoning; n **logician**

**logical** adj using logic

> **logical** adj cogent, coherent, consistent, plausible, rational, reasonable, sensible, sound, structured, valid, well-organized

**logistics** n pl science of organizing sth complicated

**logo** n design used in emblem for an organization; pl **-os**

**loiter** v linger, delay; n **loiterer**

> **loiter** v hang about, hang around, loaf about, stand about, wait around

**loll** v 1 sit, lie lazily 2 hang out tongue

**lone** *adj* solitary; isolated; *n* **-liness**; *adj* **-some**

**lone** *adj* single, unaccompanied

**lonely** *adj* 1 unhappy because of solitude 2 empty

**lonely** *adj* 1 (unhappy because of solitude) abandoned, alone, deserted, forlorn, forsaken, lonesome, solitary 2 (empty) deserted, desolate, isolated

**loner** *n coll* person who does not mix well with other people or who prefers to be alone

**long** *adj* having length; *ns* **l. jump** athletic jumping contest; **l. wave** radio using range over 1000m; *adv* for a long time; *adjs* **l.-drawn-out** lengthy; tedious; **l.-life** usable for longer than normal; **l.-range** 1 (of forecast) looking far ahead 2 able to reach far away; **l.-standing** existing for a long time already; **l.-suffering** enduring patiently; **l. term** lasting for a long time; **l.-winded** needlessly wordy and boring

**long** *adj* drawn out, elongated, endless, extended, interminable, lengthy, long-winded, never-ending, prolonged, protracted

**long** *v* desire earnestly; *phr v* **long for** want very much

**long** *v* covet, crave, dream of, hanker after, have a craving for, want, yearn for

**longevity** *n* long life
**longing** *n* strong desire; *adj* showing such desire; *adv* **-ly** yearning; desire

**longing** *n* ambition, craving, hunger, urge, wish

**longitude** *n* distance in degrees, E or W from given meridian; *adj* **-tudinal** of longitude

**look** *v* 1 use eyes 2 seem to be 3 gaze, stare; *phr vs* **look after** take care of; **look down on** despise; **look forward to; look into** investigate; **look out** 1 beware 2 search and find among one's belongings; **look up** 1 raise one's eyes 2 find and visit 3 find by consulting book; **look up to** admire; *ns* 1 act of looking; glance 2 facial expression 3 appearance; *pl* **-s** person's appearance; attractiveness; **lookout** 1 prospect 2 sentry 3 (bad) luck;

**look** *v* 1 (use eyes) browse through, cast your eye over, examine, gaze, glance, have a look, peep, peer, scan, stare, study, watch. 2 (seem) appear, give the appearance of being, strike you as being. 3 (look after) care for, keep an eye on, mind, nurse, nurture, take care of, tend
**look** *n* (act of looking) examination, gaze, glance, glare, glimpse, glower, inspection, peek, scan, stare

**loom**[1] *n* weaving machine
**loom**[2] *v* emerge indistinctly; *fig* appear important and menacing
**loop** *n* bend in cord, string, etc, made by crossing ends; *v* form loop

**loop** *n* circle, coil, curl, curve, hoop, noose, ring, spiral, turn, twist, whorl
**loop** *v* bend, coil, curl, spiral, twist, wind

**loose** *adj* 1 free from control 2 detached 3 not tight 4 vague 5 not compact 6 dissolute; of lax morals; *adj* **l.-leaf** having separate sheets of paper (**l.-leaf binder**); *adv* **-ly** (*n* **-ness**)

**loose** *adj* 1 (free from control) at large, escaped, free, out, untethered. 2 (detached) free, straggling, trailing, unattached, wobbly. 3 (not tight) baggy, floppy, hanging, slack. 4 (vague) approximate, ballpark *inf*, general, rough

a b c d e f g h i j k l m n o p q r s t u v w x y z

**loosen** v make less tight; (n **-ing**)

> **loosen** v ease off, relax, release, slacken, undo, unfasten, untie

**loot** n, v plunder
**lop** v **lops, lopping, lopped** trim, shorten by chopping (branches, etc)
**lope** v run with long, easy, bounding pace
**lopsided** adj unevenly balanced

> **lopsided** adj awry, crooked, skewed, tilting, uneven

**lord** n 1 ruler 2 any peer of realm 3 **the L.** God; adj **lordly** magnificent; haughty; ns **lordliness, lordship** power of lord; domain; title of peers

> **lord** n 1 (ruler) chief, leader, master. 2 (peer) aristocrat, baron, count, duke, earl, noble

**lore** n knowledge of special kind, often derived from tradition
**lorgnette** n Fr eyeglasses on handle
**lose** v **losing, lost** 1 not find 2 be defeated 3 suffer loss 4 get rid of 5 be bereaved of; phr v **lose out** be at a disadvantage; n **loser** adj **losing** (n **l. battle** struggle one has no chance of winning; **l. streak** sequence of bad luck)

> **lose** v 1 (not find) be unable to find, mislay, misplace. 2 (be defeated) get beaten, get hammered inf, get thrashed

**loss** n 1 act, result of losing 2 bereavement; idm **at a loss** (for words) unable to think of anything to do or say

> **loss** n (act, result of losing) cost, damage, defeat, deficit, deprivation, disappearance, failure, harm, hurt, impairment, privation

**lost** pt, pp of **lose**

**lot** 1 quantity 2 fate 3 item of auction
**lothario** n seducer of women
**lotion** n liquid for keeping skin, hair clean, healthy
**lottery** n gamble; competition in which prizes are allotted by chance drawing of tickets
**lotus** n a kind of water lily
**loud** adj 1 noisy 2 boisterous; vulgar; advs **loud, aloud, loudly**; n **-ness**

> **loud** adj (noisy) blaring, booming, deafening, ear-splitting, raucous, rowdy, shrill, thudding, thundering, tumultuous

**loudspeaker** n equipment that amplifies volume of sound on radio or recording system
**lounge** v recline lazily; n room with comfortable seats for guests

> **lounge** v flop, laze, lie about, lie back, loll, relax, sprawl
> **lounge** n drawing room, front room, living room, parlor, sitting room

**louse** n parasitic insect; pl **lice**; adj **lousy** sl unpleasant; bad
**lout** n clumsy, mannerless fellow; adj **loutish**
**love** n 1 affection 2 sexual passion 3 sweetheart 4 tennis no score; ns **l. affair**; v 1 delight in 2 desire passionately, sexually 3 show deep and lasting devotion to; adj, n **loving**

> **love** n (affection) adoration, devotion, fondness, infatuation, liking, partiality, passion, soft spot, tenderness, weakness
> **love** v 1 (delight in) adore, be keen on, be partial to, enjoy, get a kick out of, go for, have a weakness for, really like 2 (desire) be infatuated with, be keen on, be soft on, dote on, fancy, have a crush on, have a thing about, idolize 3 (show devotion) adore, be devoted to, be fond of, be in love with, think the world of, worship

**lovable** *adj* inspiring love
**lovely** *adj* 1 beautiful 2 pleasant (*n* **-iness**)

lovely *adj* 1 (beautiful) attractive, cute, good-looking, handsome, pretty, sweet. 2 (pleasant) brilliant, fabulous, gorgeous, great, marvellous, superb, terrific, wonderful

**lover** *n* 1 sexual partner 2 **lover of** enthusiast for

lover *n* (sexual partner) bit on the side *inf*, boyfriend, fiancé, fiancée, girlfriend, mistress, old flame, partner

**low**[1] *adj* 1 not high or tall 2 not loud 3 deep in sound 4 depressed 5 not intense 6 humble 7 vulgar; mean; sordid 8 inferior in order of merit or importance; *n* 1 low point 2 depression; *adj* **lowly**; *n* **-iness**

low *adj* 1 (not high or tall) dwarf, low-growing, low-lying, short, small, squat, stunted. 2 (not loud) gentle, hushed, muffled, muted, pianissimo, quiet, soft, subdued. 3 (deep in sound) bass, deep. 4 (depressed) despondent, dispirited, down, down in the dumps, downhearted, fed up, gloomy, miserable, sad, unhappy

**low**[2] *n* cry of a cow; *v* utter a sound
**lower** *adj* 1 less high 2 inferior (*n* **l. class**; *adj* **l.-class**); *v* 1 make less high 2 bring down 3 reduce
**loyal** *adj* faithful; *n* **loyalist**

loyal *adj* committed, dependable, devoted, dutiful, reliable, staunch, trustworthy

**loyalty** *n* quality of being loyal

loyalty *n* allegiance, dedication, dependability, devotion, faithfulness, fidelity, reliability, trustworthiness

**lozenge** *n* 1 diamond-shaped figure; rhombus 2 small flat medicinal tablet
**LSD** *abbr* lysergic acid diethylamide (dangerous hallucinatory drug) (*also sl* **acid**)
**lubricate** *n* make slippery, smooth with oil, grease; *ns* **lubrication, lubricant** substance used to reduce friction
**lucid** *adj* clear; easy to understand; clearheaded; *ns* **lucidity, lucidness**
**luck** *n* 1 fate 2 good fortune; *adv* **luckily**; *adj* **luckless**

luck *n* 1 (fate) chance, destiny, fluke, fortune, serendipity, the stars. 2 (good fortune) best of luck, break, good luck, prosperity, stroke of luck, success, windfall

**lucky** *adj* fortunate; *n* **l. strike** piece of good luck

lucky *adj* auspicious, charmed, fortuitous, handy, opportune, timely

**lucrative** *adj* profitable
**ludicrous** *adj* absurd

ludicrous *adj* comic, crazy, daft *inf*, farcical, incongruous, preposterous, ridiculous, silly, stupid

**luggage** *n* baggage

luggage *n* bags, belongings, cases, gear *inf*, possessions, things

**lugubrious** *adj* mournful
**lukewarm** *adj* tepid; *fig* lacking enthusiasm
**lull** *v* 1 soothe; make quiet 2 subside; *n* temporary pause; *n* **lullaby** cradle song
**lumbar** *adj* of, near loins; *n* **lumbago** rheumatic pain in loins, or lower part of spine
**lumber** *v* 1 move clumsily, heavily 2 encumber; obstruct; *n* 1 useless odds and ends 2 sawn timber; *n* **l. jack** man who fells and prepares timber for sawmill

A
B
C
D
E
F
G
H
I
J
K
**L**
M
N
O
P
Q
R
S
T
U
V
W
X
Y
Z

**luminous** *adj* bright; glowing

> **luminous** *adj* fluorescent, lustrous, phosphorescent, radiant, shining, vivid

**lump** *n* 1 shapeless mass 2 swelling, bump; *v* throw together in one mass; *n* **l. sum** single amount; *adj* **lumpy**; *n* **-iness**
**lunar** *adj* relating to moon
**lunatic** *adj* insane; *n* insane person; *n* **l. fringe** members of (*esp* political) group with eccentric ideas; *n* **lunacy**

> **lunatic** *n* madman, maniac, nut case *inf*, psychopath

**lunch** *n* midday meal; (*also* **luncheon**); *v* have lunch
**lung** *n* respiratory organ in vertebrates
**lunge** *n* sudden thrust, blow made with weapon; sudden movement of body; plunge; *v* make lunge
**lupin** *n* garden plant with long spikes of flowers
**lurch** *v* pitch, roll to one side; *n* sudden stagger

> **lurch** *v* list, lunge, reel, roll, stagger, stumble, sway, weave

**lurcher** *n* dog, cross between collie and greyhound
**lure** *n* bait used to recall hawk; decoy; *fig* anything that entices; *v* attract

> **lure** *v* beckon, draw, ensnare, entice, invite, lead on, seduce, tempt

**lurid** *adj* 1 ghastly, sensational, crude 2 glaring
**lurk** *v* remain hidden; lie in wait

> **lurk** *v* hide, linger, skulk, sneak, snoop

**luscious** *adj* delicious; excessively sweet
**lush** *adj* (of grass, etc) juicy, luxuriant

> **lush** *adj* dense, flourishing, green, luxuriant, prolific, rich, thick

**lust** *n* sexual appetite; *adjs* **lustful, lusty** vigorous, powerful
**luster** *n* 1 gloss; sheen 2 *fig* renown; glory; *adj* **lustrous** shining, luminous
**lute** *n* stringed musical instrument; *n* **lutanist**
**luxurious** *adj* extravagant

> **luxurious** *adj* affluent, comfortable, deluxe, expensive, grand, lavish, opulent, plush, rich, ritzy *inf*, sumptuous

**luxury** *n* 1 state of great ease and comfort 2 expensive but unnecessary thing; *v* **luxuriate** indulge in luxury; revel in; grow profusely; *adj* **luxuriant** abundant; exuberant (*n* **-ance**)

> **luxury** *n* 1 (state of comfort) comfort, extravagance, grandeur, indulgence, opulence, richness, splendor, sumptuousness. 2 (expensive thing) extra, extravagance, optional extra, treat, trimmings

**lychee** *n* Asiatic fruit with sweet white flesh
**lying** *v pr p of* **lie**[1], **lie**[2]
**lymph** *n* colorless fluid found in lymphatic vessels
**lynch** *v* put to death by mob violence
**lynx** *n* fierce wildcat woth short tail and tufted ears
**lyric** *n* 1 words for song 2 short emotional poem; *adj* **lyric(al)** of poems expressing emotion *adv* **-ly**, *n* **-ism**

**MA** *abbr* Master of Arts
**macabre** *adj* gruesome

> **macabre** *adj* eerie, frightening, grisly, horrible, morbid, sick, terrible

**macadam** *n* broken stone for road surfacing; *v* pave road with this
**macaroni** *n* tubular form of Italian pasta
**macaroon** *n* small sweet cake or cookie made of ground almonds or coconut
**macaw** *n* kind of parrot
**mace**[1] *n* heavy staff used in Middle Ages
**mace**[2] *n* spice used in cooking
**macerate** *v* soften by soaking; become thin through fasting
**Mach** *n* ratio of speed of aircraft, etc to speed of sound
**machete** *n* *Sp* large, heavy chopping knife
**machine** *n* **1** apparatus that applies power to perform work, or direct movement **2** organized system to carry out specific functions; *v* print, sew with machine

> **machine** *n* (apparatus) appliance, contraption, device, gadget, mechanism, robot, tool

**machinery** *n* parts of machines
**macho** *adj coll* exaggeratedly masculine
**mackerel** *n* type of edible, but bony, sea-fish
**macramé** *n* *Fr* craftwork from knotted string

**macro-** *prefix* **1** long **2** large-scale
**macrobiotic** *adj* restricted diet of whole grains, etc, thought to be extremely healthy
**macrocosm** *n* the great world; the universe
**mad** *adj* **1** insane **2** angry **3** wildly excited; *n* **madman**

> **mad** *adj* (insane) crazy *inf*, demented, mentally ill, mentally unstable, nuts *inf*, out of your mind, senile, unbalanced, unhinged

**madam** *n* formal mode of addressing women
**mad cow disease** *n* informal name for BSE
**madden** *v* drive mad; infuriate
**Madeira** *n* amber-colored dessert wine
**madeleine** *n* small, buttery shell-shaped cake
**madness** *n* **1** insanity **2** excitement
**madrigal** *n* type of part song for three or more voices
**maestro** *n* eminent composer, musician, or conductor
**Mafia** *n* Sicilian secret criminal organization
**magazine** *n* **1** publication containing articles, stories, etc by different authors **2** cartridge chamber of repeating rifle

> **magazine** *n* (publication) journal, monthly, periodical, weekly

**magenta** *adj* purplish-red in color
**maggot** *n* grub, larva, *esp* of blow-fly
**magic** *n* **1** superhuman control over natural forces and objects **2** conjuring; *adj* **-al**
**magician** *n* conjuror; wizard

> **magician** *n* illusionist, sorcerer, warlock, witch

**magistrate** *n* civil official administering law; *adj* **magisterial** of, pertaining to, magistrates
**magma** *n* molten rock below earth's crust
**magnanimous** *adj* of generous, noble character; *n* **magnanimity**
**magnate** *n* prominent, influential man, *esp* in finance, industry

a b c d e f g h i j k l **m** n o p q r s t u v w x y z

A B C D E F G H I J K L **M** N O P Q R S T U V W X Y Z

**magnesium** *n* metallic element; *n* **magnesia** alkaline compound of this, used in medicine

**magnet** *n* 1 piece of iron with property of attracting other iron objects 2 person or thing with the power to attract others; *adj* **magnetic** (**m. field** area influenced by magnetic force; **m. north** Northern pole of axis round which earth rotates; *n* **magnetism**; *v* **magnetize**

**magnificent** *adj* splendid; *n* **-ficence**

> **magnificent** *adj* brilliant, excellent, fine, glorious, gorgeous, grand, magic, marvelous, out of this world, sumptuous, superb, tremendous, wonderful

**magnify** *v* **magnifies, magnifying, magnified** cause to appear larger, as with lens; *ns* **magnification, magnifying glass**

**magnitude** *n* size, greatness, extent

**magnolia** *n* flowering tree

**magnum** *n Lat* wine bottle holding 1.6 qts

**magpie** *n* black and white bird of jay family

**Magyar** *n* dominant race in Hungary; their language

**mahatma** *n* Indian spiritual adept; one endowed with wisdom and power

**mahogany** *n* reddish-brown hard wood

**maid** *n* 1 female servant 2 *dated* young, unmarried woman

**maiden** *n lit* young unmarried woman

**mail**[1] *n* armor of metal rings or plates

**mail**[2] *n* postal system; letters conveyed at one time; *v* send by post; **mail order** order for goods sent by mail

**maim** *v* cripple; mutilate

**main** *adj* most important; *n* principal pipe or cable in water, sewage, electricity, or gas system; *pl* **mains** source of water, gas, electricity

> **main** *adj* central, chief, critical, crucial, essential, first, foremost, key, major, most important, number one, paramount, predominant, primary, principal, top, vital

**maintain** *v* 1 cause to continue 2 keep in good condition 3 support with money 4 assert; *n* **maintenance** 1 keeping in good condition 2 payment made by absent partner, husband to support family

**maize** *n* Indian corn

**majesty** *n* 1 sovereignty; dignity 2 title of sovereign

**majestic** *adj* stately, dignified

> **majestic** *adj* grand, imperial, imposing, impressive, magnificent, noble, regal, splendid

**major** *adj* 1 more important 2 greater 3 elder; *n* army rank above captain

**majority** *n* 1 greater number 2 number of votes by which one party leads in election 3 age at which full civil rights are due

**make** *v* **makes, making, made** 1 produce 2 earn 3 compel 4 add up to 5 constitute 6 reach; attain 7 appoint 8 estimate, calculate 9 complete 10 prepare for use

> **make** *v* 1 (produce) assemble, bake, build, cook, create, draw up, fashion, fix, form, manufacture, prepare, put together, synthesize. 2 (earn) bring home, bring in, clear, gain, net. 3 (compel) coerce, force, oblige, push sb into, require. 4 (add up to) come to, constitute, equal, total

**malachite** *n* green mineral

**maladjusted** *adj* unable to adapt to demands of life or other people

**maladroit** *adj* clumsy

**malady** *n* illness, *esp* of the mind or spirit

**malaise** *n Fr* slight physical discomfort

**malapropism** *n* ridiculous misuse of word

**malaria** *n* fever spread by mosquito bite

**male** *adj* belonging to sex which begets offspring; *n* male person or animal

**malevolence** *n* illwill

**malformation** *n* deformity

**malfunction** *v* fail to work properly; *n* such a failure

**malice** n illwill, spite
**malicious** adj spiteful

> **malicious** adj bitchy, bitter, hostile, hurtful, malignant, pernicious, venomous, vicious, vindictive

**malign** v say unpleasant things about; adj **malignant 1** filled with illwill **2** (of disease) likely to prove fatal
**malinger** v fake illness to escape duty, work, etc; n **malingerer**
**mall** n covered streetor area with stores
**mallard** n common wild duck
**malleable** adj **1** capable of being hammered, pressed into shape **2** able to be influenced
**mallet** n wooden-headed hammer; polo stick; croquet mallet
**malnourished** adj suffering from results of poor diet; n **-nutrition**
**malpractice** n wrong-doing
**malt** n dried fermented barley or other grain used in brewing
**maltreat** v treat with cruelty; n **-ment**
**mammal** n animal which suckles its young; adj **mammary** pertaining to breast (**m. gland** milk gland)
**mammoth** n extinct elephant; adj huge
**man** n **1** adult male person **2** human race **3** human being **4** piece used in chess, checkers etc **5** manservant; (pl **men**); v **mans, manning, manned** supply with people for defense, work, etc

> **man** n **1** (male person) bloke, chap, gentleman, guy, human being, individual, lad, male, young man. **2** (human race) Homo sapiens, human race, humankind, humans, men and women, people

**manage** v **1** control **2** succeed in doing; ns **management 1** process of managing; administration **2** body of persons managing business; **manager** one who manages; one in charge of business, etc; (fem **-ess**); adj **managerial**

> **manage** v **1** (control) administer, be in charge of, direct, head, lead, organize, oversee, pilot, run, supervise. **2** (succeed) accomplish, bring off, cope, crack it inf, deal with, get by, handle

**mandarin** n **1** former Chinese high official **2** adj form of spoken Chinese used by the court and officials **3** small sweet orange
**mandate** n command to follow specified policy, esp given by electors to their representative; adjs **mandatory, mandated** entrusted to a mandate
**mandible** n jawbone
**mandolin** n musical stringed instrument
**mandrill** n large baboon with blue face and red rump
**mane** n long hair on neck of horse, lion, etc
**maneuver** n **1** strategic movement of troops **2** clever move; pl **-s** mock warfare; v **1** manage with skillfulness **2** perform maneuvers; adj **maneuverable**
**manganese** n metallic element
**manger** n feeding-trough in stable, etc
**mangle** v mutilate, spoil, hack
**mango** n tropical fruit; pl **-os** or **-oes**
**manhandle** v use physical force on
**mania** n **1** violent madness **2** obsession; craze; adj **manic 1** suffering from mania (n **m.-depressive** person prone to sudden extreme changes of mood) **2** wildly excited; n **maniac** crazy person
**manicure** n, v care for hands and nails; n **-curist**
**manifest** adj obvious; v show; ns **-ation**; **manifesto** public declaration of policy
**manipulate** v **1** manage skilfully **2** alter fraudulently; ns **-ation, -ator**; adj **-ative**
**mankind** n the human race
**manly** adj of man; virile
**manna** n miraculous food of Israelites in wilderness; fig spiritual food; gum of Arabian tamarisk
**mannequin** n live model employed to display clothes

a
b
c
d
e
f
g
h
i
j
k
l
**m**
n
o
p
q
r
s
t
u
v
w
x
y
z

**manner** n way thing happens or is done; custom; style; pl **-s social behavior**; n **-ism** peculiarity of style; adj **-ly** polite

> **manner** n approach, means, method, procedure, process, style, technique, way

**manor** n estate, owner or lord of which retains ancient rights over land; n **m.-house** house of lord of manor

**manqué** adj Fr unfulfilled

**mansard** n roof with two angles of slope

**mansion** n large house

**manslaughter** n crime of killing without intent

**manta** n large triangular fish or ray

**mantel** n structure around fireplace; ns **mantelshelf**, **mantelpiece** shelf at top of mantel

**mantis** n predatory green or brown insect

**mantle** n 1 loose cloak 2 geol part of Earth below crust; 3 incandescent mesh covering gas flame; v cover

**mantra** n sacred word (in Hinduism, Buddhism)

**manual** adj of, done with hands; n handbook

**manufacture** n process of making articles, goods, etc; v produce goods, esp in large quantities; fig fabricate, concoct (story, etc); n **manufacturer** owner of factory; person, company making goods

**manure** n dung used to fertilize land

**manuscript** n handwritten document; draft of book, etc for printing

**many** adj numerous; n large number

> **many** adj abundant, a lot of, copious, countless, frequent, heaps of, innumerable, loads of, lots of, myriad, oodles of, plenty of, profuse, tons of, umpteen

**Maori** n New Zealand aboriginal; their language

**map** n 1 flat representation of earth's surface or part of this 2 chart of heavens; v **maps, mapping, mapped** make map

**map** n (representation of earth's surface) chart, guide, plan, street guide, road-map, town plan

**maple** n deciduous tree; its wood

**mar** v spoil, ruin

**maraca** n Latin American percussion instrument made of a gourd filled with seeds

**marathon** n long-distance footrace

**marauder** n roving thief; raider; v **maraud**

**marble** n 1 hard kind of limestone, capable of being highly polished 2 small ball used in game; pl **-s** child's game; v stain with streaks of color

**March** n third month of year

**march** v walk in steady rhythmic step, esp in military formation; n 1 act of marching 2 distance covered 3 music to accompany march

> **march** v file, parade, stride, tramp

**marchioness** n wife or widow of marquis

**Mardi Gras** n Shrove Tuesday (day before start of Lent); carnival on this day

**mare** n female horse

**margarine** n manufactured butter substitute

**margin** n 1 edge; limit 2 extra amount beyond what is necessary 3 space round printed page; adj **marginal** 1 of relatively little importance 2 adj, n polit (seat) capable of being won easily by another candidate at election; adv **marginally** by a small amount; v **marginalize** push aside, away from focus of attention

**marigold** n plant with yellow-orange flowers

**marijuana** n leaves of the hemp plant smoked as a drug

**marina** n harbor for pleasure boats

**marinade** n sauce for soaking meat, fish before cooking; meat, fish, treated this way; v soak in this way (also **marinate**)

**marine** adj of, connected with sea or shipping; n soldier serving on warship; n **mariner** seaman, sailor

**marionette** *n Fr* puppet moved on strings
**marital** *adj* of, relating to marriage
**maritime** *adj* 1 connected with, situated near sea 2 having a navy, seacoast, or sea-trade
**marjoram** *n* aromatic herb
**mark** *n* 1 visible sign 2 spot 3 symbol 4 target *v* 1 make mark 2 assign marks to (examination paper, etc) 3 observe; *adj* **marked** clear; emphatic (*adv* **-ly**)

> **mark** *n* 1 (visible sign) evidence, indication, proof, sign, symbol, token.
> 2 (spot) blemish, blot, blotch, dent, dot, impression, pockmark, scar, scratch, smear, smudge, smut, speck, stain, streak.
> 3 (symbol) badge, brand, device, emblem, hallmark, seal, signature, trademark.
> 4 (target) aim, goal, intention, objective
> **mark** *v* 1 (make mark) blemish, blot, damage, deface, disfigure, dent, dirty, draw on, scar, scrawl on, scribble on, smudge, spot, stain, streak, write on. 2 (assign marks) appraise, assess, evaluate, grade

**market** *n* 1 public gathering place for buying and selling 2 demand for goods; *v* buy, sell in, take to market; *adj* **-able** saleable
**markup** *n* proportion of increase from wholesale to retail price
**marmalade** *n* jam made of oranges
**marmoset** *n* small, bushy-tailed monkey
**maroon** *adj* dark crimson; *v* abandon on desert island, etc; *fig* desert
**marquee** *n Fr* large tent used at fêtes, etc
**marquetry** *n* inlaid woodwork
**marquis, marquess** *n* title of British nobleman between duke and earl
**marrow** *n* 1 soft blood-rich substance inside bones 2 the choices of foods
**marry** *v* **marries, marrying, married** 1 take as husband or wife 2 join in marriage; *n* **marriage** 1 state of being married 2 *fig* close union
**marsh** *n* low-lying water-logged land; *n* **m.-mallow** 1 marsh plant 2 confection made from its root; *adj* **marshy**

> **marsh** *n* bog, fen, marshland, mire, morass, quagmire, quicksand, swamp, wetland

**marshal** *n* someone who directs ceremonies; *v* **marshals, marshaling, marshaled** 1 arrange in position 2 lead with ceremony
**marsupial** *n* animal which carries young in pouch, as kangaroo, etc
**mart** *n* 1 trading-center 2 auction room
**marten** *n* weasel-like animal, valued for its fur
**martial** *adj* suitable for, relating to war; warlike *ns* **m. art** fighting sport (*eg* judo, karate) (*usu pl*); **m. law** imposition of military rule (in temporary crisis)
**Martian** *adj, n* (supposed inhabitant) of Mars
**martin** *n* species of swallow
**martinet** *n* strict, pedantic disciplinarian
**martini** *n* mixture of gin and vermouth
**martyr** *n* 1 one who dies rather than give up faith 2 *fig* sufferer (from pain, etc); *n* **martyrdom** suffering or death of martyr
**marvel** *n* something wonderful, amazing; *v* wonder; be surprised
**marvelous** *adj* wonderful

> **marvelous** *adj* amazing, astounding, breathtaking, brilliant, extraordinary, fantastic, out of this world, remarkable, sensational, stupendous, superb, terrific

**Marxism** *n* theories of Karl Marx, basis for Communism; *adj, n* **-ist**
**marzipan** *n* paste made of ground almonds, sugar, etc
**mascara** *n* cosmetic for coloring eyelashes
**masculine** *adj* 1 relating to males 2 strong 3 of gender denoting males; *n* **-linity**
**mash** *n* warm food given to animals; *v* crush into soft pulp

> **mash** *v* crush, mangle, pound, pulp, pulverize, purée, smash, squash

**mask** *n* covering for face; *v* cover with mask; conceal

a b c d e f g h i j k l m n o p q r s t u v w x y z

**mask** n camouflage, cover, disguise, façade, false colors, front, guise, pretense, screen, shield, smokescreen, veil
**mask** v cloak, cover up, disguise, hide, obscure, screen, veil

**masochism** n sexual perversion where pleasure is found in suffering physical pain and humiliation; n **masochist**
**mason** n 1 stone worker 2 Freemason; adj **masonic** of Freemasonry; n **masonry**
**masque** n verse drama with dance, music, etc; n **masquerade** masked ball; v be disguised; fig assume character of
**mass** n 1 quantity of matter in one body, lump 2 large amount, number; pl **the masses** common people; ns **m. communications**; **m. media** way of conveying facts, ideas to wide public (eg TV, radio, newspapers); adj **massive** enormous (adv **-ly**; n **-ness**)
**Mass** n act of worship in Catholic church
**massacre** v slaughter indiscriminately; n killing of helpless persons

**massacre** n annihilation, blood bath, butchery, carnage, genocide, mass execution, mass murder, slaughter

**massage** n remedial treatment consisting of rubbing and kneading affected part; v 1 treat with massage 2 polit alter (figures, etc) to give false impression; n **masseur** one who practices massage; fem **masseuse**
**mast** n 1 pole to support ship's rigging 2 flagpole
**mastectomy** n surgical removal of the breast; pl **-ies**
**master** n 1 person with authority; head of household 2 owner 3 employer 4 captain of merchant ship 5 teacher 6 expert; v 1 overcome 2 acquire knowledge of, skill in; adj **masterly** showing great talent, skill; n **mastermind** clever person, v plan and ensure success (of difficult operation); n **mastery** authority; supremacy

**master** n (person with authority) boss, chief, controller, director, employer, governor, head, lord, lord and master, ruler, top dog

**masticate** v chew with teeth; n **-ation**
**mastiff** n large, thickset guard dog
**mastitis** n inflammation of breast
**masturbate** v stimulate one's own genital organs; n **-ation**
**mat** n 1 piece of plaited straw or coconut fiber, etc for wiping feet on, or covering part of floor 2 small rug 3 tangled hair; v **mats, matting, matted** become tangled; idm **on the mat** coll reprimanded
**mat, matt** adj having dull surface
**matador** n Sp man who kills bull in bullfight
**match**[1] n 1 thing exactly like another 2 person equal to another in quality, power, etc 3 contest of skill, strength 4 marriage; v 1 be equal to in contest 2 correspond 3 pit against in fight, etc; adj **-less** unequaled

**match** n 1 (thing like another) copy, double, duplicate, look-alike, spitting image, twin. 2 (person equal to another) counterpart, equal, equivalent, peer, rival. 3 (contest) bout, competition, game, tournament. 4 (marriage) affiliation, alliance, pairing, partnership, union
**match** v 1 (be equal to) be a match for, be in the same category as, be on a level with, compare with, compete with, keep pace with, keep up with, measure up to, rival. 2 (correspond) agree with, be compatible with, be similar to, be the same as, blend with, complement, coordinate with, fit, go with, harmonize, make a set, suit

**match**[2] n small strip of wood, tipped with combustible material
**mate**[1] n, v checkmate (in chess)
**mate**[2] n 1 comrade 2 husband; wife 3 (of animals, etc) one of pair 4 officer in merchant ship; v pair, esp animals

**material** n 1 stuff of which thing is made
2 fabric; adj physical; important; ns **-ism**
theory that matter is the only reality; **-ist**
one engrossed in material interests;
adj **-istic**; v **materialize** appear; become
visible

> **material** n 1 (stuff) element, matter,
> medium, substance. 2 (fabric) cloth,
> stuff, textiles

**maternity** n motherhood; adj **maternal**
related through mother; motherly
**mathematics** n pl abstract science concerned
with properties of and relations between
quantities; adj **-tical**; n **mathematician**
**matinée** n Fr afternoon theatrical
performance
**matri-** prefix (of) mother
**matriarch** n mother as head of family or
household; n **-archy** social system where
descent is traced through female line
**matricide** n act of killing one's own mother
**matriculate** v 1 register as student in
university or college 2 pass necessary
examination; n **-ation** act of matriculating
**matrimony** n marriage; adj **-monial**
**matrix** n mold in which type is cast; rock, etc
in which gems, stones, etc are embedded;
pl **matrices**
**matron** n 1 married woman of maturity and
dignity 2 domestic superintendent in
institution or boarding- chool; adj **-ly**
dignified, plump
**matter** n 1 substance of which physical object
is made 2 subject of book, discussion, etc.
3 affair; reason 4 cause of complaint, trouble;
idm **a matter of course** taken for granted;
v be important

> **matter** n 1 (substance) material, medium,
> stuff. 2 (subject) affair, business, episode,
> event, incident, issue, occurrence,
> question, situation, topic.

**mattress** n large padded cushion for bed

**mature** adj 1 ripe; fully developed 2 prudent;
wise; v 1 ripen 2 complete 3 (of insurance
policy, etc) become due for payment;
n **maturity**
**maudlin** adj tearfully sentimental
**maul** v handle roughly
**mauve** adj pale lilac in color
**maverick** n person with unorthodox ideas
**maw** n stomach, open jaws of animal crop of
bird
**maxim** n rule of conduct; proverb

> **maxim** n adage, aphorism, axiom, motto,
> rule, saying

**maximum** n greatest size, number, degree;
adj greatest
**May** n 1 fifth month 2 hawthorn blossom;
**May Day** first day of May (spring festival)
**may** v aux expresses permission, possibility,
hope; pt **might** (no pp); adv **maybe** possibly
**mayfly** n short-lived water insect
**mayhem** n violent disorder
**mayonnaise** n Fr sauce of egg yolk, olive oil,
and vinegar
**mayor** n chief officer of city or borough;
adj **-ral**; n **-ress** mayor's wife
**maypole** n flower-topped pole round which
people dance on May Day
**maze** n network of paths, hedges or lines

> **maze** n confusion, jungle, labyrinth, mesh,
> network, puzzle, tangle, web

**MC** abbr 1 master of ceremones 2 Member
of Congress
**ME** abbr med myalagic encephalomyelitis
**me** pron objective case of **I**
**mead** n alcoholic drink made of fermented
honey, malt, and yeast
**meadow** n grassy field; hayfield; n **m.-lark**
common American songbird

> **meadow** n field, grassland, paddock, pasture

**meager** adj inadequate

a
b
c
d
e
f
g
h
i
j
k
l
m
n
o
p
q
r
s
t
u
v
w
x
y
z

**meager** *adj* deficient, measly, paltry, poor, scanty, short, skimpy, sparse, stingy

**meal**[1] *n* coarsely ground grain
**meal**[2] *n* taking of food
**mean**[1i] *n* average; midway between two extremes; *ns* **meantime, meanwhile** intervening time
**mean**[2] *adj* 1 selfish with money 2 unkind; *adv* **-ly**; *n* **-ness**

**mean** *adj* 1 (selfish with money) close-fisted, illiberal, mingy, miserly, niggardly, parsimonious, stingy, tight, tight-fisted, ungenerous. 2 (unkind) bad-tempered, callous, disagreeable, hard-hearted, obnoxious, spiteful, surly, uncharitable, unfriendly, unpleasant

**mean**[3] *v* **meaning, meant** 1 have in mind 2 signify 3 intend 4 have meaning

**mean** *v* 1 (have in mind) aim, intend, plan, propose, set out. 2 (signify) convey, denote, drive at, express, imply, indicate, insinuate, represent, say, spell, stand for, suggest, symbolize

**meaning** *n* 1 sense 2 importance 3 intention; *adjs* **meaningful** (*adv* **-ly**), **meaningless** (*adv* **-ly**)

**meaning** *n* 1 (sense) drift, essence, explanation, gist, implication, import, message, significance, substance, thrust, upshot. 2 (importance) consequence, effect, point, purpose, significance, value, worth. 3 (intention) aim, design, end, goal, object, plan

**means** *n pl* 1 method, way 2 agent, cause 3 money, resources
**measles** *n* infectious disease, characterized by red rash and fever; *adj* **measly** *coll* mean in amount

**measure** *v* 1 find the size, amount, degree, etc of sth 2 be of a certain size; *n* 1 system of measuring 2 unit of measurement 3 degree; amount 4 verse rhythm; rhythmical, musical unit 5 action taken for a purpose; *adj* **measured** 1 of certain measure 2 careful; steady; *n* **-ment**; *adj* **measurable** (*adv* **-ably**)

**measure** *v* (find size, etc) assess, calculate, calibrate, compute, count, determine, evaluate, judge, mark out, meter, quantify, rate, reckon, size, survey, take measurements, value, weigh

**meat** *n* flesh of animals used as food; *adj* **meaty** substantial
**mechanic** *n* skilled, trained worker, *esp* one working with machinery; *pl* **-s** science of motion and force; *adj* **-al** concerned with, produced by machines; *fig* acting without thinking; *adv* **-ally**
**mechanism** *n* machinery; *n* **mechanization** making; mechanical, *esp* change from manpower to machines; *v* **mechanize**; *adj* **-ized**
**med** *abbr* 1 medical 2 medium 3 medieval 4 *cap* Mediterranean
**medal** *n* small metal disk, *usu* with inscription used to mark achievement, etc; *ns* **medallion** 1 large medal 2 round panel, ornament; **medalist** one who gains medals
**meddle** *v* interfere; tamper with; *adj* **-some**
**media** *n pl* means of mass communication (TV, radio, the press)
**median** *n, adj* average
**mediate** *v* intervene as peacemaker; *ns* **-ation** reconcilement; **-ator**

**mediate** *v* act as go-between, arbitrate, conciliate, intercede, intervene, liaise, make peace, negotiate, reconcile, referee, umpire

**medic** *n coll* doctor or medical student (*also* **medico**)

**Medicaid** n government assistance to pay for medical care for those on low incomes

**medical** adj of medicine; of the treatment of illness; n examination to assess sb's physical health; n **medication** (provision of) drugs; adj **medicated** containing medicinal substance(s)

**medicine** n 1 science of preventing, treating, and curing disease 2 substance taken internally to treat illness; n **m.-man** witchdoctor; adj **medicinal** curative

> **medicine** n 1 (science) healing, therapy, treatment. 2 (substance) cure, drug, medication, remedy, panacea

**medieval** adj of, belonging to Middle Ages; n **-ism** cult, spirit of Middle Ages; n **-ist**

**mediocre** adj ordinary; not very good

**meditate** v contemplate; ponder; n **-ation** concentrated thought; solemn contemplation; adj **-ative**

> **meditate** n be lost in thought, brood, cogitate, consider, contemplate, deliberate, muse, ponder, reflect, study, think

**Mediterranean** adj of the Mediterranean Sea or the land round it

**medium** n 1 that which is between extremes 2 channel though which sth is done 3 environment 4 one who receives messages from spirit world; (pl **mediums** or **media**); adj between two extremes

> **medium** adj average, fair, intermediate, mean, median, mediocre, middle, middling, moderate

**medley** n confused, miscellaneous assortment

**meek** adj submissive; mild; humble; adv **-ly**; n **-ness**

**meet** v **meeting, met** 1 come face to face with 2 assemble 3 converge 4 satisfy 5 confront; n **meeting** 1 encounter 2 public assembly

**meet** v 1 (come face to face with) bump into, chance upon, come across, come upon, encounter, happen upon, join, make contact with, meet with, rendezvous with, run into. 2 (assemble) come together, congregate, gather, mingle, rendezvous. 3 (converge) come together, connect, intersect, join, link up, touch. 4 (satisfy) answer, comply with, correspond to, fulfill, measure up to, observe

**mega-** prefix 1 very big (eg **megadose**) 2 million (eg **megaton**)

**megabyte** n comput $2^{20}$ or 1,047,576 bytes

**megalith** n huge prehistoric stone

**megalomania** n excessive desire for power over others; n **megalomaniac**

**megaphone** n funnel-shaped device used to increase volume of sound, and carry it farther

**melancholy** n gloom, sadness; adj gloomy

> **melancholy** adj dejected, depressed, disconsolate, doleful, down, down in the dumps, down in the mouth, glum, inconsolable, melancholic, miserable, nostalgic, sad, somber, sorry for yourself, tearful, unhappy, wistful

**melanoma** n cancerous tumor of the skin

**mellow** adj 1 ripe; well-matured 2 grown gentle through age, experience 3 sl relaxed; v make, become mellow

**melodrama** n sensational sentimental play

**melodramatic** adj overemotional

> **melodramatic** adj dramatic, exaggerated, histrionic, sensational, sentimental, theatrical

**melody** n tune; adj **melodious** tuneful

> **melody** n air, descant, music, song, strain, theme

**melon** n edible gourd with sweet juicy flesh

**melt** v 1 make, become liquid by heat 2 blend 3 fig make, become tender; n **meltdown** melting and leakage of radioactivity from core of nuclear reactor

> **melt** v (make, become liquid) defrost, dissolve, liquefy, soften, thaw, unfreeze

**member** n 1 limb of human or animal body 2 single part of complex whole 3 person belonging to group, society etc; n **membership** 1 status as member 2 total number of members of club, society, etc

**membrane** n thin, supple tissue covering or lining part of organ or body

**memento** n small item that serves as a reminder of a person, place; pl **-os** or **-oes**

**memo** n coll memorandum

**memoire** n Fr biography; pl **-s** personal experiences and observations of writer

**memorabilia** n things worth remembering

**memorable** adj special and noteworthy

> **memorable** adj distinctive, extraordinary, historic, impressive, momentous, notable, remarkable, striking, unforgettable

**memorandum** n informal business communication

**memorial** n thing commemorating person, event, etc; adj bringing to mind

**memorize** v commit to memory

> **memorize** v absorb, learn, learn by heart, learn by rote, make a mental note of, remember, take in

**memory** n 1 ability to remember 2 period of recollection 3 thing remembered 4 lasting impression of dead or departed person 5 comput place where data are stored

**men** pl of **man**

**menace** n threat; v threaten

**menagerie** n Fr collection of wild animals, esp traveling exhibition

**mend** v 1 repair 2 improve in health

> **mend** v (repair) darn, fix, patch up, rebuild, reconstruct, renew, restore, sew up

**menial** adj low and unimportant

**meningitis** n med inflammation of membranes of brain

**menopause** n time in life when menstruation ceases

**menstruation** n monthly discharge from womb; v **menstruate**; adj **menstrual**

**mental** adj 1 of, relating to mind 2 sl crazy, mad; ns **m. age** measure of mental ability from the average performance of people at the age specified; n **mentality** mental quality, attitude

**menthol** n substance obtained from oil of peppermint

**mention** v speak of; n brief reference

> **mention** v acknowledge, allude to, cite, comment on, declare, disclose, divulge, indicate, quote, refer to, remark on, report, say, state, talk about, talk of

**mentor** n counselor; wise, prudent adviser

**menu** n Fr list of dishes available; list of options in computer program

**mercantile** adj connected with trade; commercial

**Mercator projection** n method of depicting the world in maps as rectangular in shape by stretching the polar regions to match the Equator

**mercenary** adj working only for payment; eager for gain; n soldier hired by foreign country

**mercer** n dealer in fabrics, cloth; n **mercery** his trade; v **mercerize** give appearance of silk to cotton fabric, by treating with chemicals

**merchant** n wholesale trader, esp with foreign countries; ns **m. bank** bank specializing in business and industrial finance; **merchandise** wares

**merchant** *n* businessman, businesswoman, capitalist, entrepreneur, exporter, importer, seller, supplier, trader, tradesman, tradesperson, vendor

**merciful** *adj* showing mercy

**merciful** *adj* compassionate, forgiving, indulgent, kind, lenient, pitying, soft-hearted, tender-hearted

**merciless** *adj* showing no mercy

**merciless** *adj* cruel, hard, pitiless, remorseless, ruthless, severe, without pity

**mercury** *n* 1 silvery fluid metallic element 2 *cap* planet nearest sun 3 *cap* Roman messenger god; *adj* **mercurial** lively; erratic

**mercy** *n* compassion shown to offender

**mercy** *n* charity, clemency, compassion, forgiveness, indulgence, kindness, lenience, pity

**mere** *adj* only; simple; nothing but

**merge** *v* join together; absorb; fade gradually into; *n* **merger** absorption of smaller thing by greater; joining of businesses

**meridian** *n Lat/Fr* 1 noon 2 line of longitude passing through poles and cutting Equator at right angles 3 zenith

**meringue** *n Fr* topping of stiffly beaten egg whites mixed with sugar and baked slowly

**merit** *n* worth; excellence; quality deserving punishment or reward; *pl* intrinsic rightness or wrongness; *v* deserve; *adj* **meritorious** praiseworthy

**meritocracy** *n* (system of government by) people with the greatest ability

**mermaid** *n* fabulous creature (half woman, half fish)

**merry** *adj* lively and joyful; *ns* **merriment, merry-go-round** carousel with brightly painted wooden horses

**merry** *adj* celebrating, cheerful, festive, happy, jolly, joyous, laughing, rejoicing

**mesa** *n* flat-topped hill with steep sides

**mesh** *n* one of open spaces in net; *pl* **meshes** 1 network 2 *fig* snares; toils, *v* catch in meshes; (of gear wheels) be engaged

**mesmerize** *v* fascinate; hold attention of

**Mesozoic** *n geol* of the period lasting from about 225 to 70 million years ago

**mess** *n* 1 muddle; disorder 2 difficult position 3 eating place for armed forces; *v* make muddle of; *adj* **messy**

**mess** *n* 1 (muddle) chaos, confusion, debris, dirt, disorder, filth, jumble, pigsty, rubbish, untidiness. 2 (difficult position) calamity, crisis, débâcle, disarray, disaster, foul-up, hole, pickle, trouble

**message** *n* 1 oral or written communication sent to a person 2 meaning

**message** *n* 1 (communication) cable, E-mail, fax, letter, memo, memorandum, missive, note, telegram, telephone call, signal, transmission. 2 (meaning) idea, import, interpretation, moral, purport, significance, theme

**messenger** *n* person who delivers a message

**Messiah** *n* expected king and deliverer of the Jews

**metabolism** *n* process of chemical changes in living organism; *adj* **metabolic**; *v* **metabolize**

**metal** *n* mineral substance that is opaque, can be shaped, and can conduct heat or electricity ; *adjs* **metallic** of metal; **metalloid** resembling metal; *ns* **metallurgy** science and technology of metals; **metalwork** skilled work in metal; product from this (*n* **-er**)

**metamorphosis** *n* transformation; remarkable change; *pl* **metamorphoses**

a b c d e f g h i j k l m n o p q r s t u v w x y z

**metaphor** n figure of speech in which word is used to denote something different from its usual meaning; adj **metaphorical** figurative

**metaphysics** n branch of abstruse study concerned with nature and causes of being and knowledge; adj **metaphysical**

**mete** v (usu **mete out**) allot, distribute

**meteor** n shooting star; adj **-ic** like meteor; dazzling but brief; ns **meteorite** stony or metallic mass fallen from outer space; **meteorology** science of weather; **-ologist**; adj **-ological**

**meter**[1] n mechanical device for measuring quantity, volume, etc

**meter**[2] n poetical rhythm; group of metrical feet; unit of length in metric system; adj **metric** measuring by meters

**methane** n inflammable hydrocarbon gas

**methanol** n methyl alcohol

**method** n way used to do sth; ordered approach

> **method** n approach, arrangement, manner, means, methodology, mode, modus operandi, plan, practice, procedure, process, rule, style, system, technique

**methodical** adj orderly; adv **-ically**

> **methodical** adj careful, deliberate, logical, meticulous, precise, step-by-step, systematic

**Methodism** n Protestant denomination founded by John Wesley

**meticulous** adj over-careful about details

> **meticulous** adj accurate, careful, conscientious, correct, detailed, exact, methodical, painstaking, punctilious

**metronome** n mus mechanical device for beating time

**metropolis** n capital, chief city of country; adj **metropolitan**

**mew** n cry of cat, gull; v utter this cry

**mezzanine** n low-ceilinged story between two higher ones

**mezzo-soprano** n mus voice between soprano and contralto 2 singer with such a voice; musical part for this

**mezzotint** n (print made by) method using metal plate with smooth and rough areas to give light and shade respectively

**mg** abbr milligram

**micro-** prefix 1 very small (eg **micro-organism**) 2 one millionth (eg **microsecond**)

**microbe** n microscopic organism, bacterium, esp as cause of disease

**microbiology** n study of minute living organisms; adj **-ological**; n **-ologist**

**microchip** n small piece of silicon or similar material marked with electric circuit

**microcosm** n miniature representation of sth larger

**microlight** n very light miniature aircraft

**micrometer** n instrument for measuring very small distances

**microorganism** n organism too small to be seen except under a microscope

**microphone** n instrument converting sound into electrical waves for transmission to a loud speaker (also coll **mike**)

**microprocessor** n comput central data processing unit

**microscope** n instrument that gives enlarged view of extremely small objects; adj **microscopic** extremely small

**microwave** n 1 very short electromagnetic wave 2 oven which cooks food rapidly by use of microwaves

**mid** adj denoting middle part or position; ns **midday** noon; **midnight** 12 o'clock at night; adj, adv **midway** half way

**midden** n dunghill; pile of refuse

**middle** adj equidistant from extremes; halfway; n middle part or point; **middling** adj average, mediocre

**midst** prep in middle of; n central part

**midwife** n person who assists women in childbirth

**might**[1] *v aux* **1** expressing doubtful possibility **2** *pt of* **may**; **might have 1** could have **2** should have; ought to have

**might**[2] *n* power; strength

**mighty** *adj* **1** powerful **2** strong; *adv* **-ily**

> **mighty** *adj* **1** (powerful) almighty, forceful, great, strong, sturdy. **2** (strong) extreme, great, heavy, intense, powerful, severe, vigorous, violent

**migraine** *n* recurrent, severe headache

**migrate** *v* move from one region to another, *esp* as certain birds, etc; *adj*, *n* **migrant**; *n* **migration** act of migrating; periodical movement of birds, fishes, etc; body of individuals migrating; *adj* **migratory** having habit of migration; wandering

**mild** *adj* **1** gentle **2** temperate **3** not strong in flavor; *n* **mildness**

> **mild** *adj* **1** (gentle) docile, inoffensive, kind, meek, mild-mannered, placid, unassertive. **2** (temperate) balmy, clement, moderate, warm. **3** (not strong in flavor) bland, insipid, soft, subtle, unobtrusive, weak

**mildew** *n* mold growing on damp food, paper, etc

**mile** *n* measure of linear distance, 1,760 yards; *n* **mileage 1** distance traveled **2** cost of travel per mile **3** *fig* possible amount of use;

**milieu** *n Fr* environment; social surroundings; *pl* **-s** or **-x**

**military** *adj* of, suitable to, or performed by soldiers, or army; *n* army; *adj* **militant** willing to use aggressive means

**milk** *n* white fluid secreted by female mammals to feed their young; *v* **1** take milk from **2** extract money, information from

**mill** *n* **1** machine for grinding grain; building containing this **2** small machine for grinding pepper, coffee, etc. **3** works, factory for processing cotton, paper, etc; *v* grind, crush in mill; *n* **miller** person who works in a flour mill

**millennium** *n Lat* period of thousand years, *esp* that of Christ's second Advent; *adj* **millennial**

**millet** *n* small-seeded cereal grass, used as food

**milli-** *prefix Lat* one thousandth (part of weight, measure in metric system); as **milligram** thousandth part of gram; **millimeter**, etc

**milliner** *n* maker, seller of women's hats, ribbons, trimmings, etc

**million** *n*, *pron*, *det* 1000 thousands; *n* **millionaire** person possessing a million dollars, etc; very rich person; *fem* **-airess**; *adj*, *n*, *pron*, *det* **millionth**

**millipede** *n Lat* wormlike creature with many pairs of legs

**mime** *n* **1** art of communication by use of gestures and facial expression **2** entertainer using mime; *v* use this means of communicating

**mimic** *v* copy; *n* one who mimics; *n* **mimicry**

> **mimic** *v* ape, caricature, do an impression of, imitate, impersonate, mime, parody, resemble

**mince** *v* **1** cut, chop in small pieces **2** speak, behave affectedly; *n* finely chopped meat; *n* **mincemeat**, mixture of raisins, candied peel, suet, brandy, etc; **m.-pie** small covered pie containing mincemeat

**mind** *n* **1** intellectual faculties **2** memory **3** opinion; thought **4** intention; *v* **1** be careful of **2** look after **3** object to; *idm* **out of one's mind** causing anxiety; *adjs* **mindful** thoughtful; attentive; or **mindless** thoughtless; stupid (*adv* **-ly**; *n* **-ness**)

> **mind** *v* **1** (be careful of) avoid, be aware, be careful, be mindful, beware, look out, pay attention, take care, watch, watch out. **2** (look after) guard, keep, keep an eye on, protect, take care of, watch, watch over. **3** (object to) be bothered, be offended, be upset, care, disapprove, take offence

a b c d e f g h i j k l **m** n o p q r s t u v w x y z

**mine**[1] n 1 deep excavation from which coal, minerals (except stone) are dug 2 buildings, machinery connected with this 3 *fig* rich source of supply; v 1 sink mine 2 extract from mine; n **miner**

> **mine** n (excavation) colliery, deep mine, open-cast mine, pit, quarry, shaft, supply, tunnel, working

**mine**[2] n charge of explosives detonated in container; v lay mines in sea, on land; n **minefield** area containing mines

**mineral** n natural, inorganic substance found in earth; anything not animal, vegetable; anything dug up by mining; n **m. water** water with natural mineral salts taken for medicinal value or refreshment

**minestrone** n rich Italian soup of vegetables and pasta

**mingle** v 1 mix; blend 2 join, combine

**mini-** *prefix* small, short

**miniature** n, adj very small (thing)

**minim** n *mus* halfnote; adj **minimal** least possible (*adv* **-ly**); v **minimize** 1 reduce to smallest possible amount 2 underestimate; understate; n **minimum** smallest, least amount, lowest point possible; adj least possible

**mining** n extracting minerals from the earth

**minion** n 1 favorite 2 subordinate

**miniscule** adj very tiny

**minister** n 1 clergyperson 2 diplomat in charge of state department; v supply; help; serve; adj **ministerial**

**miniver** n white fur, *esp* ermine, used in robes of state

**mink** n animal of weasel family; its fur

**minor** adj unimportant; n person not legally of age; n **minority** 1 state of being a minor 2 smaller number

> **minor** adj inconsequential, inferior, insignificant, lesser, negligible, slight, small, trivial

**Minotaur** n fabled monster (half man, half bull)

**minster** n large church; cathedral

**minstrel** n medieval singer; itinerant singer, musician

**mint**[1] n place where money is legally coined; v make (money); adj in new and perfect condition

**mint**[2] n 1 peppermint 2 herb used to flavor meat, etc; adj **minty**

**minus** *prep*, adj less; deducted; subtracted; lacking; n minus sign (–)

**minute**[1] n 1 ⅟₆₀th of hour or degree 2 moment; v record in the minutes

**minutes** n pl written record of meeting

**minute**[2] adj tiny; adv **-ly**; n **-ness; minutiae** small details

> **minute** adj diminutive, microscopic, mini-, miniature, miniaturized, minuscule, small

**miracle** n abnormal event that cannot be explained; adj **miraculous**

> **miracle** n marvel, mystery, phenomenon, prodigy, wonder

**mirage** n optical illusion

> **mirage** n chimera, delusion, hallucination, illusion, image, trick of the light, vision

**mirror** n polished surface which reflects image; v reflect; **m.image** image in which left and right sides are symmetrically reversed

**mirth** n merriment

**mis-** *prefix* 1 *forming ns* bad, wrong, ill (*eg* **misadventure** ill luck; accident; **misconception** wrong understanding) 2 *forming ns* lack of (*eg* **misunderstanding**) 3 *forming vs and adjs* badly; wrongly (*eg vs* **misapprehend** understand wrongly (n **-hension**); **misappropriate** use wrongly; **misbehave**, **misuse**; adj **misguided** mistaken in judgment (*adv* **-ly**)

**miscarry** v 1 go wrong 2 give birth prematurely; n **miscarriage** 1 premature birth in which fetus cannot survive 2 failure (of plan, etc); n **miscarriage of justice** unjust legal decision

**miscellaneous** adj mixed; consisting of various kinds; n **miscellany** medley of various kinds

> **miscellaneous** adj assorted, different, disparate, diverse, jumbled, motley, odd, sundry, various

**mischief** n 1 harm; injury 2 annoying but amusing behavior by children

**mischievous** adj behaving in annoying but amusing way; adv **-ly**; n **-ness**

> **mischievous** adj bad, badly behaved, cheeky, disobedient, impish, misbehaving, naughty, playful, unruly

**misconstrue** v interpret wrongly

**misdemeanor** n misdeed; minor indictable offense

**miser** n one who hoards money and lives wretchedly; adj **-ly** mean with money

**miserable** adj 1 unhappy 2 squalid 3 scanty 4 pitiable

> **miserable** adj 1 (unhappy) blue, broken-hearted, crestfallen, depressed, despondent, down, downcast, downhearted, forlorn, gloomy, glum, low, melancholy, mournful, sad, sorrowful, wretched. 2 (squalid) awful, dilapidated, filthy, foul, seedy, shabby, sordid, sorry, uncomfortable, wretched

**misery** n 1 unhappiness 2 squalor

> **misery** n (unhappiness) anguish, depression, desolation, despair, despondency, distress, gloom, grief, hardship, heartache, hell, hopelessness, melancholy, pain, sadness, sorrow, suffering, torment, torture, woe

**misfit** n person not well suited to job or social situation

**misfortune** n bad luck

> **misfortune** n accident, adversity, blow, calamity, catastrophe, disaster, hardship, harm, loss, misadventure, mishap, setback, tragedy, trial, tribulation, trouble, woe

**misgiving** n doubt, mistrust, fear

**mishap** n accident; bad luck

**mislay** v **mislaying, mislaid** lose temporarily

**mislead** v **misleading, misled** deceive; lead astray; adj **misleading** deceptive

> **mislead** v beguile, bluff, confuse, delude, fool, give sb the wrong idea, give sb the wrong impression, hoodwink, lead sb up the garden path, misdirect, misguide, misinform, take sb for a ride, take sb in, throw sb off the scent, trick

**Miss** n title of unmarried woman, girl

**miss** v 1 fail to hit, meet, catch, notice 2 omit 3 feel want of; phr v **miss out** 1 omit 2 lose an opportunity; n failure to hit, secure, etc; adj **missing** 1 lost, mislaid 2 omitted

> **miss** v 1 (fail to hit, meet, catch, notice) avoid, be too late for, blunder, botch, bungle, dodge, err, escape, evade, fail, fall short, forego, lose, side-step, skip, slip up, steer clear of. 2 (omit) fail to include, fail to mention, overlook. 3 (feel want of) grieve for, lament, long for, need, pine for, want, yearn for

**misshapen** adj badly formed

> **misshapen** adj bent, contorted, crooked, crumpled, deformed, disfigured, distorted, gnarled, grotesque, knotted, malformed, out of shape, screwed up, tangled, twisted, warped

**missile** n object thrown or shot (usu as weapon)

> **missile** n bomb, grenade, projectile, rocket, shell, torpedo, weapon

**mission** n act of sending or being sent as representative; task assigned to sb; n **missionary** one sent on religious mission
**missive** n letter
**mist** n visible watery vapor; adj **misty** covered by mist; dim; obscure

> **mist** n cloud, condensation, fog, haze, smog, spray, steam, vapor

**mistake** v **mistaking, mistaken, mistook** make error in understanding; identify wrongly; be in error; n error

> **mistake** n blunder, boob, botch, clanger, fault, faux pas, gaffe, howler, inaccuracy, miscalculation, misjudgement, misprint, misspelling, misunderstanding, omission, oversight, slip, slip-up

**Mister** n title of address to man, written **Mr.**
**mistletoe** n evergreen parasitic plant
**mistress** n 1 a man's secret or illicit lover 2 woman with power or control 3 female head of household 4 female teacher
**mistrust** v not trust; n lack of trust; adj **-ful**

> **mistrust** v be skeptical, be suspicious, be unsure, be wary, disbelieve, doubt, fear, have doubts, have misgivings, have suspicions, question, suspect

**mite** n 1 very small insect 2 anything very small 3 very small child
**mitigate** v make less severe; n **-ation**
**miter** n 1 headdress worn by pope, bishops, etc 2 angled joint between two pieces of wood; v join with miter
**mitten** n glove with finger and thumb ends open; glove with no finger partitions

**mix** v 1 put together 2 associate socially; n result of mixing

> **mix** v 1 (put together) amalgamate, blend, coalesce, combine, cross, fuse, incorporate, intermingle, interweave, join, jumble up, merge, mingle, muddle, unite. 2 (associate socially) associate, fraternize, go out with, hobnob, keep company, mingle, socialize.

**mixed** adj 1 of different sorts 2 having contradictory elements 3 of both sexes (**m. school**)

> **mixed** adj 1 (of different sorts) assorted, diverse, heterogeneous, miscellaneous, motley, varied. 2 (contradictory) ambiguous, ambivalent, confused, muddled, uncertain, unsure

**mixer** n 1 person or machine for mixing 2 drink for making cocktails
**mixture** n 1 combination 2 act of mixing 3 substances mixed

> **mixture** n (combination) amalgam, amalgamation, association, blend, brew, collection, compound, cross, fusion, hotchpotch, medley, mishmash, mix, union, variety

**mix-up** n confusion; adj mixed-up
**ml** abbr 1 mile 2 milliliter(s)
**mm** abbr millimeter(s)
**mnemonic** n (phrase, rhyme, etc.) helping memory
**moan** n low, mournful sound expressing pain, groan; v utter moan

> **moan** v groan, sigh, wail, whimper, whine

**moat** n defensive trench (usu filled with water) round castle, etc
**mob** n lawless, rough crowd; excited mass of people; v **mobs, mobbing, mobbed** jostle, attack in mob; crowd round

**mob** n body, bunch, collection, drove, flock, gang, gathering, herd, hoard, host, mass, pack, press, rabble, swarm, throng

**mobile** adj moveable; moving, changing easily; n **mobility;** v **mobilize** call up (armed forces) for service; gather resources, forces; n **-ization**

**moccasin** n soft shoe (usu deerskin) of Native Americans

**mock** v ridicule; adj imitation; n **mockery** ridicule; travesty

**mock** v deride, insult, jeer, laugh at, make fun of, parody, poke fun at, rib inf, satirize, scoff, scorn, send up inf, sneer, taunt, tease
**mock** adj artificial, bogus, counterfeit, dummy, fake, false, feigned, forged, pretend, sham, simulated, spurious

**mockingbird** n American bird of thrush family, mimic of other bird calls

**mock-up** n 1 experimental model 2 lay-out of text, pictures, etc before printing

**modal auxiliary** n verb used in front of other verb to express possibility, obligation, etc (eg **can, may, must, shall, will**)

**mode** n method; style; fashion

**model** n 1 small copy 2 pattern 3 one who wears clothes to display them 4 one who poses for artist, etc; v 1 work into shape 2 wear clothes to display them

**model** n (small copy) copy, facsimile, image, imitation, miniature, mock-up, replica, representation

**modem** n comput device allowing fast transmission of data to other computers over distances

**moderate** adj not going to extremes; restrained; medium; v make, become less extreme or violent; n one holding moderate views; n **-ation**

**modern** adj of present or recent times; up-to-date; n **-ism** movement expressing present day views, methods, etc; v **modernize** make modern; adapt to present day usage (n **-ization**)

**modern** adj avant-garde, contemporary, current, fashionable, fresh, in, in vogue, latest, modish, new, newfangled, novel, present, progressive, recent, stylish, trendy, with it

**modest** adj 1 not boastful 2 moderate 3 chaste; n **modesty**

**modest** adj 1 (not boastful) bashful, coy, demure, diffident, discreet, humble, meek, quiet, reserved, restrained, reticent, retiring, self-effacing, shy, unassuming, unpretentious. 2 (moderate) limited, medium, normal, ordinary, small

**modify** v alter slightly; n **modification**

**modicum** n small amount or quantity

**modulate** v 1 regulate; adapt; vary 2 inflect (voice, etc) 3 mus change key; n **-ation**

**module** n 1 standard part used in construction 2 part of spacecraft that can operate independently 3 unit of study that is assessed independently of other units; adj **modular** composed of modules

**modus operandi** n Lat method of working

**mogul** n very powerful and wealthy person

**moist** adj damp; v **moisten;** n **moisture** dampness; condensed watery vapor

**moist** adj clammy, dank, dewy, humid, runny, steamy, watery, wet

**molar** n double grinding tooth

**molasses** n thick dark syrup drained from raw sugar

**mold**[1] n furry, fungal growth caused by dampness; v **molder** crumble, decay

**mold**[2] n 1 hollow shape for shaping or casting soft materials 2 fig character; v give shape to

**moldy** *adj* musty, decaying

> **moldy** *adj* blighted, decayed, fusty, mildewed, moldering, rotten, rotting

**mole**[1] *n* **1** small furry animal that lives in underground tunnels **2** spy working within an organization

**mole**[2] *n* dark-colored spot on skin

**molecule** *n* **1** simplest unit of a chemical compound composed of two or more atoms **2** very small particle; *adj* **-cular**

**molest** *v* trouble; pester; accost illegally

**mollify** *v* pacify, appease

**mollusk** *n* soft-bodied animal usually having hard shell (*eg* snail, oyster)

**mollycoddle** *v* pamper

**molt** *v* shed feathers, fur, etc, periodically; *n* act or time of moulting; *n* **molting**

**molten** *adj* (of metal, rock) melted

**molto** *adv mus* much, very

**moment** *n* **1** brief period of time **2** importance

> **moment** *n* (brief time) flash, instant, jiffy, minute, second, twinkling of an eye

**momentary** *adj* brief

> **momentary** *adj* ephemeral, fleeting, hasty, passing, quick, short, short-lived, transient, transitory

**momentous** *adj* of great importance

**momentum** *n* impetus; increasing force

**monarch** *n* sovereign; supreme ruler; *ns* **monarchy** state ruled by monarch; **-ist** supporter of monarchy

> **monarch** *n* emperor, empress, king, potentate, prince, princess, queen

**monastery** *n* house lived in by religious community; *adj* **monastic** of monastery; of monks, nuns

**Monday** *n* second day of week

**monetarism** *n econ* theory that control of money supply creates stable economy; *n, adj* **-ist**

**money** *n* coins; paper money; any form of credit usable as payment

> **money** *n* bread *inf*, capital, cash, currency, dough *inf*, finance, funds, income, means, resources, revenue, savings

**mongoose** *n* small Indian animal that kills snakes; *pl* **-gooses** or **-geese**

**mongrel** *n* animal (*esp* dog) of mixed breed; hybrid; *adj* of mixed breeding or origin

**monitor** *n* **1** instrument or device for observing, checking **2** one who warns, advises **3** school prefect **4** master screen in TV studio **5** television used to display image from computer; *v* check the progress of

**monk** *n* member of religious order, living under vows of poverty, chastity, etc

**monkey** *n* **1** any of the primates (other than humans or lemurs), *esp* long-tailed **2** *coll* mischievous child

**mono-** *prefix* single, alone

**monochrome** *n* **1** with images in black, white, and shades of gray **2** using shades of one color only; *adj* **monochromatic**

**monogamy** *n* practice of marrying only one partner at a time

**monoglot** *adj* able to speak one language only

**monogram** *n* single figure made of two or more interwoven initials

**monolingual** *adj* monoglot

**monolith** *n* single block of stone as monument

**monolog** *n* speech by single actor

**mononucleosis** *n* glandular fever

**monopoly** *n* exclusive right of trading in specified commodity; *v* **monopolize** engross, enjoy to exclusion of others

**monosyllable** word of one syllable; *adj* **-syllabic**

**monotheism** *n* belief in only one God

**monotonous** *adj* lacking in variety; *n* **monotony** lack of variety; tediousness

**monotonous** *adj* boring, colorless, dreary, droning, dull, flat, humdrum, mindnumbing, plodding, repetitive, soporific, tedious, tiresome, toneless, unchanging, unexciting, uninteresting

**Monsieur** *n Fr* form of address to French-speaking man (*pl* **Messieurs**)

**monsoon** *n* seasonal wind of Indian Ocean; rainy season in India

**monster** *n* 1 person, animal, thing of abnormal shape or huge size 2 abnormally wicked, cruel person

**monstrous** *adj* 1 like a monster 2 shocking 3 hideous; *n* **monstrosity** 1 freak 2 badly made, hideous object

**montage** *n Fr* 1 final selection and arrangement of images in film 2 two or more pictures imposed on single background

**month** *n* one of twelve parts into which year is divided; period of moon's revolution; *adj* **monthly** occurring once a month; *n* magazine published monthly

**monument** *n* tombstone, building, statue, etc erected as memorial; *adj* **-al** 1 of, serving as monument 2 massive; enormous

**monument** *n* cenotaph, gravestone, mausoleum, memorial, obelisk, shrine

**mood** *n* 1 state of mind 2 angry or sullen state of mind; *adj* **moody**

**mood** *n* (state of mind) disposition, frame of mind, humor, inclination, spirit, temper

**moon** *n* 1 earth's satellite 2 satellite of another planet

**moor**[1] *n* tract of open country, usually hilly and heather-clad; *n* **m.-hen** water hen

**moor**[2] *v* fasten, secure (ship) by cables, chains etc; *n pl* **-ings** place where vessel is moored; cables, buoys etc by which it is secured

**moose** *n* huge N American deer with large antlers

**mop** *n* bundle of yarn on long handle; *v* **mops, mopping, mopped** wipe with mop

**mope** *v* be low-spirited, depressed

**moped** *n* small low-powered motorbike

**moral** *adj* relating to generally accepted ideas of right and wrong; virtuous; of right conduct; *n* lesson taught by experience, fable; *pl* **-s** principles of right and wrong conduct; *n* **morality** good moral conduct; virtue; *v* **moralize** draw moral lesson from, think on moral aspect; *n* **moralist** teacher of, writer on morals

**moral** *adj* decent, ethical, fair, good, honest, irreproachable, just, law-abiding, noble, principled, proper, pure, respectable, responsible, righteous, upright, upstandings

**morale** *n* mental state, *esp* regarding courage

**moratorium** *n* legal authorization to delay or defer payment of debt, etc

**morbid** *adj* showing abnormal interest in death and gloomy things

**morbid** *adj* brooding, ghastly, ghoulish, gloomy, grim, grisly, gruesome, hideous, horrid, macabre, sick *inf*, somber, unhealthy, unwholesome

**mordant** *adj* 1 sarcastic 2 corrosive; 3 (of dyeing) serving to fix colors

**more** *adj* greater in quantity, extent, etc; *comp* of **many, much;** *adv* in addition, to greater degree; *adv* **moreover** besides

**more** *adj* added, additional, extra, fresh, further, increased, new, other, renewed, spare, supplementary

**morello** *n* dark red, sour cherry

**mores** *n pl* customs held to be typical of social group

**morgue** *n Fr* mortuary

**moribund** *adj* dying, decaying

**Mormon** *n* member of Church of Latter-Day Saints, founded by Joseph Smith

a
b
c
d
e
f
g
h
i
j
k
l
**m**
n
o
p
q
r
s
t
u
v
w
x
y
z

**morning** *adj* first part of day, from dawn until noon

**morocco** *n* fine, flexible leather

**morose** *adj* surly; sullen; gloomy

**morphine** *n* addictive narcotic alkaloid of opium, used to relieve pain

**morphology** *n* 1 *bio* (study of) form and structure of organisms 2 *ling* (study of) changing forms of wrods according to grammatical function; *adj* **-ological**; *n* **-ologist**

**morris dance** *n* English folk dance for men in costume and bells

**Morse code** *n* system of telegraphic signals, consisting of dots and dashes

**morsel** *n* small piece; fragment

**morsel** *n* bit, bite, crumb, grain, mouthful, nibble, piece, scrap, segment, slice, titbit

**mortal** *adj* 1 liable to die 2 causing death; *n* human being; *n* **mortality** 1 condition of being subject to death 2 deathrate

**mortal** *adj* 1 (liable to die) earthly, ephemeral, fleshly, human, temporal, transient, worldly. 2 (causing death) deadly, fatal, killing, lethal, terminal

**mortar** *n* 1 vessel in which substances are pounded 2 short-barrelled cannon 3 cement of lime, sand, water for holding bricks, etc together; *n* **mortarboard** square flat college graduation cap

**mortgage** *n* conveyance of property for debt; *v* convey on mortgage

**mortify** *v* humiliate; *n* **mortification**

**mortise, mortice** *n* hole cut in piece of wood etc to receive tenon; *v* join by, make mortise in; *n* **mortise lock** one embedded in door

**mortuary** *n* building where corpses are kept before burial

**mosaic** *n* pattern made by fitting together small pieces of colored marble, stone, etc

**Moselle** *n* dry white wine from Moselle valley

**Moslem** *see* **Muslim**

**mosque** *n* Muslim temple

**mosquito** *n* biting gnat; *pl* **-oes** or **-os**

**moss** *n* low-growing tufted plant found on moist surfaces; lichen; *adj* **mossy** covered with moss

**most** *adj* greatest in number, quantity, degree; *sup* of **many, much**; *adv* to greatest degree; *adv* **mostly** generally

**motel** *n* hotel with adjacent parking

**moth** *n* night-flying insect, related to butterfly; *adj* **m.-eaten** 1 damaged by moth 2 *fig* shabby

**mother** *n* 1 female parent 2 head of convent, nunnery; *n* **m.-in-law** mother of wife or husband; *adj* **motherly**; *n* **-liness**

**motif** *n Fr* recurrent theme, *esp* in music; ornamental needlework pattern

**motile** *adj* (of organisms) capabale of moving spontaneously; *n* **motility**

**motion** *n* 1 movement 2 proposal put to meeting 3 gesture 4 *leg* application for ruling; *v* indicate; makes gesture towards

**motionless** *adj* not moving (*adv* **-ly**)

**motionless** *adj* at rest, frozen, halted, immobile, inert, lifeless, paralyzed, static, stationary, still, stopped, unmoving

**motivate** *v* give sb desire to do sth; *n* **motivation**

**motivate** *v* activate, arouse, cause, drive, encourage, galvanize, goad, impel, incite, induce, influence, inspire, instigate, lead, move, persuade, prod, prompt, provoke, push, set, spur, stimulate, stir, urge

**motive** *n* cause; incentive; that which influences behavior or action

**motive** *n* basis, grounds, inducement, influence, inspiration, intention, lure, motivation, occasion, prompting, provocation, purpose, push, rationale, reason, spur, stimulus

**mot juste** n Fr exact word or phrase
**motley** adj various colors; mixed ingredients
**motocross** n motorcycle racing over rough ground
**motor** n machine supplying motive power; engine; v travel or go at a steady pace; ns **motorcade** procession of cars; **m.cycle** (also **m.bike**) two-wheeled vehicle with engine; **m.cyclist** rider of this; **motoring** driving; **motorist** driver; **m. scooter** small engine-driven vehicle, with two/three wheels
**mottled** adj marked with irregular patches of light and dark colors

> **mottled** adj blotchy, dappled, flecked, freckled, marbled, marked, speckled, splotchy, spotted, streaked, variegated

**motto** n **-oes** or **-os** short phrase expressing maxim, rule of conduct, esp on coat-of-arms

> **motto** n adage, catch-phrase, dictum, epigram, maxim, precept, proverb, rule, saying, slogan, watchword

**mound** n raised heap of earth, stones, etc

> **mound** n bank, dune, heap, hillock, hummock, knoll, pile, rise, stack

**mount** v **1** climb **2** get on horseback **3** increase **4** provide frame, setting for (picture, etc) **5** organize (campaign, exhibition); n **1** that on which thing is mounted; **2** gun-carriage **3** mountain; high hill

> **mount** v **1** (climb) ascend, go up, rise, scale. **2** (get on horseback) climb on, get astride, get on, jump on. **3** (increase) accumulate, build, escalate, expand, grow, intensify, multiply, pile up, swell

**mountain** n large hill; n **mountaineer** dweller in, expert climber of mountains; idm **make a mountain out of a molehill** exaggerate the importance, eg of a problem

> **mountain** n alp, crest, height, mount, peak, pinnacle, range, sierra, summit

**mountainous** adj very high; enormous
**mountebank** n charletan, quack
**mourn** v grieve for; n **mourner**; n **mourning 1** grief, esp for death **2** clothes worn as sign of such grief **3** time these are worn

> **mourn** v bemoan, bewail, cry for, feel the loss of, lament, miss, pine for, regret, sorrow, wail, weep

**mournful** adj feeling or causing grief

> **mournful** adj depressing, dismal, distressing, doleful, gloomy, heart-breaking, heart-rending, melancholy, miserable, painful, piteous, pitiful, plaintive, sad, sorrowful, tragic, unhappy, woeful

**mouse** n small rodent; fig shy person (pl **mice**); v catch, hunt mice
**moustache** n hair on upper lip (also **mustache**)
**mouth** n **1** opening in animal's head by which it eats and utters sounds **2** opening; outlet; v speak with exaggerated lip and jaw movement
**move** v **1** change position of **2** affect feelings **3** set into motion **4** make formal proposal; n **1** movement **2** fig device **3** step **4** change of abode or place of work; adj **movable**

> **move** v **1** (change position) budge, carry, change places, go, shift, stir, take, transport. **2** (affect feelings) affect, arouse, fire, impassion, incite, induce, inspire, lead, motivate, persuade, prompt, provoke, push, rouse, spur, stimulate, stir, touch

**movement** n **1** act, fact, process of moving **2** moving part of mechanism, esp of watch **3** division of musical composition

a b c d e f g h i j k l **m** n o p q r s t u v w x y z

**movie** *n coll* cinematic film; *pl* **-s** cinema

**moving** *adj* 1 arousing emotions, *esp* sympathy, sadness 2 in motion

> **moving** *adj* (arousing emotion) affecting, emotional, emotive, heart-rending, heart-warming, inspiring, pathetic, poignant, powerful, rousing, stirring, touching

**mow** *v* **mowing, mowed or mown** cut down (grass, etc); *fig* **m. down** kill indiscriminately; *n* **mower** mowing machine, one who mows

**MP** *abbr* 1 Member of Parliament 2 (member of) Military Police

**mpg** *abbr* miles per gallon

**mph** *abbr* miles per hour

**Mr.** *abbr* Mister (form of address to a man)

**Mrs.** *n* form of address to a married woman

**Ms.** *n* form of address to a woman (married or unmarried)

**MS** *abbr* 1 manuscript 2 multiple sclerosis

**MSc** *abbr* Master of Science

**much** *adj* great in quantity; *n* great deal; *adv* greatly, nearly

**muck** *n* 1 filth; dirt 2 manure 3 garbage; *phr vs* **muck about/around** *coll* behave in a silly, inconsiderate way; waste time; *adj* **mucky** dirty

**mucus** *n* slimy, viscous secretion of mucous membrane; *adj* **mucous** secreting mucus

**mud** *n* very wet, moist earth

> **mud** *n* clay, dirt, mire, ooze, silt, slime, sludge, soil

**muddle** *v* 1 confuse 2 bungle; *n* disorder

> **muddle** *v* (confuse) bemuse, bewilder, confound, daze, disorient, disorientate, perplex, puzzle
> **muddle** *n* chaos, clutter, confusion, disarray, jumble, mess, mix-up, shambles *inf*, tangle

**muddy** *adj* 1 covered in mud 2 full of mud; *n* **muddiness**

**muddy** *adj* 1 (covered in mud) caked, dirty, filthy, messy, mucky. 2 (full of mud) boggy, marshy, slimy, sludgy, spongy, waterlogged

**muesli** *n* Swiss breakfast food of mixed cereals, nuts, dried fruits, etc

**muffin** *n* quick bread of egg batter baked in muffin tin

**muffle** *v* wrap with covering, for warmth or to deaden sound

**muffled** *adj* quiet, not distinct

> **muffled** *adj* dampened, deadened, dull, faint, hushed, indistinct, muted, smothered, stifled, suppressed, unclear

**mug** *n* 1 drinking cup 2 *sl* face 3 simpleton; *v* **mugs, mugging, mugged** *sl* rob with violence, in public place (*ns* **mugger, mugging**)

**muggy** *adj* warm and damp

> **muggy** *adj* clammy, close, humid, oppressive, steamy, sticky, stuffy, sultry

**mulberry** *n* tree with purple edible berries

**mule** *n* 1 hybrid between horse and donkey 2 stubborn person 3 slipper

**mull** *v* heat (wine, etc) with spices

**mullet** *n* edible seafish

**mulligatawny** *n* curried chicken soup

**multi-** *prefix* many

**multilateral** *adj* with many participants; *adv* **-ly**

**multimedia** *adj* using several types of media

**multiple** *adj* having many parts; *n* number which contains another number an exact number of times; *n* **multiplicity** great number

**multiple sclerosis** *n* chronic disease of central nervous system resulting in loss of motor control, paralysis (*also* **MS**)

**multiply** *v* 1 add (number) to itself specified number of times 2 increase in number 3 breed; *n* **-plication**

**multiply** *v* (increase in number)
accumulate, breed, expand, extend,
proliferate, propagate, reproduce, spread

**multitask** *comput adj* able to carry out several
diverse tasks simultaneously
**multitude** *n* great number; crowd of people;
*adj* **multitudinous**

**multitude** *n* army, assembly, congregation,
crowd, horde, host, legion, mass, mob,
sea, swarm, throng

**mum** *adj* silent
**mumble** *v* speak indistinctly; mutter
**mumbo-jumbo** *n* meaningless ritual or words
**mummy** *n* embalmed body, *esp* of ancient
Egyptian; *v* **mummify**; *adj* **mummified**
**mumps** *n pl* painful contagious disease causing
inflammation of patroid and salivary glands
**munch** *v* chew noisily and vigorously
**munchkin** *n* small, elflike person
**mundane** *adj* dull
**municipal** *adj* belonging to affairs of
boroughs, city, town; *n* **municipality** town,
borough, etc enjoying local government;
local authority
**munitions** *n pl* military stores
**mural** *n* wall-painting
**murder** *n* unlawful killing; *v* kill thus

**murder** *n* assassination, bloodshed,
butchery, carnage, homicide, killing,
manslaughter, massacre, slaughter, slaying
**murder** *v* assassinate, bump off *inf*, butcher,
destroy, dispatch, do away with *inf*, do in,
kill, massacre, put to death, slaughter, slay

**murderer** *n* person who kills another
unlawfully; *fem* **murderess**
**murderous** *adj* intending to murder; deadly
**murky** *adj* dark, cloudy
**murmur** *v* 1 speak in low voice 2 make low,
continuous sound 3 grumble; *n* act, sound of
murmuring

**murmur** *v* (speak in low voice) breathe,
grumble, mumble, mutter, purr, speak in
an undertone, whisper

**Murphy's law** *n coll* fatalistic outlook –
"anything that can go wrong, will go wrong"
**muscat** *n* raisin; musky grape; *n* **muscatel**
muscat; sweet wine made from it
**muscle** *n* elastic fibrous tissue on body, by
which movement is made possible; *fig* bodily
force, strength; *adj* **muscle-bound** with
muscles strained and inelastic through
overexercise
**muscular** *adj* 1 having strong muscles
2 of muscle

**muscular** *adj* (having strong muscles)
athletic, beefy *inf*, brawny, burly, hefty,
hunky, lusty, mighty, powerful, robust,
sinewy, stalwart, strapping, strong, sturdy,
tough, vigorous, well-built

**muscular dystrophy** *n* long-term illness
causing wasting muscles
**muse**[1] *v* think carefully about sth

**muse** *v* brood, cogitate, consider,
contemplate, daydream, deliberate, dream,
meditate, mull over, ponder, reflect,
ruminate, speculate, think, weigh, wonder

**muse**[2] *n* 1 *cap* one of nine goddesses
associated with the arts, sciences, and
literature 2 *fig* poetic inspiration
**museum** *n* collection of natural, scientific,
historical, or artistic objects; building
housing such collection
**mush** *n* soft, pulpy mass; *adj* **mushy** soft
**mushroom** *n* quick-growing edible fungus;
*v fig* grow, expand rapidly
**music** *n* 1 art of producing rhythmical,
melodious sounds 2 written or printed score
of musical composition 3 *fig* pleasing sound;
*n* **m.-stand** wooden or metal frame to hold
printed music for player during performance

a
b
c
d
e
f
g
h
i
j
k
l
m
n
o
p
q
r
s
t
u
v
w
x
y
z

**musical** *adj* 1 tuneful 2 of, relating to music; *n* **m. chairs** party game in which players compete for chairs to sit on when the music stops

musical *adj* (tuneful) dulcet, harmonious, lilting, melodious, sweet-sounding

**musk** *n* strong scent obtained from male muskdeer; plant with similar scent; *adj* **-y**; *ns* **m.deer** small hornless deer; **m.-ox** Arctic ox; **m.-rat** N American water rat

**Muslim** *n* follower of the religion of Islam, founded by Muhammad; *adj* of, belonging to Islam; *also* **Moslem**

**muslin** *n* fine cotton fabric

**mussel** *n* edible bivalve mollusk

**must**[1] *n* new unfermented wine

**must**[2] *v aux* expressing compulsion, obligation, certainty; *pt* **had to**; no *pp*; *n coll* an essential

**mustang** *n* 1 American wild or semiwild prairie horse 2 an officer (as in US Navy) risen from the ranks

**mustard** *n* hot, pungent powder made from pounded seeds of mustard plant, used as condiment; *n* **m. gas** poisonous irritant gas

**muster** *v* assemble, summon; *n* assembly of troops, etc for inspection, etc

**mustn't** *contracted form of* must not

**musty** *adj* moldy; *n* **-iness**

musty *adj* airless, damp, dank, decaying, fusty, mildewed, smelly, stale, stuffy, unused

**mutable** *adj* liable to change

**mutate** *v* change, *esp* genetically

**mutation** *n* 1 change 2 sudden genetic change

**mutatis mutandis** *adv Lat* after making the appropriate changes

**mute** *adj* dumb, silent; *n* 1 person unable to speak 2 device used to soften tone or reduce sound of musical instrument; *adj* **muted** muffled (sound)

mute *adj* speechless, unspoken, voiceless, wordless

**mutilate** *v* maim; *n* **mutilation**

mutilate *v* butcher, cripple, damage, deface, disable, disfigure, dismember, hack, lame, mangle

**mutiny** *n pl* **-ies**; revolt against authority, *esp* in armed forces; *pl* **-ies**; *v* **mutinies, mutinying, mutinied** revolt

mutiny *n* defiance, disobedience, insubordination, insurgence, insurrection, rebellion, resistance, revolt, revolution, riot, rising, sedition, subversion, uprising

**mutinous** *adj* refusing to obey orders

mutinous *n* defiant, disobedient, insubordinate, rebellious, restive, revolutionary, riotous, seditious, subversive, uncontrollable, ungovernable, unmanageable, unruly

**mutt** *n coll* mongrel dog

**mutter** *v* speak indistinctly in low voice; grumble

mutter *v* complain, grumble, mumble, murmur, rumble, talk under your breath

**mutton** *n* flesh of sheep used as food; *ns* **muttonchops** long wide sideburns (*also* **m.-chop whiskers**); **m.-head** *coll* stupid person

**mutual** *adj* 1 performed by joint action 2 reciprocal 3 common to both

**muu-muu** *n* Hawaiian loose, long dress

**muzzle** *n* 1 mouth and nose of animal 2 cover for these to prevent biting 3 mouth of gun; *v* 1 put muzzle on 2 impose silence on

**muzzy** *adj* daze, vague, fuddled; *n* **-ness**

**MW** *abbr* megawatt(s)

**mW** *abbr* milliwatt(s)

**my** *poss adj* belonging to **me**

**myalgic encephalomyelitis** *n* viral disease affecting nervous system, with long-lasting effect of fatigue and impaired muscular control (*also* **ME** *or* **post-viral syndrome**)

**mycology** *n* study of fungi and mushrooms

**myopia** *n* near-sightedness; *adj* **myopic**

**myriad** *n* ten thousand; endless number; *adj* countless

**myrrh** *n* strong-smelling resin used in perfumes and as incense

**myrtle** *n* evergreen, flowering shrub

**myself** *pron emphatic form of* **I**, **me**; *reflex form of* **I**, **me**

**mysterious** *adj* hard to understand or explain; *adv* **mysteriously**

> **mysterious** *adj* abstruse, baffling, bizarre, cryptic, curious, dark, enigmatic, furtive, hidden, inexplicable, inscrutable, mystifying, obscure, perplexing, puzzling, secret, strange, uncanny, unexplained, unfathomable, unknown, weird

**mystery** *n pl* **-ies** 1 anything secret, unknown, unexplained 2 secret rite 3 obscurity

> **mystery** *n* (anything secret) conundrum, enigma, paradox, problem, puzzle, riddle

**mystic** *n* having inner, secret meanings; esoteric; *n* one who believes in attainment, through contemplation, of inaccessible truths; *adj* **-al**; *n* **-ism**

**mystify** *v* puzzle; *n* **mystification**

> **mystify** *v* baffle, bemuse, bewilder, confound, confuse, elude, escape, flummox, nonplus, perplex, stump *inf*

**mystique** *n Fr* elusive quality of sth much admired but not properly understood

**myth** *n* 1 fictitious story or legend 2 imaginary person or thing

**myth** *adj* 1 (fictitious story or legend) allegory, fable, fairy-tale, legend, parable, saga, story, tale. 2 (imaginary person or thing) delusion, fabrication, falsehood, fiction, figment of sb's imagination, invention, misconception, untruth

**mythical** *adj* 1 of myths and fairy-tales 2 fictitious

> **mythical** *adj* 1 (of myths and fairy-tales) allegorical, fabled, fabulous, fantastical, legendary, mythic, mythological. 2 (fictitious) fabricated, false, fantasy, imaginary, invented, made-up, nonexistent, pretended, unreal, untrue

**mythology** *n* collection, body of myths concerning ancient religious belief; *adj* **-ological**

a b c d e f g h i j k l m n o p q r s t u v w x y z

**nab** *v* **nabs, nabbing, nabbed** *sl* catch suddenly; arrest

**nadir** *n* point opposite zenith; lowest point

**nag**[1] *n* small riding pony; horse

**nag**[2] *v* **nags, nagging, nagged** find fault persistently; scold; *fig* give constant pain

> **nag** *v* annoy, badger, be on sb's back, carp, goad, go on at, harass, harp on, hassle, hector, henpeck, pester, plague, worry

**naiad** *n* waternymph

**nail** *v* **1** horny plate at end of fingers and toes **2** talon **3** metal spike for fixing things together; *v* fix, fasten to, with nail; *adj* **n.-biting** intensely exciting

**naive, naïve** *adj Fr* natural; foolishly simple; *n* **naïveté, naïvety**

> **naive** *adj* artless, childlike, credulous, green, guileless, gullible, inexperienced, ingenuous, innocent, open, simple, trusting, unsophisticated, unsuspicious, unwary, unworldly

**naked** *adj* unclothed, bare; *n* **-ness**

> **naked** *adj* exposed, in your birthday suit, in the altogether, in the buff, in the nude, in the raw, nude, stark-naked, stripped, uncovered, undressed

**name** *n* **1** word by which person, thing, idea is known or called **2** reputation **3** lineage; family; *v* **1** give name to; identify by name **2** appoint; *adv* **-ly**; that is to say

> **name** *n* **1** (word by which sth is known) appellation, epithet, label, nickname, tag, term, title. **2** (reputation) distinction, eminence, esteem, fame, honor, note, prestige, prominence, repute, renown
> **name** *v* **1** (give name to) baptize, call, christen, designate, dub, entitle, label, nickname, style, tag, term. **2** (appoint) choose, commission, delegate, designate, elect, identify, nominate, pick, select, specify

**nanny** *n* child's nurse; **n. goat** female goat

**nano-** *prefix* **1** thousand millionth part of (*eg* **nanometer, nanosecond**) **2** of microscopically small objects and measurements (*eg* **nanotechnology**)

**nap**[1] *n* downy surface of cloth

**nap**[2] *n* short sleep; *v* doze

> **nap** *n* doze, forty winks *inf*, rest, siesta, sleep, snooze *inf*

**nape** *n* back of the neck

**napkin** *n* small cloth used at meals to protect clothes and wipe fingers, lips

**narc** *n sl* government narcotics agent

**narcosis** *n* unconsciousness induced by drugs

**narcotic** *n* drug causing sleep, insensibility; *adj* inducing sleep, etc

**narrate** *v* relate; tell story of; *ns* **-ation, -ative** story; account

**narrator** *n* person who narrates story, gives commentary, etc

> **narrator** *n* author, chronicler, commentator, reporter, storyteller, writer

**narrow** *adj* of small breadth in proportion to length; *v* become, cause to become narrow; *adv* **-ly** closely; only just

**narrow** *adj* close, confined, cramped, fine, limited, meager, pinched, restricted, scanty, slender, slim, squeezed, thin, tight

**narrow-minded** *adj* prejudiced, bigoted

**narrow-minded** *adj* biased, conservative, hidebound, inflexible, insular, intolerant, old-fashioned, parochial, petty, reactionary, rigid, small-minded, strait-laced

**nasal** *adj* of or in nose; *n* nasal sound (phonetics)

**nasty** *adj* 1 offensive to taste or smell; disgusting 2 disagreeable; *n* **-iness**

**nasty** *adj* 1 (offensive) awful, disgusting, filthy, foul, horrible, horrid, nauseating, odious, repellent, repugnant, repulsive, revolting, sickening, unpleasant, vile. 2 (disagreeable) bitchy, catty, cruel, horrible, horrid, malicious, mean, spiteful, unkind, unpleasant, vicious

**natal** *adj* of, at, belonging to birth

**natation** *n* act of swimming, floating; *adjs* **natant** floating, as of plants; **natatory** pertaining to swimming

**nation** *n* large group of people having common language, culture, etc, and living in one area under one government; *adj* **nationwide** covering the entire country

**nation** *n* country, domain, kingdom, land, people, population, power, realm, republic, society, state

**national** *adj* of, common to a nation (*n* citizen of a state); *ns* **n. debt** amount owed by country to other countries; **n. park** conservation area under care of the state; *adv* **-ally**

**nationalism** *n* 1 pride in one's native country 2 political movement for independence (*n* **-ist**; *adj* **-ist**)

**nationality** *n* status of belonging to

**nationalize** *v* take under government control (*adj* **-ized**; *n* **-ization**)

**native** *adj* relating to the place of one's birth; *n* person born in; *adj* place; original inhabitant

**nativity** *n* birth, *esp* of Christ

**NATO** *abbr* North Atlantic Treaty Organization

**natty** *adj coll* neat and smart in appearance; *adv* **-ily**

**natural** *adj* 1 arising from the physical world; not artificial (**n. gas**) 2 uncultivated; wild 3 normal (**n. manner**) 4 innate (**n. talent**); *adv* **-ly** 1 in; *adj* natural way 2 of course; *v* normal **naturalize** give officially changed nationality to immigrant (*adj* **-ized**; *n* **-ization**)

**natural** *adj* 1 (not artificial) authentic, genuine, real, sincere, spontaneous, unaffected, unfeigned. 2 (normal) common, logical, ordinary, predictable, regular, routine, standard, typical, understandable, unsurprising, usual. 3 (innate) characteristic, congenital, god-given, hereditary, inborn, inbred, inherited, instinctive, intuitive, native

**nature** *n* 1 everything created (not manmade) in the world 2 *esp cap* forces controlling events in the physical world 3 character 4 primitive state; *idm* **second nature** action performed (as if) by instinct

**nature** *n* 1 (created world) ecology, landscape, Mother Nature, natural history, scenery, the countryside, the earth, the environment, the universe, the world, wildlife. 2 (character) disposition, make-up, mood, outlook, personality, temperament, traits

**naturopath** *n* expert in treatment of illness by use of herbal remedies, natural dieting, and natural healing; *adj* **-pathic**

a b c d e f g h i j k l m **n** o p q r s t u v w x y z

**naught** n nothingness; nonexistence; arithmetical symbol nought (0) or zero

**naughty** adj 1 mischievous, disobedient 2 immoral; n **-tiness**

> **naughty** adj (disobedient) bad, badly behaved, defiant, delinquent, disruptive, impolite, mischievous, rascally, rude, stubborn, undisciplined, unmanageable, unruly, wicked, willful

**nausea** n 1 sickness 2 disgust; v **nauseate** sicken; disgust; adj **nauseous** causing, feeling nausea; loathsome

**nautical** adj pertaining to ships, sailors, etc; n **n. mile** unit of distance at sea, 6,080 ft (1,852 meters)

**nautilus** n mollusk with pearly shell

**naval** adj of, by the navy

**nave** n central part of church

**navel** n rounded depression in abdomen, umbilicus

**navigate** v 1 cause to sail or travel on set course 2 direct ship or aircraft; ns **-ation** act, science of navigating; **-ator** one skilled in science of navigation; adj **navigable**

> **navigate** v 1 (travel) cross, cruise, journey, sail, sail across, voyage 2 (direct ship) captain, drive, handle, maneuver, pilot, skipper, steer

**navy** n cap all warships of state; fleet; naval personnel; n, adj **n.blue** (of) dark blue (color)

**nay** arch no (used in dissent or refusal)

**Nazi** n member of Hitler's National Socialist party

**NB** abbr Lat nota bene (note well)

**NBC** abbr National Broadcasting Company

**NCO** abbr noncommissioned officer, or noncom

**Neanderthal man** n Stone Age man

**neapolitan** n 1 (ice cream) in different colored, flavored layers 2 cap (inhabitant) of Naples

**near** adv close to; not far from; adj 1 close in relationship, degree 2 about to come, happen; v approach; idm **near by** close at hand (adj **nearby**); adj **near-sighted** short-sighted

> **near** adj 1 (close) accessible, adjacent, adjoining, at close quarters, beside, bordering, close by, connected, handy, nearby, neighboring, next-door, touching, within reach. 2 (about to come, happen) approaching, coming, forthcoming, imminent, impending, in the offing, looming, next, round the corner

**nearly** adv almost

> **nearly** adv about, all but, approaching, approximately, around, as good as, just about, not quite, practically, roughly, virtually

**neat** adj 1 trim; well-kept 2 skillful 3 (of alcoholic liquor) pure, undiluted 4 (of utterances) apt; n **neatness**

> **neat** adj 1 (trim) accurate, clean, dapper, fastidious, methodical, meticulous, orderly, organized, precise, shipshape, smart, spick and span, spruce, straight, systematic, tidy, uncluttered, well-groomed, well-kept, well-turned-out. 2 (skillful) agile, dainty, deft, dexterous, elegant, graceful, nimble, practiced, precise, stylish. 3 (undiluted) pure, straight, undiluted

**nebula** n luminous cloudlike patch in sky; cluster of stars; adj **nebulous** 1 cloudy, misty 2 fig vague, indefinite

**necessary** adj inevitable; indispensable; obligatory; n that which is essential or indispensable; n **necessity** 1 compulsion; anything inevitable because of natural law 2 poverty; want; v **necessitate** render necessary; compel; adj **necessitous** poor, destitute

**necessary** *adj* compulsory, essential, imperative, important, mandatory, needed, required, vital

**neck** *n* 1 part of body joining head to trunk 2 narrow connecting part 3 isthmus; *ns* **neckcloth** tie; **necklace** string of jewels, beads, gold chain, etc worn around neck
**necropolis** *n* large ancient cemetery
**nectarine** *n* variety of peach with smooth skin
**nectary** *n* gland that yields nectar
**nectary** *n* gland that yields nectar
**neé** *adj Fr* (*fem*) born (with the surname)
**need** *n* 1 that which is required; necessity 2 poverty; want; *v* 1 require 2 have to; *adjs* **needful** necessary; **needless** unnecessary; **needy** poor; in want

**need** *n* 1 (sth required) demand, essential, necessity, obligation, requirement, want. 2 (poverty) deprivation, destitution, distress
**need** *v* (require) be short of, be without, call for, demand, lack, want

**needle** *n* 1 small sharp instrument with eye to take thread, for sewing 2 pointed end of hypodermic syringe 3 thin rod of metal, plastic, etc used in knitting 4 magnetized bar of compass 5 leaf of pine or fir; *ns* **-point** fine embroidery fo a pattern onto canvas; **-woman** skillful woman sewer; seamstress; **-work** sewing, embroidery
**ne'er-do-well** *n* improvident good-for-nothing
**nefarious** *adj* unlawful, wicked
**negate** *v* deny; nullify; *n* **-ation** contradictions, denial
**negative** *adj* 1 expressing denial 2 lacking in positive qualities 3 *phot* reversing light and dark; *n* word, statement which denies, refuses, forbids; *v* veto; disprove; *n* **negative equity** debt occurring when property value falls below amount of loan securing it

**neglect** *v* 1 pay no heed to 2 fail to do; *n* fact of neglecting or being neglected; *adj* **-ful**; *adv* **-ly**

**neglect** *v* 1 (pay no heed to) abandon, forget, forsake, ignore, leave alone, pay no attention to. 2 (fail to do) fail, forget, not remember, omit, overlook, shirk, skimp, skip
**neglect** *n* carelessness, forgetfulness, inattention, indifference, lack of concern, negligence

**negligence** *n* lack of care, attention
**negligent** *adj* not taking proper care

**negligent** *adj* careless, forgetful, irresponsible, neglectful, reckless, remiss, slack, slapdash, sloppy, thoughtless, unthinking

**negligible** *adj* insignificant, unimportant

**negligible** *adj* inconsequential, minor, petty, slight, small, tiny, trifling, trivial

**negotiate** *v* 1 arrange, settle business matter, by discussion 2 get cash for security 3 discuss terms of peace with 4 surmount (obstacle); *adj* **negotiable**; *ns* **-iation**, **-iator**
**neighbor** *n* one who lives next door, or nearly so; *adj* **neighboring** adjacent; placed near together; *adv* **neighborly** friendly
**neighborhood** *n* district
**neither** *adj pron* not either; also *adv conj*
**nem con** *adv Lat* unanimously
**neo** *prefix* new, modern
**neoclassical** *adj* of any modern style (in art, literature, music, etc) influenced by classical style
**neolithic** *adj* of later Stone Age
**neologism** *n* 1 new word, phrase 2 act of inventing word
**neon** *n* an inert gas occurring in atmosphere; **-light** glowing light obtained by ionizing gas in tube or bulb
**neonatal** *n* of, or relating to a newborn

a
b
c
d
e
f
g
h
i
j
k
l
m
**n**
o
p
q
r
s
t
u
v
w
x
y
z

**neophyte** *n* new convert; novice; beginner

**nephew** *n* brother's, sister's son

**nephritis** *n* inflammation of kidneys

**nepotism** *n* favoritism towards one's relatives

**Neptune** *n* Roman god of the sea; third largest planet, eighth from the sun

**nerd** *n sl* idiot; *adj* **-ish**

**nerve** *n* 1 cord-like fiber, bundle of fibers, carrying sensory and motor impulses from the brain to parts of body 2 courage 3 *coll* impudence 4 *pl* **-s** nervousness

**nerve-racking** *adj* very worrying

> **nerve-racking** *adj* anxious, difficult, distressing, frightening, harrowing, nail-biting, stressful, tense, worrying

**nervous** *adj* 1 tensely 2 timid 3 of the nerves (*adv* **-ly**; *n* **-ness**); *adj* **nervy** jumpy; easily excited

> **nervous** *adj* 1 (tense) agitated, edgy, highly strung, impatient, insecure, jumpy, on edge, on tenterhooks, restless, strained, uneasy, unnerved, uptight, worried. 2 (timid) afraid, anxious, apprehensive, fearful, trembling

**nescient** *adj* not knowing; ignorant; *n* **nescience** agnosticism

**nest** *n* structure built by bird in which it lays eggs and rears young; snug shelter; *v* build, occupy nest

**nestle** *v* lie, press closely against

**nestling** *n* young bird before it leaves nest

**net**[1] *n* 1 meshwork of knotted, woven cord, thread, etc 2 length of this used to catch anything, or for protection; *v* **nets, netting, netted** catch in, cover with net; *n* **netting** string, wire network

**net**[2], **nett** *n* free of all deductions; remaining after all necessary expenses; *v* yield as clear profit

**nether** *adj* lower, below

**nethermost** *adj* lowest

**netherworld** *n* underworld, place of the dead

**nettle** *n* plant with stinging hairs on leaves and stalks; *v* irritate, annoy

**network** *n* 1 meshed structure of wire, cords, etc 2 system of intersecting channels of communication (roads, railways, radio, TV) 3 system of interlinking operations (business, espionage, crime); *v* establish set of contacts (*n* **-ing**)

**neuralgia** *n* sharp pain along a nerve, *esp* in the face; *adj* **neuralgic**

**neurology** *n* study of nerves and nervous disease; *adj* **-ological**; *n* **-ologist**

**neurosis** *n pl* **-ses** mild mental illness that causes irrational fear or worry; *adj* **neurotic** abnormally tense, worried, or afraid

**neuter** *adj* neither masculine nor feminine; *n* 1 noun, pronoun of neuter gender 2 animal deprived of sexual organs (*v* castrate or spay)

**neutral** *adj* 1 not taking sides in dispute, *esp* war; 2 (of gears) disengaged; *n* state or subject of state taking neither side in conflict; *n* **-ity** nonparticipation, *esp* in war; *v* **-ize** make, treat as neutral; counteract, make ineffectual; *n* **-ization**

> **neutral** *adj* (not taking sides) disinterested, fair, impartial, objective, open-minded, unbiased, uncommitted, undecided, uninvolved, unprejudiced

**neutron** *n* electrically uncharged atomic particle

**never** *adv* not ever; emphatic negative; *adv* **nevertheless** notwithstanding

**new** *adj* not previously existing; newly produced; fresh; unfamiliar; novel; *adv* **newly** (*n* **newlywed** person just married, *esp pl*; *adj* **-wedded**); *n* **-ness**

> **new** *adj* advanced, brand-new, contemporary, current, different, futuristic, latest, modern, newfangled, original, recent, revolutionary, state-of-the-art, topical, trendy, unused, unusual, up-to-date

**news** *n* information, reports of recent events

> **news** *n* announcement, bulletin, dispatch, exposé, facts, headlines, leak, release, report, statement, story, tidings

**newspaper** *n* daily or weekly printed publication containing news, comment, letters, reviews, etc
**newsworthy** *adj* interesting enough to be reported
**newt** *n* small lizardlike amphibian
**next** *adj, adv* nearest in order, rank, time, etc; *adv* **n.door** in adjacent building

> **next** *adv* after, afterward, later, subsequently, then

**nib** *n* split penpoint
**nibble** *v* **1** bite gently; with small bites **2** *fig* show signs of being attracted by (offer, etc) *n* tentative bite

> **nibble** *v* bite, eat, gnaw, munch, nip, peck at, pick at, snack on

**nice** *adj* **1** pleasing **2** delicate; *n* **nicety** accuracy (*pl* **-ies** subtle details)

> **nice** *adj* (pleasing) agreeable, amiable, charming, courteous, friendly, kind, likeable, pleasant, polite, understanding

**niche** *n* small recess in wall
**nick** *n* **1** notch **2** small cut; *v* cut notch in
**nickel** *n* **1** hard, silver-white metallic element **2** five-cent coin
**nickname** *n* extra name given in affection or derision
**nicotine** *n* oily, poisonous alkaloid in tobacco
**niece** *n* brother's or sister's daughter
**nifty** *adj coll* **1** skillful **2** effective **3** stylish
**niggard** *n* covetous, miserly person; *adj* **niggardly**
**niggle** *v* fret, be fussy over petty details; *adj* **niggling** too fussy; small but persistent

**nigh** *adj, adv, prep, arch* near
**night** *n* **1** period from sunset to sunrise **2** darkness; *adj, adv* **nightly** (happening) every night
**nightfall** *n* onset of darkness after sunset

> **nightfall** *n* dusk, evening, sundown, sunset, twilight

**nightmare** *n* **1** frightening dream **2** harrowing experience (*adj* **-marish**)
**nihilism** *n* systematic rejection of all religious beliefs and moral principles; violent revolutionary beliefs, doctrines, etc; anarchism; *n* **-list**
**nil** *n* nothing
**nimble** *adj* quick, agile

> **nimble** *adj* acrobatic, active, deft, graceful, lithe, lively, skillful, sprightly, spry

**nincompoop** *n* fool
**nine** *n, pron, det* cardinal number next above eight; *adjs, ns, prons, dets* **ninth** ordinal number; 9th part; **nineteen** nine plus ten; **nineteenth**; **ninety** nine tens; **ninetieth**; *n* **ninepins** a bowling game
**nip** *v* **nips, nipping, nipped** **1** pinch sharply with fingers, claws **2** (*of wind*) affect with stinging sensation; *n* **1** pinch **2** sharp keen bite of wind or frost **3** small drink; *adj* **nippy** **1** quick; active **2** frosty; cold

> **nip** *v* (pinch) catch, clip, grip, hurt, snag, squeeze, tweak, twitch

**nipple** *n* small protuberance at center of breast in mammal; teat of woman's breast
**nisi** *conj leg* becoming valid after certain interval, unless cause is shown for rescinding it
**nit**[1] *n* egg of louse or other parasitic insect; *n* **nit-picking** concern for little trivial details as a basis for finding fault (*adj* showing such concern)
**nit**[2] *n* silly person (*also* **nitwit**)

**nitrogen** n colorless gaseous element, forming 78% of the air; adj **nitric**

**no** n refusal; negative word, vote; (pl **noes**); adj not any; adv in no respect; none

**no.** abbr number

**No, Noh** n classic, stylized Japanese drama

**Nobel prize** n any of the prizes founded by Alfred Bernhard Nobel, awarded annually for outstanding achievement in science, literature, or promotion of peace

**noble** adj 1 of high rank 2 admirable 3 famous; n person of noble birth; **nobleman** member of nobility; peer

> **noble** adj 1 (of high rank) aristocratic, blue-blooded, born with a silver spoon in your mouth, distinguished, highborn, princely, titled, upper-class. 2 (admirable) brave, gallant, heroic, honorable, magnanimous, self-sacrificing, virtuous, worthy

**nobility** n quality of being noble; body of those with hereditary titles

> **nobility** n aristocracy, elite, gentry, high society, upper class

**nobless oblige** n Fr idea of obligatory, responsible behavior associated with those nobly born or of high social status

**nobody** pron no person; n person of no account

**nocturnal** adj of, in, by night; active at night

**nod** v **nods, nodding, nodded** 1 bow head slightly, sharply in assent, greeting, etc 2 droop head when drowsy

**node** n 1 knot, joint on stem of plant 2 hard swelling on muscle 3 point of intersection; n **nodule** small rounded lump; adj **nodular** of nodes; having nodules

**noise** n clamor; loud sound; adj **-less**

> **noise** n babble, blare, cacophony, clatter, commotion, din, hubbub, hullabaloo, racket, row, sound, talk, uproar

**noisy** adj making much noise

> **noisy** adj blaring, blasting, boisterous, deafening, ear-splitting, loud, piercing, raucous, riotous, rowdy

**nomad** n member of wandering, pastoral tribe; wanderer; adj **-ic**

**no-man's-land** n neutral zone between two opposing forces, controlled by neither

**nom-de-plume** n Fr writer's assumed name; pen name

**nomenclature** n system of names or naming used in classifying; terminology

**nominal** adj 1 pertaining to name 2 existing in name only 3 inconsiderable

**nominate** v name, propose person for post, office; ns **-ator; -ation; nominee** person nominated

> **nominate** v appoint, assign, choose, designate, elect, propose, put forward, put up, recommend, select

**nominative** adj in the form used for grammatical subject

**non-** prefix not; opposite of 1 forming adjs (eg **nonaligned**) 2 forming ns (eg **nonevent** event that fails to meet expectations)

**nonagenerian** n person aged between 90 and 100

**nonce** n **for the n.** for the present; once only

**nonchalant** adj indifferent; n **nonchalance**

> **nonchalant** adj blasé, calm, casual, composed, cool, laid-back, offhand, self-possessed, unconcerned, unemotional

**noncommittal** adj refusing to take sides

**nonconformist** n dissenter

**nondescript** adj not easily classified; vague; indefinite

**none** pron no one; adv in no way

**nonentity** n unimportant person; nonexistent thing

**nonetheless** *adv* nevertheless, however
**no-no** *n* something forbidden, unacceptable
**nonplussed, nonplused** *adj* in state of
perplexity, bewilderment; taken aback
**nonsense** *n* meaningless words;
*adj* **nonsensical** absurd; ridiculous; *adv* **-ly**

> **nonsense** *n* balderdash, baloney *inf*, drivel,
> gibberish, gobbledegook *inf*, hogwash *inf*,
> rubbish, stuff and nonsense, twaddle

**noodle** *n* long thin strip of pasta
**nook** *n* corner; retreat; hiding-place
**noon** *n* midday; twelve o'clock
**noose** *n* loop of rope with slipknot, allowing
it to be drawn tight
**nor** *conj* and not
**normal** *adj* average; ordinary; conforming to
accepted standard, type; *n* **-ality**;
*v* **normalize** make normal

> **normal** *adj* accepted, common, customary,
> established, everyday, familiar, general,
> natural, predictable, regular, routine,
> run-of-the mill, standard, typical, usual

**normally** *adv* usually; a rule
**north** *n* cardinal compass point opposite
midday sun; northern parts of earth or
country generally; *adj* to, from, or in north;
*adjs* **northern** pertaining to north;
**northerly** from, to direction of north;
*n* **northerner** inhabitant of northern region
of country
**nose** *n* external organ of smell, used in
breathing; any projection like a nose
**nosh** *n sl* snack; *v sl* to eat
**nostalgia** *n* wistful longing for what is past
**nostalgic** *adj* wistful; full of longing for the
past

> **nostalgic** *adj* emotional, homesick, longing,
> pining, regretful, remembering, romantic,
> sentimental, yearning

**nostril** *n* one of two external orifices of nose

**nosy, nosey** *adj coll* inquisitive

> **nosy** *adj* curious, eavesdropping, interfering,
> intrusive, meddlesome, prying, snooping

**not** *adv* expressing denial, negation, refusal
**notable** *adj* remarkable; conspicuous;
*n* notable person; *adv* **-ably**; *n* **-ability**
person of distinction
**notary** *n* public official legally entitled to
attest, certify deeds, contracts, etc
**notation** *n* system of symbols for representing
numbers, musical notes, etc
**notch** *n* V-shaped cut, nick; *v* make notches
in
**note** *n* 1 brief letter 2 brief comment on
textual matter (*eg* footnote) 3 piece of paper
money; printed or written promise of
payment 4 single musical sound; symbol for
this on paper 5 sign, hint of specified feeling
(*eg* **note of anger**); *v* observe; record in
writing; *adjs* **noted** famous; **n.-worthy** of
interest and/or importance (*n* **-iness**)

> **note** *n* (brief letter) correspondence,
> explanation, inscription, jotting, letter,
> memo, memorandum, message, minute,
> record, reference, reminder
> **note** *v* detect, enter, indicate, jot down,
> make a note, mark, mention, notice,
> record, register, remark, see, take note,
> take notice, write down

**nothing** *n* not anything; zero; *adv* not at all
**notice** *n* 1 announcement 2 attention
3 written warning 4 dismissal (of worker)
5 review (of play, book, etc); *v* observe, heed

> **notice** *n* 1 (announcement) advertisement,
> bulletin, handout, leaflet, message, note,
> poster, sign. 2 (attention) awareness,
> observation, regard. 3 (warning) advice,
> information, notification. 4 (dismissal)
> marching orders *inf*, redundancy, the
> boot, the sack *inf*

**notice** *v* be aware, detect, discern, discover, distinguish, feel, find, make out, note, pay attention, perceive, register, see, spot, take note

**noticeable** *adj* striking; easily seen; appreciable; *adv* **-ably**

**noticeable** *adj* apparent, clear, conspicuous, discernible, distinct, evident, marked, obvious, plain, prominent, pronounced, salient, unmistakable, visible

**notify** *v* **notifies, notifying, notified** report; make known; tell officially; *n* **notification**

**notify** *v* advise, declare, inform, let sb know, make known, proclaim, publish, tell, warn

**notion** *n* idea; conception; fancy; belief; *n* **notional 1** imaginary **2** assumed for the purpose of discussion; theoretical (*adv* **-ly**)
**notoriety** *n* quality of being well-known in bad sense
**notorious** *adj* commonly known in unfavorable sense

**notorious** *adj* disgraceful, dishonorable, disreputable, ill-famed, infamous, outrageous, scandalous, well-known

**notwithstanding** *prep* in spite of; *adv, conj* although
**nougat** *n* candy of sugar paste and nuts, fruit, etc
**nought** *n* nothing; symbol 0
**noun** *n* word used to name person, thing, action, quality; substantive
**nourish** *v* **1** feed; sustain with food **2** *fig* foster, encourage; *n* **-ment**

**nourish** *v* (feed) care for, maintain, nurture, provide for, strengthen, support, sustain

**nouveau riche** *n* recently wealthy
**nova** *n* star whose brilliance flares briefly
**novel**[1] *n* fictional prose story in book form; *n* **-ist** author of novels
**novel**[2] *adj* new; unfamiliar

**novel** *adj* different, fresh, ground-breaking, imaginative, innovative, original, trail-blazing, uncommon, unconventional, unique, unusual

**novelty** *n* **1** newness **2** newly marketed ornament

**novelty** *n* **1** (newness) difference, freshness, originality, strangeness, unusualness. **2** curiosity, gadget, gimmick, knick-knack, memento, souvenir, trinket

**November** *n* the eleventh month
**novice** *n* **1** inexperienced beginner **2** monk, nun who has not taken monastic vows
**now** *adv* at present time; *adv* **nowadays** in these days

**now** *adv* at once, at present, at the moment, for the time being, immediately, instantly, just now, nowadays, promptly, right away, right now, straightaway

**nowhere** *adv* not in any place
**noxious** *adj* harmful, offensive

**noxious** *adj* corrosive, foul, nasty, poisonous, polluting, toxic, unhealthy, unwholesome

**nuance** *n* delicate distinction in color, meaning, feeling, tone of voice, etc
**nuclear** *adj* **1** of, from an atomic nucleus **2** producing nuclear energy **3** of atomic weapons **4** forming a compact unit
**nuclear energy** *n* energy released by fission or fusion of nucleus
**nucleus** *n* *Lat* **1** central core or kernel **2** *fig* starting point **3** core of atom; *pl* **nuclei**
**nude** *adj* naked, bare; *n* **nudity**

**nude** *adj* exposed, in your birthday suit *inf*, in the altogether *inf*, in the buff *inf*, in the raw *inf*, stark naked, stripped, unclothed, uncovered, undressed

**nudge** *v* push slightly with elbow; *n* such touch

**nudge** *v* bump, dig, dig sb in the ribs, elbow, jog, poke, prod, push, shove, touch

**nugget** *n* 1 small lump of metal, *esp* of natural gold 2 valuable piece of information

**nuisance** *n* something harmful, offensive, annoying

**nuisance** *n* annoyance, bore, bother, drag *inf*, hassle *inf*, inconvenience, irritation, pain *inf*, problem, trouble, worry

**null** *adj* of no effect; void

**numb** *adj* deprived of feeling, *esp* through cold; *v* make numb; deaden

**numb** *adj* anesthetized, asleep *inf*, cold, dead, deadened, frozen, paralyzed, stunned, stupefied, without feeling

**number** *n* 1 mathematical unit; symbol(s) representing this 2 countable amount (*eg* **a number of times**; *pl* large numbers of people) 3 issue of periodical 4 item in musical or variety show 5 *ling* category of singular or plural

**numeral** *adj* of, expressing number; *n* graphic symbol of number; *v* **numerate** count (*adj* able to calculate; *n* **numeracy**); *n* **numerator** number above line in a numerical fraction; *adj* **numerical** concerning numbers (*adv* **-ly**)

**numeral** *n* Arabic numeral, character, digit, figure, integer, number, Roman numeral, symbol

**numerous** *adj* many

**numerous** *adj* abundant, copious, countless, lots *inf*, multitudinous, myriad, plentiful, several, untold, various

**nun** *n* member of women's religious order, living in convent; *n* **nunnery** community of nuns; convent

**nuptial** *adj* of, relating to marriage; *n pl* **-s** wedding ceremony

**nurse** *n* 1 person trained to care for sick or injured 2 woman employed to look after children; *v* suckle (an infant); act as nurse to; *ns* **nursemaid** woman employed to look after baby or small child; **nursing** work of a medical nurse; **nursing home** home where sick or elderly people can live and be cared for

**nursery** *n* 1 room designed for small children to play in 2 place for rearing young plants

**nurture** *n* nourishment; fostering care; training; *v* rear, educate

**nurture** *v* bring up, cultivate, feed, nourish, nurse, provide for, sustain, tend, train

**nut**[1] *n* hard-shelled fruit of certain plants; *adjs* **nuts** *sl* insane; **nutty** 1 containing nuts, nutlike food 2 *sl* insane

**nut**[2] *n* hollow metal collar with internal thread to fit over bolt or screw

**nutmeg** *n* hard, fragrant seed of Indian tree; this powdered and used as spice

**nutrition** *n* process of receiving nourishment

**nutritious** *adj* nourishing; maintaining growth

**nylon** *n* synthetic plastic material with properties similar to those of silk

**nymph** *n* 1 legendary maiden deity, spirit of woods, hills, rivers, etc; 2 insect pupa; chrysalis

**oaf** n clumsy, awkward fellow; lout

**oak** n type of common tree; oak timber n **oak apple** fleshy growth on oak caused by gallwasps; *adj* **oaken** *lit* of oak wood

**oar** n long pole with flattened blade, used to propel boat

**oasis** n fertile place in desert; *pl* **oases**

**oat** n *pl usu* cereal plant; its seed; n **oatmeal**

**oath** n 1 solemn appeal to God or some sacred thing, as witness to truth of statement 2 curse; profanity

> **oath** n 1 (solemn appeal) affirmation, avowal, bond, pledge, promise, sworn statement, undertaking, vow, word of honor. 2 (curse) blasphemy, expletive, obscenity, profanity, swear word

**obedience** n submission to authority; act of obeying

**obedient** *adj* submissive; willing to obey

> **obedient** *adj* acquiescent, amenable, compliant, docile, dutiful, law-abiding, manageable, respectful, well-behaved, well-trained

**obeisance** n bow; formal gesture of respect

**obelisk** n upright, four-sided stone pillar

**obese** *adj* very fat; overweight; n **obesity**

**obey** v carry out commands of; submit; follow rules of

**obfuscate** v obscure, bewilder, confuse

**obituary** n notice of death of person, often with short biography

**object**[1] n 1 material thing 2 aim, purpose 3 *ling* noun, pronoun, noun phrase, noun clause affected by action of transitive verb or following preposition

> **object** n 1 (thing) article, item. 2 (aim) goal, idea, intention, motive, objective, point, purpose, reason

**object**[2] v be opposed to; feel dislike of; protest against; n **objection** (*adj* **-able** liable to objection; offensive); n **objector**

> **object** v argue, beg to differ, be opposed, complain, grumble, mind *inf*, oppose, protest, raise objections, take a stand against, take exception to

**objective** *adj* 1 relating to objects 2 existing outside the mind; n object, purpose aimed at

**oblate** *adj* (of sphere) flattened at both ends

**oblation** n solemn, religious offering; n **oblate** one dedicated to monastic life

**oblige** v 1 compel by legal, moral force 2 do favor to

**obligation** n binding promise, contract, etc; duty; indebtedness for kindness, favor, etc

**obligatory** *adj* compulsory; necessary to be done; v **obligate** bind legally, morally

> **obligatory** *adj* binding, essential, imperative, mandatory, necessary, required, unavoidable

**obliging** *adj* helpful; courteous

**oblique** *adj* 1 slanting 2 *fig* not straightforward

> **oblique** *adj* 1 (slanting) angled, aslant, at an angle, diagonal, inclined, slanted, sloping. 2 (not straightforward) back-handed, implicit, implied, indirect, roundabout

**obliterate** *v* blot out; efface; *n* **-ation**
**oblivion** *n* forgetfulness; being forgotten
**oblivious** *adj* unaware; not realizing

> **oblivious** *adj* absorbed, blind, careless, deaf, forgetful, heedless, ignorant, neglectful, unconcerned, unheeding

**oblong** *n*, *adj* (rectangle) longer than broad
**obloquy** *n* reproach, calumny, disgrace
**obnoxious** *adj* disagreeable, offensive
**oboe** *n* woodwind musical instrument
**obscene** *adj* indecent, lewd; *n* **obscenity**

> **obscene** *adj* blue, coarse, crude, depraved, dirty, disgusting, filthy, foul, foul-mouthed, immoral, offensive, perverted, pornographic, rude, shocking, vulgar

**obscure** *adj* 1 dim 2 not clear in meaning 3 unimportant; *n* **obscurity** 1 darkness 2 ambiguity 3 state of being unknown

> **obscure** *adj* 1 (dim) blurred, cloudy, dark, faint, fuzzy, gloomy, hazy, indistinct, masked, misty, murky, shadowy, shady, shrouded, unlit, vague. 2 (not clear in meaning) ambiguous, concealed, confusing, cryptic, deep, enigmatic, hidden, mysterious, puzzling, secret, unclear. 3 (unimportant) forgotten, hidden, insignificant, remote, undistinguished, unheard-of, unknown

**obsequious** *adj* servile; ingratiating
**observance** n 1 act of observing (laws, etc) 2 commemoration
**observant** *adj* attentive, alert, vigilant

> **observant** *adj* aware, eagle-eyed, having your eyes peeled, on the ball *inf*, on the lookout, perceptive, sharp-eyed, watchful

**observation** *n* 1 act of noticing 2 surveillance; *pl* **-s** 1 remarks 2 critical comment on action or event, etc

**observatory** *n* building with instruments for watching stars, etc
**observe** *v* 1 pay attention to; watch; consider carefully 2 comment; remark; *n* **observer** one who observes
**obsess** *v* haunt, occupy mind; *adj* **-ive**; *adv* **-ively**; *n* **-iveness**
**obsession** *n* fixed idea; exclusive preoccupation of mind

> **obsession** *n* addiction, bee in your bonnet *inf*, complex, compulsion, fetish, fixation, hang-up *inf*, infatuation, mania, phobia, preoccupation

**obsolescence** *n* state of becoming obsolete or slowly disappearing through disuse; *adj* **obsolescent**
**obsolete** *adj* disused; out-of-date
**obstacle** *n* hindrance, obstruction

> **obstacle** *n* bar, barrier, block, blockage, check, difficulty, hitch, hurdle, interruption, problem, snag, stumbling block

**obstetrics** *n pl* science and practice of childbirth; *adj* **-tric** of childbirth; *n* **-trician** specialist in childbirth
**obstinacy** *n* stubbornness, persistence
**obstinate** *adj* stubborn, persistent

> **obstinate** *adj* defiant, determined, dogged, firm, headstrong, inflexible, pigheaded, self-willed, single-minded, tenacious, unbending, unreasonable, willful

**obstreperous** *adj* noisy; unruly; turbulent
**obstruct** *v* block, impede; *n* **-ion**; *adj* **-ive** causing obstruction

> **obstruct** *v* bring to a standstill, check, choke, clog, curb, cut off, delay, frustrate, halt, hinder, hold up, interrupt, prevent, restrict, shut off, slow, stop, thwart

**obtain** *v* gain; acquire; be valid; *adj* **-able** procurable

**obtrude** *v* force upon; intrude; *n* **obtrusion**

**obtrusive** *adj* thrusting, intrusive

**obtuse** *adj* blunt; (of persons) dull, dense; (of angle) greater than a right angle

**obviate** *v* get ride of; make unnecessary

**obvious** *adj* easily seen; clear; lacking subtlety

> **obvious** *adj* apparent, blatant, conspicuous, evident, glaring, manifest, noticeable, open, overt, patent, plain, pronounced, self-evident, straight-forward, transparent, unmistakable, visible

**occasion** *n* 1 point of time when some event takes place 2 cause; reason 3 special event; *v* give rise to cause

**occasional** *adj* 1 not all the time 2 composed for special purpose

> **occasional** *adj* (not all the time) casual, incidental, infrequent, intermittent, irregular, odd, rare, sporadic

**Occident** *n* the west; Western hemisphere; *adj* **occidental**

**occipital** *adj med* of the back of skull

**occlude** *v* close, shut in or out; *n* **occlusion**; *adj* **occlusive**

**occult** *adj* hidden, esoteric, supernatural; *ns* **-ation** eclipse; **-ism** study of supernatural

**occupancy** *n* act of taking possession and residing in house, etc; term of such occupation

**occupant** *n* person who resides in house

**occupation** *n* 1 possession 2 employment

> **occupation** *n* 1 (possession) capture, colonization, conquest, invasion, overthrow, seizure, takeover. 2 (employment) business, job, profession, trade, work

**occupational** *adj* 1 of one's trade, regular employment 2 by physical or mental activity

**occupy** *v* 1 live in, have possession of (house, land, etc) 2 *mil* take, keep possession of (territory) 3 take up or fill (space or time) 4 keep busy

> **occupy** *v* 1 (live in) inhabit, move into, reside in, take up residence in. 2 (take possession) capture, colonize, conquer, invade, overrun, seize, take over. 3 (take up) fill, fill up, preoccupy, use up. 4 (keep busy) amuse, divert, engage, engross, entertain, interest

**occupied** *adj* 1 busy; active 2 being used

**occur** *v* **occurs, occurring, ocurred** 1 happen 2 (be found to) exist; *n* **occurrence** happening, incident

**ocean** *n* the great expanses of salt water on earth; *pl coll* vast amount; *adj* **-ic**; *ns* **-ology**; **-ography** branch of science concerned with oceans

**ocher** *n* earthy metallic oxide of iron, used for making yellow-brown pigments

**o'clock** *adv* (hour) by the clock

**octagon** *n* plane figure with eight sides

**octave** *n* eighth note above, below any note

**octavo** *n* size of book or page made up of sheets folded into eight

**octennial** *adj* lasting, coming every eight years

**octet, octette** *n* group or set of eight musical compositions for eight singers or instruments

**October** *n* tenth month of the year (eighth in old Roman calendar).

**octogenarian** *n* person between 80 and 90

**octopus** *n* mollusk with eight arms bearing suckers

**odd** *adj* 1 strange 2 not part of complete set 3 not even 4 not divisible by two (*also adj*); *ns* **odd-ball** eccentric person; **oddity** 1 strange person, thing 2 strangeness (*also* **oddness**); **odd one out** person, thing different from, excluded from rest of group; *adv* **oddly** 1 strangely 2 surprisingly; *pl n* **odds and ends** leftover bits, extras, assorted things

**odd** *adj* **1** (strange) abnormal, bizarre, curious, different, eccentric, extraordinary, freak, funny, idiosyncratic, incongruous, irregular, outlandish, peculiar, puzzling, rare, remarkable, uncommon, unconventional, unexpected, unusual, weird. **2** (not part of complete set) extra, leftover, lone, remaining, single, solitary, spare, surplus, uneven, unmatched, unpaired, unused

**odds** *n pl* **1** probability of sth happening (**odds in favor of/against**) **2** (in gambling) ratio between amount of prize money and size of bet

**ode** *n* lyric poem, with lines of varying lengths, *usu* addressed to a particular subject

**odometer** *n* instrument that measures distance traveled

**odontology** *n* study of teeth and their diseases

**odor** *n* **1** smell, scent; **2** *fig* reputation; *v* **odorize** perfume; *adjs* **odorous** **1** fragrant **2** *coll* bad smelling; **odoriferous** fragrant

**odor** *n* aroma, bouquet, fragrance, perfume, pong *inf*, stench, stink

**odyssey** *n* long trip, voyage with many adventures; Quest

**Oedipus complex** *n psyc* (Freudian theory of) child's subconcious sexual desire for one parent and jealousy of the other

**of** *prep* **1** belonging to **2** coming from **3** made from **4** containing **5** produced by **6** expressing quantity (250g of sth) **7** about; concerning **8** depicting; portraying

**off**[1] *adj* **1** unfriendly **2** not fresh **3** not busy **4** unsatisfactory **5** cutting off current

**off**[2] *adv* **1** disconnected; detached **2** (of fuel or energy supply) not turned on **3** leaving **4** gone on vacation, on a trip **5** canceled **6** stressing completion

**off**[3] *prep* **1** away from **2** down from **3** not far from

**offal** *n* **1** edible internal organs of animals **2** garbage; waste matter

**offense** *n* **1** wrongdoing **2** affront

**offense** *n* **1** (wrong-doing) breach, crime, felony, illegal act, misdemeanor, sin, transgression, wrong. **2** (affront) anger, annoyance, disapproval, disgust, displeasure, hurt, irritation, outrage, resentment, upset *inf*

**offend** *v* **1** annoy **2** do wrong; *n* **offender**

**offensive** *adj* **1** insulting **2** unpleasant (*adv* **-ly**; *n* **-ness**) **3** attacking *n* **1** position of attack **2** aggression

**offensive** *adj* **1** (insulting) abusive, annoying, antisocial, disgusting, embarrassing, hurtful, indecent, insolent, irritating, provocative, objectionable, outrageous, rude, tasteless, uncivil, unpleasant, vulgar, wounding. **2** (unpleasant) disgusting, distasteful, nasty, nauseating, obnoxious, odious, repellent, revolting, sickening, unsavory, vile.

**offer** *v* **1** proffer for acceptance or refusal **2** give as sacrifice or sign of worship **3** present for sale at price **4** bid as price for **5** show signs of; *n* **1** bid **2** expression of willingness to do something, *esp* to help; *n* **offering** something offered, *esp* sacrifice to God

**office** *n* **1** duty; function **2** position of trust, authority **3** public, state department **4** building, room where administrative, clerical work is done **5** form of worship; *n* **officer** one in command in armed forces; one who holds position of trust, authority

**official** *n* one holding office, *esp* in public organization; *adj* having authority; *adv* **-ly**

**official** *adj* accredited, approved, authorized, bona fide, certified, formal, legitimate, licensed, recognized, sanctioned, valid

a b c d e f g h i j k l m n **o** p q r s t u v w x y z

**officiate** *v* perform duty; preside (at); conduct divine service

**officious** *adj* meddling; offering uninvited advice; overbearing; *adv* **-ly** *n* **-ness**

**offing** *idm* **in the offing** likely to appear, happen

**offset** *n* 1 beginning 2 sideshoot 3 method of printing from rubber roller; *v* compensate for

**offside** *adj*, *adv sport* illegally ahead of puck or ball

**offspring** *n* 1 child or children 2 *fig* result

**oft, often** *adv* many times; frequently

> **oft, often** *adv* again and again, all the time, constantly, generally, much, regularly, repeatedly, time after time, time and again

**ogle** *v* make eyes at; look at amorously

**ogre** *n* imaginary, cruel, man-eating giant

**ohm** *n* unit of electrical resistance

**oil** *n* viscous organic or mineral substance, insoluble in water, and inflammable; *v* lubricate; take oil in as fuel; *adj* **oily** like oil; *fig* unctuous

**ointment** *n* oily substance for healing wounds, or softening skin

**okay, OK** *adv*, *adj coll* all right; approved; *v coll* sanction; *n coll* agreement; sanction

**okra** *n* tall annual plant with edible green pods

**old** *adj* 1 having lived, existed for a long time 2 of long standing 3 former; *comp* **older, elder**; *sup* **oldest, eldest**; *idm* **any old how** *coll* 1 carelessly, untidily 2 in a poor state of health or morale; *n* **the old** old people, things

> **old** *adj* 1 (having lived, existed a long time) aged, ageing, ancient, antiquated, antique, doddery, elderly, geriatric, getting on, gray, in your dotage, mature, prehistoric, veteran, vintage. 2 (of long standing) age-old, original, time-honored, traditional. 3 (former) erstwhile, previous

**old-fashioned** *adj* in style of former times

> **old-fashioned** *adj* antiquated, dated, obsolescent, obsolete, old-hat *inf*, outdated, outmoded, out of fashion, passé, stale, time-worn, unfashionable

**oleaginous** *adj* oily, greasy

**olfactory** *adj* pertaining to sense of smell

**olive** *n* evergreen tree; oil-yielding fruit; *adj* yellowish green

**Olympiad** *n* period of four years between Olympic Games; *adjs* **Olympian** god-like; **Olympic, O. Games** modern revival of ancient Grecian athletic meeting

**ombudsman** *n* one officially appointed to investigate and deal with individual complaints against large organizations

**omega** *n* last letter of Greek alphabet

**omelette, omelet** *n Fr* beaten eggs cooked without stirring, then folded in half

**omen** *n* sign, portent of things to come

> **omen** *n* bad sign, foreboding, harbinger, portent, sign, warning, writing on the wall

**ominous** *adj* threatening evil

> **ominous** *adj* bad, black, dark, dire, gloomy, inauspicious, menacing, sinister, unfavorable, unpromising

**omission** *n* something left out, not done

**omit** *v* **omits, omitting, omitted** leave out; fail to do or include

> **omit** *v* drop, exclude, forget, miss, miss out, neglect, overlook

**omni-** *prefix Lat* all

**omnibus** *n* large passenger-carrying road vehicle, on fixed route; *adj* having many uses

**omnipotent** *adj* all-powerful; almighty; *n* **-potence**

**omniscient** *adj* infinitely wise; *n* **-science**

**omnivorous** *adj* eating all kinds of food

**on**[1] *adj, adv* 1 forward; ahead; further 2 in progress 3 illuminated; functioning 4 being worn 5 properly fitted, attached 6 taking place as arranged 7 appearing in public; performing 8 aboard

**on**[2] *prep* 1 touching surface of; covering 2 in close proximity, adjacent to 3 aboard 4 giving day, date 5 about 6 making habitual use of, temporary use of

**once** *adv* 1 one time 2 formerly; **once more** one more time; *conj* as soon as

**oncoming** *adj* approaching

**one** *det, n* 1 lowest cardinal number (1) 2 particular person or thing 3 the same (**at one time, in one try**); *pron* 1 somebody 2 anybody ; *prons* **one another** each other; **oneself** *reflex*

**onerous** *adj* burdensome, weighty

**onion** *n* strong-smelling vegetable of the lily family

**on-line** *adj* connected to, controlled by computer (*also adv*)

**onlooker** *n* spectator

> **onlooker** *n* bystander, observer, passerby, viewer, witness

**only** *adj* single, sole; *adv* solely, exclusively; *conj* except (that)

**onomatopoeia** *n* formation of words by imitation of sounds associated with object named, as cuckoo, hiss

**onrush** *n* urgent movement ahead

**onset** *n* beginning, attack

**onslaught** *n* violent attack

**onstream** *adj, adv* in or into production

**onto** *prep* to and upon

**ontology** *n* study of the nature of existence (*adj* **ontological**)

**onus** *n* burden; responsibility

**onward** *adj, adv* forward (in space or time)

**onyx** *n* variety of agate

**oodles** *n pl coll* abundance

**ooze** *n* 1 liquid mud; slime, *esp* on sea, riverbed 2 slow trickle; *v* exude (liquid); flow slowly out

**ooze** *v* bleed, drain, dribble, emit, escape, flow, leak, secrete, seep, trickle, weep

**opal** *n* iridescent gemstone

**opaque** *n* 1 not allowing light through; dark 2 obscure

> **opaque** *adj* 1 (not allowing light through) cloudy, dirty, filmy, hazy, muddy, murky. 2 (obscure) difficult, impenetrable, incomprehensible

**open** *adj* 1 not closed 2 not enclosed (**o. country**) 3 not hidden 4 undecided (**o. verdict**); unprejudiced (**o. mind**) 5 honest; frank 6 for anyone to visit, to attend, to compete in 7 without a roof; not covered over (**o. wound** injury with broken skin) 8 not buttoned up; undone (**o. collar**) 9 (of position, vacancy) available; to be applied for 10 (of textiles) loose in texture (**o. weave**) 11 (of exhibition, public event) ready for visitors 12 (of bank account) ready to use; *v* 1 unfasten; unlock; uncover 2 begin 3 make accessible

> **open** *adj* 1 (not closed) ajar, uncovered, undone, unfastened, unlocked. 2 (not enclosed) broad, clear, exposed, free, rolling, spacious, sweeping, treeless, unenclosed, unrestricted. 3 (not hidden) available, free, public, unrestricted
> **open** *v* 1 (unfasten, etc) spread out, unbolt, uncork, uncover, undo, unfold, unfurl, unlock, unroll, untie, unwrap. 2 (begin) commence, get going, initiate, kick off *inf*, launch, set in motion, set up, start

**opening** *n* 1 gap 2 opportunity; favorable moment 3 job vacancy; *adj* first, initial

> **opening** *n* 1 (gap) aperture, chink, crack, doorway, hatch, hole, orifice, slot, split, way in. 2 (opportunity) break *inf*, chance

**open-minded** *adj* receptive to new ideas
(*adv* **-ly**; *n* **-ness**)

> **open-minded** *adj* detached, dispassionate,
> enlightened, impartial, liberal, objective,
> open to suggestions, receptive, unbiased

**opera** *n* drama set to music, sung to orchestral
accompaniment; *adj* **operatic**; *n* **operetta**
short, light opera
**operate** *v* 1 work; cause to function
2 perform act of surgery
**operation** *n* 1 action 2 plan, project,
undertaking 3 act of surgery
**operative** *adj* working, valid; *n* worker, artisan
**operator** *n* one who works machine
**ophthalmic** *adj* pertaining to eye;
*n* **ophthalmology** branch of medicine
concerned with eyes; *n* **-ologist**
**opinion** *n* personal judgment; public feeling;
professional judgment or advice; *v* **opine**
utter opinion

> **opinion** *n* assessment, belief, estimation,
> feeling, idea, impression, judgment,
> stance, view, viewpoint, way of thinking

**opinionated** *adj* obstinate in beliefs, etc;
dogmatic
**opium** *n* narcoti, intoxicant and sedative
addictive drug obtained from white poppy;
*v* **opiate** mix with opium
**opponent** *n* antagonist, rival

> **opponent** *n* adversary, competitor,
> contender, contestant, enemy, player

**opportune** *adj* seasonable, suitable,
well-timed
**opportunity** *n* lucky chance; favorable
occasion or time; *ns* **opportunism** policy for
taking advantage of circumstances; **-ist**

> **opportunity** *n* break *inf*, chance, moment,
> opening, possibility, time

**oppose** *v* place against; withstand; contend
against; *n* **opposer**

> **oppose** *v* attack, be hostile to, campaign
> against, combat, counter, defy, fight,
> obstruct, stand up to, take a stand
> against, take issue with, take on

**opposite** *adj* 1 facing 2 as different as possible

> **opposite** *adj* 1 (facing) on the other side,
> overlooking. 2 (different) conflicting,
> contradictory, converse, hostile,
> irreconcilable, opposed, rival, unlike

**opposition** *n* resistance; political party
opposing that in power
**oppress** *v* 1 crush; treat unjustly, cruelly
2 weigh heavily on; depress; *n* **oppressor**
**oppressive** *adj* 1 tyrannical 2 (of weather)
hot and heavy

> **oppressive** *adj* 1 (tyrannical) harsh,
> repressive, unjust. 2 (hot and heavy)
> airless, close, humid, muggy, stifling,
> stuffy, suffocating

**oppression** *n* harshness; tyranny
**opt (for)** *v* choose; decide (in favor of);
*phr v* **opt out** choose not to take part
**optic** *adj* of the eyes or eyesight; *adj* **optical**
**optician** *n* 1 person who makes prescriptions,
appropriate glasses, lenses 2 person who
makes and sells optical instruments
**optimism** *n* habit of looking at brighter side
of things; doctrine that good ultimately
prevails over evil; *n* **-ist**; *v* **optimize** render
as effective as possible (*n* **-ization**)
**optimistic** *adj* in the habit of looking at the
bright side of things

> **optimistic** *adj* buoyant, cheerful, confident,
> hopeful, looking on the bright side,
> looking through rose-tinted glasses,
> positive, sanguine

**optimum** *n Lat* best, most favorable state, condition

**option** *n* 1 choice 2 privilege of buying or selling at certain price within specified time

**optional** *adj* not obligatory; voluntary

> **optional** *adj* discretionary, extra, up to you

**opulent** *adj* wealthy; abundant; luxuriant; *n* **-lence**

**opus** *n Lat* work or composition, *esp* in music

**or** *conj* introduces alternative; offering choice

**oracle** *n* 1 prophecy or answer, divinely inspired, given by ancient Greek, Roman priest 2 place, shrine where answer, often ambiguous, was given; the inspired priest; *adj* **oracular** of oracle; ambiguous

**oral** *adj* 1 *med* of the mouth 2 spoken; not written; *n* test of this kind (*also* **o. test, o. examination**)

**orange** *n* large red-gold citrus fruit; tree bearing this; color of fruit

**orangutan** *n* large reddish-colored ape

**orator** *n* eloquent, public speaker; *n* **oration** set formal speech; *adj* **-ical;** *n* **oratory** eloquence, rhetoric; small private chapel

**oratorio** *n* musical composition, *usu* of sacred nature for solo voices, chorus, and orchestra

**orb** *n* 1 sphere; globe 2 ceremonial symbol of royalty

**orbit** *n* 1 path of planet or satellite around another body in space 2 *fig* area of influence; *adj* **orbital** 1 of an orbit 2 passing all around outside of city

> **orbit** *n* (path round body in space) circuit, course, path, revolution, track

**orchard** *n* plantation of fruit trees

**orchestra** *n* band of musicians playing instrumental music; front part of theater where such band plays; *adj* **orchestral;** *v* **orchestrate** compose, arrange music for orchestra; *n* **-ration**

**orchid, orchis** *n* kind of showy plant with exotic flowers; *adj* light purple color

**ordain** *v* 1 admit to holy orders 2 decree, enact, appoint

**ordeal** *n* difficult or painful experience

**order** *n* 1 relative position in series; sequence 2 state of calm 3 command 4 request for goods 5 tidiness 6 group of monks, etc 7 *cap* group of people awarded special honor; decoration awarded to them; *idm* **in order that** *conj* expressing purpose; *v* 1 command 2 request goods or service 3 arrange in organized way

> **order** *n* 1 (position) arrangement, categorization, grouping, method, pattern, plan, sequence. 2 (state of calm) calm, control, discipline, harmony, law and order, peace, symmetry. 3 (command) court order, directive, injunction, instruction, regulation, requirement. 4 (request for goods) booking, commission, requirement, requisition, selection
> **order** *v* 1 (command) decree, direct, give orders to, instruct, require, tell. 2 (request goods) ask for, book, choose, commission, put in an order for, request, reserve, send off for. 3 (arrange) categorize, classify, organize, put in order, sort out

**orderly** *adj* tidy; law-abiding; *n* **-liness**

**ordinal** *adj* indicating position in series; *n* such a number (*also* **ordinal number**)

**ordinance** *n* decree, regulation; religious ceremony

**ordinary** *adj* normal, commonplace

> **ordinary** *adj* common, common-or-garden, customary, everyday, familiar, humdrum, plain, regular, run-of-the-mill, standard, unexceptional, unremarkable

**ordination** *n* ceremony of ordaining clergy

**ordnance** *n* artillery; military stores, equipment, material

**ore** *n* metal-yielding mineral

**oregano** *n* Mediterranean herb used to season food

a
b
c
d
e
f
g
h
i
j
k
l
m
n
**o**
p
q
r
s
t
u
v
w
x
y
z

**organ** n 1 part of animal or plant performing particular function 2 keyboard wind instrument

**organic** adj 1 of the organs of the body 2 formed by living things, not from artificial chemicals 3 (of farm produce) grown without artificial fertilizer or pesticide 4 fig forming integral part of structure; developing as part of structure (adv **-ally**)

**organism** n 1 living being capable of growth and reproduction 2 system composed of interrelated elements

**organist** n player of organ

**organization** n 1 act of organizing 2 body of persons having common purpose

**organize** v arrange, group separate parts into systematic whole; make efficient; unite into society, etc; n **organizer**

> **organize** v arrange, categorize, classify, configure, order, put in order, structure

**orgasm** n excitement, peak, paroxysm, esp in sexual act

**orgy** n 1 drunken revelry 2 continous round of pleasure; adj **orgiastic**

**orient**[1] n (usu cap) Far East (esp China, Japan); adj, n **-al** (inhabitant) of the Orient

**orient**[2] v 1 enable to find sense of direction; steer 2 direct attention and interest of (n **- ation**)

**orienteering** n form of sport, using map and compass to find one's way across unfamiliar territory on foot

**orifice** n mouth, outer opening of tube, pipe, etc

**origami** n Japanese art of making objects from folded paper

**origin** n 1 source 2 ancestry

> **origin** n 1 (source) basis, derivation, provenance, root, starting point. 2 (ancestry) background, extraction, family, heritage, lineage, parentage, pedigree, stock

**original** adj 1 earliest 2 new 3 made, done for first time; n that from which copies are made; first pattern, model; eccentric person

> **original** adj 1 (earliest) first, initial, primary 2 (new) fresh, ground-breaking, imaginative, innovative, novel, unusual, untried

**originality** n 1 creative faculty 2 novelty

**originate** v bring about; have origin in (n **-ator**)

**ornament** n decoration; adornment; trinket; v decorate; embellish; adj **-al**; n **-ation**

**ornate** adj excessively adorned

> **ornate** adj busy, elaborate, fancy, flashy inf, flowery, fussy, grandiose, ornamental, pretentious, rococo, showy

**ornithology** n scientific study of birds; adj **-ological**; n **-ologist**

**orphan** n child who has lost one or both parents; n **orphanage** institution for care of orphans

**orthodontics** n med branch of dentistry concerned with correcting irregular formation of teeth (adj **-tic**)

**orthodox** adj 1 (of ideas, methods) generally accepted 2 (of people) conventional 3 cap belonging to Eastern group of Christian churches or to strict Jewish sect; n **-doxy** 1 orthodox belief 2 state of being orthodox

**orthography** n 1 (system of) spelling 2 accepted correct spelling; adj **-graphic/ -graphical**; adv **-graphically**

**orthopedics** n pl branch of surgery dealing with bone deformities; adj **-pedic** pertaining to orthopedics

**oscillate** v swing to and fro; fluctuate between extremes

**osmosis** n 1 bio, chem gradual passage of liquid through porous solid matter 2 fig imperceptible process by which ideas gradually become absorbed and accepted

**ostensible** adj apparent, pretended

**ostentation** n pretentious show of wealth
**ostentatious** adj given to showing off

> **ostentatious** adj affected, flamboyant, flashy, garish, gaudy, loud, overdone, pretentious

**osteology** n study of bones/bony structure
**osteopathy** n treatment of disease by manipulation of bones; n **-path** one who practices osteopathy
**ostracize** v refuse to associate with; banish; n **ostracism** exclusion from social group, etc
**ostrich** n large, flightless African bird
**other** adj different; additional; not the same; pron other person or thing; adv **otherwise** differently; conj if not
**otter** n web-footed aquatic mammal
**ought** v aux expressing obligation, desirability, probability
**ounce** n unit of weight, sixteenth of pound; fig small amount
**our** adj belonging to us; pron **ours**; pron **ourselves** emphatic form of **we**
**oust** v turn out; expel; eject
**out** adv 1 away from inside 2 not at home 3 away at a distance 4 revealed 5 available; published 6 no longer in power 7 no longer fashionable 8 on strike 9 unconscious 10 not acceptable; not feasible 11 extinguished 12 wrongly calculated 13 tennis (of shot) landing on wrong side of court line
**out-** prefix 1 forming vs doing better or more; surpassing 2 forming adjs, ns isolated; external; with sudden effect
**outback** n remote bush country of Australia
**outbreak** n sudden start (of illness, violence)

> **outbreak** n epidemic, eruption, explosion, flare-up, occurrence, rash, upsurge

**outburst** n sudden eruption (of emotion)
**outcast** n rejected person

> **outcast** n exile, outsider, pariah, persona non grata, refugee, reject

**outcome** n result
**outcry** n protest
**outdo** v perform better than

> **outdo** v beat, eclipse, excel, get the better of, go one better than, outclass, outshine, outsmart, overshadow, run rings around inf, show up, surpass

**outdoor** adj of the open air; adv **-s**
**outer** adj on the outside; further from the center; adj **outermost** furthest from the center
**outfit** n 1 set of equipment or clothes 2 organization; working group; v equip, esp with clothes (n **outfitter**)
**outgoing** adj 1 departing 2 ending term of office 3 extrovert; sociable; pl **-s** expenditure
**outing** n excursion

> **outing** n day-trip, expedition, jaunt, tour, trip, visit

**outlaw** n fugitive not protected by the law; v make an outlaw; ban something by law
**outlay** n total money invested in enterprise, spent on large or multiple purchase
**outlet** n 1 way out for liquid, gas, etc 2 means of relieving tension or emotion, of energy 3 comm shop; trading place
**outline** n 1 line showing shape or contour of sth 2 statement of main facts, idea; v make an outline

> **outline** n 1 (line showing shape) contour, framework, perimeter, profile, shape, sketch, skeleton, tracing. 2 (statement of main facts) bare bones, draft, résumé, rough idea, sketch, summary, synopsis

**outlook** n 1 view from a place 2 attitude to life 3 future prospects
**outmoded** adj old-fashioned
**output** n 1 product of physical or mental effort 2 rate of production 3 computer-processed data 4 telecommunications signal

a b c d e f g h i j k l m n **o** p q r s t u v w x y z

**A B C D E F G H I J K L M N O P Q R S T U V W X Y Z**

**outrage** n violation; rape; violent transgression of law; v violate; offend against
**outrageous** adj disgraceful; adv **-ly**

> **outrageous** adj disgusting, heinous, horrifying, infuriating, offensive, scandalous, shocking, terrible, upsetting

**outré** n Fr exaggerated; in bad taste
**outrider** n mounted attendant
**outright** adj 1 unmistakeable 2 complete; also adv
**outset** n start
**outside** n external part; surface; extreme limit; adj 1 external 2 unlikely 3 unconnected; adv out of doors; prep on outer side of; apart from

> **outside** adj 1 (external) exterior, open-air, out of doors, outdoor, outer, outermost, outward, surface, top. 2 (unlikely) faint, improbable, marginal, remote, slight, slim

**outsider** n 1 person not relating to, not accepted by social group 2 competitor with little chance of success
**outsize** adj unusually large
**outskirts** n pl outer areas of city
**outspoken** adj frank; not afraid to say what one thinks; adv **-ly**; n **-ness**

> **outspoken** adj blunt, direct, explicit, forthright, tactless, undiplomatic

**outstanding** n remarkable, excellent; adv **-ly**

> **outstanding** adj exceptional, great, impressive, magnificent, memorable, notable, special, stunning, superb, supreme, world-class.

**outward** adj 1 going away; away from center 2 on the outside; visible; advs going away; **-ly** externally;
**outwit** v **outwits, outwitting, outwitted** deceive or defeat by greater cunning

**outwit** v beat, deceive, dupe, get the better of, outmaneuver, outsmart, pull the wool over sb's eyes, put one over on inf

**ova** pl of **ovum**
**oval** adj egg-shaped, elliptical; n figure of this shape
**ovary** n female organ of reproduction; adj **ovarian**
**ovation** n enthusiastic welcome or applause

> **ovation** n acclaim, accolade, applause, clapping, standing ovation, tribute

**oven** n heated metal or brick receptacle, in which food is baked; small kiln, or furnace
**over** prep 1 above 2 across; from one side to the other 3 beyond; more than 4 during; throughout 5 by means of 6 because of; adv 1 above 2 across 3 finished 4 in excess; idm **over and above** in addition to
**over-** prefix 1 above 2 providing cover 3 across 4 indicating superiority 5 beyond limit 6 too much
**overcast** adj dull, cloudy

> **overcast** adj dark, grey, leaden, murky

**overcome** v **overcomes, overcoming, overcame** defeat, deal with
**overdraft** n money borrowed from bank on current account; amount overdrawn
**overdrawn** adj having drawn money beyond the credit in one's account
**overdue** adj late
**overhaul** v 1 check thoroughly and rectify 2 overtake; n thorough check
**overhear** v hear message, conversation intended for sb else
**overjoyed** adj very happy

> **overjoyed** adj delighted, ecstatic, euphoric, in raptures, jubilant, on cloud nine, on top of the world, over the moon, thrilled

**overlook** v 1 look out across 2 fail to see or do 3 ignore, forgive

> **overlook** v 1 (look out across) be opposite, face, front onto, have a view of, look out onto. 2 (fail to see or do) forget, leave out, miss, not notice, omit. 3 (ignore) excuse, let sth pass, let sth ride, turn a blind eye to inf, write off.

**overnight** adv, adj through, during the night
**overpower** v get better of, conquer
**oversight** n mistake; accidental omission
**overt** adj openly done; apparent

> **overt** adj blatant, evident, explicit, obvious, open, patent, plain, unconcealed, undisguised, visible

**overtake** v 1 pass (vehicle ahead) 2 (of misfortune, etc) affect suddenly
**overthrow** v remove from power

> **overthrow** v beat, defeat, depose, displace, oust, remove from office, throw out, topple, unseat

**overtime** adv beyond normal working hours; n extra work of this kind; money earned from this
**overtone** n 1 tinge of second color detectable in basic color 2 mus harmonic note; pl -s implication of more than literal meaning in what is said
**overtook** pt of overtake
**overture** n musical composition played at beginning of opera, etc; usu pl friendly or formal approach
**overturn** v 1 turn upside-down; upset 2 reverse (decision) 3 overthrow (regime)

> **overturn** v 1 (turn upside-down) capsize, keel over, knock over, tip over. 2 (reverse) annul, countermand, overrule, quash, reject, repeal, revoke, set aside, veto

**overweight** adj above the normal weight
**overwhelm** v overpower; make helpless with emotion
**overwhelming** adj irresistible
**overwrought** adj too excited; exhausted by emotion
**oviform** adj egg-shaped
**ovine** adj of, like sheep
**ovoid** adj egg-shaped
**ovulate** adj produce egg(s) from ovary; n -ation
**ovum** n female egg-cell; pl ova; n ovule unfertilized seed
**owe** v 1 be indebted to 2 have to repay

> **owe** v 1 (be indebted) be indebted to, be obliged to, be under an obligation to. 2 (have to repay) be in arrears, be in debt, be in the red, be overdrawn.

**owing** adj unpaid, due; **owing to** conj as a result of; caused by
**owl** n night bird of prey
**own** v 1 possess 2 admit, confess, acknowledge; adj emphasizes possession

> **own** v (possess) be the owner of, have, have in your possession, hold, keep, retain

**owner** n one who possesses; **ownership** possession
**ox** n castrated adult male of domestic cattle; pl **oxen**
**oxygen** n colorless, odorless gas in the atmosphere, essential to life
**oyster** n edible marine bivalve mollusk
**ozone** n concentrated form of oxygen, with pungent smell; coll bracing ocean air
**ozone-friendly** adj not harmful to the ozone layer
**ozone layer** n layer of ozone-rich gases in the earth's atmosphere that absorbs harmful radiation from the sun

a b c d e f g h i j k l m n **o** p q r s t u v w x y z

**pace** n 1 distance covered by a single step 2 speed (of walking, running, progress, work); v walk with slow measured steps (across sth)

**pachyderm** n thick-skinned elephant, etc

**pacify** v **pacifies, pacifying, pacified** make peaceful; appease; adj **pacific** peaceable; ns **pacification; pacifism** systematic opposition to war, or violence; **-ist** believer in pacifism

**pack** n 1 bundle of things tied together for carrying 2 bag for carrying on back (also **backpack**) 3 paper or cardboard container for selling; packet 4 set of playing cards 5 group of hunting animals 6 coll group of people with undesirable characteristic (**p. of liars**); v 1 put things into container(s) for carrying 2 fit tightly into container 3 cover or fill with protective material

**package** n 1 several things wrapped together; parcel 2 related items offered or sold as a single unit; v make into package, eg for selling; n **packaging** 1 act of packing 2 packing material 3 fig method of presentation for selling

**packet** n small package

**pact** n agreement, covenant

> **pact** n alliance, arrangement, bargain, contract, deal, settlement, treaty, understanding

**pad**[1] v **pads, padding, padded** go on foot softly; trudge along

**pad**[2] n 1 piece of soft material to prevent jarring or chafing from movement 2 thick skin under animal's foot 3 sport reinforced protection for arms, legs, etc 4 block of writing-paper sheets 5 sl place where one lives; v 1 protect with pad, pads 2 fill with pads to enlarge shape of 3 extend (writing, speech) by adding superfluous material, words; adj **padded**; n **padding**

**paddle** n short, broad oar used for propelling a canoe or kayak; v propel by paddle; move feet or hands idly in shallow water

**paddock** n small grass field, or enclosure

**padlock** n detachable lock with hinged loop to be hooked through staple, etc; v fasten thus

**paean** n song of praise

**paella** n Spanish dish of rice, chicken, seafood, etc

**pagan** n, adj heathen, barbarian; n **-ism**

**page**[1] n boy attendant or servant; v try to get sb's attention, esp by a public address system or transmitter

**page**[2] n one side of leaf of book

**pageant** n splendid, imposing display in costume; series of richly costumed, historical tableaux or scenes; n **pageantry** gorgeous display

> **pageantry** n ceremony, grandeur, magnificence, pomp, ritual, show, spectacle, splendor

**pager** n radio apparatus for calling sb by coded signal

**paginate** v number page in book, magazine

**pagoda** n Oriental temple, tapering pinnacled tower with several storeys

**paid** pt, pp of **pay**

**pail** n bucket; n **pailful**

**pain** n 1 bodily suffering 2 mental suffering, anguish; pl **-s** effort; trouble; v inflict pain on; be source of pain; adj **painstaking** careful, industrious

**pain** n 1 (bodily suffering) ache, cramp, discomfort, hurt, irritation, pang, smart, soreness, spasm, sting, tenderness, twinge. 2 (mental suffering) agony, anguish, distress, grief, heartache, misery, suffering, torment, torture, unhappiness, woe

**painful** adj 1 causing pain 2 causing distress (adv **-ly**)

**painful** adj 1 (causing pain) aching, excruciating, hurting, inflamed, smarting, sore, stinging, tender, throbbing. 2 (causing distress) disagreeable, distressing, harrowing, hurtful, nasty, traumatic, trying, unpleasant, upsetting

**painkiller** adj killer of pain, as an analgesic
**painless** adj 1 not causing pain 2 not stressful or difficult
**paint** n coloring matter used to give color to surface; pigment; v 1 color; coat; portray with paint 2 fig describe vividly; idm **paint the town red** got out and enjoy a lively time; ns **painter; painting** act of coloring with paint; painted picture, esp hand-painted

**paint** n color, coloring, dye, stain, tint

**pair** n set of two similar things normally used together; mated couple of animals; v arrange in twos; mate; match

**pair** n brace, couple, duo, match, twins, twosome

**paisley** n fabric with curved designs and intricate colored patterns
**palace** n residence of sovereign or bishop; large public hall
**palate** n roof of mouth; sense of taste; adj **palatable** 1 good to taste 2 fig acceptable
**palatial** adj like, as of a palace
**pale** adj 1 whitish 2 not bright

**pale** adj 1 (whitish) anemic, ashen, as white as a sheet, colorless, deathly pale, drained, like death, like death warmed over, pallid, pasty, peaky, wan, white, white-faced. 2 (not bright) bleached, faded, pastel, washed-out, wishy-washy

**paleolithic** adj belonging to earlier Stone Age
**paleontology** n scientific study of fossils
**palette** n small board on which colors are mixed; range of colors
**palindrome** n word, line etc, reading same backward and forward
**pall**[1] n 1 cloth spread over coffin 2 fig covering of smoke, etc; n **pallbearer** person escorting, carrying coffin
**pall**[2] v become tedious to
**pallet** n 1 portable platform used in storage and movement of goods by forklift 2 small, hard straw mattress
**pallid** adj excessively pale; n **pallor**
**palm** n 1 inner surface of hand 2 tropical tree 3 leaf of this tree as symbol of victory; v conceal in palm; transfer by sleight of hand; ns **palmistry** fortune-telling from lines on palm of hand; **palmist**
**palpable** adj capable of being felt, touched
**palpitate** v beat irregularly; flutter; throb; n **palpitation** throbbing; irregular, quickened action of heart
**paltry** adj trifling, petty, insignificant
**pampas** n grassy plains of S America (**p.grass**)
**pamper** v overindulge

**pamper** v cosset, humor, indulge, make a fuss of, mollycoddle, pet, spoil, wait on hand and foot

**pamphlet** n short unbound treatise, usu on some current topic
**pan** n broad, shallow vessel, usu for cooking; v **pans, panning, panned** wash (gravel, etc) to extract gold
**panacea** n remedy for all ills

a b c d e f g h i j k l m n o p q r s t u v w x y z

**panache** *n Fr* ostentation; swagger

**pancake** *n* thin flat cake of fried batter

**pancreas** *n* gland secreting digestive juices and insulin

**panda** *n* large black and white Himalayan bear (giant panda); small reddish bear-cat

**pandemonium** *n* complete confusion; wild disorder, uproar

**pane** *n* single sheet of glass in window

**panel** *n* 1 rectangular piece of material set into surface (of door, dress, etc) 2 list of persons called for jury service 3 group of persons taking part in quiz, or game before audience; *v* **panels, paneling, paneled** fit, ornament with panels; *n* **paneling** series of panels

**pang** *n* sudden sharp pain

**panic** *n* sudden, excessive, infectious terror

**panic** *n* alarm, dismay, fear, horror, hysteria

**panicstricken** *adj* terrified

**panicstricken** *adj* aghast, frightened, hysterical, panicky, petrified, scared out of your wits, scared stiff, scared to death

**pannier** *n Fr* basket carried on back or side (of mule, etc)

**panorama** *n* 1 wide, unbroken view 2 series of scenes, pictures showing historical or other views; *adj* **panoramic**

**panpipes** *n mus* instrument of reed pipes of different lengths

**pansy** *n* wild or garden plant of violet family

**pant** *v* gasp for breath; *n* short, labored breath

**pant** *v* blow, breathe heavily, gasp, huff and puff, puff, wheeze

**panther** *n* leopard

**pantomime** *n* 1 theatrical performance, based on legend or fairy tale, *usu* given at Christmas 2 show where words are replaced with actions and gestures

**pantry** *n* room where food, plates etc are kept

**pants** *n pl* trousers; *idm* **with one's pants down** *coll* in a state of embarrassing unreadiness

**papaya** *n* tropical tree with fleshy edible fruit (*also* **pawpaw** *or* **custard apple**)

**paper** *n* 1 substance made from pulped wood fibers, rags etc, formed into thin sheets for writing, drawing, etc 2 newspaper 3 report, as for school 4 scholarly study of topic in form of article or lecture; *idm* **on paper** in theory; *v* cover with paper

**papier mâché** *n Fr* pulped paper mixed with paste and used as modeling material

**paprika** *n* red, capsicum pepper

**papyrus** *n Gk* sedgelike plant; writing material of this

**par** *n* equality of value; nominal value (*esp* of stocks, shares); *fig* normal state of health, etc; *golf* number of strokes reckoned as perfect score for hole, course

**para-** (**par-** before vowel or h mute) *prefix* 1 beside, beyond 2 contrary; wrong 3 ancillary to 4 defense against (*eg* **parachute** *abbr* **para** *also used as prefix*: **paratroop, parafoil,** etc)

**parable** *n* brief story with moral lesson

**parabola** *n* plane curve formed by intersection of cone by plane parallel to cone's side

**parachute** *n* umbrella-like apparatus used to retard descent of falling body; *v* leap, fall to earth using parachute; *n* **parachutist**

**parade** *n* 1 proud display 2 military review 3 ground where this takes place 4 promenade; *v* 1 muster 2 march solemnly past 3 display

**paradise** *n* Garden of Eden; heaven; place of perfect happiness

**paradox** *n* statement apparently absurd or self-contradictory yet really true; *adj* **-ical**

**paraffin** *n* inflammable, waxy hydrocarbon obtained from wood, petroleum, shale, etc

**paragon** *n* model of excellence or perfection

**paragraph** *n* 1 section in prose writing 2 short, separate news item

**parakeet** *n* small, long-tailed domesticated parrot kept as a pet

**parallel** *adj* (of lines, etc) equidistant in all parts; markedly similar; *n* **1** line equidistant from another; line of latitude **2** comparison; *v* compare; *n* **parallelogram** four-sided plane figure with parallel opposite sides

**paralysis** *n pl* **-yses** loss of sensation and motive power in any part of body; *v* **paralyze 1** affect with paralysis **2** *fig* check; render inoperative; *n, adj* **paralytic** paralyzed person

**paramedic** *n* auxiliary employee of medical service (not doctor or nurse); *adj* **-al**

**parameter** *n* **1** measurable feature or characteristic **2** *usu pl* limiting factor

**paramilitary** *adj* (of a force) organized like, but not part of an official army

**paramount** *adj* having supreme authority; preeminent; chief

**paranoia** *n* mental disorder, accompanied by delusions of grandeur or power

**paranormal** *adj* not explicable by known scientific laws

**parapet** *n* low wall; *mil* rampart in front of troops

**paraphernalia** *n pl* miscellaneous belongings, accessories, equipment

**paraphrase** *n* restatement of any passage; free translation; *v* express in other words

**paraplegic** *n* person paralyzed from the waist down

**parasite** *n* useless hanger on; *bio* organism which lives on or within another organism; *adj* **parasitic** of, caused by parasite

**parcel** *n* **1** package **2** piece of land; *v* **parcels, parceling, parceled** divide into parts; wrap up

> **parcel** *n* **1** (package) bale, box, bundle, carton, pack. **2** (piece of land) lot, patch, piece, plot

**parch** *v* make, cause to become excessively dry; scorch

**parchment** *n* animal skin dressed and prepared for writing on; manuscript, etc written on this

**pardon** *n* forgiveness; excuse; remission of punishment; *v* **1** forgive **2** grant pardon to; *adj* **pardonable**

> **pardon** *v* **1** (forgive) condone, excuse, let off, overlook. **2** (grant pardon) absolve, exonerate, release, reprieve

**pare** *v* trim; cut away edge or surface; gradually reduce

**parent** *n* father or mother; *adj* **parental**; *n* **parentage** ancestry, origin

**parish** *n* smallest local unit in civil or ecclesiastical administration; *n* **parishioner** inhabitant of parish

**parity** *n* **1** equality **2** *finance* equivalent state of currencies

**park** *n* **1** public garden in town **2** area of grass and trees surrounding public building **3** country area set aside as nature reserve, etc **4** place where cars, etc may park; *v* **1** put car, etc in garage or leave elsewhere **2** *coll* leave object in one place, *usu* temporarily; *n* **parking** act of leaving stationary vehicle

**Parkinson's disease** *n* disease of nervous system causing severe lack of muscular control

**parliament** *n* supreme legislative body of UK; representative law-making body; *adj* **parliamentary**; *n* **parliamentarian**

> **parliament** *n* assembly, congress, convocation, council, legislative assembly, legislature, senate

**parlor** *n* **1** (formerly) sitting-room where visitors were received **2** room or building that provides specified goods or services

**parody** *n pl* **-dies 1** mocking imitation of author's style or work **2** bad imitation, travesty; *v* **parodies, parodying, parodied** make fun of by imitating

> **parody** *v* caricature, imitate, lampoon, mimic, satirize, send up, take off

**parrot** n 1 tropical bird with hooked beak, able to imitate human speech 2 *fig* imitator; v repeat unthinkingly

**parsimony** n undue economy; stinginess; *adj* **parsimonious**

**parsley** n culinary herb

**parsnip** n plant with edible, cream-colored root

**parson** n rector; vicar; clergyman; n **parsonage** house of parson

**part**[1] n 1 portion 2 role 3 share 4 member of organism; *pl* **-s** area (*eg* **remote parts**); *adv* **partly** in part

> **part** n 1 (portion) bit, component, constituent, element, fraction, fragment, ingredient, percentage, piece, scrap, section, segment, share, slice. 2 (role) character, lines, words

**part**[2] v 1 separate; divide 2 go different ways; n **parting** 1 departure 2 line made where hair is combed in different directions

> **part** v 1 (separate) break, break up, cleave, divide, sever, split, tear. 2 (go different ways) break up, divorce, get a separation, get divorced, go their separate ways, part company, separate, split up

**parterre** n *Fr* level space with flowerbeds

**partial** *adj* 1 forming part of whole 2 biased

**participate** v have share in; partake; *ns* **participant, participation**

> **participate** v be involved in, contribute to, engage in, join in, have a hand in, have sth to do with, play a part in, take part in

**participle** n verbal adjective, having some functions of verb

**particle** n 1 very small amount, part 2 minor, indeclinable part of speech

**particular** *adj* 1 distinct; separate 2 peculiar 3 specific 4 fussy; n *pl* **-s** detailed account; specification

**partisan** n 1 adherent of party, cause, etc 2 guerilla fighter, *esp* in resistance movement; *adj* showing blind devotion

**partition** n 1 division 2 minor dividing wall in house; v divide into parts, sections

**partner** n 1 *golf, tennis, etc* one who plays with another, against opponents 2 one person of close couple 3 member of commercial partnership 4 one who dances with another; n **-ship** 1 state of being partner 2 association of two or more persons in business, etc

> **partner** n 1 (partner in sport) accomplice, ally, associate, collaborator, colleague, comrade, companion, coworker, fellow worker, sleeping partner, teammate. 2 (one of couple) boyfriend, common-law husband, common-law wife, companion, girlfriend, husband, live-in lover, mate, significant other, spouse, wife

**partridge** n game bird related to grouse

**party** n 1 group of persons holding same opinions, *esp* in politics 2 social gathering 3 squad of soldiers, etc 4 *coll* person

> **party** n 1 (political) bloc, faction, grouping. 2 (social gathering) bash, do, get-together, orgy, reception, social, soirée

**pass** v 1 go by 2 give (by hand) 3 spend (time) 4 reach acceptable standard (in test) 5 approve (law, regulation) by voting 6 (cause to) move in specified direction 7 *sport* give (by throw, kick, etc) 8 transfer (money, goods) illegally 9 examine and find acceptable 10 utter (remark, judgment); 11 be changed (from one state to another); n 1 narrow way between mountains 2 permit (for entry, travel, etc) 3 *sport* act of giving ball, etc to another player 4 acceptable standard in test or examination 5 *fencing* thrust or lunge 6 *cards* no bid; *adj* **passable**; *ns* **passerby; passing** 1 going past 2 end; death; *adj* 1 going past 2 momentary, brief

**pass** v 1 (go by) drive by, drive past, go past, move past, overtake, pass by, run by, run past, walk by, walk past. 2 (give by hand) circulate, deal, deliver, give, hand, hand over, pass on, present, proffer, transfer. 3 (spend time) fill, occupy, spend, while away. 4 (reach acceptable standard) be successful, get through, graduate, qualify. 5 (approve law) accept, agree, approve, confirm, enact, establish, promulgate, ratify, validate, vote through

**passage** n 1 voyage; crossing 2 accommodation on ship 3 part of book, etc referred to separately 4 means of access

**passenger** n one who travels in ship, by car, train, etc but does not operate it

**passion** n 1 strong feeling 2 sexual desire 3 wrath 4 cap sufferings and death of Christ

**passion** n 1 (strong feeling) animation, ardor, devotion, emotion, enthusiasm, excitement, fervor, fire, heat, keenness, zeal. 2 (sexual desire) arousal, desire, craving, fondness, infatuation, love, lust

**passionate** adj quick-tempered, intense, ardent

**passionate** adj burning, devoted, eager, emotional, enthusiastic, excitable, excited, fervent, fiery, hot-headed, impassioned, tempestuous, vehement, zealous.

**passive** adj 1 inactive; offering no active resistance 2 ling of verb form expressing action by which grammatical subject is affected; n such a grammatical form (also **passive voice**); adv **-ly**; ns **-ness, passivity**

**passport** n official document granted to enable holder to travel abroad, etc

**password** n secret word, phrase identifying person as entitled to enter (camp, society, etc); countersign

**past** adj gone by; ended; taking place in past; n time gone by; earlier life; prep beyond; after; n **p. participle** form of verb which combines with auxiliary verbs to make perfect tenses and passive tenses

**pasta** n It food from paste of flour, eggs, and water cut into different shapes

**paste** n 1 soft, slightly moist compound 2 adhesive compound 3 vitreous compound used for artificial gems 4 compound of finely minced food, esp meat or fish, for spreading; v fasten, affix with paste

**pastel** n crayon made of powdered pigment mixed with gum, or oil; drawing in pastel; adj delicately colored

**pasteurization** n sterilization (of milk, etc) by heating; v **pasteurize**

**pastime** n recreation; amusement

**pastime** n distraction, diversion, entertainment, hobby, interest, leisure activity, pursuit, sport

**pastor** n priest; minister; adj **pastoral** 1 of office of pastor 2 connected with shepherds 3 (of land) used for pasture

**pastry** n 1 sweet baked paste of flour and fat 2 pie, tart, etc made of this 3 small rich cream-filled cake

**pasture** n grass for food of cattle; land on which cattle are grazed; v graze

**pasty** n small pie of meat and potatoes, baked without dish; adj pale, unhealthy-looking

**pat** n 1 quick light touch 2 small shaped lump of butter; v **pats, patting, patted** tap (dog, horse, etc) lightly with hand

**patch** n 1 piece of material used to cover, repair hole in garment, etc 2 black spot worn as facial ornament 3 small plot of land; v mend by means of patch; adj **patchy** not consistent in quality, etc; adv **-ily**

**patchwork** n needlework of patches of different colors

**pâté** n Fr rich paste of finely minced meat (esp liver) or fish

**patella** n Lat med kneecap

a b c d e f g h i j k l m n o p q r s t u v w x y z

**patent** *adj* 1 obvious 2 protected by patent; *adv* **-ly** clearly; *n* **p. leather** very glossy, *usu* black leather used for handbags, shoes; *v* secure patent

**paternal** *adj* of father, fatherly; *ns* **paternity** fatherhood; **paternalism** policy of controlling people by supplying their needs without giving freedom of choice; *adj* **-istic**

**paternoster** *n* The Lord's Prayer; eleventh bead of rosary

**path** *n* 1 track 2 *fig* line of conduct; *n* **pathfinder** discoverer of new route

> **path** *n* (track) alley, avenue, bridle path, bridleway, footpath, lane, pathway, pavement, road, route, trail, walkway, way

**pathetic** *adj* 1 inspiring pity 2 hopelessly ineffectual; feeble in character; *adv* **-ally**

> **pathetic** *adj* (inspiring pity) abject, abysmal, bad, dismal, feeble, hapless, hopeless, ineffectual, miserable, pitiable, pitiful, poor, sad, sorry, weak, wretched

**pathology** *n* science of diseases; *adj* **pathological** caused by, of nature of disease; morbid; *n* **pathologist**

**pathos** *n* that which evokes sympathy, sorrow, or pity

**patience** *n* 1 endurance without complaint 2 cardgame

> **patience** *n* (endurance) calm, calmness, forbearance, fortitude, passivity, resignation, stoicism, tolerance

**patient** *adj* 1 enduring provocation or pain 2 persistent in sth; *n* person under medical treatment

> **patient** *adj* 1 (enduring provocation) calm, long-suffering, passive, resigned, stoical, tolerant, waiting. 2 (persistent) indefatigable, persevering, untiring

**patio** *n* paved area close to a house

**patois** *n Fr* local, provincial form of speech

**patriarch** *n* father, head of family, clan, etc; *adj* **patriarchal** venerable

**patrician** *n* member of ancient Roman nobility; one of noble birth; *adj* of noble birth

**patricide** *n* murder of one's father

**patriot** *n* one who is devoted to and loyally supports his or her country; *n* **patriotism** love of one's country

**patriotic** *adj* inspired by patriotism

> **patriotic** *adj* flag-waving, gung-ho, jingoistic, loyal, loyalist, nationalistic

**patrol** *v* **patrols, patrolling, patrolled** walk regularly up and down (in); go the rounds; be on guard duty; *n* 1 small body of troops, police, etc patrolling 2 part of a Scout troop

> **patrol** *v* be on the beat, cruise, do the rounds, guard, inspect, keep vigil, monitor, police, watch

**patron** *n* 1 supporter 2 *fml* regular customer; *n* **patronage** special support; right to distribute jobs, benefits

> **patron** *n* 1 (supporter) backer, benefactor, contributor, donor, friend, protector, sponsor. 2 (customer) client, habitué, regular, visitor

**patronize** *v* 1 treat condescendingly (*adj* **-zing**) 2 encourage 3 support by being customer treat

> **patronize** *v* (condescend) be condescending, look down on, look down your nose at, sneer at, talk down to.

**patter** *v* 1 run with quick, light steps 2 utter, speak hurriedly; *n* 1 succession of light taps 2 speech, jargon (of thieves, conjurers, comedians, etc)

**pattern** *n* **1** model; shape as guide in constructing anything; sample **2** design

**pattern** *n* **1** (model) blueprint, guide, instructions, plan, sample, specimen, stencil, template. **2** (design) arrangement, decoration, device, figure, marking, motif, ornamentation, shape

**patty** *n* small pie

**paunch** *n* belly; *v* remove entrails (of rabbit, etc)

**pauper** *n* destitute person supported by charity or at public expense

**pause** *n* brief stop or rest; *v* stop for a while; hesitate

**pause** *n* abeyance, break, cessation, delay, gap, halt, hesitation, interlude, interruption, interval, rest, silence
**pause** *v* break off, cease, delay, interrupt, rest, stop, wait

**pave** *v* cover surface with flat stones, etc; *idm* **pave the way (for)** prepare (for); make possible; *ns* **pavement** paved walk for pedestrians; **paving 1** act of, material for laying a paved surface **2** flat smooth rectangular stone (*also* **paving stone**)

**pavilion** *n* **1** large tent **2** building attached to sportsfield **3** summerhouse

**paw** *n* foot of quadruped with claws; *v* scrape with forefoot; handle roughly and unnecessarily

**pawn** *v* deposit article with (pawnbroker); *n* **1** loan thus raised **2** chess piece; *n* **pawnbroker** one who lends money at interest on articles pledged

**pawpaw = papaya**

**pay** *v* **1** give money for goods or services **2** produce profit for **3** discharge (debt) **4** render; offer; *idm* **pay one's way** not rely on borrowing; *n* salary; wages; *adj* **payable** due to be paid (*pt, pp* **paid**); *ns* **payee** one to whom payment is made; **payer**; **payment** amount paid

**pay** *v* **1** (give money) buy, cough up, fork out, foot the bill, hand over, lay out, part with, shell out, pay out, pay up, remit, settle up, spend. **2** (produce profit) be advantageous, be profitable, be rewarding, be worthwhile, make a profit, make money, pay off. **3** (discharge debt) cancel, clear, close, discharge, liquidate, meet, repay, settle, square
**pay** *n* allowance, commission, earnings, emoluments, honorarium, income, payment, take-home pay, remittance, remuneration, reward, stipend, wage

**payload** *n* **1** part of ship's load for which payment is received; passengers and cargo **2** *mil* explosive power of missile, bomb, etc **3** amount of equipment carried by spacecraft

**paymaster** *n* person holding money and in control

**PC** *abbr* **1** personal computer **2** politically correct

**PE** *abbr* physical education

**pea** *n* leguminous climbing plant, with edible seeds enclosed in pod

**peace** *n* **1** calm **2** freedom from war

**peace** *n* **1** (calm) calmness, peacefulness, quiet, repose, rest, serenity, tranquillity. **2** (freedom from war) armistice, concord, harmony, pacification, peacetime, reconciliation, truce

**peaceable** *adj* at peace; not quarrelsome

**peaceful** *adj* **1** free from war **2** calm

**peaceful** *adj* **1** (free from war) at peace, calm, harmonious, untroubled. **2** (calm) at peace, at rest, placid, quiet, restful, serene, still, tranquil

**peach** *n* stonefruit with pink velvety skin; tree bearing this;

**peacock** *n* bird with brilliantly colored fan-shaped tail; *fem* **peahen**

a
b
c
d
e
f
g
h
i
j
k
l
m
n
o
p
q
r
s
t
u
v
w
x
y
z

**peak** n 1 pointed mountain top 2 fig highest point 3 projecting part of cap over brow; v reach high or highest point

> **peak** n 1 (mountain top) brow, crest, hilltop, pinnacle, point, summit, tip, top. 2 (high point) acme, apex, climax, height, high, high-water mark, maximum, pinnacle, top, zenith

**peaked** adj 1 having peak 2 having drawn, emaciated look

**peal** n loud ringing of bells; set of bells tuned to each other; loud, reverberant sound; v ring loudly

> **peal** v chime, clang, resound, ring, ring out, toll

**peanut** n pealike plant with pods that ripen underground (also **groundnut**)

**pear** n sweet juicy oval fruit; tree bearing this; **prickly pear** type of cactus; its edible fruit

**pearl** n lustrous concretion found in some mollusks, esp oyster, and used as jewel; cultured pearl; mother-of-pearl

**peasant** n country person, rustic; n **peasantry** peasants collectively

**peat** n fibrous, partly decomposed vegetable matter found in bogs; this used for fuel

**pebble** n small rounded stone; adj **pebbly**

**pecan** n N American hickory nut

**peck** v 1 strike with beak 2 coll kiss hurriedly; n 1 blow of beak 2 coll quick kiss

**peculiar** adj 1 individual 2 unusual; n **peculiarity** distinguishing characteristic; eccentricity; oddity; adv **-ly** strangely, specially

> **peculiar** adj 1 (individual) characteristic, distinctive, distinguishing, exclusive, own, particular, proper, special, specific, unique. 2 (unusual) bizarre, eccentric, extraordinary, funny, odd, out of the ordinary, queer, singular, strange, weird

**pedagogue, pedagog** n 1 schoolmaster 2 narrow-minded teacher

**pedal** n 1 lever, operated by foot, for transmitting power or movement 2 lever used by player's foot to modify tone of piano, organ, etc; v **pedals, pedaling, pedaled** use pedals of organ etc; work, drive by pedals

**pedant** n one who attaches exaggerated importance to minor details; one who makes tiresome display of learning; adj **pedantic**; n **pedantry** tiresome display of learning

**peddle** v retail goods from house to house

**pedestal** n base of large column or statue

**pedestrian** n person on foot; walker; adj going on foot; fig prosaic, uninspiring; v **-ize** make accessible only to pedestrians; n **-ization**

**pediatrics** n branch of medicine specializing in children; adj **-tric**; n **-trician** children's doctor

**pedicure** n chiropody; care and treatment of feet

**pedigree** n genealogy; ancestry; adj of animals bred from known stock

> **pedigree** n background, descent, family, family tree, heritage, lineage

**peddler** n itinerant vendor of small wares

**peek** n, v glance with half-closed eyes

**peel** n skin of fruit or vegetable; v strip off, remove any form of covering

**peep** v look hastily, furtively; n such a look; n **peeping Tom** voyeur

> **peep** v glance, glimpse, look, peek, sneak a look, snoop, take a butcher's inf

**peer**[1] n person or thing of equal merit, quality, etc; nobleman; adj **peerless** unrivaled, without equal; ns **peerage** rank of peer; body of peers; fem **peeress**

**peer**[2] v look closely, gaze fixedly at

> **peer** v look, squint inf, stare

**peg** n wooden or metal pin, bolt; v **pegs, pegging, pegged** fasten with pegs; fix price, etc by regulations

**pejorative** adj disparaging; depreciatory

**Pekinese** n small Chinese lapdog

**pelagic, pelagian** adj of, in deep sea

**pelican** n large, fish-eating water bird, with food-storing pouch beneath its beak

**pellet** n small ball; small shot; pill

**pelt**[1] v throw things at; (of rain, etc) beat down heavily; run quickly

**pelt**[2] n raw animal skin with fur or wool

**pelvis** n bony girdle formed by hipbones and sacrum; adj **pelvic**

**pen**[1] n small enclosure for domestic animals, fowl, etc; v **pens, penning, penned** put in pen; imprison; adj **pent** confined; repressed

> **pen** n cage, coop, corral, enclosure, pound, sheep fold, pigsty, stall, stockade, sty

**pen**[2] n instrument for writing; v write, put on paper

**penal** adj connected with punishment, esp legal; v **penalize** punish, handicap

**penalty** n legal punishment; loss, suffering as result of folly, etc; sport disadvantage imposed for breaking rule

> **penalty** n caution, endorsement, fine, forfeit, punishment, sentence

**penance** n act performed as proof of repentance

**penchant** n inclination, partiality, liking

**pencil** n instrument for writing, etc, consisting of graphite or crayon cased in wood; small brush used by painters; v **pencils, penciling, penciled** draw, write with pencil

**pendant** n hanging ornament; locket

**pendent** adj hanging, suspended

**pending** adj not decided, unfinished; prep during; awaiting

**pendulous** adj hanging freely; swinging to and fro

**pendulum** n swinging weight, esp one regulating clock mechanism

**penetrate** v pierce; enter; permeate; fig see through; reach mind of; adj **penetrable; penetrating** piercing; shrill; discerning; n **-ation** acute, subtlety of mind

**penguin** n flightless Antarctic seabird

**penicillin** n one of anti-infective class of antibiotics, obtained from mold

**peninsula** n protuberance of land bordered on three sides by water; adj **peninsular**

**penis** n male sex organ

**penitence** n sorrow for sin; adj **penitent** having sense of sin; repentant; n one who repents of sin; n **penitentiary** reformatory; prison

**penknife** n small folding pocketknife

**pen name** n pseudonym used by writer

> **pen name** n alias, assumed name, nom de guerre, nom de plume, pseudonym, stage name

**penny** n copper coin worth one cent; 100th part of one dollar; pl **pennies, pence**; adj **penniless** poor, destitute

**pension** n periodic payment made to retired workerss, old people, the aged, etc

**pensioner** n person receiving pension

> **pensioner** n old age pensioner, retired person, senior citizen, veteran

**pensive** adj immersed in sad thoughts; wistful

> **pensive** adj contemplative, day-dreaming, deep in thought, meditative, reflective, ruminating, thinking, thoughtful, withdrawn

**pentagon** n plane figure with five sides

**penultimate** adj last but one

**penury** n want, destitution; adj **penurious** poor; mean

**peony** n shrub with large red, pink, or white flowers

**people** n 1 race, nation 2 human beings in general 3 the populace 4 relatives, family; v populate

> **people** n 1 (race, nation) clan, community, ethnic group, tribe. 2 (human beings) folk, human race, humanity, humankind, man, mankind, men, mortals, individuals. 3 (the populace) citizens, common people, electorate, hoi polloi, lower orders, masses, ordinary people, plebs, population, proletariat, public, society, subjects, voters

**pepper** n pungent aromatic condiment, made from dried berries of pepper tree; v sprinkle with pepper; pelt with missiles; adj **peppery** tasting of pepper; fig irritable

**peppercorn** n dried berry of pepper plant

**peppermint** n 1 pungent aromatic herb of mint family 2 candy flavored with peppermint

**per** prep by means of; for each; advs **p. annum** each year; **p. capita** per head; **p.cent** per hundred (in percentage); **p. se** in itself

**perceive** v become aware of through senses; apprehend

**perceptible** adj that can be perceived

> **perceptible** adj apparent, appreciable, audible, detectable, discernible, observable, noticeable, palpable, perceivable, recognizable, visible

**perception** n faculty of perceiving; immediate awareness

**perceptive** adj quick to notice; aware

**percentage** n rate, allowance, proportion per hundred

**perch**[1] n edible freshwater fish

**perch**[2] n rod, branch for birds to roost on; v (of birds) alight, sit

> **perch** v balance, land, poise, position yourself, rest, roost, settle, station yourself

**percolate** v filter, ooze, drip slowly (through); ns **percolation**; **percolator** coffeepot with filter

**percussion** n 1 impact; violent collision 2 musical instruments played by being struck

**peremptory** adj imperious; dictatorial; precluding opposition, appeal, etc

**perennial** adj lasting year after year; never failing; n plant lasting more than two years

**perfect** adj faultless; complete; of highest state of excellence; n verbal tense expressing complete action; v improve; make highly competent; n **perfection** state of being perfect

> **perfect** adj consummate, flawless, ideal, immaculate, impeccable, incomparable, irreproachable, matchless, pure, spotless, sublime, unbeatable, unblemished, unmarred, untarnished

**perforate** v pierce; penetrate; make hole(s) in; n **perforation** 1 act, result, of perforating 2 holes made in paper to make tearing easy

**perform** v 1 accomplish 2 enact (play) in public 3 play on musical instrument; ns **performance**; **performer** one who performs

> **perform** v 1 (accomplish) achieve, carry out, complete, discharge, do, effect, execute, finish, fulfill, pull off. 2 (enact) act, depict, play, present, produce, put on, render, represent, stage

**perfume** n 1 pleasing smell 2 scented liquid applied to body or clothing; v impart fragrance to

> **perfume** n 1 (pleasing smell) aroma, bouquet, fragrance, odor, scent, smell. 2 (scented liquid) after-shave, cologne, eau de cologne, fragrance, scent, toilet water

**perfunctory** adj superficial, hasty, indifferent

**perhaps** *adv* possibly
**perigree** *n* point at which orbit is nearest to Earth
**peril** *n* danger, hazard
**perilous** *adj* dangerous, risky

> **perilous** *adj* hazardous, insecure, precarious, threatening, uncertain, unsafe

**perimeter** *n* distance around plane figure; outer edge; boundary

> **perimeter** *n* border, bounds, circumference, confines, edge, fringe, frontier, limit, margin, periphery, verge

**period** *n* 1 interval of time 2 era; epoch 3 phase of menstrual cycle 4 grammatical mark at end of sentence (.); *adj* characteristic of certain period of time (of furniture, dress, etc); *adj* **periodic** recurring at regular intervals

> **period** *n* (interval of time) interval, phase, season, session, space, span, spell, stage, stint, stretch, term, time, while

**periodical** *adj* periodic; *n* magazine published at regular intervals, *eg* weekly
**periphery** *n* circumference; outer surface
**periscope** *n* apparatus for seeing objects above eyelevel, where direct view is obstructed
**perish** *v* 1 die 2 decay

> **perish** *v* 1 (die) be killed, bite the dust, expire, fall, kick the bucket, lose your life, pass away, snuff it. 2 (decay) decompose, disintegrate, go bad, go off, go sour, rot, waste, wither

**perishable** *adj* liable to speedy decay; *n pl* goods specially liable to decay
**perished** *adj* 1 *coll* suffering from exposure to cold 2 (of rubber and fabrics) deteriorated in quality; no longer usable

**perjure** *v* bear false witness; forswear oneself; *n* **perjury** deliberately false testimony under oath; crime of making false statement under oath
**permafrost** *n* permanently frozen subsoil
**permanent** *adj* continuing without change; lasting; *ns* **permanence** state of being permanent; **permanency** something that is permanent

> **permanent** *adj* abiding, constant, continual, continuous, durable, endless, enduring, eternal, everlasting, fixed, immutable, indestructible, invariable, life-long, never-ending, nonstop, perpetual, persistent, steadfast, unchanging

**permeate** *v* pass through; saturate; *adj* **permeable** allowing free passage of liquids
**permission** *n* leave; sanction; *adj* **permissible** allowable; **permissive** allowing unusual freedom, *esp* in sexual behavior (*adv* **-ly** *n* **-ness**)

> **permission** *n* agreement, allowance, approval, assent, authorization, consent, dispensation, franchise, freedom, go-ahead, green light, liberty, license, thumbs-up

**permit** *v* **permits, permitting, permitted** allow, tolerate; *n* warrant; license; document giving formal permission

> **permit** *v* agree, approve, assent, authorize, consent, countenance, enable, endorse, entitle, give permission, grant, legalize, let, license, sanction

**pernicious** *adj* highly injurious; deadly
**perpendicular** *adj* exactly upright, vertical; *n* line at right angles to another line or surface
**perpetrate** *v* commit, be guilty of; *ns* **perpetration**; **perpetrator**
**perpetual** *adj* everlasting; constantly repeated; *n* **perpetuity** (**in perpetuity** for ever)

**perpetual** *adj* abiding, constant, continual, continuous, durable, endless, enduring, eternal, fixed, immutable, indestructible, invariable, lasting, life-long, never-ending, nonstop, permanent, persistent, steadfast, unchanging

**perpetuate** *v* cause to last indefinitely; preserve from oblivion; *n* **perpetuation**

**perpetuate** *v* eternalize, immortalize, keep going, maintain, preserve, sustain

**perplex** *v* puzzle; make confused; *n* **perplexity** bewilderment, confusion

**perplex** *v* baffle, bamboozle, bewilder, dumbfound, confound, confuse, flummox, mystify, nonplus, stump, throw

**perquisite** *n* profit, monetary or in kind, in addition to regular wages or salary
**perry** *n* drink of fermented pear juice
**persecute** *v* harass; treat cruelly, *esp* on account of religious or political reasons; *ns* **persecution, persecutor**

**persecute** *v* abuse, afflict, distress, hound, hunt, ill-treat, maltreat, mistreat, oppress, pursue, torment, torture, victimize

**persevere** *v* persist doggedly, patiently in attaining purpose; *n* **perseverance** prolonged, steadfast effort

**persevere** *v* carry on, continue, endure, go on, hammer away *inf*, hang on, hold on, hold out, keep at it *inf*, keep going, keep it up *inf*, maintain, persist, pursue, remain

**persiflage** *n* banter
**persimmon** *n* hardwood tree; its edible fruit
**persist** *v* continue in spite of opposition; remain; endure

**persistent** *adj* 1 obstinate 2 tending to recur; *ns* **persistence** tenacity of purpose; **persistency** obstinacy

**persistent** *adj* 1 (obstinate) assiduous, determined, dogged, hard-working, immovable, insistent, patient, persevering, relentless, resolute, steadfast, stubborn, tenacious, tireless, unflagging, untiring, unwavering. 2 (tending to recur) ceaseless, constant, continual, continuous, endless, everlasting, incessant, interminable, lasting, long-lasting, never-ending, permanent, perpetual, relentless, unending, unrelenting

**person** *n* 1 human being (*pl* **people**) 2 individual (*pl* **persons**) 3 *ling* category of pronoun or verb, *eg* **first p.** the one(s) speaking; **second p.** the one(s) spoken to; **third p.** any other individual(s)

**person** *n* (human being) being, body, character, figure, human, individual, mortal, soul

**personable** *adj* attractive in appearance and manner
**personal** *adj* 1 by, of, for a person 2 private 3 derogatory; impertinent 4 of the body
**personality** *n* 1 person's qualities and character as a whole 2 (person with) lively or forceful character 3 well-known, *usu* popular person
**personify** *v* represent as person; typify, embody; *n* **personification**
**personnel** *n* all members of staff
**perspective** *n* art of depicting three-dimensional objects on plane surface; *idm* **in perspective** in proper relations
**perspicacious** *adj* having keen mental judgment or understanding
**perspicuous** *adj* clearly expressed; lucid
**perspire** *v* sweat; exude moisture through pores; *n* **perspiration**
**persuade** *v* induce to think, believe

persuade *v* cajole, coax, coerce, convince, entice, impel, induce, influence, press, prevail upon, prompt, sway, talk into, tempt, urge, wheedle *inf*, win over

persuasion *n* creed; way of thinking; *adj* persuasive

pert *adj* jaunty, lively, flippant

pertain *v* belong to; have reference to; concern

pertinent *adj* relevant; to the point

perturb *v* disturb; throw into disorder, confusion; *n* -ation agitation of mind; disorder; deviation of planet from true orbit

peruse *v* read through; look over; *n* perusal

pervade *v* penetrate thoroughly; *adj* pervasive (*ns* -ness, pervasion)

perverse *adj* intractable; self-willed; *n* perversity

perverse *adj* awkward, contrary, difficult, headstrong, inflexible, obstinate, pig-headed, rebellious, stubborn, uncooperative, unruly, wayward

pervert *v* turn, divert from proper use; *n* perversion

pervert *v* abuse, bend, distort, falsify, misapply, misconstrue, misrepresent, misuse, twist, warp

pervious *adj* permeable, penetrable

peseta *n* Spanish coin

peso *n* unit of money in some S American countries

pessimism *n* tendency to look on dark side of things; doctrine that world is essentially evil; *n* -ist

pessimistic *adj* in the habit of looking on the dark side of things

pessimistic *adj* bleak, cynical, defeatist, fatalistic, gloomy, negative, resigned

pest *n* 1 troublesome person, animal, or thing 2 garden parasite 3 blight, mildew, etc

pest *n* 1 (troublesome person, thing) annoyance, bother, inconvenience, irritation, nuisance, pain, pain in the neck, trial. 2 (garden parasite) bug, creepy-crawly *inf*, insect, parasite

pester *v* worry, plague, *esp* with trivialities

pester *v* annoy, badger, bother, disturb, harass, harry, hassle, hound, irk, nag, torment, trouble

pestilence *n* fatal infectious, contagious disease, *esp* bubonic plague; *adj* -ilent

pestle *n* instrument for pounding substances in mortar

pet *n* tame animal kept as object of affection; favorite, cherished child; *v* pets, petting, petted treat as pet; fondle

petal *n* one section of corolla of flowers

petite *adj* Fr (of woman) of small, dainty build

petition *n* entreaty; formal application, *esp* one to sovereign, or court of law; *v* address petition to; *n* -er

petrify *v* petrifies, petrifying, petrified 1 *fig* paralyze with fear, etc 2 turn into stone

petrify *v* (paralyze with fear) fill sb with fear, frighten, horrify, panic, scare, scare sb out of his/her wits/skin, scare sb to death, stun, stupefy, terrify

petroleum *n* inflammable mineral oil from coal used for fuel, ointments, etc

pettish *adj* petulant

petty *adj* trivial; of small worth, scale

petty *adj* inconsequential, insignificant, little, minor, negligible, paltry, slight, small, trifling, unimportant

petulance *n* peevishness; irritability; *adj* petulant

**pew** n 1 fixed bench, used as seat in church 2 coll seat, chair

**pewter** n alloy of tin and lead; vessel, plate, etc made of this

**pH** n measure of alkalinity or acidity

**phalanx** n 1 body of closely-massed soldiers 2 fig resolute group of persons

**phallus** n penis; image of it used in some primitive forms of religion; adj **phallic**

**phantom** n supernatural or imaginary figure

> **phantom** n apparition, ghost, phantasm, specter, spirit, spook

**pharaoh** n title of kings of ancient Egypt

**pharmacy** n preparation and dispensing of drugs

**pharynx** n med cavity at back of nose and mouth opening into larynx

**phase** n stage in development

> **phase** n chapter, period, part, point, season, spell, stage, step, time

**PhD** abbr doctor of philosophy; (person with) higher degree of doctorate

**pheasant** n gamebird with long tail and brilliant coloring

**phenomenon** n anything perceived by senses; uncommon, remarkable event; pl **phenomena**; adj **phenomenal** relating to phenomena; extraordinary

**pheromone** n bio chemical secreted by animal, insect to attract others of species

**phil-** prefix loving; studying

**philanthropy** n love of mankind; benevolence; n **philanthropist**

**philately** n stamp-collecting; n **philatelist**

**philistine** n, adj (person) showing no understanding of, hostile to artistic creation, beauty, or culture

**philosophy** n 1 theory of knowledge 2 mental balance, calmness in dealing with events, circumstances; n **philosopher**; adj **-sophic(al)**; v **-sophize** indulge in philosophical theories; moralize

**phlegm** n 1 viscid substance secreted by mucous membranes, esp in nose and throat 2 apathy; indifference 3 calmness; adj **-atic** not easily excited; sluggish

**phobia** n morbid, irrational fear

> **phobia** n antipathy, aversion, dread, fear, hang-up, hatred, horror, loathing, neurosis, obsession, repulsion, terror

**phone** n, v, adj coll telephone

> **phone** v call, dial, give sb a buzz, give sb a call, give sb a ring, make a phone call, ring up

**phonetic** adj of, relating to vocal sounds; n pl science of vocal sounds

**phony** adj coll false; n coll insincere person

> **phony** adj artificial, assumed, bogus, counterfeit, fake, false, fictitious, forged, fraudulent, imitation, mock, pretend, pseudo, put-on, sham, spurious, trick

**phosphorus** n nonmetallic element emitting glow in the dark; ns **phosphate** salt of phosphorus acid; **phosphide** compound of phosphorous; **phosphorescence** property of emitting slight glow in dark, without heat

**photo** n, v abbr photograph

**photocopier** n machine for making multiple photographic copies of documents; n, v **photocopy** (make) such a copy

**photoelectric** adj pertaining to effect of light on electrons; n **p. cell** device that detects, measures light (also **photocell**)

**photogenic** adj having qualities that make an attractive photograph

**photograph** n picture produced by action of light on sensitized film; v take photograph of; n **-er**; adj **-ic**; n **photography**

> **photograph** n exposure, image, likeness, photo, picture, print, shot, snapshot

**photon** n minute particle of light

**photosensitive** adj affected by action of light

**photosynthesis** n (in plants) conversion of carbon dioxide and water into food by using energy from sunlight; v **-thesize**

**phrasal** adj of a phrase; n **p. verb** verb combined with preposition or adverbial particle to give new meaning

**phrase** n group of words forming part to sentence; striking remark; idiomatic expression; v express in words

**phrenology** n theory that one's character, intelligence, etc can be deduced from shape of skull; study of shape of skull; n **-ologist**

**physical** adj 1 pertaining to matter 2 pertaining to nature and natural features of universe 3 connected with human or animal body

**physician** n one trained in medical profession, who diagnoses and treats disease, but does not operate

**physics** n study of properties of matter and energy; n **physicist** one skilled in, or student of physics

**physiology** n study of functions and vital processes of living beings; n **physiologist**

**physiotherapy** n remedial treatment by massage, heat, exercise, etc; n **physiotherapist**

**physique** n Fr physical form, structure; constitution

**piano** n keyboard instrument with strings struck by hammers; n **pianist** one who plays the piano

**piccolo** n small shrill flute

**pick**[1] n tool with wooden shaft, long curved head pointed at one end and chisel-edge at other; n **pickax** tool for breaking ground

**pick**[2] v 1 pluck; gather 2 choose 3 open (lock) without key 4 remove unwanted pieces from 5 nibble; phr vs **pick up** 1 take by hand 2 take by transportation 3 acquire or learn informally 4 make a casual acquaintance, usu with person of opposite sex 5 resume (activity) after interval 6 recover 7 find by chance

**pick** v 1 (pluck) collect, cut, gather, harvest, pull. 2 (choose) decide, elect, favor, make a choice, opt for, plump for, prefer, select, settle on, single out, vote for

**picket** n 1 pointed stake 2 striker posted outside place of employment to dissuade others from working 3 mil patrol on special duty; v 1 fence with pickets 2 act as picket in strike

**pickle** n 1 brine, vinegar, etc used to preserve food 2 food so preserved 3 coll trouble; v preserve in pickle; adj sl **pickled** drunk

**pickpocket** n thief stealing directly from sb's pocket

**picnic** n casual meal eaten out-of-doors; coll thing easily done; v **picnics, picnicking, picnicked** go on, take picnic

**pictorial** adj expressed in pictures

**picture** n 1 painting; drawing; photograph 2 vivid verbal description 3 mental image 4 pl **-s** cinema; v make picture of; imagine; describe

**picture** n 1 (painting, etc) drawing, illustration, image, likeness, photograph, portrait, print, representation, sketch. 2 (verbal description) account, depiction, image, impression, report **picture** v call to mind, conceive, conjure up, envisage, evoke, think up, visualize

**picturesque** adj attractive

**picturesque** adj beautiful, charming, idyllic, lovely, pretty, quaint, scenic, striking

**pidgin** n mixture of English and native tongues to be heard in some Oriental and African countries

**pie** n dish of meat, fruit, etc, covered with pastry and baked; n **p. chart** diagram consisting of circle divided into segments to illustrate relative proportions of parts of the whole under study

a b c d e f g h i j k l m n o **p** q r s t u v w x y z

**piebald** *adj* irregularly marked in black and white blotches

**piece** *n* **1** bit **2** item **3** literary, artistic or musical composition; *v* put together; join

> **piece** *n* (bit) bite, chunk, dollop, fraction, fragment, hunk, length, lump, morsel, part, portion, quantity, section, segment, share, shred, slab, slice, sliver, unit

**pied** *adj* of two contrasting colors

**pier** *n* **1** column, mass of stone, supporting arch, etc **2** projecting wharf, or landing-place; jetty

**pierce** *v* make hole in; penetrate

> **pierce** *v* bore, drill, impale, jab, perforate, prick, puncture, spike, stab

**piercing** *adj* keen, penetrating

**piety** *n* devotion to God; dutiful, loyal feelings

**pig** *n* **1** swine; hog **2** *coll* greedy, selfish person **3** oblong casting of metal; *adj* **pigheaded** stupidly obstinate; *n* **pigsty 1** pen for pigs **2** very dirty room or house

**pigeon** *n* wild or domesticated bird of dove species

**pigment** *n* substance for coloring, paint, dye; natural color in living tissue

**pigmy** *n* = **pygmy**

**pike** *n* **1** large freshwater fish **2** short spear **3** highway

**pilaf, pilaff** *n* dish of meat, rice, and spices

**pilchard** *n* large-scaled fish of herring family

**pile**[1] *n* heap or mass; large building; *v* heap up; make into pile; stack

> **pile** *n* accumulation, agglomeration, bundle, collection, heap, mass, mound, mountain, stack, stock, store, tower
> **pile** *v* accumulate, amass, assemble, collect, gather, heap, hoard, load, pile up, stack up, stockpile, stock up, store up

**pile**[2] *n* nap, *esp* of velvet; high standing fibers of cloth

**pilfer** *v* steal small quantity; *n* **-er**

**pilgrim** *n* **1** one who visits sacred place, shrine for religious reasons **2** an English colonist settling at Plymouth, Mass. in 17th century; *n* **-age**

**pill** *n* small ball of medicinal drugs, swallowed whole

> **pill** *n* capsule, drug, lozenge, medicine, pastille, pellet, tablet

**pillage** *v* plunder; rob openly; loot

**pillar** *n* slender supporting column

> **pillar** *n* pier, pilaster, pole, post, prop, shaft, stanchion, support, upright

**pillion** *n* seat, cushion for another person placed behind rider (of horse, motorcycle)

**pillory** *n* framework with holes for neck and wrists, where offenders were secured and exposed to public ridicule; *v* punish by putting in pillory; *fig* expose to public disgrace, scorn, etc

**pillow** *n* cushion for head, *esp* in bed; *v* rest on, as on pillow

**pilot** *n* **1** one who directs course of vessels, *esp* one licensed to navigate into or out of port **2** one qualified to fly aircraft **3** *fig* guide; leader; *v* act as pilot; *adj* experimental, preliminary

**pimiento** *n* large reddish sweet pepper

**pimp** *n* man living off earnings of prostitutes

**pimple** *n* small pustule on skin; *adj* **pimply**

**PIN** *abbr banking* personal identification number

**pin** *n* short, stiff, pointed wire with head, used for fastening; wooden, metal peg or rivet; *v* **pins, pinning, pinned 1** fasten, attach with pin **2** hold firmly, *esp* under weight

> **pin** *n* bolt, brooch, clip, fastener, nail, peg, rivet, spike, staple, tack

**pinafore** *n* loose sleeveless garment

**pince-nez** *n* *Fr* armless eye glasses

**pincers** *n pl* **1** gripping tool **2** pair of sharp gripping claws (of some crustaceans)

**pinch** *v* **1** nip; squeeze **2** *coll* steal **3** *fig* cause to become thin, etc **4** *sl* arrest; *n* **1** painful squeeze, *esp* of skin, with finger and thumb **2** as much as can be taken up between finger and thumb; *adj* **pinched 1** (of face) drawn, haggard **2** miserable

**pinch** *v* **1** (nip) compress, grasp, press, squeeze, tweak. **2** (squeeze) chafe, confine, cramp, crush, hurt, rub. **3** (steal) filch, lift, make off with, nick, plunder, poach, rob, shoplift, swipe, walk off with

**pinchbeck** *n* zinc and copper alloy; jewelry of this; *adj* sham
**pine** *n* evergreen coniferous tree
**pine** *v* waste away through sorrow, etc; long intensely (for)

**pine** *v* ache, crave, hanker, hunger, long, miss, mourn, mope, sicken, yearn

**pineal gland** *n* small gland in brain
**pineapple** *n* large, cone-shaped edible fruit; plant with spiny leaves bearing this fruit
**ping** *v, n* (make) single high-pitched bell-like sound; *n* **pinger** device that makes such sounds as a warning
**Ping-Pong** *n* [TM] *coll* table-tennis
**pink** *n* **1** garden plant allied to carnation **2** acme, perfection; *adj* of pale, delicate reddish colour; *idm* **in the pink** *coll* very fit; *ns* **p.-eye** conjunctivitis; **pinking shears** scissors with zig-zag blades
**pinnacle** *n* ornamental tapering turret; slender mountain peak; *fig* culminating point
**pinpoint** *v* mark, identify precisely
**pins and needles** *n* pricking feeling caused by flow of blood after temporary stoppage
**pint** *n* liquid measure; half a quart; ⅛ gallon
**pioneer** *n* **1** early settler in new country **2** one who is first in experiments or exploration; *v* take lead in; be first to introduce

**pioneer** *n* **1** (early settler) colonist, discoverer, explorer, frontiersman, frontierswoman. **2** (one first in experiments) architect, developer, discoverer, founder, front-runner, ground-breaker, innovator, inventor, leader, originator, trail-blazer, trend-setter

**pious** *adj* faithful in religious duties

**pious** *adj* dedicated, devoted, devout, God-fearing, godly, holy, religious, reverent, righteous, saintly, spiritual, virtuous

**pip** *n* **1** seed in fruit (*eg* **apple pip**) **2** short high-pitched note used as signal; bleep
**pipe** *n* **1** long tube conveying water, gas, etc **2** tube with small bowl at end for smoking tobacco **3** tube-shaped musical wind instruments **4** measure of wine **5** shrill voice, or bird call; *v* **1** play the pipe **2** make sound like pipe **3** convey by pipe **4** make tubular ornamental shapes in icing cake or on clothing; *phr v* **pipe down** stop talking; make less noise; *n* **p.dream** unrealistic hope
**piquant** *adj* **1** pleasantly sharp to taste **2** stimulating; lively; *n* **piquancy**

**piquant** *adj* (sharp to taste) hot, peppery, pungent, salty, savoury, sharp, spicy, tart, tasty

**pique** *n Fr* resentment; sense of being slighted; *v* wound pride of
**piranha** *n* small but dangerous carnivorous freshwater fish from S America
**pirate** *n* **1** person illegally plundering vessels on high seas **2** privately owned radio transmitter operating without license **3** one who infringes another's copyright, etc; *n* **piracy**; *adj* **piratical**
**pirouette** *n, v Fr* rapid spin round on toe in dancing
**pistachio** *n Sp, It* edible green nut
**piste** *n Fr* ski slope

**pistil** n the seed-bearing female part of a flower

**pistol** n small firearm held in one hand when fired; v shoot with pistol

**piston** n 1 short cylinder within cylindrical vessel, working up and down, used to generate and apply pressure 2 sliding valve in musical instrument

**pit** n 1 hole in ground 2 coal mine 3 hollow depression 4 *dram* part occupied by musicians in front of stage 5 small scar on skin; hollow on surface of sth; *pl* **-s** *aut* place where racing cars are repaired during race; *adj* **pitted** covered with small dents

> **pit** n 1 (hole) abyss, cavity, chasm, crater, dent, depression, ditch, excavation, gulf, hollow, indentation, pothole, trench. 2 (coal mine) colliery, mine, quarry, shaft

**pitch**[1] n thick, dark, resinous substance obtained from coaltar, turpentine, etc; v coat with this; *adjs* **p.-black**, **p.-dark** very dark

**pitch**[2] v 1 set up, erect 2 hurl 3 *mus* set key 4 (of ship) plunge lengthwise 5 fall headlong; *adj* **pitched** (of roof) sloping; n 1 customary position 2 act of throwing 3 *football, hockey, etc* marked area of play

**pitcher** n 1 large, *usu* earthenware jug 2 baseball player who throws ball at batter

**piteous** adj arousing pity

**pitfall** n unsuspected danger or obstacle

**pith** n 1 soft cellular tissue in plant stems and branches 2 *fig* essential part; *adj* **pithy** 1 of, full of pith 2 *fig* terse, forceful

**pitiable** adj to be pitied (adv **-ably**)

**pitiful** adj 1 arousing pity 2 pathetic (adv **-ly**); **pitiless** ruthless (adv **-ly** n **-ness**)

> **pitiful** adj (arousing pity) affecting, distressing, grievous, heartbreaking, heart-rending, lamentable, miserable, moving, pathetic, piteous, pitiable, plaintive, poignant, sad, touching, upsetting, woeful

**piton** n Fr spike for hammering into rock to support climber

**pittance** n meager, inadequate allowance of money

**pitter-patter** n, adv (with) sound of tapping or of small footsteps

**pituitary gland** n ductless gland at base of brain

**pity** n 1 sympathy for suffering of another 2 source of disappointment, regret, etc; v **pities, pitying, pitied** feel pity for

> **pity** n 1 (sympathy) charity, clemency, commiseration, compassion, compunction, condolence, fellow feeling, forbearance, kindness, mercy, quarter, tenderness. 2 (source of disappointment) bad luck, crime, misfortune, shame
> **pity** v commiserate, feel for, feel sorry for, show compassion, show mercy, sympathize, weep for

**pivot** n shaft, fixed point on which something turns; v turn as on pivot; *adj* **-al** 1 forming pivot 2 of essential importance

**pixel** n TV single small element of picture on screen

**pixie, pixy** n elf or fairy

**pizza** n open pie of flat dough baked with topping of cheese, tomato, olives, etc

**pizzazz** n coll sparkle; energy combined with glamor

**placard** n public notice or advertisement, esp one displayed on a fence or construction site

**placate** v appease, conciliate; *adj* **placatory**

> **placate** v assuage, calm, humor, mollify, pacify, propitiate, satisfy, soothe

**place** n 1 specific position related to other people, things 2 particular town, village, building, etc 3 specific situation in life 4 seat 5 unoccupied position 6 position in competition 7 position of importance; v 1 put into a position or situation 2 arrange 3 identify; n **-ment**

**place** n (position) area, location, point, scene, setting, site, situation, spot, station, venue, whereabouts
**place** v 1 (put) deposit, dump, lay, leave, locate, plant, position, rest, settle, situate, stand, station, stick. 2 (arrange) categorize, class, classify, grade, group, order, put in order, rank, sort

**placebo** n pl **-os** or **-oes** med harmless substance given (as if of medicinal value) to comfort patient
**placenta** n mass of vascular tissue in womb connecting fetus with mother; afterbirth
**placid** adj not easily roused to anger; n **-ity**

**placid** adj calm, collected, composed, cool, easy-going, equable, even-tempered, gentle, imperturbable, mild, peaceful, phlegmatic, quiet, serene, steady, still, tranquil, unexcitable, unruffled

**plagiarize** v adopt, reproduce as one's own the work of another; ns **plagiarism** act of copying without permission; **-ist**
**plague** n 1 pestilence; serious epidemic 2 coll annoying person or thing; v vex; harass; annoy
**plaice** n edible flatfish, flounder
**plain** adj 1 clear 2 simple 3 not beautiful; n tract of flat land; adv **-ly**; n **-ness**

**plain** adj 1 (clear) apparent, audible, comprehensible, distinct, evident, lucid, manifest, obvious, patent, transparent, unambiguous, unmistakable, visible. 2 (simple) austere, bare, basic, discreet, modest, pure, restrained, stark, unadorned, spartan. 3 (not beautiful) ordinary-looking, unattractive, unprepossessing
**plain** n flatland, grassland, lowland, pampas, plateau, prairie, savanna, steppe, veld

**plainspoken** adj frank

**plainspoken** adj artless, bluff, blunt, candid, direct, explicit, forthright, guileless, honest, open, outspoken, straightforward, unvarnished, upfront

**plaintiff** n one who brings action in court of law
**plaintive** adj mournful; complaining
**plait** n 1 flattened fold, pleat 2 braid of three strands (of hair, etc); v weave into plait
**plan** n 1 drawing, diagram of structure projected on flat surface; map of district, etc 2 scheme; v **plans, planning, planned** 1 draw up plan for 2 think out beforehand

**plan** n 1 (drawing) blueprint, chart, diagram, layout, map, representation, sketch. 2 (scheme) aim, design, device, formula, idea, intention, method, plot, procedure, program, project, proposal, proposition, scenario, strategy, suggestion
**plan** v (draw up plan) arrange, concoct, contrive, design, devise, draft, draw up, formulate, map out, mastermind, organize, outline, plot, prepare, project, scheme, think up, work out

**plane**[1] n wide-spreading tree with broad leaves
**plane**[2] n 1 flat surface 2 carpenter's tool for smoothing wood; v use plane; adj completely flat, level
**plane**[3] n coll airplane
**planet** n large solid body orbiting sun or other star; adj **-ary**; n **planetarium** model of solar system; building containing such model
**plank** n long, flat, broad piece of wood
**plankton** n microscope plant and animal organisms drifting in seas, lakes, etc
**plant** n 1 vegetable organism 2 complete mechanical equipment, esp for factory 3 sl hoax; swindle; v 1 put plant, seed, etc into soil that it may grow 2 fix firmly in position 3 colonize 4 sl conceal in another's possession

**plant** n (vegetable organism) bush, flower, greenery, herb, shrub, vegetable, weed
**plant** v (plant seed) implant, scatter, seed, sow, transplant

**plantain** n 1 low-growing perennial herb 2 species of banana
**plantation** n 1 collection of growing trees 2 large estate producing cotton, tobacco, sugar, etc 3 settlement in new area (*eg* Plymouth Plantation)
**plaque** n *Fr* 1 memorial plate or wall tablet 2 a buildup of bacteria on teeth or in veins
**plasma** n 1 colorless liquid forming part of blood 2 protoplasm
**plaster** n 1 medical dressing applied to wound, etc. 2 mixture of lime, sand, and water for coating walls, etc
**plastic** n any of several synthetic materials produced from heating of chemical compounds, molded in solid blocks, pliable sheets or threads; *adj* 1 capable of being molded 2 made of some type of plastic
**plate** n 1 thin sheet of metal or other hard material 2 flat dish for serving or eating food from 3 collection of such dishes and cutlery in gold, silver, etc 4 *geol* section of earth's crust (*also* **tectonic plate**) 5 plastic molded to fit mouth and hold set of false teeth (*also* **denture**) 6 *phot* sheet of light sensitive glass 7 book illustration from photograph; *v* cover with thin coating of gold, silver, etc
**plateau** n *Fr* elevated flat stretch of land
**platelet** n tiny disk in blood that aids clotting
**platform** n 1 raised floor or stage 2 part of railroad station where passengers enter and leave trains 3 *polit* declared program, policy
**platinum** n *chem* grayish white metal used in making jewelry
**platitude** n commonplace remark; triteness; dullness; adj **-udinous**
**platonic** *adj* of, derived from Plato; **p. love** love without sex, between man and woman
**platoon** n military unit
**platter** n large flat dish or plate

**platypus** n duckbilled, egg-laying mammal
**plausible** *adj* seeming fair or reasonable; *adv* **-ibly**; *n* **-ibility**

**plausible** *adj* believable, conceivable, credible, imaginable, likely, logical, persuasive, possible, probable, rational, reasonable, sensible, tenable

**play** v 1 amuse oneself 2 take part in (game, sport, etc) 3 act part of 4 perform on musical instrument 5 (of wind, light, etc) move capriciously 6 flicker; flutter 7 gamble 8 operate (video, cassette, CD player, etc); *n* 1 stage performance 2 fun activity, *esp* for children 3 action in sport 4 freedom of movement; *idm* **bring into play** involve in action; *v* **playact** pretend (*n* **-ing**)

**play** v 1 (amuse oneself) amuse yourself, caper, cavort, enjoy yourself, frisk, frolic, have a good time, have fun, gambol, romp, sport, trifle. 2 (take part) compete, join in, participate. 3 (act part of) impersonate, perform, play the part of, portray, represent, take the part of
**play** n 1 (performance) comedy, drama, show, tragedy. 2 (fun activity) diversion, entertainment, frivolity, frolics, games, horse-play, leisure, merry-making, playing, recreation, revelry

**Playbill** [TM] theater program
**plea** n 1 urgent request or appeal 2 *leg* official declaration of guilt or innocence in court of law by or on behalf of defendant
**plead** v 1 argue before court of law; put forward as excuse 2 entreat

**plead** v 1 (argue) allege, assert, claim, declare, maintain, put forward, reason. 2 (entreat) appeal, beg, beseech, implore, petition, pray, solicit, supplicate

**pleasant** *adj* 1 agreeable 2 affable; *ns* **-ness**; **pleasantry** jocular remark, jest

**pleasant** *adj* 1 (agreeable) amusing, delightful, enjoyable, fine, gratifying, lovely, pleasing, pleasurable, satisfying, welcome. 2 (affable) agreeable, amiable, charming, cheerful, congenial, engaging, friendly, genial, good-humored, likable, nice, sympathetic, winning

**please** *v* be agreeable to; delight; impress favorably
**pleasurable** *adj* giving pleasure
**pleasure** *n* 1 enjoyment 2 desire, will

**pleasure** *n* (enjoyment) amusement, bliss, comfort, contentment, delectation, delight, diversion, entertainment, ecstasy, euphoria, fulfillment, gratification, happiness, joy, recreation, satisfaction

**pleat** *n* three-fold crease in cloth; *v* form into pleats
**pledge** *n* 1 object given as security for repayment of loan, etc 2 solemn undertaking 3 token 4 toast; *v* 1 give as security 2 promise 3 drink toast
**plenteous** *adj* plentiful; abundant
**plentiful** *adj* ample; present in large quantities; *adv* **-ly**

**plentiful** *adj* abounding, abundant, bounteous, bountiful, copious, generous, inexhaustible, lavish, liberal, overflowing, plenteous, profuse

**plenty** *n* 1 abundance 2 prosperity

**plenty** *n* 1 (abundance) loads, lots, masses, mountains, plethora, profusion, quantity, sufficiency, tons, wealth. 2 (prosperity) abundance, affluence, bounty, fruitfulness, luxury, opulence, plenitude, wealth

**plethora** *n* superabundance
**pleurisy** *n* inflammation of pleura, membraneous covering of lungs

**pliable** *adj* 1 easily bent 2 *fig* flexible; yielding; *adj* **pliant** flexible; *n* **pliancy**

**pliable** *adj* (easily bent) bendable, ductile, elastic, flexible, malleable, plastic, pliant, soft, stretchable, supple, workable

**pliers** *n pl* tool for gripping, cutting wire, etc
**plight**[1] *n* distressing condition; awkward predicament
**plight**[2] *n* **plight one's troth** *arch* make vow of marriage
**plinth** *n* square base to column or pedestal
**Pliocene** *n*, *adj* (geological formation) of the Upper Tertiary period
**plod** *v* **plods, plodding, plodded** walk laboriously; *fig* work conscientiously

**plod** *v* clump, drag, lumber, plow, slog, stomp, tramp, tread, trudge

**plop** *adv*, *n* (with) sound of small solid object dropped into water; *v* **plops, plopping, plopped** fall, let fall with a plop
**plot** *n* 1 conspiracy 2 story of play, novel, etc 3 small piece of land; *v* **plots, plotting, plotted** 1 conspire 2 make chart, map of; *n* **plotter** conspirator; one who plots course

**plot** *n* 1 (conspiracy) cabal, intrigue, machination, plan, scheme, stratagem. 2 (story) action, narrative, outline, scenario, story line, thread. 3 (piece of land) acreage, allotment, garden, lot, parcel, patch, smallholding, tract
**plot** *v* (conspire) collude, cook up, devise, hatch, intrigue, maneuver, plan, scheme

**plow** *n* implement for turning up soil; *v* 1 furrow 2 *sl* fail in exam
**ploy** *n* prank, plan
**pluck** *v* 1 pull, pick off 2 remove feathers (from bird) before cooking 3 sound by pulling and releasing strings (of instrument) with fingertips (*also* **pick**); *n* 1 courage 2 act of plucking; *adj* **plucky**; *adv* **-ily**

a
b
c
d
e
f
g
h
i
j
k
l
m
n
o
**p**
q
r
s
t
u
v
w
x
y
z

**plug** n 1 piece of rubber, plastic, wood, etc used to stop up a small hole and prevent leakage 2 device with metal pins to connect electrical appliance with source of current 3 *aut* spark plug 4 *coll* piece of media publicity to promote sth/sb

**plum** n tree bearing stone fruit with sweet juicy flesh; this fruit; *fig* best of its kind

**plumage** n feathers of a bird

**plumb** n weight, lump of lead on line used to test perpendicular; n **-ing** 1 system of waterpipes, etc 2 work of plumber

**plumber** n person whose job is to repair waterpipes, tanks, etc

**plume** n a feather, tuft

**plummet** v plunge headlong

**plump** adj of rounded form; n **-ness**

> **plump** adj ample, buxom, chubby, corpulent, dumpy, fat, fleshy, full, obese, portly, pudgy, roly-poly, rotund, round, stout, tubby

**plunder** v seize by force; loot; n booty; loot

> **plunder** v despoil, lay waste, pillage, raid, ransack, ravage, rifle, rob, sack, spoil, steal, strip

**plunge** v 1 dive 2 thrust suddenly into liquid 3 enter with violence; n dive

> **plunge** v 1 (dive) descend, dip, drop, fall, hurtle, nosedive, plummet, pitch, sink, swoop, tumble. 2 (thrust into liquid) dip, douse, immerse, sink, submerge, thrust

**plural** n, adj (form) denoting more than one

**plus** prep with addition of; n symbol (+) denoting addition, positive electric charge

**Pluto** n planet ninth in distance from sun

**plutonium** n artificially produced radioactive element

**ply**[1] n fold, layer of cloth, wood, etc; strand of wool, etc; n **plywood** thin, cross-laminated sheets of wood

**ply**[2] v **plies, plying, plied** 1 wield 2 work at 3 supply excessively, in pressing manner

**pm, PM** abbr Lat post meridiem (after noon)

**PMS** abbr premenstrual syndrome

**pneumatic** adj 1 worked by air-pressure 2 air-filled; n **p. drill** roadworker's drill run by compressed air

**pneumonia** n med inflammation of lungs

**PO** abbr post office

**poach**[1] v cook eggs, without shell, in boiling water; cook fish

**poach**[2] v 1 take game or fish illegally 2 encroach on another's sphere of action; n **poacher** one who trespasses to take game, etc

**pocket** n 1 small bag or pouch in garment for carrying money, etc 2 small cavity containing mineral ore 3 space where density of air causes aircraft to drop suddenly 4 small hollow; v put into one's pocket; take as profit; adj meant for putting in pocket; miniature

**pod** n long, narrow casing of peas, beans, etc; group of whales; v **pods, podding, podded** form seedpods; shell (peas, etc)

**podiatry** n care, treatment of foot; n **-trist**

**podium** n platform for speaker; pl **-s** or **podia**

**poem** n literary composition in metrical form, rhymed or unrhymed

> **poem** n ditty, haiku, limerick, lyric, ode, rhyme, song, sonnet, verse

**poet** n writer of poems; fem **poetess**; **poetry** work, art of poet; adj **-ic**

**poignant** adj Fr affecting with feeling of unhappiness; highly pathetic; adv **-ly**; n **poignancy**

**point** n 1 sharp end of sth 2 particular moment 3 particular place 4 main idea, purpose 5 detail in argument or statement 6 promontory 7 period at end of sentence 8 unit of scoring 9 sign preceding decimal (**decimal p.**); v 1 raise forefinger (in certain direction) 2 aim 3 sharpen 4 add fresh mortar to gaps between bricks (n **-ing**)

**point** *n* **1** (sharp end) apex, end, nib, prong, sharp end, spike, spur, tine, tip, top. **2** (moment) instant, juncture, second, stage, time. **3** (place) location, position, site, spot. **4** (idea) aim, goal, intention, motive, purpose, reason, use

**pointed** *adj* tapering; *fig* satiric, critical
**pointer** *n* **1** one who, that which points, as hand of clock, etc **2** indicator **3** dog trained to point muzzle towards bird, game, etc
**pointless** *adj* purposeless (*adv* **-ly**; *n* **-ness**)

**pointless** *adj* aimless, fruitless, futile, ineffective, irrelevant, meaningless, senseless, silly, stupid, useless, worthless

**poise** *n* **1** self-possession; calmness **2** equilibrium, balance; *v* **1** put in position; keep in balance **2** hover
**poison** *n* any substance which when absorbed by living organism will kill or seriously harm it; *v* **1** administer poison to; kill by poison **2** *fig* corrupt; pervert; *n* **poisoner**
**poisonous** *adj* containing poison

**poisonous** *adj* deadly, fatal, lethal, noxious, toxic, venomous, virulent

**poke** *v* push, thrust into; nudge; *adj* **poky** cramped

**poke** *v* elbow, hit, jab, prod, punch, stab

**polar** *adj* **1** at, near, pertaining to north, south, or magnetic poles **2** having positive and negative electricity **3** *fml* (of opposites) complete; *n* **polarity;** *v* **polarize** give polarity to; limit vibrations of light to single plane; *fig* give unity of direction to; *ns* **-ization;** **polar bear** large white Arctic bear
**pole**[1] *n* **1** either ends of earth's axis **2** either terminals of electric battery **3** *fig* opposite extreme

**pole**[2] *n* long rounded piece of wood

**pole** *n* bar, column, mast, post, prop, rod, shaft, spar, stake, stick, upright

**polecat** *n* small carnivore related to weasel; a skunk
**police** *n* civil administration for maintaining public order; force of men, women so organized; *v* control
**policy** *n* **1** course of action, *esp* of government **2** political ideals of party **3** contract of insurance

**policy** *n* (course of action) approach, code, guidelines, line, manifesto, plan, practice, procedure, program, protocol, rules, scheme, strategy, theory

**polio** *n med* infection of spinal cord often causing permanent paralysis (*also* **poliomyelitis**)
**polish** *v* **1** make smooth and glossy, *esp* by rubbing **2** *fig* make elegant; refine; *n* **1** glossiness **2** substance used for polishing **3** *fig* refinement; *n* **polisher**

**polish** *v* (make glossy) brighten, buff, burnish, clean, rub, shine, smooth, wax
**polish** *n* (glossiness) brightness, brilliance, finish, glaze, gleam, gloss, luster, sheen, shine, sparkle, veneer

**polite** *adj* well-bred, courteous; *n* **politeness**

**polite** *adj* attentive, chivalrous, civil, considerate, gracious, respectful, thoughtful, well-behaved, well-mannered, well-spoken

**politic** *adj* **1** prudent, wise **2** cunning **3** opportune; *n pl* art of government; political affairs, principles, aims, etc; *v* **politicize** make political
**political** *adj* of government or administration of state

a b c d e f g h i j k l m n o **p** q r s t u v w x y z

**politician** *n* one engaged in party politics

> **politician** *n* congressman, legislator, senator, statesman

**politics** *n* **1** activity of competing for power **2** science of government
**polka** *n* lively dance; music for this; *n* **p. dot** one of large round dots forming regular pattern on plain fabric
**poll** *n* **1** register of electors **2** act of voting at election **3** number of electors voting; *v* **1** vote **2** receive (certain number of votes)
**pollen** *n* fertilizing powder on flower anther
**pollute** *v* make foul; contaminate; *n* **pollutant** substance that pollutes

> **pollute** *v* adulterate, dirty, foul, infect, make dirty, poison, soil, spoil, stain, taint

**pollution** *n* act or result of polluting

> **pollution** *n* adulteration, contamination, dirt, dirtiness, filth, filthiness

**polo** *n* ball game resembling hockey played by two teams of four players on horseback; *n* **p. neck** (of sweater) with high round turned-over collar (*adj* **p necked**)
**poltergeist** *n* noisy hobgoblin or ghost
**poly-** *prefix* many; several
**polygamy** *n* custom of having more than one wife at same time
**polygon** *n* multisided plane figure
**polyhedron** *n* multifaceted solid figure
**polymer** *n* complex molecule made up of several similar ones; *v* **-ize**; *n* **-ization**
**polystyrene** *n* thermoplastic material
**polysyllabic** *adj* having many syllables
**polythene** *n* tough, flexible plastic material
**polyunsaturated** *adj* (of fat, oil) with chemical structure that discourages cholesterol accumulation
**polyurethane** *n, adj* resinous plastic polymer
**pomegranate** *n* reddish, many-seeded fruit of African, Asiatic tree

**pomp** *n* splendid display; pageantry

> **pomp** *n* ceremony, display, glitter, glory, grandeur, magnificence, majesty, ostentation, ritual, spectacle, show

**pompous** *adj* **1** self-important **2** (of speech) florid, bombastic; *n* **pomposity**

> **pompous** *adj* (self-important) arrogant, boastful, conceited, grandiose, ostentatious, pretentious, showy, vain

**pond** *n* small lake or pool of still water
**ponder** *v* consider, muse

> **ponder** *v* brood, contemplate, deliberate, meditate, mull over, reflect, study, think

**ponderous** *adj* **1** heavy, unwieldy, massive **2** dull
**pony** *n* **1** small horse **2** small glass
**poodle** *n* breed of curly haired dog
**pool**[1] *n* small body of still water

> **pool** *n* lagoon, lake, oasis, paddling pool, pond, puddle, swimming pool, tarn

**pool**[2] *n* **1** stakes played for in various games **2** form of billiards **3** common fund **4** commercial combination **5** *pl* **-s** system for gambling on results of football matches **6** shared resources; *v* **1** put into common fund; amalgamate
**poor** *adj* **1** having little money **2** unfortunate **3** scanty **4** of low quality

> **poor** *adj* **1** (having little money) broke, destitute, hard up, impoverished, penniless, poverty-stricken, **2** (unfortunate) ill-fated, luckless, miserable, pitiable, wretched. **3** (scanty) deficient, inadequate, insufficient, meager, sparse. **4** (of low quality) cheap, defective, faulty, inferior, rubbishy, shoddy, substandard

**poorly** adv badly; adj not in good health
**pop**[1] n 1 short, explosive sound 2 coll fizzy drink; v **pops, popping, popped** 1 make such sound 2 put on, into with sudden light movement

---

**pop** v (make sound) bang, burst, crack, detonate, explode, go off, snap

---

**pop**[2] n coll popular music of the day (also **pop music**); n **pop art** modern art form based on ideas from commercial design
**popcorn** n grains of corn heated till they burst
**pope** n head of Roman Catholic church and bishop of Rome
**poplar** n straight, slender, tall tree
**poppy** n any plant of genus Papaver
**Popsicle** [TM] flavored, colored ice frozen on a stick
**populace** n common people, the masses
**popular** adj of, pertaining to populace; liked by, suited to the average person; n **popularity** quality of being popular or being generally liked; v **popularize** make popular; make familiar to average person

---

**popular** adj accepted, approved, celebrated, famous, fashionable, favorite, in demand, sought-after, well-known, well-liked

---

**populate** v furnish with inhabitants; n **population** total number of inhabitants of country, town, etc; adj **populous** thickly inhabited
**populist** n, adj (person) declaring support for interests of ordinary people
**porcupine** n rodent covere
**porcelain** n fine, translucent white earthenware; china
**porch** n projecting, covered area adjoining building entrance with access to doorway
**porcupine** n rodent covered with sharp quills
**pore**[1] n minute opening, esp in skin; small interstice between particles of any body
**pore**[2] phr v **pore over** study very closely

**pork** n pig's flesh as food
**pornography** n indecent, obscene writing, photographs, etc; adj **-graphic**
**porous** adj full of pores; permeable by liquids; n **porosity**

---

**porous** adj absorbent, cellular, penetrable, permeable, spongelike, spongy

---

**porpoise** n blunt-nosed marine mammal, like dolphin
**porridge** n oatmeal boiled in water or milk
**port**[1] n 1 harbor 2 town having harbor 3 left side of ship 4 gateway 5 opening in side of ship 6 fig refuge
**port**[2] n strong, sweet, red wine of Portugal
**port**[3] n, comput point for linking several pieces of equipment
**portable** adj capable of being carried, moved; not fixed

---

**portable** adj compact, easy to carry, handy, lightweight, manageable, mobile, movable, pocket, pocket-sized, small, transportable

---

**portcullis** n heavy grating in castle gateway
**portentous** adj ominous
**porter** n 1 doorkeeper 2 one employed to carry burden, load 3 kind of dark brown bitter beer
**portfolio** n It flat case for carrying papers; pl **-os**
**portion** n 1 part 2 share 3 one's fate; destiny

---

**portion** n 1 (part) piece, section, segment, serving, sliver, wedge. 2 (share) allocation, allowance, measure, percentage, quantity, ration, share, whack

---

**portrait** n picture of person; **portraiture** art of portraying

---

**portrait** n drawing, image, likeness, painting, photograph, picture, portrayal, representation, self-portrait, study

---

A B C D E F G H I J K L M N O **P** Q R S T U V W X Y Z

**portray** v depict, describe vividly in words; represent on stage; n **portrayal** act of portraying

**pose** v 1 lay down 2 place in, assume attitude; n 1 held position 2 pretense 3 attitude of mind; n **poseur** one who assumes affected attitudes

> **pose** n 1 (held position) attitude, bearing, position, posture, stance. 2 (pretense) act, affectation, façade, front, masquerade, posture, role

**posh** adj sl smart, expensive-looking

> **posh** adj classy, elegant, fancy, fashionable, swanky, swish, up-market, upscale

**position** n 1 place 2 posture 3 condition 4 situation; employment; v place in position; localize

> **position** n 1 (place) area, locale, location, setting, site, situation, spot. 2 (posture) angle, pose, stance, way of sitting

**positive** adj 1 definite 2 convinced 3 absolute 4 real 5 not negative

> **positive** adj 1 (definite) absolute, affirmative, categorical, certain, decided, emphatic, incontrovertible, indisputable, real, undeniable, unmistakable. 2 (convinced) certain, confident, sure

**positron** n positive electron
**posse** n force of men a sheriff can call out for aid; group of armed men
**possess** v 1 own 2 dominate, control; n **possessor**
**possessed** adj controlled by evil spirit
**possession** n 1 act of possessing 2 ownership 3 thing owned
**possessive** adj 1 selfishly domineering 2 indicating possession; adv **-ly**; n **-ness**; n possessive case or pronoun

> **possessive** adj (selfishly domineering) clinging, controlling, dominating, jealous, overprotective, proprietorial, protective

**possible** adj capable of existing; feasible; that may or may not happen

> **possible** adj able to be done, attainable, conceivable, credible, feasible, imaginable, likely, plausible, potential, practicable, probable, realizable, reasonable, viable, within reach

**possibility** n chance, likelihood

> **possibility** n danger, odds, potential, probability, prospect, risk

**post**[1] n 1 upright stake or pole supporting structure 2 stake marking finishing point of race; v fix on post or notice board

> **post** n (stake) column, pillar, pole, shaft, support, upright.

**post**[2] n 1 official collection, transport, and delivery of mail 2 letters, parcels, etc for mailing; v place in official box for mail
**post**[3] n 1 place of duty, eg of soldier 2 job; situation of employment; v place on duty
**poster** n large advertising notice in public place

> **poster** n advertisement, flyer, notice, placard, sign

**posterior** adj situated behind; n buttocks
**posterity** n descendants; future generations
**postgraduate** adj of studies carried on after graduation
**posthaste** adv very quickly
**posthumous** adj after death
**postmortem** n Lat 1 medical examination after death 2 fig discussion following important event

**postnatal** *adj* after (giving) birth
**postpone** *v* defer, delay; *n* **-ment**

> **postpone** *v* adjourn, hold over, put back, put off, put on ice, put on the back burner, shelve, suspend

**postscript** *n* addition to letter, written after and below signature; **PS, P.S.**
**post-traumatic stress** *n* condition of recurring stress following a traumatic event
**postulant** *n* person preparing to enter religious order
**postulate** *v* stipulate; take for granted
**posture** *n* attitude of body; *v* assume affected attitude

> **posture** *n* attitude, bearing, carriage, deportment, pose, stance

**pot** *n* 1 rounded vessel of any material, for holding liquid etc 2 flowerpot 3 cooking vessel 4 teapot

> **pot** *n* (vessel) bowl, cauldron, container, dish, jar, pan, urn

**potash** *n* crude potassium carbonate; alkali used in soap and fertilizers; *n* **potassium** malleable metallic alkaline element
**potato** *n* cultivated plant with edible tuber; *pl* **-oes**
**potency** *n* power, efficiency
**potent** *adj* 1 powerful 2 convincing 3 (of men) sexually vigorous
**potentate** *n* king, ruler
**potential** *n* 1 that which has latent power 2 possibility; *adj* latent, possible

> **potential** *adj* budding, developing, embryonic, future, likely, promising, would-be

**pothole** *n* 1 deep hole in rock, *eg* in limestone (*ns* **potholer** person exploring one of these; **-holing**) 2 hole in road surface

**potion** *n* draft; dose of medicine or poison

> **potion** *n* brew, concoction, dose, drink, drug, elixir, liquid, mixture

**potter** *v* dawdle; be busy in desultory manner
**pottery** *n* earthenware; art of making it; place where it is made; *n* **potter** one who makes pottery
**pouch** *n* 1 small bag, sack 2 bag in which marsupials carry young
**poultry** *n* domestic fowls
**poultice** *n* soft mass of hot meal, mustard, etc applied to inflamed part of body; *v* apply poultice
**pounce** *v* swoop down suddenly; leap on; *n* sudden swoop, movement to take something

> **pounce** *v* ambush, attack, drop, jump, lunge, snatch, spring, strike, swoop, take sb by surprise

**pound**[1] *n* 1 measure of weight (16 oz) 2 British monetary unit (£1 or 100p)
**pound**[2] *n* enclosure for straying cattle, or dogs
**pound**[3] *v* 1 reduce to pieces, powder 2 beat 3 thump 4 run, walk with heavy steps

> **pound** *v* 1 (reduce to pieces, powder) crush, grind, mash, pulverize, smash. 2 (beat) batter, knead, press, pummel, thump. 3 (thump) bang, bump, palpitate, pulse, throb. 4 (run, walk) clump, stamp, stomp, tramp

**pour** *v* 1 flow or cause to flow freely 2 rain heavily; move in continuous stream 3 *fig* emit copiously (words, ideas, etc)

> **pour** *v* 1 (flow) cascade, course, flood, gush, jet, run, rush, spew, spill, splash, spout, spurt, stream. 2 (rain) rain hard, teem

**pout** *v* thrust out lips; look sulky; *n* act of pouting

A
B
C
D
E
F
G
H
I
J
K
L
M
N
O
P
Q
R
S
T
U
V
W
X
Y
Z

**poverty** n state of being poor; adj **p.-stricken** very poor

> **poverty** n destitution, distress, hardship, insolvency, need, penury, want

**powder** n 1 solid reduced to fine, dry particles by grinding 2 drug in this form 3 gunpowder 4 cosmetic powder; v sprinkle with powder; reduce to powder; adj **powdery**

**power** n 1 ability to do or act 2 strength 3 authority 4 energy 5 math product of number multiplied by itself 6 optics magnifying capacity

> **power** n 1 (ability) capability, competence, potential. 2 (strength) drive, energy, force, might, muscle, potency, powerfulness, vigor. 3 (authority) ascendancy, clout, command, control, dominance, domination, influence, mastery, rule, sovereignty, supremacy, sway

**powerful** adj 1 having strength 2 having authority (adv **-ly**; n **-ness**)

> **powerful** adj 1 (having strength) mighty, robust, strapping, strong, sturdy, tough. 2 (having authority) authoritative, commanding, dominant, invincible, mighty, omnipotent, sovereign, strong, supreme

**powerless** adj without power or ability (adv **-ly**; n **-ness**)

> **powerless** adj debilitated, defenseless, dependent, disabled, feeble, frail, helpless, impotent, incapable, incapacitated, ineffectual, paralyzed, unable, unarmed, vulnerable, weak

**pp** abbr past participle
**PR** abbr public relations
**practicable** adj able to be done; capable of being used (n **-ability**)

**practical** adj 1 efficient 2 of, concerning action 3 not theoretic 4 virtual; adv **-ly** 1 sensibly; 2 almost; n **-ity** realistic nature; pl **-ities** practical matters

> **practical** adj (efficient) businesslike, capable, competent, down-to-earth, expert, hands-on, hard-headed, hard-nosed, matter-of-fact, no-nonsense, practiced, pragmatic, proficient, realistic, sensible, skilled, trained

**practice**[1] n 1 habitual action 2 exercise of profession 3 clients, patients collectively 4 rules of procedures in court of law; n **practitioner** one who carries on profession, esp medicine
**practice**[2] v 1 train, exercise in skill, action, etc 2 do habitually 3 pursue profession

> **practice** v (train) drill, exercise, go over, go through, polish, prepare, refine, rehearse, repeat, run through, study, warm up, work out

**pragmatic** adj 1 concerned with practical results 2 realistic; ns **pragmatism**; **-ist**
**prairie** n wide, flat, treeless grassland
**praise** v 1 commend highly 2 glorify (God); n expression of approval; adj **praiseworthy** commendable, laudable

> **praise** v 1 (commend highly) acclaim, admire, applaud, cheer, clap, commend, compliment, congratulate, pay tribute to, rave about. 2 (glorify God) adore, exalt, glorify, honor, offer praise to, worship

**prance** v 1 move with bounds; swagger 2 (of horse) spring from hind legs

> **prance** v (move with bounds) bound, caper, cavort, dance, frisk, gambol, jump, leap, play, romp, skip

**prank** n mischievous trick; practical joke

**prattle** *v* babble; talk like child; *n* childish talk; *n* **prattler**

**prawn** *n* edible, marine crustacean

**pray** *v* 1 beg for 2 offer prayers, *esp* to God

> **pray** *v* 1 (beg for) ask, beseech, entreat, implore, petition, plead, request, urge. 2 (offer prayers) commune with God, say your prayers

**prayer** *n* act of praying to God; prescribed form of words used; formal petition, request

**pre-** *prefix* 1 prior to; before 2 superior

**preach** *v* 1 deliver sermon 2 advocate strongly 3 exhort morally; *n* **-er**

**preamble** *n* preface; opening part of speech, etc

**precarious** *adj* uncertain, risky; *adv* **-ly**

> **precarious** *adj* dangerous, dicey, dodgy, doubtful, dubious, hairy, hazardous, insecure, perilous, treacherous, unreliable, unsafe, unstable, unsure, vulnerable, wobbly

**precaution** *n* careful foresight; measure taken beforehand to guard against danger; *adj* **-ary**

**precede** *v* come, be before in time, order, rank, etc

**precedence** *n* priority derived from birth, official status, etc

**precedent** *n* 1 something that has happened before, serving as model for future conduct, etc 2 *leg* previous judicial decision, *esp* as guide for present parallel case

**precinct** *n* enclosure within outer walls of building, *esp* of cathedral, etc; *pl* **-s** environs, neighborhood

**precious** *adj* 1 of great value 2 beloved 3 affected; overrefined; *adv* **-ly**; *ns* **-ness**

> **precious** *adj* 1 (of great value) invaluable, priceless, prized, rare, valuable. 2 (beloved) adored, cherished, dear, favorite, irreplaceable, loved, treasured

**precipice** *n* sheer, perpendicular cliff face; *adj* **precipitous** sheer, steep

**precipitate** *v* 1 throw, hurl down 2 cause (vapor) to fall as rain, snow, etc 3 cause to be deposited as solid substance; from solution; *adj* rash; impetuous; *n* **-tation** 1 undue haste 2 that which is precipitated 3 act, process of precipitating

**précis** *n Fr* short summary of document

**precise** *adj* 1 exactly defined 2 punctilious 3 definite 4 formal

**precision** *n* accuracy, exactness

**preclude** *v* exclude; prevent

**precocious** *adj* prematurely developed; *ns* **precocity**; **-ness**

> **precocious** *adj* advanced, bright, developed, gifted, intelligent, mature, quick

**preconception** *n* opinion formed beforehand without actual knowledge

**precursor** *n* forerunner, harbinger

**predatory** *adj* 1 living by plunder, robbery 2 (of animals) living by preying on others; *n* **predator**

**predecessor** *n* 1 one who precedes another in office, rank, etc 2 ancestor

**predestination** *n* belief that our future lives are controlled by divine plan that cannot be changed

**predicament** *n* unfortunate or puzzling situation

> **predicament** *n* corner, crisis, difficult situation, dilemma, emergency, fix, mess, pickle, plight, quandary, scrape, tight spot

**predict** *v* foretell, prophesy; *n* **prediction**

> **predict** *v* augur, divine, forebode, forecast, foresee, foreshadow, foretell, portend, presage, prophesy

**predominate** *v* be in majority; be chief element or factor in; *adj* **predominant**; *adv* **-ly**; *n* **predominance**

a b c d e f g h i j k l m n o **p** q r s t u v w x y z

**predominate** v be dominant, be in the majority, carry weight, have the upper hand, outnumber, overrule, prevail

**preeminent** *adj* superior to, excelling all others; *n* **-nence**

**preempt** v acquire, appropriate by anticipation; *n* **-emption**; *adj* **-emptive**

**preen** v 1 (of bird) dress feathers with beak 2 *fig* show off

**preface** n initial, introductory part of book, speech, etc; v begin, introduce

**preface** n foreword, introduction, preamble, prelude, prologue

**prefect** n 1 senior pupil in school with authority over others 2 official in ancient Rome 3 *esp cap* head of administrative area, *eg* in France

**prefer** v **prefers, preferring, preferred** 1 like better 2 promote

**prefer** v (like better) be partial to, choose, desire, elect, fancy, favor, go for, incline toward, like, opt for, pick, plump for, select, vote for, want, wish

**preferable** *adj* more to be desired

**preference** n 1 favor 2 prior claim; *adj* **-ential** giving, receiving preference; *n* **-ment** advancement promotion

**prefix** n 1 word placed before personal name 2 *ling* particle forming first part of compound word; v put as introduction

**pregnant** *adj* 1 with child; with young 2 *fig* full of meaning, ideas; *n* **pregnancy**

**prehistoric** *adj* pertaining to periods before recorded history; *n* **prehistory** prehistoric archeology

**prejudge** v judge or decide upon before hearing or enquiry

**prejudice** n 1 bias 2 *leg* injury, damage, loss; v bias, influence person; *adj* **prejudicial** detrimental; causing harm; injury

**prejudice** n (bias) agism, bigotry, chauvinism, discrimination, favoritism, intolerance, jingoism, narrow-mindedness, racism, sexism, unfairness, xenophobia

**prelate** n church dignatory *esp* archbishop, etc

**preliminary** *adj* introductory, preceding

**prelude** n introductory act, performance, event; v serve, act as prelude to; usher in

**premarital** *adj* before marriage

**premature** *adj* earlier than expected

**premature** *adj* early, immature, incomplete, raw, too early, too soon, undeveloped, unripe, untimely

**premeditated** *adj* (of crimes) planned in advance

**premenstrual** *adj* occurring because of hormonal changes before menstruation

**premier** *adj Fr* first in rank, degree, etc; principal

**premise** n 1 assumption, proposition on which inference is based 2 *leg* introductory part of document, *esp* lease 3 *pl* **-s** building; house, etc with grounds; v assume

**premium** n 1 reward; bonus 2 sum paid for insurance 3 *finance* excess of market price over par

**premonition** n presentiment, foreboding

**premonition** n apprehension, fear, feeling, idea, intuition, misgiving, omen, portent, sign, suspicion, warning

**prenatal** *adj* occurring before birth

**preoccupy** v occupy and engross thoughts to exclusion of other things; *n* **preoccupation** absent-mindedness

**preparation** n 1 act of preparing 2 school work, homework done before lesson; period when this is done (*abbr* **prep**)

**prepare** v 1 make ready for use 2 teach 3 construct 4 accustom 5 lead up to; *adj* **preparatory** serving to prepare

**prepare** *v* 1 (make ready) arrange, assemble, draw up, get ready, put together. 2 (teach) brief, coach, drill, educate, equip, groom, rehearse, train, tutor

**preposition** *n* part of speech, word placed before noun or pronoun, indicating its relation to another word in sentence

**prepossess** *v* influence, *esp* favorably; *adj* **prepossessing** attractive; *n* **prepossession**

**preposterous** *adj* unreasonable

**preposterous** *adj* absurd, bizarre, crazy, excessive, impossible, incredible, ludicrous, monstrous, out of the question, outrageous, ridiculous, shocking, unbelievable

**prerogative** *n* exclusive, peculiar right or privilege

**prescribe** *v* 1 ordain; dictate 2 *med* advise treatment, or use of medicine; *n* **prescription** 1 prescribing 2 written directions given by physician 3 medicine prescribed; *adj* **prescriptive** giving exact rules about sth

**presence** *n* 1 being present 2 impressive manner 3 nearness (of danger, etc)

**presence** *n* 1 (being present) attendance, company. 2 (impressive manner) charisma, magnetism, poise, self-assurance, self-confidence, self-possession. 3 (nearness) closeness, proximity

**present**[1] *adj* 1 existing now 2 not absent; *n* present time, tense; *n* **p. participle** form of verb (ending in **-ing** in English) indicating simultaneous or causal relationship between two verbs; *adv* **presently** soon

**present** *adj* 1 (existing now) contemporary, current, immediate, present-day, up-to-date. 2 (not absent) accounted for, at hand, available, nearby, ready, to hand

**present**[2] *v* 1 introduce (person) formally 2 show 3 give 4 perform; *n* gift

**present** *v* 1 (introduce) announce, make known. 2 (show) demonstrate, display, exhibit, reveal. 3 (give) award, bestow, confer, donate, hand over, offer. 4 (perform) act, give, put on, stage
**present** *n* contribution, donation, offering

**presentable** *adj* suitable for presentation

**presentation** *n* 1 bestowal 2 formal gift 3 introduction, *esp* at court 4 performance

**presentiment** *n* apprehension, foreboding

**preserve** *v* 1 protect 2 prevent (food) from decaying; *n* 1 that which is preserved, as jam, etc 2 hunting area preserved for shooting 3 river, etc preserved for fishing; *n* **preservation**; *n*, *adj* **preservative** (substance) that keeps (food, etc) from going bad

**preserve** *v* 1 (protect) care for, conserve, defend, guard, keep, look after, maintain, perpetuate, safeguard, save, secure, uphold. 2 (prevent food from decaying) bottle, can, cure, dry, freeze, pickle, salt, smoke

**preside** *v* take control at formal meeting; superintend

**president** *n* head of republic, society, college, public corporation, etc; **presidency** office, tenure of president; *adj* **presidential**

**press** *v* 1 apply weight, force on; squeeze 2 exert pressure; *n* 1 newspapers 2 people writing for these 3 printing machine 4 apparatus for flattening, compressing, crushing

**press** *v* (apply weight, force) compress, condense, crush, jam, mash, push, reduce, squeeze, stuff

**pressing** *adj* 1 urgent 2 insistent (*n* act or result of pressing)

a b c d e f g h i j k l m n o **p** q r s t u v w x y z

**pressgang** v force sb into service (n group which does this)

**pressure** n 1 act of pressing 2 fig compulsion; constraint 3 force exerted on surroundings by solid, liquid, gas; v **pressurize** 1 (of aircraft cabin) keep at constant atmospheric pressure 2 persuade forcefully; n **-ization**

**prestige** n good repute; power to influence; adj designed to impress; adj **-gious** highly honored

> **prestige** n cachet, credit, distinction, eminence, esteem, fame, good name, honor, importance, influence, kudos, reputation, standing, status

**presume** v 1 believe as probable 2 take liberties; adj **presumable**; probable; n **presumption** 1 act of presuming 2 probability 3 effrontery; adj **presumptive** giving reasonable grounds for belief

> **presume** v (believe as probable) assume, conjecture, guess, imagine, infer, suppose, surmise, take for granted, take it, think

**presumptuous** adj overconfident; arrogant

> **presumptuous** adj audacious, bold, cheeky, cocksure, forward, insolent, pushy, too big for your britches

**presuppose** v 1 assume to be true 2 imply
**pretend** v 1 feign 2 imagine oneself as; ns **pretender** claimant to throne; **pretension** claim

> **pretend** v 1 (feign) affect, bluff, deceive, dissemble, fake it, falsify, impersonate, make out, pose, put on an act, simulate, trick. 2 (imagine) act, fantasize, make believe, play, play-act, suppose

**pretense** n 1 pretext 2 fraud
**pretentious** adj assuming great merit or importance; conceited

> **pretentious** adj affected, exaggerated, flamboyant, grandiose, ostentatious, pompous, showy, snobbish, superficial

**preternatural** adj beyond what is natural; supernatural
**pretext** n reason, motive put forward to conceal real one; excuse
**pretty** adj 1 attractive 2 coll considerable, large; adv moderately; considerably; n **prettiness** charming personal beauty

> **pretty** adj (attractive) appealing, beautiful, charming, cute, delightful, fair, good-looking, lovely, nice-looking, pleasant

**pretzel** n Ger crisp, salted, usu knot-shaped slender bread
**prevail** v 1 triumph 2 be prevalent; be in use; n **prevalence** common occurrence; frequency; adj **prevalent** widely practiced; rife
**prevaricate** v make evasive answer; quibble; ns **prevarication, prevaricator**
**prevent** v guard against; hinder; n **prevention**; adjs **-able, -ative**

> **prevent** v avert, avoid, block, check, curb, deter, fend off, foil, forestall, frustrate, hamper, impede, nip in the bud, obstruct, put a stop to, restrain, stave off, stop, thwart, ward off

**preview** n advance, private showing of pictures, film, etc
**previous** adj 1 earlier 2 coll too hasty; adv **-ly** before

> **previous** adj (earlier) erstwhile, ex-, former, one-time, past, preceding, prior

**prey** n animal hunted by another, as food; victim; v **p on, upon** kill and eat; oppress; plunder; n **bird of p.** bird that kills and eats other birds or animals

**price** n 1 cost; value 2 betting odds; v fix price; value

> **price** n (cost) amount, bill, charge, damage, estimate, expenditure, expense, fee, figure, offer, outlay, payment, quotation, rate, sum, terms, valuation, value, worth

**priceless** adj 1 very valuable 2 coll very amusing

> **priceless** adj (valuable) costly, dear, expensive, invaluable, irreplaceable, precious, worth its weight in gold

**prick** v 1 pierce with sharp pointed object 2 give or experience feeling of this; n 1 slight stab of pain on surface of skin 2 mark left by pricking sth

> **prick** v (pierce) jab, nick, perforate, puncture, spike, stab

**prickle** n small thorn; v tingle as if pricked; adj **prickly**

> **prickle** n barb, spike, spine, thorn
> **prickle** v hurt, itch, prick, smart, sting, tickle, tingle

**pride** n 1 self-respect 2 too high an opinion of oneself 3 group of lions

> **pride** n 1 (self-respect) dignity, ego, feelings, honor, self-esteem. 2 (too high opinion of oneself) arrogance, big-headedness, conceit, snobbery, vanity

**priest** n official minister of religion; fem **-ess**; n **priesthood**; adj **priestly**

> **priest** n chaplain, clergyman, clergywoman, curate, deacon, ecclesiastic, father, minister, padre, parson, pastor, priestess, rector, shaman, vicar

**prim** adj precise; stiffly formal; easily shocked

> **prim** adj demure, fastidious, formal, prissy, proper, starchy, strait-laced

**primacy** n position of being first; preeminence; adj **primal** first, original
**primary** adj 1 main; fundamental 2 earliest; n preliminary stage of election at which candidates are selected; adv **primarily** mainly

> **primary** adj 1 (main) chief, essential, foremost, most important, paramount, prime, principal. 2 (earliest) elementary, first, initial, primitive

**primate** n 1 archbishop 2 highest order of mammals, including man, monkeys, etc
**prime** adj 1 chief; fundamental 2 first or best in quality or rank 3 with all the typical features; n the best time of life; v 1 prepare (eg gun for firing, pump for pumping) 2 provide sb with essential information 3 prepare with primer before painting
**primeval** adj of first ages of world; prehistoric
**primitive** adj not elaborate; old-fashioned; simple

> **primitive** adj basic, crude, early, elementary, naïve, rough, rudimentary, uncivilized, unsophisticated

**primrose** n wild plant with pale yellow flowers
**prince** n 1 son of king, queen 2 ruler of royal status; fem **princess**; adj **princely** 1 magnificent 2 very generous
**principal** adj main; n 1 head (of college, etc) 2 sum of loan, on which interest is charged; adv **-ly**

> **principal** adj chief, first, foremost, fundamental, key, leading, major, most important, paramount, prime, top

a
b
c
d
e
f
g
h
i
j
k
l
m
n
o
p
q
r
s
t
u
v
w
x
y
z

**principle** n 1 basic general truth 2 guiding rule for behavior (*usu pl*) 3 scientific law; *adj* **principled** morally sound

**principle** n 1 (general truth) axiom, canon, creed, doctrine, law, maxim, rule, theory. 2 (guiding rule for behaviour) decency, honour, integrity, morality, morals, probity, scruples, standards

**print** n 1 stamp 2 impression 3 printed lettering 4 photographic positive 5 printed fabric; *v* 1 reproduce words or pictures on paper, etc from inked type, plates, etc 2 impress 3 obtain positive photograph from 4 stamp with colored design; *ns* **printer** one engaged in printing; *comput* machine for printing pictures or text; **printout** *comput* printed record of stored data

**print** v (reproduce words or pictures) issue, publish, reproduce, run off, send to press, write

**prior** *adj* earlier; *n* head of religious order or house; *fem* **-ess; ** *n* **priory** monastery, nunnery
**prioritize** v give priority to
**priority** n superiority, precedence
**prism** n 1 solid figure whose bases are equal, parallel planes and whose sides are parallelograms 2 transparent triangular prism for refracting light; *adj* **-atic** of, like prism
**prison** n place of captivity; jail

**prison** n cell, cooler *inf*, detention center, dungeon, lock-up, penitentiary, place of detention

**prisoner** n captive; person in custody

**prisoner** n convict, detainee, hostage, inmate, jailbird *inf*, POW

**prissy** *adj* *coll* fussy; *adv* **-ly;** *n* **-ness**
**pristine** *adj* 1 original; primitive 2 unspoiled

**privacy** n state of being undisturbed, free from interference
**private** *adj* 1 not public; belonging to a particular person or group 2 secret 3 not under state control 4 quiet; free from intruders 5 not in any official capacity; *n* lowest rank of soldier

**private** adj 1 (not public) exclusive, intimate, personal, privately owned, secret. 2 (secret) closed, confidential, off the record, restricted, top secret, unofficial

**privation** n want of necessities and comforts of life; hardship
**privatize** v sell (state enterprise) to private ownership; *n* **-ization**
**privet** n evergreen shrub, used for garden hedges
**privilege** n individual right, advantage; immunity, exemption enjoyed by some; *v* grant privilege to; *adj* **privileged** enjoying privilege; completely confidential

**privilege** n benefit, concession, entitlement, exemption, honor, perk, prerogative

**prize** n 1 reward given for merit, success in competition 2 thing won in lottery, contest, etc 3 that which is captured in war, *esp* vessel; *v* 1 value, esteem highly 2 raise by means of lever

**prize** n (reward) accolade, award, cup, jackpot, medal, purse, trophy, winnings
**prize** v (value) cherish, idolize, revere, set great store by, treasure, worship

**probable** *adj* likely to happen, to be true; *n* **probability** likelihood; likely event

**probable** adj anticipated, apparent, expected, in the cards, likely, plausible

**probate** n proving of will; certified approved copy of will

**probation** n 1 (period of) trial to decide if sb is suitable for job 2 *leg* system of keeping (*esp* young) offender out of prison under supervision; *adj* **probationary**; n **probationer** person being given probation

**probe** n 1 *med* instrument for exploring wound, etc 2 *coll* investigation 3 exploratory spacecraft; v examine thoroughly

**problem** n 1 question set for discussion, or solution 2 difficulty; *adj* **problematic(al)** doubtful; questionable

> **problem** n 1 (question) brainteaser, can of worms *inf*, conundrum, puzzle. 2 (difficulty) dilemma, headache, predicament, quandary, snag, trouble

**proboscis** n 1 elongated flexible snout 2 elephant's trunk 3 elongated mouthparts of some insects

**proceed** v 1 advance; go on; make progress 2 come forth, arise from 3 take legal action; n *pl* -**s** product; realized profit; ns **procedure** 1 mode of action 2 manner of conducting business, *esp* parliamentary 3 technique; **proceedings** n *pl* record of transactions of society, etc

**process** n 1 series of continuous actions and changes 2 method of operation 3 system of manufacture 4 whole course of legal proceedings

**procession** n 1 body of persons marching, riding in formal order 2 act of marching forward 3 progress (*adj* -**al**)

**processor** n *comput* microprocessor

**proclaim** v announce, declare officially; make known publicly; n **proclamation**

**proclivity** n inclination; tendency

**procrastinate** v delay; defer; postpone; ns -**ation**; -**ator**

**procreate** v beget; generate; n -**ation**

**procure** v 1 gain; obtain 2 *leg* act as pimp, pander; *adj* **procurable** obtainable; ns **procurator** one who manages affairs for another; **procuration**; **procurement** act of procuring

**prod** n goad, poke; v **prods, prodding, prodded** poke with pointed instrument; *fig* stir up; incite

**prodigal** *adj* lavish; wasteful; n -**ity** profusion; extravagance

**prodigy** n 1 extraordinarily gifted person 2 wonder; marvel 3 monstrosity; *adj* **prodigious** huge, vast, amazing

**produce** v 1 make 2 cause to exist 3 continue 4 yield; ns **produce** that which is yielded or made; **producer**

> **produce** v 1 (make) compose, construct, create, develop, form, generate, manufacture, put together, turn out. 2 (cause to exist) bring about, cause, create, deliver, evoke, generate, give birth to, give rise to, give, initiate, result in, spark off, trigger, yield

**product** n result of natural growth; anything manufactured

**production** n act of producing, manufacturing; that which is produced

**productive** *adj* creative, efficient; n **productivity** rate at which something is produced, *esp* in industry

> **productive** *adj* beneficial, effective, fertile, fruitful, profitable, prolific, rich, useful, worthwhile

**prof** n *coll* professor

**profane** *adj* not sacred; irreverent; pagan; v desecrate; n **profanity** blasphemous language or behavior

**profess** v 1 affirm; make public declaration of 2 practice, have as one's business

**profession** n 1 occupation requiring training and intellectual ability 2 body of persons following such occupation 3 confession (of faith)

> **profession** n (occupation) business, career, job, line of work, trade, vocation, work

**professional** *adj* practicing specified profession; engaged in sport or game for money; *n* paid player; *n* **-alism** position (*esp* in sport) of professional as distinguished from amateur

**professor** *n* university teacher of highest rank

**proffer** *v* offer

**proficient** *adj* skilled, expert; *n* **proficiency**

> **proficient** *adj* accomplished, capable, competent, effective, efficient, experienced, good, skillful, talented

**profile** *n* 1 outline of side view of object, *esp* of face 2 short biographical sketch

**profit** *n* benefit; financial gain; *v* benefit

**profitable** *adj* 1 advantageous 2 lucrative

> **profitable** *adj* 1 (advantageous) beneficial, constructive, useful, worthwhile.
> 2 (lucrative) cost-effective, money-making, rewarding, successful

**profligate** *adj* dissolute; depraved; recklessly extravagant; *n* **profligacy**

**profound** *adj* 1 deep 2 very learned; *n* **profundity**

> **profound** *adj* 1 (deep) great, intense, marked, passionate, sincere, strong.
> 2 (learned) difficult, erudite, impenetrable, intellectual, scholarly, weighty

**profuse** *adj* abundant, prodigal; *n* **profusion**

> **profuse** *adj* copious, lavish, luxuriant, plentiful, prolific, unstinting

**progeny** *n* children; descendants; *n* **progenitor**

**progesterone** *n* hormone which prepares uterus for pregnancy and prevents ovulation

**prognosis** *n* 1 act of predicting 2 *med* opinion formed as to probable future course and outcome of disease; *pl* **-ses**; *adj* **-nostic** (*v* **-ate** foretell, predict, warn; *n* **-ation**)

**program**[1] *v*, *n* *comput* (equip with) set of instructors; *adj* **-grammable** with facility for programming; *n* **-grammer**

**program**[2] *n* 1 printed details of performers, items, etc in play, concert, broadcast, etc 2 performance or broadcast of a program 3 summary of things to be done 4 data for computer; *v* prepare program of work for

> **program** *n* (printed details) agenda, bill, curriculum, listing, menu, order of events, order of the day, plan, schedule, scheme, syllabus

**progress** *n* 1 advance; forward, onward movement 2 improvement; *v* 1 go forward 2 develop favorably

> **progress** *n* advancement, development, evolution, growth, headway, improvement, movement, progression, step forward

**progression** *n* 1 act of moving forward 2 *math* series of numbers each of which increase, decrease by regular law 3 *mus* succession of notes, chords

**progressive** *adj* 1 advocating reform 2 progressing

> **progressive** *adj* (advocating reform) advanced, avant-garde, contemporary, enlightened, go-ahead, innovative, liberal, modern, radical, trendy, up-to-date

**prohibit** *v* forbid, prevent

> **prohibit** *v* ban, make illegal, make impossible, outlaw, preclude, proscribe, rule out, stop, veto

**prohibition** *n* 1 act of forbidding 2 *cap* forbidding by law of supplying and consuming alcoholic drinks

**prohibitive** *adj* 1 intended to prevent certain action (*also fml* **prohibitory**) 2 (of cost) too high (*adv* **-ly**)

**project** n plan, scheme; v 1 propel 2 jut out 3 scheme; plan 4 cast (photographic image, etc.) on screen

> **project** n enterprise, idea, job, operation, program, proposal, task, undertaking, venture
> **project** v 1 (propel) cast, direct, fire, hurl, launch, shoot, throw out, throw. 2 (jut out) bulge, extend, overhang, protrude, stick out

**projectile** n heavy missile, shell, bullet
**projection** n 1 thing that sticks out 2 estimate for future based on available facts 3 act or result of projecting sth (n **-ist** person working movie projector)

> **projection** n 1 (thing that sticks out) bulge, ledge, overhang, protrusion, protuberance, shelf. 2 (estimate for future) calculation, computation, estimate, extrapolation, forecast, prediction

**projector** n apparatus to project image on screen
**prolapse** n falling down or out of place
**proletariate** n lowest class of society; working class, esp manual workers; adj **-arian**
**proliferate** v reproduce by budding, or rapid celldivisions; n **-ation**
**prolific** adj productive, fruitful

> **prolific** adj abundant, lush, luxuriant, plentiful, profuse, riotous, vigorous

**prologue** n preface to poem, play, etc; introductory act or event
**prolong** v extend, in space or time; n **-ation**

> **prolong** v drag out, lengthen, make longer, spin out, stretch, string out

**promenade** v stroll about for pleasure, exercise; n 1 such a walk 2 seaside esplanade (coll abbr **prom**)

**prominent** adj 1 standing, jutting out; conspicuous 2 well-known; n **-nence**
**promiscuous** adj indiscriminate, esp in sexual intercourse; n **-scuity**
**promise** n 1 undertaking to do or not to do something 2 likelihood of success; v 1 make promise 2 give cause for hope; n **Promised Land** fig state of ideal happiness

> **promise** adj 1 (undertaking) assurance, commitment, guarantee, oath, pledge, vow. 2 (likelihood of success) ability, flair, potential, talent

**promising** adj 1 likely to develop well 2 likely to achieve success, etc

> **promising** adj 1 (likely to develop well) bright, encouraging, favorable, hopeful, optimistic. 2 (likely to achieve) budding, gifted, rising, talented, up-and-coming

**promissory** adj containing promise
**promontory** n headland jutting out into sea
**promote** v 1 raise, move to higher rank 2 assist in formation of (company, scheme, etc) 3 publicize; ns **promotion**; **promoter**
**prompt** adj done quickly; at right time; immediate; v help (actor, etc) by suggesting forgotten words; ns **-er**; **-itude**

> **prompt** adj direct, early, immediate, instant, on time, punctual, quick, rapid, speedy, swift, timely

**promulgate** v 1 put into effect 2 announce publicly; n **-ation**
**prone** adj 1 lying with face down 2 inclined; liable; n **-ness** inclination, tendency

> **prone** adj 1 (lying with face down) face down, horizontal, prostrate, recumbent, stretched out. 2 (inclined) apt, disposed, given, liable, likely, subject, susceptible, tending, vulnerable

a
b
c
d
e
f
g
h
i
j
k
l
m
n
o
**p**
q
r
s
t
u
v
w
x
y
z

**prong** n 1 sharp pointed piece of metal; a tine of a fork 2 point of stag's antler

**pronoun** n word used in place of noun; adj **pronominal** of, like pronoun

**pronounce** v 1 declare, utter solemnly and publicly 2 articulate, utter word, sound 3 give as expert opinion; adj **pronounced** emphasized; strongly marked; n **-ment** formal declaration

**pronto** adj coll Sp immediately

**pronunciation** n way in which word, syllable, etc is pronounced; articulation

> **pronunciation** n accent, delivery, diction, enunciation, inflection, intonation, speech, stress, way of saying sth

**proof** n 1 act of proving truth of fact, etc; demonstration 2 test, trial of quality, truth, etc 3 standard of alcoholic strength 4 trial impression from type, plates, etc; adj having standard quality of strength, hardness; idm **proof against** strong enough to be impenetrable, unmoved by; v make proof against

**proofread** v read and correct printed proofs (ns **-er**, **-ing**)

**prop**[1] n support, stay, strut; v **props, propping, propped** act as prop; furnish with support

> **prop** v brace, buttress, hold up, lean, rest, shore up, support, underpin

**prop**[2] n dram any portable article used on stage (esp pl)

**propaganda** n act, method of spreading opinions, beliefs to promote a cause; views, doctrines thus spread; n **propagandist** zealous supporter of cause, etc

> **propaganda** n brainwashing, disinformation, hype inf, indoctrination, misinformation, promotion campaign, public relations exercise, publicity

**propagate** v 1 reproduce; have offspring 2 disseminate 3 cause to multiply by reproduction; ns **propagation** act, process of propagating; **propagator 1** one who propagates 2 garden frame used for propagating plants

**propel** v **propels, propelling, propelled** drive forward; impel; ns **propellant** propelling agent (eg explosive for rocket) (also adj, n **propellent**); **propeller** (abbr **prop**) screw of ship or aircraft

> **propel** v fling, hurl, launch, move, project, push, send, shoot, thrust

**propensity** n inclination, addiction, tendency

**proper** adj 1 suitable 2 peculiar; particular 3 respectable, prim 4 one's own; n **p. noun** one denoting particular person or place

> **proper** adj (suitable) acceptable, accepted, appropriate, conventional, correct, decent, decorous, fitting, respectable, right

**property** n 1 characteristic 2 that which is owned; possessions (estate, land, goods, money) 3 object, costume used in play, etc (usu pl abbr **props**)

> **property** n 1 (characteristic) attribute, feature, power, quality. 2 (possessions) belongings, effects, gear, things

**prophecy** n prediction, foretelling of future; adj **prophetic**

> **prophecy** n forecast, fortune-telling, prognosis, second sight

**prophesy** v make predictions; foretell

> **prophesy** v forecast, foresee, predict

**prophet** n 1 interpreter, teacher of divine will; religious leader, teacher 2 one who foretells the future

**prophylactic** *adj* guarding against disease or disaster; *n* device preventing venereal infection, pregnancy, *esp* condom

**propinquity** *n* nearness, proximity in time, space, relationship

**propitiate** *v* appease, conciliate; *n* **propitiation**; *adj* **propitious** favorable

**proponent** *n* supporter; person advising in favor of sth

**proportion** *n* 1 part or share 2 comparative relation in size, number, amount, degree 3 harmonious relation of parts in whole 4 symmetry; *pl* **-s** dimensions; *adj* **-al** corresponding in amount, size, etc; *adv* **-ally**; **proportionate to** in due proportion to

**propose** *v* 1 bring forward, submit for consideration 2 offer marriage 3 intend; *ns* **proposal** plan; offer, *esp* of marriage; **proposer**; **proposition** 1 statement expressing considered opinion 2 suggestion 3 bargaining offer or proposal 4 *geom* statement of theorem or problems; *v* make direct proposal to sb

**propound** *v* put forward; offer for consideration

**proprietor** *n* owner; *fem* **proprietress**; **proprietary** 1 belonging to owner 2 made, patented, sold under exclusive ownership

**propriety** *n* correct behavior; decency

**propulsion** *n* act of propelling or driving forward; *adj* **-pulsive**

**pro rata** *Lat adj, adv fml* in proportion

**prorogue** *v* terminate (session of Parliament) without dissolution; *n* **prorogation**

**pros and cons** *n pl* arguments for and against

**prosaic** *adj* matter-of-fact; unromantic; dull

**proscenium** *n* part of stage between curtain and orchestra

**proscribe** *v* outlaw; denounce and forbid; *n* **proscription**

**prose** *n* language, spoken or written without rhyme or meter; *adj* **prosy** dull, uninspired; *n* **prosiness**

**prosecute** *v* start legal proceedings against; *ns* **prosecution**; **prosecutor** one who prosecutes, *esp* in criminal court

**prosecute** *v* accuse, bring an action against, bring before the courts, indict, prefer charges against, put on trial, take to court

**proselyte** *n* convert; *v* **-ytize**

**prosody** *n* art of versification; *n* **-odist**

**prospect** *n* 1 wide outlook 2 something expected or thought likely 3 possible customer, etc 4 *pl* **-s** future expectations, *esp* financial; *v* inspect, search for, *esp* gold, etc; *n* **prospector** one who explores for minerals, etc

**prospective** *adj* anticipated, future

**prospectus** *n* descriptive pamphlet issued by company, school, etc

**prosper** *v* succeed; flourish; be fortunate; *n* **-ity** success; good fortune

**prosper** *v* blossom, do well, get on, go from strength to strength, grow, thrive

**prosperous** *adj* doing well; rich; thriving

**prosperous** *adj* affluent, comfortable, wealthy, well-heeled, well-off, well-to-do

**prostate** *n* gland accessory to male generative organs

**prosthesis** *n med* artificial replacement for damaged part of body; *adj* **-thetic**

**prostitute** *n* person who sells his or her body for sexual intercourse; *v fig* put to base, dishonorable use; *n* **-ution**

**prostrate** *adj* 1 lying flat; prone 2 *fig* crushed; spent; utterly dejected; *v* 1 cast to ground 2 *fig* abase oneself; cringe; *n* **-ation** 1 extreme bodily exhaustion 2 extreme depression and distress

**protagonist** *n* principal character in play, etc; lead

**protect** *v* keep safe; guard

**protect** *v* conserve, cover, defend, look after, preserve, shelter, take care of

**protection** *n* **1** protecting; being protected
**2** thing that protects **3** paying money to
gangsters in return for not having one's
business destroyed; money paid in this way

**protectionism** *n* practice of protecting home
trade by taxing imported goods more heavily

**protective** *adj* giving, wishing to give
protection

**protector** *n* **1** one that protects **2** one
appointed as regent; *n* **protectorate 1** rule
by protector **2** state as ruled

**protégé** *n Fr* person under patronage of
another

**protein** *n* complex organic compound of
numerous amino-acids

**pro tem** *adv Lat* for the time being

**protest** *v* **1** raise objection **2** affirm;
*n* declaration of objection, disapproval;
*ns* **-er, protestation** solemn affirmation

> **protest** *v* (raise objection) appeal, argue,
> complain, kick up a fuss *inf*, make a stand
> against, object, take exception to

**Protestant** *adj* Christiandenominations
rejecting Roman Catholicand adhering to
Reformation principles; *n* member of such
church; *n* **Protestantism**

**proto-, prot-** *prefix* first

**protocol** *n* **1** diplomatic etiquette **2** first draft
agreement for treaty **3** *med* description of
treatment plan, etc, in clincial study

**proton** *n* positively charged particle in
nucleus of atom

**protoplasm** *n* basic material of which cells
are composed

**prototype** *n* original; model

**protozoone** *n* one-celled living creature

**protract** *v* lengthen; prolong; draw to scale;
*adj* **protracted** long drawn out; tedious;
*ns* **protraction; protractor** instrument for
measuring angles

**protrude** *v* project; stick out; *ns* **protrusion;**
*adj* **protrusive** thrusting forward

**protuberant** *adj* bulging out;
*n* **protuberance** projection; swelling

**proud** *adj* **1** feeling or displaying pride
**2** arrogant **3** splendid **4** gratified **5** jutting
out

> **proud** *adj* **1** (feeling pride) delighted, glad,
> gratified, happy, honored, pleased,
> satisfied, well pleased. **2** (arrogant) big-
> headed *inf*, boastful, cocky *inf*, conceited,
> disdainful, haughty, high-and-mighty *inf*,
> imperious, overbearing, self-important,
> snobbish, snooty *inf*, stuck up,
> supercilious, vain. **3** (splendid)
> distinguished, glorious, grand, honorable,
> illustrious, magnificent, noble, worthy

**prove** *v* **1** establish truth of **2** turn out to be
**3** test quality, accuracy; *adj* **proven** proved

**provenance** *n* place of origin; source

**proverb** *n* short, pithy, traditional saying;
*adj* **-ial** generally known

> **proverb** *n* adage, axiom, maxim, old saw,
> saying

**provide** *v* **1** procure and supply **2** equip
**3** furnish with means of support

> **provide** *v* **1** (supply) contribute, donate,
> give, grant, lay on, present. **2** (equip)
> endow, fix up with, provision, stock up,
> supply. **3** (furnish with means of support)
> care for, keep, maintain, make provision
> for, provide for, support

**providence** *n* **1** fate **2** benevolent provision
of God **3** foresight **4** thrift

**provident** *adj* looking ahead; thrifty; *adj* **-ial**
lucky, merciful, beneficial

**province** *n* **1** division of country; region
**2** sphere of knowledge, thought, action, etc;
*pl* **-s** any part of country outside capital;
*adj* **provincial 1** of the provinces
**2** countrified; unsophisticated; *n* inhabitant
of provinces; country person

**proving ground** *n* **1** place for scientific tests
**2** *fig* opportunity for testing sth new

**provision** *n* **1** act of providing, supplying **2** something provided, *esp pl* food **3** *leg* stipulation, condition; *v* supply with food; *adj* **provisional** temporary, conditional

**proviso** *n Lat* condition; *pl* **-os** or **-oes**

> **proviso** *n* exception, limitation, provision, qualification, requirement, restriction, stipulation

**provocation** *n* such as to arouse anger, sexual interest

**provocative** *adj* **1** arousing anger **2** arousing sexual interest

> **provocative** *adj* **1** (arousing anger) aggravating, annoying, exasperating, goading, infuriating, insulting, offensive, provoking, stimulating. **2** (arousing sexual interest) alluring, erotic, raunchy *inf*, seductive, sexy, suggestive, titillating

**provoke** *v* **1** give rise to; stir up **2** make angry

> **provoke** *v* **1** (give rise to) arouse, awaken, bring about, cause, elicit, evoke, excite, give rise to, incite, induce, inspire, kindle, occasion, produce, prompt, rouse, stimulate, stir up, work up. **2** (make angry) aggravate, anger, annoy, exasperate, gall, get on your nerves *inf*, harass, infuriate, insult, irritate, madden, make your blood boil *inf*, offend, outrage, pique, rile, rouse, tease, torment, upset, wind up

**prow** *n* front of ship; bow

**prowess** *n* **1** bravery; valor **2** skill **3** success

**prowl** *v* go about stealthily, furtively, *esp* in search of prey, plunder; *n* act of prowling; *n* **-er**

> **prowl** *v* creep, move stealthily, slink, sneak, stalk, steal

**proxy** *n* **1** authority given to person to act as agent **2** person acting as agent or substitute

**prude** *n* excessively prim, proper person; *adj* **prudish**

**prudence** *n* **1** careful behavior **2** sagacity

**prudent** *adj* careful, discreet, circumspect, provident; *adj* **-ial** showing prudence

**prune**[1] *n* dried plum

**prune**[2] *v* **1** cut out, shorten unwanted branches (of trees, shrubs, etc) **2** *fig* shorten by omission

**prurient** *adj* having morbidly indecent, obscene ideas, etc; *n* **-ence**

**pruritis** *n med* severe itching

**pry** *v* **pries, prying, pried** **1** search into **2** break open, as with lever

> **pry** *v* (search into) be a busybody, be inquisitive, be nosy, interfere, intrude, meddle, nose about *inf*, poke your nose in, search, snoop, stick your nose in *inf*

**PS** *abbr* postscript

**psalm** *n* sacred song or hymn; *ns* **-ist** composer of psalms; **psalmody** art of singing sacred songs; **psalter** Book of Psalms

**psephology** *n* study of elections; *n* **-ologist**

**pseudo-** *prefix* false; pretended; seeming

**pseudonym** *n* fictitious name; nom-de-plume; *adj* **-ous**

**psittacine** *adj* pertaining to parrots; *n* **psittacosis** contagious influenza of parrots

**psyche** *n* human soul or spirit; mentality; mind

**psychedelic** *adj* relating to a relaxed, ultraperceptive mental state, or to drugs causing this

**psychiatry** *n* treatment, cure of mental illness; *n* **psychiatrist** one who practices this

**psychic** *adj* **1** concerned with phenomena beyond physical, natural laws **2** (seemingly) gifted with supernatural powers **3** relating to communication with the dead; *adv* **-ally**

**psycho-** *prefix* mental

**psychoanalysis** *n* method of treating certain mental disorders; investigation of subconscious mind; *n* **psychoanalyst**

a
b
c
d
e
f
g
h
i
j
k
l
m
n
o
**p**
q
r
s
t
u
v
w
x
y
z

**psychology** n branch of science studying mental processes and motives; adj **psychological** 1 of or concerning the working of the mind 2 coll produced by the mind; imaginary; n **psychologist** one who studies, practices psychology

**psychopath** n person with mental disorder that can lead to sudden uncontrollable violence; adj **-ic**

**psychosis** n pl **-oses** chronic mental disorder; adj **psychotic**

**psychosomatic** adj physical symptoms, complaint caused by mental disorder

**psychotherapy** n psychological treatment of illness, without drugs; n **-therapist**

**pt** abbr 1 point 2 part 3 pint

**P.T.A.** abbr parent-teacher association

**pterodactyl** n extinct flying reptile

**P.T.O.** abbr please turn over (also **p.t.o.**)

**ptomaine** n poisonous alkaloid substance formed by putrefaction of animal or vegetable matter

**pub** n coll public house; n **p. crawl** visit to many different pubs in one evening

**pub** n bar, inn, saloon, tavern, wine bar

**puberty** n state of sexual maturity

**pubic** adj of or close to the private parts (**p. hair**)

**public** adj 1 not private 2 of the community 3 not kept secret; adv **publicly**; n people in general

**public** adj 1 (not private) accessible, communal, open to all, unrestricted. 2 (of the community) civic, communal, community, national, nationalized, social, state. 3 (not kept secret) acknowledged, known, notorious, obvious, open, overt, plain, published, well-known, widely known

**publication** n 1 making available for public to read 2 item printed for general distribution

**publication** n 1 (making sth available) announcement, broadcasting, declaration, disclosure, dissemination, issuing, notification, printing, production, publicizing, publishing, reporting. 2 (printed item) book, booklet, brochure, leaflet, magazine, newspaper, pamphlet, periodical, title

**publicity** n state of being generally known; advertisement; notoriety

**publicize** v make known to public, esp by advertizing

**publicize** v advertise, announce, broadcast, give publicity to, hype inf, make known, make public, market, plug inf, promote, publish, push, spotlight

**publish** v 1 make generally known 2 prepare and issue for sale (books, journals, etc); n **-er**

**publish** v 1 (make generally known) advertise, announce, break the news about, broadcast, circulate, declare, disclose, divulge, leak inf, make known, make public, publicize, report, reveal. 2 (prepare and issue for sale) bring out, issue, print, produce, put out, release

**puce** n, adj brownish purple color

**pucker** v wrinkle; fall into creases; n crease, fold

**pudding** n soft, cooked mixture of flour, milk, eggs, etc; any solid sweet dish

**puddle** n shallow muddy pool

**pudency** n modesty, bashfulness

**pudendum** n med **-enda** outer part of sexual organs, esp of female body

**pudgy** adj coll short, plump; chubby

**puerile** adj childish, silly

**puerile** adj adolescent, childish, immature, infantile, juvenile

**puff** n 1 short blast of wind, breath, etc
2 laudatory notice 3 kind of pastry; v blow
out, send out in puff; adj **puffy** swollen

**puffin** n sea-bird with large parrot-shaped
beak

**pug** n 1 breed of dog, resembling small bulldog
2 footprint of wild beast; adj **pug-nosed**
snub-nosed

**pugilist** n boxer; adj **-ic**; n **pugilism**

**pugnacious** n fond of fighting; n **pugnacity**

**puke** v sl vomit

**pull** v 1 draw toward you 2 remove by pulling
3 pluck; 4 propel (by rowing); n 1 act of
pulling 2 pulling power 3 steep climb
4 power to influence

> **pull** v 1 (draw toward you) drag, draw,
> haul, tow, trail, tug, yank. 2 (remove by
> pulling) collect, cull, extract, pick, pluck,
> pull out, pull up, uproot

**pulley** n small grooved wheel, carrying cord,
used to change direction of power

**pulmonary** adj of lungs

**pulp** n 1 soft, moist vegetable or animal
substance; flesh of fruit or vegetable
2 mixture of cellulose fibers obtained from
trees used to make paper; v reduce to pulp

**pulpit** n raised enclosed structure from which
clergy delivers sermon

**pulsar** n starlike object emitting radio signals

**pulse**[1] n 1 throb of blood in arteries, etc 2 any
regular vibration or beat; v **pulsate** 1 throb;
vibrate 2 fig throb with excitement, emotion,
etc; n **-ation**

**pulse**[2] n edible seeds of leguminous plants

**pulverize** v reduce to fine powder, dust, or
spray; fig destroy utterly; n **-ation**

**puma** n large, carnivorous feline mammal;
cougar

**pumice** n light, porous volcanic stone

**pump** n device for raising water, etc by
suction, or for taking out and putting in air,
etc, by piston and handle; v 1 raise
2 compress 3 take out, put in (air, liquids,
etc) 4 fig extract information from

**pumpernickel** n Ger dark coarse rye bread

**pumpkin** n round, orange, edible fruit of the
gourd family

**pun** n play upon words; v **puns, punning,
punned** make pun

**punch**[1] n 1 blow with fist 2 tool for
perforating, stamping 3 force; power; v 1 hit
with fist 2 make hole with tool

> **punch** v 1 (hit with fist) bash, belt, box,
> clout, pound, pummel, slug, sock, strike,
> thump, wallop. 2 (make hole) bore, drill
> hole, perforate, pierce, prick, puncture

**punch**[2] n drink of spiced spirits or wine
(usu hot)

**punctilious** adj very exact, particular

**punctual** adj in good time; prompt; n **-ity**

> **punctual** adj early, on the dot, on time,
> when expected

**punctuate** v divide up written or printed
words by periods, commas, etc; n **-ation**
commas, semicolons, etc put in writing to
help make sense clear

**puncture** v make hole in; prick; n small hole
made by sharp point

**pundit** n 1 learned person 2 one who offers
opinions; critic

**pungent** adj 1 sharp; piercing 2 highly
seasoned 3 (of mode of expression) piquant;
pointed

**punish** v 1 inflict retribution on 2 handle
roughly; adjs **-ing** exhausting; debilitating;
**-able**; n **-ment**

> **punish** v (inflict retribution) castigate,
> chasten, chastise, correct, discipline,
> exact retribution from, inflict punishment
> on, make sb pay for sth, penalize, rap sb
> over the knuckles inf, take disciplinary
> action against, teach sb a lesson inf

**punitive** adj 1 serving as punishment 2 harsh,
severe

**punk** *n* rebel against conventional tastes and ideas; *n* **punk rock** cacophonous, rebellious rock music; *adj* **punky**; *n* **-iness**

**punt**[1] *n* flat-bottomed boat with square ends, propelled by long pole thrust against riverbed; *v* convey, travel in punt

**punt**[2] *n* kick given to football dropped from hands, before it hits the ground; *v* kick thus

**punt**[3] *v* 1 *cards* lay stake against bank 2 bet, *esp* on horse

**puny** *adj* weak, feeble

> **puny** *adj* frail, sickly, small, stunted, underdeveloped, undersized, weakly

**pupa** *n* stage between larva and imago; chrysalis of insect; *pl* **-ae** or **-as**; *v* **pupate** become pupa

**pupil** *n* 1 person being taught 2 opening of iris in eye

**puppet** *n* 1 small jointed figure, moved by strings, wire 2 *fig* person who is unable to act on their own; *n* **p.-show**; **puppetry** art of manipulating puppets

**puppy, pup** *n* 1 young dog 2 conceited, impudent young man; **p. love** *coll* adolescent infatuation

**purchase** *v* 1 buy 2 *fig* obtain by effort, etc 3 move by leverage; *n* 1 that which is bought 2 leverage; *n* **purchaser**

**purdah** *n* Muslim or Hindu custom of keeping women hidden from public view

**pure** *adj* 1 perfectly clean 2 unmixed 3 chaste 4 simple; *adv* **-ly** 1 in a chaste manner 2 simply; only; *v* **purify** make pure; *n* **purification** cleansing, purifying

> **pure** *adj* 1 (perfectly clean) germ-free, immaculate, spotless, sterile, unpolluted, untainted, wholesome. 2 (unmixed) flawless, genuine, perfect, unadulterated, unalloyed, undiluted, true. 3 (chaste) blameless, decent, good, immaculate, impeccable, innocent, irreproachable, uncorrupted, unsullied, virginal, virtuous

**purée** *n Fr* finely ground solid food

**purgatory** *n* 1 state or place of torment, etc, where souls of dead are purified 2 *fig* any such state or place

**purge** *v* 1 cleanse; purify 2 *leg* clear oneself of accusation 3 cause evacuation (of bowels) 4 expel unwanted members from political party, armed forces, etc; *n* that which cleanses; *n, adj* **purgative** (medicine) causing evacuation

**Puritan** *n* extreme Protestants in 16th and 17th centuries; one holding very strict religious and moral views; *adj* **-ical**

**purity** *n* state of being pure

**purl**[1] *n* knitting stitch producing ridge; *v* knit purl stitch

**purl**[2] *v* flow with gentle murmur; babble

**purple** *n* red-blue color; *adj* of this color; *n* **p. heart** *n* durabl epurplish wood of leguminous trees

**purport** *v* mean to be; seem to signify; *n* significance, bearing

**purpose** *n* intention, aim; *v* intend

> **purpose** *n* ambition, design, end, goal, motivation, motive, object, objective, plan, target

**purr** *v* (of cats, etc) express pleasure by making low vibrating noise; *n* this sound

**purse** *n* 1 small bag, pouch for money 2 funds 3 sum of money offered as prize, etc; *v* pucker, wrinkle up (lips)

**pursue** *v* 1 follow closely 2 chase 3 follow to desired end 4 continue (speaking); *ns* **pursuer**; **pursuit** 1 chasing after; quest 2 employment, occupation

**purvey** *v* provide, supply, *esp* provisions

**purview** *n fml* scope; range of operation

**pus** *n* yellowish matter produced by suppuration; *adj* **purulent** full of, discharging pus; septic; *n* **purulence**

**push** *v* 1 use force to move (sb/sth) away from oneself, to another position 2 urge very strongly 3 *coll* sell (illegal drugs); *n* 1 act of pushing 2 concerted attack

**push** *v* 1 (use force to move sth away) barge, bustle, drive, elbow, hustle, jostle, manhandle, nudge, press, propel, ram, shoulder, shove, squeeze, thrust. 2 (urge strongly) browbeat, coerce, encourage, force, impel, incite, lean on *inf*, motivate, persuade, press, prompt, put pressure on

**pusher** *n* 1 person that pushes 2 *sl* seller of illegal drugs

**pushy** *adj* self-assertive; overambitious

**pusillanimous** *adj* cowardly; *n* **pusillanimity**

**pussyfoot** *v coll* act timidly, overcautiously

**pussy willow** *n* (tree with) silky gray catkins

**pustule** *n* pimple containing pus; *adj* **pustular**

**put** *v* **putting, put.** 1 place 2 express 3 throw 4 submit for judgment

**put** *v* (place) fix, install, locate, park, plonk, position, set, settle, situate, stand

**putative** *adj* reputed, supposed, presumed

**putrefy** *v* make, become putrid; *n* **putrefaction** process of putrefying rotten, foul-smelling substance; *adj* **putrescent** rotting; stinking (*n* **-ence**)

**putrid** *adj* decomposed, rotten

**putrid** *adj* bad, decayed, fetid, foul, off, putrefied, rancid, rotting, spoiled, stale, stinking

**putsch** *n Ger* sudden move to overthrow government by use of force

**putt** *v* 1 strike golf ball gently across green 2 *athletics* throw weight (shot) from shoulder; *n* distance that ball, weight is putted; *n* **putter** golfclub used for putting

**putty** *n* 1 soft cement made of linseed oil and clay 2 gem-polishing powder made of tin and lead

**puzzle** *v* 1 perplex, baffle 2 try to solve; *n* difficult problem

**puzzle** *n* brainteaser, conundrum, dilemma, enigma, mystery, poser *inf*, quandary, question, riddle

**puzzled** *adj* confused

**puzzled** *adj* at a loss, at sea, baffled, bewildered, flummoxed *inf*, mystified, perplexed, stumped

**puzzling** *adj* confusing

**puzzling** *adj* abstruse, baffling, bewildering, cryptic, enigmatic, incomprehensible, involved, mind-boggling *inf*, mysterious, mystifying, perplexing, unclear

**PVC** *abbr* polyvinyl chloride (form of thermoplastic, widely used in domestic articles and industry)

**pygmy, pigmy** *n* dwarf; *adj* very small, dwarfish

**pylon** *n* tall structure, *usu* of steel girders, carrying electric cables, etc

**pyorrhoea** *n med* disease of gums; discharge of pus

**pyramid** *n* 1 figure with square base and four triangular sides sloping to apex 2 Egyptian tomb of this shape; *adj* **-al**

**pyre** *n* pile of wood for burning corpse

**Pyrex** (*TM*) heatproof glass ovenware

**pyrotechnics** *n pl* 1 display of fireworks 2 *fig* display of brilliant, ironical oratory

**Pyrrhic** *adj* **P. victory** one won at enormous and ruinous cost

**python** *n* large nonvenomous snake that crushes its prey

a
b
c
d
e
f
g
h
i
j
k
l
m
n
o
p
q
r
s
t
u
v
w
x
y
z

**quack**[1] *n* cry of duck; *v* utter such sound
**quack**[2] *n* one who pretends to have skill, knowledge, *esp* in medicine; charlatan
**quad** *n coll* 1 quadrangle 2 quadruplet
**quadrangle** *n* 1 four-angled plane figure 2 square or rectangular court with buildings round it; *n* **quadrant** 1 quarter of circle 2 instrument for measuring angles
**quadraphonic** *adj* using four sound channels or speakers
**quadrilateral** *n, adj* (figure) having four sides and four angles
**quadrille** *n Fr* dance for four persons; music for this
**quadruped** *n* four-footed animal
**quadruple** *adj* fourfold; *v* multiply by four
**quadruplet** *n* one of four siblings born of the same pregnancy
**quag, quagmire** *n* soft, marshy ground
**quail**[1] *n* small game-bird related to partridge
**quail**[2] *v* 1 cower, flinch 2 lose heart
**quaint** *adj* attractively strange

> **quaint** *adj* charming, curious, droll, eccentric, fanciful, odd, offbeat, olde worlde *inf*, old-fashioned, peculiar, queer, strange, sweet, unusual, whimsical

**quake** *v* shake; tremble; rock from side to side; *n* 1 tremor 2 *coll* earthquake

> **quake** *v* quiver, rock, shake, shiver, shudder, tremble, vibrate

**Quaker** *n* member of Christian group (Society of Friends) opposed to all forms of violence
**qualification** *n* 1 limiting factor 2 act of qualifying 3 proof of having passed examination
**qualify** *v* **qualifies, qualifying, qualified** 1 obtain official qualification by study, etc 2 limit (by description) 3 become competent

> **qualify** *v* 1 (obtain qualification) be eligible, be entitled, have/gain the right, get through, go through, make the grade, meet the requirements, pass, reach the required standard, succeed. 2 (limit by description) add a rider to, mitigate, moderate, modify, restrict, soften, temper, tone down, weaken

**qualified** *adj* 1 having qualifications 2 limited

> **qualified** *adj* 1 (having qualifications) able, capable, certificated, competent, experienced, fit, proficient, skilled, trained 2 (limited) cautious, conditional, guarded, half-hearted, modified, provisional, reserved, restricted

**quality** *n* 1 essential nature 2 characteristic 3 degree of value 4 high social rank; *adj* **qualitative** having to do with quality

> **quality** *n* 1 (essential nature) character, description, essence, kind, nature. 2 (characteristic) advantage, aspect, attribute, feature, good point, hallmark, mark, property, trait. 3 (degree of value) caliber, excellence, merit, rating, standard, standing, status, value, worth

**ualm** n misgiving, scruple

**qualm** n anxiety, apprehension, conscience, disinclination, disquiet, doubt, guilt, hesitancy, hesitation, pang, reluctance, remorse, reservations, reticence, second thoughts, uncertainty, uneasiness

**uandary** n perplexing situation

**quandary** n difficulty, dilemma, fix *inf*, impasse, plight, predicament, problem, puzzle, uncertainty

**uantity** n number; amount; extent; specified amount; *adj* **quantitative**

**quantity** n aggregate, lot, sum, total

**uarantine** n isolation to prevent spreading of infection; v put, keep in quarantine
**uarrel** n **quarrelling, quarrelled** angry dispute; v disagree

**quarrel** n altercation, argument, battle, break, conflict, confrontation, difference of opinion, disagreement, dispute, falling-out, feud, fight, rivalry, row *inf*, squabble, tiff *inf*, vendetta, war, wrangle
**quarrel** v argue, battle, be estranged, be in conflict, bicker, cross, cross swords, dispute, fall out, feud, fight, row *inf*, spar, squabble, tangle, wrangle *inf*

**uarrelsome** *adj* tending to quarrel

**quarrelsome** *adj* aggressive, angry, argumentative, bad-tempered, bloody-minded, cantankerous, choleric, confrontational, contrary, disagreeable, disputatious, explosive, fractious, impatient, irascible, irritable, obstructive, pugnacious, querulous, quick-tempered, testy, truculent, unfriendly, vengeful, volatile

**quarry**[1] n person or thing that is being hunted or pursued

**quarry**[1] n goal, objective, prey, prize, target, victim

**quarry**[2] n open pit from where stone, sand, etc, is excavated; v dig, excavate from quarry

**quarry**[2] n excavation, mine, open-cast mine

**quart** n quarter of gallon; two pints
**quarter** n 1 fourth part 2 area 3 clemency 4 coin worth; v divide into quarters
**quarterly** *adj* occurring, due each quarter of year;
**quartet(te)** n 1 group of four musicians 2 musical composition for four performers
**quartz** n form of crystalline silica
**quash** v annul, suppress

**quash** v cancel, invalidate, nullify, overrule, overthrow, overturn, rescind, reverse, revoke

**quatercentenary** n 400th anniversary
**quaver** v tremble; vibrate; n *mus* note, time value of half crotchet

**quaver** v falter, fluctuate, quake, shake, waver

**quay** n pier, jetty, wharf
**queasy** *adj* 1 feeling nausea 2 easily shocked; n -**iness**

**queasy** *adj* bilious, ill, nauseous, queer, seasick, sick, unwell, woozy *inf*

**queen** n 1 wife of king 2 female sovereign 3 playing card 4 most powerful piece in chess 5 fertile female bee, wasp, etc; n **q. mother** king's widow; mother of ruling monarch; **the Q.'s English** standard Southern British English; *adj* **queenly** of or like a queen

**queer** *adj* 1 odd, strange, suspicious 2 unwell; *idm* **queer the pitch** spoil chances of success

**queer** *adj* (odd) aberrant, abnormal, bizarre, curious, deviant, eccentric, funny, inexplicable, outlandish, peculiar, singular, strange, unusual, weird

**quell** *v* suppress, stifle, allay, pacify

**quench** *v* 1 slake (thirst) 2 extinguish; put out (fire)

**quench** *v* (slake thirst) gratify, relieve, sate, satisfy, slake

**querulous** *adj* complaining; whining

**query** *n* question; interrogation mark (?); *v* question; express doubt about

**query** *n* doubt, hesitation, inquiry, problem, question mark, suspicion, uncertainty
**query** *v* call into question, challenge, contest, dispute, doubt, mistrust, suspect

**quest** *n* search; *v* search for

**quest** *n* crusade, expedition, journey, mission, pursuit

**question** *n* 1 act of asking 2 sentence requiring reply 3 point of discussion; *v* 1 ask question of 2 dispute; *ns* **q. -mark** punctuation mark showing end of question; **questionnaire** list of formal questions devised to obtain information, etc;

**question** *v* 1 (ask questions) ask, cross-examine, debrief, grill, inquire, interrogate, interview, poll, probe, pump *inf*, quiz. 2 (dispute) argue over, call into question, challenge, contest, doubt, impugn, object to, oppose, quarrel with, query

**questionable** *adj* 1 dubious 2 not completely honest

**questionable** *adj* (dubious) arguable, borderline, contestable, controversial, debatable, disputable, doubtful, open to challenge, problematic, uncertain

**queue** *n Fr* line of waiting people or vehicles; *v* wait in queue

**queue** *n* file, line, string, waiting list
**queue** *v* file, form a line, line up, queue up, stand in line, wait in line

**quibble** *n* play on words; *v* evade point

**quibble** *n* argument, complaint, criticism, dispute, nit-picking, objection, pettyfogging, point of contention, query
**quibble** *v* argue, carp, dispute, nit-pick, pettyfog, split hairs, take issue

**quiche** *n Fr* baked custard with egg, cheese, and other savory items in pastry crust

**quick** *adj* 1 rapid, brisk 2 hasty 3 prompt 4 keen 5 living; *v* **quicken** 1 cause to be quick 2 become faster 3 give life to 4 become living; *ns* **quicklime** unslaked lime; **quicksand** very loose, wet, soft sand; **quicksilver** mercury; *adjs* **quickfire** in rapid succession; **quick-tempered** quick to anger; **quickwitted** reacting quickly

**quick** *adj* 1 (rapid) brisk, fast, fast-moving, fleet of foot, headlong, high-speed, nippy *inf*, speedy, swift. 2 (hasty) abrupt, hurried, lightning, momentary, rapid, swift. 3 (prompt) instant, instantaneous, rapid, spur-of-the-moment, swift. 4 (keen) alert, astute, bright, clever, intelligent, perceptive, quick-thinking, quick-witted, sharp, shrewd, smart

**quid** *n* chew of tobacco
**quid pro quo** *n Lat* thing given in return for sth
**quiescent** *adj* still, calm, inactive, passive

**quiet** *adj* 1 peaceful; motionless;
2 monotonous; *ns* **-ness, -ude**

> **quiet** *adj* (peaceful) calm, noiseless, placid,
> restful, serene, silent, sleepy, soundless,
> still, tranquil, unexciting

**quieten** *v* make, become quiet (*also* **quiet**)

> **quieten** *v* calm, calm down, hush, lull,
> muffle, mute, pacify, shut up, silence,
> stifle, subdue

**quietism** *n* religious philosophy of calm
acceptance; *n, adj* **-ist**
**quietus** *n* riddance; final discharge; death
**quill** *n* 1 hollow stem of bird's feather 2 long
wing feather 3 spine of porcupine 4 object
made from these (*eg* a pen)
**quilt** *n* padded bedcover; *v* stitch pieces of
cloth together with padding between; *n* **-ing**
**quince** *n* pear-shaped fruit with sharp flavor
**quinine** *n* bitter-tasting drug
**quinquennial** *adj* occurring once in or lasting
five years
**quint** *n coll* quintuplet
**quintal** *n* unit of weight equal to:
1 100 pounds 2 100 kg
**quintessence** *n* purest form of some quality;
*adj* **-ential**
**quintet(te)** *n mus* 1 composition for five
instruments or voices 2 group of five
performers
**quintuplet** *n* (*abbr* **quint**) one of five
children born of the same pregnancy
**quip** *n* witty remark

> **quip** *n* bon mot, crack *inf*, epigram, gag *inf*,
> jest, joke, one-liner, wisecrack, witticism

**quire** *n* twentieth part of ream of paper
**quirk** *n* individual trait

> **quirk** *n* eccentricity, foible, idiosyncrasy,
> kink, oddity, peculiarity, whim

**quit** *v* **quitting, quit** 1 leave, abandon
2 cease from; give up

> **quit** *v* 1 (leave) depart, give notice, go
> away, hand in your notice, resign, vacate,
> withdraw. 2 (cease from) abandon,
> abstain, cease, cut out, desist, discontinue,
> drop, give up, refrain, renounce, stop

**quite** *adv* 1 to some extent (**quite good**)
2 completely (**quite right; quite
finished**); *interj* expressing agreement

> **quite** *adv* 1 (to some extent) fairly,
> moderately, pretty *inf*, rather, relatively,
> somewhat. 2 (completely) absolutely,
> altogether, entirely, fully, totally, wholly

**quiver** *v* tremble, shake

> **quiver** *v* oscillate, palpitate, pulsate, shiver,
> shudder, throb, vibrate

**quixotic** *adj* extravagantly generous and
chivalrous
**quiz** *v* **quizzing, quizzed** question closely;
*n* game of answering questions, or solving
problems, *esp* as public entertainment

> **quiz** *v* cross-examine, fire questions at, grill
> *inf*, interrogate, interview, poll, pump,
> question
> **quiz** *n* competition, contest, game show,
> questionnaire

**quizzical** *adj* (of look, smile) questioning;
with a hint of amused disbelief
**quorum** *n* minimum number of members that
must be present before meeting may proceed
**quota** *n* proportional share; allowance
**quote** *v* 1 repeat or cite something said,
written by another 2 name price, give
estimate

**rabbet** *n* groove in woodwork; *v* join by rabbet

**rabbi** *n* Jewish religious leader

**rabbit** *n* burrowing rodent akin to hare; *phr v* **rabbit on** *coll* talk at length

**rabble** *n* noisy crowd or mob; *adj, n* **r.-rousing** stirring up feelings of anger and violence in a mob

> **rabble** *n* band, crowd, gang, horde, mob, rioters, troublemakers

**rabid** *adj* 1 affected with rabies 2 violently fanatical; *n* **rabies** infectious disease of dogs

**race**[1] *n* contest of speed in running, riding, sailing, etc; *v* run swiftly; compete in speed (against); *n* **racetrack** course for races

> **race** *n* chase, competition, contest, event, heat, match, pursuit, run

**race**[2] *n* 1 group of persons descended from same original stock 2 lineage; breed; *ns* **r. relations** relations between different races in the same community; **racism** 1 belief that one's own race is superior to others 2 unjust treatment of member(s) of a particular race; *adj, n* **racist**

**rack** *n* 1 framework to hold things 2 medieval instrument of torture; *idm* **go to rack and ruin** become delapidated; *idm* **rack one's brains** make hard effort to think

**racket**[1] (also **racquet**) *n* bat used in tennis

**racket**[2] *n* 1 loud noise 2 illegal business; *n* **-eer** one who operates illegal business

> **racket** *n* 1 (loud noise) cacophony, din, disturbance, fracas, noise, sound, tumult, uproar. 2 (illegal business) corruption, extortion, fraud, graft, scam *inf*, scheme

**racy** *adj* spirited; piquant; spicy; *n* **raciness**

**radar** *n* electronic system for direction finding and observation of distant objects, by reflection of radio waves

**raddled** *adj* confused

**radial** *adj* arranged like the spokes of a wheel

**radian** *n geom* angle formed at center of circle by radii drawn from each end of arc with length of one radius

**radiant** *adj* 1 shining 2 showing delight

> **radiant** *adj* 1 (giving off light) bright, brilliant, dazzling, glittering, luminous, resplendent, shining, shiny, sparkling. 2 (showing delight) beaming, delighted, expansive, happy, serene, smiling, warm

**radiate** *v* 1 emit light, heat 2 spread from center; *n* **-ation** emission of heat, light

> **radiate** *v* (emit) emanate, exude, generate, give off, produce, send forth, shed, send out, shine, spread

**radiator** *n* 1 device for cooling car engine 2 apparatus for heating rooms, etc

**radical** *adj* 1 progressive in political belief 2 complete; *n* person of liberal views

**radii** *pl of* radius

**radio** *n* 1 transmission of sounds by electromagnetic waves, without wires 2 receiving apparatus (*also* **receiver**) 3 **the radio** (activity of) the broadcasting industry; *v* send (message) by radio; *ns* **r. astronomy** astronomy using radio telescope; **r. cab** cab or car equipped with radio intercom; **r. telephone** telephone using radio waves

**radioactivity** *n* spontaneous disintegration and emission of gamma rays, etc; *adj* **radioactive**

**radiography** *n* X-ray photography, *usu* for medical use; *n* **-pher** person qualified to do this

**radiology** *n* study of X-rays and their use in medicine; *n* **-ologist** specialist in this

**radiotherapy** *n* treatment of disease by X-rays; *n* **-therapist**

**radish** *n* plant with edible, pungent root

**radium** *n* rare, radioactive metallic element

**radius** *n* *pl* **radii, radiuses** straight line from center to circumference of circle

**radix** *n* number or quantity taken as basis for calculation

**raffia** *n* fiber from leaves of Madagascar palm, used for tying plants, etc

**raffish** *adj* rakish, disreputable

**raffle** *n* sale of article by means of lottery; *v* dispose of by raffle

**raft** *n* flat, buoyant structure of logs, planks

**rafter** *n* piece of timber supporting roof

**rag**[1] *n* shred, tatter of cloth; *pl* **-s** old clothes

**rag**[2] *v* **ragging, ragged** tease good-naturedly

**rage** *n* violent anger; *v* 1 speak, act with violent anger 2 (of storm, etc) be extremely violent, rough; *idm* **all the rage** *coll* very popular

> **rage** *n* bile, frenzy, fulmination, fury, rampage, violence, vituperation

**ragged** *adj* 1 jagged, uneven 2 clothed in torn clothes; rough

**ragoût** *n* Fr stew of meat and vegetables

**ragtime** *n* strongly syncopated music

**raid** *n* attack, invasion; police search on suspect premises, as low nightclub, etc; *v* make raid on, into; attack

**rail**[1] *n* 1 horizontal wooden or metal bar; *pl* **-s** system of railroad lines; *ns* **railing** *usu* *pl* fence of wooden or metal rails; **railroad** system of tracks for running of trains

**rail**[2] *v* utter complaints against; reproach bitterly; *n* **raillery** good-humored banter

**rain** *n* condensed moisture of atmosphere falling in drops; *idm* **right as rain** perfectly alright; completely fit and healthy; *v* fall as rain; *phr vs* **rain down** fall in abundance

> **rain** *n* cloudburst, deluge, downpour, drizzle, flood, precipitation, raindrops, rainfall, shower, storm, thunderstorm

**rainbow** *n* multicolored arc appearing in sky when sun shines through rain

**raincheck** *idm* **take a raincheck** *coll* postpone acceptance of offer or invitation

**rainfall** *n* amount of rain falling on a given area over a given period

**rain forest** *n* tropical wet forest

**raise** *v* 1 lift upward 2 increase 3 improve 4 arouse 5 bring up (question)

> **raise** *v* 1 (lift upward) elevate, hoist, hold up, jack up, lift up, pick up, pull up, push up, rear. 2 (increase) augment, boost, inflate, mark up, push up, put up, up *inf*. 3 (improve) enhance, exalt, heighten, promote, upgrade. 4 (arouse) activate, awaken, breed, cause, create, engender, evoke, excite, foment, foster, generate, incite, instigate, kindle, provoke, rouse, set off, spark, stimulate, trigger. 5 (bring up question) ask, broach, express, introduce, mention, moot, pose, present, propose, put forward, state, suggest

**raisin** *n* dried grape

**raison d'être** *n* Fr reason for existence

**raj** *n* (period of) British colonial rule in India

**rake**[1] *n* long-handled tool with cross bar set with teeth for gathering hay, leaves, etc or for breaking, scraping ground; *v* 1 use rake 2 sweep target with fire lengthwise

**rake**[2] *n* dissolute or immoral man

**rally** *v* **rallying, rallied** 1 gather together again 2 reform after repulse, etc 3 recover health, strength, etc 4 revive; *phr v* **rally round** come to the rescue; *n* 1 mass meeting 2 long car race 3 *tennis* exchange of strokes

**rally** n (mass meeting) assembly, conference, congress, convention, convocation, gathering, meeting, public meeting, reunion

**RAM** abbr comput random access memory
**ram** n 1 adult male sheep 2 device for battering or piercing; v **ramming, rammed** 1 collide forcibly with; crush by repeated blows 2 instill (ideas, etc) by persistent effort
**Ramadan** n great feast, lasting throughout ninth month of Muslim year
**ramble** v 1 wander for pleasure 2 chatter incoherently 3 (of plants) grow in long shoots; n casual walk; n **rambler** one who rambles; climbing, trailing plant, esp rose

**ramble** v 1 (wander) amble, hike, range, roam, rove, stroll, walk. 2 (chatter) digress, drone on, wander

**ramekin** n small ceramic baking dish
**ramification** n subdivision in complex system
**ramp** n inclined plane joining two level surfaces
**rampage** v rage; n wild behavior
**rampant** adj growing too fast and abundantly
**rampart** n defensive mound with parapet
**ramshackle** adj rickety; wornout

**ramshackle** adj decrepit, dilapidated, flimsy, jerry-built, shaky, unstable, unsteady, tumbledown

**ran** pt of **run**
**ranch** n large American cattle farm
**rancid** adj having offensive smell and taste, esp of fats and oils
**rancor** n deep-rooted hatred
**R and D** abbr comm research and development
**random** adj done by chance; idm **at random** in an unplanned way; **r. access** comput system allowing information to be stored or retrieved in any order; adv **-ly**

**random** adj accidental, arbitrary, casual, chance, disorganized, fortuitous, haphazard, hit-or-miss, indiscriminate, irregular, sporadic, spot, stray, unplanned, unsystematic

**randy** adj coll lustful
**range** n 1 extent; area; scope 2 distance that can be reached by weapon, vehicle, etc 3 shooting area 4 cooking stove; v 1 place, set in rows 2 wander 3 vary within limits; n **ranger** forest or park official
**rangy** adj tall and thin
**rank¹** n 1 class; position 2 line, row 3 pl **-s** body of soldiers; v classify; idm **rank and file** ordinary members, not leaders

**rank** n (class, position) grade, level, place, ranking, rating, seniority, standing, status

**rank²** adj rancid
**rankle** v cause anger, resentment
**ransack** v plunder, pillage
**ransom** n money, price paid for release of prisoner; v pay ransom for
**rant** v speak wildly, violently
**rap¹** n light, smart blow; idm **take the rap** coll be punished for sb else's wrongdoing; v **rapping, rapped** tap with quick blow
**rap²** v sl talk rhythmically and continuously to musical accompaniment
**rapacious** adj greedy; grasping
**rape¹** n plant grown as fodder for sheep and to produce oil (**rapeseed oil**)
**rape²** v assault sexually; n act of raping; n **rapist**
**rapid** adj 1 fast 2 done quickly; n, usu pl **-s** swift current in river; n **-ity** speed

**rapid** adj 1 (fast) breakneck, brisk, fast-moving, headlong, high-speed, lightning, nippy inf, quick, speedy, swift. 2 (done quickly) hasty, hurried, momentary, quick, swift

**rapier** n light, thrusting sword
**rapport** n Fr sympathetic relationship
**rapporteur** n Fr person who investigates and reports
**rapt** adj completely absorbed; intent; n **rapture** ecstasy; adj **rapturous**
**rare**[1] adj 1 uncommon 2 exceptional; adv **-ly** seldom; n **rarity** 1 state of being rare 2 rare object or quality

> **rare** adj 1 (uncommon) few and far between, infrequent, occasional, scarce, scattered, sporadic. 2 (exceptional) atypical, extraordinary, singular, uncommon, untypical, unique, unusual

**rare**[2] adj (of meat) only slightly cooked
**rarebit** n **Welsh r.** melted cheese on toast
**raring** adj very eager
**rascal** n rogue; scamp
**rash**[1] n skin eruption
**rash**[2] adj acting without caution, thought

> **rash** adj devil-may-care, foolhardy, hasty, headlong, headstrong, heedless, hot-headed, hurried, ill-advised, ill-considered, impetuous, imprudent, impulsive, incautious, injudicious, madcap, reckless, spur-of-the-moment, unthinking

**rasher** n thin slice of bacon or ham
**rasp** n 1 coarse file 2 grating sound; v 1 file, scrape with rasp 2 grate upon (ear)
**raspberry** n bright-red fruit growing on canes
**rat** n 1 small, long-tailed rodent, allied to mouse 2 fig cowardly traitor; n **r. race** competition to succeed in business; v 1 **ratting, ratted** to hunt rats 2 inform on someone; adj **ratty** sl irritable
**ratafia** n 1 liquid distilled from almonds, crushed fruit kernels 2 small macaroon
**ratchet** n set of teeth on bar or wheel, allowing motion in one direction only
**rate** n 1 amount, degree measured in relation to sth else 2 amount charged; n **ratepayer** one who pays charge for a public utility

**rather** adv 1 sooner, more, slightly, preferably 2 slightly, fairly
**ratify** v **ratifying, ratified** make valid; n **ratification**

> **ratify** v approve, certify, confirm, countersign, endorse, pass, sanction, sign, underwrite, validate

**rating** n 1 act of assessing; classification 2 pl **-s** order of popularity of TV programs
**ratio** n proportion; fixed numerical relations; pl **-os**
**ration** n fixed amount or allowance of food, goods; v limit to certain amount

> **ration** n allocation, amount, assignment, dose, helping, measure, portion, provision, quantity, quota, share, supply

**rational** adj reasonable, sensible

> **rational** adj enlightened, intelligent, logical, lucid, sane, sound

**rationale** n logical basis or reasoning
**rationalize** v 1 give rational explanation of 2 reorganize industry to make more efficient
**rattan** n species of climbing palm; cane of this
**rattle** v 1 make succession of short, sharp sounds 2 move with clatter 3 talk rapidly 4 coll disconcert; confuse; n 1 this sound 2 device or child's toy, making this sound

> **rattle** v (make short, sharp sounds) bang, clang, clank, clatter, jangle

**rattlesnake** n venomous American snake, which can rattle its tail
**raucous** adj hoarse, harsh-sounding
**ravage** v 1 devastate by violence 2 plunder; n pl **-s** destructive effect
**rave** v 1 speak very angrily 2 talk enthusiastically about; ns **r. review** enthusiastic review; **raver** dance party at changing locations

**ravel** *v* **raveling, raveled** entangle, confuse, fray

**raven** *n* large black bird related to crow

**ravenous** *adj* famished with hunger

**ravine** *n* deep narrow valley or gorge

**raving** *adj* wild; behaving wildly (*n pl* **-s** wild talk)

> **raving** *adj* crazed, crazy, delirious, demented, deranged, frenzied, hysterical, insane, irrational, mad, rabid, raging, unbalanced

**ravioli** *n pl* Italian dish of small squares of pasta holding chopped meat, cheese, etc

**ravishing** *adj* delightful

**raw** *adj* **1** uncooked **2** in natural state **3** sore **4** cold; *n* **r. deal** *coll* unfair treatment

> **raw** *adj* **1** (uncooked) fresh, rare, uncooked, underdone, unprepared. **2** (in natural state) basic, coarse, crude, natural, rough, unfinished, unprocessed, unrefined, untreated. **3** (sore) bloody, chafed, grazed, inflamed, open, scraped, scratched, sensitive, tender

**ray** *n* beam, shaft of light

> **ray** *n* flash, gleam, glint, laser, streak, stream

**ray** *n* flatfish, skate

**rayon** *n* artificial silk made from cellulose

**raze** *v* obliterate, destroy

**razor** *n* cutting instrument for shaving

**RC** *abbr* Roman Catholic

**re-** *prefix Lat* repetition, again, back

**re, in re** *prep* in the matter of; concerning

**reach** *v* **1** achieve **2** arrive at **3** extend hand to take; *n* **1** act, power of touching **2** range

> **reach** *v* **1** (achieve) accomplish, arrive at, attain, gain, get, make. **2** (arrive at) contact, extend to, get as far as, stretch to, touch. **3** (extend hand to take) outstretch, put out your hand, stretch, try to get

**react** *v* act in response to stimulus; *n* **reaction 1** response to stimulus **2** reciprocal action **3** contrary action

**reactionary** *n* one who opposes progress and reform; *adj* inclined to such action

> **reactionary** *adj* conservative, die-hard, old-fashioned, rightist, right-wing, traditionalist

**reactor** *n* (physics) apparatus for generating heat by nuclear fission; atomic pile

**read** *v* **1** see and understand writing **2** read and utter **3** (of thermometer, etc) indicate, register **4** learn by reading; *ns* **reader 1** person who reads **2** elementary reading book; **reading 1** act of reading **2** extract from book **3** interpretation **4** figure shown on measuring gauge; **readership** type or number of regular readers of publication; *pt, pp* **read**; *adj* **readable** interesting to read

> **read** *v* **1** (see and understand writing) dip into, look at, peruse, pore over, scan, skim, study. **2** (read and utter) announce, deliver, recite, speak

**ready** *adj* **1** prepared **2** available **3** willing; *ns* **r. money** cash; *adj* **r.-made** prepared beforehand; *n* **readiness**; *adv* **readily** easily, willingly, promptly

> **ready** *adj* **1** (prepared) all set *inf*, arranged, completed, equipped, fit, organized, primed, set, waiting. **2** (available) accessible, at hand, at your disposal, at your fingertips *inf*, convenient, handy, near, on call, present

**reagent** *n* substance used to produce chemical change or reaction

**real** *adj* genuine; actual; *ns* **realism** practical outlook; ability to see things as they are; attempt to depict life, etc, as it actually exists; **-ist**; *adj* **-istic**; *n* **reality** state of being real

**realize** v 1 become aware of 2 convert into money; ns **-ization** act of realizing; **reality** leg real estate, property

**realize** v (become aware of) appreciate, catch on to inf, comprehend, conceive, grasp, imagine, recognize, take in, understand

**realm** n 1 kingdom 2 fig sphere; region
**reap** v 1 cut and gather (corn, etc) 2 fig obtain as reward, result of action
**rear**[1] v 1 raise; lift up 2 bring up; educate 3 (of horse, etc) stand on hind legs
**rear**[2] n hind, back part; ns **rear admiral** naval officer above captain; **rear guard** body of troops protecting rear of army on march

**rear** n back, back end, end, rear end, stern, tail, tail end

**reason** n 1 motive for doing sth 2 ability to think logically 3 sanity; v talk, think logically; try to persuade by reasoned argument

**reason** n 1 (motive) aim, basis, cause, end, explanation, goal, grounds, impetus, incentive, intention, justification, object, objective, pretext, purpose, rationale. 2 (ability to think logically) brains, common sense, intellect, judgment, logic, reasonableness, sanity, sense, understanding, wisdom, wit

**reasonable** adj 1 fair 2 inexpensive; adv **-ably** fairly

**reasonable** adj 1 (fair) calm, intelligent, impartial, just, logical, practical, realistic, sane, sensible, sober, sound, thinking, un-biased, wise. 2 (quite good) average, fair, moderate, ordinary, passable, tolerable

**reasoning** n logical process

**reassure** v comfort; n **-surance**; adj **-suring**

**reassure** v calm, cheer, encourage, hearten, put sb at ease, restore sb's confidence, set sb's mind at rest, support, uplift

**rebate** n deduction, discount
**rebel** v **rebelling, rebelled** revolt; resent control, constraint; take up arms against; n one who rebels
**rebellion** n organized, open resistance to authority, etc

**rebellion** n defiance, disobedience, dissent, heresy, mutiny, resistance, revolt, revolution, riot, rising, uprising

**rebellious** adj showing resistance to authority

**rebellious** adj defiant, difficult, disloyal, disobedient, disorderly, insurgent, intractable, mutinous, nonconformist, obstinate, rebel, recalcitrant, revolutionary, turbulent, unruly, wild

**reborn** adj renewed in morale or religious faith
**rebound** v 1 bound, spring back 2 recoil on; n act of rebounding; idm **on the rebound** 1 when bouncing back 2 when suffering from disillusion, esp in love
**rebuff** n repulse, snub; v snub, defeat
**rebuke** v criticize for fault; n reproof
**rebut** v **rebutting, rebutted** repel, refute; n **rebuttal**
**recalcitrant** adj obstinately disobedient
**recall** v 1 remember 2 call back; n summons to return

**recall** v 1 (remember) recollect, summon up, think of. 2 (call back) call in, summon, take back, withdraw

**recant** v take back opinions, beliefs
**recap** v **recapping, recapped** coll recapitulate; restate briefly

**recapitulate** (*coll abbr* **recap**) *v* summarize; restate briefly

**recede** *v* **1** move back **2** slope backward

**receipt** *n* **1** written acknowledgment of money, goods received **2** act of receiving or getting **3** *pl* **-s** money earned in trading

**receive** *v* **1** take something given, sent, offered **2** be told **3** experience **4** welcome and entertain; *n* **receiver 1** person receiving sth **2** one receiving stolen goods **3** official appointed to collect money

> **receive** *v* **1** (take sth given, sent, offered) acquire, be given, be sent, collect, gain, get, obtain, pick up, take. **2** (be told) apprehend, be informed, be notified, be told, find out, gather, hear, learn of. **3** (experience) be subjected to, encounter, endure, go through, meet with, suffer, sustain, undergo. **4** (welcome and entertain) greet, let in, meet, show in

**recent** *adj* fresh, modern

> **recent** *adj* brand new, contemporary, current, late, latest, new, novel, up-to-date, up-to-the-minute, young

**receptacle** *n* vessel; container

**reception** *n* **1** act of receiving **2** formal act of receiving guests, clients, hotel visitors, etc **3** quality of broadcasting signals received **4** desk in entrance hall of hotel or business establishment where visitors are received (*also* **r. desk**); *ns* **receptionist** person employed to receive hotel guests, patients, etc, and arrange accommodation, appointments, etc; **r. room** room for receiving visitors, clients, patients, etc

**receptive** *adj* quick to receive new ideas, etc; *adv* **-ly**; *ns* **-ness**; **receptivity**

**recess** *n* **1** alcove **2** secret place; *adj* **recessive** *bio* not evident in an offspring because of dominant effect of other gene(s)

**recession** *n* period of reduction, slackening in industry and trade

> **recession** *n* decline, depression, downturn, drop, hard times, slump

**recessional** *n* hymn sung at end of church service

**recidivist** *n* one who relapses into crime

**recipe** *n* formula, directions for making or cooking something

**recipient** *n, adj* (person, thing) that receives

**reciprocal** *adj* felt, done in return; mutual; *v* **reciprocate 1** exchange mutually **2** alternate **3** move backward and forward

**recite** *v* repeat aloud from memory, *esp* to audience; *ns* **recital** act of reciting; *mus* performance; **recitation** recital of poetry or prose, *usu* from memory

> **recite** *v* articulate, deliver, narrate, perform, present, rattle off, recount, reel off, relate

**reckless** *adj* careless

> **reckless** *adj* crazy, foolhardy, hasty, heedless, impetuous, imprudent, impulsive, irresponsible, mad, rash, thoughtless, wild

**reckon** *v* **1** count, calculate **2** *coll* think, suppose; *phr vs* **reckon on** rely on; base one's plans on; **reckon with/without 1** consider important/unimportant **2** remember/fail to take into account

**reclaim** *v* **1** bring back **2** demand return of **3** reform from vice, etc **4** recover (land) from sea or waste state; *n* **reclaimable**

**recline** *v* sit, lean backward

**recluse** *n* hermit; one who chooses to live alone

**recognize** *v* **1** know again **2** acknowledge; *n* **recognition**

> **recognize** *v* **1** (know again) identify, place, recall, recollect, remember, spot. **2** (acknowledge) accept, admit, appreciate, avow, endorse, notice, respect

**recoil** v 1 draw back 2 retreat 3 rebound 4 *fig* feel disgust, horror; n rebound, *esp* of gun; backward motion

**recollect** v remember; n **-lection** memory

**recommend** v 1 advise 2 put forward as suitable for job 3 entrust to care of; n **-ation**

> **recommend** v 1 (advise) advocate, counsel, propose, put forward, suggest, urge. 2 (put forward as suitable for job) commend, endorse, favor, put in a good word for, speak favorably/highly/well of, support, vouch for

**recompense** v make equal return for; reward; compensate; n that which is given as reward, compensation, etc

**reconcile** v 1 settle (dispute, quarrel, etc) 2 bring into logical agreement 3 be resigned to; ns **reconciliation** restoration of friendship; act, state of being reconciled; **reconcilement**; *adj* **reconciliatory**

**reconnoiter** v *Fr* make preliminary survey (of enemy's position, etc); explore, examine beforehand; n **reconnaissance** act of reconnoitering

**reconsider** v think again about

> **reconsider** v change your mind, have a change of heart, reassess, re-examine, rethink, review, revise, think again, think better of, think twice

**reconstitute** v restore to usual state (*eg* dried foodstuff by adding water); n **-tution**

**record** v 1 write down for future information 2 store (sound) on disk or magnetic tape for subsequent reproduction; n 1 written account, document 2 past performance in work or sport 3 best achievement, *esp* in sport 4 sound recording, *esp* on vinyl disk; *idm* **for the record** for the sake of accuracy; *idm* **off the record** *coll* unofficial(ly); confidentially; *idm* **set the record straight** correct a misunderstanding

**record** v 1 (write down) catalog, chronicle, document, enter, file, minute, note, put down, register, report, transcribe. 2 (store sound) tape, tape-record, video

**record** n 1 (written account) chronicle, documentation, dossier, file, journal, log, report. 2 (past performance) background, career, curriculum vitae, history

**recorder** n 1 wooden or plastic instrument of flute family 2 machine for playing recorded tape (*also* **tape recorder**); *adj* **recorded** 1 preserved on disk, tape, or cassette; not performed live 2 written down

**recording** n 1 music or sound put onto disk, tape, etc 2 act of making written record

**recount** v 1 narrate, relate 2 count again

**recoup** v make good (financial losses)

**recourse** n act of seeking help; *idm* **have recourse to** get help from

**recover** v 1 get better after illness, weakness 2 win back what has been lost; n **recovery**

> **recover** v 1 (get better) be on the mend, convalesce, get back on your feet, get back to normal, get well, perk up, pick up, rally, recuperate, revive. 2 (win back) reclaim, recoup, redeem, regain, retrieve, salvage

**re-create** v create, form anew; restore, revive

**recreation** n relaxation; amusement; *adj* **-al**

> **recreation** n distraction, diversion, enjoyment, exercise, fun, hobby, leisure, pastime, play, pleasure, relief, sport

**recriminate** v express mutual reproach; n **-ation** mutual abuse and reproach

**recruit** n newly enlisted member of armed forces; new member of society, etc; v seek to enlist (new soldiers, members, etc); n **-ment**

> **recruit** v draft, employ, engage, enlist, enroll, sign on, sign up, take on

a b c d e f g h i j k l m n o p q **r** s t u v w x y z

**rectangle** n right-angled parallelogram;
adj **rectangular**

**rectify** v **rectifying, rectified** put right;
n **rectification**

**rectitude** n moral uprightness; integrity;
honesty of purpose

**rector** n parish priest; head of certain religious
and educational institutions; n **rectory**
rector's house

**rectum** n anat lowest, terminal part of large
intestine; pl **-tums** or **-ta**; adj **rectal**

**recumbent** adj lying down; reclining

**recuperate** v recover; n **-ation**

**recur** v **recurring, recurred** v 1 happen
again 2 return to one's mind 3 math be
repeated indefinitely

> **recur** v come back, persist, reappear, return

**recurrent** adj happening again and again;
n **recurrence**

> **recurrent** adj continued, frequent, habitual,
> periodic, persistent, recurring, repeated

**recycle** v treat used materials from
manufactured articles to make them
reusable; adj **recyclable** suitable for
recycling

**red** adj 1 of color of blood 2 (of hair) reddish-
brown or ginger 3 coll usu cap Communist;
n 1 red color 2 cap coll Communist; idm **in
the red** in debt; ns **r. carpet** ceremonial
welcome; **r. giant** enormous star, cooler
than white or yellow star; **redhead** person
with red hair; **r. herring** sth irrelevant
introduced as a distraction; **r. ink** business
loss; **r.-letter day** day made memorable by
happy event; **r. light** warning light to halt
traffic, to call for silence in recording studio,
etc; **redneck** coll bigoted, uneducated
person; **redwood** large conifer with reddish
wood; adjs **r.-blooded** full of vigor;
**r.-handed** (idm **catch sb red-handed**
catch sb doing wrong); v **redden** 1 make red
2 turn red; blush

> **red** adj crimson, rosy, ruby, ruddy, scarlet,
> vermilion

**redeem** v 1 buy back 2 fulfill 3 make amends
for 4 ransom 5 (of God, Christ) save from
damnation; n **redemption**

**redolent** adj fragrant; giving out sweet scent;
**r. of** fig reminiscent of

**redouble** v 1 double again 2 make or become
more intense

**redoubtable** adj formidable, valiant

**redress** v put right; make amends for;
idm **redress the balance** make things equal
again; n fml reparation, compensation

**reduce** v 1 decrease 2 bring by force or
necessity to some inferior position, state

> **reduce** v (decrease) contract, cut,
> diminish, lessen, limit, lower, minimize,
> moderate, shorten, shrink, slash, truncate

**reduction** n decrease

> **reduction** n contraction, cut, cutback,
> decline, drop, lessening, limit, lowering,
> minimizing, moderation, shortening,
> shrinking, slashing, truncating

**redundant** adj 1 superfluous; unnecessary
2 made unemployed; n **redundancy**

**reed** n 1 various aquatic or marsh grasses;
stem of these 2 vibrating cane or metal strip
of some musical instrument

**reef** n ridge of coral rock just below surface of
water; ns **r.-knot** double-knot that does not
slip easily; **reefer** 1 short close-fitting warm
jacket 2 sl cigarette from cannabis (also
**joint**)

**reek** n fumes, stench; v smell, stink

**reel** n 1 small spool or bobbin around which
thread is wound 2 lively Scottish dance;
music for it 3 unit of length of film; v 1 wind
on reel 2 stagger; phr v **reel off** recite
rapidly

**ref** abbr coll 1 reference 2 referee

**refectory** n room for meals, *esp* in monastery
**refer** v **referring, referred** 1 assign to
2 send to for information 3 allude 4 submit
for decision 5 introduce in business;
 ns **reference** 1 testimonial 2 act of
referring; n **r. book** book designed for easy
retrieval of information; n **referendum**
submitting of question to electorate

> **refer** v 1 (allude to) cite, hint, make
> reference to, mention, speak of. 2 (send
> to for information) direct, guide, pass on,
> point, recommend, send. 3 (look at for
> information) consult, go to, study, turn to

**referee** n 1 one to whom a thing is referred
2 umpire, *esp* in football (*coll* **ref**); v act as
umpire
**refine** v 1 remove impurities from 2 make
more elegant; ns **refinement** 1 act of
refining 2 culture 3 fineness of feeling, taste;
**refinery** place where materials are refined
or purified

> **refine** v 1 (remove impurities from)
> decontaminate, distill, filter, purify, treat.
> 2 (make more elegant) civilize, cultivate,
> elevate, improve, perfect, polish, temper

**refit** v fit new parts in; n act of doing this
**reflate** v increase supply of money in
(economy); n **-ation**; *adj* **-ationary**
**reflect** v 1 reproduce visual image 2 throw
back light, heat, etc 3 think deeply;
ns **reflection** act of reflecting; that which is
reflected (rays of light, heat, etc); reflected
visual image (by mirror, etc); meditation;
*adj* **reflective**; n **reflector** polished surface
which reflects (rays of light, etc)

> **reflect** v 1 (throw back image or idea) echo,
> mirror, reproduce, return, send back,
> scatter, throw back. 2 (think deeply)
> consider, contemplate, deliberate,
> meditate, mull over, muse, ponder, wonder

**reflex** *adj* directed backward; **r. action**
involuntary muscular, nervous reaction to
stimulus; **r. angle** angle greater than 180°
and less than 360°; *adj* **reflexive** *ling*
denoting action coming back on subject
**reflexology** n therapy using foot massage to
alleviate stress in other parts of body
**reform** v change for better; n improvement;
n **-er** person initiating social or political
change

> **reform** v correct, improve, mend, rebuild,
> reconstruct, refashion, regenerate, re-
> model, reorganize, restore, revamp, revise
> **reform** n change, conversion, correction,
> rebuilding, reconstruction, regeneration,
> remodeling, renovation, reorganization

**refract** v deflect rays or waves from direct
course; n **refraction**
**refractory** *adj* 1 unmanageable; stubborn
2 *med* resistant to treatment; hard to cure
**refrain**[1] n recurring lines at end of song
**refrain**[2] v abstain; keep oneself from

> **refrain** v avoid, cease, desist, do without,
> eschew, forbear, give up, leave off, quit
> *inf*, renounce, stop

**refresh** v revive, invigorate; *idm* **refresh sb's
memory** remind sb of important details;
n **refresher** 1 thing that refreshes 2 further
study by qualified person to bring knowledge
uo to date; *adj* **refreshing** 1 restoring
vitality 2 thirst-quenching 3 new and
stimulating; n **-ment** 1 of refreshing, being
refreshed 2 food and drink; *pl* **-ments** snacks

> **refresh** v brace, cheer, cool, energize,
> enliven, fortify, freshen, perk up, pick up,
> reanimate, renew, restore, revitalize,
> revivify, stimulate

**refrigerate** v keep at very low temperature;
ns **-ation**; **refrigerator** machine for
cooling, freezing (food, etc)

a
b
c
d
e
f
g
h
i
j
k
l
m
n
o
p
q
**r**
s
t
u
v
w
x
y
z

**refuge** n safe place; n **refugee** one who seeks refuge, *esp* in another country

> **refuge** n asylum, haven, hide-away, hideout, hiding place, protection, retreat, safety, sanctuary, security, shelter, stronghold

**refulgent** *adj* shining, radiant; n **refulgence** brightness, splendor

**refund** v repay, restore

**refurbish** v renovate

**refuse** v decline, reject; n garbage; discarded matter; n **refusal** 1 act of refusing 2 option

> **refuse** v deny, rebuff, repudiate, say no, spurn, turn down, withhold

**refute** v reject, disprove

**regain** v get back

**regal** *adj* of, like royalty

**regale** v give great delight to

**regard** v 1 consider 2 gaze at intently; n 1 look 2 esteem 3 care; attention; *pl* **-s** expression of goodwill; *idm* **with regard to** concerning; *adj* **-less** heedless; negligent

> **regard** v 1 (consider) adjudge, believe, deem, esteem, hold, imagine, judge, look upon, perceive, rate, reckon, see, suppose, think, treat, value, view. 2 (look intently at) eye, keep an eye on, observe, scrutinize, stare at, study, view, watch

**regatta** n *It* race for boats, yachts

**regenerate** v 1 bring new life to 2 reorganize after decay; *adj* **-ative**; n **-ation**

**regent** n one who rules during absence, minority, or illness of sovereign; n **regency**

**reggae** n popular dance music from Caribbean

**regicide** n killer, killing of king or sovereign

**regime** n system, method of government, administration

**regimen** n course of treatment, *esp* in matters of medicine, diet, exercise, etc

**regiment** n military unit; *fig* large quantity; *adj* **-al** of regiment

**region** n area; *idm* **in the region on** about; *adj* **-al**; *adv* **-ally**; n *pl* **-s** the provinces; v **regionalize** organize by regions

> **region** n county, department, district, division, locality, part, place, province, quarter, section, sector, state, territory, tract, zone

**register** n 1 official record of names, events, etc, kept for reference 2 range of voice or musical instrument 3 *ling* variety of language (formal/informal, spoken/written, etc) appropriate to social situation or professional use; v 1 record formally 2 have one's name recorded or checked 3 enroll for sth 4 (of machinery) give reading or measurement 5 (of face) express 6 be noted or remembered; *adj* **registered** sent by special postal service with protection against loss, etc (n **r. mail**)

**registrar** n one who keeps public records (births, deaths, etc) or educational records; n **registration** act of registering (**r. number** official code for identification of motor vehicle)

**registry** n place, office where register is kept; **r. office** local registry for births, marriages, and deaths

**regorge** v 1 vomit 2 swallow again

**regress** v go back to old ideas, behavior; n **-ive** falling back; n **regression** backward movement

**regret** v regretting, regretted be sorry for; remember with grief, sorrow; n repentance; sorrow; *adj* **regrettable** to be regretted (*adv* **-ably**)

> **regret** v feel guilty, feel remorse, feel sorry, repent, reproach yourself, rue
> **regret** n conscience, contrition, grief, guilt, penitence, remorse, ruefulness, self-reproach

**regular** *adj* 1 happening in an orderly way 2 habitual; normal; n **regular** visitor, client, etc; *adv* **-ly**; n **regularity**; v **regularize**

**regular** *adj* 1 (orderly) consistent, constant, equal, even, fixed, measured, ordered, periodic, predictable, recurring, repeated, rhythmic, set, steady, symmetrical, systematic, uniform, unvarying. 2 (habitual, normal) common, conventional, customary, daily, established, everyday, familiar, frequent, known, ordinary, orthodox, prevailing, routine, standard, typical, usual

**regulate** *v* 1 put in order 2 control by law; *adj* **regulatory**

**regulation** *n* 1 rule 2 act of regulating

**regulation** *n* 1 (rule) bylaw, commandment, decree, dictate, directive, edict, law, order, ordinance, precept, requirement, restriction, ruling, statute. 2 (act of regulating) administering, administration, control, controlling, direction, government, handling, management, monitoring, ordering, overseeing, running, steering, supervision

**regurgitate** *v* bring up again (swallowed food)

**rehabilitate** *v* restore normal capacity; reinstate; *n* **-ation**

**rehash** *v* rearrange old literary material and produce under new title

**rehearse** *v* perform, practice (play, music, etc) in private, before public performance; *n* **rehearsal**

**reign** *n* rule, supreme power of sovereign; period of ruler's reign; *v* rule as monarch; be supreme; predominate

**reimburse** *v* refund; compensate by payment; *n* **-ment**

**rein** *n* leather strap fastened to bit for leading, holding horse; *fig* that which restrains; *v* hold in, control with reins; *idm* **keep a tight rein on** control very strictly

**reincarnation** *n* return of soul to earth, after death, in fresh form; *v* **reincarnate** cause to be reborn in other form

**reindeer** *n* large domesticated deer of northern Europe; **r. moss** gray arctic lichen

**reinforce** *v* strengthen; *ns* **-ment**; **reinforced concrete** concrete strengthened by embedded steel bars

**reinforce** *v* back up, bolster, brace, buttress, emphasize, fortify, harden, prop, shore up, stiffen, stress, support, toughen, underline

**reinstate** *v* restore to former state, position; *n* **reinstatement**

**reiterate** *v* repeat many times; *n* **-ation** repetition

**reject** *v* 1 discard as imperfect, useless 2 turn down (request); *n* that which is rejected; *n* **rejection** refusal

**reject** *v* (discard as imperfect, useless) cast out, discard, dismiss, disown, eliminate, exclude, jettison, jilt, rebuff, renounce, repudiate, scrap, send back, send packing *inf*, shun, spurn, throw away, throw out

**rejoice** *v* feel, express joy

**rejoin** *v* 1 join again 2 make answer; *n* **rejoinder** retort; answer to a reply

**rejuvenate** *v* make young, fresh again

**relapse** *v* 1 fall back into former bad state 2 become ill again (*also n*)

**relate** *v* narrate; *phr v* **relate to** 1 connect, be connected with 2 *coll* show sympathy towards

**related** *adj* 1 connected 2 of the same kind, family

**related** *adj* affiliated, akin, allied, associated, correlated, coupled, interconnected, linked, relevant, similar

**relation** *n* 1 connection by blood, marriage 2 connection between things 3 narration; *n pl* **-s** links between people, groups of people

**relationship** *n* 1 connection 2 friendship or other link between people

a
b
c
d
e
f
g
h
i
j
k
l
m
n
o
p
q
**r**
s
t
u
v
w
x
y
z

A
B
C
D
E
F
G
H
I
J
K
L
M
N
O
P
Q
R
S
T
U
V
W
X
Y
Z

**relationship** n 1 (connection) affinity, association, bond, conjunction, correlation, interconnection, kinship, link. 2 (friendship) affair, alliance, intrigue, liaison, partnership, romance

**relative** n member of same family; adj comparative; not absolute; ns **r. clause** ling clause performing adjectival function relating to noun or pronoun; **r. pronoun** ling pronoun: who, which, or that used to relate relative clause to sth in main clause; **relativity** fact or state of being relative

**relax** n 1 become less tense 2 make less strict; n **-ation** act of relaxing; slackening of strain, tension, etc; recreation

**relax** v 1 (become less tense) calm down, chill out sl, cool down, laze around, loosen up, put your feet up inf, slow down, take it easy, unwind. 2 (make less strict) diminish, ease, lessen, let up, loosen, reduce, slacken, soften, weaken

**relaxed** adj calm, informal

**relaxed** adj at ease, carefree, casual, comfortable, cool, easy, easygoing, insouciant, laid-back inf, leisurely, light-hearted, nonchalant, peaceful, serene, tranquil, unconcerned, untroubled

**relay** n team of fresh men, horses, or dogs, etc replacing tired ones; v 1 pass on ( signal, information) 2 to lay again; **r. race** race between teams, each member running part of distance and handing baton to next runner

**release** v 1 set free 2 discharge 3 give up n 1 liberation 2 catch releasing mechanism

**release** v (set free) acquit, deliver, discharge, emancipate, extricate, free, let go, let out, liberate, loose, unchain, unfasten, unshackle, untie

**relegate** v send, dismiss to inferior position; n **-ation**

**relent** v become less hard, severe, stern, or obstinate; adj **-less** pitiless; inexorable

**relevant** adj bearing on point at issue;

**relevant** adj applicable, apposite, appropriate, apt, connected, germane, pertinent, related, salient, significant

**reliable** adj dependable, trustworthy; adv **-ably**; ns **reliability**; **reliance on** 1 trust in 2 dependence on; adj **reliant on** dependent on

**reliable** adj certain, consistent, constant, faithful, loyal, predictable, proven, regular, responsible, safe, secure, solid, sound, stable, staunch, sure, true, trusty, unfailing

**relic** n object surviving from past

**relief** n 1 alleviation of pain, anxiety, etc 2 help for people in distress 3 release from duty; v **relieve** 1 bring relief to 2 take over duty from 3 lessen (the effect of); idm **relieve oneself** coll urinate or defecate; phr v **relieve sb of sth** take sth, esp burden from sb; adj **relieved** freed of anxiety

**religion** n belief in and worship of God or gods; adj **religious** 1 pertaining to religion 2 devout, pious 3 fig conscientious

**relinquish** v abandon; surrender; let go

**relish** n 1 enjoyment of food 2 fig zest; enthusiasm 3 spicy sauce for flavoring food; v enjoy

**relocate** v move to new place, esp of work or residence; n **-ation**

**reluctant** adj unwilling; n **reluctance**

**reluctant** adj averse, disinclined, grudging, hesitant, loath, slow, unenthusiastic

**rely** phr v **relying, relied**; **rely on** depend on; trust; adj **reliable** dependable, trustworthy; ns **reliability**; **reliance** dependence

**rely** *v* bank on, be sure of, bet on, count on, have confidence in, lean on, put your trust in, reckon on, rely on, swear by

**REM** *abbr* rapid eye movement (occurring while dreaming)

**remain** *v* stay, be left behind; continue in same place; *n pl* **-s** what is left or survives; relics; dead body; *n* **remainder 1** remaining persons or things **2** quantity left after subtraction; *v* offer unsold books, etc, at reduced prices

**remain** *v* abide, carry on, endure, keep on, last, linger, live on, persist, prevail, stand, survive

**remand** *v* send back, *esp* into custody

**remark** *v* **1** utter comment **2** take notice of; *n* comment

**remark** *n* assertion, declaration, observation, pronouncement, reflection, statement, utterance

**remarkable** *adj* amazing; *adv* **-ably**

**remarkable** *adj* astonishing, astounding, distinctive, distinguished, exceptional, extraordinary, impressive, notable, noteworthy, outstanding, phenomenal, preeminent, rare, singular, strange, striking, surprising, uncommon, unusual

**remedy** *n* **1** substance which cures disease, etc **2** action or method tending to mitigate an evil or wrong; *pl* **-ies**; *v* **remedying, remedied** put right; *adj* **remedial** providing remedy

**remember** *v* call to mind; retain in memory; *n* **remembrance 1** memory **2** keepsake

**remember** *v* be mindful of, call up, keep in mind, recall, recognize, recollect, reminisce

**remind** *v* cause to remember; *n* **reminder** that which reminds

**remind** *v* bring to mind, call up, give a reminder, jog your memory, prompt

**reminisce** *v* talk, *usu* with enjoyment, about past memories; *n* **reminiscence** recollection; *pl* **-s** memoirs; *adj* **reminiscent of** tending to remind one of; similar to

**remiss** *adj* negligent, careless

**remission** *n* **1** forgiveness of sins or offenses **2** *med* period of less severe illness (*eg* cancer)

**remit** *n* area of control

**remittance** *n* sum of money sent as payment or allowance

**remnant** *n* **1** remaining fragment **2** short length of fabric

**remonstrate** *v* protest; plead with

**remorse** *n* repentance; regret; *adjs* **-ful**; **-less** ruthless, pitiless, relentless

**remorse** *n* conscience, contrition, guilt, penitence, self-reproach, shame, sorrow

**remote** *adj* **1** far away **2** aloof; *n* **r. control** device for controlling machine, weapon, etc from distance by radio waves

**remote** *adj* (far away) cut off, distant, far-off, inaccessible, isolated, lonely, off the beaten track, out of the way, secluded

**remove** *v* **1** take away **2** erase **3** relieve of office, rank, etc **4** move from one place to another, *esp* residence; *n* **removal** act of removing of furniture from house

**remove** *v* **1** (take away) carry away, convey, transfer, transport. **2** (get rid of) abolish, banish, delete, do away with, eliminate, eradicate, erase, excise, exterminate, kill, liquidate, obliterate, withdraw. **3** (relieve of office) depose, dislodge, dismiss, eject, expel, evict, fire, oust, replace, sack

a b c d e f g h i j k l m n o p q **r** s t u v w x y z

A B C D E F G H I J K L M N O P Q **R** S T U V W X Y Z

**remunerate** *v* pay, compensate; *n* **-ation**; *adj* **-ative** profitable

**Renaissance** *n* rebirth, revival, *esp* **the R.** revival of art and learning in 15th and 16th centuries

**renal** *adj* of the kidneys

**renascent** *adj* reviving; springing into fresh life

**rend** *v* **rending, rent** tear apart; split

**render** *v* 1 give in return 2 interpret 3 depict by art; *ns* **-ing** version, interpretation; **rendition** interpretation, performance

**rendezvous** *n Fr* meeting place

**renegade** *n* traitor, turncoat

**renege** *v* break promise

**renew** *v* 1 restore to original condition or state of freshness 2 begin again 3 prolong 4 grow again; *n* **renewal** revival; restoration; *adj* **-able**

> **renew** *v* 1 (restore) modernize, overhaul, recondition, refit, refurbish, regenerate, rejuvenate, remodel, renovate, repair, replace, resurrect, revamp, revitalize, revive, transform. 2 (renew efforts) come back to, continue, pick up, recommence, restart, resume, return to. 3 (renew a pledge) confirm, reaffirm, reiterate, repeat, restate

**renounce** *v* 1 formally give up, disclaim 2 repudiate; *n* **renunciation**

**renovate** *v* restore to good condition; *ns* **-ation**; **-ator** one who renovates

> **renovate** *v* fix up *inf*, modernize, overhaul, recondition, refit, refurbish, remake, remodel, repair, revamp

**renown** *n* fame, celebrity

**renowned** *adj* famous

> **renowned** *adj* acclaimed, celebrated, distinguished, eminent, famed, illustrious, known, prominent, well-known

**rent** *n* payment made for use of house, land, etc; *v* occupy (house, etc) for payment; rent out; lease; *n* **rental** apartment, house, etc available for rent

> **rent** *v* charter, lease, let

**rep** *n coll abbr* representative

**repair** *v* mend; *n* act or result of mending; *adjs* **reparable, repairable**; *n* **reparation** redress, amends

> **repair** *v* darn, fix, heal, patch, patch up, put right, renovate, restore

**repartee** *n Fr* witty replies or retorts

**repast** *n* meal; feast

**repatriate** *v* send back to native country; *n* **-iation**

**repay** *v* **repaying, repaid** 1 pay back, refund (money) 2 make return for; reward; *n* **-ment**

**repeal** *v* revoke, annul (law, etc)

**repeat** *v* 1 say again 2 do again; *adv* **-edly** over and over again

> **repeat** *v* 1 (say again) echo, parrot, quote, recap, recite, reiterate, retell. 2 (do again) copy, duplicate, rehearse, replay, replicate, reproduce, rerun, show again

**repel** *v* **repelling, repelled** drive back; spurn; rouse dislike, disgust in

**repellent** *adj* disgusting; revolting; *n* that which repels (insects, etc)

**repent** *v* feel penitence, regret for deed or omission

**repentant** *adj* full of regret; *n* **repentance**

> **repentant** *adj* apologetic, ashamed, chastened, conscience-stricken, contrite, guilt-ridden, penitent, remorseful, sorry

**repercussion** *n* 1 rebound, recall 2 *fig* indirect effect, consequence, *usu pl*

**repertoire** *n* stock of songs, plays that person or company can perform

**repertory** n store, stock; **r. theater** theater with permanent company of actors
**repetition** n act of repeating
**repetitive** adj tending to repeat

> **repetitive** adj boring, dull, mechanical, monotonous, recurrent, repeated, tedious, unchanging

**repetitive strain injury** n muscle injury caused by repetitive work, *esp* keyboarding
**repine** v fret; complain; be discontented
**replace** v 1 substitute sth else for 2 take place of 3 put back; n **replacement**
**replenish** v fill up again; restock; n **replenishment**
**replete** adj well-filled; n **repletion** surfeit
**replica** n exact copy
**reply** v, **replying, replied** answer; n answer in speech or writing

> **reply** v acknowledge, counter, rejoin, respond, retort, riposte, write back
> **reply** n acknowledgment, comeback inf, reaction, rejoinder, response, retort, riposte

**report** v 1 state formally 2 make official complaint about 3 present oneself for duty; n 1 account of events 2 rumor 3 sound of explosion; n **reportage** (style of) news reporting on media; adj **reported** alleged; n **reporter** journalist

> **report** v 1 (state formally) announce, broadcast, circulate, communicate, describe, disclose, document, publish, recount, reveal, tell, write about, write up. 2 (make official complaint about) accuse, denounce, inform against, inform on, rat on, squeal on, tell on. 3 (present oneself for duty) announce yourself, arrive, be present, check in, come, sign in, turn up
> **report** n (account of events) announcement, article, description, message, news, note, paper, piece, statement, story, write-up

**repose** v place; rest; n act of resting; n **repository** place where things may be deposited, stored; warehouse
**repossess** v retake possession of (mortgaged property, leased goods, etc) when borrower has not kept up payments; n **repossession**
**reprehensible** adj not good; deserving reproof
**represent** v 1 symbolize 2 act on behalf of 3 depict by painting, etc 4 be an example of, the result of 5 act as a substitute for; n **representation** 1 act of representing, being represented 2 picture or other art form which depicts sb/sth; adj **representative** 1 typical 2 of elected members (n 1 person elected to represent group 2 agent of firm, *esp* as traveling salesman)

> **represent** v 1 (symbolize) correspond to, embody, exemplify, express, mean, stand for, typify. 2 (act on behalf of) act for, be the representative of, be the spokesperson for, speak for. 3 (depict by painting, etc) depict, draw, evoke, illustrate, portray, render, show, sketch

**repress** v suppress; put down; curb; check; overcome; n **repression** suppression, restraint; *psyc* result of mental conflict
**repressive** adj cruel and harsh
**reprieve** v cancel or defer punishment, *esp* death sentence; give respite (to); n cancellation or suspension of criminal sentence; respite
**reprimand** v rebuke, censure severely; n severe reproof

> **reprimand** v castigate, criticize, lecture, reproach, scold, tell off, tick off
> **reprimand** n condemnation, criticism, lecture, reproach, telling-off, ticking-off

**reprisal** n retaliation
**reprise** n mus repeat
**reproach** v scold; upbraid; charge with some fault; n rebuke; thing bringing disgrace, etc; idm **beyond reproach** perfect; adj **-ful**

**reprobate** *adj*, *n* depraved (person); (one) without honor or principles

**reproduce** *v* 1 create afresh 2 make copy of 3 bear young; *n* **-duction** 1 process of reproducing 2 copy; facsimile; *adj* **-ductive** pertaining to, used in, reproduction; fertile

> **reproduce** *v* 1 (create afresh) copy, echo, forge, imitate, match, mirror, parallel, recreate, redo, remake, repeat, replicate. 2 (make copy of) duplicate, photocopy, print, reprint, Xerox [TM]. 3 (bear young) breed, give birth, increase, multiply, procreate, produce offspring, spawn

**reprove** *v* chide, rebuke; *n* **reproof**

**reptile** *n* cold-blooded, air-breathing vertebrate, which crawls, as snake, lizard, etc

**republic** *n* State having no monarch and governed by representatives elected by people; *adj*, *n* **republican** (person) in favor of such a system (*n* **-ism**); *n* cap member of Republican Party

**repudiate** *v* reject, disown; *n* **-ation**

**repugnant** *adj* distasteful, offensive; *n* **-ance** dislike, aversion

> **repugnant** *adj* abhorrent, disagreeable, disgusting, hateful, horrible, nauseating, objectionable, repellent, revolting, sickening, unpleasant

**repulse** *v* 1 drive, beat back 2 *fig* snub, rebuff; *n* **repulsion** aversion, dislike, disgust

**repulsive** *adj* disgusting

> **repulsive** *adj* distasteful, foul, gross, hideous, loathsome, nauseating, odious, repellent, repugnant, revolting, sickening, ugly, vile

**repute** *n* good or bad name; reputation; *idm* **of repute** of good reputation; *adjs* **reputable** of good repute; held in esteem; **reputed** considered; believed; thought of as; *n* **reputation** opinion commonly held of person or thing

**request** *n* act of asking for sth; *v* ask for

> **request** *n* appeal, call, demand, desire, entreaty, petition, plea, prayer, question

**requiem** *n* dirge; mass for the dead

**require** *v* 1 ask, claim as right; command 2 need, want

**requirement** *n* need, condition

> **requirement** *n* demand, essential, necessity, precondition, qualification, stipulation

**requisite** *n*, *adj* (something) needed, essential

**requisition** *n* formal demand or request; *v* demand supply of

**rerun** *v*, *n* (broadcast) repeat of film or TV show, or of any planned operation

**reschedule** *v* postpone repayment of loan or interest on it

**rescind** *v* cancel; make void; *n* **rescission** act of rescinding

**rescue** *v* save from danger, injury, etc; *n* **-er**

> **rescue** *v* deliver, free, get back, get out, liberate, recover, redeem, release, retrieve, salvage, save, set free

**research** *n* diligent search and investigation, *esp* with view to gaining new knowledge, etc; *v* study in depth; *n* **-er**

> **research** *n* analysis, enquiry, examination, experimentation, exploration, fact-finding, inquiry, investigation, study, tests

**resemble** *v* be like; *n* **resemblance**

> **resemble** *v* bear a resemblance to, be like, duplicate, echo, look like, mirror, put you in mind of, sound like, remind you of, take after

**resent** *v* feel and show displeasure, irritation at; regard as offensive; *n* **-ment**; *adj* **-ful**; *adv* **-fully**

**reserve** v 1 keep, hold back; keep for specific person or use 2 order in advance; n 1 that which is reserved 2 *fig* aloofness; self-restraint 3 part of army only called up in emergency; n **reservation** 1 act of reserving 2 unexpressed doubt 3 tract of land reserved for native residents or for preservation of animals; *adj* **reserved** not showing feelings

**reservist** n, adj (soldier) serving in reserve force

**reservoir** n artificial lake for water supply

**reset** v 1 set again; 2 change reading (*eg* on clock)

**reshuffle** n, v (make) changes in people holding positions of responsibility

**reside** v dwell in permanently or for long time; ns **residence** abode, habitual dwelling; **residency** period of advanced professional training (as in medicine); *adj, n* **resident** (one) dwelling permanently in given place; *adj* **residential** of part of town etc mainly of residences

**residue** n remainder; *adj* **residual**

> **residue** n dregs, excess, extra, leftovers, remains, remnant, rest, surplus

**resign** v retire from office; *idm* be **resigned sb to sth** get sb to accept sth; n **-ation** 1 act of resigning office, etc 2 submission to fate; *adj* **resigned** content to endure; uncomplaining

> **resign** v abdicate, give up, hand in your notice, hand over, leave, quit, step down

**resilient** *adj* capable of returning to original shape; adaptable; n **resilience** 1 elasticity 2 recuperative power

**resin** n sticky substance secreted by most plants, *esp* pines, firs

**resist** v withstand; oppose; n **resistance** 1 act of resisting 2 organized armed opposition by civilians in occupied country 3 *elec* opposition of conductor to flow of electricity; *adj* **resistant**

**resolute** *adj* determined; *adv* **-ly;;** n **-ution** 1 firm intention 2 vote or decision of public assembly or legislative body 3 analysis

> **resolute** *adj* adamant, bold, committed, decided, decisive, dogged, immovable, obstinate, persistent, resolved, set, singleminded, staunch, steadfast, stubborn, tenacious, unbending, undaunted, unwavering

**resolve** v 1 decide firmly 2 make clear 3 form by vote or resolutiion 4 separate component parts of; n determination; firmness of purpose; *adj* **resolvable** capable of being resolved

> **resolve** v 1 (decide firmly) agree, determine, intend, make up your mind, undertake. 2 (deal with) clear up, figure out, settle, sort out, solve, unravel, work out

**resonant** *adj* echoing; resounding; n **resonance** 1 quality of being resonant 2 sound caused by vibrations of same wavelength from another body; v **resonate** be resonant

**resort** *phr v* **resort to** have recourse to; frequent; use as means; n vacation spot or hotel, *usu* with recreational facilities

**resound** v 1 ring with prolonged sound; echo 2 be loud and clear; *adj* **resounding** 1 loud and clear 2 outstanding (*adv* **-ly**)

**resource** n inventiveness, skill in adapting thing to one's purpose; *pl* **-s** means of support; stock that can be drawn on

**resourceful** *adj* imaginative and clever in use of materials available

> **resourceful** *adj* able, bright, capable, creative, enterprising, ingenious, inspired, inventive, quick-witted, skillful, talented

**respect** v 1 hold in high esteem 2 treat as binding; n 1 esteem 2 special aspect; *idm* **with respect to** regarding, concerning

A B C D E F G H I J K L M N O P Q **R** S T U V W X Y Z

**respect** *v* 1 (hold in high esteem) admire, adore, defer to, have a high opinion of, honor, look up to, revere, think highly of. 2 (treat as binding) abide by, adhere to, comply with, follow, heed, obey, observe
**respect** *n* (esteem) admiration, approval, awe, consideration, honor, recognition, regard, reverence

**respectable** *adj* estimable, decent, moderate, passable; *n* **respectability**
**respectful** *adj* deferential
**respective** *adj* of each individually; *adv* **-ly** taken separately in the order mentioned
**respire** *v* breathe; *ns* **respiration**; **respirator** apparatus worn over mouth and nose to protect lungs from fumes, gas, etc; *adj* **respiratory** pertaining to breathing
**respite** *n* temporary rest from work, effort, duty, pain, etc; pause; reprieve
**resplendent** *adj* magnificent, splendid
**respond** *v* 1 reply, make answer 2 act as result of another's action 3 react, *usu* in good sense; *n* **response** answer; reaction to stimulus; *adj* **responsive** sympathetic; readily reacting to stimulus
**responsible** *adj* 1 legally, morally answerable for actions, etc; capable of assuming responsibility 2 at fault 3 sensible; *n* **-ibility** moral obligation, liability, duty; charge; state of being answerable

**responsible** *adj* 1 (answerable for actions) accountable, in control, liable. 2 (at fault) answerable, at fault, culpable, guilty, to blame. 3 (sensible) adult, conscientious, dependable, levelheaded, mature, reasonable, reliable, steady, trustworthy

**rest**[1] *n* 1 stopping of activity or movement 2 peacefulness 3 short sleep; *idm* **put/set sb's mind at rest/at ease** reassure sb; *idm* **lay to rest** bury; *v* 1 (let) take repose; stop working for a while 2 lean; support; *phr v* **rest with** be the responsibility of

**rest** *n* 1 (stopping of activity, movement) break, breather *inf*, halt, interlude, intermission, interval, lull, pause, respite, time off. 2 (peacefulness) calmness, ease, hush, inactivity, peace, quiet, relaxation, repose, sleep, tranquillity. 3 (short sleep) forty winks, nap, siesta

**rest**[2] *n* what is left; residue; others; *v* remain in (specified state or condition)
**restaurant** *n* place where meals can be bought and eaten; *n* **restaurateur** restaurant proprietor, owner
**restful** *adj* relaxing
**restitution** *n* act of giving back something that has been taken or lost; *v* **restitute**
**restive** *adj* restless; fidgety; stubborn; impatient of control; *adv* **-ly**; *n* **-ness**
**restless** *adj* 1 unable to sleep 2 unable to relax

**restless** *adj* 1 (unable to sleep) disturbed, fitful, fretful, sleepless, uncomfortable, uneasy, wakeful. 2 (unable to relax) agitated, edgy, fidgety, ill at ease, impatient, jittery, jumpy, nervous, restive, uneasy, unsettled, worked up, worried

**restore** *v* 1 bring back to former place, state, etc; reinstate 2 renovate, repair 3 give back; *n* **restoration** act of restoring; *n, adj* **restorative** (medicine, treatment) restoring health, etc
**restrain** *v* 1 hold back, control 2 confine legally; *adj* **restrained** calm; controlled (*adv* **-ly**); *n* **restraint** 1 control of emotions 2 limitation 3 confinement
**restrict** *v* impose limits on; limit by law; *adj* **restrictive**
**restriction** *n* law, regulation that restricts

**restriction** *n* ban, check, condition, control, curb, handicap, limit, limitation, proviso, qualification, restraint, rule, stipulation

**result** v happen, follow as consequence; *phr* v **result in** end in; n consequence; outcome; (in games) final score; *adj* **resultant** arising as result

> **result** v appear, arise, come about, derive, develop, emerge, ensue, follow, occur, proceed, spring, stem, take place, turn out

**resume** v assume, occupy again; begin again; summarize; n *Fr* **résumé** summary; n **resumption** starting again; resuming
**resurge** v rise again; n **resurgence**; *adj* **resurgent**
**resurrection** n rising again, *cap* **the R.** rising of Christ from the tomb; v **resurrect** restore to life; resuscitate
**resuscitate** v restore to life, consciousness, activity; n **-tation**
**retail** n sale in small quantities to consumer; *adj* concerned with such sale; *adv* by retail; v sell by retail; repeat (gossip, news, etc); n **r. politics** campaigning by traditional methods of town meetings, speaking face-to-face; n **-er**
**retain** v 1 keep control 2 remember 3 hold back 4 engage services; n **-er** fee to retain sb's services

> **retain** v 1 (keep) hang on to *inf*, hold, keep hold of, maintain, preserve, reserve, save. 2 (remember) keep in mind, learn, memorize, recall, recollect

**retaliate** v take vengeance; n **-iation** return of like for like; reprisals; *adj* **-atory**

> **retaliate** v avenge yourself, get even *inf*, get your own back, give as good as you get, hit back, reciprocate, repay, settle a score, strike back, take revenge

**retard** v delay, make slow or late; *adj* **retarded** slow in physical development
**retch** v try to vomit, strain as in vomiting
**retd** *abbr* 1 retired 2 retained 3 returned

**retention** n act of retaining; *adj* **retentive** having good memory
**reticent** *adj* reserved in speech; uncommunicative; secretive; n **reticence**

> **reticent** *adj* quiet, retiring, shy, silent, tight-lipped

**retina** n sensitive layer of nerve fibers at back of eye
**retinue** n suite, train of retainers, attendants
**retire** v 1 give up profession, occupation 2 go to bed; *adj* **retired** having withdrawn from active life, business, etc; n **-ment**; *adj* **retiring** shy, unobtrusive

> **retire** v (give up profession, occupation) give up work, leave, quit, stop working

**retort** v answer sharply; n sharp, witty reply
**retouch** v touch up; add finishing touches to (photograph, etc)
**retrace** v 1 go over again 2 recall
**retract** v draw back; disavow, recant; *adj* **retractable**; n **retraction** recantation
**retread** v walk over or along again; put new tread on (tire); n used tire given new tread
**retreat** v move backward; n act of retreating; military signal to retire; secluded, quiet, private place

> **retreat** v back away, back down, back off, depart, draw back, evacuate, fall back, flee, give way, go away, go back, leave, pull back, recoil, retire, run away, take flight, take to your heels *inf*, turn tail, withdraw

**retrench** v cut down, *esp* expenditure; curtail
**retribution** n punishment for evil deeds
**retrieve** v search for and fetch; regain; make good; atone; *ns* **retrieval**; **retriever** kind of dog trained to retrieve shot game; *adj* **retrievable**
**retro-** *prefix* backward in place, time, etc
**retrograde** *adj* moving, going backward; deteriorating; n **retrogression**

a
b
c
d
e
f
g
h
i
j
k
l
m
n
o
p
q
**r**
s
t
u
v
w
x
y
z

**retrospect** *n* mental review of past; *adj* **-ive** referring to past; *n* **-ion**

**retsina** *n* Greek wine flavored with resin

**return** *v* 1 come back 2 go back 3 give back 4 reelect 5 ticket for theater, concert, etc, returned before performance for resale; *idm* **return a verdict** *leg* (of jury) give verdict; *n* 1 act of returning 2 official report 3 *esp pl* profit 4 ticket for two-way journey (*also* **r. ticket**); *idm* **many happy returns (of the day)** expressing greetings for a happy birthday; *idm* **in return (for)** in exchange (for

> **return** *v* 1 (come back) come again, go back, reappear. 2 (go back) double back, retrace your steps. 3 (give back) put back, replace, restore, send back, take back

**reunion** *n* 1 joining; being joined together again 2 social gathering for former associates, friends, etc

**reunite** *v* unite after separation

**Rev** *abbr* Reverend

**rev** *n coll* revolution (of engine); *v* **revving, revved** increase speed of engine; *phr v* **rev up** run engine fast to check smoothness of running before engaging gear

**revalue** *v* give new higher value to; *n* **-ation**

**revamp** *v coll* renew; give a new appearance to

**reveal** *v* 1 make known 2 show; *n* **revelation**

> **reveal** *v* 1 (make known) announce, betray, broadcast, confess, disclose, divulge, give away, leak, let on, let out, let slip, publicize, tell. 2 (show) bare, display, expose, uncover, unmask, unveil

**revel** *v* **revelling, revelled** feast; carouse; *phr v* **revel in** enjoy; *n pl* rejoicing; merrymaking; *ns* **reveler, revelry** unrestrained merrymaking

**revelation** *n* 1 uncovering of secret 2 surprising fact made known

**revenant** *n* ghost, apparition

**revenge** *v* avenge; make retaliation for; *n* vindictiveness, vengeance; *adj* **-ful**

**revenue** *n* total income, *esp* of state

**reverberate** *v* echo, resound; throw back, reflect (sound, etc); *n* **-ation**

**revere** *v* venerate; regard with great or religious respect; *n* **reverence** feeling of awe and admiration; deference; *adj* **reverend** worthy to be revered

**reverent** *adj* showing great respect

> **reverent** *adj* adoring, awed, deferential, devout, humble, pious, religious, respectful, reverential, solemn, submissive, worshipful

**reverie** *n Fr* 1 daydream; dreamy contemplation 2 musical composition reflecting this state of mind

**reverse** *v* 1 move backward 2 cancel decision 3 put other way round; *n* 1 what is contrary, opposite 2 less important side 3 setback; defeat; financial loss; *adj* contrary; opposite; *n* **reversal** act of reversing; state of being reversed

> **reverse** *v* 1 (move backward) go backward. 2 (cancel decision) annul, change, countermand, invalidate, overrule, overturn, quash, repeal, revoke, set aside, undo, upset. 3 (put other way round) invert, put back to front, transpose, turn over, turn around, turn upside down

**revert** *phr v* **revert to** 1 go back to (former state) 2 refer to again

**revet** *v* face surface with stone to strengthen

**review** *v* 1 reconsider 2 write critical notice of book, etc 3 inspect (troops); *n* 1 revision 2 written criticism of book, etc 3 inspection of troops; *n* **reviewer**

> **review** *v* 1 (reconsider) look again at, reassess, reexamine, rethink, think over. 2 (write critical notice) analyze, appraise, assess, criticize, evaluate, judge

**revile** *v* abuse; bitterly reproach

**revise** *v* 1 change 2 look over and amend 3 study again for exam; *n* **revision** act of revising; something that has been revised

> **revise** *v* 1 (change) alter, amend, modify, reconsider. 2 (look over/amend) correct, edit, redraft, rewrite, update. 3 (study again) brush up, cram, learn, read, reread

**revival** *n* increase in popularity again

**revive** *v* come, bring back to life, consciousness, health, etc

**revoke** *v* 1 annul 2 *cards* fail to follow suit; *adj* **revocable**; *n* **revocation** act of revoking, *esp leg* repeal, annulment

**revolt** *v* 1 rebel 2 disgust; *n* rebellion

**revolting** *adj* repulsive; disgusting

> **revolting** *adj* abhorrent, distasteful, foul, horrible, nasty, nauseating, obnoxious, obscene, offensive, repellent, repugnant, shocking, sickening, vile

**revolution** *n* 1 complete rotation or turning around 2 complete overthrow of political system

**revolutionary** *adj* causing radical change of methods; *n* person taking part in revolution

**revolutionize** *v* make big changes in

**revolve** *v* 1 go round; rotate 2 move, occur in cycles; *phr v* **revolve around** have as main concern

**revolver** *n* pistol with revolving magazine

**revue** *n* theatrical entertainment, with songs, sketches, dancing, etc

**revulsion** *n* violent feelings, *esp* disgust

**reward** *v* repay, recompense for service, conduct, etc; *n* that which is given in return for goods received, or for return of lost articles; *adj* **rewarding** satisfying

> **reward** *n* award, bonus, decoration, gift, honor, medal, payment, present, prize, remuneration, tribute

**rhapsody** *n* 1 highly emotional, enthusiastic utterance 2 emotional musical composition; *idm* **go into rhapsodies** be very enthusiastic; *phr v* **rhapsodize about/over** express eager approval of; *adj* **rhapsodic**

**rhea** *n* large flightless bird of S America

**rhesus** *n* small long-tailed monkey; **rhesus factor** *med* substance in blood causing harm to Rhesus-positive fetus if mother is Rhesus-negative (*also* **Rh factor**)

**rhetoric** *n* art of oratory; flowery, high-sounding language

**rhetorical** *adj* 1 using flowery, high-sounding language 2 uttered for effect, not for a response (**r. question**); *adv* **-ally**

> **rhetorical** *adj* (using flowery language) bombastic, extravagant, flamboyant, florid, flowery, high-flown, insincere, longwinded, ostentatious, pretentious, showy, verbose, wordy

**rheumatism** *n* name of various diseases attended with painful inflammation of joints and muscles; *adjs* **rheumatic** (*n* **r. fever** severe disease that can cause damage to heart, *esp* in children); **rheumatoid** (*n* **r. arthritis** long-term disease causing inflammation of joints)

**Rh factor** *see* **rhesus factor**

**rhino** *n coll* rhinoceros

**rhinoceros** *n* large, thick-skinned, tropical quadruped, with one or two horns on nose

**rhinoplasty** *n* plastic surgery on nose

**rhizome** *n bot* rootlike stem of plants growing underground

**rhododendron** *n* evergreen flowering shrub

**rhombus** *n* equilateral parallelogram with two acute and two obtuse angles

**rhubarb** *n* perennial garden plant with thick pink stalks that are cooked and eaten as fruit in pies, etc; *coll* nonsense

**rhyme, rime** *n* close similarity of sound in words or final syllables, *esp* at ends of lines of verse; *idm* **with no/without rhyme or reason** without sense; *v* make rhymes

**rhythm** n regular increase and decrease of sounds, movements; pleasant rise and fall, *esp* of words, musical sounds; n **r. and blues** popular music based on blues
**rhythmic, rhythmical** adj having strong rhythm; adv **-ically**

> **rhythmic** adj flowing, lilting, measured, melodious, metrical, musical, pulsating, regular, repeated, steady, throbbing

**rib** n one of bones curving forward from spine, and enclosing chest; n **r. cage** structure of ribs; v **ribbing, ribbed** furnish with ribs
**ribald** adj coarse; irreverent; n **ribaldry** coarse, indecent joking
**ribbon** n narrow woven strip of silk, satin, etc; *fig* long, narrow strip
**rice** n grain from grass grown on marshy or flooded ground in tropical climates; seeds of this plant used as food; n **r. paper** edible paper used for packing candy, etc
**rich** n 1 wealthy 2 elegant and expensive 3 (of ground) fertile 4 (of food) very fatty, sweet or highly seasoned 5 (of colours, sound) full, deep intense; n pl **riches** wealth, abundance

> **rich** adj 1 (wealthy) affluent, moneyed, prosperous, well-to-do. 2 (elegant and expensive) costly, elaborate, exquisite, lavish, opulent, palatial, precious, splendid, sumptuous, valuable. 3 (fertile) abundant, ample, fruitful, lush, luxurious, plentiful, prolific. 4 (fatty, sweet, or highly seasoned) creamy, delicious, fattening, full-flavored, heavy, savory, spicy, succulent

**Richter scale** n scale measuring intensity of seismic activity
**rick** n stack of corn, hay, straw (*also* **hayrick**)
**rickets** n deficiency disease of children, marked by deformation of bones
**rickety** adj shaky, tottering
**rickshaw** n light, two-wheeled, Oriental carriage powered by a person

**rid** v **ridding, ridded** free, deliver from; clear away; *pt and pp* **rid**; *idm* **get rid of** dispose of; *phr v* **rid sb of sth** set sb free of sth; n **riddance** act of getting rid; **good r** welcome relief from unwelcome, unwanted person or thing

> **rid** v (**get rid of**) destroy, dispose of, do away with, dump, eject, eliminate, expel, jettison, remove, throw away, unload

**riddle** n 1 enigma 2 puzzling question, *esp* with pun 3 puzzling thing or person
**riddled with** *idm* full of
**ride** v **riding, rode, ridden** travel on animal, vehicle; *idm* **let things ride** take no action; *idm* **ride roughshod over** treat harshly, with contempt or without sensitivity; *phr vs* **ride out** manage to survive; **ride up** (of clothing) work its way up, out of place; n 1 journey by vehicle, on horse, or other animal 2 apparatus in fairground for carrying people

> **ride** v float, gallop, go, journey, move, progress, travel, trot

**ridge** n 1 long raised strip 2 elongated summit of mountain, etc 3 line where two slopes of roof meet 4 elevated part between furrows; v form ridges
**ridicule** v make fun of; n mockery; derision

> **ridicule** v be sarcastic about, humiliate, jeer at, laugh at, mock, parody, poke fun at, satirize, sneer at, taunt, tease
> **ridicule** n irony, laughter, sarcasm, satire, scorn, sneering, teasing, taunting

**ridiculous** adj absurd; very foolish

> **ridiculous** adj amusing, comical, crazy, droll, farcical, funny, humorous, illogical, incredible, ludicrous, nonsensical, preposterous, silly, surreal, unbelievable

**Riesling** *n* Ger medium-dry white wine

**rife** *adj* prevalent, frequent, common

**riff** *n* (in jazz) repeated phrase

**rifle** *v* search and rob; *n* type of firearm;
*n* **rifling** spiral grooves in gun barrel;
plundering

**rift** *n* **1** opening, crack, split **2** *fig* serious
disagreement between friends, colleagues, etc
*n* **r. valley** steep-sided valley formed by land
subsidence

> **rift** *n* **1** (crack) breach, break, chink, cleft,
> crevice, fault, fissure, opening, split.
> **2** (disagreement) breach, difference,
> division, feud, quarrel, separation

**rig**[1] *v* (of ship) equip with spars, ropes, etc;
*phr vs* **rig out** equip with clothes; **rig up**
arrange hastily, *esp* in makeshift way; *n* way
ship's masts and sails are arranged; style of
dress; *n* **rigging** complete system of ship's
ropes, sails, spars, etc

**rig**[2] *v* **rigging, rigged** manipulate
dishonestly; arrange by underhand means; *n*
dishonest dealing (also **rigging**)

**right** *adj* **1** morally good; just **2** correct
**3** suitable **4** on side of body opposite to heart
**5** in a healthy state; *v* **1** put right **2** set
straight or upright; *n* **1** moral goodness;
justice **2** moral claim **3** *esp pl* what one is
entitled to by law **4** right side **5** political
parties opposed to socialism; *idm* **within
one's rights** with legal justification; *idm* **in
one's own right** by one's own authority;
*idm* **in the right** morally justified;
*ns* **r. angle** *geom* angle of 90°; **r. of way**
**1** (right to walk on) road or path over
private land **2** priority over vehicles coming
from other directions; *adjs* **righteous**
**1** morally good **2** justifiable (*adv* **-ly**;
*n* **-ness**); **r.-hand** on the right; **r.-handed**
using the right hand; **r.-minded** with sound
principles, views; *adv* **1** toward the right side
**2** directly **3** completely **4** correctly
**5** certainly; *v* **1** put right **2** set straight;
restore to correct position; *adv* **-ly**

> **right** *adj* **1** (morally good) correct,
> decent, equitable, ethical, fair, honest,
> honorable, just, lawful, moral, proper,
> virtuous. **2** (correct) accurate, exact,
> precise, true. **3** (suitable) appropriate,
> convenient, ideal, opportune, proper

**rigid** *adj* **1** stiff **2** stern; severe; *adv* **-ly**; *n* **-ity**

**rigmarole** *n* long, rambling, incoherent string
of words

**rigor**[1] *n* shivering, with sense of chill;
**r. mortis** stiffening of body after death

**rigor**[2] *n* severity, inflexibility, austerity,
harshness; *adj* **rigorous**

**rile** *v* make angry; annoy; irritate

**rim** *n* **1** edge; brim **2** outer part of wheel

> **rim** *n* (brim) border, brink, circumference,
> edge, lip, margin, perimeter, verge

**rime** *n* hoarfrost; *adj* **rimy**

**rind** *n* **1** peel; bark; crust **2** tough outer layer
of bacon, cheese, etc

**ring**[1] *n* **1** line enclosing round space **2** flat
circular object with large hole in middle
**3** hoop of gold, silver, etc for finger **4** area
within roped square for boxing, etc; *v* put
ring around; put identifying ring or tag on
(bird's leg, etc); *ns* **three r. binder** binder
with metal rings for loose sheets of paper;
**r.-leader** leader of group of wrongdoers;
**ringlet** loosely hanging curl of hair;
**r.master** director of circus performance;
**r.-pull** metal ring for opening can of drink;
**r.side** area close to boxing ring (*idm* **have a
ringside seat** have good view of action);
**r.worm** disease causing red patches on skin

**ring**[2] *v* **1** cause (bell) to sound **2** (of bell)
sound **3** be filled with (ringing) sound; *pt*
**rang**; *pp* **rung**; *n* sound of ringing; telephone
call; *idm* **ring a bell** remind sb of sth; *phr vs*
**ring out** resound loudly; **ring up 1** record
(prices) on cash register **2** call by phone
**3** raise (curtain in theater); *n* **ringer** *coll* one
who closely resembles another person

a b c d e f g h i j k l m n o p q **r** s t u v w x y z

**ring** *v* (cause bell to sound) buzz, chime, clang, clink, ding-dong, jangle, jingle, peal, ping, toll

**ring-around-the-rosy** *n* children's game
**rink** *n* sheet of ice for skating or hockey
**rinse** *v* wash in clean water; *n* act of rinsing; hair dye
**riot** *n* 1 disturbance of public peace; tumult 2 *fig* unrestrained profusion; *idm* **run riot** get out of control; *v* take part in riot; *ns* **r. police**; **rioter**; **rioting**; *adj* **riotous** wild and disorderly (*adv* **-ly**; *n* **-ness**)
**RIP** *abbr Lat* requiescat in pace (rest in peace)
**rip** *v* **ripping, ripped** cut; slit; slash, tear with violence; *n* rent, tear; *idm* **let sth rip** *coll* take away all restraints; *phr v* **rip off** 1 tear off 2 *coll* defraud by overcharging (*n* **r.-off**) 3 *sl* steal ; *adj* **r.-roaring** 1 wild and noisy 2 (of success) resounding; *ns* **ripcord** cord to open parachute; **riptide** tide causing violent currents

**rip** *v* cut, gash, lacerate, pull apart, rupture, shred, slit, split, tear

**ripe** *adj* 1 ready to harvest as food, etc 2 fully matured, developed 3 ready for specific use; *v* **ripen** grow, become ripe; mature
**riposte** *n Fr* 1 quick return lunge or thrust in fencing 2 *fig* quick retort
**ripple** *v* form, flow in, small slight waves; *n* 1 slight wave 2 light, soft sound 3 ruffling of surface
**ripsaw** *n* handsaw with narrow-set teeth
**rise** *v* **rising, rose, risen** 1 stand up 2 go upward 3 increase in value, price 4 appear above horizon (of sun, moon, etc); *n* 1 increase 2 move toward situation of greater power 3 slope upward; *idm* **give rise to** lead to; *idm* **rise to the occasion** show oneself capable of success when challenged; *n* **riser** upright face of step, between two treads; person or thing that rises; *n* **rising** uprising; revolt

**rise** *v* 1 (stand up) get to your feet, get up, leap up, surface *inf*, wake up. 2 (go upward) ascend, climb, come up, go up, levitate, lift, mount, take off. 3 (increase) escalate, go up, rocket, soar, spiral

**risk** *n* 1 possibility, likelihood of danger 2 amount covered by insurance; *idm* **at risk** exposed to danger; *idm* **at one's own risk** agreeing to bear the cost of any loss or damage; *v* 1 expose to danger 2 hazard 3 accept the possibility of; *adj* **risky** hazardous (*adv* **-ily**; *n* **-iness**)
**risotto** *n It* dish of slowly cooked rice with meat, vegetables, etc
**risqué** *adj Fr* verging on, tending toward impropriety
**rissole** *n Fr* ball, cake of minced meat, fish, etc, fried in egg and breadcrumbs
**rite** *n* solemn act *usu* religious ceremony; *n* **r. of passage** ceremony in some societies marking stage of change (*eg* puberty); *adj* **ritual** of rites; *n* system of religious or magical ceremonies; book of prescribed ceremonies; *n* **ritualism** practice of, and insistence on, ritual
**ritzy** *adj coll* glamorous
**rival** *n* one who competes against another for success, favor, etc; *v* **rivaling, rivaled** vie with, equal, be comparable to

**rival** *n* adversary, antagonist, challenger, competitor, contender, contestant, enemy, opponent, opposition
**rival** *v* be as good as, challenge, compete with, match up to, measure up to, oppose

**rivalry** *n* arid competition

**rivalry** *n* adversary, competitiveness, conflict, contention, hostility, opposition

**riven** *adj* completely split apart
**river** *n* large body of water flowing in natural channel to sea; plentiful flow

**rivet** n bolt or pin for fastening metal plates; v 1 fasten with rivets 2 fig hold attention of; n **riveter**; adj **riveting** coll very interesting

**riviera** n stretch of coast with fashionable resorts

**rivulet** n small stream, brook

**roach** n 1 coll cockroach 2 sl butt of marijuana cigarette

**road** n 1 track with surface prepared for use by vehicles 2 direction; route 3 fig mode, line of action by which aim is attained; ns **r.-block** barricade across road; **r. hog** reckless or selfish driver; **roadie** organizer of tour for pop group; **r. show** entertainment by company on tour; **r.-works** (site of) repair or building of road; adj **roadworthy** in safe enough condition to be driven

> **road** n (track) avenue, bypass, drive, reeway, highway, lane, roadway, route, street, thoroughfare

**roam** v wander; ramble aimlessly

**roan** n, adj (horse, dog) of bay, sorrel, chestnut mingled with white, gray; of mixed reddish color

**roar** n loud, deep, resonant sound; bellow; burst of laughter; v make such sound

> **roar** v bawl, blare, boom, crash, cry, rumble, shout, thunder, yell

**roast** v 1 cook in hot oven, bake 2 make, be very hot; n roasted joint of meat,chicken, etc; n animal, bird suitable for roasting

**rob** v robbing, robbed steal; plunder; deprive of unlawfully; n **robbery**

**robber** n person who steals

> **robber** n bandit, burglar, cat burglar, housebreaker, looter, mugger, pickpocket, shoplifter, thief

**robe** n long, loose outer garment; (esp in pl) official, ceremonial dress; v put on robe

**robin** n small, brown songbird with red breast

**robot** n 1 automaton man 2 fig one who works mechanically with unthinking efficiency; n **robotics** use of robots in industry

**robust** adj 1 strong 2 vigorous; n **robustness**

> **robust** adj (strong) hardy, powerful, rugged, sturdy, tough, well-made

**rock**[1] n 1 mass of hard mineral matter 2 crag; boulder 3 hard candy; idm **on the rocks** 1 (of drink) with ice cubes 2 (of marriage, etc) likely to fail ns **r. bottom** the lowest point; **r. crystal** pure rock quartz; **r. salt** common salt mined in crystal form; n **rockery** mound of earth and rocks, where rock plants are grown; adj **rocky** full of, made of rocks

**rock**[2] v sway, move from side to side; shake violently; idm **rock the boat** coll upset finely balanced situation; ns **r. and roll** early form of rock music; **rocker** curved base of rocking chair, of object that rocks; idm **off one's rocker** coll insane; **rocking chair** chair with rockers; **rocking horse** wooden horse mounted on rockers as child's toy; adj **rocky** unsteady

**rocket** n 1 projectile driven through space by explosion produced in it 2 large jet-powered missile 3 explosive firework, used for signaling, display or carrying life-line 4 coll reprimand; v 1 rise straight upward 2 fig increase sharply (in price, etc)

**rococo** adj (of furniture, architecture) florid; flamboyantly ornamented in style of 17th and 18th centuries; n this style

**rod** n slender piece of wood; long, light, pole of metal, wood, etc; wand; cane

> **rod** n bar, baton, pole, shaft, stick, wand

**rode** pt of **ride**

**rodent** adj gnawing; n gnawing animal, as rat

**rodeo** n rounding-up of cattle on ranch; display of skill in rounding up cattle

a
b
c
d
e
f
g
h
i
j
k
l
m
n
o
p
q
**r**
s
t
u
v
w
x
y
z

**roe**[1] n small species of deer
**roe**[2] n mass of fish eggs
**roebuck** n male roedeer
**Rogation days** n three harvest days preceding Ascension Day
**roger** interj (message) understood
**rogue** n 1 rascal, criminal 2 mischievous child or person; n **rogues' gallery** set of pictures of criminals or villains; adj **roguish** arch, mischievous

> **rogue** n (rascal) cheat, con-man, crook, fraud, scoundrel, sharper

**role** n part played by actor; specific function or action; ns **r. model** person representing ideal to be imitated; **r.-playing** taking part in imaginary situation for practice
**roll** v 1 go around and around; turn like wheel 2 (of ship) wallow 3 form into ball or cylinder 4 pass roller over something to flatten it; phr vs **roll in** arrive in large numbers; **roll on** (of time) pass by ; **roll out** 1 unroll 2 (of pastry) spread out flat 3 fig introduce new product; **roll up** coll 1 arrive 2 come and be entertained; n 1 packet, bundle formed by folding into cylindrical shape 2 small rounded loaf, bun, bread 3 cylindrical mass 4 list of names 5 swaying motion; ns **r. call** calling of names to check absentees; **roller** 1 long powerful sea wave 2 cylindrical object for smoothing, flattening (ns **r. coaster** amusement park ride with track that rises and falls, twists and turns sharply); **r. skate** skate on wheels (v ride on this); **r. towel** towel in one continuous loop on roller; adj **rolling** (**r. pin** cyclindrical object to flatten pastry; **r. stone** person with no fixed home)

> **roll** v (go round and round) coil, curl, furl, revolve, rotate, somersault, spin, tumble, turn, twirl, wheel, wind

**rollicking** adj jolly
**roly-poly** adj coll fat and round

**ROM** abbr comput read-only memory
**Roman** adj of Rome; n **R. Catholic** member of branch of Christian church headed by the Pope
**romance** n 1 sentimental, adventurous novel 2 happy love affair 3 medieval tale of chivalry 4 glamorous charm, atmosphere; v invent fanciful stories; exaggerate
**Romanesque** adj of architectural style developed from 9th century AD, using rounded arches
**romantic** adj 1 expressing or concerning love 2 glamorous 3 (of literature, etc) seeking to rouse personal feelings, expressing sentiment and imaginative episodes, etc; n **-ism** (in literature and art) emphasis on feelings rather than objective realism; v **-ize** make seem more romantic than in reality

> **romantic** adj 1 (expressing love) affectionate, amorous, emotional, lovey-dovey inf, loving, passionate, sentimental, soppy, tender. 2 (glamorous) exciting, fabulous, fairy-tale

**Romany** n gipsy; gipsy language
**Romeo** n 1 romantic male lover 2 hero of Shakespearean tragedy Romeo and Juliet
**romp** v play noisily; idm **romp home** win easily; phr v **romp through** finish easily; n wild, noisy game
**rompers** n pl one-piece garment for baby
**rondo** n musical composition with principal theme repeated after each subordinate one
**rood** n crucifix, esp one over junction of nave and choir
**roof** n **-fs** outer covering over top of building; **roof of mouth** palate; v put roof on; n **r. rack** luggage rack on roof of car
**rook**[1] n bird of crow family; v cheat, swindle; n **rookery** colony of rooks
**rook**[2] n castle piece in chess
**room** n 1 space 2 separate apartment in a building 3 scope; opportunity; n **r. service** serving of food, drink, etc in hotel room; n pl **-s** lodgings; adj **roomy** large spacious

**roost** n perch for birds at night; v sleep on perch; n **rooster** male chicken

**root** n 1 source; origin 2 downward-growing part of plant 3 essential element 4 basic element of word 5 factor of quantity which gives that quantity when multiplied by itself; v implant roots firmly; be firmly established, esp by development of roots; n **r. beer** sweet fizzy drink flavored with roots and herbs; phr vs **root for** support enthusiastically; **root out** get rid of; n pl **roots** (one's sense of belonging to) one's place of upbringing; adj **rootless** (n **-ness**)

**rope** n thick cord; v tie with rope; phr vs **rope in** 1 bind with rope 2 persuade to take part; **rope off** separate by ropes

> **rope** n cable, halter, hawser, tether, towrope

**Roquefort** n Fr pungent, blue French cheese

**Rorschach test** n psyc test based on interpretation of random shapes made by inkblots on paper

**rosary** n 1 rose garden 2 string of beads used by Roman Catholics to count prayers

**rose** n 1 any of genus Rosa; flower of this 2 perforated nozzle 3 pinkish color; ns **rosette** rose-shaped bunch of ribbon, etc; **rosewood** dark-colored fragrant wood used in cabinetmaking; adj **rosy** 1 pink, flushed 2 fig favorable, optimistic

**rosemary** n evergreen fragrant bush

**roster** n list showing rotation of duty

**rostrum** n platform, pulpit

**rot** v **rotting, rotted** decompose naturally; n 1 decay 2 fungus disease of timber, plants, etc; 3 coll nonsense

> **rot** v crumble, decay, disintegrate, fester, go bad, go off, go sour, perish, putrefy

**rota** n roster; round of duties

**rotary** adj turning like wheel

**rotate** v revolve round axis; follow regular succession; n **rotation** act of rotating; recurrence

**Rotary Club** n one of international association of business clubs

**rote** n **by rote** by heart, from memory

**rotisserie** n Fr turning device to roast meat

**rotor** n rotating part of machine, esp of helicopter

**rotten** adj 1 decaying 2 terrible 3 ill

> **rotten** adj 1 (decaying) addled, bad, foul, moldering, off inf, perished, putrid, rotting, sour. 2 (terrible) awful, bad, disappointing, dismal, foul inf, inferior, lousy inf, miserable, nasty, poor. 3 (ill) bad, off color, poorly, rough inf, sick, under the weather, unwell

**Rottweiler** n large powerful guard dog

**rotund** adj round; plump

**rouge** n red cosmetic used to colour cheeks and lips; v colour with rouge

**rough** adj 1 uneven; not smooth 2 approximate 3 not polite in behaviour 4 arduous; difficult 5 harsh (of sound) 6 stormy; adv without comfort or amenities (**live/sleep r.**); n golf areas with unmown grass; idm **rough it** live simple life without comforts; ns **r.-and-tumble** boisterous play or fighting; **diamond in the rough** kind but unrefined person; **roughneck** 1 rowdy person 2 oil rig worker; v **roughen** make rough; adv **roughly** approximately

> **rough** adj 1 (uneven) bumpy, coarse, jagged, rocky, rugged, scratchy, stony. 2 (approximate) crude, estimated, general, quick, raw, rudimentary, sketchy, vague. 3 (not polite in behavior) badly behaved, brusque, curt, ill-mannered, loutish, rowdy, rude, surly. 4 (arduous) hard, heavy-handed, severe, spartan, tough, unfair, unjust, violent. 5 (harsh) grating, gruff, hoarse, husky, rasping. 6 (stormy) choppy, heavy, wild

**roulette** n Fr game of chance, played with revolving wheel and ball

**round** *adj* 1 spherical, circular, curved
2 approximate 3 plump 4 blunt, outspoken;
*n* 1 circle 2 thing round in shape 3 fixed
circuit 4 type of song 5 single shot from rifle
6 series of actions, duties, etc 7 game (of
golf) 8 single bout (in boxing, etc);
*n* **r. trip** journey to a place and back;
*adv* 1 converging on central point 2 to a
variety of places 3 to a place nearby; *v* turn,
as corner; *phr vs* **round down** reduce to
nearest whole unit or number; **round off**
finish; **round up** 1 increase to nearest
whole number or unit 2 gather together;
*n* **-ness**

**round** *adj* (spherical) ball-shaped, bulbous,
circular, curved, cylindrical, disk-shaped,
globular, rounded, spheroid

**roundabout** *n* 1 merry-go-round on which
people can ride in regular circular motion
2 (at road junctions) raised circular area
round which traffic must follow specified
direction; *adj* indirect
**roundelay** *n* song with refrain
**rounders** *n* European children's game similar
to baseball
**Roundhead** *n Brit* supporter of Parliament in
17th-century English Civil War (derisory
description because their hair was cut short)
**rouse** *v* stir up; wake up; cause to rise;
stimulate; excite to action; *adj* **rousing**

**rouse** *v* (stir up) arouse, awaken, egg on
*inf*, galvanize, incite, inflame, kindle,
provoke, stimulate, whip up, work up

**roustabout** *n* heavy laborer
**rout** *n* 1 rabble, mob 2 overwhelming defeat;
*v* defeat, put to flight; drag out by force
**route** *n* road; way; *mil* order to march;
*n* **r. march** long march as part of military
training (*also v*)
**routine** *n* customary actions; regular
procedure; boringly automatic procedure;
*adj* done regularly

**routine** *adj* common, everyday, familiar,
habitual, ordinary, regular, standard, usual

**roux** *n Fr* blend of melted fat, flour as base for
sauce, gravy, etc
**rove** *v* wander at random; *n* **rover** one who
wanders
**row**[1] *n* number of things or persons in straight
line

**row** *n* (line) bank, chain, column, file,
procession, queue, rank, series, string, tier

**row**[2] *v* propel (boat) by oars; transport by
rowing; *n* act of rowing; trip in rowing boat
**row**[3] *n* 1 noisy argument 2 noise; *v* argue

**row** *n* 1 (argument) altercation, controversy,
disagreement, dispute, quarrel, scrap,
spat, squabble, tiff, wrangle. 2 (noise)
commotion, din, fracas, hubbub,
hullabaloo, racket, rumpus, uproar

**rowan** *n* European mountain ash tree
**rowboat** *n* a boat designed for rowing
**rowdy** *adj* disorderly; noisy; rough;
*n* hooligan
**rowel** *n* small spiked wheel on spur
**rowing machine** *n* a piece of exercise
equipment that simulates the action of
rowing
**rowlock** *n* forked support in boat serving as
leverage for oar
**royal** *adj* pertaining to king or queen;
majestic; *n* member of the royal family;
*adv* **- ly**; *ns* **r. blue** deep rich blue colou;
**r. jelly** substance with which worker bees
nourish queen bee; *ns* **royalist** supporter of
monarchy; **royalty** 1 state of being royal
2 royal persons collectively 3 percentage
paid to author by publisher 4 payment to
owner of land for right to exploit it
5 payment to inventor for use of his
invention
**rpm** *abbr* revolutions per minute

**RSI** *abbr* repetitive strain injury
**RSVP** *abbr* Fr répondez s'il vous plaît (please reply)
**rub** *v* **rubbing, rubbed 1** apply friction to, *esp* to clean **2** abrade; make sore **3** become frayed, worn by friction; *idm* **rub it in** keep referring to fact that causes embarrassment to sb; *idm* **rub salt in the wound** add further to sb's suffering; *idm* **rub shoulders with** *coll* meet (famous person) socially, as if on equal terms; *idm* **rub up the wrong way** *coll* cause offense to; *phr vs* **rub down 1** dry by rubbing **2** smooth by rubbing; **rub off** remove, be removed from surface by rubbing; **rub off on** have influence on (through example); *n* **rubbing** impression of relief picture made by laying paper over and rubbing with crayon or charcoal

> **rub** *v* **1** (apply friction to) buff, clean, polish, scour, scrub, shine, smooth, wipe. **2** (stroke) caress, fondle, massage

**rubber**[1] *n* **1** elastic substance from sap of rubber tree **2** *coll* condom; *ns* **r. band** loop of rubber for keeping things firmly bundled together (*also* **elastic band**); **r. plant** houseplant with large thick leaves; **r. stamp** stamp with lettering or figures for printing (*v fig* give official approval without questioning anything); *adj* **rubbery**
**rubber**[2] *n* series of odd number of games
**rubbish** *n* **1** waste material **2** nonsense; *v coll* discredit; *adj* **-y** valueless

> **rubbish** *adj* **1** (waste material) debris, detritus, dross, garbage, junk, litter, rubble, scrap, trash, waste, refuse. **2** (nonsense) balderdash, claptrap, drivel, gobbledegook, rot *inf*

**rubble** *n* **1** broken, crushed pieces of stone **2** builders' trash
**rubella** *n* German measles
**rubicund** *adj* reddish, ruddy
**ruble, rouble** *n* Russian coin

**rubric** *n* **1** authoritative rule **2** liturgical direction
**ruby** *n* deep red, transparent, precious stone; its color; *adj* of this color
**rucksack** *n* bag, knapsack carried on back
**ruckus** *n* rumpus
**rudder** *n* steering device at stern of boat, or tail of aircraft
**ruddy** *adj* of fresh, red color; rosy
**rude** *adj* **1** impolite; ill-mannered; crude **2** primitive; rough; crude

> **rude** *adj* **1** (not polite) abusive, bad-mannered, cheeky, discourteous, disrespectful, impertinent, insolent, insulting, offensive, offhand, short, uncivil, uncouth. **2** (obscene) blue, coarse, crude, dirty, naughty, risqué, smutty, vulgar

**rudiment** *n* **1** beginning; first principle **2** basic elementary facts of subject; *adj* **rudimentary** in undeveloped state
**rue**[1] *n* small perennial herb with bitter leaves
**rue**[2] *v* regret; *adj* **rueful** sorry, dejected
**ruff** *n* starched frilled collar; *n* **ruffle** gathered or pleated frill; *v* **1** make uneven, untidy **2** upset, disconcert
**ruffian** *n* rough, lawless person

> **ruffian** *n* bully, hooligan, lout, rowdy, scamp, thug, tough

**rug** *n* thick, woolen wrap; floor covering
**rugby** *n* British form of football, played with oval ball that may be carried in hands
**rugged** *adj* **1** rough and rocky **2** robust, strong
**ruin** *n* **1** state of decay, collapse **2** financial failure; *pl* **-s** remains of buildings, etc; *v* **1** spoil **2** impoverish; *n* **-ation**; *adj* **-ous** tending to cause financial ruin; wasteful

> **ruin** *n* (financial failure) bankruptcy, collapse, defeat, destitution, destruction, downfall, end, failure, havoc, insolvency, undoing, wreck, wreckage

a b c d e f g h i j k l m n o p q **r** s t u v w x y z

**rule** n 1 law 2 control 3 pl **-s** regulations of society, game etc 4 bar for measuring; idm **as a rule** normally; v 1 give decision 2 govern 3 draw straight line; phr v **rule out 1** regard as impossible 2 render impossible; n **r. of thumb** rough type of calculation

**rule** n 1 (law) axiom, code, direction, formula, guideline, maxim, order, principle, regulation, ruling, standard, statute, tenet. 2 (control) administration, authority, command, dominion, government, management, power, regime, reign, sovereignty, supervision
**rule** v 1 (give decision) decree, determine, find, judge, lay down, order. 2 (govern) administer, be in power, control, hold the reigns, lead, manage, reign, run

**ruler** n 1 person who governs 2 instrument for measuring or drawing straight lines

**ruler** n (person who governs) chief, dictator, emperor, governing body, government, governor, head of state, king, leader, monarch, potentate, president, queen, regent, sovereign

**ruling** n official decision or pronouncement
**rum** n 1 alcoholic spirit distilled from sugar cane 2 general term for liquor (as **demon r.**)
**rumba, rhumba** n dance of Cuban origin; the rhythm of this music
**rumble** v make low, continuous, rolling noise, as of thunder, or heavy cart, etc
**rumbustious** adj noisy and cheerful; adv **-ly**; n **-ness**
**ruminate** v chew cud; fig mediate, think deeply over; ns **-ation** act of chewing cud; fig deep thought; **ruminant** animal that chews cud; adj thoughtful
**rummage** v grope about; turn over roughly; search thoroughly; n **rummage sale** sale of secondhand, cast-off goods at bargain prices
**rummy** n 1 card game 2 a lush, a drunk
**rumor** n story; statement without basis

**rumor** n dirt, gossip, grapevine, hearsay, news, scandal, story, talk, the latest

**rump** n 1 buttocks 2 fig last, inferior part
**rumple** v crease; wrinkle; crush
**rumpus** n noisy disturbance; confusion
**run** v 1 travel swiftly on foot 2 drip 3 be in charge of 4 extend flow; pt **ran**; phr vs **run down 1** knock down with vehicle 2 (of clockwork) lose power and slow down 3 criticize in negative way; **run into** meet by chance; **run off** print (multiple copies); **run out 1** leave abruptly 2 (of supply) be used up; **run out of** have none left; **run over 1** overflow 2 knock down with vehicle; **run through 1** repeat for practice 2 check over 3 pierce with sword; **run up 1** raise 2 make quickly 3 incur; accumulate (debt); **run up against** be confronted by; n 1 act of running 2 continuous sequence 3 animal enclosure 4 unit of score in baseball; idm **on the run** trying to escape, esp from justice; ns **r.-around** sl evasive behavior; **r.down** coll brief report; **r.-in** coll 1 time leading to event 2 quarrel; **r.-through 1** review 2 rehearsal; **r.-up** period leading to event; adjs **runaway 1** having escaped 2 out of control; **run-down 1** dilapidated 2 in poor health; **runny 1** more liquid than usual 2 producing mucus

**run** v 1 (move swiftly on foot) bolt, charge, dash, gallop, hotfoot it, hurry, jog, race, scurry, sprint, tear. 2 (drip) dissolve, go soft, melt. 3 (be in charge of) administer, control, direct, govern, head, lead, manage, operate, supervise. 4 (extend) continue, go, last, reach, stretch. 5 (flow) cascade, discharge, gush, pour, spill, spout, stream, trickle

**rune** n any of the characters of ancient alphabets (eg Teutonic); ancient magic sign
**rung**[1] n crossbar of ladder or chair
**rung**[2] pt of **ring**

**unnel** n gutter; small rivulet

**unner** n 1 person who runs 2 smooth or tubular plate making movement of sled, etc, more efficient 3 long, fast-growing shoot of plant; ns **r bean** bean with long edible pod; **r.-up** next one after the winner(s) of contest; **running** n 1 act or sport of running 2 operation or management of sth; adj 1 flowing (**r. water**) 2 continuous (**r. commentary**) 3 exuding pus (**r. sore**) 4 incurred in roperations (**r. costs**)

**unt** n 1 weakest animal, usu lastborn of litter 2 sl small disagreeable person

**unway** n strip of ground for landing and takeoff of aircraft

**upee** n Indian coin

**upture** n 1 breaking, split 2 hernia; v 1 burst, break 2 produce hernia

> **rupture** v (burst, break) breach, divide, fracture, separate, sever, split, tear

**ural** adj of country; rustic

**use** n stratagem, trick

**ush**[1] n aquatic plant, stems of which are used for basket-making, etc

**ush**[2] v move, do sth hastily; n impetuous forward movement; sudden increase; eagerness to obtain; n **r. hour** busiest time of day for commuting

> **rush** v bolt, charge, dart, dash, flood, fly, get a move on, hurry, move fast, race, run, scramble, shoot, speed, sprint, stampede, surge, tear, zoom

**ushes** n pl cinema first printing of film

**usk** n piece of crisp baked bread or cookie

**usset** adj of reddish brown; n this color; homespun fabric; kind of apple

**Russian** n 1 language of Russia 2 person whose native language is this; adj of Russia, its culture, people, or language; **R. roulette** dangerous game of chance where player fires revolver containing bullet in only one chamber at his own head

**Russo-** prefix of Russia

**rust** n 1 reddish brown coating produced on iron, etc, by oxidation 2 desease of plants, caused by fungus; v develop this; adj **rusty** 1 covered with rust 2 out of practice

> **rust** v corrode, oxidize

**rustic** adj of country life or people; rural; unsophisticated; n **rusticity**; v **rusticate** live country life; n **rustication**

> **rustic** adj agrarian, agricultural, countrified, country, countryside, pastoral, rural

**rustle** v 1 emit soft, whispering sound as of dry leaves 2 steal cattle (n **rustler**); phr v **rustle up** provide, esp at short notice

> **rustle** v crackle, hiss, swish, whisper

**rut**[1] n wheel track; groove; idm **in a rut** leading a boring, meaningless existence; adj **rutted** full of ruts

**rut**[2] n sexual excitement, esp of deer; v **rutting, rutted** be affected with rut

**rutabaga** n yellow turnip

**ruthless** adj pitiless or cruel

> **ruthless** adj brutal, callous, cold, harsh, heartless, inhuman, merciless, savage, severe, unfeeling, unrelenting, violent

**RV** abbr recreational vehicle

**rye** n cereal plant, grain used for fodder and bread; n **rye whisky** distilled from rye grains; n **rye grass** grass grown for fodder

**Sabbath** *n* day of rest and worship, observed by Jews on Saturday and most Christians on Sunday; *n* **sabbatical year** one allowed to some university teachers, clergy, etc as working holiday

**saber** *n* curved cavalry sword; *n* **s.-rattling** trying to intimidate sb by threat of attack

**sable** *n* small Arctic carnivore, having valuable dark brown fur; *adj* black

**sabotage** *n* deliberate damage to buildings, transport systems, etc done by strikers or spies; *v* cause such damage; *n* **saboteur**

> **sabotage** *v* attack, damage, disable, put out of action, thwart, vandalize, wreck

**saccharine(e)** *n* very sweet sugar substitute; *adj fig* too sweet, sentimental

**sacerdotal** *adj* priestly

**sachet** *n* small soft bag holding dried flowers

**sack**[1] *n* large rectangular bag of strong, coarse fabric; *ns* **sackcloth** coarse cloth for making sacks (**s. and ashes** sign of mourning or repentance); **sacking** pieces(s) of this

**sack**[2] *v sl* dismiss from post; *n idm* **give/get the sack** dismiss/be dismissed

> **sack** *v* ax, discharge, fire, give sb the boot *inf*, give sb the push *inf*, give sb their marching orders, lay off, make redundant

**sack**[3] *v* destroy (city) in war

**sack**[4] *n* dry, white wine

**sackbut** *n* medieval form of trombone

**sacrament** *n* **1** one of solemn religious ceremonies of Christian Church, *esp* Eucharist **2** any sacred, solemn obligation **3** *cap* bread and wine taken at Communion

**sacred** *adj* holy, dedicated to God, a god; set apart; inviolable; *n* **s. cow** person or thing felt to be byond criticsm; *n* **-ness**

> **sacred** *adj* blessed, consecrated, devotional, divine, godly, hallowed, heavenly, inviolate, religious, revered, sacrosanct, sanctified, spiritual

**sacrifice** *n* **1** making offering to God **2** thing offered **3** giving up (sth valued) for sake of someone else; *v* **1** give up (sth valued) **2** offer as sacrifice; *adj* **-ficial**

**sacrilege** *n* violation of something sacred; *adj* **sacrilegious** profane

**sacrosanct** *adj* protected from harm or change by being sacred or very important

**sacrum** *n anat* bone at lower end of spine

**sad** *adj* **1** unhappy **2** upsetting **3** terrible; *v* **sadden** made sad; *n* **sadness**

> **sad** *adj* **1** (unhappy) brokenhearted, crestfallen, dejected, depressed, desolate, despondent, disappointed, distressed, down, down in the dumps *inf*, grief-stricken, heartbroken, low, miserable, tearful, upset. **2** (upsetting) depressing, distressing, heartbreaking, heartrending, moving, poignant, touching, tragic. **3** (terrible) bad, deplorable, disastrous, disgraceful, miserable, pitiful, regrettable, sorry, unfortunate, unsatisfactory

**saddle** *n* **1** rider's seat on horse, bicycle, etc **2** joint of mutton or venison; *phr v* **saddle with** burden with (duty, responsibility)

**saddler** *n* maker of saddles

**sadism** *n* sexual perversion marked by cruelty, *n* **sadist** (*adj* **-ic**)

**sadness** n unhappiness

> **sadness** n dejection, depression,
> despondency, disappointment, grief,
> heartache, misery, regret, sorrow

**sadomasochism** n (sexual) gratification from
inflicting pain on oneself or others

**s.a.e.** abbr stamped and addressed envelope

**safari** n hunting or photographic expedition,
esp in Africa; ns **s. park** large park where
wild animals living in natural habitat can be
observed by tourists; **s. jacket** light linen
jacket with belt and breast pockets

**safe** adj 1 unharmed 2 not in danger
3 harmless 4 reliable; n strong metal box
with lock for keeping valuable objects or
documents secure; n **s. conduct** official
protection when traveling; adv **safely**

> **safe** adj 1 (unharmed) all right, in one
> piece, intact, out of danger, safe and
> sound, unhurt, uninjured. 2 (not in
> danger) impregnable, protected, secure.
> 3 (harmless) fit for human consumption,
> good, healthy, nontoxic, pure, tried and
> tested, uncontaminated, wholesome

**safeguard** n means of protection; v protect

**safety** n condition of being safe; ns **s. catch**
lock to prevent gun from being fired
accidentally; **s. net 1** net to save people
who fall from a height **2** fig safeguard; **s. pin**
pin with protective guard over sharp end

**saffron** n a variety of orange-yellow crocus;
dye and flavoring substance from this;
adj of this color

**sag** v **sagging, sagged** droop downward in
middle

> **sag** v bend, dip, drop, fall, flop, give, hang
> down, sink, slump, wilt

**saga** n ancient Norse prose epic; long novel or
series about family or group; romantic tale of
adventure and heroism

**sagacious** adj shrewd; keenly intelligent;
n **sagacity** sound judgment; quality
resembling reason in lower animals

**sage**[1] adj wise; n person of great wisdom

**sage**[2] n aromatic herb, used in cooking

**sagebrush** n bushy plant of western US

**sago** n edible starchy pith of certain Malayan
palms

**sail** n 1 piece of canvas arranged to catch
wind, to drive ship 2 voyage on ship;
idm **set sail** begin journey at sea; v travel
across water; ns **sailboard** shaped board with
sail for windsurfing; **sailing 1** sport of riding,
racing in yacht, dinghy, etc **2** time of
departure for sea voyage; **sailor** member
of ship's crew

**saint** n one recognised and venerated as holy,
etc by Christian Church

**saintly** adj good and virtuous; n **saintliness**

> **saintly** adj angelic, blessed, devout, God-
> fearing, godly, holy, pious, pure, religious,
> righteous

**sake** idm **for the sake of** in order to please,
benefit, obtain

**saké** n Japanese drink made from fermented
rice, served warm

**salaam** n ceremonial bow; Eastern mode of
greeting; v make salaam

**salacious** adj lewd, lecherous; n **salacity**

**salad** n dish of raw or cold cooked vegetables
or fruit; n **salad days** age of youth and
immaturity

**salami** n highly seasoned sausage of pork/beef

**salary** n fixed payment for work made at
regular interval; adj **salaried**

> **salary** n earnings, fee, income, pay,
> remuneration, stipend, take-home
> pay, wage

**sale** n act of selling; offering of goods for sale,
esp at reduced prices; ns **salesperson** one
engaged in selling; **salesmanship** business
skill of salesperson

**sale** n auction, deal, marketing, retailing, selling, trade, traffic, transaction

**salient** adj prominent; projecting
**saline** n metallic, alkaline salt; n **salinity** saltiness
**saliva** n fluid secreted in mouth to aid digestion; adj **salivary**
**sallow** adj having sickly, yellow color
**sally** n 1 quick repartée 2 sudden but brief attack; phr v **sallying, sallied; sally forth** set out (on campaign)
**salmon** n large edible silvery fish with pink flesh; n **s.-trout** sea trout
**salmonella** n bacteria causing food poisoning
**salon** n 1 reception room 2 private reception of people in the arts 3 private room for specific use (eg hairdressing, billiards, etc)
**saloon** n 1 bar serving alcohol 2 large reception room
**salsify** n long tapering root vegetable
**salt** n 1 chemical substance (sodium chloride) used to season and preserve food 2 chemical compound of metal and acid; idm **the salt of the earth** admirable person/people; idm **with a pinch of salt** with skepticism; v 1 flavor with salt 2 cover (roads) with salt to melt ice; phr v **salt away** save (money) secretly, stealthily; adj **salty**
**SALT** abbr Strategic Arms Limitation Talks
**saltpeter** n chem white powder used in making gunpowder, matches, etc
**salubrious** adj healthy; beneficial; promoting health
**salutary** adj wholesome; having good effect
**salute** v 1 perform military salute 2 praise; n 1 greeting 2 mil formal gesture made by hand to superior

**salute** v (praise) acknowledge, greet, honour, pay tribute to, take your hat off to

**salvage** n 1 rescue of ship, cargo, etc from shipwreck, fire, etc 2 saving goods from fire, etc; v save from shipwreck, fire, destruction

**salvage** v reclaim, recover, redeem, rescue, restore, resurrect, retrieve, save

**salvation** n fact or state of being saved
**salve** n healing, soothing ointment
**Samaritan** n helpful, charitable person
**samba** n dance of Brazilian origin
**same** adj 1 identical 2 unchanged

**same** adj 1 (identical) alike, corresponding, duplicate, equal, equivalent, interchangeable, like, matching, parallel, similar, twin. 2 (unchanged) changeless, consistent, constant, uniform, unvarying

**samosa** n triangular pastry snack filled with spicy meat or vegetables (of Indian origin)
**sampan** n light, flat-bottomed Chinese river boat
**sample** n specimen, example; v test quality of; take sample; n **sampler** piece of embroidery, needlework
**sanatorium** n hospital, esp one for treatment of tuberculosis; pl **-ia** or **-iums**
**sanctify** v regard as holy; n **sanctity** saintliness; inviolability
**sanctimonious** adj making show of piety
**sanction** n 1 measure taken to compel nation to obey international law 2 permission; v allow; permit; approve
**sanctuary** n 1 place of refuge 2 holy place; n **sanctum** any private or inviolate retreat

**sanctuary** n asylum, cover, haven, protection, refuge, safety, shelter

**sand** n fine, dry, gritty substance found on beaches and in deserts, etc; pl **-s** area of sand or sandbank; ns **sandbag** sand-filled sack used in protecting wall; **sandbank** shoal of sand in river or sea; **sandpaper** paper coated with abrasive material for smoothing wood; **sandstone** type of soft, porous rock formed from compressed sand; adj **sandy** of sand or color of sand

**sandal** *n* open shoe with sole secured by straps
**sandalwood** *n* yellowish, sweet-scented wood
**sandwich** *n* two slices of bread with meat, sheese, or other filling between them; *v* insert between two other things
**sane** *adj* 1 mentally normal 2 sensible

**sane** *adj* (mentally normal) all there *inf*, balanced, lucid, of sound mind, rational, reasonable, right-minded, stable

**sang** *pt of* **sing**
**sang-froid** *n* Fr coolness; presence of mind; composure
**sangria** *n* Spanishiced drink of red wine containing fruit juice, sodawater, etc
**sanguine** *adj* 1 ruddy, florid 2 hopeful, optimistic
**sanitary** *adj* having to do with health and cleanliness; *n* **s. napkin, s. pad** absorbent pad worn during menstruation; *v* **sanitize** 1 make hygienic 2 *fig* make less offensive; censor; *n* **sanitation** 1 public hygiene 2 system of drainage, disposal of sewage, ventilation, and pure water supply
**sanity** *n* condition of being sane

**sanity** *n* common sense, good sense, level-headedness, normality, rationality, reason

**sank** *pt of* **sink**
**Sanskrit** *n* ancient language of Hindus
**sap** *n* 1 juice, fluid circulating in plant tissue 2 *fig* vigor, vitality; *v* **sapping, sapped** *fig* drain away strength
**sapient** *adj* wise, shrewd, knowing; *n* **sapience**
**saponaceous** *adj* containing soap; soapy; *fig* unctuous
**sapphire** *n* deep blue precious stone
**sarcasm** *n* bitter, ironic remarks
**sarcastic** *adj* using irony in a scornful way

**sarcastic** *adj* caustic, derisive, ironic, mocking, satirical, scoffing, scornful

**sard** *n* semi precious stone, variety of chalcedony
**sardine** *n* small fish of herring family; *idm* **packed like sardines** packed close together
**sardonic** *adj* bitter, sneering, scornful
**sardonyx** *n* semi precious stone with layers of red sard and white chalcedony
**sari, saree** *n* robe worn by Hindu women
**sarong** *n* principal garment of Malay people and Pacific islanders
**sarsen** *n* large block of hard sandstone, as in Stonehenge
**sartorial** *adj* pertaining to work of tailor
**sash** *n* ornamental scarf worn over shoulder or around waist
**sat** *pt, pp of* **sit**
**Satan** *n* the Devil; *adj* **satanic(al)** fiendish, malignant, wicked; *n* **satanism** devil worship (*n, adj* **-ist**)
**satchel** *n* handbag
**sate** *v* satisfy; gratify to the full
**sateen** *n* glossy, imitation satin, cotton fabric
**satellite** *n* 1 planet revolving around another 2 projectile in orbit around the earth; *n* **s. dish** concave disk used as aerial for receiving satellite TV; **s. television** TV relayed by satellite to any part of earth
**satiate** *v* satisfy
**satin** *n* soft silk fabric with glossy surface
**satire** *n* 1 holding up of human follies to ridicule 2 literary work of this nature; *adj* **satiric(al)**; *n* **satirist** writer of satires; *v* **satirize** make object of satire

**satire** *n* burlesque, caricature, irony, mockery, parody, ridicule, sarcasm, skit, spoof *inf*, take-off *inf*

**satisfactory** *adj* good enough

**satisfactory** *adj* acceptable, adequate, all right, average, fair, good enough, not bad, okay, passable, quite good, reasonable, sufficient, suitable

a
b
c
d
e
f
g
h
i
j
k
l
m
n
o
p
q
r
**s**
t
u
v
w
x
y
z

**satisfy** *v* **satisfying, satisfied 1** fulfill a need **2** take away hunger or thirst **3** convince; *n* **satisfaction**

> **satisfy** *v* **1** (fulfill a need) answer, comply with, meet, resolve, supply. **2** (take away hunger or thirst) assuage, gratify, quench, satiate, suffice. **3** (convince) make happy, persuade, placate, put sb's mind at rest, reassure

**satori** *n* Zen ideal state of illumination
**saturate** *v* **1** soak thoroughly **2** *chem* cause substance tocombine completely **3** *fig* be steeped in, affected by; *n* **-ation** act, result of saturating (**s. point** stage at which greatest possible amount of something has been absorbed)
**saturated fat** *n* fat found in meat and dairy products, thought to be harmful to heath
**Saturday** *n* seventh day of week
**Saturn** *n* **1** Roman god **2** large planet surrounded by rings; *adj* **saturnine** gloomy, glowering, morose; *n* **saturnalia** revelry, orgy
**satyr** *n* woodland deity (half beast, half man)
**sauce** *n* **1** flavoured liquid served with food **2** impudence; *n* **saucepan** cooking pot; *adj* **saucy 1** impertinent **2** (of clothes) jaunty
**saucer** *n* shallow dish put under a cup
**sauerkraut** *n Ger* chopped raw cabbage fermented in brine
**sauna** *n* **1** very hot, dry room **2** period of relaxation in this, followed by ice-cold bath
**saunter** *v* stroll; *n* leisurely walk
**sausage** *n* minced, seasoned meat packed into skin; *n* **s. roll** cylinder of pastry with sausage meat filling
**sauté** *adj Fr* lightly, quickly fried in oil
**savage** *adj* **1** uncivilized **2** cruel; *v* bite and worry ferociously; *n* **savagery**

> **savage** *adj* **1** (uncivilized) fierce, primitive, untamed, wild. **2** (cruel) barbaric, brutal, ferocious, ruthless, vicious, violent

**savanna, savannah** *n* grassy treeless plain
**savant** *n Fr* person of learning; scholar
**save** *v* **1** keep **2** economize **3** rescue; *ns* **-er** person who saves money; **savings** amount saved

> **save** *v* **1** (keep) collect, conserve, hoard, hold on to, invest, put aside, put away, put back, reserve, stash away, stockpile, store. **2** (economize) cut costs, cut expenditures, find savings, make cuts, make economies. **3** (rescue) bail out, defend, deliver, free, preserve, protect, safeguard, salvage, screen, shield

**savior** *n* one who redeems; *cap* Christ
**savoir faire** *n Fr* ability to know how to behave in any situation
**savor** *n* taste; *v* enjoy taste of
**savory** *adj* **1** salty, not sweet **2** tasty; *n* light, tasty, salty food eaten before meal

> **savory** *adj* **1** (salty) piquant, spicy, tangy. **2** (tasty) appetizing, delicious, mouthwatering, scrumptious *inf*

**savoy** *n* kind of cabbage with curled leaves
**saw**[1] *pt of* see
**saw**[2] *n* tool with toothed edge, for cutting wood, etc; *v* **sawing, sawed, sawn** cut with saw; *n* **sawdust** small particles of wood made by sawing
**saxophone** *n* reeded brass wind instrument
**say** *v* **1** utter **2** state **3** express in words; *pt, pp* **said**; *idm* **have one's say** have chance to express one's views; *n* **saying** proverb

> **say** *v* **1** (utter) enunciate, mention, mouth, pronounce,voice. **2** (state) affirm, allege, announce, answer, assert, claim, comment, declare, exclaim, maintain, remark, reply, report, respond, retort, suggest. **3** (express in words) articulate, communicate, convey, enunciate, intimate, make known, put into words, tell

A B C D E F G H I J K L M N O P Q R **S** T U V W X Y Z

**scab** *n* **1** dry crust which forms over wound **2** skin disease **3** plant disease **4** *coll* worker who crosses union protests ot work

**scabbard** *n* sheath for sword or dagger

**scabies** *n* contagious itching skin disease

**scabious** *n* herbacious plant having round cushionlike mauve flowers

**scabrous** *adj* **1** having rough surface **2** knotty; difficult **3** controversial **4** indecent

**scaffold** *n* **1** temporary structure of poles and planks to support workmen **2** gallows; *n* **-ing** collective term for planks and poles used as scaffold, *esp* by builders

**scald** *v* injure skin with hot liquid, steam

**scale**[1] *n* **1** one of hard, thin plates covering fish and reptiles **2** any flaky deposit in boilers, kettles, etc

**scale**[2] *n mus* **1** series of graduated notes, *esp* in octave **2** system of grading by size, rank, amount, etc **3** ratio of size; *v* climb up

**scalp** *n* skin and hair on top of head; *v* strip, cut scalp off

**scalpel** *n* small, slender surgical knife

**scam** *n coll* scheme for swindling people

**scamp** *n* rogue, rascal

**scamper** *v* run about happily

**scamper** *v* dart, dash, frisk, frolic, gambol, romp, run, scoot, scuttle

**scampi** *n pl* dish of garlicky large prawns

**scan** *v* **scanning, scanned 1** look closely at **2** read quickly **3** *med* obtain image(s) of (parts of) body with scanner; *n* act of scanning; *n* **scanner** *med* apparatus for examining the body by producing images from many angles

**scandal** *n* malicious or idle talk, act, or thing that brings disgrace; *v* **-lize** shock

**scandalous** *adj* shocking

**scant** *adj* small, inadequate in amount

**scanty** *adj* insufficient

**scanty** *adj* inadequate, limited, meager, measly, paltry, poor, restricted, skimpy

**scapegoat** *n* one who takes blame, or is punished, for faults of others

**scapula** *n* shoulder blade

**scar** *n* mark left by wound, burn, or sore, after healing; *v* **scarring, scarred** mark, heal with scar; *adj* **scarred**

**scarce** *adj* rare; *adv* **-ly** barely; *n* **scarcity** deficiency of supply

**scarce** *adj* at a premium, few and far between, hard to come by *inf*, inadequate, infrequent, in short supply, insufficient, lacking, scanty, seldom seen, short, sparse, uncommon, unusual

**scare** *v* frighten; *n* ill-founded alarm; widespread fear; *n* **scarecrow** dummy figure used to scare birds from crops

**scare** *v* alarm, daunt, give sb a fright, intimidate, petrify, put the wind up sb, startle, terrify, terrorize, unnerve

**scared** *adj* frightened

**scared** *adj* alarmed, fearful, nervous, panicky, panic-stricken, petrified, shaken, startled, terrified

**scarf** *n* piece of material worn round neck; *pl* **scarves** or **scarfs**

**scarify** *v* **scarifying, scarified 1** scratch, cut (skin) **2** break, loosen surface (of soil) **3** *fig* lacerate feelings of; *ns* **scarification**; **scarifier** agricultural implement

**scarlet** *n* briliant, vivid red

**scarp** *n* steep slope or face below rampart or hill; escarpment

**scathing** *adj* (of remarks) cutting, bitter

**scatter** *v* **1** sprinkle **2** be dispersed

**scatter** *v* **1** (sprinkle) diffuse, disseminate, fling, litter, shower, sow, spread, strew, toss about. **2** (be dispersed) break up, disband, go off in all directions, separate

**scatterbrain** n flighty, thoughtless person

**scatty** adj coll crazy

**scavenge** v 1 feed on dead flesh of other animals 2 search among refuse for usable objects; ns **-enger, -enging**

**scavenger hunt** n game where players compete to collect items on a list

**scenario** n lt 1 written outline of action for film, play, etc 2 imagined sequence of coming events

**scene** n 1 place of action 2 background for fictional events, as in play, etc 3 coll outburst of anger, etc 4 view 5 subdivision of play within an act; idm **behind the scenes** 1 backstage 2 in secret; idm **make a scene** make a great fuss; have an emotional outburst; idm **on the scene** present; idm **set the scene** make everything ready; n **scenery** painted scenes in theater; landscape; woods, hills, etc collectively as view; adj **scenic** theatrical, picturesque; pertaining to natural scenery

> **scene** n 1 (place of action) area, backdrop, locality, location, place, position, setting, site, spot. 2 (view) landscape, panorama, prospect, scenery, vista

**scent** v 1 smell 2 track by smell 3 make fragrant; n 1 odor; pleasant smell 2 liquid perfume

**scepter** n ornamental rod carried as symbol of sovereignty

**schedule** n 1 written or printed list 2 timetable 3 tabulated statement; v set out, put into, form of schedule; idm **on schedule** on time; adj **scheduled** 1 planned for a certain time 2 regular

**schema** n diagram (pl **schemata**); adj **schematic** shown by diagrammatic representation (adj **-ally**); v **schematize** 1 simplify 2 organize schematically (n **-ization**)

**scheme** n 1 plan 2 outline; v 1 plan as scheme 2 plot dishonestly; n **schemer** one who plots schemes, esp in bad sense

> **scheme** n 1 (plan) course of action, procedure, program, project, strategy, system, tactics. 2 (outline) blueprint, design, draft, layout, plan, project, proposal

**scherzo** n mus lively, playful movement or passage

**schism** n division in church

**schist** n type of crystalline rock

**schizophrenia** n psychosis or mental disorder; adj **schizophrenic**

**schmaltz** n coll excessive sentimentality in art, music, etc; adj **-y**

**schnapps** n Ger strong alcoholic drink

**scholar** n 1 learned person 2 holder of scholarship; adj **-ly**; n **scholarship** 1 quality of learned person 2 grant of money to scholar; adj **scholastic** 1 of school, scholars 2 academic (n **-ism**)

**school**[1] n 1 place of education 2 group of artists, composers, writers sharing common ideas, methods; idm **school of thought** people sharing common ideas; v educate; n **schoolmaster/-mistress/-teacher**

> **school** n (place of education) academy, college, educational establishment, educational institution, seminary

**school**[2] n large group of fish, whales, etc

**schooner** n 1 sailing vessel 2 large glass

**science** n 1 systematized knowledge of natural or physical phenomena; investigation of this; knowledge or skill based on study, experience, and practice; n **s. fiction** stories of imaginary events set in future

**scientific** adj based on principles and methods of science

> **scientific** adj analytical, controlled, methodical, rational, regulated, rigorous, systematic

**scientist** n one trained in natural science

**scintillating** v bright and lively

**scion** n slip for grafting; young member of family, descendant

**scissors** n pl cutting instrument of two blades joined together

**sclerosis** n med hardening of body tissue

**scoff**[1] n taunt; expression of contempt; v jeer at; mock

**scoff** v belittle, deride, despise, disparage, gibe, laugh at, poke fun at, pooh-pooh inf, ridicule, scorn, sneer

**scoff**[2] v coll eat greedily and quickly

**scold** v reprove angrily, noisily

**scold** v bawl out inf, berate, blame, castigate, chide, give sb a talking-to, haul over the coals, lecture, nag, read the riot act to, rebuke, reprimand, reproach, reprove, tell off, tick off

**sconce** n metal bracket candlestick on wall

**scone** n small, rich, round bread

**scoop** n 1 article for ladling, dipping, or shoveling 2 tool for hollowing out 3 journalism exclusive news item; v 1 ladle, shovel out 2 hollow out

**scoot** v coll run quickly; run away; n **scooter** 1 low-powered motorcycle with small wheels 2 child's toy

**scope** n range or extent

**scope** n area, compass, competence, field, limit, reach, span, sphere

**scorch** v burn surface of

**scorching** adj very hot

**score** n 1 number of points made in game 2 mark drawn or scratched 3 set of 20 4 pl indefinite, large number; idm **pay/settle an old score** have revenge; v 1 notch 2 keep count of points in game 3 cross out; phr v **score out/through** draw line through; delete; n **scoreboard** board showing points scored; n **scorer** one who keeps or makes score in game

**score** n (number of points) count, marks, points, result, sum, tally, total

**scorn** n contempt; v feel, show contempt of

**scorn** v be above, deride, disdain, disparage, flout, look down on, mock, scoff at, slight, treat with contempt

**scornful** adj full of contempt

**scornful** adj contemptuous, derisive, disdainful, haughty, insolent, mocking, sarcastic, slighting, sneering, snide, supercilious, superior

**scorpion** n small arachnid insect with sting in tail and lobsterlike claws

**Scot** n native of Scotland; adjs **Scotch** contracted form of Scottish (n whisky from Scotland); **Scottish (S. highlands)**

**scotch** v 1 crush, render harmless 2 thwart, hinder; n wedge to prevent wheel, etc from slipping

**scot-free** adj unpunished, unhurt

**scoundrel** n rogue; villain

**scour** v 1 clean 2 search thoroughly

**scourge** n sth that causes great suffering

**scourge** n affliction, bane, burden, curse, evil, infliction, misery, misfortune, plague, punishment, terror, torment, visitation

**scout** n 1 child enrolled as Boy/Girl Scout 2 soldier sent to reconnoiter 3 person sent out to look for people with talent

**scowl** v look sullen, angry; n angry frown

**scowl** v frown, glare, glower, grimace

**scrabble** v scramble about; n 1 scrawl; 2 cap [TM] word-building board game

**scrag** n bony end of neck of mutton; adj **scraggy** skinny, thin, lean

a b c d e f g h i j k l m n o p q r **s** t u v w x y z

A B C D E F G H I J K L M N O P Q R **S** T U V W X Y Z

**scram** v coll go away at once

**scramble** v 1 clamber, climb using arms and legs 2 cook beaten eggs with butter, until set; n 1 act of scrambling 2 rough hill climb in motorcycle racing

**scrap** n 1 small piece 2 waste material 3 coll fight; v **scrapping, scapped** 1 dispose of as useless 2 coll fight; ns **s. book** book with plain pages for pasting in press-cuttings, etc; **s. heap** pile of waste material; **s. metal** metal for melting down and re-using; **s. paper** used paper for making notes, etc

> **scrap** n 1 (small piece) bit, crumb, fragment, grain, morsel, offcut, piece, remnant, snippet, trace. 2 (waste material) junk, rejects, rubbish

**scrape** v graze, abrade surface with sharp edge; phr v **scrape along** coll manage with difficulty; **scrape through** pass test with difficulty; **scrape together/up** collect or obtain with difficulty; n act, sound of scraping; coll awkward predicament; n **scraper** instrument for scraping

> **scrape** v abrade, bark, graze, lacerate, rub, scratch, scuff, skin

**scratch** v leave slight mark on skin or surface with claws, or anything sharp; n mark made by scratching; idm **up to scratch** satisfactory

> **scratch** v abrade, bark, claw, cut, graze, mark, score, scrape, wound

**scratch card** n game ticket on which surface is scratched off to reveal numbers

**scrawl** v scribble; n untidy handwriting

**scrawny** adj thin and thin

**scream** v utter shrill, piercing cry; n shrill cry

> **scream** v cry, howl, screech, shriek, squall, wail, yell, yowl

**screech** v utter shrill harsh cry; n scream

**screed** n long tedious speech or letter

**screen** n 1 structure giving shelter from heat, cold, wind, or concealing something 2 large surface on which films are projected; v 1 shelter, protect with screen 2 conceal 3 project (film, etc) 4 examine (person) for political motives

**screw** n cylindrical piece of metal with spiral groove running around it and used as fastening; v fasten with screw(s); phr vs **screw off** remove by turning; **screw on** fasten by turning; n **screwdriver** chisel-shaped tool with tip for turning screws

**scribble** v write, draw carelessly; n something scribbled

> **scribble** v dash off, doodle, jot down, scrawl

**scribe** n writer, author; v mark with scriber; n **scriber** tool for marking lines on stone etc

**scrimmage** n scuffle; confused struggle

**scrimp** v cut corners; adj **scrimpy** scanty

**scrip** n share- or stock-certificate

**script** n 1 handwriting 2 text of play, film, etc

**scripture** n sacred writings; the Bible

**scroll** n 1 roll of parchment or paper 2 ornamental spiral or curved design

**scrooge** n miserly person

**scrotum** n pouch of skin containing testicles

**scrounge** v sl beg; scavenge; n **scrounger** cadger

> **scrounge** v cadge, sponge

**scrub**[1] n land covered with brushwood; adj **scrubby** insignificant, undersized, inferior

**scrub**[2] v **scrubbing, scrubbed** 1 clean by rubbing 2 sl cancel; n act of scrubbing; n **scrubbing-brush** hard stiff brush

**scruff** n nape of neck

**scruffy** adj untidy in appearance

> **scruffy** adj disheveled, ragged, shabby, slovenly, tattered, unkempt

**scrum** n struggle between opposing forwards in rugby game, with ball on ground between them; n **scrum-half** rugby player who puts ball into scrum

**scrumptious** n coll delicious

**scrunch** v 1 crush; crumple 2 chew noisily (n noise of this)

**scruples** n doubts about proposed action

> **scruples** n compunction, conscience, doubt, hesitation, misgiving, qualm, second thought, twinge of conscience

**scrupulous** adj conscientious; meticulous

**scrutiny** n careful examination; v **scrutinize** examine carefully

> **scrutiny** n check, checking, examination, exploration, inspection, investigation, perusal, search, study

**scud** v **scudding, scudded** move quickly

**scuff** v scratch (shoes) by dragging feet

**scuffle** v struggle; n confused struggle

**scull** n light, small oar

**scullery** n room near kitchen, where messy chores and cleaning of pots, etc are done

**sculpture** n art of carving or chiseling stone, wood, etc to form figures; v represent by sculpture; n **sculptor** artist who models in clay, carves wood or stone figures; fem **sculptress**

**scum** n froth on liquid; waste part of anything; fig lowest, most degraded people

**scurf** n thin flakes of dried skin on scalp; adj **scurfy**

**scurrilous** adj coarsely abusive

> **scurrilous** adj defamatory, insulting, libelous, obscene, offensive, slanderous

**scurry** v run, hurry

**scurvy** n disease of malnutrition, due to lack of Vitamin C; adj mean, low

**scuttle**[1] n receptacle for holding coal

**scuttle**[2] v run away hurriedly; bolt

**scythe** n tool for mowing, with long curved blade; v cut with scythe; mow

**sea** n 1 mass of salt water covering much of earth's surface 2 fig large expanse of sth; ns **seaboard** coastal area of country; **seafood** fish and other edible sea creatures; **s. front** area above beach at seaside resort; **seagull** gull; **s.-horse** small fish with horse-like head; **s. lion** large seal; **seaman** sailor; **seaweed** any form of plant life growing in the sea; adjs **seafaring** traveling by sea (n seafarer); **seaworthy** fit for a sea voyage

> **sea** n (mass of salt water) ocean, the briny, the deep, the waves

**seal**[1] n marine, amphibious fish-eating mammal with flippers

**seal**[2] n 1 piece of metal, etc with engraved design for stamping on wax 2 disk of wax thus stamped as authentication of a document or for security 3 any substance used to fill a crack or gap preventing leakage of gas, air, water, oil, etc; idm **seal of approval** formal approval; v 1 close tightly 2 coat with protective waterproof substance 3 decide; phr v **seal off** close securely to prevent entry or exit

> **seal** v (close tightly) close up, cork, fasten, make airtight, make watertight, plug, secure, stick down, stop, stopper, stop up

**seam** n 1 join between two edges (of cloth, or planks) 2 thin layer; stratum; v join by sewing together; adj **-less**; n **seamstress, sempstress** needlewoman

**séance** n Fr meeting of spiritualists

**searing** adj (of pain) burning

**search** v go through and examine closely; n act of searching; adj **-ing** 1 penetrating (**s. look**) 2 severely testing (**s. question**); ns **searcher** person who searches; **searchlight** powerful beam of light for scanning area in darkness; **s. party** group of people searching for missing person

**search** v comb, explore, go over, go through, hunt through, investigate, poke about, pry, rummage through, sift through, turn inside out, turn upside down
**search** n check, hunt, inquiry, inspection, investigation, look, probe, pursuit, quest

**season** n 1 one of four divisions of the year (spring, summer, autumn, winter) 2 period of year associated with specific activity; *idm* **in season** 1 easily available now 2 (of female animal) ready to mate; v 1 give extra flavor to by adding salt, pepper, spice, etc 2 (of wood) make or become fit for use by gradual drying out to avoid warping; ns **seasoning** flavoring added to food; **season (ticket)** ticket valid for any number of times' use within a specified period; *adjs* **seasonable** appropriate for the time of year; **seasonal** varying with the seasons
**seat** n 1 sth made to sit on 2 right to sit (as in Congress, theater, etc) 3 buttocks; v 1 make sit down 2 provide with seating accommodation
**sebaceous** *adj* fatty
**secluded** *adj* remote and quiet

**secluded** *adj* concealed, cut off, hidden, inaccessible, isolated, lonely, off the beaten track, out of the way, solitary

**second**[1] n 1 sixtieth part of one minute 2 *coll* brief space of time
**second**[2] *det* 2nd (ordinal number of two); next after first (*also adv, pron*); n 1 helper of boxer or dullist 2 second gear (of vehicle) 3 *pl* imperfect goods sold with a reduction; *adjs* **s. best** not as good as best; **s.-class** inferior in quality to first-class; **s.-hand** 1 previously owned, used by sb else 2 (of information) obtained indirectly (*also adv*); **s.-rate** of inferior quality; ns **s. childhood** dotage; **s. thought** change of opinion; **s. wind** fresh burst of energy in activity after first onset of tiredness

**second**[3] support (proposal or nominee for post); n **-er** supporter
**secondary** *adj* 1 following what is first or primary (**s. education, s. school**) 2 less important than primary (**s. consideration, s. motive**) 3 dependent on, caused by what is primary (**s. infection**)
**secret** *adj* 1 hidden; kept from common knowledge 2 mysterious; clandestine 3 remote; secluded; n thing kept secret; n **secrecy** ability to keep sth secret; *adj* **secretive** unduly reticent; furtive

**secret** *adj* clandestine, concealed, confidential, covert, esoteric, hidden, mysterious, private, undercover, undisclosed, unknown

**secretary** n 1 employee dealing with correspondence, keep records 2 head of state department; *adj* **secretarial**
**secrete** v 1 hide, conceal 2 (of gland, etc) collect and distribute material from blood as secretion; n **secretion** process of collecting substances from blood for use of body or expulsion as excreta
**sect** n group holding minority views in religion or politics; *adj* **sectarian** characteristic of sect
**section** n 1 separate, distinct part of anything 2 department 3 drawing of an object cut vertically; *adj* **-al**

**section** n 1 (separate, distinct part) area, division, portion, region, segment, sector, unit. 2 (department) branch, division, group, subdivision, unit

**sector** n portion of circle; part of an area
**secular** *adj* worldly; not ecclesiastical
**secure** *adj* 1 made safe 2 firm; stable 3 free from care 4 certain; v 1 make safe 2 make certain 3 fasten firmly 4 get hold of; n **security** safety; protection; safeguard; guarantee; *pl* **-s** bonds, title-deeds, stock certificates, etc

**secure** adj 1 (safe) fastened, locked, locked up, secured, tight. 2 (held firmly) fast, firm, fixed, held in place, stable, supported

**sedan** n covered chair carried on two poles; large closedcar

**sedate** adj calm, staid, decorous; adv **-ly**; n **-ness**

**sedate** adj composed, decorous, deliberate, dignified, majestic, slow, solemn, staid, stately, unhurried

**sedative** adj soothing; n sedative drug; n **sedation** act of administering sedative

**sedentary** adj sitting

**sedge** n coarse perennial grasslike plant

**sediment** n matter which settles at bottom of liquid; dregs

**sedition** n offense against state authority, not amounting to treason; adj **seditious**

**seduce** v 1 entice sexually 2 corrupt; lead astray; n **seduction**; adj **seductive** alluring, attractive, persuasive

**see** v **seeing, saw, seen** 1 perceive with the eyes 2 understand 3 meet 4 verify 5 imagine; visualize 6 experience; phr vs **see about** 1 think about 2 deal with; **see off** chase away; **see out** 1 escort to the exit 2 endure to the end of; **see over/around** inspect (place); **see through** 1 not be deceived by 2 ensure completion of 3 help and support (in difficult times); **see to** attend to

**see** v 1 (perceive with the eyes) behold, catch sight of, descry, discern, distinguish, espy, glimpse, look, make out, note, notice, observe, sight, spot, spy, view, watch, witness. 2 (understand) appreciate, apprehend, comprehend, fathom, follow, grasp, perceive, realize. 3 (meet) consult, go out with, go to, have a date with, have an appointment with, interview, rendezvous with, spend time with, visit

**seed** n 1 grain of plant from which new plant grows 2 sperm; idm **go to seed** become shabby; v 1 form seed 2 arrange draw for tennis tournament so that best players do not meet in early rounds; n **seedling** young plant raised from seed; adj **seedy** shabby

**seek** v **seeking, sought** search for

**seek** v be after, be on the lookout for, chase after, go in search of, hunt, look for, pursue, want

**seem** v appear to be; adjs **-ing** apparent; **seemly** decent, proper, appropriate

**seem** v feel, give the impression, look, sound

**seen** pp of see

**seep** v trickle through slowly; n **seepage** slow seeping through

**seer** n prophet; oracle

**seersucker** n lightweight, puckered fabric

**seesaw** n 1 children's play apparatus of plank resting on central support, child sitting on each end, moving up and down alternately 2 any motion as this; v move up and down

**seethe** v bubble up; fig be violently angry

**segment** n section, portion cut or marked off; v divide into parts; n **-ation**

**segregate** v keep apart; n **-ation**

**segregate** v divide, isolate, quarantine, separate, sort

**seismic** adj pertaining to earthquakes; n **seismograph** instrument for recording earth tremors

**seize** v 1 grasp, take by force 2 grasp rapidly with mind; phr v **seize up**; (of machinery, etc) stick; not move; n **seizure** 1 forcible taking 2 sudden attack of illness, esp stroke or fit

**seldom** adv rarely; not often

**select** v choose; adj chosen, exclusive, fastidious; adj **selective** having power of selection, able to discriminate

A
B
C
D
E
F
G
H
I
J
K
L
M
N
O
P
Q
R
**S**
T
U
V
W
X
Y
Z

**select** v cull, draw, elect, pick, pick out, prefer, sample

**selection** n 1 collection of different samples 2 act of selecting

**selection** n (collection of samples) assortment, choice, range, sample, set

**self**[1] n person's own identity, and individual character; pl **selves**

**self-**[2] prefix expressing reflexive action to, by, for oneself

**self-absorbed** adj only concerned with one's own interests

**self-assured** adj confident of one's abilities

**self-centered** adj preoccupied with one's own affairs or personality

**self-confident** adj sure of oneself and one's ability; adv **-ly**; n **-fidence**

**self-confident** adj assured, brash, cocky inf, confident, self-assured, swaggering

**self-conscious** adj easily embarrassed; shy

**self-contained** adj complete within itself

**self-denial** n voluntary abstention from pleasures

**self-determination** n right of nation to decide on its own form of government

**self-devotion** n giving up one's time to cause, etc

**self-effacing** adj modest

**self-employed** adj earning money directly from one's own business

**self-evident** adj clearly so

**self-fulfilling** adj happening, likely to happen simply because it has been predicted

**self-importance** n exaggerated idea of own importance

**selfish** adj thinking only of oneself

**selfish** adj egoistic, egotistical, greedy, mean, mercenary, miserly, self-centered

**self-possessed** adj composed

**self-reliant** adj independent; n **-ance**

**self-respect** n regard for one's own character, etc

**self-righteous** adj too sure of one's own goodness

**self-righteous** adj holier-than-thou, pious, pompous, pontificating, sanctimonious, sententious, vain

**selfsame** adj identical

**self-satisfied** adj conceited

**self-seeking** adj acting only for one's own advantage

**self-service** adj (of stores, etc) where customers serve themselves

**self-styled** adj named, or cited, or titled, by oneself

**self-sufficient** adj able to supply all one's own needs for existence

**self-will** n obstinacy; being headstrong

**sell** v 1 give in return for money 2 deal in 3 be sold 4 persuade people to buy 5 persuade people that something is good; pt, pp **sold**; idm **be sold out (of)** have sold all available; idm **sell down the river** betray somebody; phr v **sell out** 1 sell one's whole supply 2 be all sold (n **sell-out** entertainment for which all tickets are sold); n **sell-by date** date marked on perishable product as last acceptable date for selling

**sell** v 1 (give in return for money) cash in, dispose of, export, find buyer for, get rid of, offload inf. 2 (deal in) advertise, dispense, have for sale, hawk inf, put on sale, offer, stock, trade in, vend

**seltzer** n carbonated water

**selvage** n edge of cloth woven to prevent fraying

**selves** pl of **self**

**semantics** n pl branch of linguistic study dealing with development of meaning of words

**semaphore** n signaling with arms, flags

**semblance** n appearance; outward show

**semen** n sperm fluid of male animal

**semester** n university term of 18 weeks

**semi**[1] n coll 18-wheel, distance-hauling truck

**semi-**[2] prefix partly, half

**semibreve** n whole note

**semicircle** n halfcircle; adj **semicircular**

**semicolon** n punctuation mark (;)

**semiconductor** n substance that conducts electricity under certain conditions

**semidetached** adj (of house) having another joined to it on one side

**semifinal** n round before the final

**seminal** adj 1 important and influential 2 containing semen

**seminar** n class for advanced students

**seminary** n college for clergy

**semiology** n study of signs and symbols; adj **-logical**; n **-logist**

**semiprecious** adj of moderate value

**semiquaver** n sixteenth note

**Semite** n member of racial group including Jews, Arabs; Jew; adj **Semitic** pertaining to Semites and their languages

**semitone** n mus half step

**semolina** n ground grains of wheat, used in making pasta

**senate** n upper legislature of US Congress; n **senator**

**send** v 1 dispatch 2 cause to go, be conveyed 3 sl delight; thrill; pt, pp **sent**; phr vs **send for** 1 order 2 request to come; **send off** 1 post 2 (sport) dismiss from field of play

---

**send** v 1 (dispatch) consign, export, forward, mail,  post, put in the mail,relay, send off, ship. 2 (cause to move) drive, force, kick, propel, throw. 3 (order to a place) assign, force, order, post, second, throw. 4 (transmit) beam, broadcast, emit, send out

---

**senile** adj showing weakness of mental faculties, due to old age; **senile dementia**; n mental deterioration in old age; n **senility**

**senior** adj older, of higher rank, position; n older person; superior; n **s. citizen** person beyond age of retirement; n **seniority**

---

**senior** adj elder, first, high, outranking, ranking, superior, top

---

**senna** n dried leaves of pealike plant used as laxative

**sensation** n effect felt by senses; very successful event

**sensational** adj amazing; wonderful; arousing great interest, curiosity; n **sensationalism** crude, melodramatic presentation of news items, esp sex and violence

**sense** n 1 one of five faculties by which one perceives the world around (sight, hearing, taste, smell, touch) 2 practical wisdom 3 meaning 4 feeling (about sth) 5 purpose; idm **bring/come to one's senses** (cause to) stop acting foolishly; idm **make sense** be intelligible; idm **make sense (out of)** understand; v become aware of; feel; detect; adj **senseless** 1 unconscious 2 foolish

---

**sense** n 1 (one of five faculties) ability, faculty, feel, feeling, instinct, gift, perception, reflex, sensitivity, talent. 2 (practical wisdom) common sense, foresight, gumption inf, intelligence, judgment, understanding, wit. 3 (meaning) connotation, denotation, implication, import, reference

---

**sensibility** n delicate feeling (pl **-ies** capacity for being shocked easily)

**sensible** adj wise (adv **-ibly**)

---

**sensible** adj intelligent, judicious, logical, meaningful, practical, rational, sober

---

**sensitive** adj 1 feeling acutely 2 aware 3 reacting quickly to slight changes; n **sensitiveness** state of being sensitive; **sensitivity** degree of sensitiveness; v **sensitize** phot make sensitive to light

**sensitive** *adj* **1** (feeling emotions deeply) delicate, easily hurt, emotional, feeling, highly strung, touchy. **2** (aware) alert, attuned, conscious, in tune, perceptive, responsive, sympathetic

**sensor** *n* device for detecting presence of heat, sound, smoke; *adj* **sensory** of the physical senses

**sensual** *adj* **1** pertaining to body senses **2** lustful, voluptuous; *ns* **sensuality** proneness to sexual indulgence; **sensualism** sexual indulgence; *adj* **sensuous** based on bodily senses

**sent** *pt, pp* of **send**

**sentence** *n* **1** decision of court, declaring punishment to be inflicted on criminal **2** combination of words which convey complete meaning; *v* condemn

**sentient** *adj* having sense or feeling

**sentiment** *n* **1** tender emotion **2** verbal expression of feeling; **sentimental** *adj* foolishly emotional; *n* **sentimentality**

**sentimental** *adj* exaggerated, gooey, gushing, pathetic, sad, sickly, sloppy, tear-jerking

**sentinel** *n* one who keeps watch; sentry

**sentry** *n* armed military guard

**separate** *v* divide; *adj* divided; distinct physically; kept apart; *n* **-ation 1** act, process of separating **2** in law, formal arrangement when married couple live apart, without divorce

**separate** *v* break up, come apart, cut off, detach, disconnect, dissociate, divorce, isolate, part, pull apart, segregate, sever, sort, split, sunder, take apart, tear asunder

**separate** *adj* detached, different, disconnected, discrete, independent, individual, separable, separated, unattached, unconnected, unrelated

**separatism** *n* policy of keeping a religious or political group separate and independent; *adj, n* **-ist**

**sepia** *n* dark brown pigment, made from ink of cuttle fish; *adj* of this color

**September** *n* 9th month

**septennial** *adj* lasting, occurring every seven years

**septet** *n* music for, group of, seven instruments or voices

**septic** *adj* of, caused by infection or putrefaction; **s. tank** underground tank where sewage is dispersed through action of bacteria; *n* **septicemia** blood poisoning

**septuagenarian** *adj* aged between 70 and 80; *n* person so aged

**sepulchre, sepulcher** *n* tomb; burial vault; *adj* **sepulchral 1** of pertaining to grave, burial, or dead; funeral **2** (of voice, etc) deep, hollow; *n* **sepulture** burial

**sequel** *n* **1** consequence **2** account, story of later events

**sequence** *n* order in which events, objects follow; series; succession; *adj* **sequential** in sequence; *adv* **-ly**

**sequence** *n* continuation, list, order, procedure, progression, series, succession

**sequester** *v* set apart; isolate; *v* **sequestrate** confiscate; *leg* take (property) by process of law and divert income to meet claims against owner; *n* **sequestration**

**sequin** *n* small ornamental disk or spangle

**seraph** *n* angel; *pl* **seraphim**

**Serbo-Croatian** *n* Slavonic language spoken in Croatia, Bosnia and Herzegovina, Serbia, and Montenegro

**serenade** *n* music sung or played at night (*esp* by lover) beneath lady's window

**serendipity** *n* good luck

**serene** *adj* calm and contented; *n* **serenity**

**serene** *adj* happy, peaceful, placid, quiet, untroubled

**serf** *n* feudal laborer; slave; *n* **serfdom**
**serge** *n* hard-wearing, twilled woolen cloth
**sergeant** *n* NCO in army; police officer;
    **s.-at-arms** ceremonial official
**serial** *adj* of, forming series; *n* story, novel, etc
    published in successive instalments; *v* **-ize**
    publish, produce as serial
**serial killer** *n* person who commits a series
    of murders, *usu* in the same way
**series** *n* 1 sequence 2 set; succession 3 linear,
    end-to-end arrangement
**serious** *adj* 1 important and worrying 2 severe
    3 not laughing 4 not joking

> **serious** *adj* 1 (important and worrying)
> critical, crucial, far-reaching, grave,
> life-and-death, major, momentous, of
> consequence, pressing, significant, urgent,
> vital, weighty. 2 (severe) acute, bad,
> chronic, critical, dangerous, grave,
> grievous, life-threatening. 3 (not
> laughing) austere, dour, earnest, grave,
> humourless, long-faced, pensive, prim and
> proper, severe, sober, solemn, somber,
> stern, thoughtful, unsmiling. 4 (not
> joking) earnest, genuine, honest, in
> earnest, sincere, truthful

**sermon** *n* speech given in church service
**serpent** *n* 1 snake 2 malevolent person
    3 obsolete wind instrument
**serrated** *adj* having notches like teeth of saw
**serum** *n* watery fluid remaining after
    coagulation of blood
**servant** *n* one who serves another

> **servant** *n* assistant, butler, companion,
> drudge *inf*, employee, factotum, footman,
> housekeeper, lackey, maid, menial,
> minion, secretary, slave, valet

**serve** *v* 1 work for; perform duty for 2 wait
    upon (with food) 3 satisfy 4 undergo (prison
    sentence) 5 deliver (writ) 6 (tennis, etc)
    deliver ball to opponent, by striking it 7 be
    useful for

**service** *n* 1 (performance of) official duty
    2 help given 3 public organization or
    department 4 organized system of transport
    or communication 5 satisfying of needs of
    clients 6 set of dishes, silverware, etc
    7 ceremony of religious worship; *ns*
    **s. charge** sum added to basic bill for service;
    **serviceman/woman** person serving in
    armed forces; **s. station** garage for gasoline;
    *adj* **-able** usable, useful; *ns* **servicing**
    maintenance; **serving** portion of food
**serviette** *n Fr* table-napkin
**servile** *adj* obsequious; cringing; *n* **servility**
**servitude** *n* slavery; bondage
**sesame** *n* annual herb, with seeds yielding oil
**session** *n* 1 formal assembly or meeting
    2 period during which legislative body sits,
    *esp* Congress
**set** *v* **setting, setted** 1 put in position
    2 adjust 3 agree 4 allocate 5 harden 6 (of
    sun, moon, etc) pass below horizon; *idm* **set
    free** liberate; *phr vs* **set about** begin; **set
    aside** keep, save for later; **set back** delay
    (*n* **set back**); **set off** 1 depart 2 cause to
    explode; **set on** (cause to) attack; **set out**
    1 depart 2 arrange in order; **set up** 1 erect
    2 prepare 3 organize; *adj* 1 fixed 2 inflexible;
    *idm* **be all set** be quite ready; *idm* **be set on**
    be determined about; *n* 1 complete group
    2 radio or TV receiver 3 arrangement of
    scenery on stage or for filming 4 *tennis*
    specified number of games; subdivision of
    match; *n* **s. piece** sequence of action
    executed according to plan

> **set** *v* 1 (put in position) apply, arrange,
> locate, lodge, put, place, plant, position,
> rest, situate, station. 2 (adjust) calibrate,
> prepare, regulate, start, synchronize.
> 3 (agree) appoint, arrange, decide,
> determine, fix, schedule, specify.
> 4 (allocate) assign, designate, give,
> prescribe, present. 5 (harden) coagulate,
> congeal, crystallize, gel, solidify, stiffen,
> thicken

**settee** n sofa, couch

**setter** n breed of dog trained to point at game

**setting** n surroundings in which sth takes place; that in which gems are set

**settle** n wooden bench with high back and arms; v **1** arrange; agree **2** pay **3** go to live **4** subside **5** make quiet **6** end (dispute); phr vs **settle down 1** make a home **2** begin to lead a quiet life **3** form a regular pattern of work; **settle for** agree to accept; **settle in** get used to new home, job etc; **settle on** agree on; decide on; **settle up** pay what one owes; adj **settled 1** calm **2** established; ns **settlement 1** movement of people to new habitat **2** small newly built village **3** agreement **4** gift of money **5** payment of required sum; **settler** colonist

**settle** v **1** (arrange, agree) conclude, decide, resolve, reconcile, sort out. **2** (pay) clear, defray, discharge, liquidate, pay off, redeem, repay, square. **3** (go to live) camp, colonize, ensconce yourself, establish yourself, install yourself, occupy, people, populate, put down roots, set up home

**seven** n, pron, det cardinal number next above six; ns, adjs, dets **seventh** ordinal number; seventh part; idm **(be in) seventh heaven** (be in) state of bliss; **seventeen** seven plus ten; **seventeenth**; **seventy** seven tens; **seventieth**

**sever** v separate; cut off

**several** adj more than two; not many

**severe** adj **1** bad **2** difficult **3** harsh **4** serious; n **severity**

**severe** adj **1** (bad) bitter, dangerous, drastic, extreme, fierce, great, heavy, intense, serious. **2** (difficult) arduous, demanding, exacting, rigorous, stringent, taxing, tough. **3** (harsh) cruel, hard, oppressive, pitiless, rigid, rigorous, strict, stringent. **4** (serious) austere, dour, forbidding, grim, humorless, sober, solemn, stern, unsmiling

**sew** v **sewing, sewed, sewn** fasten, work with needle and thread; phr v **sew up** repair by sewing; n **sewing**

**sewage** n waste matter carried away in sewers; ns **sewer** underground conduit or drain for carrying off sewage; **sewerage** public drainage

**sex** n **1** fact or quality of being male or female **2** physiological difference between male and female **3** coll sexual intercourse; ns **s. appeal** power of sexual attraction; n **sex offender** person who has committed a sexual crime; n **sex offence** sexual crime; n **sexism** discriminatory treatment of one sex by the other (adj **-ist**); adj **sexual** (**s. intercourse** act of intimacy by joining sex organs of male and female) adv **-ly**; n **-ity**; adj **sexy**

**sexennial** adj lasting, happening once in, six years

**sextet** n group of six instruments or players; music for this group

**sexton** n caretaker, gravedigger of church

**sextuplet** n any of six children born of the same pregnancy

**SF** abbr science fiction

**shabby** adj **1** well worn **2** shameful; n **-iness**

**shabby** adj **1** (well worn) dilapidated, dingy, dirty, dowdy, drab, faded, frayed, gone to seed, grubby, moth-eaten, ragged, rundown, old, scruffy, seedy, threadbare. **2** (shameful) base, contemptible, deceitful, despicable, discreditable, dishonest, dishonorable, disreputable, grubby, ignoble, mean, nasty, shoddy, sordid, squalid, treacherous, unfair, ungenerous, unkind, unworthy

**shack** n hut; shanty

**shackle** n strong metal link; pl **-s** chains

**shad** n edible marine fish of herring family

**shade** n **1** partial darkness; shadow **2** depth of color **3** something that gives shelter, protection from light; pl **-s** coll sunglasses; v **1** darken; screen from light **2** represent light and shade in drawing

**shadow** n 1 patch of shade 2 person who follows closely; v 1 cast shadow over 2 follow closely, esp as detective or bodyguard; adj **shadowy** dim; unsubstantial

**shady** adj 1 giving shade 2 coll disreputable

> **shady** adj 1 (giving shade) cool, leafy, shaded, sheltered. 2 (disreputable) crooked, dodgy, dubious, fishy inf, shifty, slippery, suspicious, untrustworthy

**shaft** n 1 handle; stem 2 arrow 3 beam (of light) 4 vertical opening to mine, etc

**shag**[1] n 1 long-napped cloth 2 fine-cut tobacco

**shag**[2] n small crested cormorant

**shaggy** adj rough, unkempt; n **shaggy-dog story** long rambling joke with pointless ending

**shagreen** n kind of untanned leather; sharkskin

**Shah** n former ruler of Iran

**shake** v **shaking, shook, shaken** 1 tremble; agitate 2 wave 3 shock; (pt **shook,** pp **shaken**); idm **shake hands (with sb)** grasp sb's right hand in greeting; phr vs **shake off** 1 elude 2 get rid of 3 remove by shaking; **shake up** 1 mix by shaking 2 rouse from apathy 3 reorganize fundamentally (n **shake-up**); adj **shaky** unsteady; insecure

> **shake** v 1 (tremble, agitate) bump, convulse, jar, quiver, rattle, rock, shiver, shudder, sway, totter, vibrate, waver, wobble. 2 (wave) brandish, flourish. 3 (shock) alarm, distress, disturb, frighten, perturb, rattle, ruffle, unnerve, unsettle, upset

**shall** v aux used to denote promise, obligation, intention, command, futurity; pt **should**; no pp

**shallot** n kind of onion

**shallow** adj 1 not deep 2 without deep thought; n esp pl shallow place in body of water

**shallow** adj (without deep thought) empty-headed, facile, foolish, frivolous, glib, ignorant, insincere, puerile, silly, simple, superficial, unintelligent, unthinking

**sham** n counterfeit, faked article

**shamble** v walk with stumbling, shuffling gait

**shambles** n pl coll confusion; mess

**shame** n 1 emotion of regret caused by consciousness of guilt, dishonour, etc 2 disgrace 3 coll unfair happening; bad luck; v 1 make ashamed 2 bring shame, disgrace on; adj **shame-faced** ashamed of oneself

> **shame** n (disgrace) condemnation, discredit, dishonor, disrepute, humiliation, ignominy, infamy, loss of face, reproach, scandal, smear, stigma, vilification

**shameful** adj disgraceful

> **shameful** adj atrocious, base, contemptible, deplorable, despicable, indecent, low, mean, outrageous, scandalous, wicked

**shameless** adj 1 impudent; brazen 2 immodest

**shampoo** v wash (hair) with shampoo; wash carpet, car, etc with special preparations; n special preparation for washing hair, carpet, etc

**shamrock** n trefoil plant, probably wood-sorrel, taken as national emblem of Ireland

**shandy** n beer mixed with lemonade or ginger-beer

**shank** n 1 lower leg; shin 2 handle; shaft

**shan't** contracted form of shall not

**shantung** n natural Chinese silk

**shanty**[1] n small hut; temporary building

**shanty**[2], **chanty** n sailor's song

**shantytown** n poor residential area consisting of rough improvised huts

**shape** n 1 external form 2 person's build; v form, fashion; adjs **shapely** well proportioned; **shapeless**

a b c d e f g h i j k l m n o p q r s t u v w x y z

**shape** n 1 (external form) configuration, contours, cut, figure, format, formation, lines, model, mold, outline, pattern. 2 (person's build) body, figure, physique, profile, silhouette

**shard** n broken fragment of pottery
**share**[1] n 1 portion 2 part played in action 3 one of equal portions into which capital of public company is divided; v give, allot, take a share; n **shareholder**

**share** n (portion) allocation, allotment, allowance, assignment, cut, division, helping, part, percentage, proportion, quota, ration, serving
**share** v allot, apportion, assign, deal out, distribute, divide, halve, quarter, split

**share**[2] n blade of plow
**sharecropper** n farmer paying part of rent in produce
**shark** n large, carnivorous, voracious sea fish; fig rapacious, grasping swindler
**sharp** adj 1 having good cutting edge or point 2 clever 3 acute 4 clear 5 hurtful; n mus note raised half note in pitch; v **sharpen** whet edge or point

**sharp** adj 1 (having good cutting edge or point) jagged, pointed, serrated, spiky. 2 (clever) alert, astute, bright, incisive, intelligent, observant, perceptive, quick, quick-witted, shrewd, smart. 3 (acute) cutting, intense, piercing, severe, shooting, stabbing, stinging, violent. 4 (clear) crisp, distinct, focused, well-defined

**shatter** v smash; fig cause to crumble
**shave** v **shaving, shaved, shaven** cut off (hair) with razor; pare; n 1 act of shaving 2 fig narrow escape; n **shaver** one who, that which shaves
**Shavian** adj after, in manner of George Bernard Shaw

**shawl** n large square of fabric worn around shoulders, or for wrapping babies in
**she** fem nom pron (3rd pers sing) female person, etc just referred to; adj female
**sheaf** n bundle of things tied together, esp cut wheat, corn stalks; pl **sheaves**
**shear** v **shearing, sheared, shorn** 1 clip, remove (fleece) from 2 cut off by one stroke; n pl **shears** large cutting implement with blades like scissors; n **shearer** one who shears, esp sheep
**sheath** n 1 close-fitting cover (eg for sharp weapon) 2 simple fitted dress; v **sheathe** cover with sheath
**shed**[1] n wooden hut; outhouse; shelter for cattle, tools, etc
**shed**[2] v 1 cast off 2 get rid of; pt, pp **shed**; idm **shed blood** cause death or injury

**shed** v 1 (cast off) discard, drop, molt, slough. 2 (get rid of) dismiss, fire, make redundant, sack inf

**she'd** contracted form of 1 she had 2 she would
**sheen** n gloss; luster
**sheep** n pl **sheep** ruminant mammal with woolly coat and edible flesh
**sheepish** adj bashful

**sheepish** adj coy, embarrassed, guilty, meek, reticent, self-conscious, shy, timid, uncomfortable

**sheer** adj 1 clear; unmixed 2 perpendicular (of cliff) 3 (of fabric) transparent; phr v **sheer away/off** turn suddenly in another direction
**sheet** n 1 large piece of fabric used to cover bed 2 broad, flat piece of any thin material 3 thin flat piece of metal, paper
**sheik, sheikh** n Arab chieftain
**shelf** n 1 horizontal projecting board on wall, etc 2 horizontal ledge of rock, etc 3 reef; pl **shelves**; idm **on the shelf** beyond the age when one is likely to get married; n **s.-life** length of time a product can remain on sale before it deteriorates

**shell** n 1 hard outer covering of animal or vegetable object 2 explosive projectile 3 ruined building with only walls standing; n idm **go into/come out of one's shell** behave/stop behaving in a shy, retiring manner; v 1 remove shell from (nut, pea, etc) 2 bombard with shells; phr v **shell out** coll pay out, esp unwillingly; n **shellfish** edible marine mollusk or crustacean

**she'll** contracted form of she will

**shellac** n colored resin used in varnishes, sealking wax, etc; v coat with shellac

**shelter** n 1 place of refuge 2 protection; v 1 protect 2 seek safety

> **shelter** n 1 (place of refuge) haven, retreat, sanctuary. 2 (protection) defense, refuge, safety, sanctuary, security

**shelve** v 1 put on shelves 2 fig postpone; abandon 3 slope gently

**shelves** pl of **shelf**

**shepherd** n one who tends sheep; fem **shepherdess**; n **shepherd's pie** baked dish of minced meat covered with mashed potato

**sherbet** n frozen fruit-flavored ice dessert

**sheriff** n chief officer enforcing law, order in county

**Sherpa** n member of Tibetan people noted as mountaineers

**sherry** n type of Spanish wine

**she's** contracted form of she is

**shiatsu** n Japanese massage technique using acupuncture pressure points

**shield** n piece of protective armor carried on arm; v protect

> **shield** v cover, defend, guard, keep safe, safeguard, screen

**shift** v 1 change position 2 change opinion; n 1 change in position or direction 2 (period of work allocated to) team of workers interchanging with other teams; n **s. key** typewriter key giving access to upper case letters; adj **shifty** evasive, dishonest; furtive

> **shift** v 1 (change position) budge, displace, move, relocate, reposition. 2 (change opinion) adjust, alter, change, modify, reverse, switch, transfer, vary

**Shiite** n Muslim of the Shia branch of Islam

**shillelagh** n Irish walking stick

**shilly-shally** n indecisioin; needless delay; v hesitate, waver

**shimmer** v shine with faint light; n faint, tremulous light; glimmer

**shin** n front of lower leg

**shindig** n 1 coll noisy party 2 disturbance

**shine** v 1 emit, reflect light 2 show great ability 3 excel 4 show great intelligence; pt, pp **shone**; n brightness; polish

> **shine** v 1 (emit, reflect light) beam, blaze, dazzle, flash, glare, gleam, glisten, glitter, glow, radiate, shimmer, sparkle, twinkle. 2 (show great ability) be excellent, be exceptional, be outstanding, do well, excel, stand out

**shingle** n pebbles found on seashore

**shingles** n acute inflammatory disease of nerve endings

**Shinto** n national religion of Japan

**shiny** adj reflecting light brightly

> **shiny** adj bright, gleaming, glistening, glittering, glossy, lustrous, polished, shimmering, shining, sparkling, twinkling

**ship** n large sea going vessel; v **shipping, shipped** 1 send (goods, etc) by ship 2 embark, serve in ship; ns **shipping** 1 ships 2 transporting by ship; **shipment** cargo; **shipwreck** destruction of ship by storm (adj **-ed**); **shipyard** place where ships are built

**shire** n county; pl rural counties of England

**shirk** v avoid (danger, duty, etc); n **shirker**

**shirt** n sleeved garment, worn under jacket

**shirty** adj coll angry; irritable

**shish kebab** *n* meat cooked on skewers

**shiver** *v* shake with cold or fear; *n* shudder, quivering movement

> **shiver** *v* quake, quiver, shudder, tremble

**shoal** *n* large mass of fish swimming together

**shock** *n* 1 feeling of horror, surprise, disgust, etc 2 that which causes such feeling 3 discharge of electric current through body 4 violent jolt; *v* cause, feeling of horror, surprise, disgust; *n* **s. wave** air pressure wave in wake of ultrasonic aircraft

> **shock** *n* 1 (feeling of surprise, disgust) astonishment, distress, fright, offense, outrage, revulsion. 2 (thing which causes such feeling) blow, bombshell, thunderbolt, trauma, upset
> **shock** *v* astonish, astound, daze, distress, frighten, horrify, jolt, offend, outrage, revolt, shake, sicken, stagger, startle, stun, stupefy, traumatize, unsettle

**shocking** *adj* distressing, disgusting

> **shocking** *adj* appalling, atrocious, awful, disgraceful, foul, ghastly, hideous, horrific, obscene, offensive, outrageous, revolting, scandalous, sickening, terrible, upsetting

**shoddy** *adj* cheap; insubstantial

**shoe** *n* 1 outer covering for foot 2 metal rim, or plate, nailed to hoof of horse; *v* protect, furnish with shoes; *pt, pp* **shod**; *n* **shoelace** string for securing shoe

**shone** *pt, pp* of **shine**

**shoo** *interj* used, *esp* to animals to go away

**shook** *pt* of **shake**

**shoot** *v* 1 kill or wound with bullet 2 fire (missile) 3 move quickly 4 *football* kick directly toward goal; *idm* **shoot one's mouth off** *coll* talk indiscreetly; *phr v* **shoot down** cause to fall by shooting; *n* 1 act of shooting 2 sprout 3 shooting party; *n* **s. star** burning meteor seen as bright streak in sky

> **shoot** *v* 1 (kill or wound with bullet) bag, bring down, gun down, hit, injure, kill, shell, snipe at, wound. 2 (fire) aim, discharge, launch. 3 (move quickly) bolt, charge, dart, dash, fly, hurtle, leap, race, rush, speed, streak, tear

**shop** *n* 1 place where goods are sold 2 *fig* one's business, etc 3 workshop; *idm* **talk shop** discuss one's work on a social occasion; *v* **shopping, shopped** visit shops to buy goods; *phr v* **shop around** compare goods and prices in shops before buying; *ns* **s.-assistant** person who serves in shop; **s.-floor** 1 production area in factory 2 workers; **shopkeeper** owner of small shop; **shopper**; **shopping** 1 act of buying 2 goods bought; *v* **shoplift** steal from shop

> **shop** *n* boutique, chain store, department store, outlet, retailer, seller, store, supermarket, wholesaler

**shore** *n* land at edge of sea or lake

**short** *adj* 1 brief 2 not tall 3 not lasting long 4 deficient; *idm* **short of** 1 lacking in; having insufficient of 2 failing to reach; *idm* **be short with** be impatient with; *idm* **stop short** stop suddenly; *n coll* strong alcoholic drink; *pl* **-s** short trousers; *adjs* **s.-lived** not lasting long; **s.-range** covering a short distance or time; **s.-sighted** 1 not able to see distant objects clearly 2 not thinking of the future; **short-term** relating to the immediate future; *ns* **s. circuit** *elec* bypassing of normal circuit through faulty insulation or loose connection (*v* **s.-circuit**); **shortcoming** failing; **s. cut** quick way; **shortfall** deficit; **shorthand** system for quick writing; **s.-list** preliminary selection of applicants from whom an appointment for a post is to be made (*v* select for such a list); **s. wave** radio broadcasting on waves of under 60 m; *adv* **shortly** 1 soon 2 briefly

**short** *adj* **1** (brief) abbreviated, abridged, compact, compressed, concise, pithy, succinct, summarized, terse, truncated. **2** (not tall) diminutive, little, midget, petite, slight, small, squat. **3** (not lasting long) brief, cursory, fleeting, momentary, passing, quick, short-lived, transitory

**shortage** *n* lack

**shortage** *n* dearth, deficiency, deficit, inadequacy, insufficiency, scarcity, shortfall, want

**shortbread** *n* crumbly sweet butter cookie
**shorten** *v* make shorter

**shorten** *v* abbreviate, abridge, compress, condense, contract, curtail, cut, decrease, dock, lessen, précis, prune, reduce, shrink, summarize, trim, truncate

**shot**[1] *pt, pp of* **shoot**
**shot**[2] *adj* fabric woven so as to change color, according to angle of light
**shot**[3] *n* **1** small lead pellet in cartridge **2** act of firing **3** noise of this **4** attempt, try **5** *sl* injection, injected dose, *esp* of drug; **s. in the dark** random guess
**should** *modal v* (*pt or conditional of* **shall**) **1** ought to **2** were to **3** 1st person was going to; *neg* **should not** (*contracted form* **shouldn't**)
**shoulder** *n* part of body to which arm is attached; *v* put on one's shoulder; *fig* undertake responsibility for; *n* **shoulderblade** shoulder bone
**shout** *n* loud outcry; *v* utter with loud voice

**shout** *v* bellow, call, cheer, clamor, cry, rant, roar, scream, screech, shriek, yell

**shove** *v, n* push
**shovel** *n* broad spade, used for lifting earth, etc; *v* lift, move with shovel

**show** *v* **showing, showed, shown, shews 1** expose to view **2** be visible **3** explain **4** guide; *phr vs* **show off 1** show to best effect **2** try to impress others by talk or behavior (*n* **show-off** person who does this); **show up 1** arrive **2** embarrass **3** outdo; *n* **1** performance, entertainment **2** display **3** ostentation **4** indication **5** effort; *ns* **s. business** work of people in theater, cinema, etc; **s. jumping** sport in which horses are ridden to jump over obstacles; *adj* **showy** ostentatious; (too) bright, etc

**show** *v* **1** (expose to view) display, exhibit, manifest, present. **2** (be visible) appear, be in view, be seen, be visible, catch the eye, make an appearance, materialize, stand out, stick out. **3** (explain) demonstrate, divulge, expose, express, indicate, make known, make plain, prove, reveal, teach, uncover. **4** (guide) accompany, conduct, direct, escort, lead, steer, usher

**showbiz** *n coll* show business
**shower** *n* **1** short fall of rain **2** copious discharge (of missiles) **3** device making bath water fall from overhead; *v* **1** fall as shower **2** give out abundantly **3** take shower; *adj* **-ly** with frequent rain-showers
**shown** *pt, pp of* **show**
**shrank** *pt of* **shrink**
**shrapnel** *n* shell casing filled with bullets or pieces of metal that scatter on bursting
**shred** *n* tattered fragment, strip; *v* **shredding, shredded** tear into shreds
**shrew** *n* **1** virago **2** mouselike carnivorous mammal; *adj* **-ish** nagging
**shrewd** *adj* clever and cunning; *n* **-ness**

**shrewd** *adj* astute, canny, crafty, intelligent, keen, knowing, observant, perceptive, quick-witted, sharp, sly, smart, wily

**shriek** *v, n* screech; scream
**shrike** *n* insect-eating bird of prey
**shrill** *adj* piercing, high-pitched in tone

a
b
c
d
e
f
g
h
i
j
k
l
m
n
o
p
q
r
s
t
u
v
w
x
y
z

**shrill** *adj* acute, ear-splitting, high, jarring, penetrating, screeching, sharp, shrieking

**shrimp** *n* small edible, long-tailed crustacean; *fig* small person; *v* fish for, catch shrimps
**shrine** *n* sacred place associated with saint
**shrink** *v* **shrinking, shrank, shrunk, shrunken** 1 contract; diminish 2 recoil; retreat; flinch; *phr v* **shrink from doing** be reluctant to do; *n coll* psychiatrist or psychoanalyst; *v* **s.-wrap** wrap in tight-fitting plastic film to exclude air; *n* **shrinkage** degree of shrinking
**shrivel** *v* **shrivelling, shrivelled** curl, roll up; wither
**shroud** *n* cloth wound around corpse; *fig* covering; *pl* ropes from masthead; *v* wrap in shroud; hide, cover, veil
**Shrovetide** *n* three days before Lent; **Shrove Tuesday** day before Ash Wednesday
**shrub** *n* low-growing bushy woody plant
**shrug** *v* **shrugging, shrugged** lift and draw up shoulders slightly, as sign of doubt
**shrunk(en)** *adj* shrivelled; contracted
**shudder** *v* tremble violently; *n* shuddering

**shudder** *v* convulse, jerk, quake, quiver, rattle, shake, shiver, vibrate

**shuffle** *v* 1 move feet without lifting them 2 mix cards up; *ns* **shuffler; shuffling**
**shun** *v* **shunning, shunned** avoid
**shunt** *v* turn, switch (train) to side line
**shush** *interj* requesting silence
**shut** *v* close; *pt, pp* **shut**; *n* **shutter** 1 hinged window screen 2 device in camera for screening lens

**shut** *v* bolt, draw, fasten, lock, seal, secure, slam

**shut-eye** *n coll* sleep
**shuttle** *n* plane, train making short regular trips over same routes; *v* move regularly back and forth between two places

**shuttle cock** *n* feathered, weighted cork, used in badminton
**shy** *adj* **shyer, shyest** timid; *phr vs* **shy at** turn away in fear; **shy away from** avoid

**shy** *adj* bashful, coy, diffident, hesitant, inhibited, introverted, nervous, reserved, reticent, retiring, self-conscious, self-effacing, sheepish, wary, withdrawn

**Siamese cat** *n* cat with short pale brown fur and blue eyes;
**Siamese twin** *n* either of two twins whose bodies are joined at birth
**sibling** *n* brother or sister
**sibyl** *n* wise woman; soothsayer
**sick** *adj* 1 nauseous 2 ill 3 (of humor) macabre; *idm* **be sick (to death) of** be fed up with; *idm* **feel sick** suffer from nausea; *v* **sicken** 1 become ill 2 disgust; *adj* **sickly** 1 often ill 2 unhealthy looking; *n* **sickness** illness

**sick** *adj* 1 (nauseous) nauseated, queasy. 2 (ill) ailing, bedridden, diseased, feeble, indisposed, infirm, poorly, sickly, under the weather *inf*, unwell, weak. 3 (macabre) black, ghoulish, grim, morbid, perverted, sadistic, unhealthy

**sickle** *n* reaping hook; *n* **s.-cell anemia** severe hereditary type of anemia
**side** *n* 1 external or internal surface 2 area 3 space that is to right or left 4 edge, margin 5 team 6 area between ribs and hip in human body; *v* support (person, party, etc); *phr v* **side with** support; act or speak in favor of; *ns* **sideboard** cupboard for dishes, glasses, etc; **sideburns** hair grown in front of man's ears; **s. effect** secondary effect; **sideline** secondary activity; **sideshow** amusement stall at fairground or circus; **sidewalk** pavement; *adj* **sidelong** directed sideways; *adv* **sideways** moving or turned toward one side; *v* **s.-track** divert sb from his/her purpose

A B C D E F G H I J K L M N O P Q R S T U V W X Y Z

**sidereal** *adj* relating to, measured by apparent motion of stars

**sidle** *v* move, walk sideways in sly manner

**siege** *n* besieging of fort or town

**sienna** *n* brownish-yellow earthy pigment

**sierra** *n Sp* mountain chain with jagged ridges

**siesta** *n Sp* short rest, sleep in early afternoon

**sieve** *n* framework of mesh or net for sifting; *v* pass through sieve; sift

**sift** *v* pass through sieve or riddle

**sigh** *v* utter long audible breath; express grief, fatigue by this act; *n* act, sound, of sighing

**sight** *n* 1 faculty of seeing; vision 2 that which is seen 3 device (on gun, etc.) for helping vision 4 view; spectacle; *idm* **a sight for sore eyes** sb/sth one is delighted to see; *idm* **be in sight of** be near to; *idm* **set one's sights on** aim to have or do; *v* **s.-read** *mus* be able to perform at first reading; *n* **s.-seer/seeing** tourist visitor/visiting

**sign** *n* 1 indication 2 board with information on 3 gesture conveying meaning 4 symbol *v* 1 write one's name on 2 ratify 3 indicate by word or gesture; *phr vs* **sign away** give up rights, property by signing document; **sign for** acknowledge receipt by signing; **sign on** 1 register one's name for activity 2 enlist in armed forces; **sign up** enroll; *n* **signpost** post with signs showing direction, distance

> **sign** *n* 1 (indication) clue, evidence, hint, manifestation, mark, proof, suggestion, symptom, token, trace. 2 (board with information on) marker, notice, placard, signpost. 3 (gesture conveying meaning) gesticulation, indication, motion, movement, signal. 4 (symbol) cipher, code, device, emblem, hieroglyph, insignia, logo, mark

**signal** *n* message conveyed to distance; indication, warning of something else; *v* **signalling, signalled** make signal to; send, notify by signals; *adj* remarkable, conspicuous

**signatory** *n* representative of party or state who signs document, treaty, etc

**signature** *n* person's name written by himself; **s. tune** one associated with program or performer on radio, etc

**signet** *n* small seal

**significant** *adj* important; *n* **significance** import; meaning

> **significant** *adj* considerable, meaningful, momentous, noteworthy, of consequence, of note, serious, valuable, weighty

**signify** *v* **signifying, signified** mean

> **signify** *adj* be a sign of, connote, denote, imply, indicate, point to, portend, represent, stand for, suggest, symbolize

**signor, signore** *n* title for Italian man; *fem* **signora** (*married*), **signorina** (*unmarried*)

**Sikh** *n* member of military sect in Punjab

**silence** *n* absence of noise or sound; refraining from speech; *v* cause to be silent

> **silence** *n* calm, hush, lull, peace, quiet, quietness, soundlessness, stillness, tranquillity

**silent** *adj* 1 quiet 2 not speaking

> **silent** *adj* 1 (quiet) calm, hushed, noiseless, peaceful, soundless, still, tranquil. 2 (not speaking) dumb, mum, mute, speechless, taciturn, tight-lipped, tongue-tied, voiceless, wordless

**silhouette** *n* outline, profile, of object seen as dark against light background; *v* show up in outline

**silica** *n* hard, white mineral; *n* **silicon** nonmetallic element; *n* **s. chip** microchip of silicon used in making integrated circuit

**silicone** *n* one of various compounds of silicon and hydrocarbon, used in lubricants, polishes, etc

a b c d e f g h i j k l m n o p q r **s** t u v w x y z

**silk** *n* thread, fabric made from fine filament produced by certain moths; *adj* **silky** glossy, fine, soft to touch; *ns* **silkiness; silkworm** silk-producing caterpillar

**sill** *n* horizontal slab at base of window or door

**silly** *adj* foolish; *n* **silliness**

> **silly** *adj* absurd, brainless, childish, crazy, daft *inf*, fatuous, frivolous, giddy, idiotic, immature, inane, infantile, meaningless, mindless, pointless, puerile, ridiculous, simple-minded, stupid

**silo** *n* pit, tower for fodder or grain; *n* **silage** cattle fodder partly fermented and stored

**silt** *n* sediment, mud, etc deposited by water

**silvan, sylvan** *adj* of woods, forests; rural

**silver** *n* 1 white precious metal element 2 objects made of this 3 coins of silver; *adj* made of, resembling silver; *v* coat with silver; *ns* **s. birch** birch with silvery white bark; **s.-fish** small, wingless insect found in houses; **silversmith** person making or selling articles in silver; **silverware** utensils made of this or similar-colored metal; **s. wedding** 25th anniversary of wedding

**simian** *adj* of, like apes

**similar** *adj* like, resembling

> **similar** *adj* akin, alike, analogous, close, comparable, corresponding, equivalent, matching, parallel, related, the same, uniform

**similarity** *n* likeness

> **similarity** *n* affinity, agreement, closeness, correspondence, equivalence, kinship, match, relation, resemblance, similitude, uniformity

**simile** *n* figure of speech in which one thing is directly compared to another

**similitude** *n* comparison, likeness, similarity

**simmer** *v* 1 boil gently 2 *coll* be in condition of suppressed rage

**simper** *v* smile affectedly; smirk

**simple** *adj* 1 easy 2 without luxury 3 naive; *adj* **s.-minded** showing lack of intelligence; *n* **simplicity** quality, state of being; simple; *adj* **simplistic** treating complex matter as if it were simple (*adv* **-ally**)

> **simple** *adj* 1 (easy) clear, comprehensible, intelligible, lucid, obvious, plain, straightforward, uncomplicated, understandable. 2 (without luxury) austere, basic, classic, modest, natural, plain, pure, restrained, unadorned, unfussy

**simplify** *v* make less complicated; *n* **simplification**

> **simplify** *v* abridge, clarify, cut, make simpler, edit, prune, shorten, streamline

**simulate** *v* imitate; pretend

**simultaneous** *adj* occurring at same time

**sin** *n* breaking of divine law, moral code; *v* **sinning, sinned** commit sin; *adj* **-ful**; *n* **sinner**

**since** *adv* from then until now; *prep* after; *conj* because

**sincere** *adj* genuine and honest; *n* **sincerity**

> **sincere** *adj* candid, earnest, frank, heartfelt, open, real, serious, truthful, unaffected, unfeigned, wholehearted

**sine** *n* perpendicular drawn from one extremity of arc to diameter drawn through other extremity; ratio of this perpendicular to radius of circle

**sinecure** *n* paid office or work with few or no duties

**sine die** *adv leg Lat* without fixed date

**sine qua non** *n Lat* essential thing

**sinew** *n* 1 tendon 2 *pl* **-s** muscles; *adj* **sinewy** muscular

**sing** *v* **singing, sang, sung** 1 utter musical notes 2 (of birds) utter melodic natural cries; *ns* **singer, singing**

**sing** *v* chant, chirp, croon, hum, pipe, serenade, trill, warble, yodel

**singe** *v* **singeing, singed** burn superficially; scorch; *n* slight burn

**single** *adj* 1 one only 2 unmarried 3 for one person 4 separate; *phr v* **single out** select for special attention; *n coll* record, CD with one song (on each side); *pl* **-s** tennis match between two players; *adjs* **s.-breasted** (of jacket) with one row of buttons; **s.-handed** unaided (*adv* **-ly**); **s.-minded** with one clear purpose in mind (*adv* **-ly**; *n* **-ness**); *n, adv* **s. file** in a line one behind the other

> **single** *adj* 1 (one only) distinct, individual, isolated, lone, separate, sole, solitary, singular, unique. 2 (unmarried) bachelor, celibate, free, lone, unattached, unwed

**singlet** *n* sleeveless, loose-fitting top worn by athletes

**singsong** *adj* with repeated rising and falling intonation (*n* such speech)

**singular** *adj* 1 of, relating to one person or thing 2 remarkable; unusual; eminent

**sinister** *adj* evil

> **sinister** *adj* dark, dire, disquieting, forbidding, foreboding, frightening, malevolent, malign, menacing, nefarious, ominous, threatening, villainous

**sink** *v* 1 be, become, submerged in liquid 2 become lower (in value, degree, health, etc); *pt* **sank**; *pp* **sunk**; *phr v* **sink in** become fully understood; *adj* **-ing** (**s. feeling** *coll* feeling of fear or helplessness); *n* kitchen basin

**Sino-** *prefix* Chinese

**sinology** *n* study of Chinese language and culture; *n* **-ologist**

**sinuous** *adj* curving, bending; snakelike

**sinus** *n med* cavity in facial bone; *n* **sinusitis** inflammation of nasal sinus

**sip** *v* **sipping, sipped** drink in very small quantities; *n* very small mouthful of liquid

**siphon** *n* 1 bent tube used for transferring liquid from one level to lower one 2 bottle with tap at top, through which carbonated water is forced by gas pressure; *v* draw off by siphon (*occasionally* **syphon**)

**sir** *n* term of respect for man; title of knight

**sire** *n* form of address to monarch; male parent, *esp* of horse, dog; *v* beget; be sire of

**siren** *n* 1 mythological sea-nymph 2 *fig* alluring woman 3 loud warning hooter or signal

**sirloin** *n* upper part of loin of beef

**sirocco** *n* hot Mediterranean wind

**sisal** *n* fiber of Mexican agave, used for making rope

**sissy** *n coll* effeminate man; timid person

**sister** *n* 1 daughter, woman, born of same parents 2 nun; *adj* closely related, of same type; *adj* **-ly**; *ns* **sisterhood** women's club; community of nuns, etc; **sister-in-law** sister of husband of wife; wife of brother

**sit** *v* 1 rest on buttocks 2 undergo examination 3 pose for portrait 4 fit, hang well 5 (of birds) sit on eggs; *pt, pp* **sat**; *idm* **sit tight** remain where one is; *phr vs* **sit back** relax and do nothing; **sit on** 1 delay action concerning 2 be a member of; **sit up** raise oneself to a sitting position; *n* period of sitting; *ns* **sitting** 1 session of parliament, committee, etc 2 serving of meal; **s. duck** one easy to take advantage of

> **sit** *v* 1 (rest on buttocks) be seated, perch, rest, settle, squat, take a seat. 2 (undergo examination) enter, go in for, take

**sitar** *n* type of Indian lute

**sitcom** *n coll* situation comedy

**site** *n* land where sth takes place

> **site** *n* area, ground, location, place, plot, position, setting, situation, spot

**situate** *v* place somewhere

**situated** *adj* placed, having particular site

**situation** *n* **1** state of affairs **2** place **3** job

> **situation** *n* **1** (circumstances) background, case, condition, position, state of affairs. **2** (place) environment, locale, location, plot, position, setting, site, spot

**six** *n, pron, det* cardinal number one above five; *adj, n, det* **sixth** ordinal number after fifth; *ns, adjs* **sixteen** six and ten; **sixteenth**; **sixty** six times ten; **sixtieth**

**size** *n* standard measure of length, weight, quantity; *v* arrange according to size

> **size** *n* amount, area, capacity, dimensions, expanse, extent, gauge, hugeness, immensity, largeness, magnitude, mass, measurements, proportions, range, scale, scope, vastness, volume

**sizzle** *v* make hissing noise; *n* hissing, spluttering sound, *esp* in frying

**skate**[1] *n* edible flat fish of ray family

**skate**[2] *n* **1** one of pair of steel blades, attached to boot, for gliding over ice **2** roller-skate; *v* move on skates; *n* **skateboard** narrow board on wheels for standing and riding on (*ns* **-er**, **-ing**)

**skein** *n* quantity of wool; flock of wild geese

**skeleton** *n* **1** bony framework of human or animal body **2** outline, draft

**skeptic** *n* one who refuses to accept statement without positive proof

**skeptical** *adj* not inclined to believe sth

> **skeptical** *adj* cynical, disbelieving, distrustful, doubting, dubious, hesitant, incredulous, mistrustful, suspicious, uncertain, unconvinced, unsure

**sketch** *n* **1** rough drawing **2** short play; *v* make sketch of; *adj* **sketchy** depicted in outline; unfinished, inadequate

**skewer** *n* pointed pin of wood or metal for keeping meat in shape; *v* fasten with skewer

**ski** *n* long wooden or fiberglass runner, fastened to foot, for moving over snow; *v* **skiing, skied** use skis for traveling over snow; *n* **skier**

**skid** *v* **skidding, skidded** (of vehicle) slip sideways out of control; *fig* slip and fall

**skiff** *n* small rowing, sculling boat

**skiffle** *n* jazz folkmusic; *n* **s. group** musical group using guitar and improvised percussion instruments

**skillful** *adj* clever, dextrous

> **skillful** *adj* able, accomplished, adept, competent, consummate, deft, efficient, expert, handy, masterful, masterly, nimble, practiced, proficient, quick, trained

**skill** *n* cleverness; *adj* **skilled** skillful; expert; trained in some specific trade, etc

> **skill** *n* ability, adeptness, adroitness, aptitude, artistry, competence, deftness, dexterity, efficiency, expertise, finesse, flair, gift, knack, mastery, proficiency, prowess, talent, technique, workmanship

**skim** *v* **skimming, skimmed 1** remove scum, fat from surface of liquid **2** pass lightly over; *fig* read through (book) rapidly

**skim milk** *n* milk from which fat, cream have been removed

**skimp** *v* supply in too small an amount; *adj* **skimpy** meager; fitting too tightly

**skin** *n* outer covering of human or animal body, fruit, etc; *v* **skinning, skinned** remove skin of; *adjs* **s. deep** superficial; **skinny** thin; **s.-tight** very close fitting; *ns* **s.-flint** miser; **s.-diving** underwater swimming with oxygen tanks

**skip** *v* **skipping, skipped 1** leap lightly **2** jump on spot, while rope passes underneath one **3** omit; not do

**skipper** *n* captain of ship; captain of team

**skirl** *n* shrill, piercing sound of bagpipes

**skirmish** *n* fight between small groups; *v* engage in skirmish

**skirmish** n affray, battle, brush, clash, conflict, confrontation, fight, fracas, fray, incident, mêlée, set-to, spat, tussle

**skirt** n woman's garment hanging below waist; v go around; n **-ing** baseboard running around bottom of walls of room

**skit** n light, satirical, humorous sketch or satire; adj **skittish** playful, lively, frolicsome

**skitter** v move rapidly, lightly

**skivvies** n pl underwear of T-shirt and shorts

**skulduggery** n coll trickery; devious behavior

**skulk** v lurk in concealment; sneak away

**skull** n bony case containing brain of animals; n **s. cap** close-fitting cap

**skunk** n small N American mammal emitting offensive odor when attacked

**sky** n upper part of earth's atmosphere; heaven; pl **skies**; ns **s.-diving** sport involving free-fall from aircraft before using parachute; **skylight** window in roof; **skyline** line in sky formed by buildings, trees on horizon; **skyscraper** very tall city building; adj, adv **s.-high** very high

**skylark** n songbird with soaring flight

**slab** n thick, squarish plate

**slab** n block, chunk, hunk, lump, piece, slice, wedge

**slack** adj 1 loose 2 lazy 3 not busy; n pl **slacks** loose sports trousers; v 1 sag 2 be idle, lazy; v **slacken** abate; diminish; reduce (speed)

**slack** adj (loose) baggy, drooping, droopy, limp, loose, sagging, saggy, soft, relaxed

**slain** pp of **slay**

**slake** v quench

**slalom** n 1 ski-race down zig-zag course 2 any similar race, eg with canoes

**slam** v **slamming, slammed** shut with bang; put down noisily; n loud bang; **grand s.** (cards) taking of all tricks in one deal

**slander** n leg malicious, false spoken statement; v utter such statement

**slanderous** adj saying malicious things

**slanderous** adj damaging, defamatory, disparaging, false, libelous, malicious, scurrilous, untrue, vicious

**slang** n colloquial language

**slant** v slope; n 1 slope 2 coll point of view

**slant** v be at an angle, be skewed, incline, lean, list, slope, tilt

**slap** v **slapping, slapped** smack with open hand; n such blow; adjs **slapdash** careless and hasty; **slaphappy** carefree and irresponsible; n **slapstick** rough knockabout farce or comedy

**slash** v 1 cut violently 2 reduce (prices) abruptly; n 1 long cut; slit 2 act of slashing

**slash** v 1 (cut violently) gash, hack, knife, lacerate, rend, rip, score, slit. 2 (reduce prices) cut, decrease, drop, lower, mark down

**slat** n thin narrow strip of wood; adj **slatted**

**slate** n hard, gray, shale-like rock that splits easily into thin layers; piece of this used for roofing, or writing upon' v 1 cover with slates 2 propose (for office)

**slaughter** n 1 butchering of animals for food 2 massacre; v 1 kill animals for meat 2 massacre; n **slaughterhouse** abattoir

**slaughter** n (massacre) bloodshed, butchery, carnage, extermination, killing, murder

**slave** n 1 one held in bondage to another; drudge 2 one dominated by desire, passion, or devoted to cause, principle; v work like slave; ns **s. driver** person who forces one to work hard; **slavery** bondage; serfdom; adj **slavish** servile

**Slav** adj of the Slavs (also **Slavonic**)

**slay** *v fml* **slaying, slew, slain** kill

**sleaze** *n* dishonest or immoral behavior, *esp* among public figures

**sleazy** *adj coll* sordid, dirty-looking

> **sleazy** *adj* cheap, disreputable, low, seedy, squalid, unwholesome

**sled, sledge** *n* vehicle on runners, for sliding on snow; *v* travel, convey by sledge

**sledgehammer** *n* large heavy hammer

**sleek** *adj* smooth and shiny

> **sleek** *adj* gleaming, glossy, lustrous, satiny, silky, well-groomed

**sleep** *n* natural unconscious state during which dreaming takes place; period during which one sleeps; *v* take rest by sleeping; *pt, pp* **slept**; *phr v* **sleep on sth** postpone decision on sth until next day; *n* **sleepover** children's party at which guests stay the night; *n* **sleeper 1** person who sleeps 2 wooden beam supporting railroad track; *n* **s. bag** bag for sleeping in; *adj* **sleepy**; *adv* **-ily**; *n* **-iness**

> **sleep** *n* catnap, doze, forty winks *inf*, nap, repose, rest, siesta, slumber, snooze
>
> **sleep** *v* be asleep, catnap, doze, drop off *inf*, drowse, fall asleep, nap, nod off *inf*, rest, slumber, snooze, snore

**sleet** *n* mixture of rain and snow falling together; *v* fall as sleet

**sleeve** *n* **1** part of garment which covers arm 2 decorative outer cover of book, CD, etc

**sleigh** *n* sled

**sleight** *n* dexterity, cunning; **s. of hand** conjuring trick, *esp* by substitution

**slender** *adj* **1** thin 2 slight, scanty

> **slender** *adj* (thin) fine, graceful, lean, narrow, slight, slim, svelte, sylph-like, willowy

**slept** *pt, pp* of **sleep**

**sleuth** *n* detective; *v* track by scent; *n* **sleuth hound** bloodhound

**slew** *pt* of **slay**

**slice** *n* **1** flat, thin piece 2 spatula for spreading ink, paint 3 slicing stroke, *esp* in ball games 4 wedge-shaped piece; *v* **1** cut in slices 2 hit ball so that it turns away

> **slice** *n* (flat, thin piece) piece, portion, segment, share, shaving, sliver, wedge

**slick** *adj* **1** smooth, sleek 2 persuasive but not always honest; *v* make smooth or glossy; *n* area of spilled oil floating on water; *n* **slicker 1** slick person; sophisticate 2 raincoat

**slide** *v* glide or move smoothly; *pt, pp* **slid**; *idm* **let sth slide** *coll* let unsatisfactory situation remain or deteriorate even further; *n* **1** act of sliding 2 angled playground toy accessed by ladder

> **slide** *v* coast, plane, skate, skid, skim, slip, slither, veer

**slight** *adj* **1** slim; slender 2 mild; trivial; *idm* **(not) in the slightest** (not) at all; *v* neglect; disregard; *n* act, utterance of disrepect; humiliation

**slightly** *adv* a little bit

> **slightly** *adv* a bit, a little, moderately, somewhat, to a small extent

**slim** *adj* **1** thin 2 small (chance); *v* make thin; reduce weight by diet etc; *n, adj* **slimming** reducing one's weight; *n* **slimmer** person doing this; *adj* **slimline 1** giving slim appearance 2 not fattening; low-calorie

> **slim** *adj* **1** (thin) fine, lean, narrow, slender, slight, svelte, sylph-like, trim, willowy. 2 (small) faint, feeble, flimsy, fragile, frail, remote, slight, tenuous, weak

**slime** n 1 soft wet dirt; liquid mud 2 moisture secreted by snails

**slimy** adj 1 wet and slippery 2 insincerely flattering

> **slimy** adj 1 (wet and slippery) clammy, glutinous, greasy, mucous, muddy, oily, slithery, squishy inf, viscous.
> 2 (insincerely flattering) creepy inf, gushing, obsequious, oily, smooth, sycophantic, unctuous

**sling** n 1 loop of leather, etc for hurling missiles 2 strip of cloth supporting injured limb; v throw; pt, pp **slung**

**slink** v move secretively; pt, pp **slunk**

**slip** v **slipping, slipped** 1 slide 2 miss one's footing 3 pass rapidly; idm **let slip** make known by inadvertent remark; n 1 act of slipping 2 moral lapse 3 petticoat; idm **give sb the slip** escape from or elude sb; ns **slippage** (degree of) slipping; **slipped disk** displacement of cartilage disk between two vertebrae; **s.-stream** 1 air vacuum that forms behind fast moving vehicle 2 air propelled backward by aircraft engines; **s.-up** coll mistake; **slipshod** done without much care and attention

**slipper** n soft indoor shoe

**slippery** adj 1 smooth and difficult to keep a firm hold of 2 elusive

> **slippery** adj (smooth) glassy, greasy, icy, oily, perilous, slimy, wet

**slit** v **slitting, slit** cut open, make incision in; n narrow opening, incision

**slither** v slide slowly along or down

**sliver** n small, narrow piece, cut, torn on anything; splinter

**slob** n sl fool, lout

**slobber** v dribble; n dribbling saliva

**sloe** n bluish-black fruit of blackthorn

**slog** v **slogging, slogged** work hard and persistently; plod heavily; persevere

**slogan** n catchword used in advertising, etc

**slop** v **slopping, slopped** spill; be spilt; overflow; phr v **slop about/around** 1 play around in mud, water, etc 2 move about idly, purposelesssly; n pl dirty water, liquid waste; food waste (garbage) used as animal feed

**slope** n inclined direction or surface; steepness; v be, have inclined (in) surface

> **slope** n angle, ascent, camber, descent, dip, drop, fall, gradient, incline, hill, mountain, pitch, ramp, rise, slant, tilt
> **slope** v dip, drop away, fall, incline, lean, pitch, rise, slant, tilt, tip

**sloppy** adj 1 wet and messy 2 careless in one's work 3 sentimental; adv **-ily**; n **-iness**

**slosh** v (of liquid) move noisily; splash; adj **-ed** coll drunk

**slot** n 1 narrow slit; aperture, esp for insertion of coins 2 niche; v **slotting, slotted** make slot(s) in; phr v **slot in(to)** fit neatly, closely (into)

> **slot** n 1 (slit) aperture, crack, gash, groove, hole, notch, opening, vent. 2 (space in programme) opening, period, place, position, space, spot, time, vacancy

**sloth** n 1 laziness 2 S American mammal

**slouch** n careless, slovenly gait; v walk thus

**slough** phr v **slough off** 1 (of snake) shed skin 2 get rid of sth unwanted

**slovenly** adj untidy in appearance; careless

**slow** adj 1 not quick or fast 2 not quick to learn; v reduce speed; n **-ness**; adv **-ly**

> **slow** adj 1 (not quick) careful, cautious, creeping, dawdling, lazy, leaden, leisurely, lingering, measured, painstaking, ponderous, prolonged, sluggish, snail-like, steady, unhurried, unwilling. 2 (not quick to learn) backward, behind, late, retarded, with special needs
> **slow** v decelerate, ease up inf, go slower, put the brakes on, slow down

**slowworm** n blindworm; limbless lizard

**sludge** n thick, greasy mud

**slug** n 1 land snail with no shell 2 small bullet for airgun, etc; v **slugging, slugged** hit hard; slog; adj **sluggish** slow, inactive, lazy

**sluice** n floodgate; v 1 provide with sluices 2 coll wash down with, splash water over

**slum** n dilapidated, squalid street or area

**slumber** v sleep

**slump** n sudden fall in prices, value, etc; v fall in price, demand

**slur** v **slurring, slurred** pass lightly over; pronounce indistinctly; mus sing, play legato; n act of slurring; stain; stigma

**slurp** v drink noisily; n noise caused by this

**slurry** n mixture of mud, clay, etc with water

**slush** n liquid, soft mud; melting snow; coll sickly sentiment; drivel; n **s. fund** money reserved secretly for dishonest use

**sly** adj cunning; idm **on the sly** secretly

> **sly** adj artful, crafty, deceitful, devious, foxy, furtive, mischievous, scheming, secret, secretive, shifty, shrewd, sneaky, stealthy, surreptitious, tricky, underhand, wily

**smack** n smart explosive sound (of lips); crack of whip; slap; v make such sound; adv 1 sudden 2 exactly

**small** adj 1 not large 2 unimportant 3 not large in amount; n **smallness**; idm **feel small** feel ashamed; ns **s. change** coins; **s.-holding** small plot of agricultural land; **smallpox** acute infectious and contagious disease leaving scars on skin; adjs **s.-minded** petty and mean; **s.-scale** limited in size or extent

> **small** adj 1 (not large) baby, dwarf, little, microscopic, mini, miniature, minute, petite, short, teeny, tiny, undersized, wee, young. 2 (unimportant) inconsequential, insignificant, minor, petty, trivial. 3 (not large in amount) inadequate, insufficient, meager, mean, measly, scanty, stingy

**smarmy** adj coll insincerely polite; flattering

**smart** adj 1 well-dressed 2 clever; v 1 feel sore and painful 2 feel hurt, resentful

> **smart** adj (well-dressed) chic, dapper, dashing inf, elegant, fashionable, neat, snazzy inf, stylish, tidy, well-groomed, well turned-out

**smart card** n credit or debit card with built-in microprocessor to record information on transactions

**smarten** v make, give spruce appearance to; adj **smartly** fashionably, quickly; n **smartness**

**smash** v 1 break to pieces; hit violently 2 defeat utterly; n 1 violent shattering 2 violent collision of vehicles; n **smash hit** coll highly popular song, film, etc

**smashing** adj devastating; coll outstanding; wonderful

**smattering** n slight, superficial knowledge

**smear** n 1 greasy stain 2 coll malicious rumor; n **Pap s,** screening for cervical cancer; v mark with smear; damage by rumor

> **smear** n (greasy stain) blot, blotch, daub, mark, smudge, splotch, spot, stain, streak

**smell** v **smelling, smelt, smelled** 1 perceive, emit odor 2 give off unpleasant odor; stink 3 fig track; discover; idm **smell a rat** coll suspect sth is wrong; n 1 fragrance; 2 unpleasant odor 3 act of smelling

> **smell** v 1 (perceive odor) get a whiff of, scent, sniff out. 2 (give off odor) reek, stink, whiff
> **smell** n 1 (fragrance) aroma, bouquet, odor, perfume, redolence, scent. 2 (unpleasant odor) reek, stench, stink, whiff

**smelt**[1] n small edible silvery fish

**smelt**[2] v extract metal from ore, by heat

**smidgin** n coll tiny amount

**smile** v curve lips in expression of pleasure, amusement; n act of smiling; facial expression showing happiness

> **smile** v beam, grin, laugh, leer, simper, smirk

**smirch** v dirty; stain; disgrace

**smirk** v smile in affected, smug manner; n conceited; knowing smile

**smite** v **smiting, smote, smitten** wound; afflict; affect strongly

**smith** n worker in metal; n **smithy** smith's workshop; forge

**smithereens** n idm **in(to) smithereens** in(to) tiny pieces

**smitten** pp of **smite**; smitten (with) 1 suddenly in love 2 deeply affected by

**smock** n loose outer protective garment, formerly worn by shepherds; v adorn with honeycomb needlework; n **-ing**

**smog** n dense mixture of smoke and fog

**smoke** n fine particles, emitted by burning matter; v 1 emit smoke 2 inhale and expel smoke from burning tobacco 3 cure (fish, etc) by exposing to wood smoke; adj **smoky**

> **smoke** n exhaust, fumes, pollution, smog, steam, vapor

**smolder** v burn slowly without flame

**smooch** v coll cuddle and kiss

**smooth** adj 1 level 2 shiny 3 calm; not moving 4 moving easily; adv **-ly**; n **-ness** v make smooth

> **smooth** adj 1 (level) even, flat, flush, horizontal, plane, unwrinkled. 2 (shiny) burnished, glossy, polished, satiny, silken, silky, sleek, soft, velvety. 3 (calm; not moving) glassy, mirrorlike, peaceful, still, tranquil, unbroken, undisturbed, unruffled. 4 (moving easily) comfortable, easy, effortless, flowing, fluent, fluid, regular, rhythmic, steady

**smorgasbord** n buffet of assorted dishes

**smote** pt of smite

**smother** v 1 suffocate 2 cover thickly 3 suppress

**smudge** n smear, blot; v make smudge

**smug** adj self-satisfied; adv **-ly**

> **smug** adj complacent, conceited, pleased with yourself, priggish, self-important, self-righteous, superior

**smuggle** v 1 import or export (goods) without payment of customs duties 2 convey secretly; n **smuggler**

**smut** n 1 particle of soot 2 obscene talk, writing, etc 3 parasitic fungus; adj **-ty**

**snack** n hasty, light meal; n **snack bar** bar in restaurant where snacks are served

**snaffle** n light bit for horse; v sl steal, pinch

**snag** n fig unexpected obstacle

> **snag** n catch, complication, disadvantage, drawback, hitch, problem, set-back, stumbling block

**snail** n shell-bearing, slow-moving mollusk

**snake** n scaly limbless reptile; serpent; idm **snake in the grass** false friend

**snap** v **snapping, snapped** 1 break suddenly with sharp sound 2 open or close with sharp sound 3 speak sharply; idm **snap out of it** coll throw off bad mood; phr vs **snap at** 1 try to catch in the mouth 2 speak sharply to; **snap up** seize or buy quickly; n 1 act or sound of snapping 2 informal photo 3 card game; adj sudden (**s. judgment**); adj **snappy** 1 hasty 2 impatient 3 coll stylish

**snapdragon** n coll antirrhinum

**snapper** n tropical fish

**snare** n device for catching birds, animals; n **s. drum** type of drum; v catch in snare

**snarl** v growl threateningly; phr vs **snarl up** (n facial expression; sound made in snarling); **snarl-up** (n confusion of traffic; traffic jam)

**snatch**[1] n bit, scrap, or fragment of something

**snatch**[2] v seize, makequick grab at; n 1 act of snatching 2 a lift in weight-lifting

A B C D E F G H I J K L M N O P Q R **S** T U V W X Y Z

**snatch** *v* 1 (seize) catch, clutch, grab, grasp, grip, pluck, pull, take, win, wrench. 2 (kidnap) abduct, hold to ransom, make off with, nab *inf*, steal

**snazzy** *adj coll* stylishly attractive (*adv* **-ily**; *n* **-iness**)
**sneak** *v* 1 creep furtively 2 *sl* inform against; *n* mean, furtive person; tell-tale; *n* **s. preview** opportunity to view before official public opening or premiere; *adj* **sneaky**

**sneak** *v* (creep) cower, lurk, pad, prowl, sidle, skulk, slink, stalk, steal

**sneer** *v* smile, speak scornfully; *n* act of sneering
**sneeze** *v* eject air through nostrils with sudden involuntary noise and spasm
**snick** *n* small, cut, notch; *v* cut thus
**snicker** *v* laugh slyly
**snide** *adj* implying criticism in an indirect, unpleasant way; sneering
**sniff** *v* inhale audibly through nose; *phr vs* **sniff out** *coll* find out (sb/sth secret); **sniff at** express scorn, etc by sniffing
**sniffle** *v* sniff repeatedly; *n* slight cold
**snigger** *n* unpleasant, surreptitious laugh
**snip** *v* **snipping, snipped** cut, clip; *n* 1 short, quick cut 2 *sl* profitable bargain; *n* **snippet** small piece

**snip** *v* crop, dock, nick, notch, prune, shave, trim

**snipe** *n* bird of plover family; *v* shoot at enemy from cover; *n* **sniper**
**snitch** *v coll* 1 inform on 2 steal
**snivel** *v* **snivelling, snivelled** whine peevishly; sniff repeatedly; *n* **snivel**
**snob** *n* one who pretends to be better than he is; one too interested in rank, wealth, etc; *n* **snobbery**
**snobbish** *adj* thinking yourself superior to others

**snobbish** *adj* arrogant, condescending, haughty, hoity-toity, patronizing, pompous, posh *inf*, proud, smug, snobby, snooty *inf*, stuck-up *inf*, superior

**snood** *n* knitted cover for hair
**snooker** *n* game played on billiard table
**snoop** *v sl* pry; peer into
**snooty** *adj coll* snobbish
**snooze** *v* take short, light nap; doze
**snore** *v* breathe heavily, noisily when asleep; *n* act, sound of snoring
**snorkel** *n* breathing tube for underwater swimmers; *v* use this
**snort** *v* make loud noise by drawing air through nostrils
**snot** *n sl* mucus from nose
**snot-nosed** *adj* snooty
**snout** *n* projecting nose of animal
**snow** *n* frozen vapour falling as flakes from sky; *v* fall as snow; *n* **snowball** snow pressed into hard ball (*v* play with snowballs; increase in size rapidly); *ns* **snowdrop** early spring flower; **snowplow** apparatus for clearing snow
**snub** *v* **snubbing, snubbed** rebuff by sneering remark; *n* snubbing
**snuff** *n* powdered tobacco for sniffing; *v* put out (candle); *idm* **snuff it** *coll* die
**snuffle** *n* 1 sniffing noise; *v* 1 make this noise 2 talk through the nose
**snug** *adj* warm and cosy; *n* **snuggle** nestle, lie close to; cuddle

**snug** *adj* comfortable, comfy *inf*, intimate, sheltered, soft

**so** *adv* 1 in such manner; thus 2 to such extent; *conj* 1 therefore 2 **so (that)** in order that; *conj* **so as to** in order to; *n* **so-and-so** 1 unnamed person 2 annoying person; *adj* **so-called** called thus
**soak** *v* steep; drench; wet thoroughly; *phr v* **soak up** absorb; *n* 1 act of soaking 2 *coll* drunkard; *adj* **-ed**

**soaking** *adj* very wet

> **soaking** *adj* drenched, dripping, saturated, soaked, soaked to the skin, sodden, sopping, waterlogged, wringing wet

**soap** *n* substance which cleans and washes; *n* **s.box** improvised stand for public speaking; **s. opera** serialized drama on radio, TV with melodramatic stories; *adj* **soapy**

**soar** *v* fly high; *fig* rise to heights of imagination, etc; *n* **soaring**

**sob** *v* **sobbing, sobbed** cry noisily

**sober** *adj* 1 not drunk 2 not garish 3 serious; *v* make, become sober; *n* **sobriety** state of being sober

**soccer** *n coll abbr* game played on field, by teams kicking ball toward goals

**sociable** *adj* friendly

> **sociable** *adj* affable, companionable, convivial, cordial, extroverted, gregarious, outgoing, social, warm, welcoming

**social** *adj* relating to society; sociable; *ns* **s. climber** person seeking acceptance by higher social class; **s. democrat** person believing in gradual move towards socialism by democratic means; **s. science** subject dealing with study of society; **s. security** government program for economic security, social services; **s. services** local services dealing with public welfare, education, health, etc; **s. work** work in giving aid to people in trouble or need

**socialism** *n* political movement advocating public ownership of means of production; *n* **-ist** member of socialist party

**socialize** *v* mix with other people socially

**society** *n* 1 civilization 2 people 3 club

> **society** *n* 1 (civilization) community, culture. 2 (people) mankind, the community, the public. 3 (club) association, circle, group, league, union

**socioeconomic** *adj* relating to both social and economic aspects

**sociology** *n* social science

**sociopath** *n* psychopath

**sock**[1] *n* short stocking

**sock**[2] *v coll* hit, thrash

**socket** *n* recess into which something fits

**sod** *n* flat piece of turf with roots

**soda** *n also* **soda water** carbonatated water

**sodden** *adj* soaked

**sodium** *n* metallic alkaline element

**sofa** *n* long padded couch with back and arms

**soft** *adj* 1 not hard 2 smooth to touch 3 faint (of light) 4 gentle (of sounds); *adv* **-ly**; *n* **-ness**; **s. drink** non-alcoholic drink; *ns* **s. landing** spacecraft landing without damage; **s. sell** use gentle persuasiion to sell; **s. spot** fond feeling; **s. touch** person easy to persuade or deceive; *adjs* **s.-hearted** kind; **s.-spoken** with gentle voice; *v* **soften** make soft; *phr v* **soften up** 1 weaken 2 render unable to resist

> **soft** *adj* 1 (not hard) doughy, elastic, flexible, gelatinous, gooey, malleable, mushy, plastic, pliable, pulpy, spongy, springy, squashy, supple, tender, yielding. 2 (smooth to touch) downy, feathery, fleecy, fluffy, furry, silky, smooth, velvety. 3 (faint) diffuse, dim, gentle, low, restful, subdued. 4 (gentle) dulcet, faint, hushed, inaudible, low, mellow, murmured, muted, quiet, soothing, subdued, whispered

**softball** *n* game similar to baseball

**softie, softy** *n* weak or sentimental person

**software** *n comput* programs that operate computer

**softwood** *n* wood from coniferous trees that cuts easily

**soggy** *adj* soaked with water, sodden

**soignée** *adj Fr* elegant

**soil**[1] *n* surface earth; land; country

**soil**[2] *v* make, become dirty; tarnish, sully

**soirée** *n Fr* evening party

**sojourn** *v* stay for a time; *n* short visit

**solace** n consolation; v comfort in distress

**solar** adj pertaining to sun; ns **solar plexus** network of nerves in pit of stomach; **solar system** system of planets, comets, asteroids, etc which revolve around the sun

**solarium** n bed with lamps for giving artificial suntan (pl **-ia** or **-iums**)

**sold** pt, pp of **sell**

**solder** n fusible metal alloy used for joining metal; v join with this; n **soldering-iron**

**soldier** n one enlisted in army; v serve as soldier; n **soldiery** soldiers collectively

> **soldier** n commando, fighter, gunner, officer, paratrooper, private, serviceman, servicewoman, warrior

**sole**[1] n 1 under surface of foot; under part of shoe, etc 2 edible marine flatfish; v (of shoes, etc) fit with (new) sole

**sole**[2] adj one and only; single

**solemn** adj serious and formal; n **solemnity**

**solicit** v 1 request earnestly 2 accost (person) for immoral purpose; n **solicitude** anxiety; concern; adj **solicitous** eager, anxious

**solid** adj 1 dense 2 strong 3 not hollow; n solid body of three dimensions; adj **s. state** elec using transistors; n **solidity**; v **solidify** make, become solid; ns **solidification**; **solidarity** unanimity

> **solid** adj 1 (dense) compact, compressed, concrete, firm, hard, impermeable, rigid, thick, unmoving. 2 (strong) durable, robust, sound, stable, sturdy, substantial, well-made

**soliloquy** n talking to oneself; monologue not addressed to anyone; v **soliloquize**

**solitary** adj alone; lonely; n **solitude** state of being alone; loneliness; n **solitaire** 1 single gemstone 2 card game for one

**solo** n mus 1 composition for single voice or instrument 2 fig display, performance by one person 3 card game like whist; pl **-os**; n **soloist**; adj **solo** alone

**solstice** n time of year when earth's orbit makes sun most distant N or S of Equator

**soluble** adj able to be dissolved in liquid

**solution** n 1 answer to problem 2 liquid containing dissolved solid

> **solution** n (answer) clarification, conclusion, explanation, key, result, solving, working out

**solve** v find answer to

> **solve** v clear up, crack inf, explain, figure out, find the solution to, resolve, sort out, unravel

**solvent** adj able to pay debts; n substance that can dissolve sth (n **s. abuse** illegal drug abuse); n **solvency** ability to pay debts

**somber** adj dark, gloomy

**sombrero** n Sp wide-brimmed hat; pl **-os**

**some** pron certain number, not specified; adj unspecified (person, thing, number); n **somebody**; adv **somehow** by means still unknown; n **something** thing not clearly defined; advs **sometimes** now and then; occasionally; **somewhat** rather; **somewhere** in unspecified place

**somersault** v turn, fall head over heels

**somnolent** adj sleepy, drowsy

**son** n male child; n **son-in-law** daughter's husband

**sonar** n apparatus used in locating underwater objects

**sonata** n musical composition

**son et lumière** n Fr outdoor spectacle with music and special flood-lighting

**song** n musical utterance by human voice, or by birds

> **song** n anthem, ballad, carol, ditty, hymn, lullaby, pop song, tune

**sonic** adj of sound; n **s. boom** sound of shock waves set up by aircraft flying through sound barrier

**sonnet** n short poem of fourteen lines

**sonorous** adj deep, resonant

**soon** adv in short time

> **soon** adv any minute now inf, before long, before you know it inf, in a minute, in a moment, in a while, in the near future, quickly, shortly, straightaway

**soot** n black flaky substance produced by burning matter; adj **sooty**; v cover with soot

**soothe** v appease; make calm

**soothsayer** n prophet, diviner

**soppy** adj coll weakly sentimental

**sophisticated** adj worldly-wise; artificial; having latest refinements; n **-ation**

**soporific** n, adj (drug) causing sleep

**soppy** adj Brit sentimental

**soprano** n person with highest singing voice; musical part for this; pl **-os**

**sorbet** n Fr water-ice flavored with fruit

**sorcerer** n wizard, magician; n **sorcery** witchcraft, enchantment

**sordid** adj 1 dirty 2 dishonorable

> **sordid** adj 1 (dirty) dingy, filthy, foul, mean, miserable, seedy, shabby, sleazy, slovenly, squalid, ugly, unpleasant, vile, wretched. 2 (dishonorable) corrupt, disreputable, immoral, mercenary, shabby, unethical

**sore** adj 1 painful 2 upset; n boil; ulcer; n **s.point** painful memory; adv **-ly** very greatly; grievously; n **-ness**

> **sore** adj (painful) aching, angry, bruised, burning, inflamed, irritated, raw, red, sensitive, smarting, tender, wounded

**sorghum** n cereal grown in tropical countries

**sorority** n society of female students

**sorrel** n herb with reddish-brown acrid tasting leaves; adj of this color

**sorrow** n grief; mental pain; regret; v grieve, mourn; adj **-ful**

**sorry** adj 1 regretful 2 unhappy 3 sympathetic

> **sorry** adj 1 (regretful) apologetic, ashamed, contrite, penitent, remorseful, repentant, shamefaced. 2 (unhappy) distressed, grieved, sad, sorrowful, upset. 3 (sympathetic) compassionate, concerned, full of pity, moved, pitying

**sort** n class, kind; idm **out of sorts** coll unwell; idm **sort of** coll rather; v 1 arrange in groups 2 put in order; phr v **sort out** 1 separate from others 2 deal with

> **sort** n brand, breed, family, genre, make, race, species, strain, style, type, variety

**sortie** n Fr attack by besieged troops

**SOS** n international signal of distress

**so-so** adj coll mediocre

**sotto voce** adv in an undertone

**soufflé** n Fr light baked dish made with beaten whites of egg

**sought** pt, pp of **seek**; adj **s.-after** popular

**soul** n 1 spiritual, non material part of man; part thought to be immortal 2 human being 3 quality of decency and sincerity 4 essence (of quality) 5 coll **s. music** type of music; ns **s. mate** person with whom one has deep understanding; **s.-searching** analysis of one's own motives; adjs **soulful** showing deep feeling; **soulless** without emotion

**sound**[1] n noise; v 1 emit noise 2 seem; n **sound barrier** moment when aircraft's speed equals the speed of sound

> **sound** n bang, blare, crash, creak, cry, din, hoot, music, scream, shout, squeak, thud, yelp, voice

**sound**[2] adj 1 healthy; in good condition 2 logical 3 reliable; strong

**sound**[3] v measure depth of (water); phr v **sound out** ascertain views of; n strait; channel; **sound bite** n short extract from an interview, eg with a politician quoted in the media

a
b
c
d
e
f
g
h
i
j
k
l
m
n
o
p
q
r
**s**
t
u
v
w
x
y
z

**soup** n thick or clear liquid food made from meat or vegetables

**soupçon** n Fr a little bit

**sour** adj 1 acid in taste 2 (of milk) bad 3 grumpy; v make, become sour; n **-ness**

> **sour** adj (acid in taste) bitter, lemony, pungent, sharp, tangy, tart, vinegary

**source** n 1 spring 2 starting point; origin

**south** n cardinal point opposite N; region in this direction; adj, adv toward south; adjs **southerly** toward, coming from south; **southern** pertaining to south; n **sou'wester** waterproof hat

**souvenir** n keepsake, memento

**sovereign** n 1 monarch, supreme ruler 2 British gold coin worth £1; adj supreme; efficacious, effectual; n **sovereignty** supreme power or rule

**sow**[1] n fully grown female pig

**sow**[2] v scatter, cast seed on ground; pt **sowed**; pp **sown** or **sowed**; n **sower**

**soy, soya** n species of oil-yielding bean; ns **soy flour** flour made from dried ground soya beans; **soy sauce** dark brown sauce made from soya beans

**spa** n health resort having mineral spring

**space** n 1 area 2 region beyond earth's atmosphere 3 empty place; v place at intervals apart; phr v **space out** leave plenty of room between; ns **spacecraft, spaceship** vehicle designed for travel outside earth's atmosphere; **spaceman** coll astronaut; **s. shuttle** vehicle traveling back and forth between earth and space station; **s. station** large satellite base from which space research can be carried out

> **space** n 1 (area) expanse, volume. 2 (region beyond earth's atmosphere) emptiness, infinity, nothingness, vacuum, void. 3 (empty place) capacity, freedom, leeway, margin, room, scope, spaciousness

**spacious** adj extensive, roomy

**spade** n digging tool with flat blade; card of suit of spades

**spaghetti** n It pasta in long strings

**span** n 1 full distance across 2 space between supports of bridge 3 extreme breadth, esp of birds or aircraft across wings; v **spanning, spanned** stretch across, over

**spangle** n small disk of brilliant metal; sequin

**Spaniard** n Spanish person

**spaniel** n breed of sporting dog

**Spanish** n, adj (language) of Spain

**spank** v slap with open hand

**spanner** n wrench; tool for tightening or loosening nuts and bolts

**spar** v **sparring, sparred** fight

**spare** adj 1 additional 2 meager; thin; lean; n spare part for machine, esp car; v 1 refrain from killing etc; show mercy; give away; do without

> **spare** adj (additional) emergency, extra, free, in reserve, leftover, odd, remaining, surplus, unoccupied, unused, unwanted

**spark** n 1 glowing particle from fire; brief flash of light accompanying electrical discharge 2 fig vitality, life; v emit sparks

**sparkle** v glitter; n brilliance; n **sparkler** small hand-held firework; adj **sparkling** shining; bubbling

> **sparkle** v beam, flash, gleam, glint, glisten, glow, shimmer, shine, twinkle, wink

**sparrow** n small common brown bird

**sparse** adj thinly scattered; scanty; adv **-ly**

> **sparse** adj light, meager, scarce, slight, thin

**spartan** adj austere, hardy, unflinching

**spasm** n involuntary muscular contraction; adj **spasmodic** jerky, intermittent

**spate** n sudden flood of river after rain; fig excessive amount

**spatial** adj pertaining to space

**spatter** v splash drops on; n shower

**spatula** *n* blunt, broad-bladed knife used for mixing paint, and in cooking

**spawn** *n* eggs of fish, frogs; *v* **1** (of fish, etc) lay eggs **2** *fig* generate in mass

**spay** *v* remove ovaries of female animal

**speak** *v* **speaking, spoke, spoken** say words; *n* **speaker** one who delivers, speech, lecture, etc

> **speak** *v* argue, communicate, converse, express yourself, give a lecture, have a chat, have a word, hold forth, pipe up *inf*, recite, say sth, talk, tell sth

**spear** *n* long-shafted weapon with pointed head; *v* pierce, catch with spear

**spearmint** *n* common garden mint

**special** *adj* exceptional, distinctive; *n* **-ist** one devoted to a particular branch of science, art, or profession; *v* **-ize** become expert at one thing; *ns* **-ization, speciality** special product, distinctive feature, etc

> **special** *adj* different, extraordinary, important, momentous, noteworthy, odd, out-of-the-ordinary, peculiar, strange, unique, unmistakable, unusual

**specie** *n* coined money

**species** *n* sort, type; *pl* **species**

**specific** *adj* **1** precise, definite; **2** *med* of or for particular disease (*n* such a remedy); *adv* **-ally**; *v* **specify** state definitely, precisely; *n* **specification** detailed description or statement

**specimen** *n* representative example or sample

**speck** *n* small spot, mark; *adj* **speckled** marked with small spots

**spectacle** *n* show; display; *pl* pair of optical lenses in frame

**spectacular** *adj* very impressive

> **spectacular** *adj* beautiful, breathtaking, dazzling, dramatic, magnificent, sensational, striking

**spectator** *n* onlooker

**specter** *n* ghost, apparition; *adj* **spectral**

**spectrum** *n* series of bands of colored light formed when beam has passed through prism; *pl* **spectra**

**speculate** *v* form theory about; *adj* **speculative** given to guessing; risky

> **speculate** *v* conjecture, consider, hypothesize, make a guess, meditate, muse, reflect, suppose, think, wonder

**sped** *pt, pp of* **speed**

**speech** *n* **1** formal public talk **2** act of speaking; *v* **speechify** make long, tedious speeches; *adj* **speechless** unable to speak

> **speech** *n* **1** (formal public talk) address, discourse, lecture, monologue, oration, sermon, soliloquy, talk. **2** (act of speaking) communication, conversation, dialogue, discussion, talk

**speed** *n* swiftness, velocity; *v* **speeding, sped** or **speeded** move quickly; *ns* **s. hump** or **bump** raised surface across width of road causing traffic to move very slowly; **s. limit** maximum legal speed; *phr v* **speed up** go faster; *n* **speedometer** instrument to show speed of vehicle; *adj* **speedy** rapid; prompt

> **speed** *n* briskness, haste, hurry, pace, quickness, rapidity, rate, speediness, tempo
> **speed** *v* **1** career, dash, flash, fly, gallop, hurtle, race, rush, scamper, sprint, streak, tear, whizz, zoom. **2** (speed up) accelerate, gather momentum, hurry up, increase speed, put your foot down *inf*, step on it

**spell**[1] *n* magic formula; *adj* **spellbound** entranced

**spell**[2] *n* bout, short period of activity

**spell**[3] *v* **spelling, spelled** say or write letter by letter; *phr v* **spell out** explain in more detail; *n* **spelling** way in which word is spelled

**spend** *v* **1** pay out **2** pass (time); *pt, pp* **spent**

> **spend** *v* **1** (pay out) fork out, fritter away, shell out, splurge, squander, use up.
> **2** (pass time) fill, occupy, while away

**sperm** *n* **1** male fertilizing fluid (*also* **semen**) **2** single male reproductive cell; *n* **spermicide** substance that kills sperm
**spew** *v* vomit
**sphere** *n* **1** ball, globe **2** scope, range, status; *adj* **spherical**
**spice** *n* aromatic pungent vegetable seasoning; *fig* that which adds interest or excitement
**spick and span** *adj* bright, fresh, tidy
**spicy** *adj* flavored with spices

> **spicy** *adj* aromatic, flavorsome, fragrant, highly flavored, hot, peppery, pungent, seasoned, sharp, well-seasoned

**spider** *n* small eight-legged animal, which spins web to catch prey; *adj* **spidery**
**spiel** *n coll* long voluble impressive speech
**spike** *n* **1** sharp pointed piece of metal, wood etc **2** ear (of corn, etc); *pl* **-s** athlete's running shoes; *v* **1** impale **2** *coll* make (drink) strong by adding alcohol to it
**spill** *v* **spilling, spilt,** or **spilled 1** cause liquid to flow out **2** tip out **3** (of liquid) flow out

> **spill** *v* **1** (cause liquid to flow out) knock over, overturn, slop, splash, tip over, upset. **2** (tip out) drop, scatter, shed, upset. **3** (flow out) brim over, discharge, disgorge, overflow, pour, slop over, spill over

**spin** *v* **spinning, spun 1** turn raound and around **2** twist wool into thread; *n* act of spinning; twist; whirl; *ns* **spin doctor** person who puts a positive slant on events on behalf of a political party or politician; **spinning** process of forming thread; **s.-off** additional indirect benefit

> **spin** *v* (turn round and round) circle, gyrate, pirouette, reel, revolve, rotate, swivel, turn, twirl, twist, wheel, whirl

**spina bifida** *n med* malformation of spine which leaves spinal cord partly exposed
**spinach** *n* green vegetable with edible leaves
**spinal** *adj* of the spine; *n* **s. cord** thick cluster of nerves enclosed within the spine
**spindle** *n* rod, axis on which anything rotates; *adj* **spindly** long and slender
**spine** *n* backbone; thin, sharp thorn, or growth on animal; back of book; *adjs* **s. chilling** terrifying; **spineless 1** without backbone **2** *fig* weak, cowardly; **spiny** prickly
**spinet** *n Fr* keyboard instrument
**spinney** *n* small wood or thicket
**spinster** *n* unmarried woman
**spiral** *adj* winding constantly about center, like thread of screw; *n* spiral curve
**spire** *n* pointed part of steeple
**spirit** *n* **1** ghost **2** courage **3** characteristic quality of sth **4** intended meaning **5** distilled alcohol **6** liveliness **7** soul; *n* **s. level** tool used by builder for checking whether surfaces are level; *adjs* **-ed** lively (*adv* **-ly**; *n* **-ness**); *phr v* **spirit away** remove secretly; *adj* **spiritual** pertaining to soul or spirit, not material (*n, adj* **-ist**); *n* **spiritualism** belief that spirits of dead can communicate with living

> **spirit** *n* **1** (ghost) apparition, phantom, poltergeist, specter, vision. **2** (courage) attitude, bravery, determination, enthusiasm, guts, mettle, optimism, pluck, resolution, vigor, willpower

**spit**[1] *n* sharp rod for roasting meat on; sandy point projecting into sea; *v* thrust through
**spit**[2] *v* **spitting, spat** eject saliva; *n* saliva; *ns* **spittle** saliva; **spittoon** vessel to spit into
**spite** *n* malice; *v* act maliciously towards; *prep* **in spite of** notwithstanding

**spite** *n* animosity, bitterness, envy, hate, hatred, ill-feeling, maliciousness, resentment, spitefulness, vindictiveness

**spiteful** *adj* full of spite

**spiteful** *adj* catty, cruel, cutting, hurtful, ill-natured, malevolent, malicious, snide, venomous, vicious, vindictive

**spitting image** *n* exact likeness
**splash** *v* 1 scatter (liquid) on 2 fall in drops on; *n* 1 sound of, result of splashing 2 impressive effect
**splatter** *v* 1 splash noisily 2 cover with splashes
**splay** *v* spread apart
**spleen** *n* ductless gland in abdomen
**splendid** *adj* magnificent, excellent; *n* **splendor** brilliance; magnificence

**splendid** *adj* admirable, beautiful, dazzling, elegant, fantastic, fine, glorious, gorgeous, grand, great, heroic, impressive, lavish, marvelous, outstanding, rich, sublime, sumpuous, superb, wonderful

**splice** *v* join by interweaving strands
**splint** *n* rigid piece of wood, etc, *esp* when keeping fractured bone in place; *v* support with splint; *n* **splinter** small, sharp broken off piece of wood, glass etc; *n* **s. group** group separated from main body; *v* break into fragments
**split** *v* **splitting, split** 1 break 2 divide into parts 3 share; *n* hole; tear

**split** *v* 1 (break) burst, crack, disintegrate, rip, separate, snap, splinter. 2 (divide into parts) bisect, break, chop, cleave, cut, rip, separate, slash, slice, slit, tear
**split** *n* breach, cleft, crack, division, fissure, gap, gash, opening, rip, slash, slit

**splotch** *n* blot or stain

**splurge** *n* ostentation
**splutter** *v* spit slightly while speaking; utter indistinctly
**spoil** *v* **spoiling, spoilt** or **spoiled** 1 damage 2 cause (a child) to become selfish, badly-behaved by over-indulgence; *n pl* **-s** 1 booty; stolen goods 2 profits; *n* **spoil sport** one who prevents others from enjoying themselves

**spoil** *v* 1 (damage) blemish, blight, deface, destroy, disfigure, harm, impair, injure, mar, mess up, ruin, undermine, undo, upset, wreck. 2 (spoil a child) baby, coddle, cosset, indulge, make a fuss of, mollycoddle, overindulge, pamper

**spoke**[1] *n* radial bar of wheel
**spoke**[2] *pt* **spoken** *pp* of **speak**
**spokesperson** *n* person chosen to represent views of group (*also* **spokesman** *pl* **-men**; **spokeswoman** *pl* **-women**)
**sponge** *n* 1 marine animal whose fibrous skeleton is used to absorb liquids, or for cleaning 2 light cake; *v* clean with sponge; *phr v* **sponge off/on sb** live at sb's expense (*n* **sponger**); *adj* **spongy** soft but resilient; having texture of sponge
**sponsor** *n* guarantor; patron
**spontaneous** *adj* done or doing things without thought; *n* **spontaneity**

**spontaneous** *adj* automatic, impromptu, impulsive, instinctive, reflex, spur-of-the-moment, unhesitating, unplanned, unrehearsed, voluntary

**spoof** *n*, *v* hoax; *n* amusing untrue copy
**spook** *n* ghost, wraith
**spooky** *adj coll* ghostly
**spool** *n* reel, bobbin
**spoon** *n* implement consisting of shallow bowl on handle, used for conveying food to mouth etc; *v* lift with spoon
**spoor** *n* track of wild animal
**sporadic** *adj* occurring in single cases

a
b
c
d
e
f
g
h
i
j
k
l
m
n
o
p
q
r
**s**
t
u
v
w
x
y
z

**sporadic** *adj* erratic, every now and then, intermittent, irregular, occasional, on and off, patchy, periodic, random, scattered, spasmodic

**spore** *n* minute reproductive organism, of flowerless plant, or as in bacteria

**sporran** *n* leather pouch worn in front of kilt

**sport** *n* 1 physical activity, *esp* outdoor, for exercise or amusement 2 particular form of this; game with set rules 3 fun 4 *coll* fairminded person with sense of fun; *adj* **sporting** 1 relating to sport 2 fond of sport 3 fair and generous; *ns* **sportscar** low fast car; **sportsman** (*pl* **-men**; *n* **-manship** respect for fairness in competing); **sportswoman** (*pl* **-women**)

**sporty** *adj* fond of, good at sport

**sporty** *adj* active, athletic, energetic, fit, healthy, muscular, outdoor

**spot** *n* 1 small mark on skin 2 small mark 3 place; *idm* **put on the spot** 1 force to act 2 cause embarrassment; *ns* **s. check** random check without warning; *v* **spotting, spotted** mark with spot; *coll* see; **spotlight** strong beam of light able to be focused on one spot; *adjs* **spotted** decorated with spots; **spotless** 1 without blemish 2 perfectly clean; **spotty** with pimples

**spot** *n* 1 (small mark on skin) blackhead, freckle, mole, pimple, pockmark, pustule, rash, whitehead, zit. 2 (small mark) blob, blotch, dot, drop, fleck, patch, speck, splash, stain. 3 (place) area, location, position, site, situation

**spouse** *n* husband or wife

**spout** *v* gush, pour out; *n* projecting lip or tube for pouring liquid; gushing jet of liquid

**sprain** *v, n* twist or wrench (of muscles, tendons, etc)

**sprat** *n* heringlike fish

**sprawl** *v* lie, be stretched out awkwardly

**spray** *n* fine droplets of liquid; wind-blown particles of sea-water; atomizer; device for spraying; *v* squirt, treat, with spray; become spray; *n* **sprayer** device for spraying

**spread** *v* 1 extend 2 increase; *pt, pp* **spread**; *n* 1 extent 2 increase 3 feast; *n* **spreadsheet** *comput* program for displaying rows of figures, *esp* in accounting

**spread** *v* 1 (extend) expand, fan out, open out, reach, sprawl, stretch. 2 (increase) broaden, develop, disperse, distribute, expand, get bigger, grow, multiply, mushroom, proliferate, swell

**spree** *n* drinking or spending bout

**sprig** *n* small twig; small nail; scion; *adj* **sprigged** ornamented with spray-like design

**sprightly** *adj* lively; *n* **sprightliness**

**spring** *v* 1 leap 2 pounce 3 bubble, gush forth 4 sprout up; *pt* **sprang**; *pp* **sprung**; *idm* **spring a leak** (of container) begin to let liquid escape; *phr v* **spring sth on sb** surprise sb with sth; *n* 1 season after winter 2 natural source of running water 3 coiled or bent length of resilient metal 4 elasticity 5 leap; *ns* **s. onion** small onion eaten raw in salad; **s. tide** strong tide occurring at time of full or new moon; *v* **s. clean** clean (house, etc) very thoroughly

**springbok** *n* S African gazelle

**sprinkle** *v* scatter in small drops; *ns* **sprinkler**; **sprinkling** small quantity of drops; few scattered people or objects

**sprinkle** *v* dribble, drizzle, pepper, scatter, shower, spatter, spray, strew

**sprint** *v* run at full speed; *n* such run; *n* **-er**

**sprite** *n* fairy, elf

**sprocket** *n* projecting tooth on wheel for engaging chain

**sprout** *v* begin to grow; *n* young shoot; *n pl* **Brussels sprouts** vegetable like miniature cabbages

**sprout** *v* come into bud, come up, germinate, grow, put out shoots, shoot

**spruce**[1] *n* type of coniferous tree

**spruce**[2] *adj* clean and neat; *phr v* **spruce up** make (oneself) clean, neat

**sprung** *pp of* **spring**

**spry** *adj* nimble, agile, alert

**spud** *n sl* potato

**spume** *n, v* foam, froth

**spun** *pt, pp of* **spin**

**spur** *n* 1 pricking wheel fixed on horseman's heel, for urging on horse 2 pointed projection on cock's leg 3 projecting ridge or part of mountain range 4 stimulus; *idm* **on the spur of the moment** without forethought; *v* **spurring, spurred** prick with spurs; urge into action

**spurious** *adj* not genuine

**spurious** *adj* artificial, bogus, false, insincere, mock, phony, pretended, pseudo, sham

**spurn** *v* reject scornfully

**spurt** *n* jet; short vigorous effort, *esp* in race; *v* gush out suddenly

**sputnik** *n* (Russian) satellite

**sputter** *v* make series of spitting noises

**sputum** *n* saliva, spittle

**spy** *n* agent employed to obtain secret information; *v* **spying, spied** act as spy; catch sight of

**spy** *n* double agent, foreign agent, informer, member of the secret service, mole *inf*, 007 *inf*, secret agent, snooper, undercover agent

**sq** *abbr* square

**squabble** *n* petty quarrel; *v* quarrel, bicker

**squad** *n* group of people working together

**squadron** *n* body of cavalry

**squalid** *adj* foul, sordid; *n* **squalor**

**squall** *n* 1 harsh shriek 2 brief, violent storm

**squander** *v* spend, use wastefully

**square** *n* 1 shape with four straight sides of equal length 2 open space in a town 3 product of number multiplied by itself; *adj* 1 of the shape of a square 2 having settled all debts (mutually); *v* 1 multiply (number) by itself 2 get cooperation of; *ns* **s. meal** *coll* meal that satisfies hunger; **s. root** number which when squared gives specified number

**squash** *v* crush; *n* 1 pulpy mass 2 game for two, played with rackets and soft ball in walled court 3 edible vegetable

**squash** *v* compress, flatten, mash, pound, press, pulp, pulverize, squeeze

**squat** *v* **sqatting, squatted** sit on heels; *adj* short and thick; *n* **squatter** illegal settler in unoccupied house or land

**squawk** *n* loud, harsh cry; *v* utter such cry

**squeak** *v* utter high, thin cry; make high, grating noise; *n* such noise

**squeak** *v* cheep, cry, peep, pipe, scream, screech, shrill, squeal, yelp

**squeal** *v* utter shrill prolonged cry; *sl* betray secrets; *n* long shrill cry

**squeamish** *adj* oversensitive

**squeegee** *n* rubber wiper for cleaning glass

**squeeze** *v* 1 press hard 2 force into small place; *n* act of squeezing

**squeeze** *v* 1 (press) clasp, compress, crush, grip, nip, pinch, pulp, squash, twist, wring. 2 (force into small place) cram, crowd, force, jam, pack, ram, squash, stuff, wedge

**squelch** *v* produce sucking, gurgling sound

**squid** *n* cuttlefish

**squiggle** *n* twisty illegible writing; *v* wriggle; squirm

**squint** *v* look in different directions with each eye; *n* problem with eye causing this

**squire** *n* county landowner

**squirm** *v, n* wriggle, writhe

**squirrel** *n* small bushy-tailed rodent

a
b
c
d
e
f
g
h
i
j
k
l
m
n
o
p
q
r
**s**
t
u
v
w
x
y
z

**squirt** *v* eject, be forced out, in jet; *n* jet (of liquid); syringe

**St** *abbr* Saint

**stab** *v* **stabbing, stabbed** pierce with pointed weapon; *n* wound so inflicted; *idm* **have a stab (at)** *coll* make an attempt (at); *idm* **stab in the back** act of betrayal; *adj* **stabbing** (of pain) sharp

> **stab** *v* cut, gash, gore, jab, knife, pierce, run through, skewer, slash, spear, spike

**stability** *n* steadiness, firmness

> **stability** *n* equilibrium, permanence, reliability, security, solidity, soundness, strength

**stabilize** *v* make stable; *n* **stabilizer** device for keeping ship, aircraft, etc in equilibrium

**stable** *adj* firmly fixed; not easily upset

> **stable** *adj* balanced, constant, firm, lasting, on a firm footing, permanent, reliable, secure, solid, sound, steadfast, steady, sturdy, unchanging, well founded

**stable** *n* building where horses are kept

**staccato** *adj mus* with each note played in sharply detached manner

**stack** *n* 1 large heap, *esp* of hay, straw 2 neat pile 3 tall chimney; *pl* **-s** *coll* large amount; *v* pile up neatly

**stadium** *n* open-air arena for athletics, etc; *pl* **-iums or -ia**

**staff** *n* tall pole; organized body of workers; servants of one employer

**stag** *n* male deer; *adj coll* for men only, as **s. party**

**stage** *n* 1 raised platform in theatere 2 scene of action 3 point of development; *ns* **s. coach** (formerly) horse-drawn public vehicle; **s. fright** nervousness felt when appearing in public; *adj* **s.-struck** ambitious to become actor; *v* 1 put (play) on stage 2 cause to happen, *esp* to create effect

> **stage** *n* 1 (raised platform) dais, platform, podium, proscenium, rostrum. 2 (point of development) juncture, lap, leg, level, phase, point, step

**stagger** *v* walk unsteadily; shock; prevent from coinciding; *n* unsteady gait

**stagnant** *adj* (of water) not flowing; stale

**stagnate** *v* be or become stagnant (*n* **-ation**)

**stagy** *adj* theatrical, exaggerated

**staid** *adj* sedate; sober; steady

**stain** *v* 1 leave dirty marks on 2 damage reputation; *n* dirty mark; *n* **stained glass** colored glass for decorative windows; *adj* **stainless** resistant to rust (*n* **s. steel**)

> **stain** *v* (leave dirty marks on) dirty, discolor, make dirty, mark, splash, spot
> **stain** *n* blotch, discoloration, mark, spot

**stairs** *n pl* series of steps, *usu* in building; *ns* **staircase, stairway** flight of stairs

**stake** *n* 1 pointed stick or post 2 prize 3 money bet 4 financial interest; *idm* **at stake** at risk; *v* bet; risk; *idm* **stake a claim** claim ownership

**stalactite** *n* tapering lime formation hanging from roof of cave, etc; *n* **stalagmite** similar formation rising from cave floor

**stale** *adj* 1 not fresh 2 no longer interesting or interested

> **stale** *adj* 1 (not fresh) dry, hard, musty, off, old, sour. 2 (no longer interesting or interested) clichéd, dull, hackneyed, jaded, tedious, tired, worn-out

**stalemate** *n* 1 chess position in which neither player can win 2 *fig* deadlock

**stalk**[1] *v* stem of plant

**stalk**[2] *v* pursue (prey, game, etc) stealthily; *n* **stalker**

**stall** *n* 1 division in stable 2 booth in market 3 front seat in theater; *v* unintentionally stop (engine); delay

**stallion** n uncastrated male horse

**stalwart** adj strong, brave, unflinching

**stamen** n pollen-bearing male organ of flower

**stamina** n strength to continue

> **stamina** n dynamism, endurance, energy, fortitude, resilience, strength, vigor

**stammer** v speak hesitantly, with repetition of speech sounds; n this speech defect

**stamp** v 1 put foot down heavily 2 affix postage stamp 3 impress mark on; phr v **stamp out** fig destroy utterly; n 1 act of stamping 2 imprinted mark, or instrument making it 3 gummed label used as evidence of postage paid

**stampede** n sudden frightened rush of animals, crowd, etc; v flee in panic

**stance** n attitude in standing; opinion

**stand** v **standing, stood** 1 put somewhere in upright position 2 move to upright position; be in upright position 3 be located 4 tolerate 5 remain in force 6 treat sb else to; pay for; idm **stand a chance** have some hope or prospect; phr vs **stand back** refrain from taking part; **stand by** 1 remain loyal to 2 be ready to act; idm **on standby** ready for action; **stand down** 1 resign 2 leg leave witness box; **stand for** 1 represent 2 be strongly in favor of; support; **stand in (for sb)** be a substitute (for sb); **stand out** 1 be clearly seen 2 be different in quality; **stand up** (of evidence) be convincing; **stand sb up** fail to keep a date with sb; **stand up for** support; **stand up to** resist; n **standing**; adj erect, lasting; ns **standpoint** position, repute; point of view; **standstill** complete cessation of progress, etc

> **stand** v 1 (put) erect, lean, place, position, set. 2 (move to upright position) get to your feet, get up, rise. 3 (be located) be, be found at, be situated, lie, sit. 4 (tolerate) abide, bear, cope with, endure, handle, put up with, stomach, take, withstand

**standard** n 1 model to measure things by 2 flag; n **s. of living** level of material comfort and wealth; v **-ize** make so as to conform with single standard (n **-ization**)

> **standard** n (model) benchmark, criterion, example, guideline, ideal, level, measure, norm, principle, quality, requirement, specification, yardstick

**standing** n 1 rank 2 reputation; idm **of long standing** well established; n **s. order** order for regular deliveries

**stank** pt of **stink**

**stanza** n group of verse-lines

**staple** n 1 U-shaped piece of metal with pointed ends, for fastening 2 basic food or raw material; v fasten with staple; n **stapler** stapling machine

**star** n 1 luminous heavenly body 2 figure, device resembling apparent shape of star 3 famous person 4 asterisk (*); ns **s.sign** any one of 12 signs of the zodiac; **s. turn** item in entertainment causing greatest attraction; adjs **s.-crossed** ill-fated; **s. studded** with many famous performers; v **starring, starred** 1 play a main role 2 mark with stars; ns **stardom** state of being famous; **starfish** flat star-shaped fish; adj **starry** full of stars (adj **s.-eyed** enthusiastic but unrealistic)

> **star** n (famous person) celebrity, film star, leading actor, leading light, name, personality, pop star, rock star, superstar

**starboard** n right-hand side of ship

**starch** n 1 carbohydrates, main food element in vegetables 2 white powder mixed with water for stiffening linen, etc; adj **starchy** containing starch; too formal

**stare** v look, gaze at intently; n long look

> **stare** v gape, gawp, gaze, glare, look, peer, scrutinize, watch

a b c d e f g h i j k l m n o p q r **s** t u v w x y z

427

A
B
C
D
E
F
G
H
I
J
K
L
M
N
O
P
Q
R
**S**
T
U
V
W
X
Y
Z

**stark** *adj* stiff; rigid; absolute; *adv* absolutely
**starkers** *adj coll* completely naked
**starling** *n* gregarious glossy black bird
**start** *v* 1 begin doing 2 create 3 begin
happening 4 set out 5 set in motion 6 jump;
*n* 1 beginning 2 advantage 3 sudden jerk

> **start** *v* 1 (begin doing) commence, get
> cracking, get going, kick off, make a
> start, set the ball rolling, set out, take the
> plunge. 2 (create) establish, form, found,
> get off the ground, inaugurate, initiate,
> instigate, introduce, launch, open,
> pioneer, set up, start up, trigger. 3 (begin
> happening) appear, arise, come into
> being, start up. 4 (set out) depart, get
> going, get under way, leave, push off, set
> off. 5 (set in motion) activate, boot, get
> going, start up, switch on, turn on
> **start** *n* (beginning) birth, commencement,
> creation, dawn, early stages, foundation,
> inception, introduction, launch, onset,
> opening, origin, outset, root, source

**startle** *v* alarm, shock, surprise
**starve** *v* die, suffer, from lack of food; suffer
from cold; *ns* **starvling** thin, underfed
person or thing; **starvation**
**stash** *v* hide; store away (*also n*)
**state** *n* 1 condition 2 predicament 3 nation
and its government; *v* **state** express in
words; *adj* **stateless** having no citizenship
of any country

> **state** *n* 1 (condition) circumstances, mode,
> position, shape, situation, status.
> 2 (predicament) chaos, condition, fluster,
> frame of mind, mess, mood, panic, plight,
> tizzy. 3 (nation) country, kingdom, land,
> republic, territory

**stately** *adj* dignified, imposing; *n* **s. home**
large historical house or estate
**statement** *n* 1 formal declaration (oral or
written) 2 summary of financial transactions,
showing present state of account

**statement** *n* (formal declaration) account,
announcement, assertion, bulletin,
comment, communiqué, disclosure,
explanation, press release, proclamation,
report, testimony

**statesman** *n* person skilled in management of
state affairs (*pl* **-men**); *adj* **-like**; *n* **-ship**
**static** *adj* not moving; **s. electricity**
electricity that accumulates in an object
**station** *n* 1 place, position where thing stops
2 walk in life; *v* place in specific spot
**stationary** *adj* not moving

> **stationary** *adj* at a standstill, fixed, moored,
> motionless, parked, standing, static, still,
> stockstill, unmoving

**stationery** *n* writing materials; *n* **stationer**
dealer in writing materials
**statistics** *n pl* systematic collection and
arrangement of numerical facts; study of
these; *n* **statistician** one skilled in dealing
with statistics; *adj* **statistic(al)**
**statue** *n* carved or molded figure
**stature** *n* bodily, height, size
**status** *n* 1 legal or social position 2 high
social position; *n* **s. quo** present or original
state of affairs
**statute** *n* law enancted by legislative branch
of government
**staunch** *v* stop flow (of blood); *adj* loyal

> **staunch** *adj* faithful, firm, steadfast, strong,
> true, unswerving

**stave** *v pt, pp* **stove** or **staved**; *phr vs* **stave
in** smash a hole in
**stay**[1] *n* prop; strut; rope supporting mast, etc;
*pl* corsets; *v* support, sustain
**stay**[2] *v* 1 remain 2 prevent; *n leg* stopping of
proceedings; *n* **staying power** stamina

> **stay** *v* (remain) hang on, linger, wait

**St. Bernard** n big powerful dog often used in mountain rescue

**std** abbr standard

**stead** n **in (one's) stead** in place of

**steady** adj 1 firm 2 regular 3 reliable; v make, become steady; adj **steadfast** unwavering, resolute; n **steadiness**

> **steady** adj 1 (firm) balanced, safe, secure, solid, stable, still, sure. 2 (regular) consistent, constant, continuous, even, nonstop, perpetual, rhythmic, round-the-clock, unbroken, unfaltering, uniform, uninterrupted, unvarying

**steak** n thick slice of meat or fish

**steal** v **stealing, stole, stolen** 1 take without permission 2 move silently

> **steal** v (take without permission) burglarize, embezzle, hijack, lift, misappropriate, nick, pilfer, pinch, pirate, poach, pocket, rob, shoplift, snatch, swipe, take, walk off with

**stealth** n secret, furtive action; adj -y

**steam** n water vapor; v cook, treat with steam; give off steam; idm **run out of steam** become exhausted; ns **steam engine** one worked or propelled by steam; **s.-roller** heavy roller for leveling roads; adjs **steamed-up** coll angry; **steaming** very hot; **steamy** 1 full of steam 2 coll erotic

**steed** n poetic horse

**steel** n iron containing carbon; tool, weapon of steel; ns **s. band** Caribbean band of steel drums made from empty oil containers; **s. wool** pad of steel strands used as scourer; v fig harden; adj **steely**

**steep**[1] adj 1 sharply inclined 2 too expensive

> **steep** adj (sharply inclined) abrupt, perpendicular, precipitous, sheer, sudden, vertical

**steep**[2] v soak, saturate; fig imbue

**steeple** n tall tapering structure on church; ns **steeplechase** cross-country horse race; **steeplejack** man employed to repair, clean steeples, tall chimney, etc

**steer**[1] v guide, direct course of (car, ship, etc); aim one's course

**steer**[2] n young ox, bullock

**stellar** adj of stars

**stem**[1] n 1 stalk; trunk 2 part of word to which inflectional endings are added; phr v **stemming, stemmed, stem from** be a result of

**stem**[2] v check flow of; resist

**Sten gun** n British light submachine gun

**stench** n offensive smell

**stencil** n thin plate of metal, etc perforated with design, or letters; pattern, design produced by applying coloring matter through holes of stencil plate; v decorate, make copy of, by using stencil

**step** v **stepping, stepped** lift and set down foot; walk; idm **in/out of step** moving one's feet in/out of line with the rest of the group; idm **step by step** gradually; phr vs **step aside** make way for sb else; **step down** resign; **step in** intervene; **step up** increase; n **stepping-stone** 1 stone laid on bed of river enabling one to cross on foot 2 fig stage in progress towards objective

> **step** n footfall, footstep, gait, pace, print, stride, tramp, tread, walk

**stepchild** n child of husband or wife by previous marriage; ns **stepfather, stepmother**

**steppe** n broad, open, treeless plain in Russia

**stereophonic** adj (of sound) giving effect of live sound, coming from many directions

**stereotype** n fixed set of ideas or expectations about a certain type of person or thing; adj **stereotypical**

**sterile** adj 1 free from germs 2 barren; n **sterility**; v **sterilize** make incapable of reproduction; destroy bacteria; n **sterilization**

a
b
c
d
e
f
g
h
i
j
k
l
m
n
o
p
q
r
**s**
t
u
v
w
x
y
z

**sterile** adj 1 (free from germs) antiseptic, aseptic, clean, disinfected, hygienic, pure, spotless, sterilized, uncontaminated. 2 (barren) infertile, sterilized, unproductive

**sterling** n British currency
**stern** adj severe, strict; n **sternness**
**stern** n after part of ship
**sternum** n breast bone; pl **-nums** or **-na**
**steroid** n chem type of medicinal drug
**stethoscope** n instrument for listening to action of heart or lungs
**stew** v cook slowly in closed vessel; n food so cooked; coll agitated condition
**steward** n catering manager; waiter; attendant; fem **-ess**
**stick**[1] n slender rod of wood

**stick** n baton, branch, cane, crook, pole, staff, stake, twig, walking stick, wand

**stick**[2] v 1 thrust into, stab 2 attach; adhere 3 coll bear bravely; pt, pp **stuck**; phr vs **stick by/with** remain loyal to; **stick out** (cause to) protrude; **stick to** 1 adhere to 2 refuse to change; **stick up** project upward; **stick up for** defend; n **sticker** adhesive label
**stickleback** n small fierce spiny-backed fish
**stickler** n one who insists on trivial points
**sticks** n pl **the s.** rural area far from big cities
**sticky** adj 1 glue-like 2 coll difficult (n **-iness**)

**sticky** adj (glue-like) adhesive, glutinous, gooey, gummed, self-adhesive, viscous

**stiff** adj 1 not moving easily 2 difficult 3 formal; idm **stiff upper lip** ability not to show fear or any other emotion; v **stiffen** make, become, stiff

**stiff** adj (not moving easily) arthritic, firm, hard, rheumatic, rigid, solid, solidified, taut, tense, unbending

**stifle** v smother
**stigma** n moral reproach; v **stigmatize** mark out (something discreditable)
**stile** n steps, rail for climbing hedge or fence
**stiletto heel** n thin high heel of woman's shoe
**still** adj 1 motionless; silent 2 (of drinks) not sparkling; v calm; quieten; n **-ness**; adj **stillborn** born dead; n **s. life** picture of inanimate objects

**still** adj (motionless, silent) at rest, calm, flat, peaceful, quiet, serene, stagnant, static, stationary, tranquil, undisturbed

**stilt** n (usu pl) pole with foot rests, for raising walker above ground
**Stilton** n strong-flavored English cheese with blue veins
**stimulus** n anything which excites action; incentive; pl **stimuli**; v **stimulate** rouse up; urge, incite; n, adj **stimulant** (drink, drug, etc) producing temporary increase of energy; n **stimulation**
**sting** n sharp, pointed defensive and offensive organ of insect, reptile, etc; sharp pain caused by sting; v thrust sting into; cause, feel sharp pain; pt, pp **stung**
**stingy** adj mean; miserly; n **stinginess**
**stink** v **stinking, stank** (or **stunk**), **stunk** give out bad smell; n offensive smell
**stint** v grudge; be stingy with
**stipend** n salary, esp of clergy
**stipple** v paint, engrave in dots
**stipulate** v insist on; n **stipulation** proviso
**stir** v **stirring, stirred** 1 mix around and around with spoon 2 move 3 inspire feelings; phr v **stir up** provoke; n great public excitement; adj **stirring** exciting

**stir** v 1 (mix with spoon) agitate, blend, churn, mingle. 2 (move) budge, come round, show signs of life, wake up

**stirrup** v metal hoop hung by strap from saddle for supporting foot of rider

**stitch** *n* movement of needle in sewing; result of such movement; sharp pain in side; *v* sew

**stoat** *n* animal of weasel family

**stock** *n* 1 supply 2 goods available for sale 3 meat or vegetable liquid used in making soup, sauces, etc 4 farm animals (*also* **livestock**) 5 lineage of family 6 portion of company's capital, held by investor; *v* keep supplies of; *adj* 1 constantly available 2 habitually produced 3 commonplace; *ns* **S. Exchange** place for trading in stocks, shares; **s.-market** (business done at) stock exchange; **s.-taking** checking of stock; *ns* **stockbroker** person trading in stocks and shares on behalf of clients; **stockpile** large supply accumulated for future use

**stockade** *n* wooden fence for defense

**stocky** *adj* short, solid in appearance

**stodgy** *adj* 1 heavy and indigestible 2 dull

> **stodgy** *adj* (heavy and indigestible) filling, solid, substantial, thick

**stoic** *n* person of calm, fortitude; *adj* **stoic(al)** calmly accepting of fate; *n* **stoicism**

**stoke** *v* fill with fuel

**stole**[1] *pt of* **steal**; *pp* **stolen**

**stole**[2] *n* long, narrow wrap of fur, etc worn about shoulders

**stolid** *adj* dull; not lively

**stomach** *n* 1 organ in abdomen in which food is digested; abdomen 2 liking; wish; *v* 1 eat without falling ill 2 tolerate

**stone** *n* 1 fairly small piece of rock 2 gem 3 hard seedcase in certain fruits 4 hard deposits formed in kidneys, bladder, etc 5 *Brit* measure of weight, 14 lbs (6,350kgs); *v* throw stones at; remove stone from fruit; *ns* **stonemason** person who prepares stone for use in building; **stoneware** pottery from clay containing flint; *adjs* **stone blind/dead/deaf** completely blind/dead/deaf; **stoned** *coll* 1 blind drunk 2 under influence of drugs; **stony** 1 full of stones 2 *fig* hard and cruel 3 (of silence) complete; *v* **stonewall** cause delay

**stood** *pt, pp of* **stand**

**stooge** *n* one who is butt of comedian's jokes; *coll* dupe, butt

**stool** *n* 1 backless seat 2 matter evacuated from bowels

**stool pigeon** *n coll* person used as decoy by police to trap criminal

**stoop** *v* 1 bend forward or down 2 be round-shouldered 3 lower one's moral standards by (doing sth); *n* position of stooping

> **stoop** *v* 1 (bend forward or down) bend, bow, lean down. 2 (lower one's moral standards) condescend, deign, demean yourself, descend to, humble yourself, lower yourself to, resort to, sink to

**stop** *v* **stopping, stopped** 1 cease moving 2 prevent 3 cease happening 4 discontinue; *n* 1 act of stopping 2 *mus* any device for altering pitch of note; *ns* **stopgap** temporary substitute; **stoppage** cessation of work ; **stopper** plug, *esp* for bottle; **s. press** late news; **s. watch** with split second start-stop facility for timing races

> **stop** *v* 1 (cease moving) come to a halt, come to a standstill, come to a stop, draw up, halt, pause, pull up, stop moving. 2 (prevent) abolish, ax, ban, block, bring to an end, call off, check, crack down on, curb, cut short, discontinue, end, finish, foil, frustrate, hamper, hinder, impede, interrupt, nip in the bud, obstruct, put a stop to, put down, quell, repress, restrain, suppress, terminate, thwart, wind up. 3 (cease happening) be over, come to an end, conclude, finish, pause, peter out. 4 (discontinue) break off, cease, desist, knock off *inf*, leave off, quit *inf*, refrain from

**store** *n* 1 reserve supply 2 warehouse 3 large general shop; *v* accumulate and keep supplies, etc; hold storage room for; *n* **storage** act of storing, being stored

**store** *n* **1** (reserve supply) cache, fund, hoard, provision, reservoir, stock, stockpile, supply. **2** (warehouse) depository, repository, storehouse, storeroom

**store** *v* hoard, keep, lay down, lay in, preserve, put away, put by, reserve, save, set aside, stash, stockpile, stock up

**stork** *n* large wading bird

**storm** *n* violent atmospheric disturbance; tempest; *idm* **take by storm 1** overcome by sudden attack **2** *fig* win enthusiastic approval of; *v* assault; *fig* express rage; *n* **s.trooper** Nazi militia man; *adj* **stormy** tempestuous, passionate

**story**[1] *n* **1** spoken or written narrative **2** account **3** item of news; *n* **storyteller 1** reciter, writer of stories **2** *coll* liar

**story** *n* **1** (spoken or written narrative) allegory, anecdote, fable, legend, myth, narrative, parable, romance, tale, yarn. **2** (account) chronicle, history, record, report, saga. **3** (item of news) article, dispatch, feature, news item, piece, report

**story**[2] *n* horizontal division, floor of building

**stout** *adj* **1** strong **2** fat; *n* strong dark beer; *adj* **stouthearted** *lit* brave (*adv* **-ly**; *n* **-ness**); *n* **stoutness**

**stove** *n* apparatus for heating/cooking food

**stow** *v* pack away; fill (hold) with goods; *phr v* **stow away** hide on board ship or plane in hope of having free journey (*n* **stowaway** person doing this)

**straddle** *v* spread legs wide over sth

**straggle** *v* be behind; *n* **straggler**

**straight** *adj* **1** not bent or crooked; *lit, fig* upright **2** in order **3** (of spirits) neat; *n* **s. away** straight stretch of road, river, etc; *adv* **1** in a straight line **2** directly; *idm* **keep to the straight and narrow** *coll* lead an honest life; *adv* **straightaway** immediately; *adj* **straightforward 1** simple **2** frank and honest (*adv* **-ly**; *n* **-ness**)

**straight** *adj* **1** (not bent or crooked) aligned, erect, even, in line, level, square, symmetrical, true, upright. **2** (in order) neat, orderly, organized, shipshape

**straighten** *v* make straight or tidy; *phr v* **straighten out** remove difficulties from

**straighten** *v* neaten, put straight, unbend, uncurl, untwist

**strain**[1] *v* **1** make taut **2** overexert; overtax **3** wrench by too sudden effort; *n* **1** tautness **2** severe physical or mental effort

**strain**[2] *n* breed, stock, ancestry

**strainer** *n* sieve; colander; *v* filter

**strait** *n* **1** narrow channel of water between two seas **2** (often *pl*) difficult position; *adj* **straitlaced** austere, strict; *n* **straitjacket** coat to confine arms of prisoners, violent patients, etc

**strand**[1] *n* shore; *v* leave, be left helpless

**strand**[2] *n* single thread of wool, rope, etc

**strange** *adj* **1** unusual **2** sinister **3** unknown **4** mad; *n* **-er** unknown person; foreigner

**strange** *adj* **1** (unusual) abnormal, bizarre, curious, funny, mystifying, odd, peculiar, perplexing, puzzling, quaint, queer, remarkable, surreal. **2** (sinister) eerie, grotesque, uncanny, weird. **3** (unknown) alien, exotic, foreign, remote, unexplored

**strangle** *v* kill by compressing windpipe; throttle; *ns* **stranglehold** powerful control that prevents action; **strangulation**

**strap** *n* strip of leather or metal for fastening; *v* **strapping, strapped** fasten with strap; beat with strap; *adj* **strapping** tall, well-made

**strata** *pl of* **stratum**

**stratagem** *n* trick, plan for deceiving enemy, opponent

**strategy** *n* art of military maneuvering; *adj* **strategic(al)**

**strategy** n design, game plan, master plan, plan of action, policy, program

**stratify** v arrange in strata; n **stratification**

**stratosphere** n uper atmospheric layer beginning approx 6 miles (9.7 km) above earth's surface

**stratum** n pl **strata** 1 geol layer 2 fig social division, class

**straw** n dry cut stalks of corn; idm **the last straw** new development that makes an already difficult situation quite intolerable; ns **strawberry** plant bearing red sweet juicy fruit; **s. poll** unofficial survey of public opinion

**stray** v wander; lose one's way; adj lost; not in correct place; n lost animal or child

**stray** v drift, meander, move aimlessly, ramble, range, roam

**streak** n 1 long line; stripe 2 (of lightning) flash; v 1 mark with streaks 2 coll rush quickly past (n **-er** person running naked in public); adj **-y**

**stream** n body of flowing water orother liquid; rivulet; brook; v 1 flow, run with liquid 2 move in large numbers 3 fly out, float on air; n **streamer** ribbon, flag to fly in air

**stream** n brook, channel, creek, rill, rivulet, tributary, watercourse
**stream** v 1 (flow) cascade, course, flood, gush, pour, run, spill, spout. 2 (move in large numbers) flood, pour, surge, swarm

**streamlined** adj of curved shape, offering minimum resistance to water or air

**street** n road in town or village with buildings on both sides; idm **on/in the street** without a home; ns **s. cleaner** sanitation worker who cleans streets and sidewalks; **streetwalker** prostitute who solicits on the streets; adj **street-smart** coll quick-witted enough to survive in a tough environment

**strength** n 1 physical power 2 effectiveness 3 determination; v **strengthen** 1 make stronger 2 make more successful

**strength** n 1 (physical power) brawn, might, muscle, power, robustness, stamina, staying power, sturdiness, toughness, vigor. 2 (effectiveness) efficacy, force, intensity, potency, power, validity, weight. 3 (determination) backbone inf, commitment, courage, firmness, fortitude, grit, resolution, resolve, spirit, tenacity

**strenuous** adj energetic, unremitting

**stress** n 1 pressure 2 emphasis 3 mech force exerted on solid body; v 1 emphasize 2 subject to mechanical stress; adj **stressed out** coll exhausted by stress

**stress** n 1 (pressure) anxiety, strain, tension, worry. 2 (emphasis) importance, significance, weight

**stressful** adj causing stress

**stressful** adj anxious, difficult, taxing, tiring, traumatic, worrying

**stretch** v 1 pull to make larger 2 become larger through pulling 3 extend; idm **stretch one's legs** exercise by walking; n **stretcher** 1 light framework for carrying disabled person 2 device for framing artists' canvases

**stretch** v 1 (pull to make larger) distend, draw out, elongate, expand, extend, inflate, lengthen, pull out, pull taut. 2 (become larger through pulling) be elastic, be stretchy, enlarge, expand, get bigger, get loose. 3 (extend) range, spread, unfold

**strew** v scatter, spread on surface; pt **strewed**; pp **strewn** or **strewed**

**stricken** adj affected by grief, illness, terror

**strict** adj 1 stern and firm 2 accurate 3 absolute; n **strictness**

a
b
c
d
e
f
g
h
i
j
k
l
m
n
o
p
q
r
s
t
u
v
w
x
y
z

**strict** adj **1** (stern and firm) authoritarian, harsh, inflexible, rigid, severe, stringent. **2** (accurate) close, exact, faithful, meticulous, precise, scrupulous, true

**stride** v **striding, strode, stridden** walk with long steps; n single step or its length

**strife** n conflict, discord

**strike** v **stricking, struck 1** hit; collide **2** (of clock) sound time **3** affect **4** ignite **5** make (coin, medal) **6** stop work to enforce demand; pt **struck**; idm **strike a balance** reach a compromise; phr vs **strike off** remove (person's name) from list; **strike up 1** initiate (friendship) **2** begin playing (music); n **1** refusal to work **2** attack, esp aerial **3** discovery of mineral deposit; n **-er**

**striking** adj **1** attractive **2** noticeable

**striking** adj **1** (attractive) arresting, dazzling, extraordinary, impressive, memorable, outstanding, stunning. **2** (noticeable) conspicuous, obvious, prominent, visible

**string** n cord, twine; series of objects; pt, pp **strung**; pl **-s** (players of) stringed instruments in orchestra; v **1** attach string to **2** thread onto string (pt, pp **strung**); idm **highly strung** very sensitive and excitable; phr v **string along 1** coll keep company for a while **2** persuade by deception; adj **stringy** fibrous

**stringent** adj strict, rigid, tight; n **stringency**

**stringent** adj exacting, inflexible, severe,

**strip** v **stripping, stripped 1** remove clothing **2** take away property; phr v **strip down** (of machine) remove detachable parts before cleaning, repairing; n **1** long thin piece of sth **2** act of stripping; ns **comic s.** comic story in pictures; **s.-tease** type of night-club entertainment where performer undresses slowly in front of spectators (n **stripper** person who does this)

**strip** v (remove clothing) disrobe, get undressed, strip off, take sb's clothes off, take your clothes off, undress, unclothe

**strip** n band, bar, belt, piece, ribbon, shred

**stripe** n narrow mark, band; chevron worn as symbol of military rank

**strive** v try earnestly; pt **strove**; pp **striven**

**strobe (light)** n rapidly flashing light

**strode** pt of **stride**

**stroke** n **1** blow **2** line made by single movement of pen, brush, etc **3** single movement of hands **4** sudden attack of illness; v caress

**stroke** v fondle, massage, pet, run your hand over, rub, soothe

**stroll** v take short leisurely walk; saunter

**strong** adj **1** physically powerful **2** healthy **3** courageous **4** unlikely to break **5** determined **6** persuasive **7** harsh **8** pungent; n **stronghold 1** fort **2** fig place where specified activity is strongly supported

**strong** adj **1** (physically powerful) athletic, brawny, burly, mighty, muscular, powerful, resilient, robust, rugged, strapping, sturdy, tough, vigorous. **2** (healthy) hale and hearty, sound, vigorous. **3** (courageous) brave, decisive, determined, firm, forceful, formidable, resolute, tough. **4** (unlikely to break) durable, hard-wearing, heavy, impenetrable, indestructible, long-lasting, solid, sturdy, tough, well-made, well-built. **5** (determined) dedicated, eager, enthusiastic, fervent, fierce, keen, loyal, passionate, staunch, steadfast, vehement, zealous. **6** (persuasive) cogent, compelling, convincing, plausible, powerful, valid, weighty. **7** (harsh) draconian, drastic, extreme, firm, forceful, severe, tough. **8** (pungent) full, highly flavored, savory, spicy, sharp, well-flavored

**strop** n leather strap for putting edge on razor

**strove** pt of **strive**

**struck** pt, pp of **strike**

**structure** n 1 formation; construction 2 that which is made up of many parts 3 building; v organize into structure; adj **structural**

**strudel** n Ger baked cake of fruit in pastry

**struggle** v 1 try hard 2 fight; n 1 fight 2 effort to achieve sth

> **struggle** v (try hard) bend over backward, do everything you can, do your utmost, endeavor, give it your best shot, labor, make a real effort, strain, toil, try
> **struggle** n 1 (fight) brush, clash, conflict, contest, encounter, scrap, set-to, skirmish, tussle. 2 (effort to achieve sth) battle, difficulty, effort, fight, grind, hassle, labor, problem, trouble

**strum** v **strumming, strummed** play on stringed instrument

**strung** pt, pp of **string**

**strut** n prop; stay; v **strutting, strutted** walk proudly; swagger

**stub** n end part (of cigarette, pencil, etc); v **stubbing, stubbed** hit one's toe accidentally; phr v **stub out** extinguish (cigarette); adj **stubby** short and thick

**stubble** n short stalks of corn, etc left in ground after reaping; short growth of hair

**stubborn** adj unwilling to change mind; n **-ness**

> **stubborn** adj adamant, defiant, determined, dogged, headstrong, inflexible, intractable, obdurate, obstinate, pig-headed, rigid, uncompromising, unreasonable, unyielding, willful

**stucco** n It fine plaster for coating walls

**stuck** pt, pp of **stick**; adj **stuck-up** conceited

**stud**[1] n large-headed projecting nail or peg; double headed button for cuff or collar of shirt; v **studding, studded** set, decorate with studs

**stud**[2] n 1 horse kept for breeding 2 coll man regarded as sexually active, virile; n **s.-farm** place for breeding horses

**student** n person studying at university

**studio** n 1 workroom of artist, photographer etc 2 room or premises where films are made or broadcasts are transmitted

**studious** adj 1 fond of study 2 careful

**study** v **studying, studied** 1 investigate 2 look closely at 3 learn about; n 1 detailed analysis 2 subjects being learned 3 room in which to study; adj **studied** premeditated

> **study** v 1 (investigate) analyze, consider, contemplate, inquire into, look into, research, survey, think about. 2 (look closely at) examine, inspect, peruse, pore over, read carefully, scrutinize. 3 (learn about) major in, read, read about, read up on, take a course in, take lessons in
> **study** n (detailed analysis) examination, inquiry, investigation, review, scrutiny, survey

**stuff** n 1 substance; material 2 textile fabric; v 1 fill 2 put stuffing inside 3 fill skin of (dead animal for preservation); n **stuffing** filling; savory seasoning used inside bird, meat; adj **stuffy** 1 lacking ventilation 2 coll too formal; stodgy

**stultify** v make ineffectual

**stumble** v trip up; **s. across/on** come upon by chance; n **stumbling-block** impediment; obstacle

**stump** n stub, remainder, remnant v walk noisily

**stun** v **stunning, stunned** 1 knock senseless 2 shock, amaze

**stunning** adj 1 beautiful, wonderful 2 causing loss of senses

> **stunning** adj (beautiful) brilliant, dazzling, fabulous, gorgeous, lovely, marvelous, ravishing, sensational, smashing, wonderful

**stung** pt, pp of **sting**

**stunk** *pp of* **stink**

**stunt**[1] *v* spectacular feat or display, *esp* involving danger

**stunt**[2] *v* stop growth of; *adj* **stunted** undersized

**stupefy** *v* **stupifying, stupified** 1 leave speechless 2 amaze; *n* **stupefaction**

**stupendous** *adj* astonishing; extra-ordinary

**stupid** *adj* 1 not intelligent 2 very foolish; *adv* **-ly;** *n* **-ity**

> **stupid** *adj* 1 (not intelligent) brainless, clueless, daft, dense, dim, foolish, gullible, half-witted, moronic, naïve, silly, simple, thick, unintelligent. 2 (very foolish) absurd, asinine, crackpot, crazy, futile, half-baked, idiotic, ill-advised, inane, irrational, ludicrous, mindless, pointless, rash, senseless, silly, unwise

**stupor** *n* dazed condition

**sturdy** *adj* robust, vigorous; *n* **-iness**

**stutter** *v* speak with hesitation and repetitions; stammer; *n* speech defect

**sty**[1] *n* pen for pigs; *fig* filthy place

**sty**[2] **stye** *n* inflamed swelling on eyelid

**style** *n* 1 elegance 2 way of doing sth 3 type 4 fashion; *v* designate; *idm* **in style** in an elegant way; *adj* **stylish** fashionable (*adv* **-ly**); *n* **-stylist** one who styles clothes, hair

> **style** *n* 1 (elegance) dash, flair, panache, polish, smartness, sophistication, stylishness. 2 (way of doing sth) approach, custom, manner, method, way. 3 (type) design, kind, pattern, variety. 4 (fashion) cut, design, look, mode, shape, vogue

**suave** *adj Fr* bland; urbane; affable

**sub** *n coll* 1 submarine 2 substitute

**sub-** *prefix forming ns, adjs, and vs* 1 under 2 almost 3 smaller than; less than 4 inferior

**subconscious** *adj* not fully realized by mind; *n* (psychoanalysis) part of mind outside personal awareness of individual

**subcontract** *v* arrange subsidiary contracts with workers for all or part of a big job

**subcutaneous** *adj* under the skin

**subdivide** *v* divide further into smaller units

**subdue** *v* overcome

**subject** *n* 1 topic 2 branch of learning 3 *ling* (word or phrase referring to) thing or person doing action of verb 4 citizen of a state; *adj* 1 under sb's political control; **subject to** 1 exposed to 2 liable to 3 depending on (specified conditions); *v* 1 bring under political control; *phr v* **subject sb to** cause sb to undergo; *adj* **subjective** 1 existing in the mind 2 based on personal feeling

> **subject** *n* 1 (topic) affair, business, gist, issue, matter, point, question, subject matter, substance, theme. 2 (branch of learning) area of study, branch of knowledge, course, discipline, field.

**sub judice** *adj Lat leg* not for public comment while being considered in a court of law

**subjugate** *v* conquer; force under control

**subjunctive** *n ling* mood of verb expressing wish, possibility; *adj* of, in that mood

**sublease, sublet** *v* lease or rent to another person, property which one is already leasing

**subliminal** *adj* at a level where the ordinary senses are not aware; *adv* **-ly**

**submarine** *n* ship designed to remain, travel, under water for long period

**submerge** *v* plunge, cause to go, beneath surface of water; *n* **submersion**

**submission** *n* surrender

**submissive** *adj* meek and docile

**submit** *v* **submitting, submitted** 1 surrender 2 put forward for consideration

> **submit** *v* 1 (surrender) bend the knee, bow, capitulate, cede, concede, give in, give way, knuckle under, lay down your arms, succumb, wave the white flag, yield. 2 (put forward) give in, hand in, present, put in, register, send in, surrender, tender

**subnormal** *adj* below normal; not normal

**subordinate** *adj* inferior in rank or importance; *adj* inferior or junior person

**subplot** *n* secondary plot in play, etc

**subpoena** *n leg* writ summoning person to attend court; *v* serve with such writ

**subscribe** *v* 1 pay regularly (eg contribution to club, payment to magazine) 2 **s. to** *fig* be in favor of; *ns* **subscriber**; **subscription** 1 act of subscribing 2 amount of money regularly paid for membership, etc

**subsequent** *adj* following as result; *adv* **-ly**

> **subsequent** *adj* consequent, ensuing, following, further, resulting, succeeding

**subservient** *adj* submissive, servile

**subside** *v* settle, sink down; diminish, abate; *n* **subsidence**

**subsidiary** *adj* additional, secondary

**subsidize** *v* support by subsidy

> **subsidize** *v* bail out, contribute to, finance, financially support, foot the bill for, fund, invest in, pay for, prop up, underwrite

**subsidy** *n* grant of money by state

> **subsidy** *n* aid, contribution, financial support, finance, funding, grant, investment, loan

**subsist** *v* sustain life; continue in being; *n* **-tence** means of supporting life

**subsoil** *n* level of soil below the surface

**subsonic** *adj* of less than speed of sound

**substance** *n* 1 matter; material 2 essential, most important elements or parts 3 considerable wealth; *v* **substantiate** give reality to; prove, establish truth

**substantial** *adj* quite large in amount

> **substantial** *adj* ample, considerable, great, large, important, marked, meaningful, notable, significant, sizable, weighty

**substitute** *n* person, thing taking place of another; deputy; *v* put, use in place of another; *n* **-tution**

**subsume** *v fml* include; consume

**subterfuge** *n* means of evasion

**subterranean** *adj* existing underground

**subtitle** *n* explanatory second title (*v* add subtitle to); *pl* **-s** visual translation of dialogue in foreign film

**subtle** *adj* 1 not obvious 2 ingenious; *n* **subtlety**

> **subtle** *adj* 1 (not obvious) complex, delicate, elusive, exquisite, fine, intricate, nuanced, refined, understated. 2 (ingenious) adroit, artful, astute, clever, crafty, cunning, devious, diplomatic, discerning, discreet, discriminating, guileful, perceptive, sensitive, shrewd, skillful, tactful, wily

**subtotal** *n* part total combining with others to make grand total

**subtract** *v* deduct; *n* **subtraction**

**subtropical** *adj* relating to regions borering on tropical zones

**suburb** *n* outlying part of town or city; *adj* **-an**

**suburbia** *n* city suburbs

**subvert** *v* try to undermine the power of; *adj* **subversive**; *adv* **-ly**; *ns* **-ness**; **subversion** act of subverting

**subway** *n* underground passage; underground commuter train

**succeed** *v* 1 accomplish purpose 2 follow in job or position

> **succeed** *v* 1 (accomplish purpose) achieve success, be successful, come up trumps *inf*, do well, flourish, get a result *inf*, hit the jackpot *inf*, make good *inf*, make it *inf*, prosper, score, thrive, win, win through. 2 (follow in job or position) accede, be next in line, come after, come next, follow, follow in sb's footsteps, inherit, replace, take over, take sb's place

a
b
c
d
e
f
g
h
i
j
k
l
m
n
o
p
q
r
**s**
t
u
v
w
x
y
z

**success** n fortunate accomplishment, attainment of desired object, or result; triumph

**successful** adj 1 enjoying wealth and social success 2 achieving desired result

> **successful** adj 1 (enjoying wealth and social success) all-conquering, booming, flourishing, profitable, prosperous, rich, strong, thriving, top, triumphant, victorious. 2 (achieving desired result) effective, fruitful, lucky, lucrative, profitable, rewarding, victorious, winning

**succession** n 1 act or right of following in job or position 2 series of things, events

**successive** adj consecutive

**successor** n one who follows another in job or position

**succinct** adj concisely expressed; terse

**succor** v, n help, aid

**succulent** adj juicy

> **succulent** adj delicious, luscious, lush, ripe, sappy, tasty

**succumb** v 1 yield 2 cease to exist

**such** adj of similar kind; adj **suchlike** similar

**suck** v 1 draw (liquid) into mouth 2 dissolve in mouth

**suckle** v feed (young) with milk from breast

**sucrose** n form of natural sugar

**suction** n creation of partial vacuum causing body to adhere to, or enter, something under atmospheric pressure

**sudden** adj done, occurring unexpectedly; adv **-ly**; n **-ness**

> **sudden** adj abrupt, hurried, impromptu, impulsive, instant, instantaneous, momentary, quick, spontaneous, unexpected

**suds** n pl froth of soap and water, lather

**sue** v bring, take legal action against

**suede** n Fr leather with napped surface

**suet** n solid fatty tissue surrounding kidneys, etc of oxen, sheep etc

**suffer** v 1 be in pain 2 be affected by illness 3 endure; n **sufferer**

> **suffer** v 1 (be in pain) ache, ail, be in distress, grieve, hurt, struggle, writhe. 2 (be affected by illness) be a victim of, be affected by, be afflicted by, be cursed with, be troubled with, have. 3 (endure) bear, experience, feel, go through, live through, put up with, sustain, undergo

**suffering** n pain, misery

> **suffering** n affliction, agony, anguish, discomfort, distress, grief, hardship, harm, heartache, hurt, torment, torture

**suffice** v be enough, adequate

**sufficient** adj enough; n **sufficiency** adequate supply

> **sufficient** adj adequate, ample, decent, plenty, satisfactory

**suffix** n syllable added to end of word

**suffocate** v kill by depriving of air; n **suffocation**

**suffrage** n vote, right to vote, esp at elections; n **suffragette** woman who campaigned for right of women to vote in elections

**suffuse** v (of fluid, colour, etc) spread over, flood, cover; n **suffusion**

**sugar** n sweet, crystalline vegetable substance; v sweeten with sugar; ns **s.-beet** variety of beetroot yielding sugar; **s.-cane** tall grass from whose juice sugar is obtained

**suggest** v 1 give advice 2 imply; adj **-ive** 1 evoking association of ideas 2 provoking indecent thoughts

> **suggest** v 1 (give advice) advise, move, propose, recommend. 2 (imply) hint, indicate, insinuate, intimate

**suggestion** n 1 proposal 2 hint

> **suggestion** n 1 (proposal) idea, motion, plan, proposition. 2 (hint) indication, intimation, remark, whisper

**suicide** n 1 act of killing oneself 2 one who intentionally kills him/herself; adj **suicidal**
**suit** n 1 action at law 2 set of clothes worn together, esp man's outer clothes 3 one of four sets in pack of cards; v 1 satisfy 2 match 3 please 4 be convenient; adj **suited** 1 appropriate 2 compatible; n **suitcase** portable flat oblong traveling case
**suitable** adj convenient; n **suitability**

> **suitable** adj acceptable, adequate, applicable, apposite, appropriate, apt, befitting, due, fit, fitting, opportune, pertinent, proper, relevant, right, satisfactory, to your liking

**suite** n Fr set (as of rooms, furniture, etc)
**suitor** n petitioner, wooer
**sulfur** n pale yellow, inflammable, nonmetallic element; adj **sulphurous**
**sulk** v feel resentful and unsociable
**sulky** adj feeling resentful and unsociable

> **sulky** adj angry, bitter, brooding, churlish, cross, gloomy, glum, grouchy, grumpy, in a huff, irritable, moody, morose, peeved, peevish, petulant, querulous, seething, sour, sullen, surly, truculent, unhappy

**sullen** adj ill-tempered, morose, surly
**sully** v **sullying, sullied** stain, defile
**sultan** n Muslim prince or king; n **sultana** 1 sultan's wife 2 kind of raisin
**sultry** adj (of weather) hot and close

> **sultry** adj heavy, humid, muggy, oppressive, sticky, stifling, sweltering

**sum** n amount, total; phr v **summing, summed, sum up** 1 summarize 2 (of judge) review and comment on evidence

**summary** n brief statement or abridgment of chief points (of document, speech, etc); adj carried out without delay; v **summarize** present briefly and concisely; n **summation** reckoning up

> **summary** n abridgment, abstract, digest, outline, précis, résumé, round-up, rundown, synopsis

**summer** n warmest season of year; adj **summery**; ns **summerhouse** small garden building for sitting in during warm weather; **s. school** short course given during summer vacation period
**summit** n 1 top, peak 2 coll political conference between heads of states
**summon** v 1 send for 2 leg order to attend court; phr v **summon up** evoke, n **summons** call; notice to appear before judge or magistrate

> **summon** v (send for) beckon, bid, call, call for, call up, convene, convoke, invite

**sumptuary** adj relating to expenditure
**sumptuous** adj lavish, splendid, costly
**sun** n 1 luminous heavenly body around which earth and other planets rotate 2 direct rays of sun; v bask in sun's rays; v **sunbathe** lie in the sun in order to have a suntan; ns **sunbeam** ray of sunshine; **sundial** device with pointer that shows time by movement of shadow across dial; **sunflower** large flower with yellow petals and seeds yielding edible oil; **s.-glasses** spectacles with dark lenses for protecting eyes from strong light **s.-lamp** lamp for giving artificial suntan by ultraviolet rays; **sunrise** time when sun rises at start of day; **sunset** time when sun sets at end of day; **sunstroke** illness caused by too much exposure to sun; **s.-tan** browning of skin from exposure to sun; **s.-trap** warm, sunny place; **s.-worship** fig coll addiction to sunbathing
**sundae** n ice cream with fruit, nuts, syrup, etc

**Sunday** n first day of week

**sundry** adj several, of indefinite number; n pl **sundries** unspecified odds and ends

**sung** pp of **sing**

**sunk** pp of **sink**

**sunken** adj 1 fallen to the bottom of the sea 2 on a lower level 3 (of cheeks, eyes, etc) hollow

**super** (adj coll) marvelous, superb

**superb** adj wonderful

> **superb** adj admirable, brilliant, excellent, exquisite, fabulous, fantastic, fine, first-class, first-rate, glorious, gorgeous, magnificent, marvelous, outstanding, splendid, sublime, superior, superlative, unrivaled, world-class

**supercilious** adj disdainful, haughty

**superficial** adj 1 done quickly 2 without deep thought 3 on surface

> **superficial** adj 1 (done quickly) casual, cursory, desultory, hasty, hurried, perfunctory, quick, rushed, sketchy, slapdash. 2 (without deep thought) facile, shallow, skin deep, silly, slight, trite, trivial

**superfluous** adj more than necessary

**superhuman** adj of more than can be expected of ordinary humans

**superimpose** v put sth on top of sth so that both can be seen (or heard) together

**superintend** v direct, control, oversee, supervise; ns **-ent** manager; one with executive oversight; **-ence**

**superior** adj 1 higher in position, rank, grade 2 above; n **-ity**

**superlative** adj of, in highest degree of excellence, or quality; n ling superlative degree of adjective or adverb

**superman** n hypothetical being possessing supreme physical and mental powers

**supermarket** n large sgrocery store

**supernatural** adj not explicable by known laws of nature

**supernatural** adj eerie, ghostly, inexplicable, magical, miraculous, mysterious, mystic, occult, out of the ordinary, paranormal, phantom, preternatural, psychic, spectral, spiritual, strange but true, uncanny, unearthly, unexplained, unnatural, weird

**superpower** n very large, powerful nation

**supersede** v replace

**supersonic** adj moving faster than speed of sound; of sound waves of too high frequency to be audible to human ear

**superstar** n coll entertainer (eg athlete) with outstanding skill and reputation

**superstition** n irrational belief in charms, omens; adj **superstitious**

**supervise** v be in charge of; ns **supervisor** (adj **-visory**); **supervision**

> **supervise** v conduct, control, direct, govern, invigilate, keep an eye on, look after, manage, mind, monitor, organize, oversee, preside over, regulate, run, watch over

**superwoman** n woman of outstanding physical and mental talents

**supine** adj lying on back, face up

**supper** n last meal of day

**supplant** v take place of, esp by fraud

**supple** adj able to bend easily; n **-ness**

> **supple** adj agile, bendable, double-jointed, elastic, flexible, lithe, malleable, nimble, plastic, pliable, pliant, soft, yielding

**supplement** n 1 something added to fill need 2 separable part of newspaper, etc; v add to; supply deficiency; adj **supplementary** extra; additional

**supplicate** v pray for; beg, ask for humbly; ns **-ation** entreaty; **suppliant** petitioner

**supply** v **supplying, supplied** 1 make sth available 2 equip (sb with sth); n 1 available store of sth 2 (system for) providing; idm **in short supply** difficult to obtain; n **supplier**

supply *v* (make available) deal in, deliver,
distribute, donate, export, furnish, give,
hand over, offer, procure, provide, purvey,
retail, sell, trade in

supply *n* (available store) amount, cache,
consignment, hoard, quantity, provision,
ration, reserve, reservoir, stock, stockpile

support *v* 1 help 2 agree with 3 help to prove
4 give money to 5 hold up; *n* 1 help
2 agreement 3 money given to help sb
4 object holding sth up; *n* **-er** 1 person loyal
to a team, political party, etc 2 person
devoted to an activity, principle, etc;
*adjs* **-ing** giving support; **-ive** ready to offer
encouragement

support *v* 1 (help) aid, assist, back, bolster,
defend, encourage, endorse, give strength
to, protect, reinforce, second, speak up for,
sponsor, stick up for. 2 (agree with)
advocate, approve of, back, be in favor of,
believe in, endorse, favor, subscribe to.
3 (help to prove) agree with, be consistent
with, bear out, bolster, boost, confirm,
corroborate, illustrate, prove, reinforce,
strengthen, substantiate, underpin. 4 (give
money to) back, bail out, contribute to,
donate to, finance, fund, invest in, keep,
maintain, provide for, sponsor, subsidize,
underwrite. 5 (hold up) bear, carry, keep
in place, prop up, shore up, withstand

support *n* 1 (help) aid, assistance, backing,
backup, endorsement. 2 (agreement)
advocacy, approval, backing, favor. 3
(money) aid, assistance, finance, funding,
grant, investment, loan, provision, relief,
sponsorship, subsidy. 4 (object holding
sth up) brace, bracket, buttress, column,
frame, mounting, pillar, prop, strut, truss

suppose *v* assume; *idm* **be supposed to** be
required, expected to; *adj* **supposed** believed
to be (*adv* **-ly**); *conj* supposing what if;
*n* **supposition** hypothesis, guess

suppose *v* conjecture, expect, guess, infer,
presume, speculate, surmise, think

suppository *n* soluble medicinal bolus
inserted in rectum or vagina

suppress *v* 1 subdue, crush by force 2 prevent
publication of; ban; *n* **-ion**

suppurate *v* produce pus; *n* **suppuration**

supreme *adj* highest, superior in rank, power,
jurisdiction, etc; utmost; *ns* **supremacy**
1 superiority 2 dominance

surcharge *n* extra charge; *v* demand extra
payment

sure *adj* 1 certain 2 guaranteed 3 reliable;
*adv, interj coll* certainly; willingly; *idm* **make
sure** 1 verify; be certain 2 guarantee;
*n* **surety** money laid down as pledge of
person's good behavior

sure *adj* 1 (certain) confident, in no doubt,
positive. 2 (guaranteed) assured, certain,
destined. 3 (reliable) infallible, trusty,
unerring, unfailing

surf *n* foam of breaking waves; *n* **surfboard**
board used in sport of surfing

surface *n* exterior; outside; top; visible side;
*adj* superficial; *v* 1 come to surface of water
2 emerge, appear after being missing

surfeit *n* excess, *esp* in eating, feeding; satiety;
repletion; *v* overindulge

surge *v* (of waves, water) swell; rise
powerfully; *n* sudden rush of electric
current in circuit

surgeon *n* doctor who performs operations;
*n* **surgery** treatment of disease and injuries
by operation or manipulation; *adj* **surgical**

surly *adj* gloomy and bad-tempered

surly *adj* churlish, crusty, gruff, grumpy,
hostile, ill-natured, irascible, irritable,
rude, sulky, sullen, uncivil, unfriendly

surmise *v* guess, infer; *n* guess
surmount *v* overcome (difficulty); *adj* **-able**

**surname** n hereditary family name

**surpass** v excel in degree, quality, etc

**surplice** n loose white vestment worn by clergy and choristers

**surplus** n excess quantity; adj forming amount over and above what is required

**surprise** v 1 astonish 2 come upon unexpectedly; n 1 astonishment 2 something unexpected

> **surprise** v 1 (astonish) amaze, astound, bewilder, dumbfound, faze, nonplus, rock, take sb aback, shock, startle, stun, throw. 2 (come upon unexpectedly) burst in on, catch sb in the act, catch sb red-handed, detect, discover, startle, take sb unawares
>
> **surprise** n 1 (astonishment) amazement, incredulity, wonder. 2 (sth unexpected) bolt from the blue inf, bombshell, revelation, shock

**surprised** adj astonished

> **surprised** adj amazed, astounded, bewildered, dumbfounded, fazed, flabbergasted, incredulous, shocked, speechless, staggered, startled, struck dumb, stunned, thrown, thunderstruck

**surprising** adj astonishing

> **surprising** adj amazing, astounding, bewildering, extraordinary, incredible, mind-blowing, remarkable, shocking, staggering, startling, unexpected, unusual

**surrealism** n movement in art or literature that believes in expressing dreamlike effects and irrational fantasies; n, adj **-ist**

**surrender** v 1 give up 2 hand over; n act of surrendering

> **surrender** v (give up) capitulate, concede, give in, lay down your arms, submit, throw in the towel inf, yield

**surreptitious** adj stealthy; clandestine; furtive

**surrogate** n substitute; deputy, esp of bishop; n **surrogate mother** woman who bears a child for another woman

**surround** v encircle; be, come all around; n pl **surroundings** material environment; circumstances

**surtax** n additiional tax on high incomes

**surveillance** n Fr constant watch

**survey** v 1 look over; review 2 inspect and assess value of (house, etc) 3 measure, map (area of land); n record of result of surveying; n **surveyor**

**survive** v continue to live or exist; n **survivor** one left alive when others are dead

> **survive** v carry on, endure, keep going, last, live on, persist, remain, subsist, succeed

**susceptible** adj highly sensitive; n **-ibility**

**suspect** v 1 believe to be true 2 doubt; mistrust 3 believe guilty; adj rousing suspicion; n suspected person

> **suspect** v (believe to be true) conjecture, consider, fancy, feel, guess, have a feeling, have a hunch, imagine, suppose, surmise, think

**suspend** v hang up; postpone; defer; debar, prohibit temporarily; n pl **suspenders** device for holding up stockings or socks

**suspense** n state of anxious uncertainty; n **suspension** state of being suspended (in various senses)

**suspicion** n 1 act of suspecting 2 feeling of doubt, mistrust

**suspicious** adj 1 not to be trusted 2 untrusting; adv **-ly**

> **suspicious** adj (not to be trusted) dubious, fishy inf, funny, shady inf, shifty, suspect, unreliable, untrustworthy

**sustain** *v* 1 support; hold up 2 undergo; *n* **sustenance** nourishment, maintenance

**suture** *n* 1 act, process of sewing up wound 2 thread, wire used for this 3 *anat* articulation of bones of skull; *v* join with suture

**suzerain** *n Fr* feudal law; state with sovereignty over another

**svelte** *adj* slender; graceful

**swab** *n med* absorbent pad; *v* **swabbing, swabbed** clean; wash out with swab

**swaddle** *v* bundle up; *n pl* **swaddling-clothes, -bands** strip of cloth formerly wrapped around baby

**swag** *n sl* booty; plunder

**swagger** *v* walk in strutting, arrogant way

**swain** *n lit* country lad; lover; admirer

**swallow**[1] *n* migratory bird with long, pointed wings and forked tail; *n* **s.-tail** kind of butterfly or humming bird; man's dresscoat

**swallow**[2] *v* 1 make (food, drink, etc) pass down gullet 2 believe implicitly; *n* act of swallowing food, etc

**swam** *pt of* **swim**

**swamp** *n* marsh; *v* cover with water; *fig* overwhelm; *adj* **swampy**

> **swamp** *n* bog, fen, mire, mud, quagmire

**swan** *n* large, long-necked aquatic bird

**swank** *v coll* behave, talk boastfully

**swap, swop** *v* **swapping, swapped** exchange

> **swap, swop** *v* barter, interchange, switch, trade

**swarm** *n* large mass of insects, *esp* cluster of bees with queen; crowd; *v* 1 (of bees) leave hive with queen 2 gather in large numbers

**swarthy** *adj* dark-complection

**swastika** *n* hooked cross, used as a badge by Nazi Party

**swat** *v* **swatting, swatted** squash insect, etc

**swathe** *v* cover, wrap with cloth or bandage

**sway** *v* swing unsteadily; move; influence; *n* swaying motion; influence; power

> **sway** *v* (swing unsteadily) bend, incline, lean, lurch, oscillate, rock, swing, wave

**swear** *v* **swearing, swore, sworn** 1 promise on oath 2 cause to take an oath 3 curse; *phr v* **swear by** have great faith in

**sweat** *n* 1 moisture exuded by pores of skin 2 hard labor; *v* 1 exude sweat 2 work hard for low wages 3 suffer great anxiety; *ns* **s.-band** strip of material worn to absorb sweat; **s.-shirt** long-sleeved sweater *usu* of cotton; **s.-shop** place where people work hard for low wages

**Swede** *n* native of Sweden

**sweep** *v* **sweeping, swept** 1 clean with brush, broom 2 move in stately manner 3 form wide curve 4 drive, move violently away; *n* 1 act of sweeping 2 wide curve or curving movement 3 person who cleans chimneys; *ns* **sweeper** 1 machine for cleaning carpets 2 person who sweeps 3 (football) player giving extra support to defenders; **sweepstake** form of gambling

**sweeping** *adj* 1 extensive 2 too generalized

**sweet** *adj* 1 tasting like sugar 2 appealing 3 fragrant 4 melodious; *n* dessert; candy; confection; *ns* **s.corn** type of corn with sweet grain; **sweetheart** person one loves; **sweetmeat** *ar* item of confectionery; **s. pea** climbing plant with colorful fragrant flowers; **s. potato** tropical plant with yellow edible roots; *adv* **-ly** *n* **-ness;** *v* **sweeten** 1 make sweet 2 *coll* bribe (*ns* **-er, -ing**)

> **sweet** *adj* 1 (tasting like sugar) sugared, sugary, sweetened. 2 (appealing) agreeable, amiable, attractive, charming, cute, endearing, engaging, good-natured, likable, lovable, winning. 3 (fragrant) aromatic, balmy, fresh, perfumed, pure

**swell** *v* **swelling, swelled, swollen** (or **swelled**) expand; increase in size; *n* 1 act of swelling 2 succession of unbroken waves; *adj coll* excellent, fine

a b c d e f g h i j k l m n o p q r s t u v w x y z

**swelter** *v* suffer discomfort from heat; *adj* **-ing** very hot

**swept** *pt, pp* of **sweep**; *adjs* **1** with front edge angled backward **2** (of hair) brushed backward

**swerve** *v* swing around; deviate from course

**swift** *adj* speedy; *adv* **-ly**; *n* bird like swallow

**swig** *v* **swigging, swigged** to drink a liquid in large mouthfuls

**swill** *v* **1** rinse; wash out with water **2** drink greedily; *n* liquid food for pig

**swim** *v* **swimming, swam, swum 1** move through water by movement of limbs, fins etc **2** feel dizzy **3** be flooded; *idm* **swim with the tide** copy what others do; *idm* **in/out of the swim** familiar/unfamiliar with what is happening in the world; *ns* **swimmer**; **swimming** (**s.pool** artificial indoor or outdoor pool for swimming; **s.-trunks** shorts for swimming); *adj* **swimmingly** *coll* smoothly; pleasantly

**swindle** *v* cheat, defraud; *n* **swindler**

> **swindle** *v* con *inf*, deceive, do, double-cross, fleece, pull a fast one, rip sb off *inf*, take sb for a ride, trick

**swine** *n* pig; *coll* unpleasant person; *pl* **swine**

**swing** *v* **swinging, swung 1** be suspended **2** move from side to side **3** turn on hinge or pivot; *n* **1** act of swinging **2** seat for children to swing on for amusement **3** sudden change or reversal; *idm* **in full swing** operating at its peak; *idm* **get into the swing (of)** *coll* become adapted (to)

> **swing** *v* **1** (be suspended) dangle, hang, suspend. **2** (move from side to side) oscillate, rock, sway, veer, wave

**swipe** *v* strike with powerful blow; *coll* steal

**swirl** *v* whirl about; *n* such motion

**swish** *v* pass, cut through air with hissing sound; *n* swishing sound, or movement

**Swiss** *adj* of Switzerland; *n* **Swiss cheese** firm pale yellow cheese with many holes

**switch** *n* **1** device for interrupting or diverting electrical current in a circuit **2** sudden change **3** substitution **4** slender, flexible twig or rod; *v* **1** change **2** exchange; transfer; *phr vs* **switch off/on 1** turn off/on (electrical device) **2** *coll* cease/begin to show interest; *n* **switchboard** control center for telephone system

**swivel** *v* turn round; *n* link consisting of ring and shank, allowing two parts to revolve independently

> **swivel** *v* gyrate, pirouette, pivot, revolve, rotate, spin, swing, twirl

**swizzle** *n* mixed drink of rum, lime juice, etc

**swollen** *pp* of **swell**

**swoon** *v, n* (have) fainting fit

**swoop** *v* descend steeply through air like hawk; *n* act of swooping; sudden attack

> **swoop** *v* dive, drop down, lunge, plunge, sweep down

**sword** *n* weapon with long sharp blade fixed in hilt; *ns* **s.-fish** fish with long, sharp upper jaw; **s.-play** fighting with swords; **swordsman** man skilled in using sword

**swore** *pt* of **swear**

**sworn** *pp* of **swear**; *adj* **1** (of statement) made under oath **2** (of friend or enemy) long-established; confirmed by pledge

**swum** *pp* of **swim**

**swung** *pt, pp* of **swing**

**sybarite** *n* one who is fond of luxurious comfort; *adj* **sybaritic**

**sycamore** *n* tree related to maple

**sycophant** *n* **1** flatterer **2** parasite; *n* **sycophancy**

**syllable** *n* division of word, as unit of pronunciation; *adj* **syllabic**

**syllabus** *n* list of subjects; program

**sylph** *n* sprite; *adj* **sylphlike** slender and graceful

**sylvan, silvan** *adj* of, in wood, forests; rustic; rural

**symbiosis** n *bio* condition of living things which depend on each other; *adj* **symbiotic**
**symbol** n sign; anything representing or typifying something; *adj* **symbolic**; **symbolize**; n **symbolism** represented by symbols

> **symbol** n badge, crest, emblem, insignia, logo, token

**symmetry** n balance of arrangement between two sides; *adj* **symmetrical** duly proportioned; harmonious
**sympathetic** *adj* feeling compassion

> **sympathetic** *adj* caring, compassionate, concerned, feeling, friendly, humane, interested, kind, responsive, supportive, understanding, warm

**sympathize** v 1 understand 2 feel pity for
**sympathy** n 1 compassion 2 agreement

> **sympathy** n 1 (compassion) caring, concern, friendliness, humanity, kindness, responsiveness, support. 2 (agreement) empathy, understanding

**symphony** n *mus* sonata or composition for full orchestra; *adj* **-phonic**
**symptom** n outward sign; change in body indicating presence of disease; *adj* **-atic**
**synagogue** n Jewish place of worship
**synchronize** v 1 make agree in time 2 (cause to) happen at same time; *adj* **synchronized** (*ns* **s. swimming** sport where swimmers aim to perform complex movements in complete synchronization)
**syncopate** v *mus* begin (note) on normally unaccented beat; n **syncopation**
**syndicate** n body of person, combining for some enterprise
**syndrome** n combination of various symptoms of disease
**synonym** n word with same meaning as another; *adj* **synonymous**

**synopsis** n summary, outline; *pl* **-opses**
**syntax** n *ling* sentence construction
**synthesis** n combination; *pl* **-theses** *adj* **-thetic** artificial; v **synthesize** combine into a whole; n **-sizer** electronic keyboard instrument with facility for producing a variety of instrumental sounds

> **synthesis** n amalgamation, blend, compound, fusion, union

**syphilis** n contagious venereal disease
**syringe** n instrument for drawing in liquid by piston and ejecting it in jet
**syrup** n thick solution obtained in refining of sugar; *adj* **syrupy**
**system** n plan, scheme for organizing, classifying objects; complex whole

> **system** n approach, means, method, procedure, process, routine, structure, technique, way

**systematic** *adj* methodical

> **systematic** *adj* efficient, logical, orderly, organized, precise, structured, well organized

**systemic** *adj* affecting entire organism
**systems analysis** n analysis of management requirements in a form which can be programmed to a computer
**systems analyst** specialist in analysis of computer systems

a
b
c
d
e
f
g
h
i
j
k
l
m
n
o
p
q
r
**s**
t
u
v
w
x
y
z

**tab** n small flap of cloth, paper, etc; idm **keep tabs on** coll keep under observation

**tabby** n striped cat

**table** n 1 piece of furniture consisting of flat board supported by legs 2 set of facts, figures, etc arranged in lines, or columns; ns **t. tennis** (also **ping-pong**) game like tennis played with wooden paddles and hollow plastic ball on table with net; **tablespoon** large spoon for serving food; **tableware** dishes and cutlery

> **table** n (set of facts, figures) chart, diagram, figure, graph, index, inventory, list, plan, register, roll, schedule

**tablet** n 1 small flat slab (as paper) 2 small flat medicinal pill or sweet

**tabloid** n small, sensational newspaper

**taboo** n ban based on religion or social custom

**tabor** n small drum

**tabulate** v arrange (words, figures) in a table; n **-ation**; adj **tabular**

**tachometer** n device for measuring speed

**tacit** adj implied by silence

> **tacit** adj implicit, inferred, taken for granted, understood, unexpressed, unspoken, unstated, unvoiced

**taciturn** adj speaking little; n **taciturnity**

**tack** n 1 small broad-headed nail 2 long temporary stitch 3 fig course of action; v 1 fasten with tacks 2 sew loosely

**tackle** n 1 equipment for task or sport 2 act of tackling in sport; v 1 attempt to do 2 attempt to solve 3 challenge opponent for ball in sport

> **tackle** v 1 (attempt to do) begin, set about, take on, undertake. 2 (attempt to solve) confront, cope with, deal with, grapple with, handle, sort out. 3 (in sport) block, challenge, intercept, take on

**tacky** adj sticky; of poor quality

**taco** n Mexican tortilla filled with meat, etc

**tact** n skill in dealing with people, situations without causing offense

**tactful** adj able to deal with people, situations without causing offense

> **tactful** adj careful, delicate, diplomatic, discreet, perceptive, sensitive

**tactic** n means of achieving sth; pl **-s** mil art of deploying troops, weapons, etc; adj **tactical** 1 of tactics 2 with calculated intent

**tactile** adj of, relating to sense of touch

**tactless** adj accidentally offensive

> **tactless** adj blundering, blunt, careless, clumsy, gauche, inconsiderate, insensitive, thoughtless, unfeeling, unsubtle

**tadpole** n young frog or toad, having gills, tail

**taffeta** n Fr stiff lustrous fabric of silk, wool

**tag** n label; v **tags, tagging, tagged** label

**tagliatelle** n It long strips of pasta

**tail** n 1 prolonged extension of animal's spine 2 pl reverse side of coin; v follow (person) closely; ns **t.-end** very end; **t.light** red light at rear of vehicle; **t.pipe** car exhaust pipe; **t.-wind** wind blowing from behind

**tailor** n one who makes men's clothing; v adapt for special purpose; adj **t.-made** precisely made for specific need

**taint** *n* stain; trace of decay; disgrace; *v* stain or spoil slightly; become infected

**taint** *n* blemish, blot, defect, fault, flaw, smear, spot, stigma

**take** *v* 1 get possession of; accept 2 carry 3 accompany 4 tolerate 5 use (transport) 6 accommodate 7 need (time) 8 imbibe; *pt* **took**; *pp* **taken**; *idm* **take place** happen; *idm* **take sides** show a bias; *phr vs* **take after** look or behave like (parent, etc); **take away** 1 subtract 2 remove; **take in** 1 provide accommodation for 2 include 3 deceive 4 understand properly 5 reduce size of (clothes); **take off** 1 remove 2 leave the ground; **take on** 1 accept a challenge from 2 start to employ 3 accept (work, etc); **take out** 1 extract 2 escort (socially) 3 obtain by official agreement; **take over** 1 gain control (of) 2 assume responsibility (for) (*n* **t.-over**); **take to** 1 like instantly 2 begin doing regularly; **take up** 1 pick up 2 begin to practice or study 3 occupy (time/space); *ns* **t.-home pay** amount of pay after deduction of tax, etc; **takings** money received from selling goods, performing in public, etc

**take** *v* 1 (get possession of; accept) get, grab, grasp, obtain, receive, seize, snatch. 2 (carry) cart, convey, ferry, transport. 3 (accompany) escort, guide, lead, usher. 4 (tolerate) abide, bear, endure, put up with, stand, stomach, suffer, undergo

**talc** *n* magnesium silicate; *n* **talcum** powdered talc used on skin; baby powder
**tale** *n* story, account, rumor, narrative
**talent** *n* special faculty; *adj* **talented** gifted

**talent** *n* aptitude, brilliance, capacity, expertise, flair, genius, gift, prowess

**talisman** *n* charm; amulet; object regarded as having magic powers

**talk** *v* 1 speak 2 discuss 3 converse; *phr vs* **talk sb into/out of** persuade sb to do/not to do; *n* 1 conversation 2 informal lecture 3 words of no special meaning; *pl* **-s** formal discussion, *esp* political; *n* **-er**; *adjs* **talkative** fond of talking; **talking** capable of speech (*ns* **t. point** subject of discussion; **t.-to** reprimand)

**talk** *v* 1 (speak) babble, chat, chatter, converse, gossip, say, tell, utter, verbalize. 2 (discuss) confer, negotiate, parley
**talk** *n* 1 (conversation) chat, chit-chat *inf*, gossip. 2 (lecture) address, oration, presentation, sermon, speech

**tall** *adj* above average in height; *ns* **t. order** *coll* unreasonable request; **t. tale** story difficult to believe

**tall** *adj* big, gangling, giant, high, lanky, lofty, soaring, towering

**tallow** *n* melted-down animal fat
**tally** *n* notched rod to county by; *v* **tallies, tallying, tallied** correspond exactly; agree
**talon** *n* claw
**tambourine** *n* small shallow drum fitted with tinkling cumbals on perimeter
**tame** *adj* 1 not wild 2 dull; *v* make tame

**tame** *adj* 1 (not wild) docile, domesticated, house-trained, manageable, obedient, submissive, tamed. 2 (dull) bland, boring, feeble, insipid, vapid, weak, wishy-washy

**tamper** *phr v* **tamper with** 1 interfere with 2 alter fraudulently
**tampon** *n* internal protection used during menstruation
**tan** *adj* of yellowish brown; *v* **tans, tanning, tanned** 1 make animal hides into leather 2 become brown, *esp* by exposure to sunlight
**tandem** *n* bicycle for two riders
**tandoori** *n* food cooked by Indian method in clay oven

447

**tang** n 1 projecting spike 2 strong flavor or smell 3 kind of seaweed

**tangent** n line touching curve at one point; n idm **fly/go off on a tangent** fig suddenly change direction; adj **tangential**

**tangerine** n small, sweet thin-skinned orange

**tangible** adj capable of being touched; fig clearly defined in mind

**tangle** v form confused mass; intertwine; n 1 intricate knot 2 disorder

**tangle** v catch, enmesh, ensnare, entangle, knot, scramble, snarl, trap, twist
**tangle** n (knot) coil, jumble, mass, mat, mesh, mess, scramble, snarl, twist

**tango** n S American dance; music for this; pl **-os**; v dance tango

**tank** n 1 receptacle for storing liquids, oil, or gas 2 heavy armored vehicle with tracked wheels and guns; n **tanker** ship, truck carrying oil, liquid fuel in bulk

**tankard** n large beer mug

**tantalize** v torment, tease

**tantamount** adj equal in value; equivalent

**tantrum** n fit, outburst of violent temper

**tap**[1] n device with turning valve for controlling flow of liquid from pipe, cask, etc; v **taps, tapping, tapped** 1 draw off (liquid) 2 listen in deliberately (to telephone conversation); n **taproot** long tapering root of plant

**tap**[2] v strike lightly; n light blow; sound of this; n **t. dance** dance with special shoes that make rhythm audible; **taps** these shoes

**tap** v (strike lightly) knock, pat, rap, touch

**tape** n 1 long narrow band of fabric, paper, etc 2 (spool holding) length of magnetic tape; recording on this; v 1 fasten with tape 2 record on tape; ns **t. deck** tape recording component of sound system; **t. measure** flexible strip of fabric or metal for measuring lengths; **t. recorder** apparatus for recording on magnetic tape

**taper** v narrow gradually to point at one end; n thin candle

**tapestry** n fabric with designs hand-worked in wool

**tar** n thick black liquid distilled from coal, etc; v **tars, tarring, tarred** cover with tar

**taramasalata** n Greek appetizer of paste from fish roe

**tarantula** n large venomous spider

**tardy** n slow, late, reluctant

**target** n 1 objective 2 butt of jokes 3 round board marked in circles, to be shot at 4 object of attack (military, verbal)

**target** n 1 (objective) aim, ambition, end, goal, hope, intention, mark, object, purpose. 2 (butt of jokes) object, prey, quarry, scapegoat, victim

**tariff** n list of duties on imports and exports; list of charges

**tarmac** n mixture of tar and macadam used as road-surfacing material

**tarnish** v 1 spoil brightness of by exposure to air, etc 2 fig stain; sully; n loss of luster

**tarot** n set of cards used by fortune-teller

**tarpaulin** n waterproof canvas

**tarragon** n aromatic herb used for flavoring

**tarry** v linger; stay in a place

**tart**[1] adj 1 sour 2 scathing (of remark)

**tart** adj 1 (sour) acid, astringent, citrus, piquant, sharp, tangy. 2 (scathing) biting, caustic, cutting, sharp, stinging

**tart**[2] n open, or covered fruit pie

**tart**[3] phr v **tart up** sl embellish in a cheap way, esp in order to conceal faults

**tartan** n woolen fabric woven in various colored plaids

**tartar** n hard deposit forming on teeth; n **t. sauce** type of mayonnaise with capers, herbs, etc

**task** n piece of work imposed or undertaken; idm **take to task** reprove; n **task force** group detailed for specific operation

**task** *n* activity, assignment, charge, chore, duty, enterprise, errand, exercise, job, mission, undertaking, work

**tassel** *n* knotted bunch of threads, used as ornament

**taste** *v* 1 test, perceive flavor of; 2 have particular flavor of; *n* 1 flavor 2 small portion of food or drink 3 appetite 4 ability to appreciate good quality

**taste** *n* 1 (flavor) relish, savor, tang. 2 (small portion of food, drink) bite, dash, drop, morsel, mouthful, nibble, sample, sip. 3 (appetite) desire, fondness, inclination, leaning, liking, love, partiality, penchant, predilection, preference, relish. 4 (ability to appreciate good quality) class, culture, discernment, discrimination, elegance, judgment, grace, polish, refinement, style

**tasteful** *adj* showing refinement; in good taste
**tasteless** *adj* insipid, tactless
**tasty** *adj* pleasant to taste; savory

**tasty** *adj* appetizing, delicious, flavorsome, mouth-watering, piquant, scrumptious

**ta-ta** *interj* good-bye
**tattered** *adj* ragged
**tatters** *n* rags; torn fragments
**tattle** *v* gossip; talk indiscreetly
**tattoo**[1] *n* military pageant or spectacle
**tattoo**[2] *v* mark (skin) by pricking and inserting indelible pigments; *n* mark so made
**tatty** *adj* old and ragged

**tatty** *adj* battered, frayed, raggedy, scruffy, shabby, shoddy, tattered, threadbare, worn

**taunt** *v* jeer at; *n* jeer, gibe

**taunt** *v* deride, goad, insult, laugh at, mock, poke fun at, revile, ridicule, tease, torment

**taut** *adj* stretched tightly; *v* **tauten** make tight
**tautology** *n* unnecessary repetition
**tavern** *n* inn where alcohol is sold/consumed
**tawdry** *adj* showy, flashy, gaudy
**tawny** *adj* of light, brownish yellow color
**tax** *n* compulsory duty imposed on income, goods, etc; *v* 1 impose tax on 2 lay heavy burden on; *ns* **t. haven** country with low tax rate; **t. return** statement of income for tax authorities; *n* **taxation** act of levying tax; *adj* **taxable**; *n* **taxpayer**

**tax** *n* charge, due, duty, excise, imposition, levy, tariff, tithe, toll

**taxi** *n* car for public hire; *v* **taxies, taxiing** or **taxying, taxied** (of aircraft) travel on ground under own power before takeoff
**taxidermy** *n* art of preparing and stuffing animal skins; *n* **-dermist**
**TB** *abbr med* tuberculosis
**T-bone** *n* thick steak with T-shaped bone
**tea** *n* 1 dried leaves of tea plant, infused to make drink 2 light afternoon meal; *ns* **teabag** paper packet containing tea leaves; **t. rose** scented China rose; **t. towel** cloth for drying wet dishes, etc
**teach** *v* **teaching, taught** instruct; train; impart knowledge

**teach** *v* advise, coach, direct, drill, educate, enlighten, give lessons, guide, impart, inculcate, inform, instill, lecture, school, show, tutor

**teacher** *n* one who teaches or instructs

**teacher** *n* adviser, coach, don, governess, guide, guru, instructor, lecturer, master, mentor, mistress, pedagogue, professor, schoolmaster, schoolmistress, schoolteacher, trainer, tutor

**teak** *n* East Indian tree with very hard wood
**team** *n* number of people working, playing together; *phr v* **t. up with** *coll* work together

**team** *n* band, bunch, company, crew, gang, group, party, set, side, squad, troupe

**teapot** *n* container with spout for serving tea

**tear**[1] *n* single drop of saline fluid coming from eye; *adj* **tearful** shedding tears; sad; *ns* **teardrop**; **tear-gas** irritant poison gas, causing abnormal watering of eyes; **t.-jerker** story or film likely to provoke tears

**tear**[2] *v* **tearing, tore, torn** 1 rip 2 rush; *idm* **be torn between** be unable to decide between; *phr v* **tear down** 1 pull down 2 run fast down 3 *fig* malign; *n* torn hole

**tear** *v* (rip) claw, gash, gore, lacerate, mangle, pull apart, rend, rupture, scratch, shred, split, sunder
**tear** *n* gash, hole, laceration, opening, rent, rip, rupture, scratch, slit, split

**tease** *v* 1 poke fun at 2 worry 3 tear apart fibers of; *n* one who torments

**tease** *v* (poke fun at) bait, goad, laugh at, make fun of, mock, needle *inf*, pester, provoke, pull sb's leg, rib, taunt, torment

**teaspoon** *n* small spoon

**teat** *n* nipple of female mammal's breast; nipple of feeding bottle

**technical** *adj* pertaining to industrial or mechanical arts; peculiar to some specific branch of science or art; not understandable by laypeople; *n* **t. school** school with emphasis on practical subjects; *ns* **-ity** detail of procedure; **technique** method of execution or performance; **technician** one skilled in mechanical art

**technnocrat** *n* scientific expert in favor of technocracy

**technology** *n* science of industrial and mechanical arts; **technologist**; *adj* **-ological**

**teddy** *n* soft stuffed toy bear (*also* **t. bear**)

**tedious** *adj* dull, long, and boring

**tedious** *adj* banal, drab, dreary, endless, humdrum *inf*, laborious, long-drawn-out, long-winded, mind-numbing, monotonous, prosaic, repetitive, tiresome, uninteresting

**tedium** *n* weariness, boredom

**tee** *n* small peg off which golf ball is first played at each hole

**tee shirt** = **T-shirt**

**teem** *v* rain heavily; *phr v* **teem with** abound with

**teenager** *n* adolescent between 13–20

**teens** *n pl* age between 13–19

**teeter** *v* move or stand unsteadily

**teeth** *pl of* **tooth**

**teethe** *v* develop or cut teeth

**teetotal** *adj* never drinking alcohol; *n* **-ler**

**Teflon** [TM] substance used on surface of nonstick pans

**tele-** *prefix* at or over a distance

**telecommunications** *n pl* communication of messages over distances, *esp* by telephone and radio

**telegraph** *n* electrical apparatus for transmitting messages over a distance; *n* **t. pole** pole supporting telephone wires

**telepathy** *n* thought transference

**telephone** *n* instrument for transmitting conversation over a distance; *v* use, communicate by, telephone

**telephone** *v* call, dial, give sb a buzz *inf*, give sb a call, give sb a ring, phone, ring

**telescope** *n* optical instrument for viewing magnified images of distant objects; *v* compress forcibly; *adj* **telescopic**

**television** *n* transmission of visible moving images by electromagnetic waves; machine for viewing such; *v* **televise** transmit by television

**tell** *v* **telling, told** 1 give information 2 order; command 3 divulge sth secret 4 perceive; comprehend; *phr v* **tell off** reprimand; *adj* **telling** impressive

**tell** *v* 1 (give information) advise, announce, communicate, disclose, divulge, explain, express, impart, inform, let sb know, make known, mention, notify, recite, recount, relate, reveal, say, speak, state, utter. 2 (order) bid, call upon, command, direct, enjoin, instruct, require. 3 (divulge sth secret) blab *inf*, inform, rat, snitch, spill the beans, squeal

**telly** *n Brit coll* television
**temerity** *n* audacity; great boldness
**temp** *n coll* person in temporary employment; *v coll* work as a temp
**temper** *v* moderate; *n* 1 frame of mind 2 angry mood; *idm* **lose your temper** become very angry

**temper** *n* 1 (frame of mind) attitude, character, disposition, humor, makeup, mood, nature, personality, temperament. 2 (angry mood) anger, annoyance, fury, hot-headedness, ill-humor, irascibility, irritability, passion, peevishness, petulance, rage, tantrum, wrath. 3 (lose your temper) blow up, blow your top *inf*, explode, flip, fly into a rage, get angry, go crazy, go mad, hit the roof *inf*, lose your cool *inf*, see red

**temperament** *n* natural disposition; emotional mood; *adj* **-al** unreliable; unstable; liable to strong changes of mood
**temperate** *adj* moderate and restrained; (of climate) not extreme; *n* **temperance** 1 abstinence, *esp* from alcohol 2 moderation
**temperature** *n* degree of heat or cold in atmosphere or body; *idm* **have a temperature** be feverish
**tempest** *n* violent storm; *fig* violent emotion; *adj* **-uous** stormy; violently excited
**template** *n* mold, pattern, used as guide in shaping
**temple**[1] *n* building, place of worship
**temple**[2] *n* flat part of head on either side of forehead

**tempo** *n* degree of speed; rate; pace
**temporal** *adj* 1 relating to time 2 secular
**temporary** *adj* lasting short time; not permanent

**temporary** *adj* brief, ephemeral, fleeting, impermanent, interim, momentary, passing, provisional, short-lived, short-term, transient, transitory

**temporize** *v* try to avoid making decision
**tempt** *v* try to persuade, *esp* to evil; *ns* **-ter**; **-tation** act of tempting; attraction

**tempt** *v* allure, attract, bait, bribe, cajole, coax, dare, entice, inveigle, invite, lure, persuade, provoke, seduce, tantalize, woo

**ten** *n, pron, det* cardinal number next after nine; 10
**tenable** *adj* (of opinions, etc) logical
**tenacious** *adj* holding fast; unyielding; *n* **tenacity**
**tenant** *n* one who holds land or house, etc on rent or lease; *n* **tenancy**
**tend**[1] *v* take care of; watch over
**tend**[2] *v* have inclination; move in certain direction
**tendency** *n* inclination, bent, trend

**tendency** *n* bias, disposition, drift, leaning, partiality, penchant, predilection, predisposition, preference, proclivity, proneness, propensity, susceptibility

**tender**[1] *v* offer; make estimate; *n* offer made to carry out work, etc at fixed price
**tender**[2] *adj* 1 delicate 2 loving 3 painful; *adj* **t.-hearted** kind; *n* **tenderness**

**tender** *adj* 1 (delicate) fragile, frail, sensitive, soft, vulnerable, weak. 2 (loving) affectionate, caring, compassionate, concerned, emotional, gentle, kind, sentimental, solicitous, sympathetic, warm

a b c d e f g h i j k l m n o p q r s **t** u v w x y z

**tenderize** *v* make (sinewy meat) more tender

**tenderloin** *n* cut of pork, beef between sirloin and ribs

**tendon** *n* sinew attaching muscle to bone

**tendril** *n* coiling stem in climbing plants

**tenement** *n* house, dwelling divided into separate apartments

**tenet** *n* opinion, belief held as true

**tennis** *n* game for two or four players, in which ball is struck over net with rackets

**tenor** *n* singing voice between baritone/alto

**tense**[1] *n* modification of verb to show time of action

**tense**[2] *adj* **1** not relaxed **2** stressful **3** stretched tight

> **tense** *adj* **1** (not relaxed) anxious, apprehensive, edgy, highly strung, jittery, jumpy, nervous, on edge, stressed, uptight *inf*, worried. **2** (stressful) exciting, fraught, nail-biting *inf*, nerve-racking, strained, worrying. **3** (stretched tight) firm, flexed, rigid, strained, taut, tight

**tension** *n* **1** emotional strain **2** tightness

> **tension** *n* **1** (emotional strain) anxiety, apprehension, excitement, nervousness, pressure, stress, suspense, unease, worry. **2** (tightness) pull, strain, tautness

**tent** *n* portable canvas shelter

**tentacle** *n* long, flexible organ of feeling

**tentative** *adj* cautious; not definite

> **tentative** *adj* doubtful, faltering, hesitant, indecisive, indefinite, nervous, preliminary, provisional, shy, timid, uncertain, unsure

**tenterhooks** *idm* **on tenterhooks** in state of anxiety; suspense

**tenth** *adj, n, pron, det* ordinal number of ten; next after ninth

**tenuous** *adj* **1** thin, fine, flimsy **2** too subtle

**tenure** *n* act of holding land, office, etc

**tepid** *adj* lukewarm; not enthusiastic

**tequila** *n* Mexican strong alcoholic drink

**term** *n* **1** word or expression **2** period of time **3** period when schools are open; *v* designate, call

> **term** *n* **1** (word) appellation, denomination, designation, name, phrase, title. **2** (period of time) duration, season, span, spell

**terminal** *n* **1** (passenger building at) airport or end station of rail, bus line **2** place of connection to electric circuit **3** *comput* apparatus for input to and output from central computer; *adj* of, near the end; *n* **t. disease** incurable, fatal illness

**terminate** *v* bring to an end

**terminology** *n* special, technical words

**terminus** *n* station at end of railway, bus line; *pl* **-ni** or **-nuses**

**termite** *n* one of order of destructive insects; so-called white ant

**terms** *n pl* conditions of agreement or sale; *idm* **come to terms with** reach agreement; *idm* **on good/bad, etc terms (with)** having a good/bad, etc relationship (with)

**terrace** *n* raised level platform of earth, etc; colonnaded porch, promenade; *v* build up, cut, into form of terrace; *adj* **terraced** arranged in terraces (*n* **t. house** row house)

**terracotta** *n It* hard reddish brown pottery

**terrain** *n Fr* tract of land

**terrapin** *n* edible fresh-water turtle

**terrarium** *n* closed container for growing plants; *pl* **-iums** or **terraria**

**terrestrial** *adj* earthly; of, living on dry land

**terrible** *adj* **1** of poor quality **2** very unpleasant; *adv* **-ibly 1** badly **2** *coll* very

> **terrible** *adj* **1** (of poor quality) abysmal, appalling, dire, dreadful, no good, poor, rotten, useless. **2** (very unpleasant) awful, dreadful, frightful, ghastly, gruesome, harrowing, horrible, horrific, horrendous, hideous, loathsome, nasty, outrageous, shocking, unspeakable, unthinkable, vile

**terrier** n one of several breeds of dog
**terrific** adj coll wonderful, excellent; adv **-ally** extremely

terrific adj amazing, brilliant, fabulous, fantastic, fine, good, great, marvelous, outstanding, superb

**terrify** v fill with terror; adjs **-ified, -ifying**

terrify v alarm, frighten, horrify, make sb's blood run cold inf, paralyze, petrify, scare sb to death, shock, terrorize

**territory** n region; district ruled by state or ruler; adj **territorial** of territory
**terror** n extreme fear

terror n alarm, dread, fear, fright, horror, panic, shock, trepidation

**terrorist** n (person) using violence for political ends; n **-ism**
**terrorize** v intimidate with violent threats
**terse** adj concise; curt, abrupt in speech
**tertiary** adj of third rank or order
**test** n critical, searching examination; v prove, examine the quality, extent, reliability of; ns **t. case** lawsuit which establishes precedent; **t. tube** small tubular container used in scientific experiments (n **t.-tube baby** baby conceived by artificial insemination, esp in vitro fertilization); v **t.-drive** take on trial drive before deciding whether to purchase

test n analysis, appraisal, assessment, check, checkup, evaluation, exam, investigation, questionnaire, quiz, research, trial
test v analyze, appraise, assess, check, evaluate, experiment, investigate, put to the test, question, research, study, try out, verify

**testament** n 1 one of two major divisions of Bible 2 leg will

**testicle** n sperm-secreting gland in male animals, typically paired
**testify** v **testifies, testifying, testified** give evidence; ns **testimony** solemn statement; evidence; **testimonial** document setting forth person's character, ability, etc
**testis** n anat testicle; pl **testes**
**testosterone** n hormonecontroling development of secondary sex characteristics in males
**testy** adj irritable, irascible
**tetanus** n disease causing muscle spasms
**tetchy** adj coll irritable; bad-tempered
**tête-à-tête** n Fr private talk, meeting
**tether** v fasten, tie up with rope; n rope, chain for fastening grazing animal
**text** n 1 main part of book 2 verse, short passage of Scripture; n **textbook** book used for study; adj **textual** of, based on, text
**textile** adj woven; n woven fabric
**texture** n degree of coarseness, fineness, etc as felt by touch

texture n appearance, composition, consistency, feel, grain, quality, structure, surface, touch, weave

**than** prep used after compound adjectives and adverbs before nouns and pronouns
**thank** v express gratitude to; interj **t. you** expressing gratitude

thank v offer thanks, say thank you, show appreciation, show gratitude

**thankful** adj grateful

thankful adj appreciative, glad, happy, pleased, relieved

**thankless** adj unlikely to bring gratitude
**thanks** n pl words of gratitude

thanks n acknowledgment, appreciation, credit, gratefulness, gratitude, recognition

a
b
c
d
e
f
g
h
i
j
k
l
m
n
o
p
q
r
s
**t**
u
v
w
x
y
z

**thanksgiving** n expression of thanks
**that** adj, dem pron (thing, person) just
mentioned, or pointed out; pl **those**;
conj introduces noun, or adverbial clause
**thatch** v cover (roof) with reeds, straw, etc;
n **thatch, thatching** straw, reeds, etc used
as covering
**thaw** v 1 (of snow, etc) melt; 2 fig become
more friendly
**the** definite art indicating particular person or
thing
**theater** n 1 place where plays are performed
2 room in hospital where operations are
performed 3 drama; dramatic works
collectively; adj **theatrical** 1 relating to
theater 2 affected, insincere
**theft** n act of stealing

> **theft** n burglary, embezzlement, fraud,
> larceny, pilfering, robbery, shoplifting,
> stealing, swindling, thieving

**their** poss adj of **them**; poss pron belonging to
them
**them** pron objective case of **they**; those
persons or things; pron **themselves**
emphatic and reflexive form; idm **by
themselves** (they) alone
**theme** n important idea in talk or writing;
n **t. park** open-air enclosure with
entertainments based on a single subject

> **theme** n argument, idea, matter, subject,
> text, topic

**then** adv 1 at that time 2 next 3 that being
so; therefore; n that time.
**thence** adv ar 1 from that place 2 for that
reason; therefore; **thenceforth** from that
time on (also **thenceforward**)
**theodolite** n surveying instrument for
measuring angles
**theology** n systematic study of religion;
adj **theological**
**theorem** n proposition to be established by
reasoning

**theoretical** adj based on theory; speculative
(adv **-ly**); n **theorist** unpractical person;
v **theorize** form, put forward theories
**theory** n set of ideas or opinion put forward
to explain sth

> **theory** n argument, assumption, belief,
> conjecture, explanation, guess,
> hypothesis, notion, speculation, view

**therapeutic** adj 1 promoting better health or
mental state 2 of, for healing; pl **-s** branch of
medicine concerned with curing disease
**therapy** n curative treatment; n **therapist**
**there** adv in that place; adv **thereabouts**
1 approximately 2 in that vicinity;
**thereafter** fml always after that; **thereby**
by this means; **therefore** for this reason;
**thereupon** fml immediately
**therm** n unit of heat; adj **thermal** of, by heat
**thermo-** prefix of, by heat
**thermodynamics** n branch of science dealing
with relation between thermal and
mechanical energy
**thermometer** n instrument for measuring
temperature
**Thermos** n [TM] vacuum flask
**thermostat** n device for regulating
temperature automatically
**thesaurus** n lexicon of words grouped by
meaning
**these** pron pl of **this**
**thesis** n 1 theory 2 long essay; pl **theses**

> **thesis** n 1 (theory) argument, assertion,
> contention, hypothesis, idea, opinion,
> proposition, view. 2 (essay) composition,
> dissertation, paper, treatise

**thespian** adj of acting; n actor
**they** pron 3rd person pl nom
**they'd** contracted form of 1 they had
2 they would
**they'll** contracted form of **they will**
**they're** contracted form of **they are**
**they've** contracted form of **they have**

**thiamine, thiamin** n Vitamin B$_1$
**thick** adj 1 wide; not thin 2 (of liquid) not flowing easily 3 dense 4 closely packed 5 sl stupid; adv (**-ly**); idm **be thick with** coll habitually associate with sb; idm **thick and fast** coll very frequently; idm **thick with** covered, filled with; idm **through thick and thin** despite all hardship; adj **t.-skinned** insensitive to pain/ criticism; v **-en**; n **-ness** 1 state of being thick 2 layer

**thick** adj 1 (wide) broad, bulky, chunky, deep, fat, large, solid, stout. 2 (not flowing easily) clotted, coagulated, concentrated, firm, dense, solid, sticky, stiff, viscous. 3 (dense) heavy, impenetrable, murky. 4 (closely packed) dense, impassable, impenetrable

**thicket** n dense growth of shrubs, trees
**thief** n one who steals; pl **thieves**; v **thieve** steal

**thief** n bandit, burglar, cheat, embezzler, housebreaker, looter, mugger, pickpocket, pirate, robber, shoplifter, stealer, swindler

**thigh** n thick upper part of leg
**thimble** n small cap for protecting finger when sewing
**thin** adj 1 narrow 2 fine 3 slim 4 watery; v make, become thin; adv **-ly**; n **-ness**; n **thinner** liquid used to dilute paint

**thin** adj 1 (narrow) fine. 2 (fine) delicate, diaphanous, filmy, flimsy, gauzy, gossamer, see-through, sheer. 3 (slim) bony, gaunt, lanky, lean, scraggy, skinny, slender, slight, svelte, underweight, wiry. 4 (watery) dilute, diluted, runny, sloppy, weak

**thine** poss pron lit, ar 2nd person sing of **thou**
**thing** n any object, material or immaterial; idm **have a thing about** coll have strong like or dislike for; pl **-s** 1 personal possessions 2 general situation

**think** v 1 believe 2 reflect 3 imagine; pt, pp **thought**; phr vs **think out/through** plan in detail; idm **think over** consider carefully; **think up** invent; n **t. tank** group of experts meeting to advise on national problems

**think** v 1 (believe) conclude, consider, feel, guess inf, imagine, judge, presume, reckon, suppose. 2 (reflect) brood, chew things over, concentrate, daydream, deliberate, meditate, mull things over, muse, ponder, reminisce, worry. 3 (imagine) anticipate, envisage, expect, foresee, plan, visualize

**third** det, pron ordinal number of three; next after second; n third part; ns **t. party** person or body other than those involved in a relationship or contract; **t. person** form of verb or pronoun used for someone other than the speaker/writer or addressee; **T. World** underdeveloped countries
**thirst** n 1 craving for liquid 2 fig strong desire; v suffer thirst; adj **thirsty**
**thirteen** n, pron, det cardinal number three and ten; 13 (n, adj, pron, det **thirteenth** ordinal number 13th)
**thirty** n three times ten; 30; adj, n pron, det **thirtieth** ordinal number 30th
**this** dem adj, pron denotes thing, person near, just mentioned; pl **these**
**thistle** n prickly leaved flowering plant
**thither** adv ar to, toward that direction
**thong** n narrow strip of leather, strap
**thorn** n prickly spine on plant

**thorn** n barb, needle, prickle, spike, spine

**thorough** adj complete, absolute, careful; adj **thoroughbred** pure-bred; n purebred animal; n **thoroughfare** public road
**those** pron pl of **that**
**thou** pron lit, ar 2nd pers. sing. nom. of **you**
**though** conj in spite of; although; conj **as though** as if
**thought** pt, pp of **think**; n 1 careful consideration 2 idea 3 regard

a
b
c
d
e
f
g
h
i
j
k
l
m
n
o
p
q
r
s
t
u
v
w
x
y
z

**thought** n 1 (careful consideration) contemplation, deliberation, meditation, reflection, thinking, worrying. 2 (idea) notion, observation, opinion, plan

**thoughtful** adj thinking deeply; attentive to others

**thoughtless** adj careless; not thinking of others

**thousand** n, pron, det cardinal number, ten hundreds; 1,000; pl **-s** a large number adj, n, det **thousandth** ordinal number 1,000th

**thrash** 1 beat, flog 2 thresh; phr v **thrash out** fig clear up (problem, etc.) by discussion

**thread** n fine cord used for sewing; spiral groove cut in screw; v put thread into (needle, etc); adj **-bare** very worn

**threat** n 1 menace 2 statement of intention to injure

**threaten** v 1 put in danger 2 state intention to injure 3 give warning of danger, disaster

**threaten** v 1 (put in danger) endanger, imperil, jeopardize, put at risk. 2 (state intention to injure) bully, intimidate, issue threats to, lean on inf, pressurize

**three** n, pron, det cardinal number, one more than two; 3; adj **t-dimensional** with length, width and height (also **3-D**); ns **t.-legged race** race in which each competitor has one leg tied to leg of partner; **t. Rs** reading, writing, and arithmetic; basic educational skills

**thresh** v separate grain from chaff mechanically or by beating

**threshold** n stone or plank below door, at entrance to house, etc; (fig) beginning

**threw** pt of **throw**

**thrice** adv lit, ar three times

**thrift** n economy with money; adj **-y** frugal

**thrill** v stir emotions of; n exciting event

**thrill** v arouse, electrify, excite, stir, titillate

**thriller** n book or film of exciting, usu crime story

**thrilling** adj exciting

**thrive** v **thriving, thrived** grow well; prosper

**throat** n front part of neck; gullet; wind pipe

**throb** v **throbs, throbbing, throbbed** beat, pulsate strongly; n beat, palpitation (of heart, etc)

**throb** v palpitate, pound, thump, vibrate

**thrombosis** n med clotting of blood in blood vessel

**throne** n seat of state, esp of regent

**throng** n large number of people; v crowd

**throttle** n valve in engine regulating flow of steam, gas, etc; v strangle

**throttle** v asphyxiate, choke, smother, stifle, suffocate

**through** prep 1 from end to end 2 by means of; 3 across; adv from end to end; adv, prep **throughout** right through; in every particular

**throughput** n quantity of work or material produced in given time

**throw** v **throwing, threw, thrown** 1 hurl 2 dislodge (from saddle) 3 form (pottery) on wheel; phr vs **throw away** discard; **throw in** add without extra charge; **throw off** 1 escape from 2 resist (illness); **throw together** coll construct hastily; **throw up** coll vomit; n 1 act of throwing 2 distance thrown; adj **t.-away** 1 expendable 2 casual (remark); n **t. back** example of regression

**throw** v 1 (hurl) cast, chuck inf, fling, heave, launch, lob, pitch, project, propel, shy, sling, toss. 2 (throw away) chuck out inf, discard, dispense with, dispose of, dump inf, jettison, reject, scrap, throw out

**thrum** v **thrums, thrumming, thrummed** drum, strum, or repeat monotonously

**hrush**[1] n one of several varieties of songbirds

**hrush**[2] n fungal infection with candida fungus, *esp* in mouth (*also* throat and vagina)

**hrust** v **thrusting, thrust** push; lunge; stab with violent action; n lunge

**hud** n dull, sound as of heavy body falling on ground; v **thuds, thudding, thudded** make such sound

> **thud** n bang, clunk, crash, smack, thump
> **thud** v bang, clump, crash, knock, smack, thump

**hug** n murderous ruffian; robber; n **thuggery**

**humb** n short thick inner finger of hand; *idm* **thumbs up/down** sign of approval/disapproval; *idm* **under sb's thumb** ruled by sb; *idm* **thumb a ride** obtain ride from passing motorist; ns **t. nail** nail of thumb; **thumbscrew** former instrument of torture; v make dirty (pages of book, etc) by handling

**hump** v strike with heavy blow; n such blow, or sound of it

> **thump** v bang, batter, beat, clobber *sl*, crash, hit, knock, pound, punch, rap, smack, strike, thrash, thud, whack *inf*

**hunder** n 1 loud rumbling sound following flash of lightning 2 any such noise (as of applause, etc); v 1 emit thunder 2 utter with loud, powerful voice; ns **thunderbolt** 1 flash of lighting 2 *fig* startling news or event; **thunderclap** single crash of thunder

**Thursday** n fifth day of week

**hus** *adv lit, ar* in this way; accordingly

**hwack** v, n whack

**hwart** v hinder

> **thwart** v check, defeat, foil, frustrate, impede, obstruct, oppose, outwit, prevent, stand in the way of, stop, stump

**hy** *poss pron lit, ar* of **thee**; *pron* **thyself** emphatic form of **thou**

**thyme** n aromatic herb used in cooking

**thyroid** n large endocrine gland in neck

**tiara** n 1 jeweled small crown worn by women 2 triple crown of pope

**tibia** n shin bone; *pl* **-biae** or **-bias**

**tic** n convulsive twitching of facial muscles

**tick**[1] n blood-sucking parasite

**tick**[2] n 1 slight clicking, tapping noise, as of clock 2 *Brit* mark (✓) indicating that sth has been checked, *esp* for correctness; v 1 make sound of tick 2 mark with symbol ✓; *idm* **make sb tick** *coll* cause sb to behave as he/she does; *phr vs* **tick off** 1 check (items on list) by marking with ✓ 2 reprimand 3 annoy; anger

**tick**[3] n outer covering of mattress, pillow, etc

**ticket** n marked card or paper entitling holder to admission, travel, view, etc; v mark with ticket; label

> **ticket** n coupon, docket, label, pass, permit, slip, sticker, tab, tag, token, voucher

**tickle** v 1 itch; touch or stroke lightly to cause tingling sensation 2 amuse; *adj* **ticklish** 1 sensitive to tickling 2 difficult to deal with

**tidbit** n 1 choice morsel 2 spicy item of news

**tiddlywinks** n game in which flat circular disks are flipped into a cup

**tide** n 1 ebb and flow of surface of sea 2 *fig* trend; tendency; *phr v* **tide over** help through difficult period; *adj* **tidal** (n **t. wave** massive wave of great destructive power)

**tidings** n *pl* news

**tidy** *adj* 1 keeping things neat 2 neatly arranged; v **tidies, tidying, tidied** put in order

> **tidy** *adj* 1 (keeping things neat) careful, house-proud, methodical, neat, organized, presentable, systematic. 2 (neatly arranged) clean, in good order, shipshape, spick and span, spruce, trim, uncluttered, well-kept, well-ordered

**tie** *v* **tying, tied** 1 fasten with rope, etc formed into knot 2 (in games, etc) make equal score; *phr vs* **tie down** 1 restrict 2 force to make a clear statement or decision; **tie in** be connected with, consistent with; *n* necktie; connecting piece; equality of scores in contest; *n* **t.-breaker** means of finding winner from contestants with equal scores (*also* **tiebreak**)

**tie** *v* (fasten with rope) attach, bind, chain, connect, couple, hitch, join, knot, lash, link, moor, rope, secure, splice, tether

**tier** *n* 1 row, rank 2 several rows placed one above the other
**tiff** *n* trifling dispute; passing quarrel
**tiger** *n* large, carnivorous mammal, having tawny back with black stripes; *fem* **tigress**
**tight** *adj* 1 firm, taut 2 cramped 3 close fitting 4 mean 5 *sl* drunk; *n pl* close fitting knitted garment covering legs and lower part of body; *adjs* **t.-fisted** stingy; **t.-lipped** 1 with lips pressed close together 2 refusing to speak; *n* **tightrope** rope stretched horizontally for sb to walk along as acrobatic feat; *v* **tighten** make, become tighter

**tight** *adj* 1 (firm, taut) fixed, rigid, secure, stiff, strained, stretched. 2 (cramped) compact, constricted, inadequate, limited, restricted, small. 3 (close fitting) figure-hugging, snug, tight-fitting, too small

**tile** *n* flat cake of baked clay used for roofing; one of finer clay, plastic, etc. for inside use; *v* cover with tiles; *adj* **tiled**
**till**¹ *prep* up to time of; *conj* to time that
**till**² *n* small drawer or box where cash is kept
**till**³ *v* cultivate (ground)
**tilt** *v* slope; slant; tip up; *n* slope, slant
**timber** *n* 1 wood cut and prepared for building 2 trees; *v* furnish with timber; *adj* **timbered** built of or with timber
**timbre** *n mus* quality of sound of different musical instruments or voices

**time** *n* 1 concept of past, present, and future 2 hour 3 period of history 4 period of time 5 moment; *idm* **behind the times** out-of-date; *idm* **in time** 1 not too late 2 after some time has passed; *idm* **on time** punctual(ly); *idm* **take one's time** make no attempt to hurry; *n* **t. bomb** bomb set to explode at given moment; *v* measure time taken by; plan time for sth to happen

**time** *n* 1 (period of history) age, epoch, era, period. 2 (period of time) interval, spell, stretch, term, while. 3 (moment) juncture, occasion, opportunity, point

**timing** *n* choosing of appropriate moment
**timeless** *adj* 1 never ending 2 unchanging
**timely** *adj* well-timed; opportune
**timetable** *n* 1 (list of) times for public transport 2 (list of) times for lessons, lectures, etc 3 (plan of) timing for business operation; *v* plan sequence of events
**timid** *adj* shy; easily frightened

**timid** *adj* afraid, apprehensive, bashful, coy, fearful, nervous, scared, spineless, unadventurous, wimpish *inf*

**timorous** *adj fml* timid; easily frightened
**tin** *n* 1 white malleable metal 2 container made of tin or tin-coated iron; *ns* **tinfoil** thin flexible metallic sheet; **t. hat** metal helmet worn by soldiers
**tincture** *n* medicinal solution
**tinge** *v* color, flavor slightly; *n* slight trace
**tingle** *v* feel prickling or stinging sensation; *n* such sensation

**tingle** *v* itch, prickle, sting, tickle

**tinker** *n* mender, *esp* itinerant, of pots and pans; *v* mend, patch, *esp* clumsily
**tinkle** *v* give out series of light sounds like small bell; *n* this action or sound
**tinnitus** *n med* hearing disorder causing ringing sound

**tinsel** *n* glittering material made of thin strips of metal, used for decoration

**tint** *v* color, tinge; *v* dye; give color to

**tiny** *adj* very small

> **tiny** *adj* diminutive, infinitesimal, insignificant, little, microscopic, mini, miniature, minute, negligible, teeny-weeny *inf*, wee

**tip** *n* **1** pointed end of anything **2** useful piece of information **3** gratuity given to waiter, etcfor service; *v* **tips, tipping, tipped 1** tilt, pour, upset **2** lean over; be tilted **3** give tip to; *phr v* **tip off** *coll* give advance, *esp* secret warning (*n* **t.-off**)

> **tip** *n* **1** (pointed end) apex, cap, cover, crown, end, head, nib, peak, pinnacle, point, summit, top. **2** (useful piece of information) hint, piece of advice, pointer, recommendation, suggestion, tip-off

**tipple** *v* take strong drink frequently; *n* **tippler**

**tipster** *n* person giving advice on likely results of (*esp* horse, dog) races

**tipsy** *adj* drunk; mildly intoxicated

**tiptoe** *v* **tiptoes, tiptoeing, tiptoed** walk on toes; walk softly

**tire**[1] *n* ring of metal, rubber, etc, on a round wheel

**tire**[2] *v* make or become weary or fatigued; *adj* needing rest, sleep

> **tired** *adj* dead on your feet, dog-tired *inf*, done in *inf*, drained, drowsy, exhausted, fatigued, shattered *inf*, sleepy, weary, worn out, zonked *sl*

**tiresome** *adj* **1** annoying **2** tedious

**tissue** *n* **1** structural material of body of animals or plants **2** light woven fabric; *n* **tissue-paper** very thin wrapping paper

**tit** *n* small, brightly colored bird

**titan** *n* person of great strength, intellect

**titanic** *adj* huge, gigantic

**titanium** *n* gray-coloued metallic element

**titchy** *adj coll* tiny

**tithe** *n* tenth part, *esp* of profit from land, produce, etc paid to church

**titillate** *v* stimulate pleasurably; *n* **-lation**

**titivate** *v* smarten up; adorn

**title** *n* **1** heading of book, picture, etc **2** appellation of distinction or honor **3** name showing rank, occupation; *adj* **titled** having title of nobility; *n* **t.** legal document establishing ownership of land, etc

> **title** *n* (heading) caption, credit, headline, inscription, label, name

**titter** *v* utter quiet laugh; giggle; *n* such laugh

**tittle-tattle** *n* gossip; *also v*

**titular** *adj* having title but no real power

**tizzy** *n coll* state of nervous excitement

**T-junction** *n* T-shaped road junction

**TNT** *abbr* trinitrotoluene (powerful explosive)

**to** *prep* **1** toward **2** expressing comparison, contrast **3** introducing infinitive mood of verb; *adv* to, into normal, desired position, etc; *adv* **to and fro** back and forth

**toad** *n* amphibianlike large frog; *n* **toadstool** any fleshy fungus other than mushroom, *esp* if poisonous

**toast** *v* **1** drink health of **2** make brown by heat; *n* **1** slice of bread browned by heat **2** proposal to drink health of **3** person toasted

> **toast** *v* **1** (drink health of) raise your glass to, salute. **2** (make brown) crisp, cook, grill, heat, warm

**tobacco** *n* plant whose leaves are used for smoking; its prepared and dried leaves; *n* **tobacconist** one who sells tobacco, etc

**toboggan** *n* sled for sliding down snowy slopes; *v* **toboggans, tobogganing, tobogganed** use, slide on toboggan

**today** *n* this day; *adv* on this day

**toddle** *v* walk unsteadily, as small child;
*n* **toddler** young child just starting to walk

**toe** *n* one of five digits of foot

**toffee** *n* candy of boiled sugar with butter

**tofu** *n* bean curd

**toga** *n* flowing robe of ancient Romans

**together** *adv* 1 in company 2 happening at
same time, place, etc

**toggle** *n* short metal or wooden pin fixed
through loop (of rope, etc) to secure it

**togs** *n sl* clothes, dress

**toil** *n* difficult work; *v* work hard

> **toil** *n* drudgery, effort, exertion, grind *inf*,
> hard work, industry, labor, slaving, work

**toilet** *n* bathroom; *ns* **t. paper** paper for
cleaning oneself in a lavatory; **t. roll** roll of
toilet paper; **t. water** scented water; dilute
form of perfume; **toiletries** articles used for
personal cleanliness, etc

**token** *n* symbol; coin, disk, or voucher

**tolerable** *adj* fairly good; bearable

**tolerant** willing to tolerate others;
broadminded; *n* **tolerance**

> **tolerant** *adj* charitable, easygoing,
> magnanimous, open-minded, patient,
> sympathetic, understanding, unprejudiced

**tolerate** *v* put up with; *n* **-ation**

> **tolerate** *v* accept, allow, bear, condone,
> countenance, endure, permit, sanction,
> stand, stomach, submit to, suffer, swallow,
> take, undergo

**toll**[1] *n* tax, duty paid for use of road, etc

**toll**[2] *v* cause (bell) to ring slowly at regular
intervals, *esp* at funeral

**tomahawk** *n* light hatchet used by Native
Americans in war or hunting

**tomato** *n* plant with red edible fruit; *pl* **-oes**

**tomb** *n* grave; vault; *n* **t.stone** memorial
stone on grave

**tombola** *n* kind of lottery

**tomboy** *n* romping, athletic girl

**tomcat** *n* male cat

**tome** *n* volume; large book

**tommy-gun** *n* short-barreled submachine gun

**tomorrow** *adv* on, during day after this;
*n* day after today

**tom-tom** *n* primitive African/Oriental drum

**ton** *n* 1 measure of weight, 2,000 lbs; 2 unit of
ship's carrying capacity; *pl* **-s** very large
amount (*also adv*); *n* **tonnage** freight-
carrying capacity of ship; ships collectively

**tone** *n* 1 pitch of voice 2 prevailing mood
3 shade of color 4 musical sound 5 vigor;
*v* give tone to; *adj* **t.-deaf** unable to
distinguish between notes of different
musical pitch

> **tone** *n* (pitch of voice) accent, emphasis,
> force, inflection, intonation, modulation,
> phrasing, pitch, sound, sound quality,
> stress, timbre, tone of voice, volume

**tongs** *n pl* hinged or jointed grasping device

**tongue** *n* 1 fleshy muscular organ in mouth;
chief organ of taste, speech, etc 2 language;
speech; *idm* (**with**) **tongue in cheek**
insincerely; *adj* **t.-tied** unable to speak;
*n* **t.-twister** phrase difficult to pronounce

**tonic** *n* 1 *med* st that invigorates 2 tonic
water; *n* **t. water** carbonated mineral water
flavored with quinine

**tonight** *n* this night; night after today;
*adv* on, during this night

**tonnage** *n* cargo capacity of ship (in tons)

**tonne** *n* measure of weight equal to 1,000
kilograms

**tonsil** *n* oval mass of tissue in throat;
*n* **tonsillitis** inflammation of tonsils

**too** *adv* 1 in addition 2 excessively; as well

**took** *pt of* **take**

**tool** *n* implement, appliance; *v* shape, mark
with tool

> **tool** *n* aid, contrivance, device, gadget,
> instrument, machine, utensil

**toot** *n* sound of horn or trumpet; *v* make this sound

**tooth** *n pl* **teeth 1** one of hard growths inside jaws of vertebrates **2** prong **3** cog; *adjs* **toothless** without teeth; **toothsome** *coll* tasty; *ns* **toothbrush/paste** brush/paste for cleaning teeth; **toothpick** small pointed stick for removing food from between teeth

**tootle** *v coll* play wind instrument casually

**top**[1] *n* **1** highest part **2** cover **3** highest rank; *v* **tops, topping, topped 1** be higher, better than **2** provide top for; *ns* **t. brass** *coll* high-ranking military officers; **t. dog** person in most powerful position; **t. hat** man's formal tall cylindrical black or gray hat; **topspin** spinning action causing ball to shoot forward as it hits the ground; *adjs* **t.-notch** *coll* of the best; **t.-secret** highly confidential; *adj* **-less** with breasts uncovered

> **top** *n* **1** (highest part) apex, crest, crown, head, height, peak, pinnacle, summit, tip, vertex, zenith. **2** (cover) cap, cork, covering, lid, stopper

**top**[2] *n* small spinning toy

**topaz** *n* yellowish semiprecious stone

**topiary** *n* art of cutting living shrubs, trees into shapes of animals, birds, etc; *n* **-arist**

**topic** *n* subject of thought or discussion; *adj* **-al** connected with subject of current interest

> **topic** *n* issue, matter, point, question, subject, text, theme

**topography** *n* detailed features of district; *n* **grapher**; *adj* **-graphical**

**topper** *n coll* top hat

**topping** *n* garnish on food

**topple** *v* fall over; overbalance

**topsy-turvy** *adj* upset; upside-down

**torch** portable flame; *n* **torchlight** light shed by torches

**tore** *pt of* **tear**

**torment** *n* suffering; anguish of mind or body; *v* **1** torture **2** tease; *n* **-tor**

> **torment** *v* **1** (torture) distress, harrow, hurt, pain, persecute, plague, victimize. **2** (tease) aggravate, annoy, bother, harass, hassle, irritate, persecute, pester, provoke

**tornado** *n* violent storm; *pl* **-oes** or **-os**

**torpedo** *n* self-propelled underwater missile used for destroying shipping; *pl* **-oes**

**torpid** *adj* sluggish; apathetic; *ns* **-ity** state of being torpid; **torpor** inactivity of mind

**torque** *n* **1** twisted collar, necklace, or chain **2** *mech* twisting force or movement

**torrent** *n* **1** violently rushing stream **2** *fig* rush of words; *adj* **-ial** falling with great violence

> **torrent** *n* (violently rushing stream) cascade, current, deluge, downpour, flood, flow, gush, rush, spate, stream, tide

**torrid** *adj* **1** (of climate) very hot and dry **2** passionate; **t. zone** that between tropics

**torsion** *n* state of being twisted

**torso** *n* **1** trunk of human body **2** limbless, headless statue; *pl* **-sos**

**tortilla** *n* Mexican flat bread

**tortoise** *n* reptile with complete scaly covering for body; *n* **tortoiseshell** mottled brown shell of tortoise, polished and used commercially

**tortuous** *adj* **1** twisting; winding **2** (of mind, aims, etc) devious

**torture** *n* **1** deliverate infliction of severe pain **2** great mental anguish; *v* subject to torture; *n* **torturer**

> **torture** *n* abuse, agony, cruelty, distress, hell, humiliation, martyrdom, persecution, punishment, suffering, torment

**Tory** *n* member of British Conservative party

**toss** *v* **1** throw up; fling; pitch **2** be flung, thrown **3** toss a coin with someone; *n* act of tossing; *n* **t.-up** uncertain situation

**tot** n **1** tiny child **2** small quantity, *esp* of drink; dram

**tot up** v **tots, totting, totted** add up

**total** n whole amount; complete number; *adj* entire, complete; v **totals, totaling, totaled 1** add up **2** amount to as whole; n **-ity** entirety

> **total** n answer, mass, sum, totality

**totalitarian** *adj* applied to state run by dictator or single political party, allowing no opposition or other political representation

> **totalitarian** *adj* absolute, authoritarian, autocratic, despotic, dictatorial, fascist, oppressive, tyrannical, undemocratic

**totem** n tribal symbol or emblem; n **t. pole** post supporting this

**totter** v **1** walk unsteadily **2** (of building, etc) be about to fall

**toucan** n large billed S American bird

**touch** v **1** put hand on **2** come into contact **3** move to pity, etc; n **1** act of touching **2** sense of feeling **3** characteristic method of technique; *idm* **touch wood** expressing hope of avoiding bad luck; *phr vs* **touch down** land (n **touchdown** score in football); **touch on/upon** mention briefly; *adj* **t.-and-go** risky; uncertain; n **touchstone** sth used to measure quality, integrity; *adj* **touchy** easily offended

> **touch** v **1** (put hand on) brush, caress, feel, finger, fondle, handle, pat, push, rub, stroke, tap. **2** (come into contact) abut, border, come together, converge, join, meet. **3** (move to pity) affect, disturb, get to, influence, make sad, soften, stir, upset

**touché** *interj Fr* acknowledging a hit in fencing or the aptness of an insult

**tough** *adj* **1** strong **2** difficult **3** needing effort to chew **4** ruthless; n *sl* hooligan; criminal; n **toughness**; v **toughen**

**tough** *adj* **1** (strong) durable, firm, hard, hard-wearing, indestructible, lasting, leathery, rigid, rugged, solid, sound, stiff, stout, sturdy, substantial, unbreakable, well-made. **2** (difficult) arduous, challenging, demanding, grueling, hard, strenuous. **3** (needing effort to chew) chewy, hard, gristly, leathery, rubbery, stringy. **4** (ruthless) grim, hard, harsh, macho, rough, rowdy, severe, strong, vicious, violent, wild

**toupée** n *Fr* artificial wig, *usu* worn by men

**tour** n journey around district; excursion; v make tour; travel; ns **-ist** one who travels for pleasure; **-ism** business of organizing, operating tours, and catering for tourists

> **tour** n jaunt, journey, outing, ride, trip

**tour de force** n *Fr* highly skillful achievement

**tournament** n **1** medieval contest between mounted knights **2** (of games) contest of skill, *usu* for championship

**tourniquet** n *Fr* tight bandage to stop arterial bleeding

**tousle** v make untidy; rumple; ruffle

**tout** v pester in order to sell; n one who touts

**tow** v pull along (vehicle, etc) by rope; n act of towing; *idm* **in tow** following closely behind

> **tow** v drag, draw, haul, lug, trail, tug

**toward** *adj* imminent, at hand; *prep* **toward** in direction of

**towel** n cloth used for drying (skin, china, etc) after washing; v dry, rub with towel; n **toweling** absorbent cloth for making towels

**tower** n tall strong structure often forming part of church or other building; v rise, stand very high; n **t. of strength** person that can be relied on for moral support

**town** *n* group of houses and other buildings, larger than village; *n* **t. hall** public building, headquarters of local government; *n* **township** town and surrounding area

**towpath** *n* path along bank of river or canal

**toxic** *adj* poisonous; *ns* **toxemia** blood poisoning; **toxicology** study of poisons and their effects; **toxin** poisonous organic substance

> **toxic** *adj* dangerous, deadly, lethal, noxious

**toy** *n* plaything; *phr v* **toy with** 1 consider without serious thought 2 handle in an aimless way; *n* **t. boy** young man with whom older woman has amorous relationship

**trace** *n* 1 visible signs left by anything 2 slight tinge; *n* **t. element** any chemical element found only in minute quantities in an organism, but essential to its healthy development; *v* 1 find 2 follow course, track of 3 draw, copy exactly, *esp* by use of tracing paper; *ns* **tracery** intricate decorative pattern of lines; **tracing** traced copy of drawing; **t. paper** thin, transparent paper on which tracings are made

> **trace** *v* 1 (find) detect, dig up, discover, get back, recover, retrieve, track down, turn up, uncover, unearth. 2 (follow) pursue, track, track down, trail, tail

**trachea** *n anat* windpipe; *pl* **-eae**

**track** *n* 1 mark, marks left by passing animal, person, vehicle 2 rough path 3 railway line 4 course for racing 5 *mus* any of the sections that make up the contents of a record, cassette, or CD; *idm* **keep/lose track of** manage/not manage to have up-to-date information about; *v* 1 follow the track of 2 (of camera) move while filming; *phr vs* **track down** find by searching; *ns* **tracker** person tracking wild animals (**t. dog** dog used by police to track down criminal); **t. event** (sport) athletic running contest; **t. record** past record of achievement

**tract**[1] *n* 1 expanse of country 2 *anat* system of related organs

**tract**[2] *n* pamphlet, treatise

**tractable** *adj* 1 easily managed 2 docile 3 easily wrought

**traction** *n* 1 act, process of drawing along 2 *med* artificial stretching of spine, etc; *n* **t. engine** steam engine for use on road

**tractor** *n* motor vehicle for drawing plow

**trad** *n coll* traditional; jazz (*also* **trad jazz**)

**trade** *n* 1 commerce; buying and selling of goods 2 skilled job; *v* 1 buy and sell goods 2 barter; *idm* **do good/bad trade** be successful/unsuccessful in business; *phr v* **trade in** offer in part exchange for sth new; *ns* **trader, trading; t. mark** 1 official design of manufacturer 2 *fig* characteristic thing by which one can be identified; **t. name** name given by manufacturer to identify brand; **t. union** labor organization that protects interests of workers (*ns* **t. unionism, -ist**); **t. wind** strong steady wind blowing toward the Equator

> **trade** *n* 1 (buying and selling) barter, business, commerce, dealing, exchange, marketing, merchandising, trading, traffic, trafficking, transactions. 2 (skilled job) business, calling, career, job, line of work, occupation, profession, skill

**tradition** *n* belief, custom, law, etc handed down verbally from one generation to another

> **tradition** *n* habit, institution, practice, rite, ritual, usage

**traditional** *adj* handed down from generation to generation; *adv* **-ly**

> **traditional** *adj* conventional, customary, established, familiar, fixed, habitual, historic, old, time-honored, usual

**traduce** *v* slander

**traffic** n 1 passing to and fro of vehicles, etc in street 2 trade; v **-ficking, -ficked** trade; ns **trafficker** person trading, *esp* in sth illicit or immoral; **t. jam** congested state of traffic in which vehicles come to a standstill; **t.-light** light that controls flow of traffic automatically; **t. police** officers appointed to monitor illegal parking of vehicles and to cite offenders

**tragedy** n 1 very sad event, calamity, *esp* one causing death 2 drama dealing with human misfortunes and sorrows

**tragic** adj 1 causing death or great suffering 2 showing great sorrow 3 relating to tragedy

**tragic** adj (causing death or great suffering) appalling, awful, catastrophic, disastrous, dreadful, fatal, ill-fated, ill-starred, miserable, sad, shocking, unfortunate

**trail** v 1 drag along ground 2 follow track of; shadow; n 1 track or trace 2 rough ill-defined road; n **trailer** 1 vehicle towed by another one 2 advertisement of forthcoming film, etc

**train** v 1 teach 2 practice, *esp* for sport 3 aim (gun); n 1 series of cars, etc drawn by locomotive 2 retinue 3 trailing part of dress hem ; ns **trainee** one who is being trained in certain skill, etc; **training** 1 process of educating 2 art of preparing (persons for athletic contests, or horses for racing)

**train** v 1 (teach) coach, drill, educate, guide, indoctrinate, instruct, prepare, school, tutor. 2 (practice) exercise, learn, prepare, rehearse, study, work out

**traipse** v walk around aimlessly

**trait** n characteristic feature

**traitor** n one who betrays one's country or another person

**traitor** n back-stabber, deceiver, deserter, double-crosser, informer, Judas, renegade

**trajectory** n path of missile fired or thrown through air

**tram** n public vehicle running on rails on road

**tramp** v 1 walk, tread heavily 2 travel as vagabond 3 travel on foot; n 1 homeless vagrant 2 long walk

**tramp** n (homeless person) bag lady, beggar, bum *inf*, dosser *inf*, down-and-out, drifter, vagrant, wanderer

**trample** v tread under foot

**trample** v crush, flatten, squash, squish *inf*, stamp on, stand on, step on, walk on

**trampoline** n frame with sheet of strong fabric stretched by springs where people can jump, bounce, and perform gymnastic exercises; v perform on this; n **-lining**

**trance** n state of suspended consciousness

**tranquil** adj calm, serene, peaceful, unruffled; n **tranquillity**; v **tranquilize** make calm (n **-izer** sedative)

**trans-** *prefix* across, through, beyond

**transact** v to carry through (negotiations, etc); n **-ion** piece of business; *pl* proceedings

**transcend** v go beyond; surpass

**transcribe** v copy out; write out (notes) in full

**transcript** n written version of speech

**transept** n part of church which crosses nave

**transfer** v **transfers, transferring, transferred** 1 move from one place to another 2 pass from one person to another; n 1 act of transferring; conveyance 2 design, etc transferred from one surface to another by heat, pressure, etc; adj **-able**; n **-ference**

**transfer** v 1 (move from one place to another) carry, change over, convey, ferry, move, relocate, transplant, transport. 2 (pass from one person to another) give, hand over, pass on, pass over, sell

**transfix** v 1 impale 2 *fig* root to the spot

**transform** *v* change shape, character, nature of; *n* **-ation**

> **transform** *v* alter, change, convert, make over, metamorphose, remodel, reshape, restructure, revolutionize

**transfuse** *v* transfer (blood) from veins of one person or animal to another; *n* **-fusion**

**transgress** *v* 1 violate (law) 2 sin; *ns* **-gression**; **-gressor**

**transient** *adj* brief, momentary

> **transient** *adj* ephemeral, fleeting, passing, short, short-lived, temporary, transitory

**transistor** *n* small electrical device; small portable radio containing this

**transit** *n* passage, crossing

**transition** *n* change; *adj* **-al**

> **transition** *n* conversion, development, evolution, progress, progression, shift, transformation

**transitory** *adj* of short duration; not lasting

**translate** *v* render into another language; *ns* **-lator**; **-lation**

**translucent** *adj* letting light pass through

**transmit** *v* **transmits, transmitting, transmitted** 1 communicate by radio, television 2 pass on 3 hand down (by heredity, etc); *ns* **-mitter** apparatus for sending out radio waves; **transmission** act of transmitting; that which is transmitted

**transparent** *adj* 1 able to be seen through 2 obvious; *ns* **-ence**; **-ency** 1 quality of being transparent 2 picture on transparent material, visible when lit from behind

> **transparent** *adj* 1 (able to be seen through) crystal-clear, glassy, see-through, sheer, translucent 2 (obvious) blatant, clear, evident, open, patent, plain, unambiguous, unequivocal, unmistakable, visible

**transpire** *v* 1 become known 2 *coll* happen

**transplant** *v* 1 dig up (plant) and replant elsewhere 2 *med* remove (healthy organ, tissue) and graft elsewhere; *n* **-ation**

**transport** *v* carry from one place to another; *n* 1 act, method of conveying persons, goods 2 vehicle, ship, etc. so used

> **transport** *v* bring, carry, convey, fetch, move, shift, ship, take, transfer

**transpose** *v* 1 change order of 2 *mus* put into different key

**transsexual** *n* person who feels he/she belongs to the opposite sex

**transvestism** *n* seeking of sexual pleasure from wearing clothes usually associated with opposite sex; *n* **transvestite** person who does this

**trap** *n* 1 device for catching, snaring animals, etc; pitfall 2 two-wheeled carriage; *v* **traps, trapping, trapped** catch or deceive by a trap or by cunning; *ns* **t.-door** hinged door in floor, ceiling, etc; **trapper** one who traps animals for their fur

> **trap** *v* block, catch out, confine, corner, cut off, hold back, imprison, inveigle, lure, shut in, snare, trick, trip up

**trapeze** *n* swinging horizontal bar for gymnastic and acrobatic use

**trapezium** *n* quadrilateral figure with only two sides parallel

**trappings** *n pl* equipment; ornaments

**trash** *n* 1 rubbish; useless matter 2 worthless person; *adj* **trashy** cheap, shoddy

**trashcan** *n* garbage receptacle

**trauma** *n* 1 injury 2 emotional injury caused by shock, etc; *v* **traumatize**

**traumatic** *adj* very distressing

> **traumatic** *adj* difficult, frightening, harrowing, nerve-racking, painful, stressful, upsetting

**travel** *v* **travels, traveling, traveled** move along; make journey; *n* **t. agent** person who takes responsibility for making travel arrangements and reservations; *n pl* **-s** 1 journeys 2 tour, *esp* abroad

> **travel** *v* backpack, cross, fly, go, go on a trip, go on vacation, journey, move, proceed, sail, tour, trek, visit, walk

**traveler** *n* one who travels; *n* **traveler's check** check issued by bank to client for use abroad
**traverse** *v* pass across; swivel
**travesty** *n* parody; distortion
**trawl** *n* open-mouthed fishing net drawn along ocean bottom; *v* fish with one; *n* **trawler** fishing vessel using trawl
**tray** *n* flat board, slab of wood, metal, etc, with rim, for carrying things
**treacherous** *adj* 1 dangerous 2 likely to betray others

> **treacherous** *adj* 1 (dangerous) hazardous, perilous, unsafe. 2 (likely to betray others) deceitful, disloyal, double-crossing, false, unfaithful, untrustworthy

**treachery** *n* betrayal; perfidy; breach of trust

> **treachery** *n* back-stabbing, deceit, disloyalty, double-dealing, duplicity, treason

**treacle** *n* thick syrup obtained from unrefined sugar, molasses
**tread** *v* 1 walk; step; set foot on 2 press, crush (*eg* grapes); *pt* **trod**, *pp* **trodden** or **trod**; *idm* **tread water** remain afloat by moving one's arms and legs; *n* manner, sound of walking; part of tire in contact with ground
**treason** *n* betrayal of sovereign or state
**treasure** *n* valuables, money; riches; *v* regard; store; cherish; *ns* **treasurer** person in charge of funds of club, society, etc; **treasury** department of state, collecting and controlling public money and taxation

**treasure** *n* booty, cache, gold, hoard, jewels, riches, treasure trove, valuables

**treat** *v* 1 behave toward, use 2 seal with chemically 3 pay expenses of; *n* special pleasurable event
**treatise** *n* systematic written account of something
**treatment** *n* 1 way of dealing with sth 2 method of curing sth

> **treatment** *n* 1 (way of dealing with sth) conduct, coverage, handling, management. 2 (method of curing sth) care, cure, first aid, healing, medicine, operation, remedy, surgery, therapy

**treaty** *n* agreement between states, etc
**treble** *adj* high pitched; *n* treble part of voice
**tree** *n* large perennial plant having woody trunk; **family t.** diagram showing descent from common ancestor
**trek** *v* make long journey; *n* long journey
**trellis** *n* structure of crossed wooden strips
**tremble** *v* shiver, quake; *n* shaking

> **tremble** *v* judder, quiver, shake, shudder, vibrate, wobble

**tremendous** *adj* 1 vast, amazing, awe-inspiring 2 *coll* very exciting; *adv* **-ly** extremely
**tremolo** *n* quivering effect in playing or singing
**tremor** *n* 1 shaking 2 thrill
**tremulous** 1 shaky, trembling 2 timid, fearful
**trench** *n* long furrow, dug in ground
**trenchant** *adj* keen, incisive, biting; *adv* **-ly**
**trend** *n* 1 general tendency 2 fashion; *n* **t.-setter** person leading the way in fashion

> **trend** *n* 1 (tendency) bias, development, direction, inclination, movement, shift. 2 (fashion) craze, fad, look, style, vogue

**trepidation** n state of alarm

**trespass** n 1 go unlawfully on another's land 2 commit an offense; n act of trespassing

**tress** n lock of hair; pl hair of head

**trestle** n wooden table

**tri-** prefix three

**trial** n 1 judicial inquiry 2 act of trying, testing 3 source of irritation; idm **stand trial** be tried in court

> **trial** n (judicial inquiry) case, court case, court-martial, court proceedings, hearing, inquiry, lawsuit, legal proceedings, litigation, prosecution, tribunal

**triangle** n figure with three angles; musical instrument; adj **triangular**

**triathlon** n athletic contest in running, swimming, and cycling

**tribe** n social unit; class; group; adj **tribal**; n **tribesman** member of tribe

**tribulation** n grief; affliction; mental distress

**tribunal** n court of justice or inquiry

**tributary** n stream flowing into larger one

**tribute** n act performed, words uttered as sign of respect

> **tribute** n accolade, acknowledgment, appreciation, compliment, honor, praise

**trice** n instant; brief space of time

**triceps** n large muscle at back of upper arm

**trick** n 1 deception 2 illusion 3 special way of doing sth; v cheat, deceive; n **trickery**

> **trick** n (deception) cheat, con inf, dodge, hoax, ploy, practical joke, prank, ruse, scam inf, stunt, swindle
> **trick** v con inf, diddle, double-cross, fool, pull a fast one inf, swindle, take sb in

**trickle** v flow slowly; n thin flow

**tricky** adj shifty; ingenious

**tricycle** n three-wheeled cycle

**trident** n three-pronged fork

**tried** pt, pp of **try**; adj well tested

**trifle** n 1 small, insignificant thing of no value 2 sweet dish of sponge cake, wine, and whipped cream, etc; phr v **trifle with** treat casually, without respect; adj **trifling** trivial

**trigger** n catch which releases spring to fire gun; phr v **trigger off** initiate large scale process by small act

**trigonometry** n branch of mathematics dealing with triangles

**trilateral** adj having three sides

**trilby** n man's soft felt hat

**trill** v sing, with vibrating sound; warble; n such singing

**trillion** n one million million; pl enormous quantity; a very large number

**trilogy** n series of three connected works

**trim** v trims, trimming, trimmed 1 prune 2 decorate (garment, etc); adj neat; tidy; n 1 act of trimming 2 decorative finish; n pl **trimmings** usual extras

> **trim** v (prune) clip, cut, cut back, even up, lop, pare, peel, shape, snip, tidy up
> **trim** adj smart, well-groomed

**trinity** n 1 the three divine persons of Godhead 2 state of being threefold

**trinket** n bauble; worthless trifle

**trio** n group of three; music for three voices or instruments; pl **-os**

**trip** v trips, tripping, tripped 1 stumble; make false step 2 skip; phr v **trip up** make a mistake; n short journey; n 1 short journey 2 act of tripping 3 sl sensations experienced from taking hallucinatory drug

> **trip** n (short journey) excursion, expedition, holiday, outing, ride, tour, visit

**tripartite** adj of, in three parts

**tripe** n 1 stomach of ruminant animal, prepared as food 2 coll nonsense, rubbish

**triple** adj threefold; v increase threefold; ns **t. jump** athletic contest of hop, stride and jump; **triplet** three of a kind, esp one of three siblings born together

a b c d e f g h i j k l m n o p q r s t u v w x y z

**tripod** *n* three-legged stand, support, etc
**trip wire** *n* stretched wire that activates alarm when tripped accidentally
**trite** *adj* banal; commonplace

> **trite** *adj* clichéd, dull, hackneyed, insincere, overused, stale, tired, unimaginative, uninspired, unoriginal

**triumph** *n* victory, success, exultation; *v* achieve success
**triumphant** *adj* happy because of success
**trivet** *n* three-legged stand for pot or kettle
**trivia** *n pl* things of little or no importance
**trivial** *adj* of no importance; *v* **-ize**

> **trivial** *adj* insignificant, minor, paltry, petty, trifling, unimportant, worthless

**trod** *pt, pp of* **tread**
**trodden** *pp of* **tread**
**Trojan** *n* person of courage and endurance
**troll** *n* legendary goblin, giant, or dwarf
**trolley** *n* light low cart or wheeled table, pushed by hand; **t. car** bus powered by overhead electric cable
**trollop** *n* slovenly disreputable woman
**trombone** *n* powerful brass wind-instrument with sliding tube; *n* **-bonist** trombone player
**troop** *n* number of people; subdivision of cavalry squadron; *pl* soldiers; *v* move as troop; crowd; *n* **-er** cavalry soldier

> **troop** *n* band, bunch, company, contingent, crowd, flock, gang, group, horde, pack, squad, team, unit

**trophy** *n* token of victory; prize
**tropic** *n* one of two parallels of latitude 23° 28' N and S of equator; *pl* hot regions of earth between these parallels; *adj* **-al** extremely hot; growing occurring in tropics
**trot** *v* **trots, trotting, trotted** (of horse, etc) run easily with short steps; *n* rapid pace of horse, etc; quick walk
**trotter** *n* animal foot, *esp* a pig's, used as food

**trouble** *v* disturb; worry; *n* **1** difficulty **2** unrest; disturbance; *ns* **t.-maker** person who causes trouble; **t.-shooter** person who helps to solve mechanical problems or to settle disputes; *adj* **troublesome** annoying; unruly

> **trouble** *v* afflict, bother, concern, distress, plague, torment, upset
> **trouble** *n* **1** (difficulty) affliction, anxiety, hassle, misfortune, nuisance, problem, suffering, tribulation, worry. **2** (unrest) bother, commotion, discontent, disorder, disturbance, fighting, fuss, rioting

**trough** *n* **1** long narrow container for food or water for animals **2** narrow channel between waves
**trounce** *v* beat, defeat, censure
**troupe** *n Fr* band of actors; touring company
**trouper** *n* performer of long experience
**trousers** *n pl* two-legged outer garment, enclosing legs from waist to ankles
**trousseau** *n Fr* bride's outfit
**trout** *n* edible freshwater fish
**trowel** *n* small flat-bladed tool for spreading mortar; small hollow-bladed tool for lifting, planting
**truant** *n* person who stays away from school, work, etc, without permission; *phr v* **play truant** be a truant
**truce** *n* temporary agreement to stop fighting

> **truce** *n* armistice, ceasefire, cessation, pact, peace, respite, suspension of hostilities

**truck** *n* motor vehicle for carrying heavy load
**truculent** *adj* aggressive, violent
**trudge** *v* walk wearily, with effort; *n* long tedious walk
**true** *adj* **1** in accordance with fact **2** genuine **3** correct **4** loyal; *adjs* **t.-blue** totally loyal; **t.-love** sweetheart; **t.-life** based on real events and people; *n* **truism** statement of something obviously true; *adv* **truly** really, loyally, sincerely

**true** *adj* 1 (in accordance with fact) correct, honest, legitimate, right, truthful, valid. 2 (genuine) actual, authentic, bona fide. 3 (correct) accurate, close, exact, precise

**truffle** *n* 1 exotic edible fungus, growing below ground 2 small chocolate confection
**trump** *n* card of suit temporarily ranking above others; *n* **t. card** 1 card of suit that is trump 2 *fig* way of gaining advantage; *adj* **trumped up** fabricated, concocted; *v* take trick with trump
**trumpet** *n* metal wind instrument; *v* sound on trumpet; *fig* announce widely
**truncate** *v* cut off; lop off
**truncheon** *n* short thick staff or cudgel
**trundle** *v* cause to roll along; move on wheels
**trunk** *n* 1 stem of tree 2 person's body not including head or limbs 3 large suitcase 4 long flexible snout of elephant; *n* **t. road** important main road
**truss** *v* bind, tie up, tie wings (of fowl, etc) before cooking; *n* surgical support for ruptured organ
**trust** *n* 1 faith 2 custody 3 group of persons administering fund; *v* have faith in; rely on; *ns* **trustee** one legally holding property in trust for another; **t. fund** money under control of a trust; *adjs* **trusting** willing to trust other people; **trustworthy** deserving to be trusted; **trusty** *fml* dependable

**trust** *n* 1 (faith) belief, confidence, expectation, reliance. 2 (custody) care, charge, guardianship, protection, responsibility, safekeeping
**trust** *v* be sure of, count on, depend on, have confidence in, put your faith in

**truth** *n* quality, state of being true; honesty

**truth** *n* accuracy, authenticity, candour, correctness, fact, genuineness, legitimacy, reality, truthfulness, validity, veracity

**try** *v* **tries, trying, tried** 1 attempt 2 conduct judicial inquiry into; *phr vs* **try on** put on (garment) to see if size, color, etc are right; **try out** test by experience; *n* attempt; (rugby football) touch-down; *adjs* **tried** proved, reliable; **trying** provoking, painful, wearisome

**try** *v* (attempt) aim, do your best, endeavor, have a go, have a stab at *inf*, make an attempt, make an effort, undertake

**tsar** *n* formerly emperor of Russia; *fem* **tsarina** (*also* **csar, csarina**)
**T-shirt** casual shirt with short T-shaped sleeves
**tub** *n* 1 wooden vessel, often shaped like half barrel 2 bath
**tuba** *n* low-pitched brass wind instrument
**tube** *n* long, hollow cylinder; underground electric railway; *adj* **tubular** shaped like tube

**tube** *n* conduit, duct, hose, pipe, roll

**tuber** *n* swollen part of underground stem, *eg* potato
**tuberculosis** *n* infectious disease
**tuck** *v* gather up; fold; *phr vs* **tuck in/into** 1 push end in, so that it is neatly hidden 2 *coll* eat heartily; **tuck up** make comfortable in bed; *n* stitched fold
**Tuesday** *n* third day of week
**tuft** *n* bunch, bundle. *esp* of grass, hair, etc
**tug** *v* **tugs, tugging, tugged** pull violently; *n* 1 act of tugging 2 small boat for towing; *n* **t. of war** contest of strength between two teams pulling in different directions on rope

**tug** *v* drag, haul, heave, jerk, wrench, yank

**tuition** *n* teaching; instruction
**tulip** *n* bulbous plant of lily family
**tumble** *v* 1 fall 2 decrease dramatically; *n* fall; *ns* **t. drier** machine with rotating drum for drying clothes; **tumbler** 1 acrobat 2 drinking glass without stem

A B C D E F G H I J K L M N O P Q R S **T** U V W X Y Z

tumble *v* 1 (fall) fall over, overbalance, pitch, roll, somersault, topple.
2 (decrease) collapse, crash, dive, drop, fall, nosedive, plummet, plunge, slump

tumor *n* abnormal growth in body
tumult *n* uproar, disturbance; *adj* **-uous** noisy
tumulus *n* ancient burial mound; *pl* **-li**
tuna *n* large edible ocean fish with dark flesh
tundra *n* frozen treeless plain
tune *n* 1 melody 2 harmony 3 correctness of pitch; *idm* **change one's t.** *fig* speak, act very differently; *idm* **in/out of tune** at correct musical pitch; *v* adjust to correct pitch; adjust radio, etc to receive programs on certain wave length

tune *n* (melody) ditty, music, song

tuneful *adj* pleasantly melodious

tuneful *adj* attractive, catchy, easy listening, lilting, lyrical, melodic, musical, sweet

tuneless *adj* with no melody
tunic *n* loose-belted, knee-length garment
tunnel *n* 1 underground passage, *esp* one for cars, trains 2 burrow (of mole, etc); *n* **t. vision** 1 sight defect from which sufferer can only see straight ahead 2 *fig* tendency to see only one aspect of a question; *v* **tunnels, tunneling, tunneled** make tunnel through
turban *n* Oriental head-covering made by coiling long strip of cloth around head
turbid *adj* muddy, opaque; *fig* confused
turbine *n* motor driven by jets of steam, water, etc playing on blades
turbojet *n, adj* (engine) using exhaust gas to drive turbine
turbot *n* large edible flat seafish
turbulent *adj* riotous, disorderly

turbulent *adj* rough, rowdy, stormy, tempestuous, unruly, unstable, volatile

tureen *n* deep, covered dish for serving soup
turf *n* area of earth covered by grass; sod; peat; *pl* **-fs** or **-ves**
turgid *adj* swollen, inflated, pompous
turkey *n* large, domestic edible fowl of pheasant family; *idm* **talk turkey** *coll* speak openly, negotiate seriously
Turkish *adj* pertaining to Turkey, the Turks
turmeric *n* aromatic plant of ginger family
turmoil *n* uproar, confusion

turmoil *n* bedlam, chaos, commotion, disorder, hubbub, pandemonium, tumult, turbulence, upheaval

turn *v* 1 move around; rotate 2 move to reverse side 3 change direction 4 go around (corner) 5 aim 6 become 7 go sour; *idm* **turn a blind eye/deaf ear** pretend not to see/hear; *idm* **turn one's stomach** make one feel sick; *phr vs* **turn down** 1 (turn controls to) reduce (heat, noise, etc) 2 refuse (request); **turn in** 1 fold inward 2 *coll* go to bed; **turn off** 1 cause to stop operating 2 cause to lose interest, *esp* sexually; **turn on** 1 cause to start operating 2 attack without warning 3 *sl* arouse with excitement, *esp* sexual; **turn out** 1 empty 2 extinguish 3 expel 4 happen; **turn over** 1 move to next page 2 ponder 3 (of engine) idle 4 do trade; **turn up** 1 arrive 2 find or be found 3 fold up, *esp* to shorten garment 4 raise in heat, volume, etc by turning controls; *n* 1 act of turning 2 change of direction 3 rightful time or opportunity 4 move from one period or condition to another 5 attack of illness 6 short theatrical performance; *idm* **(done) to a turn** (cooked) exactly right; *idm* **give sb a turn** shock sb; *idm* **in turn** 1 in rightful order 2 one after the other; *idm* **out of turn** 1 before one's proper time 2 in a tactless way; *ns* **t.around** time taken trequired to complete and return a job; **turnstile** revolving gate to control admission, *eg* to sports event; **t.-table** revolving flat surface for playing records

**turn** *v* **1** (move around) circle, coil, curl, go around, gyrate, loop, pivot, revolve, roll, rotate, spin, spiral, swivel, twirl, wind. **2** (move to reverse side) bend, flip, fold, invert, reverse. **3** (change direction) change course, go, head, move, steer, swerve, swing round, veer, wheel. **4** (go around corner) negotiate, round, take. **5** (aim) direct, point, train. **6** (become) change to, get, go. **7 turn down** (refuse) decline, reject, say no to, throw out, veto

**turning** *n* corner, curve, or branch in road; *n* **t. point** time when most important change occurs

**turning** *n* crossroads, exit, fork, junction, left turn, right turn, road, side road, turn, turn-off

**turnip** *n* plant with large white edible root
**turnover** *n* **1** amount of business done or rate of selling **2** changes in staff
**turpentine** *n* liquid solvent
**turquoise** *n* semiprecious greenish-blue stone; this color
**turret** *n* small tower
**turtle** *n* marine tortoise
**turtledove** *n* wild dove
**turtleneck** *n* (shirt or sweater with) high close-fitting neck band
**turves** *pl of* **turf**
**tusk** *n* long pointed tooth in some animals, as elephants, etc
**tussle** *n* scuffle; rough struggle; *v* engage in rough struggle
**tussock** *n* clump of grass; tuft
**tut** *interj* expressing annoyance or disapproval
**tutelage** *n* stage of acting as guardian, or being under guardianship
**tutor** *n* teacher, private instructor

**tutor** *n* coach, guru, lecturer, mentor, supervisor

**tutorial** *adj* informal discussion session for students
**tutu** *n* short, full, ballet skirt; *pl* **-us**
**tuxedo** *n* dinner jacket (*also* **tux**)
**TV** *abbr* television
**twaddle** *n* empty, foolish talk; nonsense
**twang** *n* **1** nasal speech **2** vibrating metallic sound; *v* pluck strings of musical instrument
**tweak** *n, v* nip, pinch
**twee** *adj* excessively dainty or sentimental
**tweed** *n* Scottish woolen cloth; *pl* **-s** suit of tweed; tweed clothes
**tweet** *v, n* chirp
**tweezers** *n pl* small metal instrument used for plucking, etc
**twelfth** *det, pron* ordinal number of twelve; next after eleventh; **T.-night** evening of January 6
**twelve** *n, adj* cardinal number one above eleven; 12
**twenty** *n, pron, det* cardinal number, twice ten; 20; *adj* **twentieth** ordinal number 20th
**twice** *adv* two times
**twig**[1] *n* small branch; shoot
**twig**[2] *v* **twigs, twigging, twigged** *coll* understand
**twilight** *n* **1** (fading light at) time after sunset before complete darkness **2** *fig* declining years (of life, career)

**twilight** *n* dusk, early evening, half-light, sundown, sunset, the end of the day

**twill** *n* diagonally ribbed fabric
**twin** *n* one of two babies born at one birth; *adj* **1** double **2** closely connected; resembling; *n* **t. bed** bed for one person; single bed; *v* **1** link, match closely **2** establish special offical relationship between (places in different countries); *n* **t. town** such a town
**twine** *v* twist, coil round; *n* strong string

**twine** *v* climb, entwine, intertwine, snake, spiral, weave, wind, worm, wrap

**twinge** *n* sudden, sharp, shooting pain

a b c d e f g h i j k l m n o p q r s **t** u v w x y z

**twinkle** v flash, sparkle intermittently; (of eyes) show sudden gleam of mirth; n **twinkling** intermittent sparkle; brief moment

**twirl** v turn or twist quickly; spin around

> **twirl** v coil, gyrate, pirouette, pivot, revolve, rotate, spiral, twiddle, whirl, wind

**twist** v 1 wind around 2 make, become bent 3 distort; idm **twist sb's arm** use physical or moral pressure to persuade sb; idm **twist sb round one's little finger** be able to get from somebody anything one wants; n 1 act of twisting 2 spiral 3 bend 4 unexpected turn of events; n **-er** coll 1 swindler 2 tornado 3 difficult puzzle

> **twist** v 1 (turn around) coil, corkscrew, curl, meander, screw, snake, spin, spiral, swivel, twine, weave, wind, worm, wrap, wring, zigzag. 2 (make, become bent) bend, buckle, contort, distort, kink, screw up, warp, wrinkle

**twisty** adj winding

**twitch** v pluck, pull jerkily; n spasmodic movement of body; adj **-y** showing signs of nervousness; adv **-ily**; n **twitcher** one who twitches

**twitter** v, n (of birds) chirp intermittently; idm **all of a twitter** coll nervously excited

**two** n, pron, det cardinal number next above one (2); pair; adjs **t.-faced** insincere; **t.-way** moving, communicating in both directions; n **twosome** couple; v **t.-time** deceive

> **two** n brace, duet, duo, pair, twosome

**tycoon** n coll powerful business man

> **tycoon** n baron, businessperson, capitalist, entrepreneur, fat cat inf, financier, industrialist, magnate, millionaire, mogul, wheeler-dealer

**type** n 1 kind 2 print block of wood, metal with letter or symbol on surface; v 1 classify 2 print with typewriter; vs **t. cast** (repeatedly) give actor/actress role that corresponds with his/her natural character; **t.-set** set for printing (ns **t.-setter, t.-setting**); ns **t.-face** style of lettering for printing; **typewriter** writing machine with keys to make individual letters and signs; **typist** person able to type; adj **t.-written**

> **type** n (kind) category, character, class, genre, group, nature, order, sort, species, variety

**typhoid** n med infectious fever

**typhoon** n violent whirlwind, hurricane

**typical** adj 1 usual 2 characteristic; v **typify, -fying, -fied** serve as type or model of

> **typical** adj 1 (usual) archetypal, average, conventional, model, normal, ordinary, orthodox, regular, routine, run-of-the-mill, standard, stock. 2 (characteristic) in character, normal, predictable, unsurprising, usual, to be expected

**typography** n art of style of printing; adj **typographical**; n **typographer**

**tyrant** n 1 harsh, unjust ruler 2 one who rules others cruelly; adj **tyrannical**; v **tyrannize** rule, exert authority harshly; n **tyranny** despotism

> **tyrant** n 1 (harsh ruler) absolute ruler, authoritarian, autocrat, despot, dictator. 2 (one who forces his will on others) bully, martinet, oppressor, slavedriver

**ubiquitous** *adj* present, existing everywhere
**udder** *n* external milk gland of cow, etc
**UFO** *abbr* unidentified flying object
**ugh** *interj* expressing disgust, horror
**ugly** *adj* 1 unpleasant to look at 2 hostile; threatening; *n* **ugliness**

> **ugly** *adj* 1 (unpleasant to look at) grotesque, hideous, horrible, inelegant, misshapen, nasty, plain, unattractive, unsightly.
> 2 (hostile, threatening) angry, dangerous, menacing, nasty, ominous, sinister

**UHF** *abbr rad* ultrahigh frequency
**UHT** *abbr* (of dairy products) ultra heat treated
**UK** *abbr* United Kingdom (Great Britain and N Ireland)
**ukulele** *n* small stringed musical instrument
**ulcer** *n* 1 open sore, discharging pus, on skin or mucous membrane 2 *fig* corrupting influence; *v* **-ate** infect with ulcer
**ulna** *n* **ulnae** inner bone of forearm
**ulterior** *adj* (of motive) undisclosed

> **ulterior** *adj* concealed, covert, hidden, private, secret, underlying

**ultimate** *adj* 1 final 2 best; *n* **ultimatum** final demand, terms offered by person or power; *adv* **ultimo** (*abbr* **ult**) in preceding month

> **ultimate** *adj* 1 (final) closing, concluding, eventual, extreme, last, terminal.
> 2 (best) greatest, highest, paramount, supreme, unsurpassed

**ultra-** *prefix* beyond; excessively
**ultrahigh frequency** *adj* (of radio waves) over 300 million hertz
**ultramarine** *adj* of bright blue color
**ultrasonic** *adj* (of sounds) beyond limit of human hearing; *n* **ultrasound**
**ultrasound** *n* pressure waves with frequency above 20,000 hertz (hz)
**ultraviolet** *adj* of electromagnetic waves between visible violet and X-rays
**umbilicus** *n anat* navel; *n* **umbilical cord** structure joining foetus to placenta
**umbrage** *idm* **take umbrage** be offended
**umbrella** *n* 1 folding shade or cover, for protection against rain or sun 2 agency or group that coordinates work of other groups in an organization
**umpire** *n* person who enforces rules in game; *v* act as umpire
**umpteen** *det, pron coll* an indefinite large number of
**un-** *prefix* expressing negation before simple words or reversal of action before verbs
**unable** *adj* not having ability, opportunity or permission

> **unable** *adj* incapable, incompetent, ineffectual, not equal to, not up to, powerless, unfit, unqualified

**unaccountable** *adj* inexplicable; not responsible
**unanimous** *adj* being of one mind; all agreeing; *n* **unanimity**
**unarmed** *adj* carrying no weapons

> **unarmed** *adj* defenseless, exposed, helpless, unprotected, vulnerable, weaponless

**unassuming** *adj* modest

a
b
c
d
e
f
g
h
i
j
k
l
m
n
o
p
q
r
s
t
**u**
v
w
x
y
z

A
B
C
D
E
F
G
H
I
J
K
L
M
N
O
P
Q
R
S
T
**U**
V
W
X
Y
Z

**unattached** *adj* 1 not married or committed to relationship 2 independent 3 not attached

> **unattached** *adj* (not married) available, footloose and fancy free, free, independent, on your own, single, unmarried, without a partner

**unattractive** *adj* not attractive
**unavailing** *adj* ineffectual, useless.
**unaware** *n* ignorant; not noticing; *adv* **-s** without warning; inadvertently

> **unaware** *adj* ill-informed, oblivious, unconscious, uninformed, unknowing, unsuspecting

**unbalance** *v* 1 throw off balance 2 affect the mental stability of; *adj* **-anced** 1 unevenly arranged 2 insane
**unbearable** *adj* impossible to tolerate

> **unbearable** *adj* insufferable, intolerable, more than flesh and blood can stand *inf*, too much *inf*, unacceptable, unendurable

**unbeknownst to** *adv* without it being known by
**unbelievable** *adj* incredible

> **unbelievable** *adj* beyond belief, far-fetched, implausible, impossible, improbably, inconceivable, preposterous

**unbend** *v* 1 straighten 2 behave less formally; *adj* **-ing** not yielding; stubborn
**unbidden** *adv* 1 uninvited 2 voluntarily
**unbowed** *adj fml* not defeated
**unbridled** *adj* uncontrolled, extravagant
**uncalled-for** *adj* not necessary or deserved
**uncanny** *adj* mysterious; extraordinary
**unceremonious** *adj* without formality or politeness
**uncertain** *adj* 1 not knowing for certain 2 not certain to happen or succeed 3 likely to change; *n* **uncertainty**

**uncertain** *adj* 1 (not knowing for certain) ambivalent, distrustful, doubtful, dubious, hesitant, indecisive, not convinced, not sure, of two minds, skeptical, tentative, unconvinced, undecided, unsure, vague, wavering. 2 (not certain to happen or succeed) chancy, dicey *inf*, doubtful, iffy *inf*, in the balance, precarious, questionable, risky, unclear, undecided, unpredictable, up in the air. 3 (likely to change) changeable, erratic, fitful, inconstant, not dependable, unpredictable, unreliable, unsettled, variable

**uncharitable** *adj* unkind, harsh
**uncharted** *adj* 1 not marked on map 2 *fig* unexplored
**uncle** *n* 1 brother of father or mother 2 husband of aunt
**unclean** *adj* 1 not clean 2 impure
**unclear** *adj* 1 not clearly visible 2 not obvious

> **unclear** *adj* 1 (not clearly visible) dim, blurred, faint, fuzzy, hazy, indistinct, out of focus, opaque. 2 (not obvious) ambiguous, confused, garbled, imprecise, muddled, obscure, uncertain, vague

**uncommon** *adj* not common or usual
**uncompromising** *adj* unwilling to compromise
**unconscionable** *adj* unscrupulous; excessive.
**unconscious** *adj* 1 not conscious 2 not aware 3 unintentional; *adv* **-ly**; *n* **-ness**

> **unconscious** *adj* 1 (not conscious) comatose, dead to the world *inf*, in a coma, insensible, knocked out, out cold *inf*, out for the count *inf*, senseless. 2 (not aware) ignorant, insensible, oblivious, unaware, unsuspecting. 3 (unintentional) accidental, inadvertent, unintended, unpremeditated, unwitting

**unconsidered** *adj* spoken thoughtlessly
**unconventional** *adj* not usual or conventional

> **unconventional** *adj* atypical, bizarre, different, eccentric, idiosyncratic, irregular, odd, offbeat, peculiar, queer, strange, unorthodox, unusual, way-out, weird, zany

**uncouple** *v* separate
**uncouth** *adj* awkward; unrefined in manner

> **uncouth** *adj* bad-mannered, boorish, churlish, coarse, crude, loutish, rough, rude, uncivilized

**uncover** *v* 1 remove cover from 2 find out (truth)

> **uncover** *v* 1 (remove cover from) bare, expose, lay bare, open, show, strip. 2 (find out) bring to light, detect, disclose, discover, reveal, unearth, unmask

**uncrowned** *adj* not officially appointed
**unctuous** *adj* excessively polite, flattering
**undaunted** *adj* bold; intrepid; not frightened
**undecided** *adj* 1 not yet decided 2 not sure

> **undecided** *adj* 1 (not decided) indefinite, in the balance, not decided, not known, not settled, pending, uncertain, unresolved. 2 (not sure) ambivalent, dithering, doubtful, hesitant, indecisive, in two minds, not convinced, uncertain, unsure

**undeniable** *adj* certainly true
**under**[1] *prep* 1 beneath; below 2 ruled, protected by 3 working for 4 subject to; in the process of 5 less than; *adv* 1 below 2 less
**under-**[2] *prefix* lower; insufficiently; beneath
**underarm** *adj, adv sport* with the hand below shoulder level
**undercarriage** *n* wheels on which aircraft lands; framework for these
**undercharge** *v* charge too little

**underclass** *n* group of poor people excluded from normal society
**undercoat** *n* coat of paint applied before top coat
**undercover** *adj* acting secretly, *esp* as spy
**undercurrent** *n* current flowing beneath surface; subtle underlying trend, feeling
**undercut** *v comm* charge less than (competitor)
**underdeveloped** not fully developed; *n* **u. country** country where economic potential (*eg* in industry) has not been fully exploited
**underdog** *n* person regarded as weaker or likely to lose

> **underdog** *n* little fellow *inf*, loser, victim, weaker party

**undergo** *v* **undergoing, underwent, undergone** experience

> **undergo** *v* be subjected to, endure, experience, go through, submit to, suffer

**undergraduate** *n* student at college, university not yet awarded degree
**underground** *adj* below surface of earth; secret; *idm* **go underground** *fig* hide; go into hiding; *n* 1 underground railway 2 secret resistance movement
**undergrowth** *n* bushes and other low plants, *esp* growing among trees
**underhand** *adj* sly

> **underhand** *adj* crafty, crooked, deceitful, devious, dishonest, fraudulent, sneaky, treacherous, unscrupulous

**underlay** *n* material laid under carpet
**underline** *v* 1 mark (word, etc) with line underneath 2 *fig* emphasize
**underling** *n* subordinate
**underlying** *adj* 1 basic 2 hidden
**undermine** *v* 1 wear away by erosion 2 weaken gradually

**undermine** *v* (weaken gradually) damage, impair, sabotage, sap, subvert, threaten

**underneath** *adv* beneath, below

**underpants** *n pl* garment worn underneath trousers (*also* **underwear**)

**underpass** *n* tunnel or covered route taking one road under another

**underpin** *v* support; *n* **underpinning**

**underplay** *v* give too little importance to

**underrate** *v* underestimate

**underrate** *v* not appreciate, not do justice to, sell short *inf*, undervalue

**underscore** *v* underline

**undersell** *v* 1 sell too cheaply 2 undervalue

**understand** *v* 1 comprehend 2 sympathize with 3 assume; (*pt, pp* **-stood**); *adj* **-able**

**understand** *v* 1 (comprehend) appreciate, catch on *inf*, fathom, figure out, follow, get, get sb's drift *inf*, get the hang of *inf*, get the message *inf*, get the picture *inf*, get to the bottom of, grasp, interpret, see, take in, tumble to, work out. 2 (sympathize with) empathize with, feel compassion toward, know how sb feels, sympathize with. 3 (assume) believe, conclude, gather, hear, learn, presume, suppose, think

**understanding** *n* 1 ability to understand 2 sympathy 3 assumption 4 agreement; *adj* sympathetic

**understanding** *n* 1 (ability to understand) acumen, awareness, comprehension, grasp, insight, intelligence, interpretation, judgment, knowledge, perceptiveness, percipience, sense, wisdom. 2 (sympathy) compassion, empathy, insight, kindness, tolerance. 3 (assumption) belief, conclusion, feeling, idea, perception, supposition, view

**understanding** *adj* compassionate, considerate, forgiving, kind, patient, perceptive, sensitive, sympathetic, tolerant

**understate** *v* 1 say sth is less than it is 2 show strong feeling ironically by less strong expression; *n* **-ment**

**understudy** *v* learn part (of actor, etc) in order to deputize for him, if necessary

**undertake** *v* **undertaking, undertook, undertaken** promise

**undertaker** *n* one whose business is to arrange funerals

**undertaking** *n* an enterprise; guarantee

**undertone** *n* 1 low voice 2 *esp pl* concealed meaning

**undertow** *n* undercurrent of wave breaking on shore

**underwear** *n* clothes worn beneath others

**underwear** *n* lingerie, underclothes, undergarments, undies *inf*

**underwent** *pt of* **undergo**

**underworld** *n* criminals as social group; place of departed spirits

**underwrite** *v* 1 insure shipping 2 promise to finance

**undesirable** *adj* unpleasant

**undies** *n coll* women's underwear

**undisputed** *adj* recognized, accepted by all

**undo** *v* **undoing, undid, undone** 1 unfasten 2 cancel 3 defeat 4 ruin; *n* **undoing** cause, source of ruin; unfastening; *adj* **undone** 1 untied 2 ruined 3 not done

**undo** *v* 1 (unfasten) detach, disconnect, disentangle, loosen, open, uncouple, unlock, untie, unwrap. 2 (cancel) annul, invalidate, nullify, quash, repeal, rescind, reverse, revoke, set aside

**undoubted** *adj* acknowledged as certain; *adv* **-ly**

**undress** *v* remove clothing

> **undress** *v* change, get changed, get undressed, peel off, strip, strip off

**undue** *adj* excessive, improper

> **undue** *adj* disproportionate, extreme, inappropriate, inordinate, undeserved, unjustified, unnecessary, unreasonable, unwarranted

**undulate** *v* rise and fall like waves
**undying** *adj* everlasting

> **undying** *adj* constant, deathless, eternal, immortal, perpetual, unceasing

**unearth** *v* dig up; discover
**unearthly** *adj* 1 not of this world; supernatural 2 weird; unreasonable
**uneasy** *adj* (of person) anxious; (of situation) worrying; *adv* **-ily**; *ns* **unease, uneasiness** apprehension
**uneconomic** *adj* not profitable
**unemployed** *adj* without a job; **unemployment** state of having no job

> **unemployed** *adj* idle, jobless, laid off, on the dole *inf*, out of a job, out of work, redundant, resting, unemployable, unoccupied

**unequivocal** *adj* clear, certain
**unerring** *adj* reliably accurate; *adv* **-ily**
**unethical** *adj* wrong, immoral
**uneven** *adj* 1 not level 2 not constant

> **uneven** *adj* 1 (not level) bumpy, jagged, lumpy, pitted, pockmarked, rough, rutted, undulating, up-and-down. 2 (not constant) erratic, fitful, inconsistent, intermittent, irregular, spasmodic, up-and-down, variable, varying

**uneventful** *adj* with no excitement

**unexceptionable** *adj* beyond criticism or objection
**unexpected** *adj* not expected

> **unexpected** *adj* like a bolt from the blue, sudden, surprising, unannounced, unanticipated, unforeseen, unheralded, unpredicted

**unfailing** *adj* 1 constant 2 totally reliable
**unfair** *adj* 1 not just 2 biased

> **unfair** *adj* 1 (not just) arbitrary, dishonest, sneaky *inf*. undeserved, unethical, unjust, unmerited, unreasonable, wrong, wrongful. 2 (biased) discriminatory, inequitable, one-sided, partial, partisan, prejudiced, unbalanced, unequal, uneven

**unfaithful** *adj* 1 adulterous 2 not loyal

> **unfaithful** *adj* 1 (adulterous) flighty, flirtatious, inconstant, philandering, promiscuous, two-timing. 2 (not loyal) deceitful, disloyal, double-crossing, double-dealing, faithless, false, perfidious, traitorous, treacherous

**unfashionable** *adj* behind the times; old-fashioned; out of date
**unfasten** *v* undo, untie
**unfeeling** *adj* insensitive, cruel; *adv* **-ly**
**unfettered** *adj* free
**unfit** *adj* not healthy or fit; *adjs* **unfitted** unsuited; **unfitting** inappropriate

> **unfit** *adj* below par, ill, injured, out of shape *inf*, sick, unhealthy, unwell, weak

**unflappable** *adj* always able to keep calm in a crisis
**unfold** *v* 1 open out from folded state 2 be revealed
**unforeseen** *adj* **unexpected**
**unfortunate** *adj* 1 unlucky 2 regrettable; *adv* **-ly**

a
b
c
d
e
f
g
h
i
j
k
l
m
n
o
p
q
r
s
t
**u**
v
w
x
y
z

**unfortunate** *adj* 1 (unlucky) hapless, ill-fated, ill-starred, luckless, unsuccessful. 2 (regrettable) annoying, deplorable, infelicitous, lamentable, untimely

**unfounded** *adj* without justification

**unfounded** *adj* baseless, false, groundless, idle, invalid, unjustified, unproven, unsupported, untrue, without foundation

**ungainly** *adj* awkward, clumsy
**ungrateful** *adj* not showing gratitude

**ungrateful** *adj* churlish, discourteous, impolite, mercenary, rude, unthankful

**ungrounded** *adj* false, unjustified
**unhand** *v lit* release from hold with hand
**unhappy** *adj* 1 sad 2 dissatisfied 3 regrettable

**unhappy** *adj* 1 (sad) depressed, disconsolate, distressed, downcast, downhearted, inconsolable, melancholy, miserable. 2 (dissatisfied) aggrieved, annoyed, discontented, disgruntled, resentful

**unhealthy** *adj* 1 not in good health 2 harmful to health

**unhealthy** *adj* 1 (not in good health) ailing, delicate, frail, ill, infirm, invalid, sick, unfit, unwell, weak. 2 (harmful to health) detrimental, insalubrious, insanitary, noxious, unwholesome

**unheard-of** *adj* very unusual; unprecedented
**unholy** *adj* 1 wicked 2 *coll* terrible, dreadful
**uni-** *prefix* one, single
**unicorn** *n* mythic horse like animal with one horn in middle of forehead
**uniform** *adj* not changing; similar in every way; *n* distinctive dress worn by members of organized body; *adj* **-ed** wearing uniform; *adv* **-ly** evenly; *n* **-ity** sameness

**uniform** *n* costume, dress, livery, outfit, regalia, robes, suit

**unify** *v* **unifying, unified** cause to be one, combine; *n* **unification**
**unilateral** *adj* one-sided; *adv* **-ly**
**unimpeachable** *adj* that cannot be doubted
**unintentional** *adj* accidental

**unintentional** *adj* casual, chance, coincidental, inadvertent, subconscious, unconscious, unintended

**union** *n* 1 act of uniting 2 group formed by uniting 3 trade union; *n* **U. Jack** national flag of UK; *v* **unionize** organize into, (cause to) become member of trade union

**union** *n* 1 (act of uniting) amalgamation, association, combination, conjunction, fusion, intermingling, marriage, merger, unification, uniting. 2 (group formed by uniting) alliance, association, brotherhood, coalition, confederacy, confederation, federation, fellowship, fraternity, guild, league, partnership, society

**unique** *adj* having no like or equal; unparalleled; *adv* **-ly** *n* **-ness**

**unique** *adj* incomparable, inimitable, matchless, one of a kind, original, peerless, unequaled, unprecedented, unrepeatable, unrivaled

**unisex** *adj* of style suited to both men and women
**unison** *n* harmony; concord
**unit** *n* 1 single complete thing 2 group of people or things forming complete whole 3 least whole number
**unite** *v* 1 join people or things 2 come together; *n* **unity** state of being unit; agreement of aims, interests, etc; harmony; *adj* **united** joined; in alliance

**unite** *v* **1** (join people or things) amalgamate, associate, blend, bring together, combine, fuse, harmonize, join, link, marry, meld, merge, unify, wed. **2** (come together) ally, associate, band together, close ranks, collaborate, cooperate, gang up, join forces, pool your resources, work together

**universal** *adj* relating to all things or all people; *adv* **-ly**

**universe** *n* whole system of created things viewed as whole; the cosmos

**university** *n* institution for higher education, empowered to confer degrees; governing body of such institution

**unkempt** *adj* of untidy appearance

**unkind** *adj* unfriendly or hurtful

**unkind** *adj* beastly *inf*, callous, cruel, harsh, impolite, inconsiderate, insensitive, malicious, mean, nasty *inf*, rough, rude, sadistic, savage, severe, sharp, spiteful, uncaring, unchristian, unfair, unpleasant, unsympathetic, vicious

**unknown** *adj* not known; *n* **u. quantity** sb/sth whose true qualities are yet to be discovered

**unlawful** *adj* illegal

**unleash** *v* release from control

**unless** *conj* if not; except that

**unlettered** *adj fml* **1** unable to read **2** not well educated

**unlike** *prep* not like; not similar to

**unlikely** *adj* **1** not likely to happen **2** not likely to be true

**unlikely** *adj* **1** (not likely to happen) doubtful, impossible, improbable, inconceivable. **2** (not likely to be true) dubious, farfetched, implausible, improbable, incredible, suspect, unbelievable, unconvincing

**unload** *v* remove load or cargo from

**unlock** *v* open lock of

**unlucky** *adj* experiencing bad luck

**unlucky** *adj* down on your luck, hapless, ill-fated, ill-starred, luckless, out of luck, star-crossed, unfortunate,, unsuccessful

**unmarried** *adj* not married; single

**unmistakable** *adj* obvious, clear

**unmitigated** *adj* absolute

**unmoved** *adj* not emotionally affected

**unnatural** *adj* strange; not natural or normal

**unnecessary** *adj* **1** not necessary **2** more than necessary

**unnerve** *v* take away (sb's) confidence; frighten; *adj* **unnerving** (*adv* **-ly**)

**unnerve** *v* agitate, alarm, daunt, demoralize, deter, disconcert, discourage, dishearten, disquiet, fluster, perturb, put off, rattle *inf*, scare, shake, take aback, throw off balance, trouble, unman, unsettle, worry

**unnumbered** *adj* **1** not marked with a number **2** countless

**unobtrusive** *adj* not obvious or standing out

**unofficial** *adj* done without official permission

**unpick** *v* remove (stitches from)

**unplaced** *adj* **1** not one of the first three in race or contest **2** not accepted on course **3** having no accommodation

**unpleasant** *adj* **1** horrible **2** unkind

**unpleasant** *adj* **1** (horrible) disagreeable, disgusting, foul, nasty, nauseating, offensive, repellent, repugnant, unsavory, unspeakable. **2** (unkind) bad-tempered, churlish, cruel, disagreeable, hostile, ill-natured, insulting, obnoxious, offensive, repulsive, rude, unfriendly, unspeakable

**unpopular** *adj* not popular

**unprecedented** *adj* not having happened before

a
b
c
d
e
f
g
h
i
j
k
l
m
n
o
p
q
r
s
t
**u**
v
w
x
y
z

**unpredictable** *adj* likely to behave in irregular way that cannot be predicted

**unprintable** *adj* too offensive to publish in print

**unproductive** *adj* not producing desired result

> **unproductive** *adj* fruitless, futile, idle, ineffective, pointless, time-wasting, unprofitable, unrewarding, useless, vain, wasted, worthless

**unqualified** *adj* 1 with no qualifications 2 absolute

**unravel** *v* take tangles, knots out of

**unreal** *adj* 1 imaginary 2 very strange

**unrealistic** *adj* not realistic or practical

> **unrealistic** *adj* foolish, half-baked *inf*, impossible, impracticable, impractical, improbable, unreasonable, unworkable

**unreasonable** *adj* 1 illogical 2 excessive 3 refusing to listen to reasonable arguments

> **unreasonable** *adj* 1 (illogical) absurd, irrational, ludicrous, meaningless, nonsensical, senseless. 2 (excessive) disproportionate, exorbitant, extortionate, extreme, inordinate, extravagant, outrageous, preposterous, steep, unconscionable, unfair. 3 (refusing to listen to reasonable arguments) cruel, harsh, inflexible, intolerant, obstinate, opinionated, pig-headed *inf*, prejudiced, stubborn, unfair

**unremitting** *adj* persistent; *adv* **-ly**

**unrequited** *adj* (*esp* of love) not reciprocated

**unrest** *n* political disturbance

> **unrest** *n* agitation, discontent, discontentment, discord, dissatisfaction, dissension, dissent, protest, rebellion, rioting, strife, trouble, turmoil, violence

**unruly** *adj* disorderly; ungovernable

**unsafe** *adj* 1 in danger 2 dangerous

**unsavory** *adj* 1 unpleasant 2 offensive in character

**unscathed** *adj* unharmed

**unscrew** *v* loosen (screw)

**unscrupulous** *adj* dishonest

> **unscrupulous** *adj* bad, corrupt, deceitful, devious, evil, exploitative, immoral, ruthless, unethical, untrustworthy, wicked

**unsettle** *v* make uneasy; worry; disturb

**unsettled** *adj* tense, agitated

**unsightly** *adj* ugly; *n* **-ness**

**unsound** *adj* not reliable or certain; flawed

**unspeakable** *adj* too bad to mention; outrageous; *adv* **-ably**

**unstable** *adj* 1 not strong 2 offensive in character; likely to change suddenly

> **unstable** *adj* 1 (not strong) flimsy, insecure, precarious, rickety, rocky, shaky, tottering, unsafe, unsteady, wobbly. 2 (likely to change suddenly) changeable, erratic, fitful, fluctuating, inconsistent, shifting, unpredictable, variable, volatile

**unsteady** *adj* 1 not firm or steady 2 (of voice) shaking due to emotion

**unstinting** *adj* given freely; *adv* **-ly**

**unstuck** *adj* not held by glue; *idm* **come unstuck** 1 fall apart 2 *fig coll* fail

**unstudied** *adj* natural

**unsuitable** *adj* not suitable

> **unsuitable** *adj* ill-judged, inappropriate, inapt, incompatible, incongruous, out of keeping, unacceptable, unfitting, unsuited

**unsure** *adj* not certain or convinced

> **unsure** *adj* doubtful, dubious, hesitant, irresolute, of two minds, skeptical, suspicious, unconvinced, wavering

**unthinkable** *adj* too bad to contemplate
**untidy** *adj* not neat or tidy

> **untidy** *adj* cluttered, disorderly, in a mess, in a state, in disarray, jumbled, like a pig sty, littered, messy, rumpled

**untie** *v* unfasten
**until** *prep* so far as; up to; *conj* up to time when
**untimely** *adj* 1 before time 2 at an unsuitable time
**unto** *prep lit, ar* to
**untold** *adj* 1 very great 2 very many

> **untold** *adj* 1 (very great) indescribable, inexpressible, unimaginable, unthinkable, unutterable. 2 (very many) countless, immeasurable, incalculable, innumerable

**untouchable** *adj* 1 that cannot be touched, reached, equaled 2 of lowest Hindu caste (*n* such a person)
**untoward** *adj* inconvenient, unlucky
**untrammeled** *adj* able to develop freely
**untrue** *adj* not true

> **untrue** *adj* erroneous, fallacious, false, inaccurate, incorrect, mistaken, spurious, wrong

**unusual** *adj* not usual or normal

> **unusual** *adj* abnormal, atypical, bizarre, curious, different, extraordinary, irregular, odd, out of the ordinary, rare, remarkable, strange, surprising, unexpected, weird *inf*

**unutterable** *adj* too great to be put in words; inexpressible; *adv* **-ably**
**unvarnished** *adj* plain; without embellishment
**unveil** *v* uncover; announce
**unversed in** *adj* having no skill or experience of
**unwarranted** *adj* not justified

**unwell** *adj* ill; not well

> **unwell** *adj* ailing, groggy, in poor health, not very well, off-color, out of sorts, poorly, sick, sickly, under the weather

**unwieldy** *adj* too large to be carried or moved easily; too complicated to be managed or controlled easily
**unwind** *v* 1 unroll 2 relax
**unwise** *v* foolish

> **unwise** *adj* foolhardy, ill-advised, ill-judged, improvident, imprudent, inadvisable, injudicious, irresponsible, rash, reckless, senseless, silly, stupid, thoughtless

**unwitting** *adj* unintentional; *adv* **-ly**
**unworthy** *adj* of no value
**unyielding** *adj* adamant; stubborn
**up** *adv, prep* 1 to, at higher or better position 2 to, in the north 3 in phrasal denoting completion 4 out of bed 5 on, at the top (of) 6 at the far end (of); *prep* **up to** until; *idm* **be up to** 1 be busy doing or planning 2 be capable of 3 be the responsibility of; *adjs* **up-and-coming** new and promising; **up-market** *comm* of better quality
**upbeat** *n mus* unaccented beat
**upbraid** *v* reproach, scold
**upbringing** *n* way in which a child is educated and disciplined

> **upbringing** *n* breeding, education, instruction, raising, rearing, training

**update** *v* revise; bring up to date; *n* revision
**upend** *v* turn upside down
**upfront** *adj* frank and direct
**upgrade** *v* raise to higher status, quality
**upheaval** *n* violent disturbance

> **upheaval** *n* chaos, commotion, confusion, difficulty, disorder, disruption, disturbance, revolution, to-do *inf*, turmoil, upset

**upheld** *pt, pp of* **uphold**

**uphill** *adj* ascending; *fig* difficult

**uphold** *v* **upholding, upheld** support

**upholster** *v* 1 stuff and cover chairs, etc; *ns* **-sterer** one who repairs covers chairs, etc or sells such goods; **-stery** trade of upholsterer; goods supplied by him

**upkeep** *n* (cost of) maintenance

**upland** *n* (often *pl*) higher ground of region

**uplifting** *adj* inspiring; raising, *esp* spiritually or culturally

> **uplifting** *adj* cheering, encouraging, feel-good, heartening

**upon** *prep* on

**upper** *adj* higher; nearer the top; *n* top part of shoe; *n, adj* **u. case** capital (letters); *ns* **u. class** privileged class; **u. hand** control; *adv* **uppermost** in highest position

**uppity** *adj* arrogant; stuck-up

**upright** *adj* 1 erect 2 *fig* honest; *n* upright post, beam, support, etc

**uprising** *n* rebellion or revolt

> **uprising** *n* coup, coup d'état, disturbance, insurgence, insurrection, mutiny, revolution, riot, rising

**uproar** *n* noisy tumult; clamor; *adj* **-ious** noisy, rowdy (*adv* **-ly**; *n* **-ness**)

**upset** *v* 1 distress 2 disrupt 3 knock over; *adj* distressed; *n* state of disorder; cause of distress

> **upset** *v* 1 (distress) bother, dismay, disturb, hurt, ruffle, sadden, shake, trouble, worry. 2 (disrupt) disturb, hinder, interfere with, jeopardize, mess up, spoil. 3 (knock over) overturn, tip over, topple, turn over, upend
>
> **upset** *adj* anxious, bothered, dismayed, distressed, disturbed, hurt, ruffled, saddened, shaken, troubled, worried

**upshot** *n* result, consequence

**upside down** *adj* with upper part underneath

**upstairs** *adj, adv* on, to higher floor; *n* upper floor

**upstanding** *adj* 1 strong and vigorous 2 honest; marked by integrity

**upstart** *n* one who has risen suddenly to high position or wealth, etc

**upsurge** *n* sudden increase

**uptake** *n* rate of acceptance, absorption; *idm* **quick/slow on the uptake** quick/slow to understand

**uptight** *adj* anxious and inhibited

**up-to-date** *adj* 1 modern 2 having all the latest news, developments

**upturn** *n* improvement in business or fortune; *adj* **-ed** turned upside-down

**upward** *adj* going higher; *adv* **upward** to higher position; *prep* **upward of** more than; *adj* **upwardly mobile** able to, seeking to improve one's economic and social status

> **upward** *adj* ascending, climbing, rising, uphill

**uranium** *n* white metallic radioactive element

**Uranus** *n* planet seventh in distance from the Sun

**urban** *adj* relating to town; *v* **-ize** change from rural to urban condition; *n* **-ization**

> **urban** *adj* built-up, city, civic, innercity, metropolitan, municipal, suburban, town

**urbane** *adj* courteous, affable, refined

**urchin** *n* mischievous, roguish child

**urge** *v* 1 encourage 2 advise; *n* strong desire

> **urge** *n* compulsion, drive, hunger, impulse, itch, longing, need, thirst, wish, yearning

**urgent** *adj* requiring immediate attention; *n* **-ency**

> **urgent** *adj* compelling, crucial, imperative, important, pressing, toppriority

**urine** *n* fluid secreted by kidneys; *v* **urinate** pass urine; *n* **urinal** place for urinating

**urn** *n* **1** large, lidded, metal vessel for serving tea or coffee **2** vase for ashes of dead

**us** *pron* objective case of **we**

**US, USA** *abbr* United States of America

**usage** *n* **1** way of using **2** way of speaking **3** custom

**use** *n* **1** act of employing anything **2** advantage; purpose served; *v* **1** employ **2** consume **3** behave toward; *idm* **make use of** take advantage of; *idm* **of use** useful; *idm* **put to good use** use profitably; *phr v* **use up** exhaust supply of; *adjs* **us(e)able** fit for use; **used** not new; **used to** familiar with; accustomed to

> **use** *v* **1** (employ) exploit, make use of, operate, ply, put into service, utilize, wield, work. **2** (consume) deplete, exhaust, expend, fritter away, get through, waste

**useful** *adj* of practical use

> **useful** *adj* advantageous, beneficial, effective, fruitful, helpful, of help, of use, productive, rewarding, successful, valuable, worthwhile

**useless** *adj* **1** not achieving desired result **2** incompetent

> **useless** *adj* **1** (not achieving desired result) fruitless, futile, hopeless, ineffective, of no help, of no use, pointless, unavailing, unproductive, unprofitable, unrewarding, unsuccessful, vain. **2** (incompetent) hopeless, inadequate, incapable, inept, no good *inf*, poor,

**user** *n* one who uses sth; *adj* **u.-friendly** designed for easy use by any user

**usher** *n* **1** official in charge of entrance to court, etc **2** person showing people to seats in cinema, theater, etc (*fem* **-ette**); *v* escort (sb) in specified direction; *idm* **usher in** *fig* mark beginning of

**usual** *adj* commonplace; habitual; *adv* **usually** generally; as a rule

> **usual** *adj* conventional, customary, established, expected, familiar, normal, ordinary, orthodox, regular, routine, set, standard, stock, traditional, typical

**usurp** *v* take possession of without right or by force; *n* **usurper**

**usury** *n* lending of money at excessive interest

**utensil** *n* vessel, container for domestic use

**uterus** *n* womb

**utilitarian** *adj* **1** serving useful purpose **2** based on belief in action that benefits the largest possible number of people (*n* **-ism**)

**utility** *n* **1** usefulness **2** useful thing; *pl* **utilities** public services, as supplying of water, gas, electricity, etc

**utilize** *v* put to use; make profitable use of

**utmost** *adj* most extreme; *n* most possible

> **utmost** *adj* extreme, greatest, highest, maximum, paramount, supreme

**Utopia** *n* imaginary state with ideally perfect social and political system; *adj* **utopian**

**utter**[1] *adj* complete, total, absolute; *adv* **-ly**

> **utter** *adj* absolute, complete, downright, out-and-out, outright, perfect, sheer, total, unmitigated, unqualified

**utter**[2] *v* produce audibly with voice; say; express by word of mouth, or in writing; *n* **utterance** act of speaking; spoken words

**U-turn** *n* **1** smooth, unbroken turn by vehicle to go in opposite direction **2** (of politics) complete reversal of policy

a b c d e f g h i j k l m n o p q r s t **u** v w x y z

**vacant** *adj* 1 empty; unoccupied
2 expressionless; *n* **vacancy** vacant job, etc

> **vacant** *adj* 1 (empty) available, free, idle,
> unfilled, unused. 2 (expressionless)
> absent-minded, blank, dreamy, faraway,
> inane, inattentive, vacuous

**vacate** *v* leave empty; resign from; *n* **-ation**
act of vacating; fixed holiday period
**vaccinate** *v* inoculate with vaccine;
*ns* **-ation**; **vaccine** preparation of virus used
as inoculation against disease
**vacillate** *v* hesitate, be undecided; *n* **-lation**
**vacuous** *adj* stupid, expressionless
**vacuum** *n* 1 space empty of all matter or
content 2 space from which air has been
partially exhausted; *n* **v.cleaner** apparatus
for removing dirt, etc by suction
**vagabond** *n* tramp, vagrant
**vagary** *n* caprice, whim, freak
**vagina** *n* female genital passage; *adj* **vaginal**
**vagrant** *n* tramp; *n* **vagrancy**
**vague** *adj* 1 blurred 2 not clearly expressed
3 absentminded

> **vague** *adj* 1 (blurred) dim, fuzzy, hazy,
> indistinct, misty, nebulous, obscure, out of
> focus, shadowy, unclear. 2 (not clearly
> expressed) ambiguous, doubtful, imprecise,
> inexact, uncertain, unclear, woolly *inf*

**vain** *adj* 1 conceited 2 futile

> **vain** *adj* 1 (conceited) arrogant, big-headed
> *inf*, boastful, egotistical, proud, swaggering.
> 2 (futile) fruitless, hopeless, ineffective,
> pointless, unproductive, unprofitable,
> unrewarding, unsuccessful, useless

**vainglorious** *adj* inordinately proud or
boastful; *adv* **-ly**
**valance** *n* short curtain above window or
around bed, table, shelf, etc
**vale** *n* valley
**valentine** *n* sweetheart chosen on February
14 ; card or gift sent on that day
**valet** *n* *Fr* manservant
**valiant** *adj* brave; heroic; *adv* **-ly**
**valid** *adj* having legal force; *n* **-ity** soundness;
legal force; *v* **-ate** make valid

> **valid** *adj* acceptable, approved, authentic,
> authorized, bona fide, current, genuine,
> legitimate, official

**valise** *n* *Fr* small suitcase
**Valium** [TM] drug used as tranquilizer
**valley** *n* tract of land lying between hills
**valor** *n* bravery; *adj* **-ous**; *adv* **-ously**
**valuable** *adj* 1 worth a lot of money 2 useful;
*n* *usu pl* valuable objects, goods, etc

> **valuable** *adj* 1 (worth a lot of money)
> costly, dear, expensive, precious, priceless.
> 2 (useful) advantageous, beneficial,
> helpful, of help, of use, worthwhile

**value** *n* 1 worth 2 benefit; *pl* **-s** principles;
*v* estimate worth of; rate highly; *n* **valuation**
estimated worth

> **value** *n* 1 (worth) cost, price, rate.
> 2 (benefit) advantage, help, importance,
> merit, profit, use, usefulness, worth

**valve** *n* device which regulates flow of air,
liquid, gas, etc. through opening, pipe, etc

**vampire** *n myth* corpse that revives itself by drinking human blood; *fig* ruthless blackmailer or money-lender; *n* **vampire bat** American bloodsucking bat

**van** *n* enclosed small truck

**vandal** *n* person who willfully damages property; *v* **-ize** damage in this way; *n* **-ism**

> **vandal** *n* hooligan, looter, raider, ruffian, thug, troublemaker

**vane** *n* web of feather; blade of propeller

**vanguard** *n* **1** leading part of army **2** leaders of political, social movement, or fashion

**vanilla** *n* plant pod used for flavoring

**vanish** *v* disappear; cease to exist

**vanity** *n* conceit

> **vanity** *n* arrogance, big-headedness, boastfulness, egotism, narcissism, pride

**vanquish** *v* conquer; be victorious

**vantage point** *n* favorable position

**vapid** *adj* insipid, lifeless

**vapor** *n* steam, mist; *v* **vaporize** convert into or pass off in vapor

**variable** *adj* changing; liable to change; *n* **1** thing that can be changed, substituted **2** *math* unspecified value; *n* **-ability**

> **variable** *adj* changeable, erratic, fickle, fitful, fluctuating, fluid, inconstant, shifting, unpredictable, unstable, unsteady, up and down *inf*, volatile, wavering

**variance** *n* **at variance (with)** in conflict (with)

**variant** *n* alternative version or form

**variation** *n* **1** degree of varying **2** variant **3** one of set of stylistic elaborations on musical, literary theme

**varicose** *adj* (of veins) abnormally swollen

**varied** *adj* various

**variegated** *adj* marked with different colors

**variety** *n* **1** diversity **2** group of different things **3** type

**variety** *n* **1** (diversity) change, variation. **2** (group of different things) assortment, collection, combination, mixture, range

**variform** *adj* found in various forms

**various** *adj* of several different kinds

> **various** *adj* assorted, different, diverse, heterogeneous, miscellaneous, mixed, sundry, varied

**varnish** *n* substance applied to surface to make it shiny; *v* apply varnish to

**vary** *v* **varying, varied** change, alter

**vascular** *adj* containing, concerning vessels conveying fluid in plants and animals

**vase** *n* ornamental container for flowers

**vasectomy** *n* operation to remove vas deferans from male to induce sterility

**Vaseline** [TM] soft petroleum jelly

**vast** *adj* huge; *n* **-ness**; *adv* **-ly** *coll* extremely

**vat** *n* large cask or tub

**vault**[1] *n* **1** arched cellar **2** strongroom

**vault**[2] *v* leap over with support of hands or pole; *n* such leap or jump

**vaunt** *v* boast, brag about

**VD** *abbr* venereal disease

**VDU** *abbr* visual display unit (computer screen)

**veal** *n* flesh of calf, used for food

**veer** *v* change in direction

> **veer** *v* change course, dodge, sheer, shift, swerve, swing, turn

**vegan** *n* person with strict vegetarian diet, not using or consuming animal products

**vegeburger, veggie-burger** *n* burger of vegetables with no meat

**vegetable** *n* edible plant

**vegetarian** *n* one who does not eat meat

**vegetate** *v* live dull monotonous life

**vegetation** *n* plant growth and development

**vehement** *adj* passionate; *adv* **-ly**; *n* **vehemence**

a b c d e f g h i j k l m n o p q r s t u **v** w x y z

**vehement** *adj* ardent, eager, earnest, fervent, fierce, intense, keen, vigorous

**vehicle** *n* means of conveyance, *usu* on wheels; means of expression; *adj* **vehicular**

**veil** *n* covering for face or head; *fig* that which conceals; *v* cover with veil; conceal; *adj* **-ed** 1 covered by veil 2 *fig* with implied meaning

**vein** *n* 1 blood vessel conveying blood to heart 2 layer containing metallic ore 3 *fig* mood; disposition

**Velcro** *n* [TM] fastener of fabric strips that stick when pressed together

**velocity** *n* speed; rapidity/rate of motion

**velour, velours** *n* Fr soft velvety material

**velvet** *n* 1 fabric with soft thick pile or nap on one side 2 *fig* soft downy surface; *adj* **velvety** like velvet; *n* **velveteen** imitation velvet made of cotton

**venal** *adj* influenced by hope of reward

**vend** *v* sell; *ns* **vendor**; **vending machine** automatic selling machine

**vendetta** *n* It blood feud

**veneer** *v* 1 thin layer of fine wood laid over inferior kind 2 superficial polish concealing defects; *v* cover with veneer

**veneer** *n* (superficial polish concealing defects) appearance, façade, front, guise, pretence, semblance, show

**venerable** *adj* worthy of deep respect; *v* **venerate** revere, respect, worship; *n* **-ation**

**venereal** *adj* pertaining to sexual intercourse; *n* **v. disease** (*also* **VD**)

**venetian blind** *n* one made of horizontal movable slats

**vengeance** *n* revenge; *idm* **with a vengeance** *coll* much more than is normal or desirable; *adj* **vengeful** filled with desire for revenge

**vengeance** *n* pay-back, reprisal, retaliation, retribution, revenge, tit for tat

**venison** *n* deer's flesh, as food

**venom** *n* 1 poison secreted by snake, etc 2 *fig* spite; *adj* **-ous** poisonous; spiteful

**vent** *n* slit, hole, outlet; *v* pour forth; utter; *idm* **give vent to** express openly; *idm* **vent one's anger/feelings, etc on** find target for one's anger/feelings, etc in

**ventilate** *v* supply with fresh air; *n* **-ation**

**ventricle** *n* main pumping chamber of heart

**ventriloquist** *n* one who can speak without apparent movement of lips

**venture** *n* risky course of action; *v* risk; dare to do or go

**venture** *n* chance, endeavor, enterprise, experiment, gamble, project, risk, speculation, undertaking

**venue** *n* Fr 1 placefixed for trial 2 *fig* meetingplace

**Venus** *n* planet second nearest to sun

**veranda** *n* open portico outside house

**verb** *n* part of speech expressing action, existence in present, past, or future; *adj* **-al** relating to words; literal; spoken, not written; *v* **-ize** express in words

**verbatim** *adj, adv* in exactly the same words

**verbiage** *n* Fr use of too many words

**verbose** *adj* using too many words

**verdant** *adj* green, as of fresh young grass

**verdict** *n* decision of jury; judgment

**verdict** *n* adjudication, assessment, conclusion, decision, finding, opinion, ruling

**verdigris** *n* greenish blue deposit formed on copper or brass

**verge** *n* edge; brink; *phr v* **verge on** approach; border on

**verify** *v* **verifying, verified** prove, confirm, check; *adj* **verifiable**; *n* **verification**

**verisimilitude** *n* appearance of truth

**veritable** *adj* real; genuine; true; actual; *adv* **-ly**

**vermicelli** *n* It thin, stringlike macaroni

**vermilion** *adj* of brilliant red color
**vermin** *n* destructive, harmful animals (*usu* small) collectively
**vermouth** *n* Fr fortified white wine
**vernacular** *n* commonly spoken language
**verruca** *n* infectious wart of the foot
**versatile** *adj* adaptable; *n* **versatility**

> **versatile** *adj* all-around, flexible, handy, multipurpose, resourceful, variable

**verse** *n* 1 subdivision of poem or chapter of Bible 2 poetry; *adj* **versed** (**in**) skilled (in)
**version** *n* personal account, statement

> **version** *n* description, interpretation, portrayal, reading, rendering, rendition, report, translation

**versus** *prep* (*abbr* **v.**) *Lat* against
**vertebra** *n pl* **-brae** one of joints of spine; *adj* **-brate** having backbone; *n* vertebrate animal
**vertex** *n* summit, zenith; *pl* **vertices**
**vertical** *adj* perpendicular; *adv* **-ly**

> **vertical** *adj* erect, on end, standing, straight, upright

**vertigo** *n* giddiness; *adj* **vertiginous**
**verve** *n* vigor; liveliness of spirit
**very** *adj* actual; real; *adv* extremely

> **very** *adv* decidedly, deeply, eminently, enormously, especially, extremely, greatly, highly, hugely, most, outstandingly, particularly, really, remarkably, terribly *inf*, truly, unbelievably, unusually, vastly

**vespers** *n pl* evensong
**vessel** *n* 1 ship 2 duct for fluid or sap, etc
**vest** *n* sleeveless garment, *usu* worn under jacket ; *phr v* **vest in/with sb** confer (legal right or power) on sb; *idm* **have a vested interest** (**in**) be likely to benefit from; *n* **vestment** ceremonial garment worn by clergy

**vestibule** *n* lobby; antechamber
**vestige** *n* visible trace or mark; *adj* **vestigial**
**vestry** *n* room in church where vestments and Communion vessels are kept
**vet** *n coll abbr* of **veterinary** (**surgeon**); *v* **vetting, vetted** *coll* examine critically

> **vet** *v* check out, inspect, investigate, review, scan, scrutinize

**veteran** *n* one with long experience, *esp* in armed services
**veterinary** *adj* of, concerned with diseases of animals; *n* **v. surgeon**, **veterinarian** one trained to treat sick animals
**veto** *n Lat* absolute prohibition; *pl* **-oes**; *v* **vetoing, vetoed** forbid

> **veto** *n* bar, block, boycott, embargo, interdict, prohibition, refusal, rejection
> **veto** *v* ban, bar, block, boycott, dismiss, prohibit, proscribe, refuse, reject, rule out, turn down, vote against

**vex** *v* irritate; cause worry to; *n* **-ation** mental distress; worry
**VHF** *abbr rad* very high frequency
**via** *adv* by way of; by means of
**viable** *adj* capable of maintaining separate existence; practicable; *n* **viability**

> **viable** *adj* achievable, feasible, operable, possible, realistic, reasonable, sound, sustainable, usable, valid, workable

**viaduct** *n* long, high bridge carrying railway, road, etc over valley
**vial** *n* small glass bottle
**vibrant** *adj* bright and exciting; *n* **vibrancy**
**vibrate** *v* shake; quiver; *n* **-ation**

> **vibrate** *v* oscillate, pulsate, resonate, reverberate, shiver, throb, tremble, wobble

**vibrator** *n* vibrating electrical device, *esp* used in massage

a
b
c
d
e
f
g
h
i
j
k
l
m
n
o
p
q
r
s
t
u
**v**
w
x
y
z

**vicar** *n* clergyman in charge of parish;
  *n* **vicarage** house of vicar

**vicarious** *adj* acting as substitute; done, felt
  on behalf of another; *adv* **-ly**

**vice**[1] *n* **1** wickedness **2** bad habit

> **vice** *n* **1** (wickedness) corruption, depravity,
> evil, immorality, iniquity, sin, turpitude,
> wrongdoing. **2** (bad habit) defect, failing,
> flaw, foible, imperfection, weakness

**vice-**[2] *prefix forms compounds with meaning of*
  second to; in place of

**vice president** *n* officer just under president
  in rank

**viceroy** *n* one who rules as representative of
  sovereign; *fem* **vicereine** wife of viceroy;
  *adj* **viceregal**; *n* **vicerroyalty**

**vice versa** *adv Lat* conversely

**vicinity** *n* nearness; neighborhood

**vicious** *adj* **1** using great violence **2** very
  unkind; *n* **v. cycle** cycle of bad events each
  causing the next to go on recurring

> **vicious** *adj* **1** (using great violence) barbaric,
> brutal, callous, cruel, diabolical, fiendish,
> foul, heinous, inhuman, monstrous,
> pitiless, ruthless, sadistic, savage, vile.
> **2** (very unkind) bitchy *inf*, catty, cruel,
> malicious, mean, nasty, poisonous, savage,
> spiteful, venomous, vindictive, vitriolic

**vicissitudes** *n pl Fr* ups and downs of life

**victim** *n* one who suffers through no fault of
  his own; *v* **victimize** make to suffer,
  penalize, *esp* unjustly; *n* **victimization**

**victor** *n* conqueror; winner

**Victorian** *adj* **1** of the time of Queen Victoria
  (1837–1901) (*n* person of this time) **2** (of
  moral attitude) based on principles of self-
  control, respectability, and thrift

**victory** *n* conquest; act of winning;
  *adj* **victorious** triumphant; winning

> **victory** *n* mastery, success, triumph, win

**victual** (*n usual pl*) food

**video** *n* **1** videotape recording **2** machine for
  recording and replaying this; *pl* **-os**;
  *v* **videoing, videoed** make video recording
  of; *ns* **v. cassette recorder** machine for
  videoing TV broadcasts (*also* **video**
  (**recorder**)); *abbr* **VCR**; **videotape**
  magnetic tape for recording moving pictures
  and sound (*v* record in this way)

**vie** *v* **vying, vied** strive with; rival

**view** *n* **1** scene; scenery **2** opinion; *v* look at;
  consider; hold specified opinion; *idm* **in
  view of** because of; *idm* **on view** being
  exhibited; *idm* **with a view to** with the
  hope, intention of; *ns* **viewpoint** point of
  view; opinion; **viewer 1** one who watches
  **2** device for looking st photographic slides

> **view** *n* **1** (scene; scenery) aspect, landscape,
> outlook, panorama, picture, prospect,
> sight, vision, vista. **2** (opinion) attitude,
> belief, conviction, feeling, idea, notion,
> perception, position, sentiment, thought

**vigil** *n* act of keeping watch or of praying all
  night

**vigilant** *adj* watchful, alert; *n* **-ance**

**vigilante** *n* member of self-appointed group
  seeking to prevent crime

**vigor** *n* strength, vitality; *adj* **-ous** strong,
  active, forceful (*adv* **-ly**)

**Viking** *n* medieval Scandinavian pirate

**vile** *adj* **1** morally bad **2** extremely unpleasant;
  *v* **vilify** speak ill of; slander; *n* **vilification**

> **vile** *adj* **1** (morally bad) bad, base,
> contemptible, debased, degenerate,
> depraved, despicable, detestable, evil,
> ignoble, immoral, impure, loathsome,
> low, perverted, shocking, sinful, ugly,
> vicious, wicked. **2** (extremely
> unpleasant) disgusting, foul, horrible,
> horrid, loathsome, nasty, nauseating,
> repellent, repugnant, repulsive, revolting

**villa** *n* country house in Italy or France

**village** n small rural community with cottages, shops, church, etc; n **villager**

**villain** n scoundrel; adj **-ous** wicked; vile; n **villainy**

**villein** n feudal serf

**vinaigrette** n Fr salad dressing

**vindicate** v prove truth or innocence of; n **vindication**

> **vindicate** v confirm, corroborate, justify, prove sb right, substantiate, verify

**vindictive** adj revengeful; punitive

**vine** n climbing plant with tendrils, esp one bearing grapes; ns **-yard** grapevine plantation; **vinery** hot-house for growing grapes

**vinegar** n acid liquid got from fermented wine, beer, etc

**vintage** n 1 yield of wine grapes in given year 2 fig date, as criterion of quality

**vinyl** n any of various tough flexible plastics

**viola**[1] n family of plants including pansy

**viola**[2] n stringed instrument slightly larger and lower pitched than violin

**violate** v desecrate, rape, infringe; n **-ation** act of, thing which violates

**violent** adj 1 aggressive 2 very powerful; adv **-ly**; n **violence**

> **violent** adj 1 (aggressive) attacking, bellicose, belligerent, bloodthirsty, brutal, destructive, ferocious, fierce, hot-headed, hot-tempered, intemperate, savage, vicious, warlike. 2 (extremely powerful) fierce, fiery, forceful, intense, passionate, powerful, raging, strong, tempestuous, unbridled, uncontrollable, uncontrolled, unrestrained, vehement, wild

**violet** n small flowering plant; adj of bluish purple color

**violin** n four-stringed soprano musical instrument; n **-ist** player of violin

**VIP** abbr very important person

**viper** n venomous snake, adder

**viral** adj of or caused by virus

**virgin** n one who has never had sexual intercourse; adj 1 sexually inexperienced 2 (of land) never before cultivated; adj **virginal** of, like virgin; pure; fresh; n **virginity**

**viridescence** n greenness, verdure, freshness

**virile** adj strong and manly; n **virility** masculinity; sexual potency in men

> **virile** adj lusty, macho, male, masculine, potent, red-blooded, rugged, vigorous

**virtual** adj in effect but not in name; adv **-ly** to all intent and purposes

**virtual reality** n environment simulated by computer software in which a user can interact as if it were the real world

**virtue** n 1 moral goodness 2 female chastity 3 advantage; idm **by virtue of** thanks to

> **virtue** n 1 (moral goodness) honesty, honor, innocence, integrity, morality, probity, rectitude, righteousness, uprightness. 2 (advantage) asset, attribute, credit, good point, merit, quality, strength

**virtuoso** n one with high degree of technical skill, esp in music; pl **-sos or -si**; n **-osity**

**virtuous** adj 1 morally good 2 chaste

> **virtuous** adj (morally good) blameless, decent, ethical, exemplary, good, honest, honorable, incorruptible, principled, pure, righteous, upright, worthy

**virulent** adj 1 (of disease, poison) very powerful 2 fml bitterly hostile; n **virulence**

**virus** n one of minute parasitic organisms causing infectious diseases; such a disease; pl **-ses**

**visa** n endorsement on passport; v endorse passport with visa

**vis-à-vis** adv, prep Fr with regard to

**viscose** n viscose rayon

**viscount** n noble rank below earl; fem **-ess**

**viscous** *adj* sticky; semifluid; *n* **viscosity**

**vise** *n* device for holding, gripping an object in given position

**visible** *adj* able to be seen; obvious; *n* **-bility** 1 state, quality of being visible 2 degree of atmospheric clarity, *esp* in navigation

> **visible** *adj* apparent, clear, conspicuous, detectable, discernible, distinct, distinguishable, evident, manifest, noticeable, observable, open, palpable, perceivable, plain, recognizable, unconcealed, undisguised, unmistakable

**vision** *n* 1 sight 2 intuition 3 something seen 4 apparition or phantom; *adj* **-ary** idealistic; perceptive (*n* impractical idealist)

**visit** *v* go to see; call upon socially; *n* temporary stay; social or professional call; *n* **visitor** one who calls to see sb

> **visit** *v* call on, drop in on *inf*, go to see, look up, pay a call on, pay a visit to, pop in on *inf*, see, stay with, stop by

**visor** *n* movable front part of helmet or hat

**vista** *n Sp, It* distant view

**visual** *adj* to do with sight; *n* **v. aid** picture, film, or video used as teaching aid; **v. display unit** screen for computer (*abbr* **VDU**); *adv* **-ly**; *v* **-ize** form a mental picture of

**vital** *adj* 1 extremely important; necessary 2 lively; *ns* **v. statistics** statistics regarding population changes; **v. signs** signs of life: pulse, respiration, temperature, blood pressure; **vitality** liveliness

> **vital** *adj* (extremely important) basic, cardinal, critical, crucial, decisive, essential, fundamental, imperative, indispensable, key, mandatory, requisite, urgent

**vitamin** *n* organic substance present in food

**vitreous** *adj* pertaining to glass

**vitriol** *n fig* biting sarcasm; *adj* **-lic**

**vituperate** *v* abuse loudly; *adj* **-ative**

**vivacious** *adj* lively and full of fun

**vivacity** *n* liveliness

**vivid** *adj* 1 (of color) very bright 2 (of description) animated; graphic; *adv* **-ly**

> **vivid** *adj* 1 (of color) bright, brilliant, clear, colorful, dazzling, glowing, intense, rich, strong, vibrant. 2 (of description) detailed, evocative, graphic, lifelike, memorable, powerful, realistic, striking

**viviparous** *adj* bringin forth young alive

**vivisection** *n* operating or experimenting on living animals

**vixen** *n* female fox; *fig* spiteful woman

**V-neck** *n* neckline of dress, sweater, etc shaped like V; *adj* **-ed**

**vocabulary** *n* stock or list of words

**vocal** *adj* uttered by voice; stated strongly; *adv* **-ly**; *v* **-ize** (*n* **-ization**); *n* **-ist** singer

**vocation** *n* occupation, job done for moral or spiritual reasons; job; *adj* **-al** (*adv* **-ly**)

**vociferate** *v* shout; bawl, utter loud cries

**vociferous** *adj* stated forcefully

> **vociferous** *adj* blunt, forthright, insistent, outspoken, strident, vehement, vocal

**vodka** *n* Russian spirit distilled from rye

**vogue** *n Fr* fashion, custom; popularity

**voice** *n* 1 sound produced by organs of speech 2 quality of such sound 3 wish, desire expressed as vote; *v* express; *n* **v.-over** (TV, film) voice of unseen person; *adj* **-less** without speaking aloud

**void** *adj* empty; lacking; legally invalid; *n* empty space; *v* excrete from body; nullify

> **void** *n* blank, emptiness, gap, lacuna, nothingness, space, vacuum

**voile** *n Fr* thin cotton or silken material

**volatile** *adj* 1 likely to change suddenly; unstable 2 evaporating quickly; *n* **-tility**

**vol-au-vent** *n Fr* small pie of puff pastry

**volcano** *n* mountain formed by eruption of molten lava through opening in earth's crust; *pl* **-oes**; *adj* **volcanic** of, like volcano

**vole** *n* mouselike rodent

**volition** *n* act or faculty of willing; choosing.

**volley** *n* 1 number of missiles thrown or shot at once 2 *fig* torrent of words 3 (tennis, etc) striking of ball before it touches ground; *v* fire, hit volley; *n* **v. ball** ball game played over high net

**volt** *n* unit of electromotive force; *n* **-age** such force measured in units

**volte-face** *n Fr* reversal of opinion/direction

**voluble** *adj* talkative

**volume** *n* 1 mass 2 book 3 intensity of sound

> **volume** *n* (mass) amount, body, bulk, capacity, dimensions, mass, quantity, size

**voluminous** *adj* bulky

**voluntary** *adj* 1 made, done freely 2 given, supported by private donations; *adv* **-ily**

**volunteer** *n* one who offers services of own free will; *v* offer freely

**voluptuous** *adj* shapely and sexually attractive

**vomit** *v* discharge digested food from stomach through mouth; *n* that which has been vomited

> **vomit** *v* be sick, bring sth up, chuck *inf*, disgorge, heave, puke, regurgitate, retch, spew *inf*, throw up *inf*

**voodoo** *n* religion derived from African polytheism and ancestor worship

**voracious** *adj* greedy, ravenous; *n* **voracity**

**vortex** *n pl* **vortices** whirlpool; whirling mass

**vote** *n* formal expression of one's wish, opinion, etc; right to vote at elections, etc; *v* choose, select by voting; *n* **voter**

> **vote** *v* cast your vote, elect, have your say, nominate, opt, pick, return

**vouch** *phr v* **vouch for** guarantee; be responsible for

**voucher** *n* document confirming fact or authenticity of something; ticket acting as substitute for cash

**vow** *n* solemn promise; *v* promise faithfully

**vowel** *n* speech sound produced by unhindered passage of breath through mouth; letter representing such sound

**voyage** *n* long journey by water or in space; *v* travel on water or in space; *n* **voyager**

**voyeur** *n Fr* one who derives pleasure from observing others, *usu* secretly

**vulcanize** *v* treat (rubber) by sulfur, under heat; *ns* **vulcanite** hard substance so made; **vulcanization**

**vulgar** *adj* 1 having coarse manners 2 showing bad taste 3 obscene; *n* **-ity** coarseness; lack of refinement; bad taste

> **vulgar** *adj* 1 (having coarse manners) common, crude, dirty, foul, gross, ill-bred, ill-mannered, impolite, indecent, naughty, offensive, rude, uncouth, unseemly.
> 2 (showing bad taste) flashy, gaudy, in bad taste, inelegant, nasty, showy, tasteless, tawdry

**Vulgate** *n* 4th-century Latin translation of Bible

**vulnerable** *adj* easily attacked, hurt, wounded; *n* **-ability**

> **vulnerable** *adj* at risk, defenseless, exposed, helpless, open, powerless, sensitive, susceptible, tender, unguarded, unprotected, weak, wide open

**vulture** *n* 1 large carrion-eating bird of prey 2 *fig* rapacious extortioner

**vulva** *n anat* external opening of female genitals

**vying** *pr, p of* **vie**

**wacky** *adj* crazy, zany

**wad** *n* small pad of fibrous material; bundle of paper, *esp* bank notes; *n* **wadding** soft material used for stuffing, etc

**waddle** *v* walk heavily with swaying motion, like duck; *n* this gait

**wade** *v* walk through water; *phr vs* **wade in** begin with determination; **wade into** attack with vigor; **wade through** read through (sth long and tedious); *n* **wader** one that wades (*pl* long waterproof boots)

**wadi, wady** *n* dried-up desert watercourse

**wafer** *n* 1 light thin biscuit; 2 small round disk of special bread eaten at Communion service; *adj* **w.-thin** very thin

**waffle**¹ *n* thin crisp cake of batter

**waffle**² *v coll* talk or write lengthily in a meaningless way

> **waffle** *v* babble, blather *inf*, jabber, prattle, ramble

**waft** *v* carry lightly and smoothly through air or over water; *n* breath of air; faint odor, whiff

**wag** *v* **wagging, wagged** move or shake up and down or from side to side; as of dog's tail; *n* humorous, joking person; *adj* **waggish** comical, droll (*adv* **-ly**; *n* **-ness**)

**wage** *n* payment for labor; *n* **w.-claim** demand by workers for specified increase in wages; *v* carry on (war)

**wage** *n* allowance, earnings, fee, income, pay, payment, remuneration, salary

**wager** *n*, *v* bet

**waggle** *v* wag; *adj* **waggly**

**wagon** *n* four-wheeled vehicle for heavy loads

**wagtail** *n* small long-tailed bird

**waif** *n fig* homeless or neglected child

**wail** *v* howl in grief; *n* cry of grief

> **wail** *v* bawl, caterwaul, cry, howl, lament, shriek, sob, weep

**wainscot** *n* wooden panelling on walls of room

**wainwright** *n* builder of wagons

**waist** *n* narrow part of body between thorax and hips; *ns* **waistband** strip of fabric enclosing waist at top of trousers, skirt, etc; **waistcoat** sleeveless garment worn under jacket; **waistline** measurement around waist

**wait** *v* 1 delay or hesitate before doing sth 2 serve at table; *phr v* **wait on** 1 serve food to 2 act as servant to; *n* act of waiting; *n* **waiter** person serving in restaurant (*fem* **waitress**); *adj* **waiting** (*ns* **w. list** list of people waiting their turn; **w. room** room where one waits to be attended to)

> **wait** *v* (delay or hesitate) be patient, bide your time, hang fire, hang on, hold back, hold your horses, linger, pause, sit tight, stay, stop

**waive** *v* relinquish (claim, etc); *n* **waiver** legal renunciation

**wake**¹ *v* **waking, woke, woken** 1 rouse from sleep 2 stir up; excite; *phr v* **wake up to** realize; *v* **waken** wake up; rouse; *adj* **wakeful** vigilant

> **wake** *v* 1 (rouse from sleep) disturb, rouse, waken, wake up. 2 (become awake) get up, rise, stir, wake up

**wake**[2] *n* aftermath; *idm* **in the w. of**
following as consequence of; close behind
**wake**[3] *n* meeting to lament dead person
before burial
**walk** *v* move along on foot at moderate pace;
*n* **1** journey on foot **2** way of walking; *phr vs*
**walk away/off with** *coll* **1** remove by theft
**2** win with ease; **walk out 1** leave suddenly
without further comment **2** go on strike
(*n* **w.-out**); **walk out on** abandon;
*ns* **walker**; **walkie-talkie** portable radio
receiver/transmitter; **walking** (*n* **w.-stick**
stick to support person walking); **walkover**
easy victory; **walkway** passage for walking
along

> **walk** *v* amble, plod, saunter, stroll, traipse,
> tramp, troop, trudge
> **walk** *n* **1** (journey on foot) hike,
> promenade, ramble, stroll, trek.
> **2** (way of walking) gait, step, stride

**Walkman** [TM] personal stereo
**wall** *n* **1** upright structure of brick, stone, etc
forming part of building or room, or as fence
**2** *fig* barrier; *idm* **go to the wall** fail; *idm* **go
up the wall** *coll* be furious; *phr vs* **wall off**
separate with wall; **wall up** enclose by walls;
*n* **wallpaper** decorative paper for interior
walls of house; *adjs* **walled** having wall(s);
**wall-to-wall** covering whole floor area
**wallaby** *n* species of small kangaroo
**wallet** *n* flat leather case for money
**wall-eyed** *adj* having eye(s) with whitish iris;
squinting
**wallflower** *n* **1** perennial plant **2** *coll* girl who
has no partners at dance
**Walloon** *adj*, *n* French-speaking Belgian
**wallop** *v* beat severely; thrash; *n* **walloping**
thrashing, beating; *adj coll* of large size
**wallow** *v* **1** roll about in water, mud **2** enjoy

> **wallow** *v* **1** (roll about in water, mud) lie,
> roll, splash around, tumble, wade.
> **2** (enjoy) bask, glory, indulge, revel

**Wall Street** *n* center of American business
**walnut** *n* **1** edible nut with crimpled surface;
**2** tree bearing this; **3** decorative hardwood
used in cabinetry
**walrus** *n* large amphibious mammal
**waltz** *n* dance in ⅓ time, performed by couple;
*v* dance waltz; whirl, twirl round;
*phr v* **waltz off with** *coll* run away with
**wan** *adj* pale, sickly
**wand** *n* long, slender rod
**wander** *v* **1** roam **2** be delirious;
*ns* **wanderer**; **wanderlust** urge to travel

> **wander** *v* (roam) cruise, drift, meander,
> ramble, range, rove, saunter, stray, stroll,
> walk

**wane** *v* diminish in amount, intensity, power
**wangle** *v coll* use irregular means to obtain
sth; *n coll* something obtained by guile or
dishonesty
**want** *v* **1** desire **2** need; *n* deficiency; need

> **want** *v* **1** (desire) aspire to, covet, crave,
> fancy, hanker after, like, long for, pine for,
> prefer, set your heart on *inf*, wish, yearn
> for. **2** (need) be in need of, be short of,
> call for, demand, lack, miss, require

**wanton** *adj* uncontrolled; purposeless; without
morals
**war** *n* armed conflict between nations;
hostility; *v* fight; *ns* **w. cry** sth shouted in
battle; **w.-paint 1** body make-up used by
Native American warriors **2** *coll* cosmetics;
*adj* **warlike** to do with war; aggressive

> **war** *n* battle, campaign, combat, conflict,
> crusade, fight, fighting, hostilities, warfare

**warble** *v* sing with trills, as bird; *n* **warbler**
genus of small wild songbirds
**ward** *n* **1** minor under care of guardian
**2** division of city **3** section of hospital,
prison, etc; *phr v* **ward off** defend oneself
against; *n* **warder** prison officer

**warden** n governor; person having authority
**wardrobe** n cupboard in which clothes are kept; stock of clothes
**wardroom** n naval officers' messroom
**ware-house** n storehouse for goods
**wares** n articles for sale; goods

> **wares** n merchandise, produce, stock, stuff

**warfare** n (fighting in) war
**warlock** n wizard; sorcerer
**warm** adj 1 (of weather) pleasantly hot 2 fairly hot 3 friendly; v make, become warm; idm **keep sb's seat warm** reserve seat for sb (by occupying it); idm **make things warm/hot for** punish or reprimand severely; phr vs **warm to** begin to like; **warm up** 1 make or become warmer 2 prepare for more energetic activity; adjs **w.-blooded** 1 having constantly warm body temperature 2 fig passionate; **w.-hearted** kind; n **warmth** 1 mild heat 2 fig cordiality 3 anger

> **warm** adj 1 (pleasantly hot) balmy, mild, 2 (fairly hot) heated, lukewarm, tepid. 3 (friendly) affectionate, caring, emotional, enthusiastic, heartfelt, hearty, loving, passionate, sincere

**warmonger** n person that provokes war
**warn** v caution as to dangers of sth

> **warn** v advise, alert, counsel, forewarn, give notice, inform, let sb know, tell, tip off inf

**warning** n 1 notice, hint of possible danger, consequences 2 premonition

> **warning** n 1 (notice, hint of danger) advice, caution, forewarning, notification, threat, tip, tip-off. 2 (premonition) omen, portent, sign, signal, token

**warp** v twist, distort; become twisted; n threads running lengthwise in fabric

**warpath** idm **on the warpath** in fighting mood
**warrant** n document that authorizes; v justify; guarantee; n **warranty** guarantee
**warren** n group of rabbit burrows
**warrior** n lit fighter
**warship** n naval vessel used in war
**wart** n small hard growth on surface of skin; n **w.-hog** large wild African pig with tusks
**wary** adj attentive for danger

> **wary** adj alert, careful, cautious, distrustful, guarded, on the lookout, on your guard, prudent, suspicious, vigilant, watchful

**was** 1st, 3rd person sing pt of **be**
**wash** v 1 clean with water or other liquid 2 (of sea, river, etc) flow over, against; idm **wash one's hands of** refuse to have further interest in or responsibility for; phr vs **wash away** (of water) carry elsewhere; **wash out** 1 (of dirt) be removed by washing 2 clean inside of; **wash over sb** coll fail to stir sb emotionally; **wash up** 1 wash onself 2 wash face and hands 3 (of sea) bring to shore; n 1 act of washing 2 load of clothes, etc (to be) washed 3 waves made by passing boat, etc; ns **w.-basin** bowl for washing hands, etc; **washroom** coll lavatory; adj **washed-out** 1 faded 2 exhausted; ns **washing** 1 act of washing 2 clothes, etc (to be) washed; **w.-machine/-powder** machine/powder for washing clothes; **w.-stand** (formerly) bedroom table with jug and basin for washing; **washerwoman** (formerly) woman who washes clothes, etc; **washy** 1 pale 2 watery 3 insipid

> **wash** v 1 (clean with water) bath, bathe, cleanse, flush, launder, moisten, mop, rinse, scrub, shampoo, shower, soap, sponge, swab, swill, wet, wipe. 2 (flow over, against) beat, break, dash, lap, splash

**washout** n coll complete failure
**wasn't** contracted form of was not

**wasp** n stinging insect; adjs **-ish** spiteful, biting; **w.-waisted** having very slender waist

**waste** v 1 use extravagantly or uselessly 2 lose strength; become emaciated 3 cause to shrink 4 devastate; adj 1 left over and useless 2 desolate; n 1 refuse; useless things left over 2 extravagant expenditure 3 desert; phr v **waste away** become weak and thin; ns **w. disposal unit** sink attachment for shredding and washing away waste vegetable matter; **w.-paper** used paper; **w.-pipe** pipe carrying used water to drain; ns **wastage** amount lost by waste; loss; n **wasteland** 1 barren or desolate area; 2 fig unproductive situation in life; adj **wasteful** extravagant

**waste** v (use extravagantly) be wasteful with, blow, fritter away, misspend, misuse, splurge, squander, throw away, use up
**waste** n 1 (junk) debris, dregs, dross, excess, garbage, leavings, leftovers inf, litter, refuse, remnants, rubbish, scrap, trash. 2 (extravagant expenditure) loss, misuse, squandering, wastage, wastefulness

**watch** v 1 observe 2 pay attention 3 guard; supervise; idm **watch it/watch one's step** be careful; phr vs **watch (out) for** look out for; beware; **watch over** guard and protect; n 1 small, portable clock, usu worn on wrist 2 act of watching 3 person, group of people employed to watch or protect sth; ns **watch-dog** dog that guards; group set up to protect people's rights; **watchman** person employed to protect property at night; adj **watchful** vigilant; observant

**watch** v 1 (observe) eye, gaze at, look, note, peer at, regard, see, stare at, view. 2 (pay attention) attend to, be watchful, keep your eyes on, take care. 3 (guard; supervise) keep an eye on, look after, mind, protect, take care of

**water** n 1 clear, tasteless liquid for drinking (oxide of hydrogen) 2 body of water (sea, river, lake etc); pl **-s** 1 sea, river, lake (**coastal/inland w.**) 2 amniotic fluid surrounding fetus in womb; idm **make/pass water** urinate; v 1 pour water on (plants, land) 2 produce tears or saliva; phr v **water down** 1 dilute 2 reduce strength of; ns **w. bed** bed with water-filled mattress; **w. closet** lavatory ; **w. lily** floating pond plant with large round leaves; **w. pistol** toy gun that squirts water; **w. table** underground water level; adj **watery**

**water** v (pour water on) dampen, douse, drench, flood, hose, irrigate, moisten, saturate, soak, spray, sprinkle, wet

**watercolor** n (picture painted with) paint made to be mixed with water
**watercourse** n (channel of) stream, river, etc
**watercress** n cress grown in water
**watered silk** n glossy silk fabric with wavy markings
**waterfall** n cascade of water
**waterfront** n harbor side
**waterhole** n pool at which animals drink
**watering can** n vessel for sprinkling water on plants
**waterlogged** adj saturated, soaked with water
**Waterloo** idm **meet one's Waterloo** be finally defeated
**watermark** n faint design in paper
**waterproof** adj (garment) proof against water

**waterproof** adj damp-proof, water-repellent, water-resistant, watertight, weatherproof

**watershed** n 1 geog ridge of high land on either side of which streams and rivers flow in opposite directions 2 fig moment of important change in life or career
**waterspout** n funnel-shaped column of water drawn up from the ocean by strong winds
**watertight** adj tightly fitting to ensure exclusion of water; fig flawless, unassailable

a
b
c
d
e
f
g
h
i
j
k
l
m
n
o
p
q
r
s
t
u
v
w
x
y
z

**waterworks** n pl 1 place from where public water supply is controlled 2 *coll* person's urinary system; *idm* **turn on the waterworks** weep intentionally

**watt** n unit of electrical power

**wattle** n fencing of woven twigs and wicker

**wave** v 1 hold in hand and shake 2 move to and fro in air 3 greet by raising and moving hand; n 1 act of, gesture of waving 2 swelling ridge on surface of water 3 (of specified activity) sudden, temporary increase 4 form of each vibration of light, sound, etc 5 curve of line of hair; ns **waveband** *rad* specified range of wavelengths; **wavelength** *rad* signal using particular frequency (*idm* **on the same wavelength** having a mutual understanding)

> **wave** v 1 (hold in hand and shake) brandish, flourish, shake, swing, wag, waggle, wield. 2 (move to and fro in air) billow, flap, flutter, ripple, stir, undulate. 3 (greet) beckon, gesticulate, gesture, indicate, signal

**waver** v fluctuate; hesitate; yield, give way

**wavy** adj curved, curly

**wax**[1] v increase in size (chiefly of moon)

**wax**[2] n solid insoluble substance used for candles; secretion of ear, bees; adj **waxy**; n **waxwork** wax model of person

**way** n 1 method 2 path 3 manner of behaving 4 aspect; *idm* **by the way** incidentally; *idm* **by way of** 1 going past, through 2 as a form of; *idm* **get/have one's own way** do or get what one wants; *idm* **give way** collapse; *idm* **have a way with one** have pleasant, persuasive personality; *idm* **make one's way** progress; *idm* **make way (for)** 1 allow to pass 2 give scope to; *idm* **out of the way** conveniently absent; *idm* **under way** 1 moving 2 happening; adj **w.-out** *coll* bizarre; unorthodox; ns **waybill** list of passengers and goods; **wayside** side of road or path; **wayfarer** traveler; v **wayward** perverse, willful

> **way** n 1 (method) approach, means, mode, plan, procedure, scheme, technique. 2 (path) access, avenue, channel, course, direction, lane, road, roadway, route, street, track, trail. 3 (manner of behaving) conduct, custom, habit, mannerism, nature, personality, routine, temperament, trait, wont. 4 (aspect) circumstance, detail, feature, particular, point, respect, sense

**we** pron 1st pers pl nom of I

**weak** adj 1 not strong 2 likely to break 3 vulnerable 4 indecisive 5 not loud 6 dim 7 not believable 8 diluted; n **weakling** person or animal lacking strength; adj **weakly** not robust

> **weak** adj 1 (not strong) decrepit, delicate, exhausted, faint, feeble, fragile, frail, infirm, puny, sickly, tender, tired, unsteady, wasted, weedy, worn out. 2 (likely to break) breakable, brittle, fragile, inadequate, insubstantial, rickety, shaky, thin, unsafe. 3 (vulnerable) defenseless, exposed, open, unguarded, unprotected. 4 (indecisive) impotent, ineffective, powerless, spineless, timid, unassertive. 5 (not loud) distant, dull, faint, low, muffled, quiet, small, soft. 6 (dim) fading, faint, poor, small. 7 (not believable) feeble, flimsy, lame, pathetic, unconvincing, unsatisfactory. 8 (dilute) insipid, runny, tasteless, thin, watery

**weaken** v 1 make weaker 2 become weaker

> **weaken** v 1 (make weaker) destroy, dilute, diminish, erode, exhaust, lessen, lower, make weaker, reduce, sap, soften, thin down, tire, undermine, water down, wear out. 2 (become weaker) abate, become weaker, decline, decrease, dwindle, ease up, ebb, fade, flag, give in, give way, let up, tire, wane

**weakness** *n* **1** lack of strength **2** fault

> **weakness** *n* **1** (lack of strength)
> cowardliness, feebleness, frailty,
> impotence, powerlessness, vulnerability. **2**
> (fault) Achilles' heel, defect, failing, flaw,
> imperfection, shortcoming, weak point

**weal** *n* mark left on flesh by blow from lash
**wealth** *n* riches; abundance
**wealthy** *adj* rich; *n* **wealthiness**

> **wealthy** *adj* affluent, comfortable, flush *inf*,
> loaded, prosperous, well-heeled, well-to-do

**wean** *v* accustom to food other than mother's
milk; *phr v* **wean sb (away) from** help sb
by gradual process to give up
**weapon** *n* object used for attack or defense
**wear** *v* **wearing, wore, worn** **1** to be
clothed in **2** be reduced by use; **wear off**
become less intense, less effective; **wear out**
**1** exhaust **2** make or become unserviceable
through great use; *n* **1** clothes **2** damage from
usage

> **wear** *v* (be clothed in) be dressed in,
> clothe yourself in, have on, put on, sport

**wearing** *adj* tiring, stressful
**weary** *adj* **1** tired **2** bored by; *v* **1** tire
**2** become bored by; *adj* **-ily**; *n* **-iness**;
*adj* **wearisome** tiresome, tedious
**weasel** *n* carnivorous animal resembling ferret
**weather** *n* general atmospheric conditions;
*v* **1** expose to action of weather **2** show effect
of such exposure **3** come safely through;
*idm* **under the weather** slightly ill or
depressed; *ns* **weathercock** weathervane
shaped like cockerel; **w. forecast**
description of expected weather; **w.-vane**
device on top of building pointing to where
wind is coming from; *adjs* **w.-beaten** having
rough, sunburned skin; showing effects of
exposure; **weatherproof** able to keep out
wind and rain

**weave** *v* **weaving, wove** (or **weaved**),
**woven** (or **weaved**) form (threads) into
web or fabric by intertwining; braid; wind in
and out; *ns* **weaver**; **weaving** act of doing
this; fabric so made

> **weave** *v* braid, criss-cross, entwine,
> interlace, intermingle, intertwine, knit,
> merge, plait, sew, twist, unite

**web** *n* **1** something woven; net; cobweb spun
by spider **2** membrane between digits of
aquatic bird, frog, etc; *adjs* **webbed** having
skin between toes to assist swimming;
**w.-footed** with webbed feet; *n* **webbing**
strong woven fabric used to make straps, etc
**we'd** *contracted form of* **1** we had **2** we would
**wed** *v* **wedding, wedded** **1** marry **2** *fig* unite
**wedding** *n* ceremony where people get
married; *ns* **w. cake** white cake,
traditionally in tiered layers; **w. ring**
ring worn as sign of being married
**wedge** *n* V-shaped piece of wood, metal, etc;
*v* make firm with wedge; fix immovably
**wedlock** *n* *fml* state of being married;
*idm* **born out of wedlock** born to
unmarried parents
**Wednesday** *n* fourth day of week
**wee** *adj* very small; tiny; *n* *sl* urine; *v* urinate
**weed** *n* wild plant, *esp* one which tends to
choke cultivated ones; *v* free (ground) from
weeds; *n* **w.-killer** chemical for killing
weeds; *adj* **weedy** **1** full of weeds **2** lanky
**week** *n* period of seven days, *esp* from Sunday
to Saturday; *ns* **weekday** any day except
Sunday; **weekend** from Friday or Saturday
until Monday; *adj, adv* **weekly** once a week
**weep** *v* shed tears; *pt, pp* **wept**

> **weep** *v* bawl, blubber, cry, lament, moan,
> mourn, sob, wail, whimper

**weevil** *n* small beetle harmful to corn, etc
**weigh** *v* **1** have certain weight **2** measure
weight of; *phr v* **weigh up** consider (by
balancing facts, arguments)

a
b
c
d
e
f
g
h
i
j
k
l
m
n
o
p
q
r
s
t
u
v
**w**
x
y
z

**weight** n 1 heaviness of sth 2 sth heavy 3 piece of metal used as standard for weighing other things 4 importance; idm a **weight off one's mind** a cause of anxiety removed; ns **w.-lifting** contest in lifting heavy weights (**w.-lifter** person doing this); **w.-watcher** person trying to lose weight by dieting, etc; adjs **weightless** (n **-ness**); **weighty** 1 heavy 2 serious

**weir** n dam in river to divert flow

**weird** adj very strange; eerie, uncanny; very strange; adv **-ly**; n **-ness**; n **weirdo** coll strange person

**welcome** adj pleasant; appreciated; n cordial greeting on arrival; v greet

> **welcome** adj acceptable, agreeable, cheering, delightful, desirable, much-needed, pleasurable, refreshing, wanted

**weld** v unite (hot metal) by fusion

**welfare** n 1 well-being; comfort, health, and happiness 2 social care for well-being of individuals, families, etc (ns **w. work**, **w. worker**) 3 money paid by government to those in need

**well**[1] adj in good health; comp **better**, sup **best**; adv 1 in a good way 1 skillfully 3 kindly; idm **as well** 1 also 2 equally well; adjs **w.-adjusted** at ease in society; **w.-connected** related to or friendly with influential people; **w.-done** thoroughly cooked; **w.-heeled** rich; **w.-lined** coll full of money or food; **w.-off** 1 rich 2 fortunate; **w.-to-do** rich

> **well** adj fit, healthy, hearty, in good health, sound, strong, thriving
> **well** adv 1 (in a good way) nicely, pleasantly, satisfactorily, smoothly, successfully.
> 2 (skillfully) ably, carefully, conscientiously, correctly, effectively, excellently, expertly, proficiently, properly, thoroughly. 3 (kindly) civilly, fairly, generously, hospitably, nicely, politely

**well**[2] n 1 shaft sunk to obtain water or oil 2 natural spring 3 elevator shaft

**wellingtons** n pl knee-high waterproof boots

**Welsh** adj of Wales, its people or language; n **W. rabbit (rarebit)** toasted cheese

**welt** n 1 strip fixed to shoe to strengthen join between sole and upper 2 ribbed edging to top of sock, etc 3 mark left on skin from blow by lash; v 1 provide with welt 2 coll thrash

**wen** n sebaceous cyst on skin

**wench** n young woman

**wend** v **w. one's way** proceed slowly

**went** pt of **go**

**wept** pt, pp of **weep**

**were** pt of **be**

**we're** contracted form of **we are**

**werewolf** n myth person changed into wolf

**west** n 1 direction of setting sun 2 one of four points of compass 3 usu cap capitalist as opposed to Communist countries; America and Europe as opposed to Asia; adj pertaining to west; situated in or facing west; adjs **westerly**; **western** (n film of cowboy life; v **-ize** adapt to lifestyle of US and Europe); **westward** towards the west (adv **-s**); n, adj **W Indian** of W Indies

**wet** adj **wetter, wettest** 1 covered, moistened with liquid 2 rainy; v **wetting, wetted** make wet; n moisture; rain; ns **w. nurse** woman employed to feed another's baby; **w. suit** rubberized body garment to keep swimmer warm

> **wet** adj 1 (covered, moistened with liquid) bedraggled, clammy, damp, dank, dewy, dripping, moist, saturated, soaking, sodden, soggy, sopping, waterlogged, watery, wet through. 2 (rainy) drizzling, humid, pouring, raining, showery
> **wet** v dampen, dip, douse, drench, irrigate, moisten, put water on, saturate, soak, splash, spray, sprinkle

**we've** contracted form of **we have**

**whack** v hit hard; n such blow; coll due, share

**whale** *n* huge aquatic mammal; *idm* **have a whale of a time** *coll* enjoy oneself a lot; *ns* **whalebone** thin, horny substance growing in upper jaw of some whales

**wham** *n* heavy blow; *v* **whammed, whamming** hit violently

**wharf** *n* berth where ships tie up, load and unload

**what** *pron* that, those which; which thing? how much? *adj* which? of which kind? how much, how great?

**what(so)ever** *pron, adj* anything at all; no matter which; emphatic form of **what**

**wheat** *n* grain plant; edible grain, ground into flour; *n* **wheat germ** part of wheat kernel rich in vitamins

**wheedle** *v* coax, cajole

**wheel** *n* circular frame with spokes or solid disk, revolving around axle; *v* 1 move on wheels 2 cause (line of people) to turn as on pivot; *idm* **wheel and deal** *coll* negotiate in cunning way (*n* **wheeler-dealer**); *ns* **wheelbarrow** small one-wheeled cart; **wheelchair** mobile chair for invalids; **w. clamp** device for immobilizing illegally parked car

**wheelie** *n coll* stunt of riding bike, motorcycle with front wheel raised

**wheeze** *v* breathe with audible friction; *n* noisy breathing; *adj* **wheezy**

> **wheeze** *v* cough, gasp, hiss, pant, puff, rasp

**whelk** *n* edible marine mollusk

**whelp** *n* puppy; cub; ill-bred youth

**when** *adv* at what time? how soon? *conj* on the occasion that; at the time that; *adv, conj* **whenever** as soon as; as often as

**whence** *adv, conj* from where

**where** *adv, conj* to, at, or in which place or part? *adv* **whereabouts** in what place? *n* locality; situation; *conj* **whereas** in view of the fact that; but on the contrary; while; *advs* **wherever** 1 in, to, at, any place 2 no matter where; **wherefore** why? for which reason?

**whereby** *adj fml* by means of which

**whereupon** *conj* (immediately) after which

**wherewithal** *n* resources; money needed

**whet** *v* **whetting, whetted** stimulate (appetite, curiosity); *n* **whetstone** stone for sharpening knives, etc

**whether** *pron ar* which of two; *conj* expressing doubt, alternative possibility

**whey** *n* watery part of milk separated from curds

**which** *adj* what person or thing? *pron* the thing(s) that; what person, thing?

**whichever** *det, pron* 1 the one which 2 no matter which

**whiff** *v* puff; emit slight unpleasant smell; inhale odor; strike out; *n* 1 puff; breath; slight gust 2 scent, flavor

**while** *n* space of time; period; *conj* as long as; during; *phr v* **while away** pass (time) idly; *conj* **whilst** while

**whim** *n* passing fancy; impulse; caprice; *n* **whimsicality**; *adj* **whimsical** capricious; quaint

> **whim** *n* craze, desire, idea, impulse, notion, urge

**whimper** *n* feeble, fretful cry; *v* cry thus

**whine** *n* high-pitched noise (in motors) or long, drawn-out thin wail; *v* cry; complain

> **whine** *v* bleat, fuss, gripe *inf*, groan, grouch *inf*, grumble, moan, sob, wail, whimper

**whinny** *v* (of horse) neigh gently

**whip** *v* **whipping, whipped** 1 strike with lash 2 whisk (eggs, cream) 3 move fast and suddenly 4 *coll* defeat; overcome; *n* lash attached to handle; *phr v* **whip up** 1 stir up (feelings) 2 quickly enlist (support); *ns* **whipcord** 1 thin strong cord 2 ribbed cloth; **whiplash** 1 blow from whip 2 sudden violent jerk to head and neck as in road accident; **whippersnapper** impudent person; small, impudent boy

**whippet** n small swift slender racing dog

**whir(r)** v **whirring, whirred** revolve, move with rapid buzzing sound; n this sound

**whirl** v spin rapidly on axis; n 1 rapid rotation 2 bewilderment; idm **give sth a whirl** coll try sth; idm **in a whirl** bewildered; ns **whirligig** top; spinning toy; merry-go-round; **w.pool** rapid circular eddy; **w.wind** column of rapidly rotating air

> **whirl** v circle, gyrate, pirouette, pivot, reel, revolve, roll, rotate, spin, swirl, turn, twist

**whisk** v 1 sweep lightly, briskly 2 twitch; beat lightly; phr v **whisk off** carry away suddenly; n 1 light, stiff brush 2 instrument for beating eggs, etc

**whisker** n one of long bristles growing from side of animal's mouth; pl **-s** hair growing on man's face; idm **by a whisker** by the narrowest margin

**whisky** n alcoholic liquor distilled from malted grain, esp barley; **whiskey** Irish whisky

**whisper** v speak in low voice; fig tell as secret; n such speech

> **whisper** v breathe, murmur, mutter, say under your breath, speak softly

**whist** n card game for two pairs of players.

**whistle** v produce shrill piping sound from wind instrument or through pursed lips; n 1 shrill, piercing sound 2 device, instrument producing such sound; n **w.-stop** brief visit by politican in election campaign

**whit** n particle; bit

**white** adj 1 of color of snow 2 (of sb's face) very pale 3 of fair complexion; of Caucasian race; ns **w. elephant** sth useless; **w. flag** sign of surrender; **w. lie** trivial lie, esp one that avoids hurt to sb; **w. paper** Government paper on policy; adjs **w.-collar** of office work; working in an office; **w.-tie** (of social occasion) when men wear tails and white bow ties; v **whiten** make white

> **white** adj 1 (of color of snow) cream, ivory, off-white, snow-white. 2 (very pale) ashen, bloodless, pale, pallid, pasty, wan, white as a sheet

**whitebait** n type of small fish

**whitewash** n 1 white liquid for wall decor 2 fig attempt to conceal fault or error

**whither** adv 1 to what place or purpose? 2 to whatever place, or purpose

**whitlow** n inflammation of finger or toe

**Whitsunday** n seventh Sunday after Easter

**whittle** v 1 shape, pare (wood) with knife 2 fig reduce gradually

**whiz, whizz** n buzzing sound; v **whizzing, whizzed** move very quickly; make buzzing sound; n **w. kid** brilliant person; one who very quickly becomes successful

**who** pron (obj **whom** poss **whose**) which or what person? that person who; pron **who(so)ever** anyone (at all) who

**WHO** abbr World Health Organization

**whoa** interj used to stop horse moving

**whodunit** adj coll detective story

**whoever** pron 1 no matter who 2 anyone at all

**whole** adj 1 intact 2 entire; complete; n complete sum, amount; adv **wholly**; idm **on the whole** generally; n, adj **wholemeal** (of) flour made from whole unrefined grain of wheat, etc; adjs **w.-hearted** without doubt or restraint; **wholesale** of selling goods in bulk to retailers; **wholesome** 1 (of food) good for health 2 (of people) looking healthy and morally sound

> **whole** adj full, in one piece, perfect, sound, total, unabbreviated, unabridged, unbroken, uncut, undamaged, unharmed

**whom** pron fml object form of **who**

**whoop** n loud cry or yell; v utter such sound; n **whooping cough** infectious respiratory disease

**whoops** *interj* used after mistake

**whoosh** *n* noise of rushing wind, etc

**whop** *v* **whopping, whopped** hit; **whopper** *n coll* big thing; *adj* **whopping** *coll* big

**whore** *n* prostitute

**whorl** *n* circular group of petals, leaves, etc; single coil of spiral

**whose** *det, pron* of who; of which

**why** *adv* for what reason? because of which; *interj* expressing surprise; *idm* **whys and wherefores** explanations

**WI** *abbr* 1 Women's Institute 2 West Indies

**wick** *n* length of thread in candle or oil lamp

**wicked** *adj* 1 evil, bad 2 *coll* mischievous; *n* **wickedness**

> **wicked** *adj* (evil, bad) amoral, blasphemous, corrupt, criminal, diabolical, dishonorable, foul, immoral, malicious, mischievous, murderous, naughty, obscene, perverted, scandalous, shameful, sinful, unholy, unscrupulous, vicious, vile, villainous, violent, wrong

**wicker** *n* fabric made of interwoven canes; *adj, n* **wickerwork** (made of) woven wickers

**wicket** *n* 1 small gate 2 set of three cricket stumps and bails 3 arch, hoops in croquet

**wide** *adj* 1 broad 2 having broad scope; *idm* **wide of the mark** badly mistaken; *adjs* **w.-ranging** extending in many directions; **widespread** extended over a large area; *adv* **-ly**

> **wide** *adj* 1 (broad) ample, expansive, full, large, roomy, spacious, vast, yawning. 2 (having broad scope) all-embracing, broad, encyclopedic, far-ranging, general, inclusive, wide-ranging

**widen** *v* make wider

> **widen** *v* broaden, dilate, enlarge, expand, extend, flare, open out, spread, stretch

**widow** *n* woman whose husband has died; *masc* **-er**; *v* make widow of

**width** *n* distance from side to side

**wield** *v* handle; make use of (implement, weapon, etc) control

**wife** *n* married woman; *pl* **wives**; *adj* **wifely**

**wig** *n* artificial hair for head

**wiggle** *v* move from side to side; wriggle

**wigwam** *n* Native American's conical tent

**wild** *a* 1 not domesticated 2 uncultivated 3 uncivilized 4 uncontrolled 5 stormy; *ns* **the w.** natural habitat (*pl* **-s** remote area); **wildfowl** game bird(s); *adv* **-ly**; *n* **-ness**

> **wild** *adj* 1 (not domesticated) feral, ferocious, fierce, free, savage, unbroken, untamed. 2 (uncultivated) desolate, godforsaken, natural, overgrown, remote, uncivilized, unpopulated, unsettled, waste

**wildebeest** *n* large African antelope (*pl* **wildebeest(s)**)

**wilderness** *adj* desolate expanse of land; *idm* **in(to) the wilderness** out of active, *esp* political, life

**wile** *n* (*usu pl*) cunning stratagem

**will**[1] *n* 1 faculty of deciding what one will do; volition 2 determination; wish 3 document making disposition of property after death; *idm* **at will** at any time one wishes; *v* 1 wish 2 leave as bequest

**will**[2] *v aux* forms moods and tenses expressing future, intention, etc; *pt* **would**

**willful** *adj* 1 stubborn 2 deliberate

**willing** *adj* ready, eager to help; *adv* **-ly**

> **willing** *adj* cooperative, enthusiastic, happy, helpful, keen, obliging

**willow** *n* genus of trees, yielding osiers; *adj* **willowy** slender, graceful

**wilt** *v* (of plants) fade, droop, wither

**wily** *adj* cunning (*n* **-iness**)

**wimp** *n coll* weak, ineffectual person; *adj* **-ish**

**win** *v* **winning, won** 1 be winner 2 obtain as prize; *n* victory, success, *esp* in contest

**win** *v* **1** (be winner) be victorious, come first, overcome, prevail, succeed, triumph. **2** (obtain as prize) achieve, acquire, attain, collect, earn, gain, get, pick up, receive, secure, walk away with

**wince** *v* shrink away; flinch; *n* involuntary recoil

**winch** *n* machine for hoisting; windlass; crank used as handle

**wind**[1] *n* **1** air in motion **2** breath **3** flatulence; *idm* **break wind** expel air from bowels; *idm* **get wind of** hear about by chance; *ns* **w.-break** line of trees giving shelter from the wind; **windfall 1** fruit blown off tree **2** *fig* piece of unexpected good fortune; **w. instrument** *mus* instrument played by blowing (brass, woodwind); **wind-mill** mill, water-pump driven by force of wind; **windshield** front window of vehicle; **windsurfer 1** flat board with keel and sail **2** person using this (*v* **windsurf**; *n* **windsurfing**); *adj* **w.-swept 1** exposed to strong wind **2** (of hair) untidy

**wind**[1] *n* (air in motion) air, blast, breath, breeze, current, draft, gale, gust, hurricane, monsoon, squall, tornado, whirlwind, zephyr

**wind**[2] *v* **winding, wound 1** twist **2** tighten (watch spring) by turning; *phr vs* **wind down 1** (of machinery) go slow and stop **2** *coll* relax after stress, etc; **wind up 1** finish **2** *coll* tease or provoke

**wind**[2] *v* (twist) coil, curl, furl, loop, reel, roll, spiral, twine, wrap, wreathe

**winding** *adj* bending, twisting

**window** *n* opening in wall, roof, vehicle, etc to admit light, air, etc, *usu* filled by glass panes; *n* **w.-dressing** art of arranging goods in shop window; *fig* attractive presentation; **w.-sill** ledge under window

**Windows** *n* [TM] computer operating system

**windy** *adj* with strong winds

**windy** *adj* blowy, blustery, breezy, drafty, fresh, gusting, gusty, squally, stormy, tempestuous, wild, windswept

**wine** *n* fermented grape juice

**wing** *n* **1** limb by which bird, insect, etc flies **2** projecting part of aircraft's structure by which it is supported in air **3** side, flank **4** side projection from building; *idm* **under the wing of** protected, helped by; *pl* **-s** hidden area at sides of stage in theater; *ns* **w. chair** high-backed chair with projecting arms; **w.-nut** nut with flanges for easier turning; **w.-span** distance between tips of wings; *adjs* **-ed**, **-less**; *n* **winger** (sport) person playing on left or right wing

**wink** *v* open and close eye rapidly

**winkle** *n* edible shellfish

**winner** *n* person who wins; *pl* **-s** money won

**winner** *n* champion, conquering hero, conqueror, prizewinner, title-holder, victor

**winsome** *adj* engaging; attractive; charming

**winter** *n* coldest season of year; *v* spend winter in; *adj* **wintry** of, like winter; cold

**wipe** *v* clean, dry by rubbing with cloth; *phr v* **wipe out** eliminate; *n* **wiper**

**wipe** *v* brush, dust, mop, polish, sponge, swab, wash

**wire** *n* fine-drawn slender flexible thread of metal; *v* **1** fasten with wire **2** equip or connect with electric wiring; *n* **wiring** connection or system of wires; *adj* **wiry** slim and tough

**wire service** *n* news agency

**wise**[1] *adj* **1** intelligent and experienced **2** sensible; *n* **w. guy** *coll* person who gives impression of being very knowledgeable; *ns* **wisdom** sound judgment; **w. tooth** one cut during adult years

**wise** *adj* 1 (intelligent and experienced) clever, deep-thinking, educated, fair, informed, just, knowledgeable, perceptive, philosophical, well-informed, well-read. 2 (sensible) clever, diplomatic, good, logical, prudent, smart, thoughtful

**wise**[2] *n* way, manner, fashion
**wisecrack** *n coll* smart remark; witticism
**wish** *v* desire, want; *n* desire; *adj* **wishful** expressing desire or hope (**w. thinking** belief based on unrealistic desire)

**wish** *n* ambition, aspiration, craving, fondness, hope, liking, longing, request, requirement, yearning

**wishy-washy** *adj coll* weak, insipid (*n* **-iness**)
**wisp** *n* small bunch of straw, etc; thin, straggly lock of hair
**wistful** *adj* yearning; sadly pensive
**wit** *n* 1 clever, amusing use of words 2 person able to do this 3 *esp pl* mental capacity; quick understanding; *idm* **at wit's end** desperate and anxious; *adv* **wittingly** knowingly; deliberately

**wit** *n* (clever, amusing use of words) banter, fun, funniness, humor, jokes, puns, quips, repartee, witticisms, wittiness

**witch** *n* sorceress; *ns* **witchcraft** magic; **w. doctor** medicine man in tribe; **w.-hunt** 1 hunt to destroy witches 2 *fig* campaign to persecute those with unorthodox views
**witch hazel** *n* N American shrub whose bark yields astringent medicinal substance
**with** *prep* against; in company of; beside; possessed of; by means of
**withdraw** *v* **-drawing, -drew, -drawn** 1 draw, take back 2 retire; not take part
**withdrawn** *adj* aloof; uncommunicative
**wither** *v* become weaker and die; *adj* **-ing** contemptuous (**w. look**; *adv* **-ly**)

**wither** *v* decay, decline, disintegrate, droop, fade, go limp, languish, perish, shrink, shrivel, waste away, wilt

**withhold** *v* **-holding, -held** keep back
**within** *prep, adv* in, inside; *adv* **without** outside; *prep* lacking
**withstand** *v* **-standing, -stood** resist
**witness** *n* one who gives evidence; person or thing furnishing proof; *v* see; *n* **w. box** area in court where witness sits, stands

**witness** *n* bystander, eyewitness, observer, onlooker, spectator, viewer, watcher
**witness** *v* behold, be present at, notice, observe, view, watch

**witticism** *n* witty remark
**witty** *adj* clever and amusing in use of words

**witty** *adj* brilliant, comic, droll, facetious, funny, humorous, sarcastic

**wives** *pl* of wife
**wizard** *n* s1 orcerer; magician 2 *fig* expert; ingenious person
**wizened** *adj* shrivelled; dried up
**wobble** *v* move, sway unsteadily; *n* oscillation; unsteady movement

**wobble** *v* quake, quaver, quiver, rock, see-saw, shake, stagger, teeter, totter, tremble, vibrate, waver

**woe** *n* cause of sorrow; misfortune; *adj* **woeful** sorrowful; pitiful (*adv* **-ly**)
**wok** *n* deep curved pan used in Chinese cuisine
**woke** *pt*, **woken** *pp* of wake
**wolf** *n* large wild carnivorous animal of dog family; *pl* **wolves**; *ns* **w. cub** 1 young wolf 2 junior boy scout; **wolfhound** large hunting dog; *n*, *v* **w. whistle** (give) loud whistle to seek attention of sexually attractive female

**wolverine** *n* small carnivorous animal
**woman** *n* adult human female; *pl* **women**; *ns* **-hood** condition of being a woman; **-kind** women in general; *adjs* **-ly** having good qualities of woman; **-ish** effeminate; *v* **-ize** (of man) have affairs with many different women (*ns* **-izer**; **-izing**)

> **woman** *n* female, girl, lady

**womb** *n* uterus; female organ in which embryo develops
**wombat** *n* small Australian wild animal
**won** *pt, pp of* **win**
**wonder** *n* **1** marvel, prodigy **2** emotion; feeling of awe, excited by marvellous object, person, etc; *v* **1** be curious **2** be amazed; *n* **wonderment 1** astonishment **2** deep admiration

> **wonder** *v* (be curious) ask yourself, conjecture, deliberate, ponder, puzzle, reflect, speculate, think

**wonderful** *adj* amazing; very good; *adv* **-ly**

> **wonderful** *adj* brilliant, excellent, fantastic, great, incredible, magnificent, marvelous, outstanding, remarkable, sensational, smashing, stunning, superb, terrific

**wondrous** *adj* inspiring wonder; *adv* **-ly**
**wonk** *n coll* nerd; egghead
**wont** *adj* accustomed; *n* usual practice
**won't** *contracted form of* will not
**woo** *v* court, seek to win love of; *n* **-er** suitor
**wood** *n* **1** area of tree-covered land **2** solid substance of trees; timber; *adjs* **-ed** covered with trees; **wooden 1** made of wood **2** *fig* stiff; inhibited; **woody 1** wooded **2** like wood, *adj, n* **woodland**

> **wood** *n* (area of tree-covered land) coppice, copse, forest, grove, jungle, orchard, rain forest, tree plantation, trees

**woodcock** *n* woodland game bird with long straight beak
**woodcut** *n* engraving on wood block; print from this
**woodlouse** *n* small insect (*pl* **woodlice**)
**woodpecker** *n* bird that pecks holes in trees
**woodwind** *n* musical instruments, *usu* made of wood and played by being blown
**woodwork** *n* carpentry; wooden part of structure
**woodworm** *n* **1** larva that eats wood **2** holes in wood made by this
**woof**[1] *n, interj, v coll* (sound of dog's) bark
**woof**[2] *n* threads crossing warp in woven fabric
**wool** *n* fleece, coat of sheep, angora goat, alpaca, etc; *adj* **woolen** (cloth) made of wool; *n, adj* **woolly** (garment, jersey) made of wool; *n* **-iness**; **w-headed** not thinking clearly; *ns* **w.-gathering** letting the mind wander instead of concentrating **woolsack** sack or bale of wood
**woozy** *adj coll* **1** dizzy, *eg* from drinking alcohol **2** mentally confused
**word** *n* **1** unit of language serving as name of object, etc **2** brief conversation **3** promise; *v* express in words; *idm* **word for word** using exactly the same words; *n* **w. processor** computer program for editing text; *v* **w.-process** edit in this way; *adj* **wordy** verbose

> **word** *n* **1** (unit of language) expression, name, term. **2** (brief conversation) chat, talk, discussion, brief exchange

**work** *n* **1** occupation **2** labor **3** sth made by labor or artistic activity; *v* **1** do job; do activity needing effort **2** function **3** be effective **4** manipulate **5** gradually move or turn to specified position or condition; *phr vs* **work off** reduce by working; **work out 1** calculate **2** develop **3** decide **4** *coll* do physical exercise (*n* **w.-out**); **work up 1** develop by stages **2** arouse **3** make nervous, excited; *adj* **-able** able to be achieved, used; *n* **-er**

**work** n 1 (occupation) business, career, employment, field, job, line, livelihood, living, post, profession, trade. 2 (labor) drudgery, effort, elbow grease, exertion, graft, grind, hassle *inf*, slog, trouble

**work** v 1 (do job) be busy, be employed, earn a living, go to work, have a job, labor, make an effort, slave, toil. 2 (function) go, operate, perform, run. 3 (be effective) have the desired effect, succeed, be successful, go according to plan. 4 **work out** (calculate) estimate, solve

**workaday** adj ordinary, routine

**workaholic** n person unhealthily obsessed with work

**workbench** n table where mechanic, artisan, etc works

**workbook** n supplementary book with practice exercises

**work force** n total number of workers

**workhorse** n 1 useful machine 2 sb doing routine jobs

**workhouse** n penal institution for offenders

**working** n functioning; way in which process works; *pl* **-s** way in which sth operates; *idm* **in (full) working order** functioning properly; *adj* 1 of, at, for work 2 used at, spent in work; *ns* **w. class** proletariat (*adj* **w.-class**); **w. knowledge** sufficient practical knowledge to put to some use; **w. party** 1 group appointed to investigate and report on special area of concern 2 group of manual workers

**workload** n amount of work expected from machine or employee in specified time

**workman** n manual laborer; *adj* **-like** of, like a good workman; *n* **-ship** skillful working

**workout** n concentrated spell of physical exercise

**workshop** n 1 room or building where goods are made or repaired 2 group meeting where members exchange ideas and develop skills, methods, projects, etc

**work station** n work area for one person, often with computer

**world** n 1 the Earth 2 humanity 3 sphere of human activity; *idm* **out of this world** *coll* wonderful; *idm* **worlds apart** *coll* totally different; *adjs* **w.-class** among the best in the world; **w.-famous** well-known everywhere; **w.-wide** found, happening in all parts of the world (*also adv*); *ns* **w. view** 1 attitude to life 2 philosophy; **w. war** war involving many major countries

**world** n 1 (Earth) globe, planet. 2 (humanity) everybody, human race, international community, mankind, people, public, whole world. 3 (sphere of activity) domain, field, province, realm

**worldly** adj 1 to do with the material rather than the spiritual world 2 experienced in the ways of society (*n* **-iness**; **w. wise** shrewd in handling of human affairs)

**worldly** adj 1 (to do with material world) earthly, material, materialistic, physical, secular, temporal, terrestrial. 2 (experienced in ways of society) cosmopolitan, experienced, shrewd, smart, sophisticated, streetwise *inf*, worldly wise

**world wide web** n body of data stored in computers world-wide, accessible using the Internet

**worm** n 1 long invertebrate, earthworm, grub, maggot 2 *fig* weak, obsequious person; *v* wriggle, edge along slowly

**wormwood** n aromatic bitter herb

**worn** pt, pp of **wear**; adj 1 much used 2 threadbare( **w.-out**); adj 1 exhausted 2 too worn to be used

**worn** adj decrepit, frayed, moth-eaten, old, ragged, scruffy, shabby, tattered, tatty *inf*, threadbare, tired, weary, worn-out

**worried** adj agitated, concerned

**worried** *adj* anxious, apprehensive, bothered, distraught, distressed, fearful, fretful, nervous, on edge, perturbed, stressed-out *inf*, tense, troubled, uneasy, uptight *inf*

**worry** *v* **worrying, worried 1** feel concerned, anxious **2** bother; concern **3** pester; *n* **1** anxiety **2** problem; *adj* **worrying**

**worry** *v* **1** (feel concerned) agonize, be agitated, be anxious, be concerned, bother, feel uneasy, fret, get worked up. **2** (bother) concern, disturb, hassle, irritate, nag, pester, torment, trouble, unsettle, upset
**worry** *n* **1** (anxiety) agitation, apprehension, concern, disquiet, distress, nervousness, stress, tension, trouble, uneasiness. **2** (problem) bother, burden, doubt, irritation, nuisance

**worse** *adj comp* of **bad**; *v* **worsen** make, grow worse; deteriorate
**worship** *v* **worshipping, worshipped** revere; pray to as God; idolize; *n* **worshipper**
**worst** *adj sup* of **bad**
**worsted** *adj, n* (made of) woolen yarn
**worth** *adj* having specified value; *n* merit; material value; *idm* **for all one's worth** with maximum effort
**worthless** *adj* of no value
**worthwhile** *adj* useful

**worthwhile** *adj* advantageous, beneficial, fruitful, good, helpful, productive, profitable, rewarding, valuable

**worthy** *adj* **1** virtuous **2** deserving; *n* eminent person (*adv* **-ily**; *n* **-iness**)
**would** *pt* of **will**; *adj* **w.-be** aspiring (*usu* in vain)
**wouldn't** contracted form of **would not**
**wound**[1] *n* cut in skin or tissue of body; *v* **1** injure **2** upset deeply

**wound** *n* gash, graze, injury, laceration, lesion, scar
**wound** *v* **1** (injure) cut, damage, harm, hurt, lacerate, stab. **2** (upset) damage, distress, hurt, injure, offend, shock, traumatize

**wound**[2] *pt, pp* of **wind**; *adj* **w.-up** intensely excited or anxious
**wove** *pt,* **woven** *pp* of **weave**
**wow**[1] *interj* expressing surprise; *n coll* great success
**wow**[2] *mus* distortion in reproduced sound
**wpm** *abbr* words per minute
**wrack** *n* ruin
**wrangle** *v* quarrel angrily; *n* noisy quarrel
**wrap** *v* **wrapping, wrapped** cover (person, thing) in material or covering; *phr v* **wrap up 1** put on warm clothes **2** complete (task, agreement); *n* garment covering woman's shoulders; *idm* **under wraps** *coll* being kept secret; *ns* **wrapper** protective outer covering (*esp* for goods on sale or sent by mail); **wrapping** material used to cover or wrap sth (**w. paper** paper for wrapping parcel or gift)

**wrap** *v* bind, encase, enfold, envelop, fold, lag, muffle, package, wrap

**wrath** *n* anger; *adj* **-ful**
**wreak** *v* give vent to (anger, etc); exact (vengeance)
**wreath** *n* circle of intertwined leaves or flowers; garland; wisp of smoke; *v* **wreathe** twist, wind into wreath; surround; wind round
**wreck** *n* destruction, *esp* of ship by wind and waves; ship fast on rocks; ruin; broken remains of structure; *v* destroy completely

**wreck** *v* dash, demolish, devastate, play havoc with, ruin, scuttle, smash, spoil, write off

**wreckage** *n* remains of sth destroyed

**wreckage** n debris, pieces, remains, rubble

**wren** n species of small songbird
**wrench** n 1 violent twist 2 adjustable tool to turn nuts 3 fig grief felt at separation; v twist; seize forcibly

**wrench** v jerk, pull, rip, tear, tug, yank

**wrest** v tear away, take by force
**wrestle** v grapple with and try to throw opponent; fig strive with (difficulties, etc)
**wretch** n miserable unfortunate person
**wretched** adj 1 miserable 2 terrible
**wriggle** n squirming, twisting movement; v move thus
**wring** v **wringing, wrung** twist; squeeze out moisture; idm **wringing wet** very wet
**wrinkle** n 1 small crease, fold, esp of skin 2 coll useful hint; v pucker

**wrinkle** v crease, crinkle, crumple, fold, ruck up, rumple

**wrist** n joint between forearm and hand
**writ** n leg document giving instructions to do or refrain from doing, something
**write** v **writing, wrote, written** 1 put words on paper 2 compose 3 correspond; phr vs **write down** record in writing; **write off** 1 acknowledge as irretrievable or irreparable (n **w.-off**) 2 treat (debt) as no longer existing; **write up** give full written account of (n **w.-up** report or review); n **writing** 1 act of writing (adj of or for writing) 2 written symbols; handwriting 3 form of written expression

**write** v 1 (put words on paper) jot down, note down, put in writing, record, scrawl, scribble, sign. 2 (compose) compile, create, dash off, draft, draw up, pen, produce, put together. 3 (correspond) communicate, drop sb a line, write sb a letter

**writer** n one who composes literary works

**writer** n author, biographer, columnist, compiler, contributor, correspondent, creator, diarist, dramatist, editor, essayist, ghostwriter, hack, journalist, novelist, playwright, poet, scriptwriter, wordsmith

**writhe** v twist, contort body about in pain
**written** pp of **write**
**wrong** adj 1 incorrect 2 wicked 3 mistaken in opinion, etc 4 unsuitable; idm **go wrong** 1 miscalculate; make errors 2 stop functioning properly; n 1 that which is wrong 2 harmful act; idm **in the wrong** responsible for error; v do wrong to; ns **-doer, -doing**; adj **wrongful** unjust or illegal

**wrong** adj 1 (incorrect) false, inaccurate, mistaken, untrue. 2 (wicked) against the law, bad, criminal, dishonest, evil, ill-advised, illegal, illicit, ill-judged, immoral, improper, inappropriate, misguided, unacceptable, unethical, unfair, unlawful, unsuitable

**wrote** pt of **write**
**wrought** adj worked; **w. iron** iron hammered, beaten into shape
**wrung** pt, pp of **wring**
**wry** adj 1 twisted 2 fig ironical; expressing distaste; adv **-ly**; n **-ness**; n **wryneck** bird related to woodpecker; adj **wry-necked** with deformed, twisted neck

a
b
c
d
e
f
g
h
i
j
k
l
m
n
o
p
q
r
s
t
u
v
**w**
x
y
z

**X** *n math* unknown quantity; *fig* any person, anything unknown

**xen-, xeno-** *prefix* relating to hospitality; external, foreign

**xenon** *n* inert, heavy gas present in air

**xenophobia** *n* irrational hate or fear of foreigners, strangers

**xer(o)-** *prefix* dry, dryness

**Xerography** *n* [TM] photocopying process

**xerophilous** *adj* able to thrive in conditions of drought; *n* **xerophyte** drought-loving plant

**Xerox** [TM] **1** dry process for making multiple photocopies **2** photocopy thus made; *v* produce photocopy by this method; *n* **X. machine**

**Xmas** *n coll* Christmas

**X-rated** *adj* (of film, video) classified as unsuitable for young people under 18 years of age; *n* **X-rating**

**X-ray** *n* **1** *usu pl* electromagnetic short wave radiation capable of penetrating matter **2** photograph taken with this **3** medical examination by this method; *v* take such a photograph or examine by this method

**xyl(o)-** *prefix* wood; pertaining to wood

**xylograph** *n* an engraving on wood; *n* **-grapher**; *adj* **-graphic**

**xyloid** *adj* of, like wood

**xylophone** *n* musical percussion instrument of graduated wooden bars, which vibrate when struck

**yacht** n light sailing vessel used for racing or pleasure-cruising; n **-sman** owner or sailor of yacht

**yak¹**, **yack** v sl talk noisily and continuously on trivial matters; n sl chat; ns **-ing**; **yackety-yack** sl incessant chatter

**yak²** n long-haired ox of Central Asia

**yam** n fleshy edible root of tropical climbing plant; sweet potato

**yammer** v coll talk incessantly in complaining manner; n **-ing**

**yang** n (in Chinese philosophy) active male principle

**yank** v coll pull sharply, jerk; n sharp tug

**Yankee** n (also **Yank**) inhabitant of New England states; coll American

**yap** n bark of small dog; v **yapping**, **yapped** yelp, bark; coll chatter

**yard¹** n unit of length, 36 ins

**yard²** n 1 enclosed space, often paved, adjoining building 2 enclosure for some specific purpose

> **yard** n (enclosed space adjoining building) back yard, compound, court, courtyard, enclosure, farmyard, gardens, quadrangle

**yardstick** n standard of comparison

> **yardstick** n benchmark, criterion, gauge, guide, measure, standard

**yarn** n continuous thread of twisted fibres (of wool, cotton, etc); coll tale

**yarrow** n white-flowered perennial herb

**yashmak** n veil worn by Muslim women

**yawn** v 1 open mouth widely and breathe in involuntarily 2 fig open wide; gape

**yawning** adj with very wide opening

> **yawning** adj cavernous, deep, gaping, huge, massive, vast, wide

**ye** pron lit, ar pl of **thou**

**yea** interj, n yes; affirmative statement

**year** n period of time taken by earth to revolve once round sun; unit of time, 365 ¼ days; idm **year in, year out** continually; n **y.book** book of information revised each year; adj **y.long** lasting all year; n **yearling** animal one year old; adj **yearly** every year; adv annually

**yearn** v desire strongly; n **yearning**

> **yearn** v covet, crave, desire, hanker after, hunger for, long for, pine for, want

**yeast** n fungoid substance used as ferment in brewing, bread-making etc; adj **yeasty** frothy, fermenting

**yell** v cry loudly and sharply; n piercing cry

> **yell** v bawl, bellow, howl, roar, scream, screech, shout, whoop, yelp, yowl

**yellow** adj 1 of color of ripe lemons 2 sl cowardly; ns **y. fever** serious infectious tropical disease; **y.hammer** yellow feathered bird; **Y. Pages** telephone directory arranged under categories of business, etc; v turn yellow, esp with age (adj **-ed**)

**yelp** v give short sharp bark of pain or anger; n such cry.

**yen** n 1 Japanese dollar 2 sl intense desire

**yeoman** n hist small landowner cultivating his own land; n **yeomanry** yeomen collectively; territorial volunteer cavalry force recruited mainly from country districts

**yes** *interj* expressing affirmation; is that so?

**yesterday** *n* day before today; *pl* **-s** past times

**yesteryear** *n lit* recent past

**yet** *adv* until now; now; besides; *conj* nevertheless, but still

**yeti** *n* hairy humanoid creature believed to live in Himalayan mountains (*also* **Abominable Snowman**)

**yew** *n* evergreen coniferous tree; its wood

**Yiddish** *n* mixed dialect of German, Hebrew and Slavonic, used by Jews in Europe and America

**yield** *v* **1** produce as crop **2** bring in (as financial return) **3** concede defeat; give up; *n* amount produced; profit; *adj* **-ing** **1** flexible **2** easily persuaded

> **yield** *v* **1** (bring in as financial return) bear, earn, generate, pay, produce, provide, return. **2** (concede defeat) accede, acquiesce, admit defeat, capitulate, comply, give in, give up, give way, relinquish, submit, surrender, throw in the towel *inf*

**yin** *n* (in Chinese philosophy) inactive female principle

**yip** *v* bark sharply

**yippee** *interj* shout of delight

**yob** *n Brit* aggressive, ill-mannered youth

**yodel** *v* **yodeling, yodeled** warble, changing rapidly from natural voice to falsetto; *n* wordless song or cry in this style

**yoga** *n* Hindu system of meditation, controlling the body and mind

**yogurt, yoghurt** *n* thick milk preparation, fermented by bacterial action

**yoke** *n* **1** crosspiece shaped to fit necks of animals, to which plow, etc may be attached **2** part of garment cut to fit shoulders **3** *fig* authority; dominion; *v* harness with yoke

**yokel** *n* countryman; rustic.

**yolk** *n* yellow central part of egg

**Yom Kippur** *n* Jewish holiday (Day of Atonement) marked with fasting and prayer

**yon** *adj lit* that, those over there; *adj ar* **yonder** over there; *adv* in that direction

**Yorkshire pudding** *n* baked batter eaten with roast beef

**you** *pron* 2nd pers sing, pl) **1** person(s) lately spoken to **2** one, anyone

**you'd** *contracted form of* **you had, you would**

**you'll** *contracted form of* **you will**

**young** *adj* in early stages of life; not yet old; *n* offspring; *n* **-ster** child, *esp* boy

> **young** *adj* adolescent, baby, growing, immature, infant, junior, juvenile, new,

**your** *adj* belonging to you; *pron* **yours** *poss of* **you**; *idm* **yours truly 1** formally polite phrase for ending letter **2** *coll* myself; *pron* **yourself** emphatic form of **you** (*pl* **yourselves**); *idm* (**all**) **by yourself 1** alone **2** unaided

**you're** *contracted form of* **you are**

**youth** *n* **1** early life **2** young man **3** young people

> **youth** *n* **1** (early life) adolescence, childhood, formative years. **2** (young man) adolescent, teenager. **3** (young people) children, kids *inf*, the younger generation

**youthful** *adj* young in appearance or behavior; *n* **-ness**

> **youthful** *adj* childish, fresh, sprightly, well-preserved, young at heart, young-looking

**you've** *contracted form of* **you have**

**yowl** *v, n* (make) loud wailing cry

**yo-yo** [TM] toy consisting of double disc with groove between that runs up and down on a string; *pl* **-os**

**yucca** *n* tall plant with white bell-like flowers

**yuck** *interj* expressing disgust

**Yule** *n* Christmas season or festival; **Yuletide** Christmas time

**yuppie, yuppy** *n coll* ambitious young person in well-paid professional or business job; *adj* typical of such people and their lifestyle

zabaglione *n It* rich creamy sauce made of egg yolk, sugar, and sweet wine

zany *adj* crazy; *adv* -ly; *n* -ness; 1 clown 2 idiot, fool

> zany *adj* absurd, daft *inf*, eccentric, mad, off the wall *inf*, wacky *inf*, wild

zap *v* zapping, zapped *coll* 1 move suddenly with great force 2 attack with destructive force; *adj* zappy lively and vigorous

zeal *n* great enthusiasm

> zeal *n* ardor, dedication, determination, enthusiasm, fanaticism, fervor, gusto, passion, vehemence, zest

zealous *adj* fanatical, full of zeal; *n* zealot fanatic

> zealous *adj* ardent, dedicated, determined, devoted, enthusiastic, fervent, passionate, vehement

zebra *n* striped African quadruped

Zen *adj, n* (of) Japanese Buddhist sect seeking truth through meditation

zenith *n fig* highest point; climax

> zenith *n* culmination, height, peak, pinnacle, summit, top

zephyr *n lit* gentle breeze

zeppelin *n* German dirigible airship used in World War I

zero *n* 1 figure 0; nought 2 starting point in scale of measurement 3 *fig* lowest point; *phr v* zero in on 1 aim (missile, etc) at 2 *fig* direct one's attention to; *n* z.-hour exact time at which important operation (*esp mil*) is due to begin

> zero *n* (nought) love, nil, nothing, zilch *inf*, zip *inf*

zest *n* 1 enthusiasm 2 relish, flavoring 3 orange or lemon peel; *adj* -ful *adv* -ly

> zest *n* (enthusiasm) determination, gusto, keenness, relish, zeal

zigzag *n* line having repeated sharp bends in alternate directions; *adj* forming zigzag; *adv* with such course; *v* zigzagging, zigzagged move in such course

zillion *det, n, pron* extremely large number

zimmer frame [TM] *n* metal walking frame

zinc *n* bluish white metallic element

zincograph *n* design in relief on zinc plate; print made from this

zinnia *n* annual plant of aster family

Zion *n* hill in Jerusalem; *fig* City of Jerusalem; religious system of Jews; Christianity

Zionism *n* political and military movement that established independent Jewish state of Israel

zip *n* 1 light whizzing sound 2 *coll* energy, vigor; *v* zipping, zipped fasten with zipper; whizz; *n* Z. code numerical code used to sort mail; *adj* zippy *coll* fast

zipper *n* device for fastening with two rows of interlocking teeth, opened by sliding grip

zit *n sl* spot on skin

zither *v* flat, stringed musical instrument

zodiac *n* imaginary belt in heavens, divided into twelve sections or signs, within which moon, sun, and chief planets have their paths; *adj* -al

**nbie** n 1 corpse revived and controlled by witchcraft in voodoo belief 2 *coll* one who acts mechanically, without feeling or intelligence; *adjs* **-ish**; **-like**

**zone** n belt, band; one of five regions of earth differentiated by climate; specified area or region with particular features or for particular purpose; *adj* **zonal**; n **zoning** designated areas of town, etc

**zone** n area, district, locality, quarter, region, section, sector

**zonked** *adj sl* 1 exhausted 2 drunk or drugged

**zoo** n park where wild animals are kept and exhibited

**zoolite** n fossil animal

**zoology** n scientific study of animals; n **-logist**; *adj* **-logical** of, for zoology (n **z. gardens** place where wild animals are kept for exhibition); *ns* **zoo-dynamics** animal physiology; **zoogeography** study of distribution of animals on surface of earth

**zoom** v 1 move quickly 2 *fig* rise sharply in price 3 compel aircraft to ascend rapidly at sharp angle; n **zoom** zooming; n **z. lens** camera lens allowing quick focus change, making distant subject suddenly seem much closer

**zoom** v (move quickly) bolt, career, charge, dash, flash, fly, gallop, hare, hurry, hurtle, run, rush, shoot, speed, tear, whiz, zip

**zoophyte** n plantlike invertebrate animal (*eg* sponge)

**zucchini** n *sing* or *pl* green summer squash

**Zulu** n member, language of Bantu or Kaffir people of S Africa

**zygote** n fertilized ovum

**zymotic** *adj* (of diseases) induced by propagation of living germs